Multicolour Illustrative Edition

CONCRETE TECHNOLOGY
THEORY AND PRACTICE

M.S. SHETTY
BE, ME, FICI, FIIBE, FIE, MACCE

Technical Advisor, MC Bauchemie (Ind) Pvt. Ltd.
Principal Technical Consultant, Grasim Industries, Ltd.
Consultant to IMCC Delhi Metro Corporation
Formerly Senior Prof. and Head of Department of Construction Engineering
College of Military Engineering (CME), Pune
Ministry of

S. CHAND & COMPANY LTD.
(An ISO 9001 : 2000 Company)
Ram Nagar, New Delhi - 110 055

S. CHAND & COMPANY LTD.

(An ISO 9001 : 2000 Company)

Head Office : 7361, RAM NAGAR, NEW DELHI - 110 055
Phones : 23672080-81-82; Fax : 91-11-23677446
Shop at: **schandgroup.com**
E-mail: **schand@vsnl.com**

Branches :

- 1st Floor, Heritage, Near Gujarat Vidhyapeeth, Ashram Road,
  Ahmedabad-380 014. Ph. 27541965, 27542369
- No. 6, Ahuja Chambers, 1st Cross, Kumara Krupa Road,
  Bangalore-560 001. Ph : 22268048, 22354008
- 152, Anna Salai, Chennai-600 002. Ph : 28460026
- S.C.O. 6, 7 & 8, Sector 9D, Chandigarh-160017, Ph-2749376, 2749377
- 1st Floor, Bhartia Tower, Badambadi, Cuttack-753 009, Ph-2332580; 2332581
- 1st Floor, 52-A, Rajpur Road, Dehradun-248 011. Ph : 2740889, 2740861
- Pan Bazar, Guwahati-781 001. Ph : 2522155
- Sultan Bazar, Hyderabad-500 195. Ph : 24651135, 24744815
- Mai Hiran Gate, Jalandhar - 144008 , Ph. 2401630
- 613-7, M.G. Road, Ernakulam, Kochi-682 035. Ph : 2381740
- 285/J, Bipin Bihari Ganguli Street, Kolkata-700 012. Ph : 22367459, 22373914
- Mahabeer Market, 25 Gwynne Road, Aminabad, Lucknow-226 018. Ph : 2626801, 2284815
- Blackie House, 103/5, Walchand Hirachand Marg , Opp. G.P.O., Mumbai-400 001.
  Ph : 22690881, 22610885
- 3, Gandhi Sagar East, Nagpur-440 002. Ph : 2723901
- 104, Citicentre Ashok, Govind Mitra Road, Patna-800 004. Ph : 2300489, 2302100

Marketing Offices :

- 238-A M.P. Nagar, Zone 1, Bhopal - 462 011. Ph : 5274723.
- A-14 Janta Store Shopping Complex, University Marg, Bapu Nagar, Jaipur - 302 015,
  Phone : 0141-2709153

© 1982, M.S. Shetty

First Edition 1982
Subsequent Editions and Reprints 1986, 88, 89, 91, 94, 95, 96, 97, 98, 99
2000, 2001, 2002, 2003, 2004
Reprint with Corrections 2005

First Multicolour Illustrative Revised Edition 2005

ISBN : 81-219-0003-4

PRINTED IN INDIA
By Rajendra Ravindra Printers (Pvt.) Ltd., 7361, Ram Nagar, New Delhi-110 055
and published by S. Chand & Company Ltd. 7361, Ram Nagar, New Delhi-110 055

Dedicated
To
My Beloved Father

V. VENKAPPA SHETTY

FOREWORD

As one who has closely watched the author's interest and involvement in concrete technology for the past several years, I have great pleasure in writting this foreword.

Concrete is by far the most widely used construction material today. The versatility and mouldability of this material, its high compressive strength, and the discovery of the reinforcing and prestressing techniques which helped to make up for its low tensile strength have contributed largely to its widespread use. We can rightly say that we are in the age of concrete.

It is easy to make concrete. There is an old saying that broken stone, sand, and cement make good concrete. But the same proportion of broken stone, sand and cement also make bad concrete. This is mainly because the quality of the end product depends as much, and perhaps more, on the man on the job as on the constituent materials. The difference between good concrete and bad concrete lies in quality control. Extensive research work was, therefore, carried out almost from the beginning of this century not only on the materials but also on the methods used for concrete making. Still, not many men on the job seem to make use of the known techniques for making good concrete which is necessary for achieving strong, durable, and economical construction. This textbook by Prof. M.S. Shetty will, therefore, help to generate a better awareness of the potential of concrete.

The book deals with several aspects of concrete technology and also covers the latest developments that have taken place in India and abroad. The coverage is comprehensive and complete. The properties of the constituent materials of concrete have been explained very lucidly in the text. The information on admixtures and on special concretes, such as air-entrained concrete, vacuum concrete, light-weight concrete, and gap-graded concrete, will be very useful to concrete engineers and those engaged in precast concrete construction. At many places in the text, the author touches upon some important, down-to-earth problems and gives specific recommendations based on his own knowledge and vast experience. The chapter on mix design gives simple and scientific procedures for the benefit of practising engineers and concrete technologists.

One of the welcome features of this book is the inclusion of detailed information on recent developments relating to fibre-reinforced concrete, sulphur-impregnated concrete, and different types of polymer concrete. The author has highlighted the potential of these new materials and has laid emphasis on the need for further research.

The text has been written in simple language and is supplemented by numerous illustrative examples, charts, and tables. The author has succeeded in presenting all the relevant information on concrete technology in a very effective manner. I am sure the book will be well received by students of concrete technology as well as practising engineers and research workers.

M. RAMAIAH
Director
Structural Engineering
Research Centre
Madras

ACKNOWLEDGMENTS

What made me interested in concrete technology was my association with Shri M.R. Vinayaka of Associated Cement Company, when he was working at Koyna Dam Concrete Research Laboratory. My interest was further enhanced while teaching this fascinating subject to the graduate and postgraduate students at the College of Military Engineering. I am grateful to them.

I gratefully acknowledge the following institutions and societies in the reproduction of certain tables, charts and information in my book:

The American Concrete Institute, the American Society for Testing and Materials, the Cement and Concrete Association, the Portland Cement Association, the Institute of Civil Engineers, London, Department of Mines, Ottawa, Canada, the Concrete Association of India, the Cement Research Institute of India, the Central Building Research Institute, Roorkee, the Structural Engineering Research Centre, Madras, the Central Road Research Institute, Delhi, and the Bureau of Indian Standards.

A book of this nature cannot be written without the tremendous background information made available by various research workers, authors of excellent books and articles which have been referred to and listed at the end of the chapters and at the end of this book. I am thankful to them.

I also wish to express my sincere thanks to the Commandant, College of Military Engineering for extending all facilities and words of encouragement while working on this book.

My special gratefulness is due to Smt. Brinda Balu and Dr. Balasubramanian for going through the manuscript with such diligence as to bring it into the present state.

My special thanks are due to Dr. M. Ramaiah, Director, Structural Engineering Research Centre, Madras, who obliged with a foreword to this book.

Lastly I am grateful to M/s S. Chand and Co., Ltd., for taking the responsibility of publishing this book.

Place: Pune, 1982   **M.S. SHETTY**

PREFACE TO THE SIXTH EDITION

It gives me immense pleasure that the book first published in 1982, has seen more than 25 reprints. The popularity of this book amongst students and practicing engineers has given me the encouragement to revise this book to make it more useful to them. The proposal and encouragement given by officers of S. Chand & Company to bring this Sixth Edition in multicolour should make the book more useful and attractive

Concrete technology is becoming a major branch of civil engineering. It is becoming the backbone of infrastructural developments of every country. It has made tremendous advancement in the western and the eastern world. Though India is lagging behind, we are catching up fast with the rest of the world.

It can be recalled that in the preface to the first edition (1982) I had mentioned that the cement production in India was 22 million tons. This was about eight decades after we first started manufacturing Portland Cement (1904). It is heart warming to note that in the subsequent two decades after 1982 i.e. in 2004, the production of cement has crossed 120 million tons. Today we are the second largest producer of cement in the world, only behind China.

The quantity of concrete and other cement products made, utilising over 120 million tons of cement to cater for the tremendous infrastructural development that is taking place in the country, is making the concrete industry one of the biggest in monetary terms. Western and Eastern countries have been making concrete of strength M40, M80, M100 and over. In the recent past, we in India have started using concrete of strength M30, M50 and even M75. We have a long way to go to learn and practice the art and science of making High Performance Concrete (HPC) yet. The recent revision of IS 456, code of practice for plain and reinforced concrete is guiding concrete technologists to make strong and durable concrete.

I have grown older by twenty three years since I wrote the first edition. During these 23 years and especially in the last 15 years, I have had opportunities to deliver numerous lectures, training site engineers, conducting trials at large project sites, throughout the country which has made me once again a student of concrete technology and motivated me to revise this book.

Major revision has been carried out in Fifth and Sixth Edition. Topics, such as blended cements, use of admixtures and their use, field trials to find out their suitability, compatibility and dosage, RMe, pumping of concrete, latest methods mix design step by step, and extensive unconventional deliberation on durability, have been included.

Another special feature of this Sixth Edition is the inclusion of SELF COMPACTING CONCRETE, a revolutionary method of concrete construction. This innovative method which is found only in journals and seminar proceedings is rarely incorporated in text books. Similarly, other latest research information on Bacteria Concrete Geopolymer Concrete and Basalt fibre concrete are also included.

The book incorporates relevant information on numerous Indian standard specifications and code of practices relating to cement and concrete, including the latest revision of IS 456 of 2000 in respect of section 2 on materials, workmanship, inspection, testing and acceptance criteria. The book should serve as a vehicle to disseminate the information to all those who are interested in concrete construction.

I am sure that this multicolour revised edition will prove to be very useful to students of engineering, architects, practicing engineers and teachers in all engineering colleges. If this book helps to enthuse the readers and enable them to make better concrete at our construction sites, I would feel that my efforts are well rewarded.

I would like to express my sincere thanks to Shri Samir Surlaker, an authority on admixtures and construction chemicals in India, for helping me to enhance the technical content of this book. I am also thankful to the officers and staff of M/s S. Chand & Company Ltd. who were extremely amicable and helpful to bringing out this sixth edition in Multicolour.

Place: Pune
May 2005   **M.S. SHETTY**

PREFACE TO THE FIRST EDITION

Cement mortar and concrete are the most widely used construction materials. It is difficult to point out another material of construction which is as versatile as concrete. It is the material of choice where strength, permanence, durability, impermeability, fire resistance and abrasion resistance are required. It is so closely associated now with every human activity that it touches every human being in his day to day living.

Cement concrete is one of the seemingly simple but actually complex materials. Many of its complex behaviours are yet to be identified to employ this material advantageously and economically. The behaviour of concrete with respect to long-term drying shrinkage, creep, fatigue, morphology of gel structure, bond, fracture mechanism and polymer modified concrete, fibrous concrete are some of the areas of active research in order to have a deeper understanding of the complex behaviour of these materials.

In any country, construction accounts for about 60 per cent of the plan outlay. Out of this, cement and cement product would account for more than 50 per cent. Today in India the annual consumption of cement is in the order of 22 million tonnes. It is estimated that the cost of mortar and concrete made from 22 million tons of cement would work out to about Rs. 4,000 crores which is about 1/5 of the plan outlay for the year 1982–83. It is in this context that the knowledge of concrete technology assumes importance.

Concrete is a site-made material unlike other materials of construction and as such can vary to a very great extent in its quality, properties and performance owing to the use of natural materials except cement. From materials of varying properties, to make concrete of stipulated qualitites, an intimate knowledge of the interaction of various ingredients that go into the making of concrete is required to be known, both in the plastic condition and in the hardened condition. This knowledge is necessary for concrete technologists as well as for site engineers.

This book is written mainly to give practical bias into concrete-making practices to students of engineering and site engineers. Practical bias needs good theoretical base. Approach to practical solution should be made on the basis of sound theoretical concept. Sometimes, theory, however good, may not be applicable on many practical situations. This is to say, that particularly in concrete-making practices both theory and practice go hand in hand more closely than in many other branches of Engineering mainly because it is a site made material.

There are many good books written on this subject. But there are only a few books dealing with conditions, practice and equipment available in this country. Moreover, most of the books refer to only British and American standards. It has been the endeavour of the author to give as much information as possible about the Indian practice, Indian standard specifications and code of practices for concrete making. If this book helps the reader to make better concrete in the field, my efforts, I feel, are rewarded.

Place: Pune

M.S. SHETTY

CONTENTS

7. STRENGTH OF CONCRETE   298-324

8. ELASTICITY, CREEP AND SHRINKAGE — 325-348

9. DURABILITY OF CONCRETE — 349-419

(xxv)

CONCRETE
IN THE UNENDING SERVICE
OF NATION BUILDING

LET US LEARN THIS SUBJECT TO BE A PART OF THE NATION BUILDING TEAM

SARDAR SAROVAR DAM : Sardar Sarovar Project is an Inter-State Multi-Purpose project of National importance. It is one of the largest projects under implementation anywhere in the world.

THE IDUKKI HYDROELECTRIC PROJECT, KERALA : The reservoir covers nearly 60 square kilometres and has a catchment of 649 square km. Water from the reservoir is taken down to the underground power house at Moolamattom through an underground tunnel, yielding an average gross head of 2182 feet (665 metres). The project has an installed capacity of 780 MW with firm power potential of 230 MW at 100 per cent load factor.

THE BHAKRA DAM is a majestic monument across river Sutlej. The construction of this project was started in the year 1948 and was completed in 1963 . It is 740 ft. high above the deepest foundation as straight concrete dam being more than three times the height of Qutab Minar. Bhakra Dam is the highest Concrete Gravity dam in Asia and Second Highest in the world.

SAI GANGA approach canal for water supply to Chennai Metro.

DELHI METRO Railway Station under construction.

THE BAHÁ'Í HOUSE OF WORSHIP known as the Lotus Temple, built near New Delhi.

Diamond shaped 'MANI KANCHAN' – Gem & Jewellery Park at Kolkata.

Unconventional building with pleasing architecture.

TARAPUR ATOMIC POWER PROJECT : Reactor Building no. 3 & 4.

Fully automatic construction of concrete pavement.

A view of large oval shaped dome under construction over Connaught Place Metro Railway Station. It is going to be a new landmark over Delhi Metro. It will be a modern version of Palika garden – A pride feature of Delhi Metro Project.

Sky Bus Metro, Goa

SOME LANDMARK HIGHRISE BUILDINGS IN THE WORLD

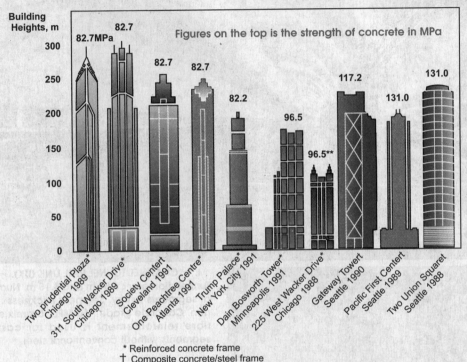

Building Heights, m

Figures on the top is the strength of concrete in MPa

* Reinforced concrete frame
† Composite concrete/steel frame
** Also includes one experimental column of 117 MPa

SOME HIGHRISE BUILDINGS AROUND THE WORLD

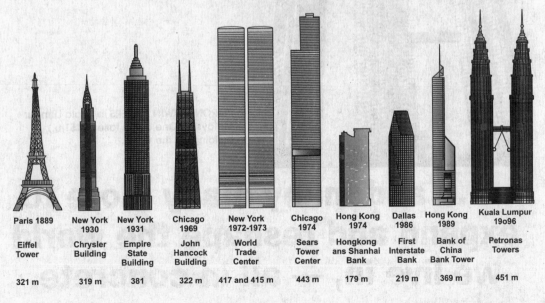

Paris 1889	New York 1930	New York 1931	Chicago 1969	New York 1972-1973	Chicago 1974	Hong Kong 1974	Dallas 1986	Hong Kong 1989	Kuala Lumpur 19o96
Eiffel Tower	Chrysler Building	Empire State Building	John Hancock Building	World Trade Center	Sears Tower Center	Hongkong ans Shanhai Bank	First Interstate Bank	Bank of China Bank Tower	Petronas Towers
321 m	319 m	381	322 m	417 and 415 m	443 m	179 m	219 m	369 m	451 m

▲ CHANNEL TUNNEL RAIL LINK (UK).
Tunnel diameter : 6.84 m and 8.15 m. Number of segments 9+key. Segment thickness : 350 mm. Concrete grade : 60 MPa. Dramix steel fibre reinforcement is used for casting segments without conventional steel.

◄ PETRONAS TWIN TOWERS in Kuala Lumpur Malaysia : One of the tallest (451m.) buildings in the world.

. . . . and many many more to expand and reshape the world we live in, — all in concrete.

Modern Cement Factory
Courtesy : Grasim Industries Cement Division

Cement

General

The history of cementing material is as old as the history of engineering construction. Some kind of cementing materials were used by Egyptians, Romans and Indians in their ancient constructions. It is believed that the early Egyptians mostly used cementing materials, obtained by burning gypsum. Not much light has been thrown on cementing material, used in the construction of the cities of Harappa and Mohenjadaro.

An analysis of mortar from the Great Pyramid showed that it contained 81.5 per cent calcium sulphate and only 9.5 per cent carbonate. The early Greeks and Romans used cementing materials obtained by burning limestones. The remarkable hardness of the mortar used in early Roman brickworks, some of which still exist, is presenting sufficient evidence of the perfection which the art of cementing material had attained in ancient times. The superiority of Roman mortar has been attributed to thoroughness of mixing and long continued ramming.

The Greeks and Romans later became aware of the fact that certain volcanic ash and tuff, when mixed with lime and sand yielded mortar possessing superior strength and better durability in fresh or salt water. Roman builders used volcanic tuff found near Pozzuoli village near Mount Vesuvius in Italy. This volcanic tuff or ash mostly siliceous in nature thus acquired the name Pozzolana. Later on, the name Pozzolana was applied to any other material, natural or artificial, having nearly the same composition as that of volcanic tuff or ash found at Pozzuoli. The Romans, in the absence of natural volcanic ash, used powered tiles or pottery as pozzolana. In India. powered brick named *surkhi* has been used in mortar. The Indian practice of through mixing and long continued ramming of lime mortar with or without the addition of *Surkhi* yielded strong and impervious mortar which confirmed the secret of superiority of Roman mortar.

It is learnt that the Romans added blood, milk and lard to their mortar and concrete to achieve better workability. Haemoglobin is a powerful air-entraining agent and plasticizer, which perhaps is yet another reason for the durability of Roman structures. Probably they did not know about the durability aspect but used them as workability agents. The cementing material made by Romans using lime and natural or artificial Pozzolana retained its position as the chief building material for all work, particularly, for hydraulic construction. Belidor, a principal authority in hydraulic construction, recommended an initimate mixture of tiles, stone chips, and scales from a black-smith's forge, carefully ground, washed free from coal and dirt, dried and sifted and then mixed with fresh slaked lime for making good concrete.

When we come to more recent times, the most important advance in the knowledge of cements, the forerunner to the discoveries and manufacture of all modern cements is undoubtedly the investigations carried out by John Smeaton. When he was called upon to rebuild the Eddystone Light-house in 1756, he made extensive enquiries into the state of art existing in those days and also conducted experiments with a view to find out the best material to withstand the severe action of sea water. Finally, he concluded that lime-stones which contained considerable proportion of clayey matter yielded better lime possessing superior hydraulic properties. In spite of the success of Smeaton's experiments, the use of hydraulic lime made little progress, and the old practice of mixture of lime and pozzolana remained popular for a long period. In 1976 hydraulic cement was made by calcining nodules of argillaceous lime-stones. In about 1800 the product thus obtained was called Roman cement. This type of cement was in use till about 1850 after which this was outdated by portland cement.

Early History of Modern Cement

The investigations of L.J. Vicat led him to prepare an artificial hydraulic lime by calcining an intimate mixture of limestone and clay. This process may be regarded as the leading knowledge to the manufacture of Portland cement. James Frost also patented a cement of this kind in 1811 and established a factory in London district.

Joseph Aspdin's first cement works, around 1823, at Kirkgate in Wakefield, UK.
Courtesy : Ambuja Technical Literature

The story of the invention of Portland cement is, however, attributed to Joseph Aspdin, a Leeds builder and bricklayer, even though similar procedures had been adopted by other inventors. Joseph Aspdin took the patent of portland cement on 21st October 1824. The fancy name of portland was given owing to the resemblance of this hardened cement to the natural stone occurring at Portland in England. In his process Aspdin mixed and ground hard limestones and finely divided clay into the form of slurry and calcined it in a furnace similar to a lime kiln till the CO_2 was expelled. The mixture so calcined was then ground to a fine powder. Perhaps, a temperature lower than the clinkering temperature was used by Aspdin. Later in 1845 Isaac Charles Johnson burnt a mixture of clay and chalk till the clinkering stage to make better cement and established factories in 1851.

Oldest surviving kiln, northeast Kent, UK, (1847AD).
Courtesy : Ambuja Technical Literature

In the early period, cement was used for making mortar only. Later the use of cement was extended for making concrete. As the use of Portland cement was increased for making concrete, engineers called for consistently higher standard material for use in major works. Association of Engineers, Consumers and Cement Manufacturers have been established to specify standards for cement. The German standard specification for Portland cement was drawn in 1877. The British standard specification was first drawn up in 1904. The first ASTM specification was issued in 1904.

In India, Portland cement was first manufactured in 1904 near Madras, by the South India Industrial Ltd. But this venture failed. Between 1912 and 1913, the Indian Cement Co. Ltd., was established at Porbander (Gujarat) and by 1914 this Company was able to deliver about 1000 tons of Portland cement. By 1918 three factories were established. Together they were able to produce about 85000 tons of cement per year. During the First Five-Year Plan (1951-1956) cement production in India rose from 2.69 million tons to 4.60 million tons. By 1969 the total production of cement in India was 13.2 million tons and India was then occupying the 9th place in the world, with the USSR producing 89.4 million tonnes and the USA producing 70.5 million tonnes[1.1]. Table 1.1 shows the Growth of Cement Industry through Plans.

Prior to the manufacture of Portland cement in India, it was imported from UK and only a few reinforced concrete structures were built with imported cement. A three storeyed structure built at Byculla, Bombay is one of the oldest RCC structures using Portland cement in India. A concrete masonry building on Mount Road at Madras (1903), the har-ki-pahari bridge at Haridwar (1908) and the Cotton Depot Bombay, then one of the largest of its kind in the world (1922) are some of the oldest concrete structures in India.[1.2]

Table 1.1. Growth of Cement Industry through Plans

Five Year Plan	At the end of the Year	Capacity (*)	%age Growth	Production (*)	%age Growth Cement	GDP Growth
Pre Plan	50-51	3.28		2.20		
I Plan	55-56	5.02		4.60		
II Plan	60-61	9.30	13.12	7.97	11.62	7.1
III Plan	65-66	12.00	5.23	10.97	6.60	3.4
There were Annual Plans for 1966-67, 67-68 and 68-69						
IV Plan	73.74	19.76	10.49	14.66	5.97	4.6
V Plan	78-79	22.58	2.70	19.42	5.78	5.5
VI Plan	84-85	42.00	13.22	30.13	9.18	3.8
VII Plan	89-90	61.55	7.94	45.41	8.55	6.9
Annual	90-91	64.36	0.90	48.90	1.49	5.4
Plans	91-92	66.56	3.42	53.61	9.63	5.3
VIII Plan	92-93	70.19	5.45	54.08	0.88	4.1
	93-94	76.88	9.53	57.96	7.17	6.0
	94-95	83.69	8.86	62.35	7.57	7.2
	95-96	97.25	16.20	69.57	11.58	7.1
	96-97	105.25	8.23	76.22	9.56	6.8
IX Plan	97-98	109.30	3.85	83.16	9.10	5.2

(*) Includes mini cement plants
Source: Indian Cement Industry Emerging Trends — P. Parthsarathy and S.M. Chakravarthy

Table 1.2. Per Capita Cement Consumption of Selected Countries of the World (1982, 1994 and 1997)

Country	Per Capita Cement Consumption (Kg.)		
	1982	1994	1997
USA	256	328	347
China	92	333	388
Taiwan	590	1285	966
Japan	617	642	622
Malaysia	290	512	831
Thailand	132	491	595
Argentina	198	184	145 (1996)
Brazil	201	165	240
Venezuela	356	222	169 (1996)
Turkey	251	436	511
World	**188**	**241**	**252 (1995)**

India 78 kg (1996), 82 kg (1997)

The perusal of table 1.2 shows that per capita cement consumption in India is much less than world average. Considerable infrastructural development is needed to build modern India. Production of more cement, knowledge and economical utilisation of cement is the need of the day.

The early scientific study of cements did not reveal much about the chemical reactions that take place at the time burning. A deeper study of the fact that the clayey constituents of limestone are responsible for the hydraulic properties in lime (as established by John Smeaton) was not taken for further research. It may be mentioned that among the earlier cement technologists, Vicat, Le Chatelier and Michaelis were the pioneers in the theoretical and practical field.

Systematic work on the composition and chemical reaction of Portland cement was first begun in the United States. The study on setting was undertaken by the Bureau of Standards and since 1926 much work on the study of Portland cement was also conducted by the Portland Cement Association, U.K. By this time, the manufacture and use of Portland cement had spread to many countries. Scientific work on cements and fundamental contributions to the chemistry of Portland cements were carried out in Germany, Italy, France, Sweden, Canada and USSR, in addition to Britain and USA. In Great Britain with the establishment of Building Research Station in 1921 a systematic research programme was undertaken and many major contributions have been made. Early literatures on the development and use of Portland cements may be found in the Building Science Abstracts published by Building Research Station U.K. since 1928, "Documentation Bibliographique" issued quarterly since 1948 in France and "Handbuch der Zement Literature" in Germany.

Manufacture of Portland Cement

The raw materials required for manufacture of Portland cement are calcareous materials, such as limestone or chalk, and argillaceous material such as shale or clay. Cement factories are established where these raw materials are available in plenty. Cement factories have come up in many regions in India, eliminating the inconvenience of long distance transportation of raw and finished materials.

The process of manufacture of cement consists of grinding the raw materials, mixing them intimately in certain proportions depending upon their purity and composition and burning them in a kiln at a temperature of about 1300 to 1500°C, at which temperature, the material sinters and partially fuses to form nodular shaped clinker. The clinker is cooled and ground to fine powder with addition of about 3 to 5% of gypsum. The product formed by using this procedure is Portland cement.

There are two processes known as "wet" and "dry" processes depending upon whether the mixing and grinding of raw materials is done in wet or dry conditions. With a little change in the above process we have the semi-dry process also where the raw materials are ground dry and then mixed with about 10-14 per cent of water and further burnt to clinkering temperature.

For many years the wet process remained popular because of the possibility of more accurate control in the mixing of raw materials. The techniques of intimate mixing of raw materials in powder form was not available then. Later, the dry process gained momentum with the modern development of the technique of dry mixing of powdered materials using compressed air. The dry process requires much less fuel as the materials are already in a dry state, whereas in the wet process the slurry contains about 35 to 50 per cent water. To dry the slurry we thus require more fuel. In India most of the cement factories used the wet process. Recently a number of factories have been commissioned to employ the dry process method. Within next few years most of the cement factories will adopt dry process system.

In the wet process, the limestone brought from the quarries is first crushed to smaller fragments. Then it is taken to a ball or tube mill where it is mixed with clay or shale as the case may be and ground to a fine consistency of slurry with the addition of water. The slurry is a liquid of creamy consistency with water content of about 35 to 50 per cent, wherein particles, crushed to the fineness of Indian Standard Sieve number 9, are held in suspension. The slurry is pumped to slurry tanks or basins where it is kept in an agitated condition by means of rotating arms with chains or blowing compressed air from the bottom to prevent settling of limestone and clay particles. The composition of the slurry is tested to give the required chemical composition and corrected periodically in the tube mill and also in the slurry tank by blending slurry from different storage tanks. Finally, the corrected slurry is stored in the final storage tanks and kept in a homogeneous condition by the agitation of slurry.

The corrected slurry is sprayed on to the upper end of a rotary kiln against hot heavy hanging chains. The rotary kiln is an important component of a cement factory. It is a thick steel cylinder of diameter anything from 3 metres to 8 metres, lined with refractory materials, mounted on roller bearings and capable of rotating about its own axis at a specified speed. The length of the rotary kiln may vary anything from 30 metres to 200 metres. The slurry on being sprayed against a hot surface of flexible chain loses moisture and becomes flakes. These flakes peel off and fall on the floor. The rotation of the rotary kiln causes the flakes to move from the upper end towards the lower end of the kiln subjecting itself to higher and higher temperature. The kiln is fired from the lower end. The fuel is either powered coal, oil or natural gass. By the time the material rolls down to the lower end of the rotary kiln, the dry material

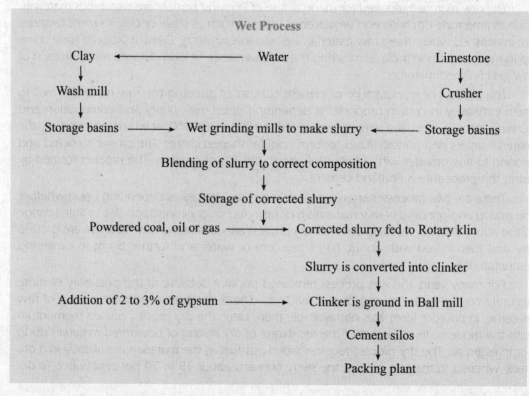

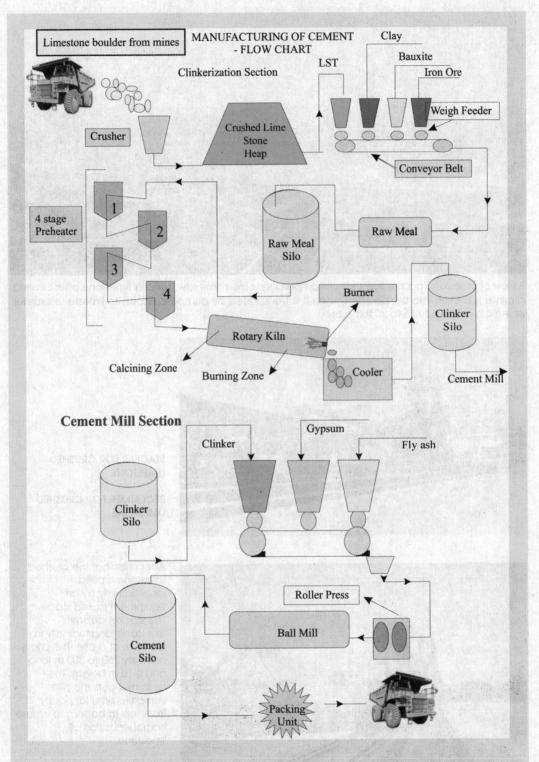

Fig. 1.1. Diagrammatic representation of the dry process of manufacure of cement.

(Courtesy : Grasim Industries Cement Division)

A view of Limestone quarry, *raw material preparation* : The prime raw material limestone after blasting in mines is broken into big boulders. Then it is transported by dumpers, tippers to limestone crusher where it is crushed to 15 to 20 mm size.

◄

STACKER FOR CRUSHED LIMESTONE

RECLAIMER FOR CRUSHED LIMESTONE

After crushing, the crushed limestone is piled longitudinally by an equipment called stacker. The stacker deposits limestone longitudinally in the form of a pile. The pile is normally 250 to 300 m long and 8-10 m height. The reclaimer cuts the pile vertically, simultaneously from top to bottom to ensure homogenization of limestone.

Reclaimer for homogenization of crushed limestone.

undergoes a series of chemical reactions until finally, in the hottest part of the kiln, where the temperature is in the order of 1500°C, about 20 to 30 per cent of the materials get fused. Lime, silica and alumina get recombined. The fused mass turns into nodular form of size 3 mm to 20 mm known as clinker. The clinker drops into a rotary cooler where it is cooled under controlled conditions The clinker is stored in silos or bins. The clinker weighs about 1100 to 1300 gms per litre. The litre weight of clinker indicates the quality of clinker.

The cooled clinker is then ground in a ball mill with the addition of 3 to 5 per cent of gypsum in order to prevent flash-setting of the cement. A ball mill consists of several compartments charged with progressively smaller hardened steel balls. The particles crushed to the required fineness are separated by currents of air and taken to storage silos from where the cement is bagged or filled into barrels for bulk supply to dams or other large work sites.

In the modern process of grinding, the particle size distribution of cement particles are maintained in such a way as to give desirable grading pattern. Just as the good grading of aggregates is essential for making good concrete, it is now recognised that good grading pattern of the cement particles is also important.

The Fig. 1.1 shows the flow diagram of dry process of manufacture of cement.

Dry Process

In the dry and semi-dry process the raw materials are crushed dry and fed in correct proportions into a grinding mill where they are dried and reduced to a very fine powder. The dry powder called the raw meal is then further blended and corrected for its right composition and mixed by means of compressed air. The aerated powder tends to behave almost like liquid and in about one hour of aeration a uniform mixture is obtained.

The blended meal is further sieved and fed into a rotating disc called granulator. A quantity of water about 12 per cent by wright is added to make the blended meal into pellets. This is done to permit air flow for exchange of heat for further chemical reactions and conversion of the same into clinker further in the rotary kiln.

The equipments used in the dry process kiln is comparatively smaller. The process is quite economical. The total consumption of coal in this method is only about 100 kg when compared to the requirement of about 350 kg for producing a ton of cement in the wet process. During March 1998, in India, there were 173 large plants operating, out of which 49 plants used wet process, 115 plants used dry process and 9 plants used semi-dry process.

Since the time of partial liberalisation of cement industry in India (1982), there has been an upgradation in the quality of cement. Many cement companies upgraded their plants both in respect of capacity and quality. Many of the recent plants employed the best equipments, such as cross belt analyser manufactured by Gamma-Metrics of USA to find the composition of limestone at the conveyor belts, high pressure twin roller press, six stage preheater, precalciner and vertical roller mill. The latest process includes stacker and reclaimer, on-line X-ray analyser, Fuzzy Logic kiln control system and other modern process control. In one of the recently built cement plant at Reddypalayam near Trichy, by Grasim Indistries, employed Robot for automatic collection of hourly samples from 5 different places on the process line and help analyse the ame, throughout 24 hours, untouched by men, to avoid human errors in quality control. With all the above sophisticated equipments and controls, consistent quality of clinker is produced.

The methods are commonly employed for direct control of quality of clinker. The first method involves reflected light optical microscopy of polished and etched section of clinker,

RAW MILL

The proportioned raw materials are transported by belt conveyor to Raw Mill for grinding into powder form before burning.

RAW MEAL SILO

After grinding, the powdered raw mix, is stored in a raw meal-silo where blending takes place. Blending is done by injecting compressed air. Generally blending ratio is 1:10. This powder material (Raw meal) is fed to the kiln for burning.

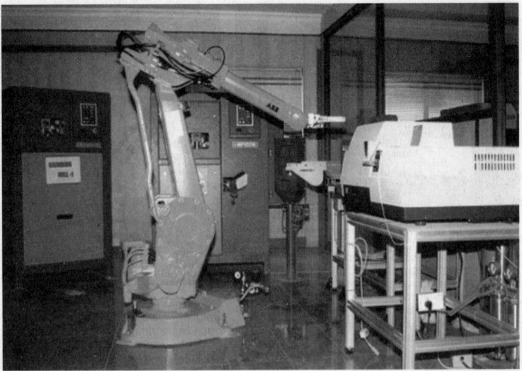

ROBO LAB

Consists of automatic sampling and sending station located at different locations in the plant. Samples are being sent through pneumatic tubes to Robo lab. This avoids human error in sampling and ensures accurate quality in semi finished and finished products. 1st of its kind in India has been used at Grasim Cement plant at Reddypalayam.

Robot receiving samples.

Close circuit grinding technology is most modern grinding system for raw mix as well as for clinker grinding. The systems are in compound mode and are equipped with high efficiency Roller press and separators. The above mentioned system enables to maintain low power consumption for grinding as well as narrow particle size distribution. With this circuit, it is possible to manufacture higher surface area of product as per customers, requirement.

Electronic packers: it has continuous weighing system and it ensures that the bags separating from the nozzles have accurate weight of cement. The weight of filled bag is also displayed on the packer.

Multi-compartment silo.

Cross section of multi-compartment silo.

Jumbo bag transportation.

Jumbo bag packing.

followed by point count of areas occupied by various compounds. The second method, which is also applicable to powdered cement, involves X-ray diffraction of powder specimen. Calibration curves based on known mixtures of pure compounds, help to estimate the compound composition. As a rough and ready method, litre weight (bulk density) of clinker is made use of to ascertain the quality. A litre weight of about 1200 gms. is found to be satisfactory.

It is important to note that the strength properties of cement are considerably influenced by the cooling rate of clinker. This fact has of late attracted the attention of both the cement manufacturers and machinery producers. The experimental results reported by Enkegaard are shown in table 1.3.

Table 1.3. Influence of Rate of Cooling on Compressive Strength[1.3]

Type of cement	Cooling conditions	Compressive Strength MPa		
		3 days	7 days	28 days
Normal Cement	Quick	9.9	15.3	26
	Moderate	9.7	21.0	27
	Slow	9.7	19.3	24
	Very slow	8.7	18.7	23
High early strength cement	Quick	10.2	18.8	29
	Moderate	14.2	26.7	33
	Slow	10.2	21.0	29
	Very Slow	9.1	18.1	28

It can be seen from the table that a moderate rate of cooling of clinker in the rotary cooler will result in higher strength. By moderate cooling it is implied that from about 1200°C, the clinker is brought to about 500°C in about 15 minutes and from the 500°C the temperature is brought down to normal atmospheric temperature in about 10 minutes.

The rate of cooling influences the degree of crystallisation, the size of the crystal and the amount of amorphous materials present in the clinker. The properties of this amorphous material for similar chemical composition will be different from the one which is crystallined.

Chemical Composition

The raw materials used for the manufacture of cement consist mainly of lime, silica, alumina and iron oxide. These oxides interact with one another in the kiln at high temperature to form more complex compounds. The relative proportions of these oxide compositions are responsible for influencing the various properties of cement; in addition to rate of cooling and fineness of grinding. Table 1.4 shows the approximate oxide composition limits of ordinary Portland cement.

Table 1.4. Approximate Oxide Composition Limits of Ordinary Portland Cement

Oxide	Per cent content
CaO	60–67
SiO_2	17–25
Al_2O_3	3.0–8.0
Fe_2O_3	0.5–6.0
MgO	0.1–4.0
Alkalies (K_2O, Na_2O)	0.4–1.3
SO_3	1.3–3.0

Indian standard specification for 33 grade cement, IS 269-1989, specifies the following chemical requirements:

(a) Ratio of percentage of lime to percentage of silica, alumina and iron oxide; known as Lime Saturation Factor, when calculated by the formula

$$\frac{CaO - 0.7\,SO_3}{2.8\,SiO_2 + 1.2\,Al_2O_3 + 0.65\,Fe_2O_3}$$ Not greater than 1.02 and not less than 0.66

(b) Ratio of percentage of alumina to that of iron oxide	Not less tan 0.66
(c) Weight of insoluble residue	Not more than 4 per cent
(d) Weight of magnesia	Not more than 6 per cent
(e) Total sulphur content, calculated as sulphuric when	Not more than 2.5%
anhydride (SO_3)	C_3A is 5% or less. Not more than 3%, when C_3A is more than 5%
(f) Total loss on ignition	Not more than 5 per cent

As mentioned earlier the oxides persent in the raw materials when subjected to high clinkering temperature combine with each other to form complex compounds. The identification of the major compounds is largely based on R.H. Bogue's work and hence it is called "Bogue's Compounds". The four compounds usually regarded as major compounds are listed in table 1.5.

Table 1.5. Bogue's Compounds

Name of Compound	Formula	Abbreviated Formula
Tricalcium silicate	$3\,CaO.SiO_2$	C_3S
Dicalcium silicate	$2\,CaO.Sio_2$	C_2S
Tricalcium aluminate	$3\,Cao.Al_2O_3$	C_3A
Tetracalcium aluminoferrite	$4\,CaO.Al_2O_3.Fe_2O_3$	C_4AF

It is to be noted that for simplicity's sake abbreviated notations are used. C stands for CaO, S stands for SiO_2, A for Al_2O_3, F for Fe_2O_3 and H for H_2O.

The equations suggested by Bogue for calculating the percentages of major compounds are given below.

$$C_3S = 4.07\,(CaO) - 7.60\,(SiO_2) - 6.72\,(Al_2O_3) - 1.43\,(Fe_2O_3) - 2.85\,(SO_3)$$

$$C_2S = 2.87\,(SiO_2) - 0.754\,(3CaO.SiO_2)$$

$$C_3A = 2.65\,(Al_2O_3) - 1.69\,(Fe_2O_3)$$

$$C_4AF = 3.04\,(Fe_2O_3)$$

The oxide shown within the brackets represents the percentage of the same in the raw materials.

Table 1.6. The Oxide Composition of a Typical Portland Cement and the Corrosponding Calculated Compound Composition.

Oxide composition Per cent		Calculated compound composition using Bogue's equation per cent	
CaO	63	C_3S	54.1
SiO_2	20	C_2S	16.6
Al_2O_3	6	C_3A	10.8
Fe_2O_3	3	C_4AF	9.1
MgO	1.5		
SO_2	2		
K_2O	1.0		
Na_2O			

In addition to the four major compounds, there are many minor compounds formed in the kiln. The influence of these minor compounds on the properties of cement or hydrated compounds is not significant. Two of the minor oxides namely K_2O and Na_2O referred to as alkalis in cement are of some importance. This aspect will be dealt with later when discussing alkali-aggregate reaction. The oxide composition of typical Portland cement and the corresponding calculated compound composition is shown in table 1.6.

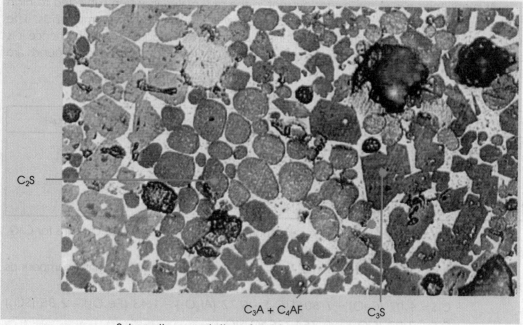

Schematic presentation of various compounds in clinker
Courtesy : All the photographs on manufacture of cement are by Grasim Industries Cement Division

Tricalcium silicate and dicalcium silicate are the most important compounds responsible for strength. Together they constitute 70 to 80 per cent of cement. The average C_3S content in modern cement is about 45 per cent and that of C_2S is about 25 per cent. The sum of the contents of C_3A and C_4AF has decreased slightly in modern cements. The calculated quantity of the compounds in cement varies greatly even for a relatively small change in the oxide composition of the raw materials. To manufacture a cement of stipulated compound composition, it becomes absolutely necessary to closely control the oxide composition of the raw materials. An increase in lime content beyond a certain value makes it difficult to combine with other compounds and free lime will exist in the clinker which causes unsoundness in cement. An increase in silica content at the expense of the content of alumina and ferric oxide will make the cement difficult to fuse and form clinker. Cements with a high total alumina and high ferric oxide content is favourable to the production of high early strengths in cement. This is perhaps due to the influence of these oxides for the complete combining of the entire quantity of lime present to form tricalcium silicate.

The advancement made in the various spheres of science and technology has helped us to recognise and understand the micro structure of the cement compounds before hydration and after hydration. The X-ray powder diffraction method, X-ray fluorescence method and use of powerful electron microscope capable of magnifying 50,000 times or even more has helped to reveal the crystalline or amorphous structure of the unhydrated or hydrated cement.

Both Le Chatelier and Tornebohm observed four different kinds of crystals in thin sections of cement clinkers. Tornebohm called these four kinds of crystals as Alite, Belite, Celite and Felite. Tornebohm's description of the minerals in cement was found to be similar to Bogue's description of the compounds. Therefore, Bogue's compounds C_3S, C_2S, C_3A and C_4AF are sometimes called in literature as Alite, Belite, Celite and Felite respectively.

Cement and hydration of Portland cement can be schematically represented as below:

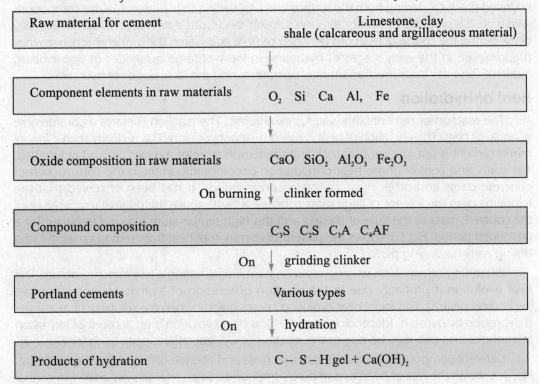

| Raw material for cement | Limestone, clay
shale (calcareous and argillaceous material) |

↓

| Component elements in raw materials | O_2 Si Ca Al, Fe |

↓

| Oxide composition in raw materials | CaO SiO_2 Al_2O_3 Fe_2O_3 |

On burning ↓ clinker formed

| Compound composition | C_3S C_2S C_3A C_4AF |

On ↓ grinding clinker

| Portland cements | Various types |

On ↓ hydration

| Products of hydration | C – S – H gel + $Ca(OH)_2$ |

Hydration of Cement

Anhydrous cement does not bind fine and coarse aggregate. It acquires adhesive property only when mixed with water. The chemical reactions that take place between cement and water is referred as hydration of cement.

The chemistry of concrete is essentially the chemistry of the reaction between cement and water. On account of hydration certain products are formed. These products are important because they have cementing or adhesive value. The quality, quantity, continuity, stability and the rate of formation of the hydration products are important.

Anhydrous cement compounds when mixed with water, react with each other to form hydrated compounds of very low solubility. The hydration of cement can be visualised in two ways. The first is "through solution" mechanism. In this the cement compounds dissolve to produce a supersaturated solution from which different hydrated products get precipitated. The second possibility is

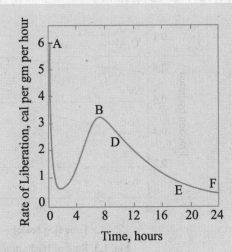

Fig. 1.2. Heat Liberation from a Setting Cement.[1.4]

that water attacks cement compounds in the solid state converting the compounds into hydrated products starting from the surface and proceeding to the interior of the compounds with time. It is probable that both "through solution" and "solid state" types of mechanism may occur during the course of reactions between cement and water. The former mechanism may predominate in the early stages of hydration in view of large quantities of water being available, and the latter mechanism may operate during the later stages of hydration.

Heat of Hydration

The reaction of cement with water is exothermic. The reaction liberates a considerable quantity of heat. This liberation of heat is called heat of hydration. This is clearly seen if freshly mixed cement is put in a vaccum flask and the temperature of the mass is read at intervals. The study and control of the heat of hydration becomes important in the construction of concrete dams and other mass concrete constructions. It has been observed that the temperature in the interior of large mass concrete is 50°C above the original temperature of the concrete mass at the time of placing and this high temperature is found to persist for a prolonged period. Fig 1.2 shows the pattern of liberation of heat from setting cement[1.4] and during early hardening period.

On mixing cement with water, a rapid heat evolution, lasting a few minutes, occurs. This heat evolution is probably due to the reaction of solution of aluminates and sulphates (ascending peak A). This initial heat evolution ceases quickly when the solubility of aluminate is depressed by gypsum. (decending peak A). Next heat evolution is on account of formation of ettringite and also may be due to the reaction of C_3S (ascending peak B). Refer Fig. 1.2.

Different compounds hydrate at different rates and liberate different quantities of heat. Fig. 1.3 shows the rate of hydration of pure compounds. Since retarders are added to control the flash setting properties of C_3A, actually the early heat of hydration is mainly contributed from the hydration of C_3S. Fineness of cement also influences the rate of development of heat but not the total heat. The total quantity of heat generated in the complete hydration will depend upon the relative quantities of the major compounds present in a cement.

Analysis of heat of hydration data of large number of cements, Verbec and Foster[1.5] computed heat evolution of four major compounds of cement. Table 1.7. shows the heats of hydration of four compounds.

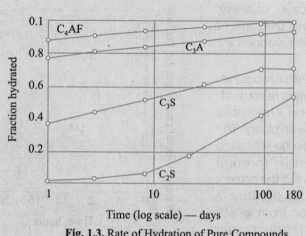

Fig. 1.3. Rate of Hydration of Pure Compounds.

Table 1.7. Heat of Hydration[1.5]

Compound	Heat of hydration at the given age (cal/g)		
	3 days	90 days	13 years
C_3S	58	104	122
C_2S	12	42	59
C_3A	212	311	324
C_4AF	69	98	102

Since the heat of hydration of cement is an additive property, it can be predicted from an expression of the type $\quad H = aA + bB + cC + dD$

Where H represents the heat of hydration, A, B, C, and D are the percentage contents of C_3S, C_2S, C_3A and C_4AF. and a, b, c and d are coefficients representing the contribution of 1 per cent of the corresponding compound to the heat of hydration.

Normal cement generally produces 89-90 cal/g in 7 days and 90 to 100 cal/g in 28 days.

The hydration process is not an instantaneous one. The reaction is faster in the early period and continues idenfinitely at a decreasing rate. Complete hydration cannot be obtained under a period of one year or more unless the cement is very finely ground and reground with excess of water to expose fresh surfaces at intervals. Otherwise, the product obtained shows unattacked cores of tricalcium silicate surrounded by a layer of hydrated silicate, which being relatively impervious to water, renders further attack slow. It has been observed that after 28 days of curing, cement grains have been found to have hydrated to a depth of only 4μ. It has also been observed that complete hydration under normal condition is possible only for cement particles smaller than 50μ.

A grain of cement may contain many crystals of C_3S or others. The largest crystals of C_3S or C_2S are about 40μ. An average size would be 15-20μ. It is probable that the C_2S crystals present in the surface of a cement grain may get hydrated and a more reactive compound like C_3S lying in the interior of a cement grain may not get hydrated.

The hydrated product of the cement compound in a grain of cement adheres firmly to the unhydrated core in the grains of cement. That is to say unhydrated cement left in a grain of cement will not reduce the strength of cement mortar or concrete, as long as the products of hydration are well compacted. Abrams obtained strength of the order of 280 MPa using mixes with a water/cement ratio as low as 0.08. Essentially he has applied tremendous pressure to obtain proper compaction of such a mixture. Owing to such a low water/cement ratio, hydration must have been possible only at the surface of cement grains, and a considerable portion of cement grains must have remained in an unhydrated condition.

The present day High Performance concrete is made with water cement ratio in the region of 0.25 in which case it is possible that a considerable portion of cement grain remains unhydrated in the core. Only surface hydration takes place. The unhydrated core of cement grain can be deemed to work as very fine aggregates in the whole system.

Calcium Silicate Hydrates

During the course of reaction of C_3S and C_2S with water, calcium silicate hydrate, abbreviated C-S-H and calcium hydroxide, $Ca(OH)_2$ are formed. Calcium silicate hydrates are the most important products. It is the essence that determines the good properties of concrete.

It makes up 50-60 per cent of the volume of solids in a completely hydrated cement paste. The fact that term C-S-H is hyphenated signifies that C-S-H is not a well defined compound. The morphology of C-S-H shows a poorly crystalline fibrous mass.

It was considered doubtful that the product of hydration of both C_3S and C_2S results in the formation of the same hydrated compound. But later on it was seen that ultimately the hydrates of C_3S and C_2S will turn out to be the same. The following are the approximate equations showing the reactions of C_3S and C_2S with water.

$$2 (3\ CaO.SiO_2) + 6H_2O \rightarrow 3\ CaO.2\ SiO_2.\ 3H_2O + 3Ca(OH)_2$$

or it can be written as $2C_3S \quad + \quad 6H \quad \rightarrow \quad C_3S_2H_3 \quad + 3Ca(OH)_2$

The corresponding weights involved are

$$100 \quad + \quad 24 \quad \rightarrow \quad 75 \quad + \quad 49.$$

Similarly, $\quad 2 (2\ CaO.SiO_2) + 4\ H_2O \rightarrow 3Cao.2\ SiO_2.\ 3H_2O + Ca(OH)_2$

or it can be written as

$$2\ C_2S \quad + \quad 4\ H \rightarrow \quad C_3S_2H_3 \quad + \quad Ca\ (OH)_2$$

The corresponding weights involved are

$$100 \quad + \quad 21 \rightarrow \quad 99 \quad + \quad 22$$

However, the simple equations given above do not bring out the complexities of the actual reactions.

It can be seen that C_3S produces a comparatively lesser quantity of calcium silicate hydrates and more quantity of $Ca(OH)_2$ than that formed in the hydration of C_2S. $Ca(OH)_2$ is not a desirable product in the concrete mass, it is soluble in water and gets leached out making the concrete porous, particularly in hydraulic structures. Under such conditions it is useful to use cement with higher percentage of C_2S content.

C_3S readily reacts with water and produces more heat of hydration. It is responsible for early strength of concrete. A cement with more C_3S content is better for cold weather concreting. The quality and density of calcium silicate hydrate formed out of C_3S is slightly inferior to that formed by C_2S. The early strength of concrete is due to C_3S.

C_2S hydrates rather slowly. It is responsible for the later strength of concrete. It produces less heat of hydration. The calcium silicate hydrate formed is rather dense and its specific surface is higher. In general, the quality of the proudct of hydration of C_2S is better than that produced in the hydration of C_3S. Fig 1.4 shows the development of strength of pure compounds.

Calcium Hydroxide

The other products of hydration of C_3S and C_2S is calcium hydroxide. In contrast to the C-S-H, the calcium hydroxide is a compound with a distinctive hexagonal prism morphology. It constitutes 20 to 25 per cent of the volume of solids in the hydrated paste. The lack of durability of concrete, is on account of the presence of calcium hydroxide. The calcium hydroxide also reacts with sulphates present in soils or water to form calcium sulphate which further reacts with C_3A and cause deterioration of concrete. This is known as sulphate attack. To reduce the quantity of $Ca(OH)_2$ in concrete and to overcome its bad effects by converting it into cementitious product is an advancement in concrete technology. The use of blending materials such as fly ash, silica fume and such other pozzolanic materials are the steps to overcome bad effect of $Ca(OH)_2$ in concrete. This aspect will be dealt in greater detail later.

The only advantage is that $Ca(OH)_2$, being alkaline in nature maintain pH value around 13 in the concrete which resists the corrosion of reinforcements.

Calcium Aluminate Hydrates

The hydration of aluminates has been the subject of numerous investigations, but there is still some uncertainty about some of the reported products. Due to the hydration of C_3A, a calcium aluminate system $CaO - Al_2O_3 - H_2O$ is formed. The cubic compound C_3AH_6 is probably the only stable compound formed which remains stable upto about 225°C.

The reaction of pure C_3A with water is very fast and this may lead to flash set. To prevent this flash set, gypsum is added at the time of grinding the cement clinker. The quantity of gypsum added has a bearing on the quantity of C_3A present.

The hydrated aluminates do not contribute anything to the strength of concrete. On the other hand, their presence is harmful to the durability of concrete particularly where the concrete is likely to be attacked by sulphates. As it hydrates very fast it may contribute a little to the early strength.

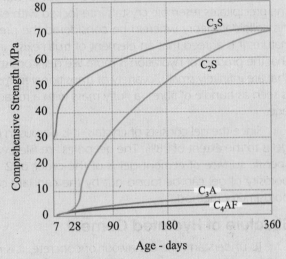

Fig. 1.4. Development of Strength of Pure Compounds

On hydration, C_4AF is believed to form a system of the form $CaO - Fe_2O_3 - H_2O$. A hydrated calcium ferrite of the form C_3FH_6 is comparatively more stable. This hydrated product also does not contribute anything to the strength. The hydrates of C_4AF show a comparatively higher resistance to the attack of sulphates than the hydrates of calcium aluminate.

From the standpoint of hydration, it is convenient to discuss C_3A and C_4AF together, because the products formed in the presence of gypsum are similar. Gypsum and alkalies go into solution quickly and the solubility of C_3A is depressed. Depending upon the concentration of aluminate and sulphate ions in solution, the pricipitating crystalline product is either the calcium aluminate trisulphate hydrate $(C_6A\overline{S}_3H_{32})$ or calcium aluminate monosulhphate hydrate $(C_4A\overline{S}H_{18})$. The calcium aluminate trisulphate hydrate is known as ettringite.

Ettringite is usually the first to hydrate and crystallise as short prismatic needle on account of the high sulphate/aluminate ratio in solution phase during the first hour of hydration. When sulphate in solution gets depleted, the aluminate concentration goes up due to renewed hydration of C_3A and C_4AF. At this stage ettringite becomes unstable and is gradually converted into mono-sulphate, which is the final product of hydration of portland cements containing more than 5 percent C_3A.

The amount of gypsum added has significant bearing on the quantity of aluminate in the cement. The maintenance of aluminate-to-sulphate ratio balance the normal setting behaviour of cement paste. The various setting phenomena affected by an imbalance in the $A/\overline{S}$ ratio is of practical significance in concrete technology.

Many theories have been put forward to explain what actually is formed in the hydration of cement compounds with water. It has been said earliiar that product consisting of $(CaO.SiO_2.H_2O)$ and $Ca(OH)_2$ are formed in the hydration of calcium silicates. $Ca(OH)_2$ is an unimportant product, and the really significant product is $(CaO.SiO_2.H_2O)$. For simplicity's sake this product of hydration is sometime called tobermorite gel because of its structural similarity to a naturally occurring mineral tobermorite. But very commonly the product of hydration is referred to as C – S – H gel.

It may not be exactly correct to call the product of hydrations as gel. Le chatelier identified the products as crystalline in nature and put forward his crystalline theory. He explained that the precipitates resemble crystals interlocked with each other. Later on Michaelis put forward his colloidal theory wherein he considered the precipitates as colloidal mass, gelatinous in nature. It is agreed that an element of truth exists in both these theories. It is accepted now that the product of hydration is more like gel, consisting of poorly formed, thin, fibrous crystals that are infinitely small. A variety of transitional forms are also believed to exist and the whole is seen as bundle of fibres, a fluffy mass with a refractive index of 1.5 to 1.55, increasing with age.

Since the gel consists of crystals, it is porous in nature. It is estimated that the porosity of gel is to the extent of 28%. The gel pores are filled with water. The pores are so small that the specific surface of cement gel is of the order of 2 million sq. cm. per gm. of cement. The porosity of gel can be found out by the capillary condensation method or by the mercury porosimetry method.

Structure of Hydrated Cement

To understand the behaviour of concrete, it is necessary to acquaint ourselves with the structure of hydrated hardened cement paste. If the concrete is considered as two phase material, namely, the paste phase and the aggregate phase, the understanding of the paste phase becomes more important as it influences the behaviour of concrete to a much greater extent. It will be discussed later that the strength, the permeability, the durability, the drying shrinkage, the elastic properties, the creep and volume change properties of concrete is greatly influenced by the paste structure. The aggregate phase though important, has lesser influence on the properties of concrete than the paste phase. Therefore, in our study to understand concrete, it is important that we have a deep understanding of the structure of the hydrated hardened cement paste at a phenomenological level.

Transition Zone

Concrete is generally considered as two phase material *i.e.*, paste phase and aggregates phase. At macro level it is seen that aggregate particles are dispersed in a matrix of cement paste. At the microscopic level, the complexities of the concrete begin to show up, particularly in the vicinity of large aggregate particles. This area can be considered as a third phase, the transition zone, which represents the interfacial region between the particles of coarse aggregate and hardened cement paste. Transition zone is generally a plane of weakness and, therefore, has far greater influence on the mechanical behaviour of concrete.

Although transition zone is composed of same bulk cement paste, the quality of paste in the transition zone is of poorer quality. Firstly due to internal bleeding, water accumulate below elongated, flaky and large pieces of aggregates. This reduces the bond between paste and aggregate in general. If we go into little greater detail, the size and concentration of crystalline compounds such as calcium hydroxide and ettringite are also larger in the transition zone. Such a situation account for the lower strength of transition zone than bulk cement paste in concrete.

Due to drying shrinkage or temperature variation, the transition zone develops microcracks even before a structures is loaded. When structure is loaded and at high stress levels, these microcracks propagate and bigger chracks are formed resulting in failure of bond. Therefore, transition zone, generally the weakest link of the chain, is considered strength limiting phase in concrete. It is because of the presence of transition zone that concrete fails at considerably lower stress level than the strength of bulk paste or aggregate.

Sometimes it may be necessary for us to look into the structure of hardening concrete also. The rate and extent of hydration of cement have been investigated in the past using a variety of techniques. The techniques used to study the structure of cement paste include measurements of setting time, compressive strength, the quantity of heat of hydration evolved, the optical and electron microscope studies coupled with chemical analysis and thermal analysis of hydration products. Continuous monitoring of reactions by X-ray diffractions and conduction calorimetry has also been used for the study.

Measurements of heat evolved during the exothermic reactions also gives valuable insight into the nature of hydration reactions. Since approximately 50% of a total heat evolution

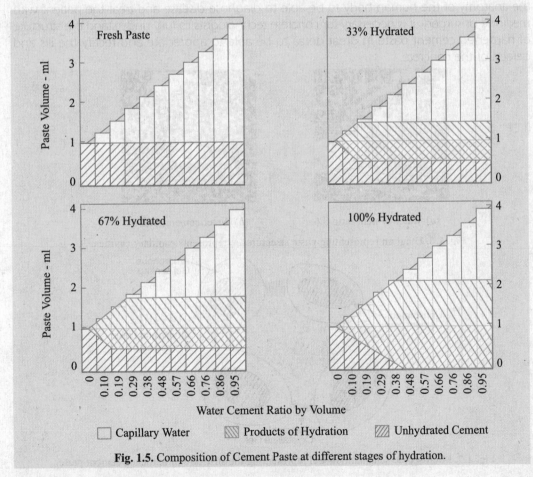

Fig. 1.5. Composition of Cement Paste at different stages of hydration.

occurs during the first 3 days of hydration, a continuous record of the rate of heat liberation during this time is extremely useful in understanding the degree of hydration and the resultant structure of the hardening cement paste. Fig. 1.5 shows the composition of cement pastes at different stages of hydration.

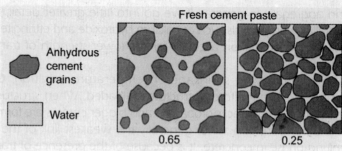

Schematic representation of two fresh cement pastes having a water/cement ratio of 0.65 and 0.25.

The mechanical properties of the hardened concrete depend more on the physical structure of the products of hydration than on the chemical composition of the cement. Mortar and concrete, shrinks and cracks, offers varying chemical resistance to different situations, creeps in different magnitude, and in short, exhibits complex behaviour under different conditions. Eventhough it is difficult to explain the behaviour of concrete fully and exactly, it is possible to explain the behaviour of concrete on better understanding of the structure of the hardened cement paste. Just as it is necessary for doctors to understand in great detail the anatomy of the human body to be able to diagnose disease and treat the patient with medicine or surgery, it is necessary for concrete technologists to fully understand the structure of hardened cement paste in great detail to be able to appreciate and rectify the ills and defects of the concrete.

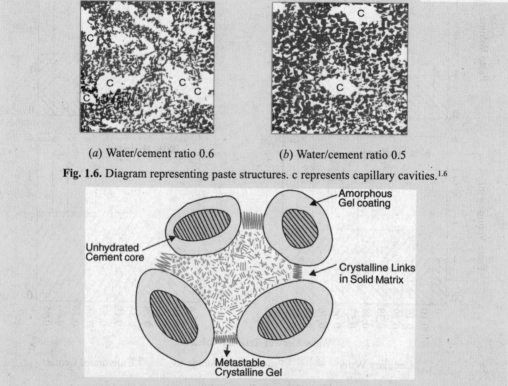

(a) Water/cement ratio 0.6   (b) Water/cement ratio 0.5

Fig. 1.6. Diagram representing paste structures. c represents capillary cavities.[1.6]

Fig. 1.7. Microscopic schematic model representing the structure of hardened cement paste.

For simplicity's sake we will consider only the structure of the paste phase. Fresh cement paste is a plastic mass consisting of water and cement. With the lapse of time, say one hour, the hardening paste consists of hydrates of various compounds, unhydrated cement particles and water. With further lapse of time the quantity of unhydrated cement left in the paste decreases and the hydrates of the various compounds increase. Some of the mixing water is used up for chemical reaction, and some water occupies the gel-pores and the remaining water remains in the paste. After a sufficiently long time (say a month) the hydrated paste can be considered to be consisting of about 85 to 90% of hydrates of the various compounds and 10 to 15 per cent of unhydrated cement. The mixing water is partly used up in the chemical reactions. Part of it occupies the gel-pores and the remaining water unwanted for hydration or for filling in the gel-pores causes capillary cavities. These capillary cavities may have been fully filled with water or partly with water or may be fully empty depending upon the age and the ambient temperature and humidity conditions. Figure 1.6 (*a*) and (*b*) schematically depict the structure of hydrated cement paste. The dark portion represents gel. The small gap within the dark portion represents gel-pores and big space such as marked "*c*" represents capillary cavities.[1.6] Fig. 1.7 represents the microscopic schematic model of structure of hardened cement paste.

Water Requirements for Hydration

It has been brought out earlier that C_3S requires 24% of water by weight of cement and C_2S requires 21%. It has also been estimated that on an average 23% of water by weight of cement is required for chemical reaction with Portland cement compounds. This 23% of water chemically combines with cement and, therefore, it is called bound water. A certain quantity of water is imbibed within the gel-pores. This water is known as gel-water. It can be said that bound water and gel-water are complimentary to each other. If the quantity of water is inadequate to fill up the gel-pores, the formations of gel itself will stop and if the formation of gel stops there is no question of gel-pores being present. It has been further estimated that about 15 per cent by weight of cement is required to fill up the gel-pores. Therefore, a total 38 per cent of water by weight of cement is required for the complete chemical reactions and to occupy the space within gel-pores. If water equal to 38 per cent by weight of cement is

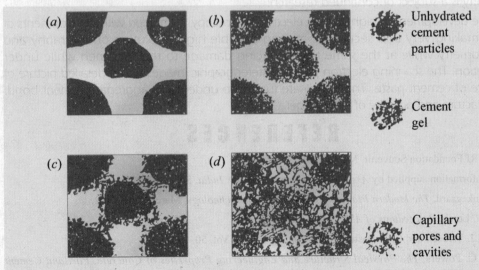

(*a*)   (*b*)   Unhydrated cement particles

Cement gel

(*c*)   (*d*)   Capillary pores and cavities

Fig. 1.8. Diagrammatic representation of the Hydration process and formation of cement gel.

only used it can be noticed that the resultant paste will undergo full hydration and no extra water will be available for the formation of undesirable capillary cavities. On the other hand, if more than 38 per cent of water is used, then the excess water will cause undesirable capillary cavities. Therefore greater the water above the minimum required is used (38 per cent), the more will be the undesirable capillary cavities. In all this it is assumed that hydration is taking place in a sealed container, where moisture to and from the paste does not take place.

It can be seen that the capillary cavities become larger with increased water/cement ratio. With lower w/c ratio the cement particles are closer together. With the progress of hydration, when the volume of anhydrous cement increases, the product of hydration also increases. The increase in the volume of gel due to complete hydration could fill up the space earlier occupied by water upto a w/c ratio of 0.6 or so. If the w/c ratio is more than 0.7, the increase in volume of the hydrated product would never be sufficient to fill up the voids created by water. Such concrete would ever remain as porous mass. This is to say that gel occupies more and more space, that once occupied by mixing water. It has been estimated that the volume of gel would be about twice the volume of unhydrated cement.

The diagrammatic representation of progress of hydration is sown in Fig. 1.8. Fig. 1.8 (*a*) represents the state of cement particles immediately when dispersed in an aqueous solution. During the first few minutes, the reaction rate is rapid and the calcium silicate hydrate forms a coating around the cement grains See Fig. 1.8 (*b*). As hydration proceeds, hydration products, including calcium hydroxide are precipitated from the saturated solution and bridge the gap between the cement grains, and the paste stiffens into its final shape, see Fig. 1.8 (*c*). Further hyudration involving some complex form of diffusion process results in further deposition of the cement gel at the expense of the unhydrated cement and capillary pore-water Fig. 1.8 (*d*).

What has been described briefly is the approximate structure of hardened cement paste on account of the hydration of some of the major compounds. Very little cognisance is taken of the product of hydration of the other major and minor compounds in cement. The morphology of product of hydration and the study of structure of hardened cement paste in its entirety is a subject of continued research.

The development of high voltage electron microscopy, combined with developments of skill in making very thin sections is making possible high resolution photography and diffractometry while at the same time reducing damage to the specimen while under observation. The scanning electron provides stereographic images and a detailed picture of structure of cement paste. These facilitate further to understand aggregate cement bond, micro fracture and porosity of cement gel.

REFERENCES

1.1   CRI Foundation Souvenir, March 1970.

1.2   Information supplied by *Associated Cement Company, India,* Sept. 1978.

1.3   Enkegaard, *The Modern Planetary Cooler, Cement Technology*, March/April 1992.

1.4   W. Lerch, *Proceedings of ASTM,* Vol. 46–1946.

1.5   G.J. Verbeck and C.W. Foster, *Proceedings of ASTM*, Vol. 50–1958

1.6   T.C. Powers, *The Physical Structure and Engineering Properties of Concrete, Portland Cement Association Research Department Bulletin* 90, July 1958.

1.7   Grasim Industries Cement Division : Technical Literature.

Part view of Cement Factory
Courtesy : Grasim Industries Cement Division

CHAPTER 2

Types of Cement and Testing of Cement

In the previous chapter we have discussed various properties of Portland cement in general. We have seen that cements exhibit different properties and characteristics depending upon their chemical compositions. By changing the fineness of grinding or the oxide composition, cement can be made to exhibit different properties. In the past continuous efforts were made to produce different kinds of cement, suitable for different situations by changing oxide composition and fineness of grinding. With the extensive use of cement, for widely varying conditions, the types of cement that could be made only by varying the relative proportions of the oxide compositions, were not found to be sufficient. Recourses have been taken to add one or two more new materials, known as additives, to the clinker at the time of grinding, or to the use of entirely different basic raw materials in the manufacture of cement.

The use of additives, changing chemical composition, and use of different raw materials have resulted in the availability of many types of cements

27

to cater to the need of the construction industries for specific purposes. In this chapter we shall deal with the properties and use of various kinds of cement. These cements are classified as Portland cements and non-Portland cements. The distinction is mainly based on the methods of manufacture. The Portland and Non-Portland cements generally used are listed below: Indian standard specification number is also given against these elements.

Types of Cement

(a) Ordinary Portland Cement
   (i)   Ordinary Portland Cement 33 Grade– IS 269: 1989
   (ii) Ordinary Portland Cement 43 Grade– IS 8112: 1989
   (iii) Ordinary Portland Cement 53 Grade– IS 12269: 1987
(b) Rapid Hardening Cement   – IS 8041: 1990
(c) Extra Rapid Hardening Cement   –   –
(d) Sulphate Resisting Cement   – IS 12330: 1988
(e) Portland Slag Cement   – IS 455: 1989
(f) Quick Setting Cement   –   –
(g) Super Sulphated Cement   – IS 6909: 1990
(h) Low Heat Cement   – IS 12600: 1989
(j) Portland Pozzolana Cement   – IS 1489 (Part I) 1991 (fly ash based)
                               – IS 1489 (Part II) 1991 (calcined clay based)
(k) Air Entraining Cement   –   –
(l) Coloured Cement: White Cement   – IS 8042: 1989
(m) Hydrophobic Cement   – IS 8043: 1991
(n) Masonry Cement   – IS 3466: 1988
(o) Expansive Cement   –   –
(p) Oil Well Cement   – IS 8229: 1986
(q) Rediset Cement   –   –
(r) Concrete Sleeper grade Cement   – IRS-T 40: 1985
(s) High Alumina Cement   – IS 6452: 1989
(t) Very High Strength Cement   –   –

ASTM Classification

Before we discuss the above cements, for general information, it is necessary to see how Portland cement are classified under the ASTM (American Society for Testing Materials) standards. As per ASTM, cement is designated as Type I, Type II, Type III, Type IV, Type V and other minor types like Type IS, Type IP and Type IA IIA and IIIA.

Type I

For use in general concrete construction where the special properties specified for Types II, III, IV and V are not required (Ordinary Portland Cement).

Type II

For use in general concrete construction exposed to moderate sulphate action, or where moderate heat of hydration is required.

Type III

For use when high early strength is required (Rapid Hardening Cement).

Type IV

For use when low heat of hydration is required (Low Heat Cement).

Type V

For use when high sulphate resistance is required (Sulphate Resisting Cement).

ASTM standard also have cement of the type IS. This consist of an intimate and uniform blend of Portland Cement of type I and fine granulated slag. The slag content is between 25 and 70 per cent of the weight of Portland Blast-Furnace Slag Cement.

Type IP

This consist of an intimate and uniform blend of Portland Cement (or Portland Blast Furnace Slag Cement) and fine pozzolana in which the pozzolana content is between 15 and 40 per cent of the weight of the total cement.

Cross Section of Multi-compartment Silo for storing different types of cement.

Courtesy : Grasim Industries Cement Division

Type IA, IIA and IIIA

These are type I, II or III cement in which air-entraining agent is interground where air-entrainment in concrete is desired.

Ordinary Portland Cement

Ordinary Portland cement (OPC) is by far the most important type of cement. All the discussions that we have done in the previous chapter and most of the discussions that are going to be done in the coming chapters relate to OPC. Prior to 1987, there was only one grade of OPC which was governed by IS 269-1976. After 1987 higher grade cements were introduced in India. The OPC was classified into three grades, namely 33 grade, 43 grade and 53 grade depending upon the strength of the cement at 28 days when tested as per IS 4031-1988. If the 28 days strength is not less than 33N/mm², it is called 33 grade cement, if the strength is not less than 43N/mm², it is called 43 grade cement, and if the strength is not less then 53 N/mm², it is called 53 grade cement. But the actual strength obtained by these cements at the factory are much higher than the BIS specifications.

The physical and chemical properties of 33, 43 and 53 grade OPC are shown in Table 2.5 and 2.6.

It has been possible to upgrade the qualities of cement by using high quality limestone, modern equipments, closer on line control of constituents, maintaining better particle size distribution, finer grinding and better packing. Generally use of high grade cements offer many advantages for making stronger concrete. Although they are little costlier than low grade cement, they offer 10-20% savings in cement consumption and also they offer many other hidden benefits. One of the most important benefits is the faster rate of development of strength. In the modern construction activities, higher grade cements have become so popular that 33 grade cement is almost out of the market. Table 2.9 shows the grades of cement manufactured in various countries of the world.

The manufacture of OPC is decreasing all over the world in view of the popularity of blended cement on account of lower energy consumption, environmental pollution, economic and other technical reasons. In advanced western countries the use of OPC has come down to about 40 per cent of the total cement production. In India for the year 1998-99 out of the total cement production *i.e.*, 79 million tons, the production of OPC in 57.00 million tons *i.e.*, 70%. The production of PPC is 16 million tone *i.e.*, 19% and slag cement is 8 million tons *i.e.*, 10%. In the years to come the use of OPC may still come down, but all the same the OPC will remain as an important type for general construction.

The detail testing methods of OPC is separately discribed at the end of this chapter.

Rapid Hardening Cement (IS 8041-1990)

This cement is similar to ordinary Portland cement. As the name indicates it develops strength rapidly and as such it may be more appropriate to call it as high early strength cement. It is pointed out that rapid hardening cement which develops higher rate of development of strength should not be confused with quick-setting cement which only sets quickly. Rapid hardening cement develops at the age of three days, the same strength as that is expected of ordinary Portland cement at seven days.

The rapid rate of development of strength is attributed to the higher fineness of grinding (specific surface not less than 3250 sq. cm per gram) and higher C_3S and lower C_2S content.

A higher fineness of cement particles expose greater surface area for action of water and also higher proportion of C_3S results in quicker hydration. Consequently, capid hardening cement gives out much greater heat of hydration during the early period. Therefore, rapid hardening cement should not be used in mass concrete construction.

The use of rapid heading cement is recommended in the following situations:

(a) In pre-fabricated concrete construction.

(b) Where formwork is required to be removed early for re-use elsewhere,

(c) Road repair works,

(d) In cold weather concrete where the rapid rate of development of strength reduces the vulnerability of concrete to the frost damage.

The physical and chemical requirements of rapid hardening cement are shown in Tables 2.5 and 2.6 respectively.

Extra Rapid Hardening Cement

Extra rapid hardening cement is obtained by intergrinding calcium chloride with rapid hardening Portland cement. The normal addition of calcium chloride should not exceed 2 per cent by weight of the rapid hardening cement. It is necessary that the concrete made by using extra rapid hardening cement should be transported, placed and compacted and finished within about 20 minutes. It is also necessary that this cement should not be stored for more than a month.

Extra rapid hardening cement accelerates the setting and hardening process. A large quantity of heat is evolved in a very short time after placing. The acceleration of setting, hardening and evolution of this large quantity of heat in the early period of hydration makes the cement very suitable for concreting in cold weather, The strength of extra rapid hardening cement is about 25 per cent higher than that of rapid hardening cement at one or two days and 10–20 per cent higher at 7 days. The gain of strength will disappear with age and at 90 days the strength of extra rapid hardening cement or the ordinary portland cement may be nearly the same.

There is some evidence that there is small amount of initial corrosion of reinforcement when extra rapid hardening cement is used, but in general, this effect does not appear to be progressive and as such there is no harm in using extra rapid hardening cement in reinforced concrete work. However, its use in prestress concrete construction is prohibited.

In Russia, the attempt has been made to obtain the extra rapid hardening property by grinding the cement to a very fine degree to the extent of having a specific surface between 5000 to 6000 sq. cm/gm. The size of most of the particles are generally less than 3 microns[2.1]. It is found that this very finely ground cement is difficult to store as it is liable to air-set. It is not a common cement and hence it is not covered by Indian standard.

Sulphate Resisting Cement (IS 12330–1988)

Ordinary Portland cement is susceptible to the attack of sulphates, in particular to the action of magnesium sulphate. Sulphates react both with the free calcium hydroxide in set-cement to form calcium sulphate and with hydrate of calcium aluminate to form calcium sulphoaluminate, the volume of which is approximately 227% of the volume of the original aluminates. Their expansion within the frame work of hadened cement paste results in cracks and subsequent disruption. Solid sulphate do not attack the cement compound. Sulphates in solution permeate into hardened concrete and attack calcium hydroxide, hydrated calcium aluminate and even hydrated silicates.

The above is known as sulphate attack. Sulphate attack is greatly accelerated if accompanied by alternate wetting and drying which normally takes place in marine structures in the zone of tidal variations.

To remedy the sulphate attack, the use of cement with low C_3A content is found to be effective. Such cement with low C_3A and comparatively low C_4AF content is known as Sulphate Resisting Cement. In other words, this cement has a high silicate content. The specification generally limits the C_3A content to 5 per cent.

Tetracalcium Alumino Ferrite (C_3AF) varies in Normal Portland Cement between to 6 to 12%. Since it is often not feasible to reduce the Al_2O_3 content of the raw material, Fe_2O_3 may be added to the mix so that the C_4AF content increases at the expense of C_3A. IS code limits the total content of C_4AF and C_3A, as follows.

$$2C_3A + C_4AF \text{ should not exceed } 25\%.$$

In many of its physical properties, sulphate resisting cement is similar to ordinary Portland cement. The use of sulphate resisting cement is recommended under the following conditions:

(a) Concrete to be used in marine condition;
(b) Concrete to be used in foundation and basement, where soil is infested with sulphates;
(c) Concrete used for fabrication of pipes which are likely to be buried in marshy region or sulphate bearing soils;
(d) Concrete to be used in the construction of sewage treatment works.

Portland Slag Cement (PSC) (IS 455–1989)

Portland slag cement is obtained by mixing Portland cement clinker, gypsum and granulated blast furnace slag in suitable proportions and grinding the mixture to get a thorough and intimate mixture between the constituents. It may also be manufactured by separately grinding Portland cement clinker, gypsum and ground granulated blast furnace slag and later mixing them intimately. The resultant product is a cement which has physical properties similar to those of ordinary Portland cement. In addition, it has low heat of hydration and is relatively better resistant to chlorides, soils and water containing excessive amount of sulphates or alkali metals, alumina and iron, as well as, to acidic waters, and therefore, this can be used for marine works with advantage.

The manufacture of blast furnace slag cement has been developed primarily to utilize blast furnace slag, a waste product from blast furnaces. The development of this type of cement has considerably increased the total output of cement production in India and has, in addition, provided a scope for profitable use for an otherwise waste product. During 98-99 India produced 10% slag cement out of 79 million tons.

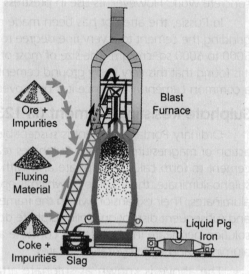

Schematic representation of production of blast furnace slag.

The quantity of granulated slag mixed with portland clinker will range from 25-65 per cent. In different countries this cement is known in different names. The quantity of slag mixed also will vary from country to country the maximum being upto 85 per cent. Early strength is mainly due to the cement clinker fraction and later strength is that due to the slag fraction. Separate grinding is used as an easy means of verying the slag clinker proportion in the finished cement to meet the market demand. Recently, under Bombay Sewage disposal project at Bandra, they have used 70% ground granulated blast furnace slag (GGBS) and 30% cement for making grout to fill up the trench around precast sewer 3.5 m dia embedded 40 m below MSL.

Portland blast furnace cement is similar to ordinary Portland cement with respect to fineness, setting time, soundness and strength. It is generally recognised that the rate of hardening of Portland blast furnace slag cement in mortar or concrete is somewhat slower than that of ordinary Portland cement during the first 28 days, but thereafter increases, so that at 12 months the strength becomes close to or even exceeds those of Portland cement. The heat of hydration of Portland blast furnace cement is lower than that of ordinary Portland cement. So this cement can be used in mass concrete structures with advantage. However, in cold weather the low heat of hydration of Portland blast furnace cement coupled with moderately low rate of strength development, can lead to frost damage.

Extensive research shows that the presence of GGBS leads to the enhancement of the intrinsic properties of the concrete both in fresh and hardened states. The major advantages currently recognised are:

   (a) Reduced heat of hydration;

   (b) Refinement of pore structure;

   (c) Reduced permeability;

(d) Increased resistance to chemical attack.

It is seen that in India when the Portland blast furnace slag cement was first introduced it met with considerable suspicion and resistance by the users. This is just because some manufacturers did not use the right quality of slag. It has been pointed out that only glassy granulated slag could be used for the manufacture of slag cement. Air-cooled crystallined slag cannot be used for providing cementitious property. The slag which is used in the manufacture of various slag cement is chilled very rapidly either by pouring it into a large body of water or by subjecting the slag stream to jets of water, or of air and water. The purpose is to cool the slag quickly so that crystallisation is prevented and it solidifies as glass. The product is called granulated slag. Only in this form the slag should be used for slag cement. It the slag prepared in any other form is used, the required quality of the cement will not be obtained.

Portland slag cement exhibits very low diffusivity to chloride ions and such slag cement gives better resistance to corrosion of steel reinforcement.

Table 2. 1. Diffusion of chloride ions at 25°C in cement pastes of w/c 0.5

Type of cement	Diffusivity (x 10^{-9} cm²/s)
SRPC*	100.0
OPC	44.7
70% OPC/30% Fly ash	14.7
35% OPC/ 65% GGBS	4.1

SRPC* – Sulphate resisting Portland cement.

Application of GGBS Concrete

In recent years the use of GGBS concrete is well recognised. Combining GGBS and OPC at mixer is treated as equivalent to factory made PSC. Concrete with different properties can be made by varying the proportions of GGBS.

While placing large pours of concrete it is vital to minimise the risk of early age thermal cracking by controlling the rate of temperature rise. One of the accepted methods is through the use of GGBS concrete containing 50% to 90% GGBS. Generally, a combination of 70% GGBS and 30% OPC is recommended. Resistance to chemical attack may be enhanced by using GGBS in concrete. Resistance to acid attack may be improved through the use of 70% GGBS. To counter the problem of sulphate and chloride attack 40% to 70% GGBS may be used. There is a general consensus among concrete technologists that the risk of ASR can be minimised by using at least 50% GGBS. GGBS concrete is also recommended for use in water retaining structures. Aggressive water can affect concrete foundations. In such conditions GGBS concrete can perform better.

Quick Setting Cement

This cement as the name indicates sets very early. The early setting property is brought out by reducing the gypsum content at the time of clinker grinding. This cement is required to be mixed, placed and compacted very early. It is used mostly in under water construction where pumping is involved. Use of quick setting cement in such conditions reduces the pumping time and makes it economical. Quick setting cement may also find its use in some typical grouting operations.

Super Sulphated Cement (IS 6909–1990)

Super sulphated cement is manufactured by grinding together a mixture of 80-85 per cent granulated slag, 10-15 per cent hard burnt gypsum, and about 5 per cent Portland cement clinker. The product is ground finer than that of Portland cement. Specific surface must not be less than 4000 cm^2 per gm. The super-sulphated cement is extensively used in Belgium, where it is known as "ciment metallurgique sursulfate." In France, it is known as "ciment sursulfate".

This cement is rather more sensitive to deterioration during storage than Portland cement. Super-sulphated cement has a low heat of hydration of about 40-45 calories/gm at 7 days and 45-50 at 28 days. This cement has high sulphate resistance. Because of this property this cement is particularly recommended for use in foundation, where chemically aggressive conditions exist. As super-sulphated cement has more resistance than Portland blast furnace slag cement to attack by sea water, it is also used in the marine works. Other areas where super-sulphated cement is recommended include the fabrication of reinforced concrete pipes which are likely to be buried in sulphate bearing soils. The substitution of granulated slag is responsible for better resistance to sulphate attack.

Super-sulphated cement, like high alumina cement, combines with more water on hydration than Portland cements. Wet curing for not less than 3 days after casting is essential as the premature drying out results in an undesirable or powdery surface layer. When we use super sulphated cement the water/cement ratio should not be less than 0.5. A mix leaner than about 1:6 is also not recommended.

Low Heat Cement (IS 12600-1989)

It is well known that hydration of cement is an exothermic action which produces large quantity of heat during hydration. This aspect has been discussed in detail in Chapter 1. Formation of cracks in large body of concrete due to heat of hydration has focussed the attention of the concrete technologists to produce a kind of cement which produces less heat or the same amount of heat, at a low rate during the hydration process. Cement having this property was developed in U.S.A. during 1930 for use in mass concrete construction, such as dams, where temperature rise by the heat of hydration can become excessively large. A low-heat evolution is achieved by reducing the contents of C_3S and C_3A which are the compounds evolving the

Low heat cement is made use of in construction of massive dams.

maximum heat of hydration and increasing C_2S. A reduction of temperature will retard the chemical action of hardening and so further restrict the rate of evolution of heat. The rate of evolution of heat will, therefore, be less and evolution of heat will extend over a longer period. Therefore, the feature of low-heat cement is a slow rate of gain of strength. But the ultimate strength of low-heat cement is the same as that of ordinary Portland cement. As per the Indian Standard Specification the heat of hydration of low-heat Portland cement shall be as follows:

7 days — not more than 65 calories per gm.

28 days — not more than 75 calories per gm.

The specific surface of low heat cement as found out by air-permeability method is not less than 3200 sq. cm/gm. The 7 days strength of low heat cement is not less than 16 MPa in contrast to 22 MPa in the case of ordinary Portland cement. Other properties, such as setting time and soundness are same as that of ordinary Portland cement.

Portland Pozzolana Cement (IS 1489-1991)

The history of pozzolanic material goes back to Roman's time. The descriptions and details of pozzolanic material will be dealt separately under the chapter 'Admixtures'. However a brief description is given below.

Portland Pozzolana cement (PPC) is manufactured by the intergrinding of OPC clinker with 10 to 25 per cent of pozzolanic material (as per the latest amendment, it is 15 to 35%). A pozzolanic material is essentially a silicious or aluminous material which while in itself possessing no cementitious properties, which will, in finely divided form and in the presence of water, react with calcium hydroxide, liberated in the hydration process, at ordinary temperature, to form compounds possessing cementitious properties. The pozzolanic materials generally used for manufacture of PPC are calcined clay (IS 1489 part 2 of 1991) or fly ash (IS 1489 part I of 1991). Fly ash is a waste material, generated in the thermal power station, when powdered coal is used as a fuel. These are collected in the electrostatic precipitator. (It is called pulverised fuel ash in UK). More information on fly ash as a mineral admixture is given in chapter 5.

It may be recalled that calcium silicates produce considerable quantities of calcium hydroxide, which is by and large a useless material from the point of view of strength or durability. If such useless mass could be converted into a useful cementitious product, it considerably improves quality of concrete. The use of fly ash performs such a role. The pozzolanic action is shown below:

$$\text{Calcium hydroxide + Pozzolana + water} \rightarrow C - S - H \text{ (gel)}$$

Portland pozzolana cement produces less heat of hydration and offers greater resistance to the attack of aggressive waters than ordinary Portland cement. Moreover, it reduces the leaching of calcium hydroxide when used in hydraulic structures. It is particularly useful in marine and hydraulic construction and other mass concrete constructions. Portland pozzolana cement can generally be used where ordinary Portland cement is usable. However, it is important to appreciate that the addition of pozzolana does not contribute to the strength at early ages. Strengths similar to those of ordinary Portland cement can be expected in general only at later ages provided the concrete is cured under moist conditions for a sufficient period. In India there is apprehension in the minds of the user to use the Portland pozzolana cement for structural works. It can be said that this fear is not justified. If the Portland pozzolana cement is manufactured by using the right type of reactive pozzolanic material, the Portland pozzolanic cement will not be in any way inferior to ordinary Portland cement except for the rate of development of strength upto 7 days. It is only when inferior pozzolanic materials, which are not of reactive type and which do not satisfy the specifications limit for pozzolanic materials, are used the cement would be of doubtful quality. The advantages of PPC can be summerised as follows.

Technically PPC has considerable advantages over OPC when made by using optimum percentage of right quality of fly ash.

Advantages of PPC

(a) In PPC, costly clinker is replaced by cheaper pozzolanic material - Hence economical.

(b) Soluble calcium hydroxide is converted into insoluble cementitious products resulting in improvement of permeability. Hence it offers, alround durability characteristics, particularly in hydraulic structures and marine construction.

(c) PPC consumes calcium hydroxide and does not produce calcium hydroxide as much as that of OPC.

(d) It generates reduced heat of hydration and that too at a low rate.

(e) PPC being finer than OPC and also due to pozzolanic action, it improves the pore size distribution and also reduces the microcracks at the transition zone.

(f) Reduction in permeability of PPC offers many other alround advantages.

(g) As the fly ash is finer and of lower density, the bulk volume of 50 kg bag is slightly more than OPC. Therefore, PPC gives more volume of mortar than OPC.

(h) The long term strength of PPC beyond a couple of months is higher than OPC if enough moisture is available for continued pozzolanic action.

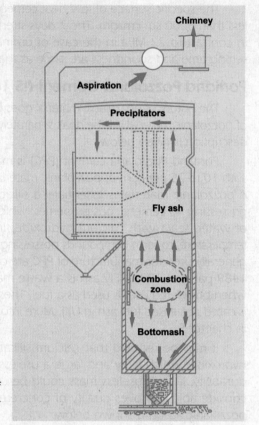

Schematic representation of the formation of fly ash.

All the above advantages of PPC are mainly due to the slow conversion of calcium hydroxide in the hydrated cement paste into cementitious product. In one investigation, 20 per cent calcium hydroxide in one year old OPC paste was found to be only 8.4 per cent calcium hydroxide in a similarly hydrated paste containing 30 per cent pozzolana. It may be noted that due to the dilution and leaching also certain reduction in calcium hydroxide may have taken place. Giving consideration to that effect, the calcium hydroxide should have been 14%. But the fact is that only 8.4% has remained goes to prove that 5.6% of calcium hydroxide was converted by the pozzolanic activity. Fig. 2.1 shows the typical reduction of Ca(OH)$_2$.

Fig. 2.1. Shows typical reduction of Ca(OH)$_2$

A few of the disadvantages are that the rate of development of strength is initially slightly slower than OPC. Secondly reduction in alkalinity reduces the resistance to corrosion of steel reinforcement. But considering the fact that PPC significantly improve the permeability of concrete, increases the resistance to corrosion of reinforcement. The setting time is nominally longer.

Status of PPC in India

Over 60 million tones of fly ash is generated from over 75 thermal power stations. But the qualities of such fly ash are generally not satisfactory to be used in PPC. In western countries fly ash generated in thermal power plants are further processed to render it fit for using in PPC. Because of the poor quality of fly ash, lack of awareness and fear psychics on the part of users, PPC is not popular. In India only 19% of total cement production is PPC. (1998-1999) and about 10% is slag cement. Government of India has set up an organisation called Fly Ash mission to promote the use of fly ash as mineral admixture or in manufacturing PPC. It has been realised by all experts in the world that more and more blended cement has to be used for sustainable development of any country.

Due to the shortage of electrical power, many cement factories have their own dedicated thermal power plant. They use their own fly ash for manufacturing PPC. As they know the importance of the qualities of fly ash, they take particular care to produce fly ash of good qualities to be used in PPC. The PPC produced by such cement plant is of superior quality. The chemical and physical qualities of properties of such PPC show much superior values than what is prescribed in BIS standard. The physical and chemical properties of PPC as given in IS: 1489 (part-I) 1991 is given in table 2.5

Birla Plus, Suraksha, Silicate Cement, Birla Bonus are some of the brand names of PPC in India.

Grading of PPC

In many countries, PPC is graded like OPC depending upon their compressive strength at 28 days. In India, so far PPC is considered equivalent to 33 grade OPC, strengthwise, although some brand of PPC is as good as even 53 grade OPC. Many cement manufacturers have requested BIS for grading of PPC just like grading of OPC. They have also requested for upper limits of fly ash content from 25% to 35%. Recently BIS has increased the fly ash content in PPC from 10–25% to 15–35%.

Application

Portland pozzolana cement can be used in all situations where OPC is used except where high early strength is of special requirement. As PPC needs enough moisture for sustained pozzolanic activity, a little longer curing is desirable. Use of PPC would be particularly suitable for the following situations:

(a) For hydraulic structures;

(b) For mass concrete structures like dam, bridge piers and thick foundation;

(c) For marine structures;

(d) For sewers and sewage disposal works etc.

Air-Entraining Cement

Air-entraining cement is not covered by Indian Standard so far. This cement is made by mixing a small amount of an air-entraining agent with ordinary Portland cement clinker at the time of grinding. The following types of air-entraining agents could be used:

(a) Alkali salts of wood resins.

(b) Synthetic detergents of the alkyl-aryl sulphonate type.

(c) Calcium lignosulphate derived from the sulphite process in paper making.

(d) Calcium salts of glues and other proteins obtained in the treatment of animal hides.

These agents in powder, or in liquid forms are added to the extent of 0.025–0.1 per cent by weight of cement clinker. There are other additives including animal and vegetable fats, oil and their acids could be used. Wetting agents, aluminium powder, hydrogen peroxide could also be used. Air-entraining cement will produce at the time of mixing, tough, tiny, discrete non-coalesceing air bubbles in the body of the concrete which will modify the properties of plastic concrete with respect to workability, segregation and bleeding. It will modify the properties of hardened concrete with respect to its resistance to frost action. Air-entraining agent can also be added at the time of mixing ordinary Portland cement with rest of the ingredients. More about this will be dealt under the chapter "Admixtures."

Coloured Cement (White Cement IS 8042–1989)

For manufacturing various coloured cements either white cement or grey Portland cement is used as a base. The use of white cement as a base is costly. With the use of grey cement only red or brown cement can be produced.

Coloured cement consists of Portland cement with 5-10 per cent of pigment. The pigment cannot be satisfactorily distributed throughout the cement by mixing, and hence, it is usual to grind the cement and pigment together. The properties required of a pigment to be used for coloured cement are the durability of colour under exposure to light and weather, a fine state of division, a chemical composition such that the pigment is neither effected by the cement nor detrimental to it, and the absence of soluble salts.

The process of manufacture of white Portland cement is nearly same as OPC. As the raw materials, particularity the kind of limestone required for manufacturing white cement is only available around Jodhpur in Rajasthan, two famous brands of white cement namely Birla White and J.K. White Cements are manufactured near Jodhpur. The raw materials used are high purity limestone (96% $CaCo_3$ and less than 0.07% iron oxide). The other raw materials are china clay with iron content of about 0.72 to 0.8%, silica sand, flourspar as flux and selenite as retarder. The fuels used are refined furnace oil (RFO) or gas. Sea shells and coral can also be used as raw materials for production of white cement.

The properties of white cement is nearly same as OPC. Generally white cement is ground finer than grey cement. Whiteness of white cement as measured by ISI scale shall not be less than 70%. Whiteness can also be measured by Hunters Scale. The value as measured by Hunters scale is generally 90%. The strength of white cement is much higher than what is stated in IS code 8042 of 1989. A typical test result of Birla White is shown in Table 2.2.

Table 2.2. Typical Properties of Birla White Portland Cement[2.2]

Characteristics	IS: 8042. 1989	Birla White
1. CHEMICAL		
a. Insoluble residue %	Max 2.0	0.60
b. Iron Oxide %	Max 1.0	0.20
c. Magnesium Oxide %	Max 6.0	0.80
d. Sulphur Trioxide %	Max 3.0	2.90
e. Alumina/Iron Oxide %	Min 0.66	9.00
f. Lime Saturation Factor	0.66-1.09	0.90
g. Loss on Ignition %		< 3%

2. PHYSICAL		
a. Degree of Whitenesses %		
ISI scale	Min 70	88+
Hunters scale		91+
b. Fineness, Blaine M²/kg.	Min 225	450*
(Specific Surface)		
c. Setting Time		
1. Intial-minutes	Min 30	80
2. Final-minutes	Max 600	120
d. Compressive Strength		
(Cement and Std. Sand Mortar 1:3)		
3 days (Mpa)	Min 14.4	45
7 days (Mpa)	Min 19.8	55
28 days (Mpa)	Min 29.7	67
e. Soundness		
1. Lechateliers method (mm)	Max 10	1.00
2. Autoclave expansion %	Max 0.8	Negligible
f. Retentión of 63 micron sieve %	—	1.00

Hydrophobic cement (IS 8043-1991)

Hydrophobic cement is obtained by grinding ordinary Portland cement clinker with water repellant film-forming substance such as oleic acid, and stearic acid. The water-repellant film formed around each grain of cement, reduces the rate of deterioration of the cement during long storage, transport, or under unfavourable conditions. The film is broken out when the cement and aggregate are mixed together at the mixer exposing the cement particles for normal hydration. The film forming water-repellant material will entrain certain amount of air in the body of the concrete which incidentally will improve the workability of concrete. In India certain places such as Assam, Shillong etc., get plenty of rainfall in the rainy season had have high humidity in other seasons. The transportation and storage of cement in such places cause deterioration in the quality of cement. In such far off places with poor communication system, cement perforce requires to be stored for long time. Ordinary cement gets deteriorated and loses some if its strength, whereas the hydrophobic cement which does not lose strength is an answer for such situations.

The properties of hydrophobic cement is nearly the same as that ordinary Portland cement except that it entrains a small quantity of air bubbles. The hydrophobic cement is made actually from ordinary Portland cement clinker. After grinding, the cement particle is sprayed in one direction and film forming materials such as oleic acid, or stearic acid, or pentachlorophenol, or calcium oleate are sprayed from another direction such that every particle of cement is coated with a very fine film of this water repellant material which protects them from the bad effect of moisture during storage and transporation. The cost of this cement is nominally higher than ordinary Portland cement.

Masonry Cement (IS 3466 : 1988)

Ordinary cement mortar, though good when compared to lime mortar with respect to strength and setting properties, is inferior to lime mortar with respect to workability, water-retentivity, shrinkage property and extensibility.

Masonry cement is a type of cement which is particularly made with such combination of materials, which when used for making mortar, incorporates all the good properties of lime mortar and discards all the not so ideal properties of cement mortar. This kind of cement is mostly used, as the name indicates, for masonry construction. It contains certain amount of air-entraining agent and mineral admixtures to improve the plasticity and water retentivity.

Expansive Cement

Concrete made with ordinary Portland cement shrinks while setting due to loss of free water. Concrete also shrinks continuously for long time. This is known as drying shrinkage. Cement used for grouting anchor bolts or grouting machine foundations or the cement used in grouting the prestress concrete ducts, if shrinks, the purpose for which the grout is used will be to some extent defeated. There has been a search for such type of cement which will not shrink while hardening and thereafter. As a matter of fact, a slight expansion with time will prove to be advantageous for grouting purpose. This type of cement which suffers no overall change in volume on drying is known as expansive cement. Cement of this type has been developed by using an expanding agent and a stabilizer very carefully. Proper material and controlled proportioning are necessary in order to obtain the desired expansion. Generally, about 8-20 parts of the sulphoaluminate clinker are mixed with 100 parts of the Portland cement and 15 parts of the stabilizer. Since expansion takes place only so long as concrete is moist, curing must be carefully controlled. The use of expanding cement requires skill and experience.

One type of expansive cement is known as shrinkage compensating cement. This cement when used in concrete, with restrained expansion, induces compressive stresses which approximately offset the tensile stress induced by shrinkage. Another similar type of cement is known as Self Stressing cement. This cement when used in concrete induces significant compressive stresses after the drying shrinkage has occurred. The induced compressive stresses not only compensate the shrinkage but also give some sort of prestressing effects in the tensile zone of a flexural member.

IRS-T 40 Special Grade Cement

IRS-T-40 special grade cement is manufactured as per specification laid down by ministry of Railways under IRS-T40: 1985. It is a very finely ground cement with high C_3S content designed to develop high early strength required for manufacture of concrete sleeper for Indian Railways. This cement can also be used with advantage for other applications where high early strength concrete is required. This cement can be used for prestressed concrete elements, high rise buildings, high strength concrete.

IRS-T 40 special grade cement was originally made for manufacturing concrete sleeper for railway line.

Oil-Well Cement (IS 8229-1986)

Oil-wells are drilled through stratified sedimentary rocks through a great depth in search of oil. It is likely that if oil is struck, oil or gas may escape through the space between the steel casing and rock formation. Cement slurry is used to seal off the annular space between steel casing and rock strata and also to seal off any other fissures or cavities in the sedimentary rock layer. The cement slurry has to be pumped into position, at considerable depth where the prevailing temperature may be upto 175°C. The pressure required may go upto 1300 kg/cm^2. The slurry should remain sufficiently mobile to be able to flow under these conditions for periods upto several hours and then hardened fairly rapidly. It may also have to resist corrosive conditions from sulphur gases or waters containing dissolved salts. The type of cement suitable for the above conditions is known as Oil-well cement. The desired properties of Oil-well cement can be obtained in two ways: by adjusting the compound composition of cement or by adding retarders to ordinary Portland cement. Many admixtures have been patented as retarders. The commonest agents are starches or cellulose products or acids. These retarding agents prevent quick setting and retains the slurry in mobile condition to facilitate penetration to all fissures and cavities. Sometimes workability agents are also added to this cement to increase the mobility.

Rediset Cement

Acclerating the setting and hardening of concrete by the use of admixtures is a common knowledge. Calcium chloride, lignosulfonates, and cellulose products form the base of some of admixtures. The limitations on the use of admixtures and the factors influencing the end properties are also fairly well known.

High alumina cement, though good for early strengths, shows retrogression of strength when exposed to hot and humid conditions. A new product was needed for use in the precast concrete industry, for rapid repairs of concrete roads and pavements, and slip-forming. In brief, for all jobs where the time and strength relationship was important. In the PCA laboratories of USA, investigations were conducted for developing a cement which could yield high strengths in a matter of hours, without showing any retrogression. Regset cement was the result of investigation. Associated Cement Company of India have developed an equivalent cement by name "REDISET" Cement.

Properties of "Rediset"[2.3]

(*i*) The cement allows a handling time of just about 8 to 10 minutes.

(*ii*) The strength pattern of REDISET and regset in mortar and concrete is given below:

Table 2.3. Compressive Strength MPa[2.3]

	4 hours	*24 hours*	*28 days*
ACC "REDISET" mortar, 1:3 mix	20	42	42 (Actual tests)
ACC "REDISET" 1: 5.5 mix concrete	21	25	32 (Actual tests)
USA Regset mortar 1: 2.75 mix	7.0	18	42 (From literature)
USA Regset concrete, 6 bags	9.0	16	42 (From literature)

(*iii*) The strength pattern is similar to that of ordinary Portland cement mortar or concrete after one day or 3 days. What is achieved with "REDISET" in 3 to 6 hours can be achieved with normal concrete only after 7 days.

(*iv*) "REDISET" releases a lot of heat which is advantageous in winter concreting but excess heat liberation is detrimental to mass concrete.

(*v*) The rate of shrinkage is fast but the total shrinkage is similar to that of ordinary Portland cement concrete.

(*vi*) The sulphate resistance, is however, very poor.

Applications

"REDISET" can be used for:

(*a*) very-high-early (3 to 4 hours) strength concrete and mortar,

(*b*) patch repairs and emergency repairs,

(*c*) quick release of forms in the precast concrete products industry,

(*d*) palletisation of iron ore dust,

(*e*) slip-formed concrete construction,

(*f*) construction between tides.

High Alumina Cement (IS 6452 : 1989)

High alumina cement is obtained by fusing or sintering a mixture, in suitable proportions, of alumina and calcareous materials and grinding the resultant product to a fine powder. The raw materials used for the manufacture of high alumina cement are limestone and bauxite. These raw materials with the required proportion of coke were charged into the furnace. The furnace is fired with pulverised coal or oil with a hot air blast. The fusion takes place at a temperature of about 1550-1600°C. The cement is maintained in a liquid state in the furnace. Afterwards the molten cement is run into moulds and cooled. These castings are known as pigs. After cooling the cement mass resembles a dark, fine gey compact rock resembling the structure and hardeness of basalt rock.

The pigs of fused cement, after cooling are crushed and then ground in tube mills to a finess of about 3000 sq. cm/gm.

Hydration of High Alumina Cement

The important reaction during the setting of the high alumina cement (HAC) is the formation of monocalcium aluminate decahydrate (CAH_{10}), dicalcium aluminate octahydrate (C_2AH_8) and alumina gel (AH_n). These aluminates give high strength to HAC concrete but they are metastable and at normal temperature convert gradually to tricalcium alumina hexahydrate (C_3AH_6) and gibbsite which are more stable. The change in composition is accompanised by a loss of strength and by a change in crystal form from hexagonal to cubical form with the release of water which results in increased porosity of concrete. The precise manner in which these changes take place depends on the temperature, water/cement ratio and chemical environment.

The change in composition accompanied by loss of strength and change in crystal form from hexagonal to cubic shape is known as conversion.

Experimental evidence suggests that in the important reaction of the conversion from CAH_{10} to C_3AH_6 and alumina hydrate, temperature effects the decomposition. The higher the temperature, the faster the rate of conversion. Experimental studies have also shown that the higher the water/cement ratio, the greater is the rate of conversion. The hydration and conversion can be shown as follows:

$$CA + 10H \longrightarrow CAH_{10}; \qquad \qquad ...(1)$$

$$3CA H_{10} \longrightarrow C_3AH_6 + 2 AH_3 + 18H \qquad \qquad ...(2)$$

It should be noted that this reaction liberates all the water needed for the conversion process to continue. The conversion reaction will result in a reduction in volume of the solids and an increase in the porosity, since the overall dimensions of specimens of cement paste or concrete remain sensibly constant.

High Alumina Cement Concrete

The use of high alumina cement concrete commenced in the U.K. in 1925 following its introduction in France where it had been developed earlier to make concrete resistant to chemical attack, particularly in marine conditions. The capability of this concrete to develop a high early strength offers advantages in structural use. However, its high cost prevented extensive use of high alumina cement for structural purposes. All the same during 1930's many structures were built in European countries using high alumina cement. Following the collapse of two roof beams in a school at Stepney in U.K. in February 1974, the Building Research Establishment (BRE) of U.K. started field studies and laboratory tests to establish the degree of risk likely in buildings with precast prestressed concrete beams made with high alumina cement. The results of the BRE investigations are summarised below:

1. Measurements of the degree of conversion of the concrete used in the buildings indicated that high alumina cement concrete reaches a high level of conversion within a few years. The concrete specimens cut from beams indicated that some concrete suffered substantial loss of strength when compared to one day strength on which the design was earlier based, (Fig. 2.2).

2. Long term laboratory tests have shown that:

(a) If concrete with a free water/cement ratio less than 0.4 is stored in water at 18°C throughout its initial curing period and its subsequent life, a minimum strength will

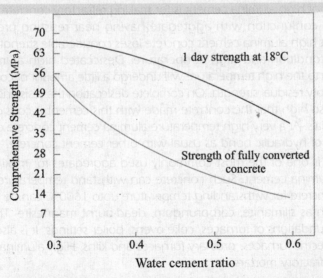

Fig. 2.2. Comparative strengths of converted and unconverted high alumina cement concretes.

be reached after about 5 years and this minimum will not be appreciably less than the strength at one day.

(b) If concrete is stored in water at 38°C, after one day at 18°C, it converts rapidly to high limit and reaches a minimum strength in about 3 months which is very substantially less than the strength at one day.

(c) If concrete is stored in water at 18°C for a long period (upto $8^1/_2$ years) and is immersed in water at 38°C it will rapidly convert and lose strength to the minimum level, reached for continuous storage at 38°C.

(d) Since the temperature at 38°C represents an upper limit of what is likely to be reached during curing of these sections or in normally heated

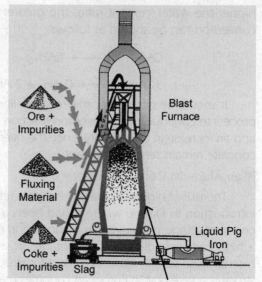

Refractory concrete made with High Alumina cement is used as refactory lining in furnaces and fire pits.

building, and the precise level is not critical, it is recommended that design should be based on the minimum strength at this temperature.

(e) Highly converted high alumina cement concrete is vulnerable to chemical attack in the presence of long term wetness and a chemically aggressive agent, which may be more serious risk for concretes with greater water/cement ratio.

One of the most advantages of high alumina cement concrete is the very high rate of strength development. About 20 per cent of the ultimate strength is achieved in one day. It also achieves a substantial strength even at 6 to 8 hours.

Refractory Concrete

An important use of high alumina cement is for making refractory concrete to withstand high temperatures in conjunction with aggregate having heat resisting properties. It is interesting to note that high alumina cement concrete loses considerable strength only when subjected to humid condition and high temperature. Desiccated high alumina cement concrete on subjecting to the high temperature will undergo a little amount of conversion and will still have a satisfactory residual strength. On complete desiccation the resistance of alumina cement to dry heat is so high that the concrete made with this cement is considered as one of the refractory materials. At a very high temperature alumina cement concrete exhibits good ceramic bond instead of hydraulic bond as usual with other cement concrete.

Crushed firebrick is one of the most commonly used aggregates for making refractory concrete with high alumina cement. Such concrete can withstand temperature upto about 1350°C. Refractory concrete for withstanding temperature upto 1600°C can be produced by using aggregates such as silimanite, carborundum, dead-burnt magnesite. The refractory concrete is used for foundations of furnaces, coke ovens, boiler settings. It is also used in fire pits, construction of electric furnaces, ordinary furnaces and kilns. High alumina cement can be used for making refractory mortars.

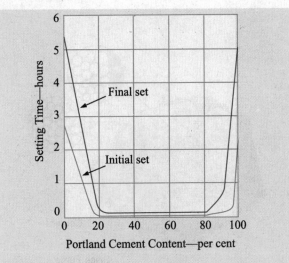

Fig. 2.3. Setting time of portland-aluminous cement mixtures.

High alumina cement is a slow setting but rapid hardening cement. Its setting time can be reduced considerably by mixing it with certain proportions of ordinary Portland cement. In situations such as stopping of ingress of water or for construction between tides or for reducing pumping time in some underwater construction a particular mixture of high alumina cement and ordinary Portland cement is adopted. Fig. 2.3 shows setting time of mixtures of Portland and alumina cement. It can be seen from Fig. 2.3 that when either cement constitutes between 20-80 per cent of mixture, flash set may occur. The values shown in the graph is only approximate. The actual proportioning and the resultant setting time are required to be actually found out by trial when such a combination is practised.

Very High Strength Cement

(a) Macro-defect-free cements (MDF)[2.4]. The engineering of a new class of high strength cement called Macro-defect-free (MDF) cements is an innovation. MDF refers to the absence of relatively large voids or defects which are usually present in conventional mixed cement pastes because of entrapped air and inadequate dispersion. Such voids and defects limit the strength. In the MDF process 4-7% of one of several water-soluble polymers (such as hydroxypropylmethyle cellulose, polyacrylamide of hydrolysed polyvinylacetate) is added as rheological aid to permit cement to be mixed with very small amount of water. Control of particle size distribution was also considered important for generating the strength. At final processing stage entrapped air is removed by applying a modest pressure of 5 MPa.

With this process a strength of 300 MPa for calcium aluminate system and 150 MPa for Portland cement system can be achieved.

(b) Densely Packed System (DSP). New materials termed DSP (Densified system containing homegeneously arranged ultre-fine particles) is yet another innovation in the field of high strength cement. Normal Portland cement and ultra-fine silica fume are mixed. The size of cement particles may very from 0.5 to 100μ and that of silica fume varies from 0.005 to 0.5μ. Silica fume is generally added from 5 to 25 %. A compressive strength of 270 MPa have been achieved with silica fume substituted paste.

The formation of typical DSP is schematically represented in Fig. 2.4.

(c) Pressure Densification and Warm Pressing. For decades uncertainties existed regarding the theoretical strength of hydrated cement paste. Before 1970, the potential strength of cement paste at theoretical density (What T.C. Powers called "intrinsic strength") had never been achieved because of considerable porosity (20 to 30% or more) always remain ofter completing hydration of cement. A new approach has ben developed for achieving very high strength by a method called "Warm Pressing" (applying heat and pressure simultaneously) to cement paste.

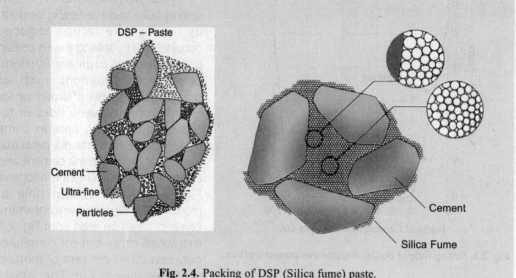

Fig. 2.4. Packing of DSP (Silica fume) paste.

Some modest increase in strength was achieved by application of pressure alone. Compressive strength as much as 650 MPa and tensile strength up to 68 MPa have been obtained by warm pressing Portland and calcium aluminate cements. Enormous increases in strength resulted from the removal of most of the porosity and generation of very homogeneous, fine micro-structures with the porosities as low as 1.7%.

(*d*) **High Early Strength Cement.** Development of high early strength becomes an important factor, sometimes, for repair and emergency work. Research has been carried out in the recent past to develop rapid setting and hardening cement to give materials of very high early strength.

Lithium salts have been effectively used as accelerators in high alumina cement. This has resulted in very high early strength in cement and a marginal reduction in later strength. Strength as high as 4 MPa has been obtained within 1 hour and 27 MPa has been obtained within 3 hours time and 49 MPa in one day.

(*e*) **Pyrament Cement.** Some cement industries in USA have developed a super high early strength and durable cement called by trade name "Pyrament Cement". This product is a blended hydraulic cement. In this cement no chlorides are added during the manufacturing process. Pyrament cement produces a high and very early strength of concrete and mortar which can be used for repair of Air Field Run-ways. In India Associated Cement Company in collaboration with R & D Engineers, Dighi, Pune have also produced high early strength cement for rapid repair of airfields.

The Pyrament cement showed the following strength. Refer Table 2.4.

(*f*) **Magnesium Phosphate Cement (MPC).** Magnesium Phosphate Cement, an advanced cementing material, giving very high early strength mortar and concrete has been developed by Central Road Research Institute, New Delhi. This cement can be used for rapid repair of damaged concrete roads and airfield pavements. This is an important development for emergency repair of airfields, launching pads, hard standing and road pavements suffering damage due to enemy bombing and missile attack.

Table. 2.4. Typical Properties of Conctete and Mortar with Pyrament Cement.

Material	Compressive strength MPa	Flexural Strength MPa
Hardened Concrete		
4 hours	17	3.45
1 day	34	5.52
28 days	69	8.27
Hardened Mortar		
2 hours	17	—
3 hours	24	4.1
1 day	41	6.9
7 days	69	10.3

The MPC has been found to possess unique hydraulic properties, in particular, a controlled rapid set and early strength development. MPC is a prepacked mixture of dead burnt magnesite with fine aggregate mixed with phosphate. It sets rapidly and yields durable high strength cement mortar. This new cement has a bright future as an alternative to costly synthetic resins currently in use for emergency repair of concrete pavements.

The following materials are used for making MPC:

Magnesite ($MgCO_3$) when calcined at or above 1500°C gives dead burnt magnesite (DBM). This material is ground to a fineness of 300-350 m²/kg (Blaines). This is mixed with commercially available crystalline Mono Ammonium Phosphate after grinding into fine powder passing 600µ seive, and other ingredients like sodium tri-polyphosphate in the form of fine powder, di-sodium tetraborate (Borax), fine aggregate (crushed dolomite sand) and water.

The DBM and sand mixture is added into cold phosphate and borax solution (12-15°C) and mixed for one minute. This mix is applied for the purpose of repair. It is air cured and is ready for opening traffic within 4-5 hours.

TESTING OF CEMENT

Testing of cement can be brought under two categories:

(a) Field testing

(b) Laboratory testing.

Field Testing

It is sufficient to subject the cement to field tests when it is used for minor works. The following are the field tests:

(a) Open the bag and take a good look at the cement. There should not be any visible lumps. The colour of the cement should normally be greenish grey.

(b) Thrust your hand into the cement bag. It must give you a cool feeling. There should not be any lump inside.

(c) Take a pinch of cement and feel-between the fingers. It should give a smooth and not a gritty feeling.

(d) Take a handful of cement and throw it on a bucket full of water, the particles should float for some time before they sink.

(e) Take about 100 grams of cement and a small quantity of water and make a stiff paste. From the stiff paste, pat a cake with sharp edges. Put it on a glass plate and slowly take it under water in a bucket. See that the shape of the cake is not disturbed while taking it down to the bottom of the bucket. After 24 hours the cake should retain its original shape and at the same time it should also set and attain some strength.

If a sample of cement satisfies the above field tests it may be concluded that the cement is not bad. The above tests do not really indicate that the cement is really good for important works. For using cement in important and major works it is incumbent on the part of the user to test the cement in the laboratory to confirm the requirements of the Indian Standard specifications with respect to its physical and chemical properties. No doubt, such confirmations will have been done at the factory laboratory before the production comes out from the factory. But the cement may go bad during transportation and storage prior to its use in works. The following tests are usually conducted in the laboratory.

(a) Fineness test.   (b) Setting time test.

(c) Strength test.   (d) Soundness test.

(e) Heat of hydration test.   (f) Chemical composition test.

Fineness Test

The fineness of cement has an important bearing on the rate of hydration and hence on the rate of gain of strength and also on the rate of evolution of heat. Finer cement offers a greater surface area for hydration and hence faster the development of strength, (Fig. 2.5). The fineness of grinding has increased over the years. But now it has got nearly stabilised. Different cements are ground to different fineness. The disadvantages of fine grinding is that it is susceptible to air-set and early deterioration. Maximum number of particles in a sample of cement should have a size less than about 100 microns. The smallest particle may have a size of about 1.5 microns. By and large an average size of the cement particles may be taken as about 10 micron. The particle size fraction below 3 microns has been found to have the predominant effect on the strength at one day while 3-25 micron fraction has a major influence on the 28 days strength. Increase in fineness of

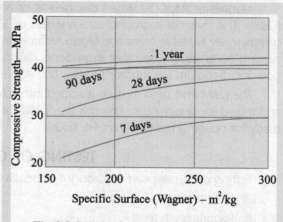

Fig. 2.5. Relation between strength of concrete at different ages and fineness of cement.

cement is also found to increase the drying shrinkage of concrete. In commercial cement it is suggested that there should be about 25-30 per cent of particles of less than 7 micron in size.

Fineness of cement is tested in two ways :

(a) By seiving.

(b) By determination of specific surface (total surface area of all the particles in one gram of cement) by air-premeability appartus. Expressed as cm²/gm or m²/kg. Generally Blaine Airpermeability appartus is used.

Sieve Test

Weigh correctly 100 grams of cement and take it on a standard IS Sieve No. 9 (90 microns). Break down the air-set lumps in the sample with fingers. Continuously sieve the sample giving circular and vertical motion for a period of 15 minutes. Mechanical sieving devices may also be used. Weigh the residue left on the sieve. This weight shall not exceed 10% for ordinary cement. Sieve test is rarely used.

Air Permeability Method

This method of test covers the procedure for determining the fineness of cement as represented by specific surface expressed as total surface area in sq. cm/gm. of cement. It is also expressed in m²/kg. Lea and Nurse Air Permeability Appartus is shown in Fig. 2.6. This appartus can be used for measuring the specific surface of cement. The principle is based on the relation between the flow of air through the cement bed and the surface area of the particles comprising the cement bed. From this the surface area per unit weight of the body material can be related to the permeability of a bed of a given porosity. The cement bed in the permeability cell is 1 cm. high and 2.5 cm. in diameter. Knowing the density of cement the weight required to make a cement bed of porosity of 0.475 can be calculated. This quantity of cement is placed in the permeability cell in a standard manner. Slowly pass on air

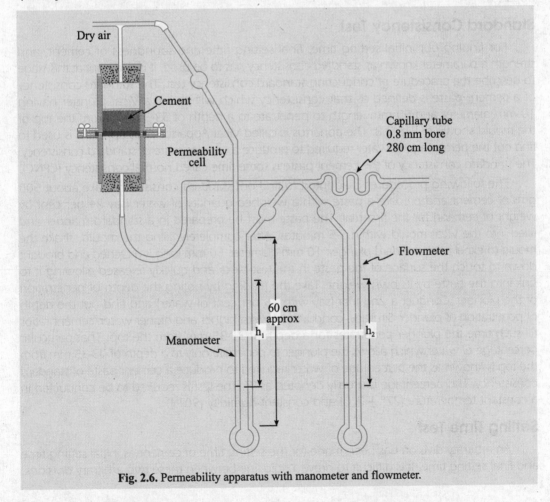

Fig. 2.6. Permeability apparatus with manometer and flowmeter.

through the cement bed at a constant velocity. Adjust the rate of air flow until the flowmeter shows a difference in level of 30-50 cm. Read the difference in level (h_1) of the manometer and the difference in level (h_2) of the flowmeter. Repeat these observations to ensure that steady conditions have been obtained as shown by a constant value of h_1/h_2. Specific surface S_w is calculated from the following formula:

$$S_w = K\sqrt{h_1/h_2} \quad \text{and} \quad K = \frac{14}{d(1-x)}\sqrt{\frac{x^3 A}{CL}}$$

where, ξ = Porosity, *i.e.*, 0.475
   A = Area of the cement bed
   L = Length (cm) of the cement bed
   d = Density of cement, and
   C = Flowmeter constant.

The specific surface for various cements is shown in Table 2.5.

Fineness can also be measured by Blain Air Permeability apprartus. This method is more commonly employed in India. Fig. 2.7 shows the sketch of Blaine type Air Permeability appartus.

Standard Consistency Test

For finding out initial setting time, final setting time and soundness of cement, and strength a parameter known as standard consistency has to be used. It is pertinent at this stage to describe the procedure of conducting standard consistency test. The standard consistency of a cement paste is defined as that consistency which will permit a Vicat plunger having 10 mm diameter and 50 mm length to penetrate to a depth of 33-35 mm from the top of the mould shown in Fig. 2.8. The appartus is called Vicat Appartus. This appartus is used to find out the percentage of water required to produce a cement paste of standard consistency. The standard consistency of the cement paste is some time called normal consistency (CPNC).

The following procedures is adopted to find out standard consistency. Take about 500 gms of cement and prepare a paste with a weighed quantity of water (say 24 per cent by weight of cement) for the first trial. The paste must be prepared in a standard manner and filled into the Vicat mould within 3-5 minutes. After completely filling the mould, shake the mould to expel air. A standard plunger, 10 mm diameter, 50 mm long is attached and brought down to touch the surface of the paste in the test block and quickly released allowing it to sink into the paste by its own weight. Take the reading by noting the depth of penetration of the plunger. Conduct a 2nd trial (say with 25 per cent of water) and find out the depth of penetration of plunger. Similarly, conduct trials with higher and higher water/cement ratios till such time the plunger penetrates for a depth of 33-35 mm from the top. That particular percentage of water which allows the plunger to penetrate only to a depth of 33-35 mm from the top is known as the percentage of water required to produce a cement paste of standard consistency. This percentage is usually denoted as 'P'. The test is required to be conducted in a constant temperature (27° ± 2°C) and constant humidity (90%).

Setting Time Test

An arbitraty division has been made for the setting time of cement as initial setting time and final setting time. It is difficult to draw a rigid line between these two arbitrary divisions.

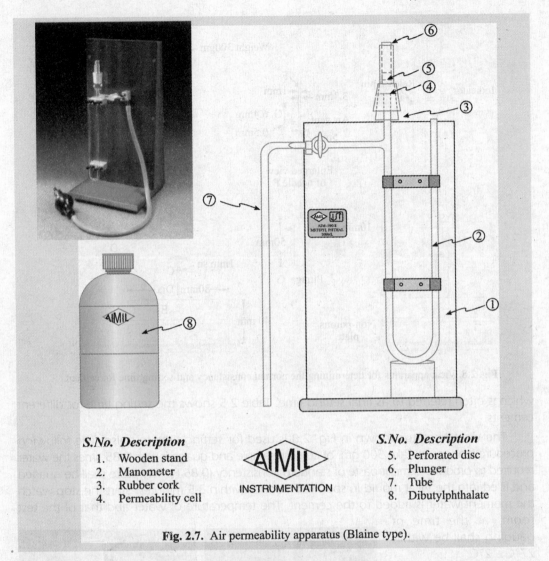

S.No.	Description
1.	Wooden stand
2.	Manometer
3.	Rubber cork
4.	Permeability cell

AIMIL
INSTRUMENTATION

S.No.	Description
5.	Perforated disc
6.	Plunger
7.	Tube
8.	Dibutylphthalate

Fig. 2.7. Air permeability apparatus (Blaine type).

For convenience, initial setting time is regarded as the time elapsed between the moment that the water is added to the cement, to the time that the paste starts losing its plasticity. The final setting time is the time elapsed between the moment the water is added to the cement, and the time when the paste has completely lost its plasticity and has attained sufficient firmness to resist certain definite pressure.

In actual construction dealing with cement paste, mortar or concrete certain time is required for mixing, transporting, placing, compacting and finishing. During this time cement paste, mortar, or concrete should be in plastic condition. The time interval for which the cement products remain in plastic condition is known as the initial setting time. Normally a minimum of 30 minutes is given for mixing and handling operations. The constituents and fineness of cement is maintained in such a way that the concrete remains in plastic condition for certain minimum time. Once the concrete is placed in the final position, compacted and finished, it should lose its plasticity in the earliest possible time so that it is least vulnerable to damages from external destructive agencies. This time should not be more than 10 hours

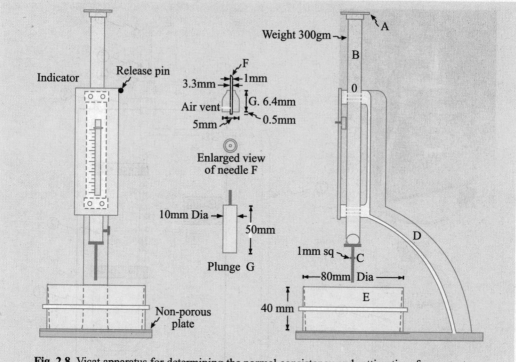

Fig. 2.8. Vicat apparatus for determining the normal consistency and setting time for cement.

which is often referred to as final setting time. Table 2.5 shows the setting time for different cements.

The Vicat Appartus shown in Fig. 2.8 is used for setting time test also. The following procedure is adopted. Take 500 gm. of cement sample and guage it with 0.85 times the water required to produce cement paste of standard consistency (0.85 P). The paste shall be guaged and filled into the Vicat mould in specified manner within 3-5 minutes. Start the stop watch the moment water is added to the cement. The temperature of water and that of the test room, at the time of gauging shall be within 27°C ± 2°C.

Initial Setting Time

Lower the needle (C) gently and bring it in contact with the surface of the test block and quickly release. Allow it to penetrate into the test block. In the beginning, the needle will completely pierce through the test block. But after some time when the paste starts losing its plasticity, the

Vicat Apparatus and Accessories.

Automatic Vicat Apparatus.

needly may penetrate only to a depth of 33-35 mm from the top. The period elapsing between the time when water is added to the cement and the time at which the needle penetrates the test block to a depth equal to 33-35 mm from the top is taken as initial setting time.

Final Setting Time

Replace the needle (C) of the Vicat appartus by a circular attachment (F) shown in the Fig 2.8. The cement shall be considered as finally set when, upon, lowering the attachment gently cover the surface of the test block, the centre needle makes an impression, while the circular cutting edge of the attachment fails to do so. In other words the paste has attained such hardness that the centre needle does not pierce through the paste more than 0.5 mm.

Strength Test

The compressive strength of hardened cement is the most important of all the properties. Therefore, it is not surprising that the cement is always tested for its strength at the laboratory before the cement is used in important works. Strength tests are not made on neat cement paste because of difficulties of excessive shrinkage and subsequent cracking of neat cement. Strength of cement is indirectly found on cement sand mortar in specific proportions. The standard sand is used for finding the strength of cement. It shall conform to IS 650-1991. Take 555 gms of standard sand (Ennore sand), 185 gms of cement (*i.e.*, ratio of cement to sand is 1:3) in a non-porous enamel tray and mix them with a trowel for one minute, then add water of quantity $\frac{P}{4}$ + 3.0 per cent of combined weight of cement and sand and mix the three ingredients thoroughly until the mixture is of uniform colour. The time of mixing should not be less than 3 minutes nor more than 4 minutes. Immediately after mixing, the mortar is filled into a cube mould of size 7.06 cm. The area of the face of the cube will be equal to 50 sq cm. Compact the mortar either by hand compaction in a standard specified manner or on the vibrating equipment (12000 RPM) for 2 minutes..

Moulding of 70.7 mm Mortar Cube Vibrating Machine.

Keep the compacted cube in the mould at a temperature of 27°C ± 2°C and at least 90 per cent relative humidity for 24 hours. Where the facility of standard temperature and humidity room is not available, the cube may be kept under wet gunny bag to simulate 90 per cent relative humidity. After 24 hours the cubes are removed from the mould and immersed in clean fresh water until taken out for testing.

Three cubes are tested for compressive strength at the periods mentioned in Table 2.5. The periods being reckoned from the completion of vibration. The compressive strength shall be the average of the strengths of the three cubes for each period respectively. The strength requirements for various types of cement is shown in Table 2.5.

Soundness Test

It is very important that the cement after setting shall not undergo any appreciable change of volume. Certain cements have been found to undergo a large expansion after setting causing disruption of the set and hardened mass. This will cause serious difficulties for the durability of structures when such cement is used. The testing of soundness of cement, to ensure that the cement does not show any appreciable subsequent expansion is of prime importance.

The unsoundness in cement is due to the presence of excess of lime than that could be combined with acidic oxide at the kiln. This is also due to inadequate burning or insufficiency in fineness of grinding or thorough mixing of raw materials. It is also likely that too high a proportion of magnesium content or calcium sulphate content may cause unsoundness in cement. For this reason the magnesia content allowed in cement is limited to 6 per cent. It

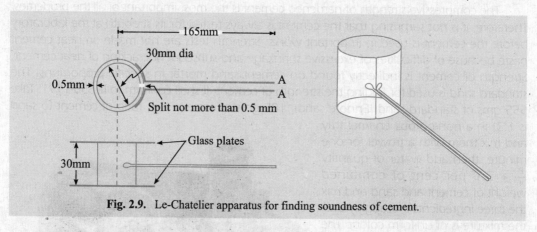

Fig. 2.9. Le-Chatelier apparatus for finding soundness of cement.

can be recalled that, to prevent flash set, calcium sulphate is added to the clinker while grinding. The quantity of gypsum added will vary from 3 to 5 per cent depending upon C_3A content. If the addition of gypsum is more than that could be combined with C_3A, excess of gypsum will remain in the cement in free state. This excess of gypsum leads to an expansion and consequent disruption of the set cement paste.

Unsoundness in cement is due to excess of lime, excess of magnesia or excessive proportion of sulphates. Unsoundness in cement does not come to surface for a considarable period of time. Therefore, accelerated tests are required to detect it. There are number of such tests in common use. The appartus is shown in Fig. 2.9. It consists of a small split cylinder of spring brass or other suitable metal. It is 30 mm in diameter and 30 mm high. On either side of the split are attached two indicator arms 165 mm long with pointed ends. Cement is gauged with 0.78 times the water required for standard consistency (0.78 P), in a standard manner and filled into the mould kept on a glass plate. The mould is covered on the top

Autoclave.

with another glass plate. The whole assembly is immersed in water at a temperature of 27°C – 32°C and kept there for 24 hours.

Measure the distance between the indicator points. Submerge the mould again in water. Heat the water and bring to boiling point in about 25-30 minutes and keep it boiling for 3 hours. Remove the mould from the water, allow it to cool and measure the distance between the indicator points. The difference between these two measurements represents the expansion of cement. This must not exceed 10 mm for ordinary, rapid hardening and low heat Portland cements. If in case the expansion is more than 10 mm as tested above, the cement is said to be unsound.

The Le Chatelier test detects unsoundness due to free lime only. This method of testing does not indicate the presence and after effect of the excess of magnesia. Indian Standard Specification stipulates that a cement having a magnesia content of more than 3 per cent shall be tested for soundness by Autoclave test which is sensitive to both free magnesia and free lime. In this test a neat cement specimen 25   25 mm is placed in a standard autoclave and the steam pressure inside the autoclave is raised in such a rate as to bring the gauge pressure of the steam to 21 kg/sq cm in $1 - 1^{1}/_{4}$ hour from the time the heat is turned on. This pressure is maintained for 3 hours. The autoclave is cooled and the length measured again. The expansion permitted for all types of cements is given in Table 2.5. The high steam pressure accelerates the hydration of both magnesia and lime.

No satisfactory test is available for deduction of unsoundness due to an excess of calcium sulphate. But its content can be easily determined by chemical analysis.

Automatic / Manual 5 litre Mortar Mixer.

Heat of Hydration

The reaction of cement with water is exothermic. The reaction liberates a considerable quantity of heat. This can be easily observed if a cement is gauged with water and placed in a thermos flask. Much attention has been paid to the heat evolved during the hydration of cement in the interior of mass concrete dams. It is estimated that about 120 calories of heat is generated in the hydration of 1 gm. of cement. From this it can be assessed the total quantum of heat produced in a conservative system such as the interior of a mass concrete dam. A temperature rise of about 50°C has been observed. This unduly high temperature developed at the interior of a concrete dam causes serious expansion of the body of the dam and with the subsequent cooling considerable shrinkage takes place resulting in serious cracking of concrete.

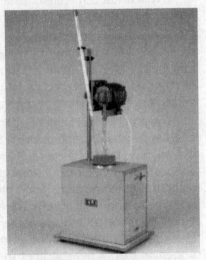

Heat of hydration Apparatus.

The use of lean mix, use of pozzolanic cement, artificial cooling of constituent materials and incorporation of pipe system in the body of the dam as the concrete work progresses for circulating cold brine solution through the pipe system to absorb the heat, are some of the methods adopted to offset the heat generation in the body of dams due to heat of hydration of cement.

Test for heat of hydration is essentially required to be carried out for low heat cement only. This test is carried out over a few days by vaccum flask methods, or over a longer period in an adiabatic calorimeter. When tested in a standard manner the heat of hydration of low heat Portland cement shall not be more than 65 cal/gm. at 7 days and 75 cal/g, at 28 days.

Chemical Composition Test

A fairly detailed discussion has been given earlier regarding the chemical composition of cement. Both oxide composition and compound composition of cement have been discussed. At this stage it is sufficient to give the limits of chemical requirements. The Table 2.6 shows the various chemical compositions of all types of cements.

Ratio of percentage of lime to percentage of silica, alumina and iron oxide, when calculated by the formulae,

$$\frac{CaO - 0.7\,SO_3}{2.8\,SiO_2 + 1.2\,Al_2O_3 + 0.65\,Fe_2O_3} : \text{Not greater than } 1.02 \text{ and not less than } 0.66$$

The above is called lime saturation factor per cent.

Table 2.5 gives the consolidated physical requirements of various types of cement.

Table 2.6 gives the chemical requirements of various types of cement.

Test Certificate

Every cement company is continuously testing the cement manufactured in their factory. They keep a good record of both physical and chemical properties of the cement manufactured applying a batch number. Batch number indicates date, month and year.

They also issue test certificate. Every purchaser is eligible to demand test certificate.

A typical test certificate of Birla super 53 grade cement for the week number 35 is given in Table 2.7 for general information.

Some cement companies also work out the standard deviation and coefficient of variation for 3 months or 6 months or for one year period subjecting the various parameters obtained from their test results. Table 2.8 shows the typical standard deviation for 3 days, 7 days and 28 days strength in respect of 53 grade cement Birla super. Standard deviation has been worked out for the whole year from Jan. 99 to Dec. 99.

The properties of cements, particularly the strength property shown in Table No. 2.5 is tested as per the procedures given by BIS. In different countries cement is tested as per their own country's code of practice. There are lot of variations in the methods of testing of cement with respect to w/c ratio, size and shape of specimen, material proportion, compacting methods and temperature. Strength of cement as indicated by one country may not mean the same in another country. This will present a small problem when export or import of cement from one country to another country is concerned. Table No. 2.9. Shows the cements testing procedure and various grades of cement manufactured in some countries. There is suggestion that all the countries should follow one method recommended by International standards organisation for testing of cement. If that system is adopted properties indicated by any one country will mean the same to any other country.

Table 2.5. Physical Characteristics of Various Types of Cement.

Sl.No.	Type of Cement	Fineness (m²/kg) Min.	Soundness By Le chatelier (mm) Max.	Soundness By Autoclave (%) Max.	Setting Time Initial (mts) min.	Setting Time Final (mts) max.	Compressive Strength 1 Day min. MPa	Compressive Strength 3 Days min. MPa	Compressive Strength 7 Days min. MPa	Compressive Strength 28 Days min. MPa
1.	33 Grade OPC (IS 269-1989)	225	10	0.8	30	600	N S	16	22	33
2.	43 Grade OPC (IS 8112-1989)	225	10	0.8	30	600	N S	23	33	43
3.	53 Grade OPC (IS 12269-1987)	225	10	0.8	30	600	N S	27	37	53
4.	SRC (IS 12330-1988)	225	10	0.8	30	600	N S	10	16	33
5.	PPC (IS 1489-1991) Part I	300	10	0.8	30	600	N S	16	22	33
6.	Rapid Hardening (IS 8041-1990)	325	10	0.8	30	600	16	27	N S	N S
7.	Slag Cement (IS 455-1989)	225	10	0.8	30	600	N S	16	22	33
8.	High Alumina Cement (IS 6452-1989)	225	5	N S	30	600	30	35	N S	N S
9.	Super Sulphated Cement (IS 6909-1990)	400	5	N S	30	600	N S	15	22	30
10.	Low Heat Cement (IS 12600-1989)	320	10	0.8	60	600	N S	10	16	35
11.	Masonry Cement (IS 3466-1988)	*	10	1	90	1440	N S	N S	2.5	5
12.	IRS-T-40	370	5	0.8	60	600	N S	N S	37.5	N S

*N S – Not specified.

Table. 2.6. Chemical Characteristics of Various Types of Cement.

Sr. No.	Type of Cement	Lime Saturation Factor (%)	Alumina Iron Ratio (%) Min.	Insoluble Residue (%) Max.	Mag-nesia (%) Max.	Sulphuric Anhydride	Loss on Ignition (%) Max.
1	33 Grade OPC (IS 269-1989)	0.66 Min. 1.02 Max.	0.66	4	6	2.5% Max. When C_3A is 5 or less 3% Max. When C_3A is greater than 5	5
2	43 Grade OPC (IS 8112-1989)	0.66 Min. 1.02 Max.	0.66	2	6	2.5% Max. When C_3A is 5 or less 3% Max. When C_3A is greater than 5	5
3	53 Grade OPC (IS 12269-1987)	0.8 Min. 1.02 Max.	0.66	2	6	2.5% Max. When C_3A is 5 or less 3% Max. When C_3A is greater than 5	4
4	Sulphate Resisting Cement (IS 12330-1988)	0.66 Min. 1.02 Max.	N S	4	6	2.5% Max.	5
5	Portland Pozzolana Cement (IS 1489-1991) Part I	N S	N S	$x + \dfrac{4(100-x)}{100}$	6	3% Max.	5
6	Rapid Hardening Cement (IS 8041-1990)	0.66 Min. 1.02 Max.	0.66	4	6	2.5% Max. When C_3A is 5 or less 3% Max. When C_3A is greater than 5	5
7	Slag Cement (IS 455-1989)	N S	N S	4	8	3% Max.	5
8	High Alumina Cement (IS 6452-1989)	N S	N S	N S	N S	N S	N S
9	Super Sulphated-Cement (IS 6909-1990)	N S	N S	4	10	6% Min.	N S
10	Low Heat Cement (IS 12600-1989)	N S	0.66	4	6	2.5% Max. When C_3A is 5 or less 3% Max. When C_3A is greater than 5	5
11	IRS-T40	0.8 Min. 1.02 Max.	0.66	2	5	3.5% Max.	4

x – Declared percentage of flyash.   N S – Not specified.

Table 2.7. Typical Test Certificate

53 Grade Portland Cement
Birla Super

Week no. 35

Physical Analysis

Fineness:		Requirements of I.S. 12269-1987	
Specific Surface	303 m²/kg	Should not be less than	225 m²/kg
Soundness			
Expansion of unaerated cement			
a) By Le chatelier mould	0.50 m.m.	Should not exceed	10 m.m.
b) By Autoclave	0.0936 %	Should not exceed	0.8%
Setting Time:			
a) Initial set	130 mts.	Should not be less than	30 mts.
b) Final set	195 mts.	Should not exceed	600 mts.
Compressive strength:			
a) 3 days	42.3 MPa	Should not be less than	27 M Pa
b) 7 days	51.6 MPa	Should not be less than	37 M Pa
c) 28 days (Week No. 32)	71.3 MPa	Should not be less than	53 M Pa
Temperature during testing	27.0 °C	Should be	27°C ∓ 2°C
Standard Consistencey	29.7 %		

Chemical Analysis

Particulars			
Lime Saturation Factor (L.S.F.) not	0.92	Should not be less than	0.80 and exceed 1.02
Alumina Iron Ratio	1.16	Should not be less than	0.66
Loss on Ignition (LOI)	1.29 %	Should not exceed	4%
Insoluble Residue (I.R.)	0.84 %	Should not exceed	2%
Sulphuric Anhydride (SO₃)	2.03 %	Should not exceed	3%
Magnesia (MgO)	1.16 %	Should not exceed	6%
Alkalies	0.46 %	Should not exceed	0.6%
Chlorides	0.0162 %	Should not exceed	0.05%

Issued to: Marketing Division

sd/–

OFFICER (QC)

sd/–

Sr. MANAGER (QC)

Table 2.8. Consistency Curves for the year 1999

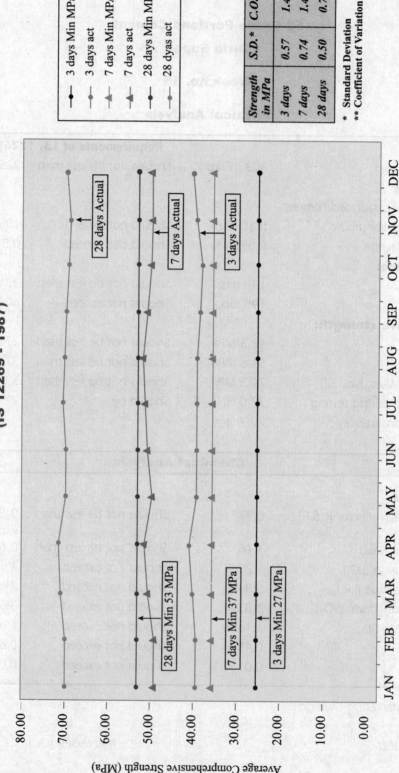

Birla Super Cement - OPC 53 Grade
(IS 12269 - 1987)

Strength in MPa	S.D.*	C.O.V.**
3 days	0.57	1.41
7 days	0.74	1.46
28 days	0.50	0.71

* Standard Deviation
** Coefficient of Variation

Legend:
- 3 days Min MPa
- 3 days act
- 7 days Min MPA
- 7 days act
- 28 days Min MPa
- 28 dyas act

Table 2.9. Brief Summary of Cement Testing Procedure and grades of Cement in various contries.

Country	Grade	TESTING PROCEDURE				COMPRESSIVE STRENGTH MPa			
		Material	Size of Cube mm.	Compaction	W/C ratio	1 day	3 days	7 days	28 days
India	33	1:3 Mortar	70.6 (50 cm²)	Vibration 12000/min For 2 min	0.39 to 0.45	-	16	22	33
	43	-	-	-	-	-	23	33	43
	53	-	-	-	-	-	12	37	53
Germany	30	Mortar	Prism 40 40 160 (25 cm²) **	Vibration	0.5	-	12	-	30
	35	-	-	-	-	-	15	-	35
	40	-	-	-	-	-	20	-	40
	45	-	-	-	-	-	25	-	45
	50	-	-	-	-	25	-	-	50
	55	-	-	-	-	25	-	-	55
China	275	1:2.5 Mortar	-	-	0.44	-	-	16	28
	325	-	-	-	-	-	12	19	33
	425	-	-	-	-	-	16	25	43
	525	-	-	-	-	-	21	32	53
	625	-	-	-	-	-	27	41	63
	725	-	-	-	-	-	36	-	73
U.S.S.R.	400	1:3 Mortar	Prism 40 40 160 **	-	0.4	-	-	-	40
	500	-	-	-.	-	-	-	-	50
	550	-	-	-	-	-	-	-	55
	600	-	-	-	-	-	-	-	60
U.K.	OPC	Mortar 1:3	70.6	Vibration 12000 ± 400 for 2 min	0.4	-	23	-	42
	-	Concrete 1:2.5:3.5	101.6	Tamping	0.6	-	13	-	30
U.S.A.	OPC Type 1	Mortar 1:2.75	50	Tamping	0.485	-	13	20	29

* P/4 + 3%, where P is standard consistency.

** After bending test, one half of the prism is stressed along the longer edges with loading area restricted to 25cm².

Additional General Information on Cement and other Pozzolanic Materials

Comparison of Physical Characteristics of OPC

Item	ASTM C-150, Type			EN 197-1, Strength Class			BIS, Strength Grades			
	I	III	V	32.5	42.5	52.5	33	43	53	SRC
Fineness, m²/kg	280	– @	280				225			
IST, minutes	45			75	60	45	30			
FST, minutes	375 (Maximum)						600 (Maximum)			
Compressive Strength, Mpa (Minimum) at										
1 day	–	12	–	–	–	–	–	–	–	–
2 days	–	–	–	–/10*	10/20	20/30	–		–	–
3 days	12	24	8	–	–	–	16	23	27	10
7 days	19	–	15	16		–	22	33	37	16
28 days	28	–	21	32.5	42.5	52.5	33	43	53	33
28 days (max)	–			52.5	62.5	–	–			

@ denotes no value specified

* first values for N (Normal), next for R (Rapid)

Comparison of Low heat Cements

Cement	Fineness, m²/kg	Heat of hydration, Cal/gm, at		Compressive strength, Mpa, at		
		7 days	28 days	3 days	7 days	28 days
ASTM type IV	280	60	70	–@	7	17
IS : 12600	320	65	75	10	16	35

@ – denotes not specified.

Comparison of Chemical Characteristics of OPC

Items (mad values)	ASTM C150, Types					EN 197-1	BIS OPC grades			
	I	II	III	IV	V		33	43	53	SRC
IR	0.75	3	0.75	0.75	0.75	5	4	3	3	4
LOI	3	-	3	2.5	3	5	5	5	4	5
MgO	6	6	6	6	6	5	6	6	6	6
Chloride	–@	@	–	–	–	0.10*	0.10#	0.10#	0.10#	0.10
Alkalis $	0.6	0.6	0.6	0.6	0.6	–	0.6	0.6	0.6	–
C_3A	–	8	15	7	5	–	–	–	–	5
$2C_3A + C_4AF$	–	–	–	–	25	–	–	–	–	25
C_3S	–	–	–	35	–	–	–	–	–	–
C_2S (min)	–	–	–	40	–	–	–	–	–	–

@ – denotes no value specified

* – for pre-stressing applications, a lower value may be prescribed

– 0.05% for prestressed concrete

$ – limits of alkali are optional, recommended in case of reactive aggregates.

Comparison of Physical properties of Portland Pozzolana Cements

Item	ASTM C-150, Type IP	EN 197-1, Strength Classes 32.5, 42.5, 52.5	IS: 1489-Part I
Fineness, m²/kg	–@	All requirements are identical to OPC as in Table 3	300
IST, minutes	45 (Min.)		30 (Min.)
FST, minutes	420 (Max.)		600 (Max.)
Compressive Strength, Mpa (Minimum) at			
3 days	13		16
7 days	20		22
28 days	25		33

Comparison of Physical properties
of Portland Slag Cements

Item	ASTM C-150, Type IP	EN 197-1, Strength Classes 32.5, 42.5, 52.5	IS: 455
Fineness, m²/kg	–@	All requirements are	225
IST, minutes	45 (Min.)	identical to OPC as in	30 (Min.)
FST, minutes	420 (Max.)	Table 3	600 (Max.)
Compressive Strength, Mpa (Minimum) at			
3 days	13		16
7 days	20		22
28 days	25		33

@ - Denotes no value specified

Comparison of Specifications
for Granulated Slag

S.No.	Item	EN 197-1	ASTM C-989	IS: 12089
1.	(C+M+1/3A)/(S+2/3A) Or	–@	–	1.0
	(C + M + A)/S, min	–	–	1.0
2.	(C + M + S), % mi n	67	–	–
3.	(C + M)/S, min	1.0	–	–
4.	MgO, % max	–	–	17
5.	MnO, % max	–	–	5.5
6.	Sulphide Sulphur, % max	–	2.5	2
7.	Insoluble Residue, % max	–	–	5
8.	Glass Content, % min	67	–	85

@ - denotes not specified.

(C=CaO, M = MgO, A = Al_2O_3, S = SiO_2)

Specifications for Fly ash in Cement and Concrete

(values are %, unless other units are indicated)

Item	ASTM C-618	European Specifications			IS : 3812	
		EN-450	EN-197-1	BS 3892-I	Existing 1981	Proposed
SiO$_2$, min					35	35
Reactive/soluble SiO$_2$, min.		25	25			25
S + A + F, min.	70				70	70
MgO, max.					5	5
LOI (1 hour) max.	6	5 - 7	5 - 7	7	12	5
Total Alkalis, max.	1.5				1.5	1.5
SO$_3$, max	5	3		2	2.75	2.75
Free CaO, max		1	1			
Total/reactive CaO max.		10	10	10		
Fineness, 45 micron, max.	34#	40@		12		34
Blaine's m^2/kg min.					320	320
Cement activity, 28 days	75*	75*		80**	80***	80***
Lime reactivity, N/mm^2					4	4.5
Soundness, Lechatelier, mm	10	10	10		10	10
Autoclave, %	0.8				0.8	0.8

Note

i) @ Permitted variation + 10 % of average

ii) # Permitted variation ± 5 % of average

iii) *   25 % fly ash

   **   30 % fly ash

   *** 20 % fly ash

iv) Drying shrinkage < 0.15 in IS 3812

REFERENCES

2.1.   *Fast Setting Cement, Engineering News Records*, Jan. 1956.

2.2   Product Literature of Birla White.

2.3   Information Supplied by CAI letter no. MISCEL/ENG/244 dated 7th Sept. 78.

2.4   Della, M. Roy, *Advanced Cement System, including CBC, DSP, MDF*, 9th International Congress on the Chemistry of Cement, New Delhi - 1992.

2.5   Comparison of BIS, ASTM and EN Cement Standards Compiled by Grasim Industries Ltd. (Cement Business) Mumbai.

**For Production of well Shaped and well Graded Aggregates.
Barmac Rock on Rock VSI Crusher**

Aggregates and Testing of Aggregates

General

Aggregates are the important constituents in concrete. They give body to the concrete, reduce shrinkage and effect economy. Earlier, aggregates were considerd as chemically inert materials but now it has been recognised that some of the aggregates are chemically active and also that certain aggregates exhibit chemical bond at the interface of aggregate and paste. The mere fact that the aggregates occupy 70–80 per cent of the volume of concrete, their impact on various characteristics and properties of concrete is undoubtedly considerable. To know more about the concrete it is very essential that one should know more about the aggregates which constitute major volume in concrete. Without the study of the aggregate in depth and range, the study of the concrete is incomplete. Cement is the only factory made standard component in concrete. Other ingredients, namely, water and aggregates are natural materials and can vary to any extent in many of their properties. The depth and range of studies that are required to be made in respect of aggregates to understand their widely varying effects and influence on the properties of concrete cannot be underrated.

Concrete can be considered as two phase materials for convenience; paste phase and aggregate phase. Having studied the paste phase of concrete in the earlier chapters, we shall now study the aggregates and aggregate phase in concrete in this chapter. The study of aggregates can best be done under the following sub-headings:

(a) Classification	(b) Source
(c) Size	(d) Shape
(e) Texture	(f) Strength
(g) Specific gravity and bulk density	(h) Moisture content
(i) Bulking factor	(j) Cleanliness
(k) Soundness	(l) Chemical properties
(m) Thermal properties	(n) Durability
(o) Sieve analysis	(p) Grading

Classification

Aggregates can be classified as (i) Normal weight aggregates, (ii) Light weight aggregates and (iii) Heary weight aggregates. Light weight aggregate and heavy weight aggregate will be discussed elsewhere under appropriate topics. In this chapter the properties of normal weight aggregates will only be discussed.

Normal weight aggregates can be further classified as natural aggregates and artificial aggregates.

Natural	*Artificial*
Sand, Gravel, Crushed	Broken Brick,
Rock such as Granite,	Air-cooled Slag.
Quartzite, Basalt,	Sintered fly ash
Sandstone	Bloated clay

Aggregates can also be classified on the basis of the size of the aggregates as coarse aggregate and fine aggregate.

Source

Almost all natural aggregate materials originate from bed rocks. There are three kinds of rocks, namely, igneous, sedimentary and metamorphic. These classifications are based on the mode of formation of rocks. It may be recalled that igneous rocks are formed by the cooling of molten magma or lava at the surface of the crest (trap and basalt) or deep beneath the crest (granite). The sedimentary rocks are formed originally below the sea bed and subsequently lifted up. Metamorphic rocks are originally either igneous or sedimentary rocks which are subsequently metamorphosed due to extreme heat and pressure. The concrete making properties of aggregate are influenced to some extent on the basis of geological formation of the parent rocks together with the subsequent processes of weathering and alteration. Within the main rock group, say granite group, the quality of aggregate may vary to a very great extent owing to changes in the structure and texture of the main parent rock from place to place.

Aggregates from Igneous Rocks

Most igneous rocks make highly satisfactory concrete aggregates because they are normally hard, tough and dense. The igneous rocks have massive structure, entirely crystalline or wholly glassy or in combination in between, depending upon the rate at which they were cooled during formation. They may be acidic or basic depending upon the percentage of silica content. They may occur light coloured or dark coloured. The igneous rocks as a class are the most chemically active concrete aggregate and show a tendency to react with the alkalies in cement. This aspect will be discussed later. As the igneous rock is one of the widely occurring type of rocks on the face of the earth, bulk of the concrete aggregates, that are derived, are of igneous origin

Aggregates from Sedimentary Rocks

Igneous rocks or metamorphic rocks are subjected to weathering agencies such as sun, rain and wind. These weathering agencies decompose, fragmantise, transport and deposit the particles of rock, deep beneath the ocean bed where they are cemented together by some of the cementing materials. The cementing materials could be carbonaceous, siliceous or argillaceous in nature. At the same time the deposited and cemented material gets subjected to static pressure of water and becomes compact sedimentary rock layer.

The deposition, cementation and consolidation takes place layer by layer beneath the ocean bed. These sedimentary rock formations subsequently get lifted up and becomes continent. The sedimentary rocks with the stratified structure are quarried and concrete aggregates are derived from it. The quality of aggregates derived from sedimentary rocks will vary in quality depending upon the cementing material and the pressure under which these rocks are originally compacted. Some siliceous sand stones have proved to be good concrete aggregate. Similarly, the limestone also can yield good concrete aggregate.

The thickness of the stratification of sedimentary rocks may vary from a fraction of a centimetre to many centimetres. If the stratification thickness of the parent rock is less, it is likely to show up even in an individual aggregate and thereby it may impair the strength of the aggregate. Such rocks may also yield flaky aggregates. Sedimentary rocks vary from soft to hard, porous to dense and light to heavy. The degree of consolidation, the type of cementation, the thickness of layers and contamination, are all important factors in determining the suitability of sedimentary rock for concrete aggregates.

Aggregates from Metamorphic Rocks

Both igneous rocks and sedimentary rocks may be subjected to high temperature and pressure which causes metamorphism which changes the structure and texture of rocks. Metamorphic rocks show foliated structure. The thickness of this foliation may vary from a few centimetres to many metres. If the thickness of this foliation is less, then individual aggregate may exhibit foliation which is not a desirable characteristic in aggregate. However, many metamorphic rocks particularly quartzite and gneiss have been used for production of good concrete aggregates.

It may be mentioned that many properties of aggregates namely, chemical and mineral composition, petro-graphic description, specific gravity, hardness, strength, physical and chemical stability, pore structure etc. depend mostly on the quality of parent rock. But there are some properties possessed by the aggregates which are important so far as concrete making is concerned which have no relation with the parent rock, particularly, the shape and size. While it is to be admitted that good aggregates from good parent rocks can make good concrete, it may be wrong to conclude that good concrete cannot be made from slightly inferior aggregates obtained from not so good parent rocks. Aggregates which are not so good can be used for making satisfactory concrete owing to the fact that a coating of cement paste on aggregates bring about improvement in respect of durability and strength characteristics. Therefore, selection of aggregates is required to be done judiciously taking the economic factor into consideration. Several factors may be considered in making the final selection of aggregates where more than one source is available. The relative cost of material in the several sources is the most important consideration that should weigh in making a choice. Records of use of aggregate from a particular source, and examination of concrete made with such aggregates, if such cases are there, provide valuable information.

The study will include appraisal of location and the amount of processing which each source may require. The aggregate which can be delivered to the mixing plant directly may not be the most economical one. It may require a cement content more than that of another source. Also very often the cost of some processing, such as correction of aggregate, may be fully recovered, when the processing accomplishes the reduction in cement content of the concrete. In general, that aggregate which will bring about the desired quality in the concrete with least overall expense, should be selected.

Size

The largest maximum size of aggregate practicable to handle under a given set of conditions should be used. Perhaps, 80 mm size is the maximum size that could be conveniently used for concrete making. Using the largest possible maximum size will result in (*i*) reduction of the cement content (*ii*) reduction in water requirement (*iii*) reduction of drying shrinkage. However, the maximum size of aggregate that can be used in any given condition may be limited by the following conditions:

(*i*) Thickness of section;   (*ii*) Spacing of reinforcement;

(*iii*) Clear cover;   (*iv*) Mixing, handling and placing techniques.

Generally, the maximum size of aggregate should be as large as possible within the limits specified, but in any case not greater than one-fourth of the minimum thickness of the member. Rubbles 160 mm size or upto any reasonable size may be used in plain concrete. In such concrete, called plum concrete, the quantity of rubble up to a maximum limit of 20 per cent by volume of the concrete, is used when specially permitted. The rubbles are placed on about 60 cm thick plastic concrete at certain distance apart and then the plastic concrete is vibrated by powerful internal vibrators. The rubbles sink into the concrete. This method of incorporating large boulders in the concrete is also called displacement concrete. This method is adopted in the construction of Koyna dam in Maharashtra. For heavily reinforced concrete member the nominal maximum size of aggregate should usually be restricted to 5 mm less than the minimum clear distance between the main bars or 5 mm less than the minimum cover to the reinforcement, whichever is smaller. But from various other practical considerations, for reinforced concrete work, aggregates having a maximum size of 20 mm are generally considered satisfactory.

Aggregates are divided into two categories from the consideration of size (*i*) Coarse aggregate and (*ii*) Fine aggregate. The size of aggregate bigger than 4.75 mm is considered as coarse aggregate and aggregate whose size is 4.75 mm and less is considered as fine aggregate.

Shape

The shape of aggregates is an important characteristic since it affects the workability of concrete. It is difficult to really measure the shape of irregular body like concrete aggregate which are derived from various rocks. Not only the characteristic of the parent rock, but also the type of crusher used will influence the shape of aggregates, *e.g.*, the rocks available round about Pune region are found to yield slightly flaky aggregates, whereas, good granite rock as found in Banglore will yield cubical aggregate. The shape of the aggregate is very much influenced by the type of crusher and the reduction ratio *i.e.*, the ratio of size of material fed into crusher to the size of the finished product. Many rocks contain planes of parting or jointing which is characteristic of its formation. It also reflects the internal petrographic structure. As a consequence of these tendencies, schists, slates and shales commonly produce flaky forms, whereas, granite, basalt and quartzite usually yield more or less equidimensional particles. Similarly, quartizite which does not posses cleavage planes produces cubical shape aggregates.

From the standpoint of economy in cement requirement for a given water/cement ratio, rounded aggregates are preferable to angular aggregates. On the other hand, the additional cement required for angular aggregate is offset to some extent by the higher strengths and sometimes by greater durability as a result of the interlocking texture of the hardened concrete and higher bond characteristic between aggregate and cement paste.

Flat particles in concrete aggregates will have particularly objectionable influence on the workability, cement requirement, strength and durability. In general, excessively flaky aggregate makes very poor concrete.

Classification of particles on the basis of shape of the aggregate is shown in Table 3.1.

One of the methods of expressing the angularity qualitatively is by a figure called Angularity Number, as suggested by Shergold [3.1]. This is based on the percentage voids in the aggregate after compaction in a specified manner. The test gives a value termed the angularity number. The method of determination is described in IS: 2386 (Part I) 1963.

Table 3.1 Shape of Particle

Classification	Description	Examples
Rounded	Fully water worn or completely shaped by attrition	River or seashore gravels; desert, seashore and wind-blown sands
Irregular or Partly rounded	Naturally irregular or partly shaped by attrition, having rounded edges	Pit sands and gravels; land or dug flints; cuboid rock
Angular	Possessing well-defined edges formed at the intersection of roughly planar faces	Crushed rocks of all types; talus; screes
Flaky	Material, usually angular, of which the thickness is small relative to the width and/or length	Laminated rocks

| Round (spherical) concrete aggregate. | Flaky concrete aggregate. | Crushed concrete aggregate. |

A quantity of single sized aggregate is filled into metal cylinder of three litre capacity. The aggregates are compacted in a standard manner and the percentage of void is found out. The void can be found out by knowing the specific gravity of aggregate and bulk density or by pouring water to the cylinder to bring the level of water upto the brim. If the void is 33 per cent the angularity of such aggregate is considered zero. If the void is 44 per cent the angularity number of such aggregate is considered 11. In other words, if the angularity number is zero, the solid volume of the aggregate is 67 per cent and if angularity number is

Poorly shapped crushed aggregate. It will make poor concrete.

Barmac crushed 20 mm cubical aggregate. It will make good concrete.

Good aggregate resulted from Barmac crusher.

20 mm crushed angular aggregates not so good for concrete.

Courtesy : Durocrete Pune

11, the solid volume of the aggregate is 56 per cent. The normal aggregates which are suitable for making the concrete may have angularity number anything from zero to 11. Angularity number zero represents the most practicable rounded aggregates and the angularity number 11 indicates the most angular aggregates that could be tolerated for making concrete not so unduly harsh and uneconomical.

Murdock suggested a different method for expressing the shape of aggregate by a parameter called Angularity Index '*fA*'.[3.2]

Angularity Index $\quad fA = \dfrac{3\,fH}{20} + 1.0 \quad$ where *fH* is the Angularity number.

There has been a lot of controversy on the subject whether the angular aggregate or rounded aggregate will make better concrete. While discussing the shape of aggregate, the texture of the aggregate also enters the discussion because of its close association with the shape. Generally, rounded aggregates are smooth textured and angular aggregates are rough textured. Some engineers, prohibit the use of rounded aggregate on the plea

Shape Size	Rounded	Irregular	Angular
40mm			
20mm			
10mm			
4.75mm			

Shape and size of aggregates
Courtesy : Ambuja Cement

that it yields poor concrete, due to lack of bond between the smooth surface of the aggregate and cement paste. They suggest that if at all the rounded aggregate is required to be used for economical reason, it should be broken and then used. This concept is not fully justified for the reason that even the so called, the smooth surface of rounded aggregates is rough enough for developing a reasonably good bond between the surface and the submicroscopic cement gel. But the angular aggregates are superior to rounded aggregates from the following two points of view:

(a) Angular aggregates exhibit a better interlocking effect in concrete, which property makes it superior in concrete used for roads and pavements.

(b) The total surface area of rough textured angular aggregate is more than smooth rounded aggregate for the given volume. By having greater surface area, the angular aggregate may show higher bond strength than rounded aggregates.

The higher surface area of angular aggregate with rough texture requires more water for a given workability than rounded aggregates. This means that for a given set of conditions from the point of view of water/cement ratio and the consequent strength, rounded aggregate gives higher strength. Superimposing plus and minus points in favour and against these two kinds of aggregates it can be summed up as follows:

For water/cement ratio below 0.4 the use of crushed aggregate has resulted in strength up to 38 per cent higher than the rounded aggregate. With an increase in water/cement ratio the influence of roughness of surface of the aggregate gets reduced, presumably because the strength of the paste itself becomes paramount, and at a water/cement ratio of 0.65, no difference in strength of concrete made with angular aggregate or rounded aggregate has been observed.

The shape of the aggregates becomes all the more important in case of high strength and high performance concrete where very low water/cement ratio is required to be used. In such cases cubical shaped aggregates are required for better workability. To produce mostly cubical shaped aggregate and reduce flaky aggregate, improved versions of crushers are employed, such as Hydrocone crushers, Barmac rock on rock VSI crusher etc. Sometimes ordinarily crushed aggregates are further processed to convert them to well graded cubical aggregates.

In the years to come natural sand will not be available in large quantity for big infrastructural projects. One has to go for manufactured sand. When rock is crushed in the normal way it is likely to yield flaky fine aggregate. Improved version of crushers are used to produce cubical shaped well graded fine aggregate. This method of production of good fine aggregate is being practised for high rise building projects at Mumbai and for construction of Mumbai-Pune express highway. On realising the importance of shape of aggregates for producing high strength concrete the improved version of crushers are being extinsively employed in India.

Texture

Surface texture is the property, the measure of which depends upon the relative degree to which particle surfaces are polished or dull, smooth or rough. Surface texture depends on hardness, grain size, pore structure, structure of the rock, and the degree to which forces acting on the particle surface have smoothed or roughend it. Hard, dense, fine-grained materials will generally have smooth fracture surfaces. Experience and laboratory experiments have shown that the adhesion between cement paste and aggregate is influenced by several complex factors in addition to the physical and mechanical properties.

As surface smoothness increases, contact area decreases, hence a highly polished particle will have less bonding area with the matrix than a rough particle of the same volume. A smooth particle, however, will require a thinner layer of paste to lubricate its movements with respect to other aggregate particles. It will, therefore, permit denser packing for equal workability and hence, will require lower paste content than rough particles. It has been also shown by experiments that rough textured aggregate develops higher bond strength in tension than smooth textured aggregate. The beneficial effects of surface texture of aggregate on flexural strength can be seen from Table 3.2.

Table 3.2. Influence of Texture on Strength[3.3]

Per cent of Particles		Water/Cement Ratio	Strength 28 days MPa	
Smooth	Rough		Flexural	Compressive
100	0	0.54	4.3	34.8
50	50	0.57	4.6	32.1
0	100	0.60	4.8	29.5

Surface texture characteristics of the aggregate as classified in IS: 383: 1970 is shown below.

Table 3.3. Surface Characteristics of Aggregate

Group	Surface Texture	Examples
1.	Glassy	Black flint
2.	Smooth	Chert; slate; marble; some rhyolite
3.	Granular	Sandstone; oolites
4.	Crystalline	Fine : Basalt; trachyte; medium : Dolerite; granophyre; granulite; microgranite; some limestones; many dolomites. Coarse : Gabbro; gneiss; granite; granodiorite; syenite
5.	Honeycombed and porous	Scoria; Pumice, trass.

Measurement of Surface Texture

A large number of possible methods are available and this may be divided broadly into direct and indirect methods. Direct methods include (*i*) making a cast of the surface and magnifying a section of this, (*ii*) Tracing the irregularities by drawing a fine point over the surface and drawing a trace magnified by mechanical, optical, or electrical means, (*iii*) getting a section through the aggregates and examining a magnified image. Indirect methods include: (*i*) measurement of the degree of dispersion of light falling on the surface, (*ii*) determining the weight of a fine powder required to fill up the interstices of the surface to a truly smooth surface, (*iii*) the rock surface is held against rubber surface at a standard pressure and the resistance to the flow of air between the two surfaces is measured.

Aggregate Crushing Value Apparatus.

Strength

When we talk of strength we do not imply the strength of the parent rock from which the aggregates are produced, because the strength of the rock does not exactly represent the strength of the aggregate in concrete. Since concrete is an assemblage of individual pieces of aggregate bound together by cementing material, its properties are based primarily on the quality of the cement paste. This strength is dependant also on the bond between the cement paste and the aggregate. If either the strength of the paste or the bond between the paste and aggregate is low, a concrete of poor quality will be obtained irrespective of the strength of the rock or aggregate. But when cement paste of good quality is provided and its bond with the aggregate is satisfactory, then the mechanical properties of the rock or aggregate will influence the strength of concrete. From the above it can be concluded that while strong aggregates cannot make strong concrete, for making strong concrete, strong aggregates are an essential requirement. In other words, from a weak rock or aggregate strong concrete cannot be made. By and large naturally available mineral aggregates are strong enough for making normal strength concrete. The test for strength of aggregate is required to be made in the following situations:

(*i*)   For production of high strength and ultra high strength concrete.

(*ii*)   When contemplating to use aggregates manufactured from weathered rocks.

(*iii*) Aggregate manufactured by industrial process.

Aggregatte Crushing Value

Strength of rock is found out by making a test specimen of cylindrical shape of size 25 mm diameter and 25 mm height. This cylinder is subjected to compressive stress. Different rock samples are found to give different compressive strength varying from a minimum of about 45 MPa to a maximum of 545 MPa. As said earlier, the compressive strength of parent rock does not exactly indicate the strength of aggregate in concrete. For this reason assessment of strength of the aggregate is made by using a sample of bulk aggregate in a standardised manner. This test is known as aggregate crushing value test. Aggregate crushing value gives a relative measure of the resistance of an aggregate sample to crushing under gradually applied compressive load. Generally, this test is made on single sized aggregate passing 12.5 mm and retained on 10 mm sieve. The aggregate is placed in a cylindrical mould and a load of 40 ton is applied through a plunger. The material crushed to finer than 2.36 mm

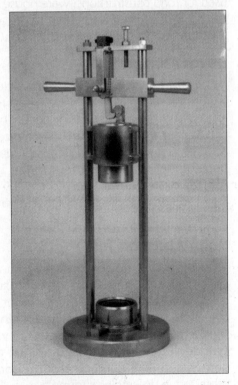

is separated and expressed as a percentage of the original weight taken in the mould. This percentage is referred as aggregate crushing value. The crushing value of aggregate is restricted to 30 per cent for concrete used for roads and pavements and 45 per cent may be permitted for other structures.

The crushing value of aggregate is rather insensitive to the variation in strength of weaker aggregate. This is so because having been crushed before the application of the full load of 40 tons, the weaker materials become compacted, so that the amount of crushing during later stages of the test is reduced. For this reason a simple test known as "10 per cent fines value" is introduced. When the aggregate crushing value become 30 or higher, the result is likely to be inaccurate, in which case the aggregate should be subjected to "10 per cent fines value" test which gives a better picture about the strength of such aggregates.

This test is also done on a single sized aggregate as mentioned above. Load required to produce 10 per cent fines (particles finer than 2.36 mm) is found out by observing the

Aggregate Impact Value Apparatus.

penetration of plunger. The 10 per cent fines value test shows a good correlation with the standard crushing value test for strong aggregates while for weaker aggregates this test is more sensitive and gives a truer picture of the differences between more or less weak samples.

It should be noted that in the 10 per cent fines value test unlike the crushing value test, a higher numerical result denotes a higher strength of the aggregate. The detail of this test is given at the end of this chapter under testing of aggregate.

Aggregate Impact Value

With respect to concrete aggregates, toughness is usually considered the resistance of the material to failure by impact. Several attempts to develop a method of test for aggregates impact value have been made. The most successful is the one in which a sample of standard aggregate kept in a mould is subjected to fifteen blows of a metal hammer of weight 14 Kgs. falling from a height of 38 cms. The quantity of finer material (passing through 2.36 mm) resulting from pounding will indicate the toughness of the sample of aggregate. The ratio of the weight of the fines (finer than 2.36 mm size) formed, to the weight of the total sample taken is expressed as a percentage. This is known as aggregate impact value IS 283-1970 specifies that aggregate impact value shall not exceed 45 per cent by weight for aggregate used for concrete other than wearing surface and 30 per cent by weight, for concrete for wearing surfaces, such as run ways, roads and pavements.

Aggregate Abrasion Value

Apart from testing aggregate with respect to its crushing value, impact resistance, testing the aggregate with respect to its resistance to wear is an important test for aggregate to be used for road constructions, ware house floors and pavement construction. Three tests are in common use to test aggregate for its abrasion resistance. (*i*) Deval attrition test (*ii*) Dorry abrasion test (*iii*) Los Angels test.

Deval Attrition Test

In the Deval attrition test, particles of known weight are subjected to wear in an iron cylinder rotated 10000 times at certain speed. The proportion of material crushed finer than 1.7 mm size is expressed as a percentage of the original material taken. This percentage is taken as the attrition value of the aggregate. This test has been covered by IS 2386 (Part IV) – 1963. But it is pointed out that wherever possible Los Angeles test should be used.

Dorry Abrasion Test

This test is not covered by Indian Standard Specification. The test involves in subjecting a cylindrical specimen of 25 cm height and 25 cm diameter to the abrasion against rotating metal disk sprinkled with quartz sand. The loss in weight of the cylinder after 1000 revolutions of the table is determined. The hardeness of the rock sample is expressed in an empirical formula

Los Angeles Abrasion Testing Machine.

$$\text{Hardness} = 20 - \frac{\text{Loss in Grams}}{3}$$

Good rock should show an abrasion value of not less than 17. A rock sample with a value of less than 14 would be considered poor.

Los Angeles Test

Los Angeles test was developed to overcome some of the defects found in Deval test. Los Angeles test is characterised by the quickness with which a sample of aggregate may be tested. The applicability of the method to all types of commonly used aggregate makes this method popular. The test involves taking specified quantity of standard size material along with specified number of abrasive charge in a standard cylinder and revolving if for certain specified revolutions. The particles smaller than 1.7 mm size is separated out. The loss in weight expressed as percentage of the original weight taken gives the abrasion value of the aggregate. The abrasion value should not be more than 30 per cent for wearing surfaces and not more than 50 per cent for concrete other than wearing surface. Table 3.4 gives average values of crushing strength of rocks, aggregate crushing value, abrasion value, impact value and attrition value for different rock groups.

Modulus of Elasticity

Modulus of elasticity of aggregate depends on its composition, texture and structure. The modulus of elasticity of aggregate will influence the properties of concrete with respect to shrinkage and elastic behaviour and to very small extent creep of concrete. Many studies have been conducted to investigate the influence of modulus of elasticity of aggregate on the properties of concrete. One of the studies indicated that the '*E*' of aggregate has a decided effect on the elastic property of concrete and that the relation of '*E*' of aggregate to that of the concrete is not a linear function, but may be expressed as an equation of exponential type.[3.4]

Table 3.4. Average Test Values For Rocks of Different Groups

Rock Group	Crushing Strength MPa	Aggregate crushing value	Abrasion value	Impact value	Attrition value		Specific gravity
					Dry	Wet	
Basalt	207	12	17.6	16	3.3	5.5	2.85
Flint	214	17	19.2	17	3.1	2.5	2.55
Gabbro	204	-	18.7	19	2.5	3.2	2.95
Granite	193	20	18.7	13	2.9	3.2	2.69
Gritstone	229	12	18.1	15	3.0	5.3	2.67
Hornfels	354	11	18.8	17	2.7	3.8	2.88
Limestone	171	24	16.5	9	4.3	7.8	2.69
Porphyry	239	12	19.0	20	2.6	2.6	2.66
Quartizite	339	16	18.9	16	2.5	3.0	2.62
Schist	254	-	18.7	13	3.7	4.3	2.76

Bulk Density

The bulk density or unit weight of an aggregate gives valuable informations regarding the shape and grading of the aggregate. For a given specific gravity the angular aggregates show a lower bulk density. The bulk density of aggregate is measured by filling a container of known volume in a standard manner and weighing it. Bulk density shows how densely the aggregate is packed when filled in a standard manner. The bulk density depends on the particle size distribution and shape of the particles. One of the early methods of mix design make use of this parameter bulk density in proportioning of concrete mix. The higher the bulk density, the lower is the void content to be filled by sand and cement. The sample which gives the minimum voids or the one which gives maximum bulk density is taken as the right sample of aggregate for making economical mix. The method of determining bulk density also gives the method for finding out void content in the sample of aggregate.

For determination of bulk density the aggregates are filled in the container and then they are compacted in a standard manner. The weight of the aggregate gives the bulk density calculated in kg/litre or kg/m³. Knowing the specific gravity of the aggregate in saturated and surface-dry condition, the void ratio can also be calculated.

$$\text{Percentage voids} = \frac{Gs - \gamma}{Gs} \times 100$$

where Gs = specific gravity of the aggregate   and γ = bulk density in kg/litre.

Bulk density of aggregate is of interest when we deal with light weight aggregate and heavy weight aggregate. The parameter of bulk density is also used in concrete mix design for converting the proportions by weight into proportions by volume when weigh batching equipments is not available at the site.

Specific Gravity

In concrete technology, specific gravity of aggregates is made use of in design calculations of concrete mixes. With the specific gravity of each constituent known, its weight can be converted into solid volume and hence a theoretical yield of concrete per unit volume can be calculated. Specific gravity of aggregate is also required in calculating the compacting factor in connection with the workability measurements. Similarly, specific gravity of aggregate is required to be considered when we deal with light weight and heavy weight concrete. Average specific gravity of the rocks vary from 2.6 to 2.8.

Absorption and Moisture Content

Some of the aggregates are porous and absorptive. Porosity and absorption of aggregate will affect the water/cement ratio and hence the workability of concrete. The porosity of aggregate will also affect the durability of concrete when the concrete is subjected to freezing and thawing and also when the concrete is subjected to chemically aggressive liquids.

The water absorption of aggregate is determined by measuring the increase in weight of an oven dry sample when immersed in water for 24 hours. The ratio of the increase in weight to the weight of the dry sample expressed as percentage is known as absorption of aggregate. But when we deal with aggregates in concrete the 24 hours absorption may not be of much significance, on the other hand, the percentage of water absorption during the time interval equal of final set of cement may be of more significance. The aggregate absorbs water in concrete and thus affects the workability and final volume of concrete. The rate and amount of absorption within a time interval equal to the final set of the cement will only be

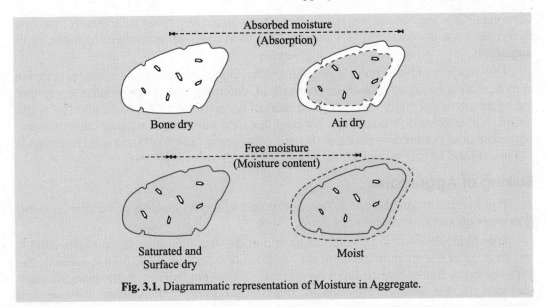

Fig. 3.1. Diagrammatic representation of Moisture in Aggregate.

a significant factor rather than the 24 hours absorption of the aggregate. It may be more realistic to consider that absorption capacity of the aggregates which is going to be still less owing to the sealing of pores by coating of cement particle particularly in rich mixes. In allowing for extra water to be added to a concrete mix to compensate for the loss of water due to absorption, proper appreciation of the absorption in particular time interval must be made rather than estimating on the basis of 24 hours absorption.

In proportioning the materials for concrete, it is always taken for granted that the aggregates are saturated and surface dry. In mix design calculation the relative weight of the aggregates are based on the condition that the aggregates are saturated and surface dry. But in practice, aggregates in such ideal condition is rarely met with. Aggregates are either dry and absorptive to various degrees or they have surface moisture. The aggregates may have been exposed to rain or may have been washed in which case they may contain surface moisture or the aggregates may have been exposed to the sun for a long time in which case they are absorptive. Fine aggregates dredged from river bed usually contains surface moisture. When stacked in heap the top portion of the heap may be comparatively dry, but the lower portion of the heap usually contains certain amount of free moisture. It should be noted that if the aggregates are dry they absorb water from the mixing water and thereby affect the workability and, on the other hand, if the aggregates contain surface moisture they contribute extra water to the mix and there by increase the water/cement ratio. Both these conditions are harmful for the quality of concrete. In making quality concrete, it is very essential that corrective measures should be taken both for absorption and for free moisture so that the water/cement ratio is kept exactly as per the design.

Very often at the site of concrete work we may meet dry coarse aggregate and moist fine aggregate. The absorption capacity of the coarse aggregate is of the order of about 0.5 to 1 per cent by weight of aggregate. A higher absorption value may be met with aggregates derived from sand stone or other soft and porous rocks. Recently it was observed that the rocks excavated in the cuttings of Pune-Mumbai express highway, showed absorption of around 4% unusualy high for rock of the type Deccan trap. The high absorption characteristic has presented plenty of problems for using such stone aggregate for 40 MPa Pavement Quality

Concrete (PQC). The natural fine aggregates often contain free moisture anything from one to ten per cent or more. Fig. 3.1 shows a diagrammatic representation of moisture in aggregates.

Free moisture in both coarse aggregate and fine aggregate affects the quality of concrete in more than one way. In case of weigh batching, determination of free moisture content of the aggregate is necessary and then correction of water/cement ratio to be effected in this regard. But when volume batching is adopted, the determination of moisture content of fine aggregate does not become necessary but the consequent bulking of sand and correction of volume of sand to give allowance for bulking becomes necessary.

Bulking of Aggregates

The free moisture content in fine aggregate results in bulking of volume. Bulking phenomenon can be explained as follows:

Free moisture forms a film around each particle. This film of moisture exerts what is known as surface tension which keeps the neighbouring particles away from it. Similarly, the force exerted by surface tension keeps every particle away from each other. Therefore, no point contact is possible between the particles. This causes bulking of the volume. The extent of surface tension and consequently how far the adjacent particles are kept away will depend upon the percentage of moisture content and the particle size of the fine aggregate. It is interesting to note that the bulking increases with the increase in moisture content upto a certain limit and beyond that the further increase in the moisture content results in the decrease in the volume and at a moisture content representing saturation point, the fine aggregate shows no bulking. It can be seen from Fig. 3.2 that fine sand bulks more and coarse sand bulks less. From this it follows that the coarse aggregate also bulks but the bulking is so little that it is always neglected. Extremely fine sand and particularly the manufactured fine aggregate bulks as much as about 40 per cent.

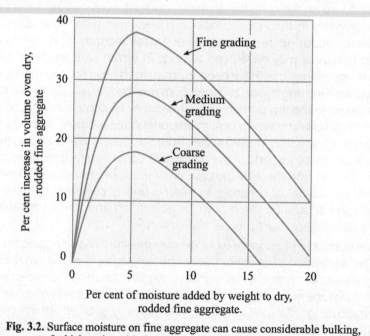

Fig. 3.2. Surface moisture on fine aggregate can cause considerable bulking, the amount of which varies with the amount of moisture and the aggregate grading.

Due to the bulking, fine aggregate shows completely unrealistic volume. Therefore, it is absolutely necessary that consideration must be given to the effect of bulking in proportioning the concrete by volume. If cognisance is not given to the effect of bulking, in case of volume batching, the resulting concrete is likely to be undersanded and harsh. It will also affect the yield of concrete for a given cement content.

The extent of bulking can be estimated by a simple field test. A sample of moist fine aggregate is filled into a measuring cylinder in the normal manner. Note down the level, say h_1. Pour water into the measuring cylinder and completely inundate the sand and shake it. Since the volume of the saturated sand is the same as that of the dry sand, the inundated sand completely offsets the bulking effect. Note down the level of the sand say, h_2. Then $h_1 - h_2$ shows the bulking of the sample of sand under test.

$$\text{Percentage of bulking} = \frac{h_1 - h_2}{h_2} \times 100$$

In a similar way the bulking factor can be found out by filling the wet sand in a water tight measuring box (farma) up to the top and then pour water to inundate the sand. Then measure the subsidence of sand and express it as a percentage. This gives a more realistic picture of the bulking factor.

The field test to find out the percentage of bulking is so simple that this could be conducted in a very short time interval and the percentage of bulking so found out could be employed for correcting the volume of fine aggregate to be used. This can be considered as one of the important methods of field control to produce quality concrete. Since volume batching is not adopted for controlled concrete, the determination of the percentage of moisture content is not normally required. The quantity of water could be controlled by visual examination of the mix and by experience. The percentage of free moisture content is required to be determined and correction made only when weigh batching is adopted for production of quality concrete.

Measurement of Moisture Content of Aggregates

Determination of moisture content in aggregate is of vital importance in the control of the quality of concrete particularly with respect to workability and strength. The measurement of the moisture content of aggregates is basically a very simple operation. But it is complicated by several factors. The aggregate will absorb a certain quantity of water depending on its porosity. The water content can be expressed in terms of the weight of the aggregate when absolutely dry, surface dry or when wet. Water content means the free water, or that held on the surface of the aggregate or the total water content which includes the absorbed water plus the free water, or the water held in the interior portion of aggregate particles.

The measurement of the moisture content of aggregate in the field must be quick, reasonably accurate and must require only simple appartus which can be easily handled and used in the field. Some of the methods that are being used for determination of moisture content of aggregate are given below:

(*i*) Drying Method   (*ii*) Displacement Method

(*iii*) Calcium Carbide Method   (*iv*) Measurement by electrical meter.

(*v*) Automatic measurement

Drying Method

The application of drying method is fairly simple. Drying is carried out in a oven and the loss in weight before and after drying will give the moisture content of the aggregate. If the drying is done completely at a high temperature for a long time, the loss in weight will include not only the surface water but also some absorbed water. Appropriate corrections may be made for the saturated and surface dry condition. The oven drying method is too slow for field use. A fairly quick result can be obtained by heating the aggregate quickly in an open pan. The process can also be speeded up by pouring inflammable liquid such as methylated spirit or acetone over the aggregate and igniting it.

Displacement Method

In the laboratory the moisture content of aggregate can be determined by means of pycnometer or by using Siphon-Can Method. The principle made use of is that the specific gravity of normal aggregate is higher than that of water and that a given weight of wet aggregate will occupy a greater volume than the same weight of the aggregate when dry. By knowing the specific gravity of the dry aggregate, the specific gravity of the wet aggregate can be calculated. From the difference between the specific gravities of the dry and wet aggregates, the moisture content of the aggregate can be calculated.

Calcium Carbide Method

A quick and reasonably accurate method of determining the moisture content of fine aggregate is to mix it with an excess of calcium carbide in a strong air-tight vessel fitted with pressure gauge. Calcium carbide reacts with surface moisture in the aggregate to produce acetylene gas. The pressure of acetylene gas generated depends upon the moisture content of the aggregates. The pressure gauge is calibrated by taking a measured quantity of aggregate of known moisture content and then such a calibrated pressure gauge could be used to read the moisture content of aggregate directly. This method is ofen used to find out the moisture content of fine aggregate at the site of work. The equipment consists of a small balance, a standard scoop and a container fixed with dial gauge. The procedure is as follows: Weigh 6 grams of representative sample of wet sand and pour it into the container. Take one scoop full of calcium carbide powder and put it into the container. Close the lid of the container and shake it rigorously. Calcium carbide reacts with surface moisture and produces acetylene gas, the pressure of which drives the indicator needle on the pressure gauge. The pressure gauge is so calibrated, that it gives directly percentage of moisture. The whole job takes only less than 5 minutes and as such, this test can be done at very close intervals of time at the site of work.

Electrical Meter Method

Recently electrical meters have been developed to measure instantaneous or continuous reading of the moisture content of the aggregate. The principle that the resistance gets changed with the change in moisture content of the aggregate has been made use of. In some sophisticated batching plant, electrical meters are used to find out the moisture content and also to regulate the quantity of water to be added to the continuous mixer.

Automatic Measurement

In modern batching plants surface moisture in aggregates is automatically recorded by means of some kind of sensor arrangement. The arrangement is made in such a way that the quantity of free water going with aggregate is automatically recorded and simultaneously that much quantity of water is reduced. This sophisticated method results in an accuracy of ± 0.2 to 0.6%.

Cleanliness

The concrete aggregates should be free from impurities and deletrious substances which are likely to interfere with the process of hydration, prevention of effective bond between the aggregates and matrix. The impurities sometimes reduce the durability of the aggregate.

Generally, the fine aggregate obtained from natural sources is likely to contain organic impurities in the form of silt and clay. The manufactured fine aggregate does not normally contain organic materials. But it may contain excess of fine crushed stone dust. Coarse aggregate stacked in the open and unused for long time may contain moss and mud in the lower level of the stack.

Sand is normally dredged from river beds and streams in the dry season when the river bed is dry or when there is not much flow in the river. Under such situation along with the sand, decayed vegetable matter, humus, organic matter and other impurities are likely to settle down. But if sand is dredged when there is a good flow of water from very deep bed, the organic matters are likely to get washed away at the time of dredging. The organic matters will interfere with the setting action of cement and also interfere with the bond characteristics with the aggregates. The presence of moss or algae will also result in entrainment of air in the concrete which reduces its strength.

To ascertain whether a sample of fine aggregate contains permissible quantity of organic impurities or not, a simple test known as colorimetric test is made. The sample of sand is mixed with a liquid containing 3 per cent solution of sodium hydroxide in water. It is kept for 24 hours and the colour developed is compared with a standard colour card. If the colour of the sample is darker than the standard colour card, it is inferred that the content of the organic impurities in the sand is more than the permissible limit. In that case either the sand is rejected or is used after washing.

Sometimes excessive silt and clay contained in the fine or coarse aggregate may result in increased shrinkage or increased permeability in addition to poor bond characteristics. The excessive silt and clay may also necessitate greater water requirements for given workability.

The quantity of clay, fine silt and fine dust are determined by sedimentation method. In this method, a sample of aggregate is poured into a graduated measuring jar and the aggregate is nicely rodded to dislodge particles of clay and silt adhering to the aggregate particles. The jar with the liquid is completely shaken so that all the clay and silt particles get mixed with water and then the whole jar is kept in an undisturbed condition. After a certain time interval, the thickness of the layer of clay and silt standing over the fine aggregate particles will give a fair idea of the percentage of clay and silt content in the sample of aggregate under test. The limits of deleterious materials as given in IS 383-1970 are shown in Table 3.5.

Fine aggregate from tidal river or from pits near sea shore will generally contain some percentage of salt. The contamination of aggregates by salt will affect the setting properties and ultimate strength of concrete. Salt being hygroscopic, will also cause efflorescence and unsightly appearance. Opinions are divided on the question whether the salt contained in aggregates would cause corrosion of reinforcement. But studies have indicated that the usual percentage of salt generally contained in the fine aggregate will not cause corrosion in any appreciable manner. However, it is a good practice to wash sand containing salt more than 3 per cent.

Table 3.5. Limits of Deleterious Materials (IS: 383-1970)

Sr. No.	Deleterious substances	Method of test	Fine aggregate percentage by weight, max		Coarse aggregate percentage by weight, max	
			uncrushed	crushed	uncrushed	crushed
(1)	(2)	(3)	(4)	(5)	(6)	(7)
(i)	Coal and lignite	IS:2386 (Part II)-1963	1.00	1.00	1.00	1.00
(ii)	Clay lumps	IS:2386 (Part II)-1963	1.00	1.00	1.00	1.00
(iii)	Materials finer than 75-micron IS Sieve	IS:2386 (Part I)-1963	3.00	15.00	3.00	3.00
(iv)	Soft fragments	IS:2386 (Part II)-1963	-	-	3.00	-
(v)	Shale	IS:2386 (Part II)-1963	1.00	-	-	-
(vi)	Total of percentages of all deleterious materials (except mica) including Sr. No. (i) to (v) for col. 4, 6 and 7 and Sr. No. (i) and (ii) for col. 5 only	-	5.00	2.00	5.00	5.00

Notes:

(i) The presence of mica in the fine aggregate has been found to reduce considerably the durability and compressive strength of concrete and further investigations are underway to determine the extent of the deleterious effect of mica. It is advisable, therefore, to investigate the mica content of fine aggregate and make suitable allowances for the possible reduction in the strength of concrete or mortar.

(ii) The aggregate shall not contain harmful organic impurities (tested in accordance with IS:2386 (Part II-1963) in sufficient quantities to effect adversely the strength or durability of concrete. A fine aggregate which fails in the test for organic impurities may be used, provided that, when tested for the effect of organic impurities on the strength of mortar, the relative strength at 7 and 28 days, reported in accordance with clause 7 of IS:2386 (Part VI)-1963 is not less than 95 per cent.

Aggregates from some source may contain iron pyrites, clay nodules, soft shale particles and other impurities which are likely to swell when wetted. These particles also get worn out when concrete is subjected to abrasion and thereby cause pitting in concrete. Such unsound particles cause damage to the concrete particularly, when subjected to alternate freezing and thawing or wetting and drying. A limitation to the quantity of such impurities is already shown in Table 3.5.

Soundness of Aggregate

Soundness refers to the ability of aggregate to resist excessive changes in volume as a result of changes in physical conditions. These physical conditions that affect the soundness of aggregate are the freezing the thawing, variation in temperature, alternate wetting and drying under normal conditions and wetting and drying in salt water. Aggregates which are porous, weak and containing any undesirable extraneous matters undergo excessive volume change when subjected to the above conditions. Aggregates which undergo more than the specified amount of volume change is said to be unsound aggregates. If concrete is liable to be exposed to the action of frost, the coarse and fine aggregate which are going to be used should be subjected to soundness test.

The soundness test consists of alternative immersion of carefully graded and weighed test sample in a solution of sodium or magnesium sulphate and oven drying it under specified conditions. The accumulation and growth of salt crystals in the pores of the particles is thought to produce disruptive internal forces similar to the action of freezing of water or crystallisation of salt. Loss in weight, is measured for a specified number of cycles. Soundness test is specified in IS 2386 (Part V). As a general guide, it can be taken that the average loss of weight after 10 cycles should not exceed 12 per cent and 18 per cent when tested with sodium sulphate and magnesium sulphate respectively.

It may be pointed out that the sulphate soundness test might be used to accept aggregates but not to reject them, the assumption being that aggregates which will satisfactorily withstand the test are good while those which breakdown may or may not be bad. Unfortunately, the test is not reliable. Certain aggregates with extremely fine pore structure show almost no loss of weight. Conversely, certain aggregates that disintegrate readily in the sulphate test but produce concrete of high resistance to freezing and thawing. A low loss of weight usually. but not always, an evidence of good durability, whereas a high loss of weight places the aggregate in questionable category.

Alkali Aggregate Reaction

For a long time aggregates have been considered as inert materials but later on, particularly, after 1940's it was clearly brought out that the aggregates are not fully inert. Some of the aggregates contain reactive silica, which reacts with alkalies present in cement *i.e.,* sodium oxide and potassium oxide.

In the United States of America it was found for the first time that many failures of concrete structures like pavement, piers and sea walls could be attributed to the alkali-aggregate reaction. Since then a systematic study has been made in this regard and now it is proved beyond doubt that certain types of reactive aggregates are responsible for promoting alkali-aggregate reaction.

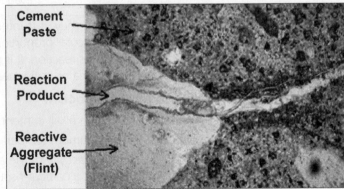

Typical Alkali - Aggregate reaction. Alkali silicate gels of unlimited swelling type are formed under favourable conditions.

The types of rocks which contain reactive constituents include traps, andesites, rhyolites, siliceous limestones and certain types of sandstones. The reactive constituents may be in the form of opals, cherts, chalcedony, volcanic glass, zeolites etc. The reaction starts with attack on the reactive siliceous minerals in the aggregate by the alkaline hydroxide derived from the alkalies in cement. As a result, the alkali silicate gels of unlimited swelling type are formed. When the conditions are congenial, progressive manifestation by swelling takes place, which results in disruption of concrete with the spreading of pattern cracks and eventual failure of concrete structures. The rate of deterioration may be slow or fast depending upon the conditions. There were cases where concrete has become unserviceable in about a year's time. In India, the basalt rocks occurring in the Deccan plateau, Madhya Pradesh, Kathiawar, Hyderabad, Punchal Hill (Jammu and Kashmir), Bengal and Bihar should be viewed with caution.[3.6]

Similarly, limestones and dolomites containing chert nodules would be highly reactive. Indian limestones of Bijawar series are known to be highly cherty. Regions of occurrence include Madhya Pradesh, Rajasthan, Punjab and Assam.

Sandstones containing silica minerals like chalcedony, crypto to microcrystalline quartz or opal are found to be reactive. Regions of occurrence include Madhya Pradesh, Bengal, Bihar and Delhi. Some of the samples obtained from Madhya Pradesh, West Bengal and Kashmir were found to be containing reactive constituents which could be identified by visual examination. These contain substantial quantities of minerals like opals, chalcedony and amorphous silica. Quartzite samples of rock obtained from Kashmir were also found to be highly reactive.

Geographically India has a very extensive deposit of volcanic rocks. The Deccan traps covering the western part of Maharashtra and Madhya Pradesh, the dolomites of Madhya Pradesh, Punjab and Rajasthan, limestones of Jammu and Kashmir would form extensive source of aggregate for concrete construction. The aggregates from these rocks should be

Typical example of the alkali-aggregate reaction product (swellable gel).

studied cautiously to see how far reactive are they. It is interesting to note that only such aggregates which contain reactive silica in particular proportion and in particular fineness are found to exhibit tendencies for alkali-aggregates reaction. It is possible to reduce its tendency by altering either the proportion of reactive silica or its fineness.

Factors Promoting the Alkali-Aggreate Reaction

(*i*) Reactive type of aggregate; (*ii*) High alkali content in cement;

(*iii*) Availability of moisture; (*iv*) Optimum temperature conditions.

It is not easy to determine the potential reactivity of the aggregates. The case history of aggregates may be of value in judging whether a particular source of aggregate is deleterious or harmless. The petrographic examination of thin rock sections may also immensely help to asses the potential reactivity of the aggregate. This test often requires to be supplemented by other tests.

Mortar Bar Expansion Test devised by Stanton has proved to be a very reliable test in assessing the reactivity or otherwise of the aggregate. A specimen of size 25 mm x 25 mm and 250 mm length is cast, cured and stored in a standard manner as specified in IS : 2386 (Part VII 1963). Measure the length of the specimen periodically, at the ages of 1, 2, 3, 6, 9, and 12 months. Find out the difference in the length of the specimen to the nearest 0.001 per cent and record the expansion of the specimen. The aggregate under test is considered harmful if it expands more than 0.05 per cent after 3 months or more than 0.1 per cent after six months.

The potential reactivity of aggregate can also be found out by chemical method. In this method the potential reactivity of an aggregate with alkalies in Portland cement is indicated by the amount of reaction taking place during 24 hours at 80°C between sodium hydroxide solution and the aggregate that has been crushed and sieved to pass a 300 micron IS Sieve and retained on 150 micron IS Sieve. The solution after 24 hours is analysed for silica dissolved and reduction in alkalinity, both expressed as millimoles per litre. The values are plotted as shown in Fig 3.3 reproduced from IS : 2386 (Part VII 1963). Generally, a potentially deleterious reaction is indicated if the plotted test result falls to the right of the boundary line of Fig. 3.3 and if plotted result falls to the left side of the boundary line, the aggregate may be considered as innocuous. The above chemical test may also be employed for finding out the effectiveness of adding a particular proportion of pozzolanic material to offset the alkali-aggregate reaction. Table 3.6 shows dissolved silica and reduction in alkalinity of some Indian aggregates.

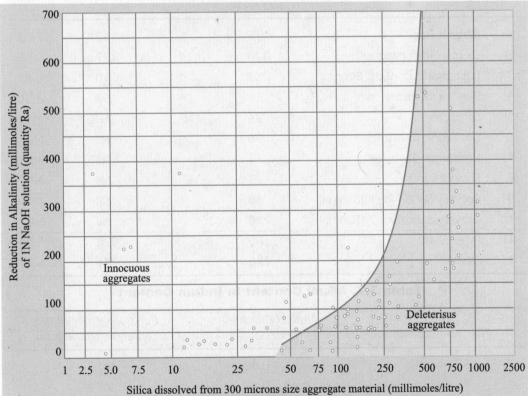

Fig. 3.3. Illustration of division between innocuous and deleterious aggregates on basis of reduction in alkalinity test.

High Alkali Content in Cement

The high alkali content in cement is one of the most important factors contributing to the alkali-aggregate reaction. Since the time of recognition to the importance of alkali-aggregate reaction phenomena, a serious view has been taken on the alkali content of cement. Many specifications restrict the alkali content to less than 0.6 per cent. Their total amount, expressed as Na_2O equivalent ($Na_2O + 0.658\ K_2O$). A cement, meeting this specification is designated as a low alkali cement. Field experience has never detected serious deterioration of concrete through the process of alkali-aggregate reaction when cement contained alkalies less than 0.6 per cent. In exceptional cases, however, cement with even lower alkali content have caused objectionable expansion. Generally, Indian cements do not contain high alkalies as in U.S.A. and U.K. The result of investigations done to find out the alkali content in the sample of Indian cement is shown in Table 3.7. Table 3.7 shows that 11 out of 26 Indian cement samples have total alkali content higher than 0.6 per cent. This is the statistics of cement manufactured prior to 1975. The present day cement manufactured by modern sophisticated methods will have lower alkali content than what is shown in Table 3.7.

Table 3.6. Dissolved silica and reduction in alkalinity of some Indian aggregates[3.5]

Sl. No.	Description of Aggregate	Reduction in Alkalinity millimoles per litre — Ra	Dissolved Silica Millimoles Per litre Si	Ratio Si/Ra
1.	Banihal Trap	16	42	2.63
2.	Deccan Trap (Nagpur)	320	177	0.55
3.	Rajmahal Trap (West Bengal)	252	210	0.83
4.	Banihal Quartizite	16	57	3.56
5.	Limestone	24	Nil	Nil
6.	Limestone (Balasore)	96	Nil	Nil
7.	Limestone (Banswara)	32	Nil	Nil
8.	Ennore Sand	4	Nil	Nil
9.	Grevelly Sand No. 1 (Banihal)	68	Nil	Nil
10.	Gravelly Sand No. 2 (Banihal)	100	Nil	Nil
11.	Pyrex Glass	160	926	5.79
12.	Opal	120	721	6.01

Table 3.7. Alkali Content in Indian Cement

No. of samples	Alkali content per cent	Percentage of number of sample to the total
8	Below – 0.40	30.8
7	0.40 – 0.60	26.9
5	0.60 – 0.80	19.2
6	0.80 – 1.00	23.1
Nil	Above – 1.00	Nil

Availability of Moisture

Progress of chemical reactions involving alkali-aggregate reaction in concrete requires the presence of water. It has been seen in the field and laboratory that lack of water greatly reduces this kind of deterioration. Therefore, it is pertinent to note that deterioration due to alkali-aggregate reaction will not occur in the interior of mass concrete. The deterioration will be more on the surface. It is suggested that reduction in deterioration due to alkali-aggregate reaction can be achieved by the application of waterproofing agents to the surface of the concrete with a view to preventing additional penetration of water into the structure.

Temperature Condition

The ideal temperature for the promotion of alkali-aggregate reaction is in the range of 10 to 38°C. If the temperatures condition is more than or less than the above, it may not provide an ideal situation for the alkali-aggregate reaction.

Mechanism of Deterioration of Concrete Through the Alkali-Aggregate Reaction

The mechanism of alkali aggregate reaction has not been perfectly understood. However, from the known information, the mechanism of deterioration is explained as follows:

The mixing water turns to be a strongly caustic solution due to solubility of alkalies from the cement. This caustic liquid attacks reactive silica to form alkali-silica gel of unlimited swelling type. The reaction proceeds more rapidly for highly reactive substances. If continuous supply of water and correct temperature is available, the formation of silica gel continues unabated. This silica gels grow in size. The continuous growth of silica gel exerts osmotic pressure to cause pattern cracking particularly in thinner sections of concrete like pavements. Conspicuous effect may not be seen in mass concrete sections.

The formation of pattern cracks due to the stress induced by the growth of silica gel results in subsequent loss in strength and elasticity. Alkali-aggregate reaction also accelerates other process of deterioration of concrete due to the formation of cracks. Solution of dissolved carbon dioxide, converts calcium hydroxide to calcium carbonate with consequent increase in volume. Many destructive forces become operative on the concrete disrupted by alkali-aggregate reaction which will further hasten the total disintegration of concrete.

Control of Alkali-Aggregate Reaction

From the foregoing discussion it is apparent that alkali-aggregate reaction can be controlled by the following methods:

(i) Selection of non-reactive aggregates;

(ii) By the use of low alkali cement;

(iii) By the use of corrective admixtures such as pozzolanas;

(iv) By controlling the void space in concrete;

(v) By controlling moisture condition and temperature.

It has been discussed that it is possible to identify potentially reactive aggregate by petrographic examination, mortar bar test or by chemical method. Avoiding the use of the reactive aggregate is one of the sure methods to inhibit the alkali-aggregate reaction in concrete.

In case avoidance of suspicious reactive aggregate is not possible due to economic reasons, the possibility of alkali-aggregate reaction can be avoided by the use of low alkali cement. restricting the alkali content in cement to less than 0.6 per cent or possibly less than 0.4 per cent, is another good step.

In the construction of nuclear power project at Kaiga in Karnataka, initially, they did not make proper investigation about the coarse aggregate they are likely to use in the power project. When they investigated, they found that the coarse aggregate was showing a tendency for alkali-aggregate reaction. They could not change the source for economical reason. Therefore, they have gone for using, special low-alkali cement. with alkali content less than 0.4 per cent.

It has been pointed out earlier that generally the aggregate is found to be reactive when it contains silica in a particular proportion and in particular fineness. It has been seen in the laboratory that if this optimium condition of silica being in particular proportion and fineness is disturbed, the aggregate will turn to be innocuous. This disturbance of optimum content and fineness of silica can be disturbed by the addition of pozzolanic materials such as crushed stone dust, diatomaceous earth, fly ash or surkhi. The use of pozzolanic mixture has been found to be one of practical solutions for inhibiting alkali-aggregate reaction.

It has been said that development of osmotic pressure on the set-cement gel by the subsequently formed alkali-silica gel is responsible for the disruption of concrete. If a system is introduced to absorb this osmotic pressure, it is probable that the disruption could be reduced. The use of air-entraining agent has frequently been recommended as a means of absorbing the osmotic pressure and controlling expansion due to alkali-aggregate reaction in mortar and concrete.

For the growth of silica gel a continuous availability of water is one of the requirements. If such continuous supply is not made available, the growth of silica gel is reduced. Similarly, if the correct range of temperature is not provided, the extent of expansion is also reduced.

Thermal Properties

Rock and aggregate possesses three thermal properties which are significant in establishing the quality of aggregate for concrete constructions. They are:

(*i*) Coefficient of expansion;   (*ii*) Specific heat;   (*iii*) Thermal conductivity.

Out of these, specific heat and conductivity are found to be important only in mass concrete construction where rigorous control of temperature is necessary. Also these properties are of consequence in case of light weight concrete used for insulation purpose. When we are dealing with the aggregate in general it will be sufficient at this stage to deal with only the coefficient of expansion of the aggregate, since it interacts with the coefficient of thermal expansion of cement paste in the body of the set-concrete.

An average value of the linear thermal coefficient of expansion of concrete may be taken as 9.9×10^{-6} per °C, but the range may be from about 5.8×10^{-6} per °C to 14×10^{-6} per °C depending upon the type and quantities of the aggregates, the mix proportions and other factors. The range of coefficient of thermal expansion for hydrated cement paste may vary from 10.8×10^{-6} Per °C to 16.2×10^{-6} per °C. Similarly, for mortar it may range from 7.9×10^{-6} per °C to 12.6×10^{-6} per °C.

The linear thermal coefficient of expansion of common rocks ranges from about 0.9×10^{-6} per °C to 16×10^{-6} per °C. From the above it could be seen that while there is thermal compatibility between the aggregate and concrete or aggregate and paste at higher range, there exists thermal incompatibility between aggregate and concrete or aggregate and paste at the lower range. This thermal incompatibility between the aggregate and concrete at the lower range causes severe stress which has got damaging effect on the durability and integrity of concrete structures.

Many research workers have studied the interaction of aggregates with different coefficient of thermal expansion with that of concrete. The result of the experiments does not present a very clear cut picture of the effects that may be expected, and some aspects of the problem are controversial. However, there seems to be a fairly general agreement that the thermal expansion of the aggregate has an effect on the durability of concrete, particularly under severe exposure conditions or under rapid temperature changes. Generally, it can be taken that, where the difference between coefficient of expansion of coarse aggregate and mortar is larger, the durability of the concrete may be considerably lower than would be predicted from the results of the usual acceptance tests. Where the difference between these coefficients exceeds 5.4×10^{-6} per °C caution should be taken in the selection of the aggregate for highly durable concrete.

If a particular concrete is subjected to normal variation of atmospheric temperature, the thermal incompatibility between the aggregates and paste or between the aggregate and matrix may not introduce serious differential movement and break the bond at the interface of aggregate and paste or aggregate and matrix. But if a concrete is subjected to high range of temperature difference the adverse effect will become acute. If quartz is used as aggregate for concrete that is going to be subjected to high temperature the concrete is sure to undergo disruption as quartz changes state and suddenly expands 0.85 per cent at a temperature of 572.7°C. It is also necessary to take care of the peculiar anisotropic behavior *i.e.*, the property of expanding more in one direction or parallel to one crystallographic axis than another. The most notable example is calcite which has a linear thermal coefficient expansion of 25.8×10^{-6} per °C parallel to its axis and -4.7×10^{-6} per °C perpendicular to this direction[3.7]. Potash feldspars are another group of minerals exhibiting anisotropic behaviour.

Therefore, in estimating the cubical expansion of concrete, care must be taken to this aspect of anisotropic behaviour of some of the aggregates. The study of coefficient of thermal expansion of aggregate is also important, in dealing with the fire resistance of concrete.

Grading of Aggregates

Aggregate comprises about 55 per cent of the volume of mortar and about 85 per cent volume of mass concrete. Mortar contains aggregate of size of 4.75 mm and concrete contains aggregate upto a maximum size of 150 mm.

Thus it is not surprising that the way particles of aggregate fit together in the mix, as influenced by the gradation, shape, and surface texture, has an important effect on the workability and finishing characteristic of fresh concrete, consequently on the properties of hardened concrete. Volumes have been written on the effects of the aggregate grading on the properties of concrete and many so called "ideal" grading curves have been proposed. In spite of this extensive study, we still do not have a clear picture of the influence of different types of aggregates on the plastic properties of concrete. It has been this much understood that there is nothing like "ideal" aggregate grading, because satisfactory concrete can be made with various aggregate gradings within certain limits.

It is well known that the strength of concrete is dependent upon water/cement ratio provided the concrete is workable. In this statement, the qualifying clause "provided the concrete is workable" assumes full importance. One of the most important factors for producing workable concrete is good gradation of aggregates. Good grading implies that a sample of aggregates contains all standard fractions of aggregate in required proportion such that the sample contains minimum voids. A sample of the well graded aggregate containing minimum voids will require minimum paste to fill up the voids in the aggregates. Minimum paste will mean less quantity of cement and less quantity of water, which will further mean increased economy, higher strength, lower-shrinkage and greater durability.

The advantages due to good grading of aggregates can also be viewed from another angle. If concrete is viewed as a two phase material, paste phase and aggregate phase, it is the paste phase which is vulnerable to all ills of concrete. Paste is weaker than average aggregate in normal concrete with rare exceptions when very soft aggregates are used. The paste is more permeable than many of the mineral aggregates. It is the paste that is susceptible to deterioration by the attack of aggressive chemicals. In short, it is the paste which is a weak link in a mass of concrete. The lesser the quantity of such weak material, the better will be the concrete. This objective can be achieved by having well graded aggregates. Hence the importance of good grading.

Many research workers in the field of concrete technology, having fully understood the importance of good grading in making quality concrete in consistent with economy, have directed their studies to achieve good grading of aggregate at the construction site.

Fuller and Thompson[3.8] concluded that grading for maximum density gives the highest strength, and that the grading curve of the best mixture resembles a parabola. Talbot and Richart from their works found that aggregate graded to produce maximum density gave a harsh mixture that is very difficult to place in ordinary concreting operations. Edwards and Young proposed a method of proportioning based on the surface area of aggregate to be wetted. Other things being equal, it was concluded that the concrete made from aggregate grading having least surface area will require least water which will consequently be the strongest.

Abrams and others in course of their investigations have also found that the surface area of the aggregate may vary widely without causing much appreciable difference in the concrete strength, and that water required to produce a given consistency is dependent more on other characteristics of aggregate than on surface area. Therefore, Abrams introduced a parameter known as "fineness modulus" for arriving at satisfactory gradings. He found that any sieve analysis curve of aggregate that will give the same fineness modulus will require the same quantity of water to produce a mix of the same plasticity and gives concrete of the same strength, so long as it is not too coarse for the quantity of cement used. The fineness modulus is an index of the coarseness or fineness of an aggregate sample, but, because different grading can give the same fineness modulus, it does not define the grading.

Waymouth introduced his theory of satisfactory grading on the basis of "particle interference" considerations[3.9]. He found out the volume relationships between successive size groups of particles based on the assumption that particles of each group are distributed throughout the concrete mass in such a way that the distance between them is equal to the mean diameter of the particles of the next smaller size group plus the thickness of the cement film between them. He stated that particle interference occurred between two successive sizes when the distance between particles is not sufficient to allow free passage of the smaller particles. The determination of grading by Waymouth method usually results in finer gradings.

Many other methods have been suggested for arriving at an optimum grading. All these procedures, methods and formulae point to the fact that none is satisfactory and reliable for field application. At the site, a reliable satisfactory grading can only be decided by actual trial and error, which takes into consideration the characteristics of the local materials with respect to size fraction, shape, surface texture, flakiness index and elongation index. The widely varying peculiarities of coarse and fine aggregates cannot be brought under formulae and set procedure for practical application.

One of the practical methods of arriving at the practical grading by trial and error method is to mix aggregates of different size fractions in different percentages and to choose the one sample which gives maximum weight or minimum voids per unit volume, out of all the alternative samples. Fractions which are actually available in the field, or which could be made available in the field including that of the fine aggregate will be used in making samples.

Sieve Analysis

This is the name given to the operation of dividing a sample of aggregate into various fractions each consisting of particles of the same size. The sieve analysis is conducted to determine the particle size distribution in a sample of aggregate, which we call gradation.

A convenient system of expressing the gradation of aggregate is one which the consecutive sieve openings are constantly doubled, such as 10 mm, 20 mm, 40 mm etc. Under such a system, employing a logarithmic scale, lines can be spaced at equal intervals to represent the successive sizes.

The aggregates used for making concrete are normally of the maximum size 80 mm, 40 mm, 20 mm, 10 mm, 4.75 mm, 2.36 mm, 600 micron, 300 micron and 150 micron. The aggregate fraction from 80 mm to 4.75 mm are termed as coarse aggregate and those fraction from 4.75 mm to 150 micron are termed as fine aggregate. The size 4.75 mm is a common fraction appearing both in coarse aggregate and fine aggregate (C.A. and F.A.).

Grading pattern of a sample of C.A. or F.A. is assessed by sieving a sample successively through all the sieves mounted one over the other in order of size, with larger sieve on the top. The material retained on each sieve after shaking, represents the fraction of aggregate coarser than the sieve in question and finer than the sieve above. Sieving can be done either manually or mechanically. In the manual operation the sieve is shaken giving movements in all possible direction to give

Set of Sieves assembled for conducting Sieve analysis.

Set of Sieves.

chance to all particles for passing through the sieve. Operation should be continued till such time that almost no particle is passing through. Mechanical devices are actually designed to give motion in all possible direction, and as such, it is more systematic and efficient than hand-sieving. For assessing the gradation by sieve analysis, the quantity of materials to be taken on the sieve is given Table 3.8.

Table 3.8. Minimum weight of sample for Sieve Analysis (IS: 2386 (Part I) – 1963)

Maximum size present in substantial proportions	Minimum weight of sample to be taken for sieving
mm	kg
63	50
50	35
40 or 31.5	15
25	5
20 or 16	2
12.5	1
10	0.5
6.3	0.2
4.75	0.2
2.36	0.1

From the sieve analysis the particle size distribution in a sample of aggregate is found out. In this connection a term known as "Fineness Modulus" (F.M.) is being used. F.M. is a ready index of coarseness or fineness of the material. Fineness modulus is an empirical factor obtained by adding the cumulative percentages of aggregate retained on each of the standard sieves ranging from 80 mm to 150 micron and dividing this sum by an arbitrary number 100. The larger the figure, the coarser is the material. Table No. 3.9 shows the typical example of the sieve analysis, conducted on a sample of coarse aggregate and fine aggregate to find out the fineness modulus.

Many a time, fine aggregates are designated as coarse sand, medium sand and fine sand. These classifications do not give any precise meaning. What the supplier terms as fine sand may be really medium or even coarse sand. To avoid this ambiguity fineness modulus could be used as a yard stick to indicate the fineness of sand.

The following limits may be taken as guidance:

Fine sand	:	Fineness Modulus	:	2.2 - 2.6
Medium sand	:	F.M.	:	2.6 - 2.9
Coarse sand	:	F.M.	:	2.9 - 3.2

A sand having a fineness modulus more than 3.2 will be unsuitable for making satisfactory concrete.

Combining Aggregates to Obtain Specified Gradings

Sometimes aggregates available at sites may not be of specified or desirable grading. In such cases two or more aggregates from different sources may be combined to get the desired

Table 3.9. The typical Example of the Sieve Analysis

IS Sieve Size	Coarse Aggregate				Fine Aggregate			
	Weight retained weight kg	Cumulative weight retained kg	Cumulative percentage retained	Cumulative percentage passing	Weight retained gm	Cumulative weight retained gm	Cumulative percentage weight retained	Comulative percentage passing
80 mm	0	0	0	100	-	-	-	-
40 mm	0	0	0	100	-	-	-	-
20 mm	6	6	40	60	-	-	-	-
10 mm	5	11	73.3	26.7	0	0	0	100
4.75 mm	4.0	15.00	100	00	10	10	2	98
2.36 mm	-	-	100	00	50	60	12	88
1.18 mm	-	-	100	00	50	110	22	78
600 micron	-	-	100	00	95	205	41	59
300 micron	-	-	100	00	175	380	76	24
150 micron	-	-	100	00	85	465	93	7
lower than 150 micron	-	-	-	00	35	500	-	-
Total	15 kg		713.3		500 gm	—	246	-

$$F.M. = \frac{713.3}{100} = 7.133$$

$$F.M. = \frac{246}{100} = 2.46$$

grading. Often, mixing of available fine aggregate with available coarse aggregate in appropriate percentages may produce desirable gradings. But sometimes two or more fractions of coarse aggregate is mixed first and then the combined coarse aggregate is mixed with fine aggregate to obtain the desired gradings. Knowing the grading of available aggregates, proportions of mixing different sizes can be calculated, either graphically or arithmetically. This aspect will be dealt in more detail under the chapter Mix Design. At this stage a simple trial and error arithmetical method of combining coarse and fine aggregate is illustrated. Table 3.10 shows the grading pattern of the available coarse and fine aggregate at site. This table also shows the specified combined grading.

Table 3.11 shows the grading of different combination of fine and coarse aggregate for first trial and second trial. The combined grading of first trial and second trial is compared with the specified combined grading. Whichever trial gives the combined aggregate grading equal or nearly equal to the specified grading is adopted.

Specific Surface and Surface Index

The importance of a good grading of the coarse and fine aggregate has already been discussed. The quantity of water required to produce a given workability depends to a large extent on the surface area of the aggregate.

Table 3.10. Shows the grading pattern of the available coarse and fine aggregate and specified combined grading

I.S. Sieve size	Percentage passing		
	C.A.	*F.A.*	*Specified combined aggregate (From Table No. 3.11)*
40	100	100	100
20	96	100	98
10	35	100	61
4.75	6	92	42
2.36	0	85	35
1.18	0	75	28
600	0	60	22
300	0	10	5
150	0	0	0

The surface area per unit weight of the material is termed as specific surface. This is an indirect measure of the aggregate grading. Specific surface increases with the reduction in the size of aggregate particle so that fine aggregate contributes very much more to the surface area than does the coarse aggregate. Greater surface area requires more water for lubricating the mix to give workability. The workability of a mix is, therefore, influenced more by finer fraction than the coarser particles in a sample of aggregates.

The foregoing paragraph gives the impression that smaller particles of aggregate contribute more surface area and hence require more water for wetting the surface of aggregates; and for a given quantity of water, the presence of smaller particles reduces the workability. This impression is correct upto a certain extent of the finer fraction. This will not hold good for very fine particles in F.A. The every fine particles in F.A. *i.e.*, 300 micron and 150 micron particles, being so fine, contribute more towards workability. Their over-riding influence

Table 3.11. Showing the Grading of Different Combination of Fine and Coarse Aggregate for Different Trials

I.S. Sieve	C.A.	F.A.	Specified combined grading	Percentage passing						
				1st Trial			2nd Trial			
				70% C.A.	30% F.A.	Combined grading	60% C.A.	40% F.A.	Combined grading	
1	2	3	4	5	6	7	8	9	10
40	100	100	100	70	30	100	60	40	100
20	96	100	98	67.2	30	97.2	60	40	97.6
10	35	100	61	24.5	30	54.5	57.6	40	61.0
4.75	6	92	42	4.2	27.6	31.8	21.0	36.8	40.6
2.36	0	85	35	-	25.5	25.5	3.6	34.0	34.0
1.18	0	75	28	-	22.5	22.5	-	30.0	30.0
600	0	60	22	-	18.00	18.00	-	24.0	24.0
300	0	10	5	-	3.00	3.00	-	4.0	4.0
150	0	0	0	-	-	-	-	-	-

It is seen that the combined grading obtained by the mixture of C.A. and F.A. in the ratio of 60:40 closely conform the specified grading shown in column 4.

in contributing to the better workability by acting like ball bearings to reduce the internal friction between coarse particles, far out-weigh the reduction in workability owing to the consumption of mixing water for wetting greater surface area.

Consideration of specific surface gives a somewhat misleading picture of the workability to be expected. To overcome this difficulty Murdock has suggested the use of "Surface Index" which is an empirical number related to the specific surface of the particle with more weightage given to the finer fractions. The empirical numbers representing the surface index of aggregate particles within the set of sieve size are given in Table 3.12.

The total surface index (fx) of a mixture of aggregate is calculated by multiplying the percentage of material retained on its sieve by the corresponding surface index and to their sum is added a constant of 330 and the result is divided by 1000. The method of computing the total surface for any given grading is shown in Table 3.13

Table 3.12. Surface Index of Aggregate Particles[3.2]

Sieve size within which particles lie	Surface Index for Particles within Sieve Size indicated
80–40 mm	– 2.5
40–20 mm	– 2
20–10 mm	– 1
10–4.75 mm	+ 1
4.75–2.36 mm	4
2.36–1.18 mm	7
1.18–600 micron	9
600–300 micron	9
300–150 micron	7
Smaller than 150 micron	2

Table 3.13. Surface Index of Combined Grading

Sieve size within which Particles lie	Percentage of particles within sieve size	Surface Index for particles within sieve size	Surface Index (fx)
20—10 mm	55	–1	–55
10—4.75 mm	15	1	15
4.75—2.36 mm	7	4	28
2.36—1.18 mm	7	7	49
1.18—600 micron	7	9	63
600—300 micron	7	9	63
300—150 micron	2	7	14
		Total	177
		Add constant	330
			507

$$\text{Surface Index } (fx) = \frac{507}{1000} = 0.507$$

Similarly, surface index can be calculated for standard grading curve, and this value of surface index can be taken as the desirable surface index of the combined aggregate.

This parameter of surface index can be made use of for finding out the proportion of fine aggregate to coarse aggregate available in the field to obtain specified or desirable surface index in the following way.

Let x = surface index of fine aggregate

y = surface index of coarse aggregate

z = surface index of combined aggregate

a = proportion of fine to coarse aggregate

Then $a = \dfrac{(z-y)}{(x-z)}$

The following example will show how to combine the available fine aggregate with available coarse aggregate whose grading patterns are known to get the desirable surface index of the combined aggregate. The desirable surface index of the combined aggregate could be calculated from the grading pattern of the standard grading curve.

Sieve size within which particles lie	Percentage of particles within sieve size	Surface index for partcles for sieve size	Surface Index (fx)
Coarse Aggregate			
20 mm — 10 mm	65	−1	−65
10 mm — 4.75	35	1	35
		Total =	−30
		Add constant =	330
		=	300

$$\text{Surface Index of Corase Aggregate} = \frac{300}{1000} = 0.30$$

Fine Aggregate			
4.75 mm — 2.36	10	4	40
2.36 mm — 1.18	20	7	140
1.18 mm — 600 micron	20	9	180
600 micron — 300 micron	30	9	270
300 micron — 150 micron	15	7	105
		Total =	735
		Add constant =	330
		=	1065

$$\text{Surface Index of fine Aggregate} = \frac{1065}{1000} = 1.065$$

Let the surface index of combined aggregate required = 0.6.

x = surface index of F.A. = 1.065

y = surface index of C.A. = 0.30

z = surface index of combined aggregate = 0.60

If a = proportion of fine to coarse aggregate, $a = \dfrac{(z-y)}{(x-z)} = \dfrac{(0.60-0.30)}{(1.065-0.60)} = \dfrac{1}{1.55}$

Therefore, F.A. : C.A. = 1 : 1.55

Standard Grading Curve

The grading patterns of aggregate can be shown in tables or charts. Expressing grading limits by means of a chart gives a good pictorial view. The comparison of grading pattern of a number of samples can be made at one glance. For this reason, often grading of aggregates is shown by means of grading curves. One of the most commonly referred practical grading curves are those produced by Road Research Laboratory (U.K.).[3.10] On the basis of large number of experiments in connection with bringing out mix design procedure, Road Research

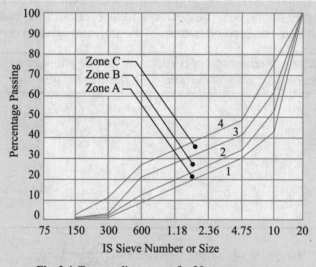

Fig. 3.4. Type grading curves for 20 mm aggregate.

Laboratory has prepared a set of type grading curve for all-in aggregates graded down from 20 mm and 40 mm. They are shown in figure 3.4 and Fig 3.5 respectively. Similar curves for aggregate with maximum size of 10 mm and downward have been prepared by McIntosh and Erntory. It is shown in Fig. 3.6. Fig. 3.7 shows the desirable grading limit for 80 mm aggregate.

Four curves are shown for each maximum size of aggregate except 80 mm size. From values of percentage passing it can be seen that the lowest curve *i.e.*, curve No. 1 is the coarsest grading and curve No. 4 at the top represents the finest grading. Between the curves No. 1 to 4 there are three zones: A, B, C. In practice the coarse and fine aggregates are supplied separately. Knowing their gradation it will be possible to mix them up to get type grading conforming to any one of the four grading curves.

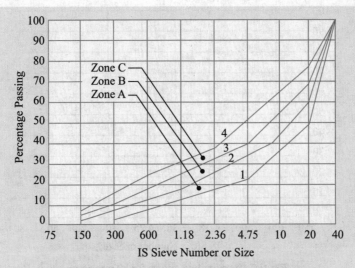

Fig. 3.5. Type grading curves for 40 mm aggregate.

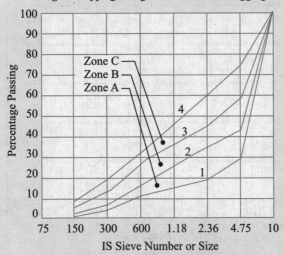

Fig. 3.6. McIntosh and Erntroy's Type Grading Curves for
10mm aggregate

In practice, it is difficult to get the aggregate to conform to any one particular standard curve exactly. If the user insists on a particular pattern of grading, the supplier may quote very high rates. At the same time the user also cannot accept absolutely poor grading pattern of aggregates. As a via media, grading limits are laid down in various specifications rather than to conform exactly to a particular grading curve. Table 3.14 shows the grading limits of coarse aggregates.

Table 3.15 shows the grading limits of fine aggregates. Table 3.16 shows the grading limits of all-in-aggregate.

It should be noted that for crushed stone sands, the permissible limit on 150 micron I.S. Sieve is increased to 20 per cent. Figs. 3.8 *a, b, c* and *d* show the grading limits of F.A.

Fine aggregate complying with the requirements of any grading zone in Table 3.15 is suitable for concrete but the quality of concrete produced will depend upon a number of factors including proportions.

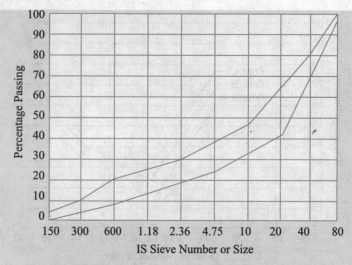

Fig. 3.7. Type grading curves for 80 mm aggregate.

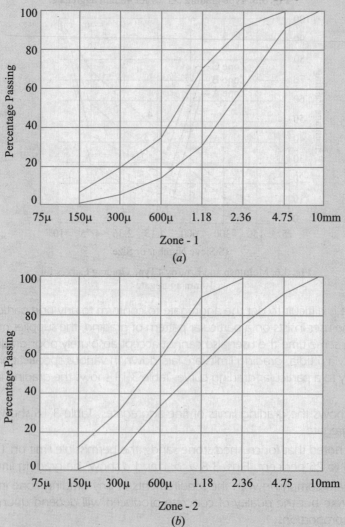

Fig. 3.8. Grading limits for sand in zones 1 and 2 of I.S. : 383-1970. (Contd.)

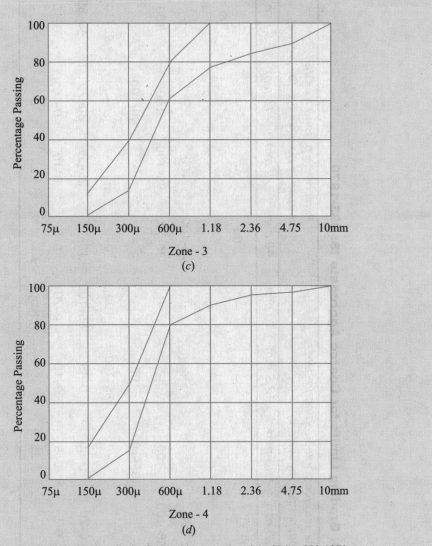

Fig. 3.8. Grading limits for sand in zones 3 and 4 of I.S. : 383-1970.

Where concrete of high strength and good durability is required, fine aggregate conforming to any one of the four grading zones may be used, but the concrete mix should be properly designed. As the fine aggregate grading becomes progressively finer, that is from Grading Zones I to IV, the ratio of the fine aggregate to coarse aggregate should be progressively reduced. The most suitable fine to coarse ratio to be used for any particular mix will, however, depend upon the actual grading, particle shape and surface texture of both fine and coarse aggregates.

It is recommended that fine aggregate conforming to Grading Zone IV should not be used in reinforced concrete unless tests have been made to ascertain the suitability of proposed mix proportions.

Table 3.14. Grading Limits for Coarse Aggregate IS: 383-1970

IS Sieve Designation	Percentage passing for single-sized aggregate nominal size (by weight)						Percentage passing for Graded aggregate of nominal size (by weight)			
	63 mm	40 mm	20 mm	16 mm	12.5 mm	10 mm	40 mm	20 mm	16 mm	12.5 mm
80 mm	100	–	–	–	–	–	100	–	–	–
63 mm	85–100	100	–	–	–	–	–	–	–	–
40 mm	0–30	85–100	100	–	–	–	95–100	100	–	–
20 mm	0–5	0–20	85–100	100	–	–	30–70	95–100	100	100
16 mm	–	–	–	85–100	100	–	–	–	90–100	–
12.5 mm	–	–	–	–	85–100	100	–	–	–	90–100
10 mm	–	0–5	0–20	0–30	0–45	85–100	10–35	25–55	30–70	40–85
4.75 mm	–	–	0–5	0–5	0–10	0–20	0–5	0–10	0–10	0–10
2.36 mm	–	–	–	–	–	0–5	–	–	–	–

Table 3.15. Grading limits of fine aggregates IS: 383-1970

I.S. Sieve Designation	Percentage passing by weight for			
	Grading Zone I	Grading Zone II	Grading Zone III	Grading Zone IV
10 mm	100	100	100	100
4.75 mm	90–100	90–100	90–100	95–100
2.36 mm	60–95	75–100	85–100	95–100
1.18 mm	30–70	55–90	75–100	90–100
600 micron	15–34	35–59	60–79	80–100
300 micron	5–20	8–30	12–40	15–50
150 micron	0–10	0–10	0–10	0–15

Table 3.16. Grading limits of all-in-aggregates

I.S. Sieve Designation	Percentage by weights passing for all in-aggragrate of	
	40 mm Nominal size	20 mm Nominal size
80 mm	100	–
40 mm	95–100	100
20 mm	45–75	95–100
4.75 mm	25–45	30–50
600 micron	8–30	10–35
150 micron	0–6	0–6

It must be remembered that the grading of fine aggregates has much greater effect on workability of concrete than does the grading of coarse aggregate. Experience has shown that usually very coarse sand or very fine sand is unsatisfactory for concrete making. The coarse sand results in harshness bleeding and segregation, and the fine sand requires a comparatively greater amount of water to produce the necessary fluidity. For fine aggregates, a total departure of 5 per cent from zone limits may be allowed. But this relaxation is not permitted beyond the coarser limit of zone I or the finer limit of zone IV.

Crushed Sand

All along in India, we have been using natural sand. The volume of concrete manufactured in India has not been much, when compared to some advanced countries. The infrastructure development such as express highway projects, power projects and industrial developments have started now. Availability of natural sand is getting depleted and also it is becoming costly. Concrete industry now will have to go for crushed sand or what is called manufactured sand.

Advantages of natural sand is that the particles are cubical or rounded with smooth surface texture. The grading of natural F.A. is not always ideal. It depends on place to place. Being cubical, rounded and smooth textured it gives good workability.

So far, crushed sand has not been used much in India for the reason that ordinarily crushed sand is flaky, badly graded rough textured and hence they result in production of harsh concrete for the given design parameters. We have been also not using superplasticizer widely in our concreting operations to improve the workability of harsh mix. For the last about 4–5 years the old methods of manufacturing ordinary crushed sand have been replaced by modern crushers specially designed for producing, cubical, comparatively smooth textured, well graded sand, good enough to replace natural sand.

Many patented equipments are set up in India to produce crushed sand of acceptable quality at project site. Pune-Mumbai express highway is one of the biggest projects undertaken in India recently. Enough quantities of natural sand is not available in this region. The total quantity of concrete involved is more than 20,000,00 m³ of concrete. The authorities have decided to use crushed sand.

A company by name Svedala is one of the concrete aggregate manufacturers who have been in the forefront for supplying crusher equipments by trade name Jaw master crusher, or Barmac Rock on Rock VSI crushers incorporating rock-on-rock crushing technology that has revolutionised the art of making concrete aggregates. This imported technology has been used for producing coarse and fine aggregates of desired quality in terms of shape, texture and grading.

Dust is a nuisance and technically undesirable in both coarse aggregate and more so in fine aggregate. Maximum permissible particles of size finer than 75µ is 15% in fine aggregate and 3% in coarse aggregate. There are provision available in these equipments to control and seal the dust.

Barmac Rock-On-Rock VSI Crusher.

In one of the high rise building sites in western suburb of Mumbai, M 60 concrete was specified. The required slump could not be achieved by natural sand with the given parameter of mix design. But with the use of manufactured sand with proper shape, surface texture, desirable grading to minimise void content, a highly workable mix with the given parameter of mix design, was achieved.

The following is the grading pattern of a sample collected from a sand crushing plant on a particular date and time at Pune-Mumbai Road Project:

Table 3.17. Grading Pattern of Crushed Sand (Typical)

I.S. Sieve mm	Percentage passing			Remarks
	As per actual test	IS Requirements for		
		Zone I	Zone II	
10	100	100	100	
4.75	97.58	90–100	90–100	Falling
2.36	82.36	60–95	75–100	in
1.18	55.27	30–70	55–90	Zone II
600	40.56	15–34	35–59	
300	29.33	5–20	8–30	
150	18.78	0–20	0–20	
75	10.09	Max 15	Max 15	

The introduction of modern scientifically operated crushers which are operating all over the world, will go a long way for making quality aggregates in all cities in India. Ordinary crushers cannot give the desired shape, surface texture or grading of both coarse and fine aggregate.

Cone Crushers.

Gap grading

So far we discussed the grading pattern of aggregates in which all particle size are present in certain proportion in a sample of aggregate. Such pattern of particle size distribution is also referred to as continuous grading.

Originally in the theory of continuous grading, it was assumed that the voids present in the higher size of the aggregate are filled up by the next lower size of aggregate, and similarly, voids created by the lower size are filled up by one size lower than those particle and so on. It was realised later that the voids created by a particular fraction are too small to accommodate the very next lower size. The next lower size being itself bigger than the size of the voids, it will create what is known as "particle size interference", which prevents the large aggregates compacting to their maximum density.

It has been seen that the size of voids existing between a particular size of aggregate is of the order of 2 or 3 size lower than that fraction. In other words, the void size existing between 40 mm aggregate is of the size equal to 10 mm or possibly 4.75 mm or the size of voids occurring when 20 mm aggregate is used will be in the order of say 1.18 mm or so. Therefore, along with 20 mm aggregate, only when 1.18 mm aggregate size is used, the sample will contain least voids and concrete requires least matrix. The following advantages are claimed for gap graded concrete:

(*i*) Sand required will be of the order of about 26 per cent as against about 40 per cent in the case of continuous grading.

(*ii*) Specific surface area of the gap graded aggregate will be low, because of high percentage of C.A. and low percentage of F.A.

(*iii*) Requires less cement and lower water/cement ratio.

(*iv*) Because of point contact between C.A. to C.A. and also on account of lower cement and matrix content, the drying shrinkage is reduced.

It was also observed that gap graded concrete needs close supervision, as it shows greater proneness to segregation and change in the anticipated workability. In spite of many claims of the superior properties of gap graded concrete, this method of grading has not become more popular than conventional continuous grading.

TESTING OF AGGREGATES

Test for Determination of Flakiness Index

The flakiness index of aggregate is the percentage by weight of particles in it whose least dimension (thickness) is less than three-fifths of their mean dimension. The test is not applicable to sizes smaller than 6.3 mm.

This test is conducted by using a metal thickness gauge, of the description shown in Fig. 3.9. A sufficient quantity of aggregate is taken such that a minimum number of 200 pieces of any fraction can be tested. Each fraction is gauged in turn for thickness on the metal gauge. The total amount passing in the guage is weighed to an accuracy of 0.1 per cent of the weight of the samples taken. The flakiness index is taken as the total weight of the material passing the various thickness gauges expressed as a percentage of the total weight of the sample taken. Table 3.18 shows the standard dimensions of thickness and length gauges.

Table 3.18. Shows Dimensions of Thickness and Length Gauges
(IS: 2386 (Part I) – 1963)

Size of Aggregate Thickness		Length of Gauge* mm	Gauge† mm
Passing through IS Sieve	Retained on IS Sieve		
63 mm	50 mm	33.90	–
50 mm	40 mm	27.00	81.0
40 mm	25 mm	19.50	58.5
31.5 mm	25 mm	16.95	–
25 mm	20 mm	13.50	40.5
20 mm	16 mm	10.80	32.4
16 mm	12.5 mm	8.55	25.6
12.5 mm	10.0 mm	6.75	20.2
10.0 mm	6.3 mm	4.89	14.7

* This dimension is equal to 0.6 times the mean Sieve size.

† This dimension is equal to 1.8 times the mean Sieve size.

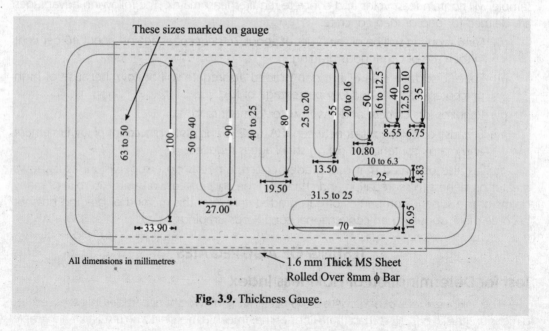

Fig. 3.9. Thickness Gauge.

Test for Determination of Elongation Index

The elongation index on an aggregate is the percentage by weight of particles whose greatest dimension (length) is greater than 1.8 times their mean dimension. The elongation index is not applicable to sizes smaller than 6.3 mm.

This test is conducted by using metal length guage of the description shown in Fig. 3.10. A sufficient quantity of aggregate is taken to provide a minimum number of 200 pieces of any fraction to be tested. Each fraction shall be gauged individually for length on the metal guage. The guage length used shall be that specified in column of 4 of Table 3.18 for the appropriate size of material. The total amount retained by the guage length shall be weighed to an accuracy of at least 0.1 per cent of the weight of the test samples taken. The elongation index is the total weight of the material retained on the various length gauges expressed as a percentage of the total weight of the sample gauged. The presence of elongated particles in excess of 10 to 15 per cent is generally considered undesirable, but no recoganised limits are laid down.

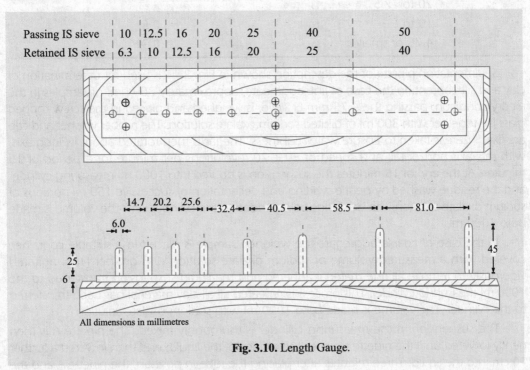

| Passing IS sieve | 10 | 12.5 | 16 | 20 | 25 | 40 | 50 | |
| Retained IS sieve | 6.3 | 10 | 12.5 | 16 | 20 | 25 | 40 | |

14.7 20.2 25.6 32.4 40.5 58.5 81.0
6.0
25
6
45

All dimensions in millimetres

Fig. 3.10. Length Gauge.

Length Gauge.

Indian standard explain only the method of calculating both Flakiness Index and Elongation Index. But the specifications do not specify the limits. British Standard BS 882 of 1992 limits the flakiness index of the coarse aggregate to 50 for natural gravel and to 40 for crushed corase aggregate. However, for wearing surfaces a lower values of flakiness index are required.

Test for Determination of clay, fine silt and fine dust

This is a gravimetric method for determining the clay, fine silt and fine dust which includes particles upto 20 microns.

The sample for test is prepared from the main sample, taking particular care that the test sample contains a correct proportion of the finer material. The amount of sample taken for the test is in accordance with Table 3.19.

Table 3.19. Weight of Sample for Determination of Clay, Fine Silt and Fine Dust

Maximum size present in substantial proportions mm	Approximate weight of sample for Test kg
63 to 25	6
20 to 12.5	1
10 to 6.3	0.5
4.75 or smaller	0.3

Sedimentation pipette of the description shown in Fig. 3.11 is used for determination of clay and silt content. In the case of fine aggregate, approximately 300 gm. of samples in the air-dry condition, passing the 4.75 mm IS Sieve, is weighed and placed in the screw topped glass jar, together with 300 ml of diluted sodium oxalate solution. The rubber washer and cap are fixed. Care is taken to ensure water tightness. The jar is then rotated about its long axis, with this axis horizontal, at a speed of 80 ± 20 revolutions per minute for a period of 15 minutes. At the end of 15 minutes the suspension is poured into 1000 ml measuring cylinder and the residue washed by gentle swirling and decantation of successive 150 ml portions of sodium oxalate solution, the washings being added to the cylinder until the volume is made upto 1000 ml.

In the case of coarse aggregate the weighed sample is placed in a suitable container, covered with a measured volume of sodium oxalate solution (0.8 gm per litre), agitated vigorously to remove all fine material adhered and the liquid suspension transferred to the 1000 ml measuring cylinder. This process is repeated till all clay material has been transferred to the cylinder. The volume is made upto 1000 ml with sodium oxalate solution.

The suspension in the measuring cylinder is thoroughly mixed. The pipette A is then gently lowered until the pipette touches the surface of the liquid, and then lowered a further 10 cm into the liquid. Three minutes after placing the tube in position, the pipette A and the bore of tap B is filled by opening B and applying gentle suction at C. A small surplus may be drawn up into the bulb between tap B and tube C, but this is allowed to run away and any solid matter is washed out with distilled water from E. The pipette is then removed from the measuring cylinder and its contents run into a weighed container. The contents of the container is dried at 100°C to 110°C to constant weight, cooled and weighed.

The percentage of the fine slit and clay or fine dust is calculated from the formula.

$$\frac{100}{W_1}\left(\frac{1000\,W_2}{V}-0.8\right)$$

where W_1 = weight in gm of the original sample.

W_2 = weight in gm of the dried residue

V = volume in ml of the pipette and

0.8 = weight in gm of sodium oxalate in one litre of diluted solution.

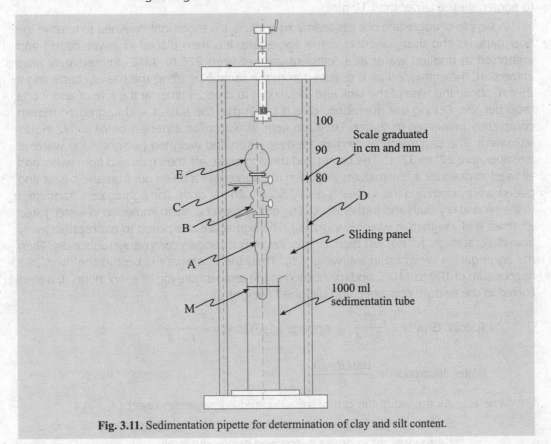

Fig. 3.11. Sedimentation pipette for determination of clay and silt content.

Test for Determination of Organic Impurities

This test is an approximate method for estimating whether organic compounds are present in the natural sand in an objectionable quantity or within the permissible limit. The sand from the natural source is tested as delivered and without drying. A 350 ml graduated clear glass bottle is filled to the 75 ml mark with 3 per cent solution of sodium hydroxide in water. The sand is added gradually until the volume measured by the sand layer is 125 ml. The volume is then made up to 200 ml by adding more solution. The bottle is then stoppered and shaken vigorously. Roding also may be permitted to dislodge any organic matter adhering to the natural sand by using glass rod. The liquid is then allowed to stand for 24 hours. The colour of this liquid after 24 hours is compared with a standard solution freshly prepared, as follows:

Add 2.5 ml of 2 per cent solution of tannic acid in 10 per cent alcohol, to 97.5 ml of a 3 per cent sodium hydroxide solution. Place in a 350 ml. bottle, stopper, shake vigorously and allow to stand for 24 hours before comparison with the solution above and described in the preceding paragraph. Alternatively, an instrument or coloured acetate sheets for making the comparison can be obtained, but it is desirable that these should be verified on receipt by comparison with the standard solution.

Test for Determination of Specific Gravity

Indian Standard Specification IS : 2386 (Part III) of 1963 gives various procedures to find out the specific gravity of different sizes of aggregates. The following procedure is applicable to aggregate size larger than 10 mm.

A sample of aggregate not less than 2 kg is taken. It is thoroughly washed to remove the finer particles and dust adhering to the aggregate. It is then placed in a wire basket and immersed in distilled water at a temperature between 22° to 32°C. Immediately after immersion, the entrapped air is removed from the sample by lifting the basket containing it 25 mm above the base of the tank and allowing it to drop 25 times at the rate of about one drop per sec. During the operation, care is taken that the basket and aggregate remain completely immersed in water. They are kept in water for a period of 24 ± 1/2 hours afterwards. The basket and aggregate are then jolted and weighed (weight A_1) in water at a temperature 22° to 32° C. The basket and the aggregate are then removed from water and allowed to drain for a few minutes and then the aggregate is taken out from the basket and placed on dry cloth and the surface is gently dried with the cloth. The aggregate is transferred to the second dry cloth and further dried. The empty basket is again immersed in water, jolted 25 times and weighed in water (weight A_2). The aggregate is exposed to atmosphere away from direct sunlight for not less than 10 minutes until it appears completely surface dry. Then the aggregate is weighed in air (weight B). Then the aggregate is kept in the oven at a temperature of 100 to 110°C and maintained at this temperature for 24 ± 1/2 hours. It is then cooled in the air-tight container, and weighed (weight C).

$$\text{Specific Gravity} = \frac{C}{B-A}; \quad \text{Apparent Sp. Gravity} = \frac{C}{C-A}$$

$$\text{Water absorption} = \frac{100\,(B-C)}{C}$$

Where, A = the weight in gm of the saturated aggregate in water ($A_1 - A_2$),
  B = the weight in gm of the saturated surface-dry aggregate in air, and
  C = the weight in gm of oven-dried aggregate in air.

Test for Determination of Bulk Density and Voids

Bulk density is the weight of material in a given volume. It is normally expressed in kg per litre. A cylindrical measure preferably machined to accurate internal dimensions is used for measuring bulk density. The size of the container for measuring bulk density is shown in Table, 3.20.

Table 3.20. Size of Container for Bulk Density Test

Size of Largest Particles	Nominal Capacity	Inside Diameter	Inside Height	Thickness of Metal
	litre	cm	cm	mm
4.75 mm and under	3	15	17	3.15
Over 4.75 mm				
to 40 mm	15	25	30	4.00
Over 40 mm	30	35	31	5.00

The cylindrical measure is filled about 1/3 each time with thoroughly mixed aggregate and tamped with 25 strokes by a bullet ended tamping rod, 16 mm diameter and 60 cm long. The measure is carefully struck off level using tamping rod as a straight edge. The net weight of the aggregate in the measure is determined and the bulk density is calculated in kg/litre.

$$\text{Bulk dinsity} = \frac{\text{net weight of the aggregate in kg}}{\text{capacity of the container in litre}}; \qquad \text{Percentage of voids} = \frac{G_s - \gamma}{G_s} \times 100$$

where, G_s = specific gravity of aggregate and γ = bulk dinsity in kg/litre.

Mechanical Properties of Aggregates
IS: 2386 Part IV – 1963

Test for determination of aggregate crushing value

The "aggregate crushing value" gives a relative measure of the resistance of an aggregate to crushing under a gradually applied compressive load. With aggregates of 'aggregate crushing value' 30 or higher, the result may be anomalous and in such cases the "ten per cent fines value" should be determined and used instead.

The standard aggregate crushing test is made on aggregate passing a 12.5 mm I.S. Sieve and retained on 10 mm I.S. Sieve. If required, or if the standard size is not available, other sizes upto 25 mm may be tested. But owing to the nonhomogeneity of aggregates the results will not be comparable with those obtained in the standard test.

About 6.5 kg material consisting of aggregates passing 12.5 mm and retained on 10 mm sieve is taken. The aggregate in a surface dry condition is filled into the standard cylindrical measure in three layers approximately of equal depth. Each layer is tamped 25 times with the tamping ord and finally levelled off using the tamping rod as straight edge. The weight of the sample contained in the cylinder measure is taken (*A*). The same weight of the sample is taken for the subsequent repeat test.

The cylinder of the test appartus with aggregate filled in a standard manner is put in position on the base-plate and the aggregate is carefully levelled and the plunger inserted horizontally on this surface. The plunger should not jam in the cylinder.

Aggregate Crushing Value Apparatus.

The appartus, with the test sample and plunger in position, is placed on the compression testing machine and is loaded uniformly upto a total load of 40 tons in 10 minutes time. The load is then released and the whole of the material removed from the cylinder and sieved on a 2.36 mm I.S. Sieve. The fraction passing the sieve is weighed (*B*),

The aggregate crushing value = $\dfrac{B}{A} \times 100$

where, B = weight of fraction passing 2.36 mm sieve,

A = weight of surface-dry sample taken in mould.

The aggregate crushing value should not be more than 45 per cent for aggregate used for concrete other than for wearing surfaces, and 30 per cent for concrete used for wearing surfaces such a runways, roads and air field pavements.

Test for determination of 'ten per cent fines value'

The sample of aggregate for this test is the same as that of the sample used for aggregate crushing value test. The test sample is prepared in the same way as described earlier. The cylinder of the test appartus is placed in position on the base plate and the test sample added in thirds, each third being subjected to 25 strokes by tamping rod. The surface of the aggregate is carefully levelled and the plunger inserted so that it rests horizontally on this surface.

The appartus, with the test sample and plunger in position is placed in the compression testing machine. The load is applied at a uniform rate so as to cause a total penetration of the plunger in 10 minutes of about:

15.00 mm for rounded or partially rounded aggregates (for example uncrushed gravels)

20.0 mm for normal crushed aggregates, and

24.0 mm for honeycombed aggregates (for example, expanded shales and slags).

These figure may be varied according to the extent of the rounding or honeycombing.

After reaching the required maximum penetration, the load is released and the whole of the material removed from the cylinder and sieved on a 2.36 mm I.S. Sieve. The fines passing the sieve is weighed and the weight is expressed as a percentage of the weight of the test sample. This percentage would fall within the range 7.5 to 12.6, but if it does not, a further test shall be made at a load adjusted as seems appropriate to bring the percentage fines with the range of 7.5 to 12.5 per cent. Repeat test is made and the load is found out which gives a percentage of fines within the range of 7.5 to 12.5

Load required for 10 per cent fines = $\dfrac{14 \times X}{Y + 4}$

where, X= load in tons, causing 7.5 to 12.5 per cent fines.

Y = mean percentage fines from two tests at X tons load.

Test for determination of aggregate impact value

The aggregate impact value gives relative measure of the resistance of an aggregate to sudden shock or impact. Which in some aggregates differs from its resistance to a slow compressive load.

Aggregate Impact Value Apparatus.

The test sample consists of aggregate passing through 12.5 mm and retained on 10 mm I.S. Sieve. The aggregate shall be dried in an oven for a period of four hours at a temperature of 100°C to 110°C and cooled. The aggregate is filled about one-third full and tamped with 25 strokes by the tamping rod. A further similar quantity of aggregate is added and tamped in the standard manner. The measure is filled to over-flowing and then struck off level. The net weight of the aggregate in the measure is determined (weight A) and this weight of aggregate shall be used for the duplicate test on the same material.

The whole sample is filled into a cylindrical steel cup firmly fixed on the base of the machine. A hammer weighing about 14 kgs. is raised to a height of 380 mm above the upper surface of the aggregate in the cup and allowed to fall freely on the aggregate. The test sample shall be subjected to a total 15 such blows each being delivered at an interval of not less than one second. The crushed aggregate is removed from the cup and the whole of it is sieved on 2.36 mm I.S. Sieve. The fraction passing the sieve is weighed to an accuracy of 0.1 gm. (weight B). The fraction retained on the sieve is also weighed (weight C). If the total weight $(B + C)$ is less than the initial weight A by more than one gm the result shall be discarded and a fresh test made. Two tests are made.

The ratio of the weight of fines formed to the total sample weight in each test is expressed as percentage.

Therefore, Aggregate Impact Value = $\dfrac{B}{A} \times 100$

where, B = weight of fraction passing 2.36 mm I.S. Sieve.

A = weight of oven-dried sample.

The aggregate impact value should not be more than 45 per cent by weight for aggregates used for concrete other than wearing surfaces and 30 per cent by weight for concrete to be used as wearing surfaces, such as runways, roads and pavements.

Test for determination of aggregate abrasion value

Indian Standard 2386 (Part IV) of 1963 covers two methods for finding out the abrasion value of coarse aggregates: namely, by the use of Deval abrasion testing machine and by the use of Los Angeles abrasion testing machine. However, the use of Los Angeles abrasion testing machine gives a better realistic picture of the abrasion resistance of the aggregate. This method is only described herein.

Table 3.21 gives the detail of abrasive charge which consists of cast iron spheres or steel spheres approximately 48 mm in diameter and each weighing between 390 to 445 gm.

Table 3.21. Specified Abrasive Charge

Grading	Number of spheres	Weight of charge (gm)
A	12	5000 ± 25
B	11	4584 ± 25
C	8	3330 ± 20
D	6	2500 ± 15
E	12	5000 ± 25
F	12	5000 ± 25
G	12	5000 ± 25

The test sample consist of clean aggregate which has ben dried in an oven at 105°C to 110°C and it should conform to one of the gradings shown in Table 3.22.

Table 3.22. Gradings of Test Samples

Sieve Size		Weight in gm. of Test Sample For Grade						
Passing	Retained on	A	B	C	D	E	F	G
mm	mm							
80	63	-	-	-	-	2500	-	-
63	50	-	-	-	-	2500	-	-
50	40	-	-	-	-	5000	5000	-
40	25	1250	-	-	-	-	5000	5000
25	20	1250	-	-	-	-	-	5000
20	12.5	1250	2500	-	-	-	-	-
12.5	10	1250	2500	-	-	-	-	-
10	6.3	-	-	2500	-	-	-	-
6.3	4.75	-	-	2500	-	-	-	-
4.75	2.36	-	-	-	5000	-	-	-

Test sample and abrasive charge are placed in the Los Angeles Abrasion testing machine and the machine is rotated at a speed of 20 to 33 rev/min. For gradings *A, B, C* and *D*, the machine is rotated for 500 revolutions. For gradings *E, F* and *G*, it is rotated 1000 revolutions. At the completion of the above number of revolution, the material is discharged from the machine and a preliminary separation of the sample made on a sieve coarser than 1.7 mm IS Sieve. Finer portion is then sieved on a 1.7 mm IS Sieve. The material coarser than 1.7 mm IS Sieved is washed, dried in an oven at 105° to 110°C to a substantially constant weight and accurately weighed to the nearest gram.

The difference between the original weight and the final weight of the test sample is expressed as a percentage of the original weight of the test sample. This value is reported as the percentage of wear. The percentage of wear should not be more than 16 per cent for concrete aggregates.

Typical properties of some of the Indian aggregate sample are shown in table 3.23.

Los Angeles Abrasion Testing Machine.

Table 3.23. Typical Properties of Some of the Indian Aggregates[3.11]

Sr. No. (1)	Name of Place (2)	Flakiness Index % (3)	Elongation Index % (4)	Specific gravity (5)	Water Absorption (6)	Crushing Value % (7)	Impact Value % (8)	Abrasion Value % (9)	Sound ness % (10)	Remarks (11)
1.	Kirkee	16.8	20.8	2.84	1.20	16.97	18.65	18.54	4.2	20 mm aggregate
2.	Uterlai	22.8	23.9	2.79	0.80	—	17.80	21.0	2.4	40 mm aggregate
	Rajasthan	28.0	25.2	2.76	0.60	23.0	25.47	19.7	3.1	20 mm aggregate
3.	Bhatinda	20.89	17.50	2.5	1.01	22.62	31.54	29.1	10.0	40 mm aggregate
4.	Jammu	40.13	38.90	2.73	0.75	17.8	17.6	26.0	2.4	40 mm aggregate
		35.06	37.68	2.71	0.50	18.32	20.41	25.1	2.84	20 mm aggregate
5.	Bhuj	25.2	14.2	2.90	0.90	18.80	13.25	11.2	10.0	20 mm aggregate
6.	Nasik	27.8	31.3	2.67	0.75	24.83	—	21.00	4.00	40 mm aggregate
7.	Ranchi	13.28	25.28	2.69	0.50	27.47	29.58	38.9	3.0	Unreactive 20 mm
		23.60	21.0	2.66	0.50	33.68	—	18.8	1.0	40 mm aggregate
8.	Cochin	14.0	20.0	2.85	0.2	27.0	23.0	20.0	2.0	40 mm aggregate
		23.0	11.0	2.84	0.2	28.0	27.0	32.0	8.0	20 mm aggregate
9.	Wellington	30.0	19.0	2.87	0.44	26.0	21.0	19.0	6.0	40 mm aggregate
		14.0	29.0	2.85	0.50	27.6	19.0	31.3	6.0	20 mm aggregate
10.	Premnagar	39.0	25.00	2.62	1.20	27.30	27.40	31.96	3.5	20 mm aggregate
	(Dehradun)	36.30	25.70	2.60	1.25	29.90	25.00	20.00	4.0	12.5 mm aggregate
11.	Sulur	8.0	9.0	2.70	0.50	26.0	33.0	35.7	2.0	20 mm aggregate
	Coimbatore									
12.	Trivandrum	22.44	25.42	2.72	0.25	22.70	17.05	15.2	1.50	20 mm aggregate
		9.38	15.74	2.71	0.50	20.28	15.23	24.1	1.30	40 mm aggregate
13.	Muzzafarpur	14.0	18.0	2.69	0.20	23.2	22.9	17.80	3.90	20 mm aggregate
14	Belgaum	20.20	38.80	2.94	0.65	20.80	17.20	8.90	0.85	40 mm Type I aggregate
		31.80	29.20	2.98	0.47	22.30	14.80	10.10	0.87	40 mm Type II aggregate
		15.70	38.40	3.00	1.31	21.80	10.15	10.35	0.66	20 mm .. I aggregate
		24.00	29.30.	3.00	1.00	12.40	13.10	9.95	0.63	20 mm Type II ..

REFERENCES

3.1   Shergold FA, *The Percentage Voids in Compacted Gravel as a Measure of its Angularity, Magazine of Concrete Research*, Aug. 1953.

3.2   Murdock L.J., *The Workability of Concrete, Magazine of concrete Research*, Nov. 1960.

3.3   Bryant Mather, *Shape, surface texture, and coatings, concrete and concrete-making materials ASTM, STP* 169 – A.

3.4   Woolf D.O., *Toughness, Hardness, Abrasion, Strength and Elastic Properties, ASTM* STP 169 A.

3.5   Investigation work carried out by SEMT of College of Military Engineering (CME), Pune.

3.6   Jagus P.J., *Alkali Aggregate Reaction in Concrete Construction, Road Research Paper No. 11 of* 1958.

3.7   Cook H.K., *Thermal properties, ASTM, STP* 169 A.

3.8   Fuller W.B. and Thompson S.E., *The Laws of Proportioning of Concrete, Transactions, American Society of Civil Engineers Vol. LIX*, 1907.

3.9   Weymouth CAG, *Designing Workable Concrete, Engineering News Record*, Dec. 1938.

3.10. *Road Research Laboratory, Design of Concrete Mixers*, DSIR Road, Note No. 4, HMSO, London 1950

3.11. *Investigation work carried out by SEMT of college of Military Engineering (CME) Pune.*

Water requires to be tested to find out its suitability for large projects.

4

Water

- Qualities of Water
- Use of Sea Water for Mixing Concrete

ater is an important ingredient of concrete as it actively participates in the chemical reaction with cement. Since it helps to form the strength giving cement gel, the quantity and quality of water is required to be looked into very carefully. It has been discussed enough in chapter 1 about the quantity of mixing water but so far the quality of water has not been discussed. In practice, very often great control on properties of cement and aggregate is exercised, but the control on the quality of water is often neglected. Since quality of water affects the strength, it is necessary for us to go into the purity and quality of water.

Qualities of Water

A popular yard-stick to the suitability of water for mixing concrete is that, if water is fit for drinking it is fit for making concrete. This does not appear to be a true statement for all conditions. Some waters containing a small amount of sugar would be suitable for drinking but not for mixing concrete and conversely water suitable for making concrete may not necessarily be fit for drinking. Some specifications require that if the water is not obtained from source that has proved satisfactory, the strength of concrete or mortar made with questionable water should be compared with similar concrete or mortar made with pure water. Some specification also accept water for making concrete if the pH value of water lies between 6 and 8 and the water is free from organic matter. Instead of depending upon pH value and other chemical composition, the best course to find out whether a particular source of water is suitable for concrete making or not, is to make concrete with this water and compare its 7 days' and 28 days' strength with companion cubes made with distilled water. If the compressive strength is upto 90 per cent, the source of water may be accepted. This criteria may be safely adopted in places like coastal area of marshy area or in other places where the available water is brackish in nature and of doubtful quality. However, it is logical to know what harm the impurities in water do to the concrete and what degree of impurity is permissible is mixing concrete and curing concrete.

Underground water is sometime found unsuitable for mixing or even for
curing concrete.
The quality of underground water is to be checked.

Carbonates and bi-carbonates of sodium and potassium effect the setting time of cement. While sodium carbonate may cause quick setting, the bi-carbonates may either accelerate or retard the setting. The other higher concentrations of these salts will materially reduce the concrete strength. If some of these salts exceeds 1,000 ppm, tests for setting time and 28 days strength should be carried out. In lower concentrations they may be accepted.

Brackish water contains chlorides and sulphates. When chloride does not exceed 10,000 ppm and sulphate does not exceed 3,000 ppm the water is harmless, but water with even higher salt content has been used satisfactorily.

Salts of Manganese, Tin, Zinc, Copper and Lead cause a marked reduction in strength of concrete. Sodium iodate, sodium phosphate, and sodium borate reduce the initial strength of concrete to an extra-ordinarily high degree. Another salt that is detrimental to concrete is sodium sulphide and even a sulphide content of 100 ppm warrants testing.

Silts and suspended particles are undesirable as they interfere with setting, hardening and bond characteristics. A turbidity limit of 2,000 ppm has been suggested. Table 4.1 shows the tolerable concentration of some impurities in mixing water.

The initial setting time of the test block made with a cement and the water proposed to be used shall not differ by ±30 minutes from the initial setting time of the test block made with same cement and distilled water.

Table 4.1. Tolerable Concentrations of Some Impurities in Mixing Water

Impurity		Tolerable Concentration
Sodium and potassium carbonates and bi-carbonates	:	1,000 ppm (total). If this is exceeded, it is advisable to make tests both for setting time and 28 days strength
Chlorides	:	10,000 ppm.
Sulphuric anhydride	:	3,000 ppm
Calcium chloride	:	2 per cent by weight of cement in non-pre-stressed concrete
Sodium iodate, sodium sulphate, sodium arsenate, sodium borate	:	very low
Sodium sulphide	:	Even 100 ppm warrants testing
Sodium hydroxide	:	0.5 per cent by weight of cement, provided quick set is not induced.
Salt and suspended particles	:	2,000 ppm. Mixing water with a high content of suspended solids should be allowed to stand in a s ettling basin before use.
Total dissolved salts	:	15,000 ppm.
Organic material	:	3,000 ppm. Water containing humic acid or such organic acids may adversely affect the hardening of concrete; 780 ppm. of humic acid are reported to have seriously impaired the strength of concrete. In the case of such waters there- fore, further testing is necessary.
pH	:	shall not be less than 6

The following guidelines should also be taken into consideration regarding the quality of water.

(a) To neutralize 100 ml sample of water using phenoplhaline as an indicator, it should not require more than 5 ml of 0.02 normal NaOH.

(b) To neutralise 100 ml of sample of water, using mixed indicator, it should not require more than 25 ml of 0.02 normal H_2So_4.

(c) Permissible limits for solids is as given below in table 4.2.

Table 4.2. Permissible limit for solids as per IS 456 of 2000

Material	Tested as per	Permissible limit Max.
Organic	IS 3025 (pt 18)	200 mg/l
Inorganic	IS 3025 (pt 18)	3000 mg/l
Sulphates (as So$_3$)	IS 3025 (pt 24)	400 mg/l
Chlorides (as Cl)	IS 3025 (pt 32)	2000 mg/l for concrete work not containing embedded steel and 500 mg/l for reinforced concrete work
Suspended	IS 3025 (pt 17)	2000 mg/l

Algae in mixing water may cause a marked reduction in strength of concrete either by combining with cement to reduce the bond or by causing large amount of air entrainment in concrete. Algae which are present on the surface of the aggregate have the same effect as in that of mixing water.

Use of Sea Water for Mixing Concrete

Sea water has a salinity of about 3.5 per cent. In that about 78% is sodium chloride and 15% is chloride and sulphate of magnesium. Sea water also contain small quantities of sodium and potassium salts. This can react with reactive aggregates in the same manner as alkalies in cement. Therefore sea water should not be used even for PCC if aggregates are known to be potentially alkali reactive. It is reported that the use of sea water for mixing concrete does not appreciably reduce the strength of concrete although it may lead to corrosion of reinforcement in certain cases. Research workers are unanimous in their opinion, that sea water can be used in un-reinforced concrete or mass concrete. Sea water slightly accelerates the early strength of concrete. But it reduces the 28 days strength of concrete by about 10 to 15 per cent. However, this loss of strength could be made up by redesigning the mix. Water containing large quantities of chlorides in sea water may cause efflorescence and persistent dampness. When the appearance of concrete is important sea water may be avoided. The use of sea water is also not advisable for plastering purpose which is subsequently going to be painted.

Divergent opinion exists on the question of corrosion of reinforcement due to the use of sea water. Some research workers cautioned about the risk of corrosion of reinforcement particularly in tropical climatic regions, whereas some research workers did not find the risk of corrosion due to the use of sea water. Experiments have shown that corrosion of reinforcement occurred when concrete was made with pure water and immersed in pure water when the concrete was comparatively porous, whereas, no corrosion of reinforcement was found when sea water was used for mixing and the specimen was immersed in salt water when the concrete was dense and enough cover to the reinforcement was given. From this it could be inferred that the factor for corrosion is not the use of sea water or the quality of water where the concrete is placed. The factors effecting corrosion is permeability of concrete and lack of cover. However, since these factors cannot be adequately taken care of always at the site of work, it may be wise that sea water be avoided for making reinforced concrete. For

Sea water is not to be used for prestressed concrete or for reinforced concrete.
If unavoidable, it could be used for plain cement concrete (PCC).

economical or other passing reasons, if sea water cannot be avoided for making reinforced concrete, particular precautions should be taken to make the concrete dense by using low water/cement ratio coupled with vibration and to give an adequate cover of at least 7.5 cm. The use of sea water must be avoided in prestressed concrete work because of stress corrosion and undue loss of cross section of small diameter wires. The latest Indian standard IS 456 of 2000 prohibits the use of Sea Water for mixing and curing of reinforced concrete and prestressed concrete work. This specification permits the use of Sea Water for mixing and curing of plain cement concrete (PCC) under unavoidable situation..

It is pertinent at this point to consider the suitability of water for curing. Water that contains impurities which caused staining, is objectionable for curing concrete members whose look is important. The most common cause of staining is usually high concentration of iron or organic matter in the water. Water that contains more than 0.08 ppm. of iron may be avoided for curing if the appearance of concrete is important. Similarly the use of sea water may also be avoided in such cases. In other cases, the water, normally fit for mixing can also be used for curing.

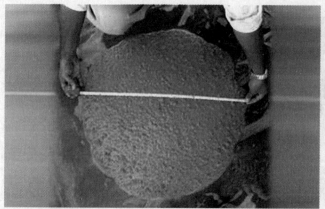

Such a flow is the result of the use of Superplasticizer

5

Admixtures and Construction Chemicals

General

Admixture is defined as a material, other than cement, water and aggregates, that is used as an ingredient of concrete and is added to the batch immediately before or during mixing. Additive is a material which is added at the time of grinding cement clinker at the cement factory.

These days concrete is being used for wide varieties of purposes to make it suitable in different conditions. In these conditions ordinary concrete may fail to exhibit the required quality performance or durability. In such cases, admixture is used to modify the properties of ordinary concrete so as to make it more suitable for any situation.

Until about 1930 additives and admixtures though used, were not considered an important part of concrete technology. Since then, there has been an increase in the use of admixtures. Though the use of admixtures and additives is being frowned upon or scorned by some technologists, there are many on the contrary, who highly commend and foster the use and development of admixtures as it imparts many desirable characteristics and effect economy in concrete construction. It should be remembered, however, that admixtures are no substitute for good concreting practices.

The history of admixtures is as old as the history of concrete. It embraces a very vast field as shown in table 5.22. But a few type of admixtures called Water Reducers or High Range Water Reducers, generally referred as plasticizers and superplasticizers, are of recent interest. They are specifically developed in Japan and Germany around 1970. Later on they were made popular in USA and Europe even in Middle East and Far East. Unfortunately, the use of plasticizers and superplasticizers have not become popular in India till recently (1985). There are many reasons for non acceptance for wider use of plasticizers in India: Ninety per cent of concreting activities are in the hands of common builders or Government departments who do not generally accept something new. Plasticizers were not manufactured in India and they were to be imported, and hence costly. Lack of education and awareness of the benefits accrued by the use of plasticizers, and we were used to making generally low strength concrete of the type M15 to M30, which do not really need the use of plasticizers.

Now, since early 1980's, some internationally renowned companies collaborated with Indian companies and have started manufacturing chemical admixtures in India. As a part of marketing they started educating consultants, architects, structural engineers and builders about the benefits of using admixtures. We, in India have also started using higher strength concrete for high rise buildings and bridges. Use of Ready mix concrete has really promoted the use of admixtures in India, in recent times.

It will be slightly difficult to predict the effect and the results of using admixtures because, many a time, the change in the brand of cement, aggregate grading, mix proportions and richness of mix alter the properties of concrete. Sometimes many admixtures affect more than one property of concrete. At times, they affect the desirable properties adversely. Sometimes, more than one admixture is used in the same mix. The effect of more than one admixture is difficult to predict. Therefore, one must be cautious in the selection of admixtures and in predicting the effect of the same in concrete.

As per the report of the ACI Committee 212, admixtures have been classified into 15 groups according to type of materials constituting the admixtures, or characteristic affect of the use. When ACI Committee 212 submitted the report in 1954, plasticizers and superplasticizers, as we know them today, were not existing. Therefore, in this grouping of admixtures, plasticizers and superplasticizers and a few variations in them have now been included under admixtures.

Classification of admixtures as given by M.R. Rixom (slightly modified to include a few new materials) is given in table 5.22.

In this chapter, the following admixtures and construction chemicals are dealt with.

Admixtures

- Plasticizers
- Superplasticizers
- Retarders and Retarding Plasticizers
- Accelerators and Accelerating Plasticizers
- Air-entraining Admixtures
- Pozzolanic or Mineral Admixtures
- Damp-proofing and Waterproofing Admixtures
- Gas forming Admixtures

- Air-detraining Admixtures
- Alkali-aggregate Expansion Inhibiting Admixtures
- Workability Admixtures
- Grouting Admixtures
- Corrosion Inhibiting Admixtures
- Bonding Admixtures
- Fungicidal, Germicidal, Insecticidal Admixtures
- Colouring Admixtures

Construction Chemicals

- Concrete Curing Compounds
- Polymer Bonding Agents
- Polymer Modified Mortar for Repair and Maintenance
- Mould Releasing Agents
- Protective and Decorative Coatings
- Installation Aids
- Floor Hardeners and Dust-proofers
- Non-shrink High Strength Grout
- Surface Retarders
- Bond-aid for Plastering
- Ready to use Plaster
- Guniting Aid
- Construction Chemicals for Water-proofing
  1. Integral Water-proofing Compounds
  2. Membrane Forming Coatings
  3. Polymer Modified Mineral Slurry Coatings
  4. Protective and Decorative Coatings
  5. Chemical DPC
  6. Silicon Based Water-repellent Material
  7. Waterproofing Adhesive for Tiles, Marble and Granite
  8. Injection Grout for Cracks
  9. Joint Sealants

Plasticizers (Water Reducers)

Requirement of right workability is the essence of good concrete. Concrete in different situations require different degree of workability. A high degree of workability is required in situations like deep beams, thin walls of water retaining structures with high percentage of steel reinforcement, column and beam junctions, tremie concreting, pumping of concrete, hot weather concreting, for concrete to be conveyed for considerable distance and in ready mixed concrete industries. The conventional methods followed for obtaining high workability is by improving the gradation, or by the use of relatively higher percentage of fine aggregate or by increasing the cement content. There are difficulties and limitations to obtain high workability in the field for a given set of conditions. The easy method generally followed at the site in most of the conditions is to use extra water unmindful of the harm it can do to the strength and durability of concrete. It has been stressed time and again in almost all the chapters of this book to the harmful effect of using extra water than necessary. It is an abuse, a criminal act, and unengineering to use too much water than necessary in concrete. At the same time, one must admit that getting required workability for the job in hand with set conditions and available materials is essential and is often difficult. Therefore, engineers at the site are generally placed in conflicting situations. Often he follows the easiest path and that is adding extra water to fluidise the mix. This addition of extra water to satisfy the need for workable concrete is amounting to sowing the seed of cancer in concrete.

Today we have plasticizers and superplasticizers to help an engineer placed in intriguing situations. These plasticizers can help the difficult conditions for obtaining higher workability without using excess of water. One must remember that addition of excess water, will only improve the fluidity or the consistency but not the workability of concrete. The excess water will not improve the inherent good qualities such as homogeneity and cohesiveness of the mix which reduces the tendency for segregation and bleeding. Whereas the plasticized concrete will improve the desirable qualities demanded of plastic concrete. The practice all over the world now is to use plasticizer or superplasticizer for almost all the reinforced concrete and even for mass concrete to reduce the water requirement for making concrete of higher workability or flowing concrete. The use of superplasticizer has become almost an universal

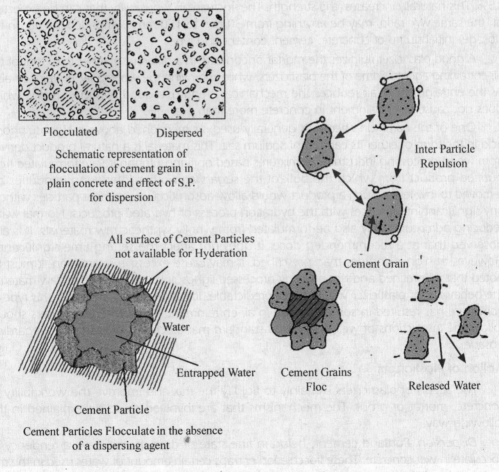

Flocculated   Dispersed

Schematic representation of
flocculation of cement grain in
plain concrete and effect of S.P.
for dispersion

Inter Particle
Repulsion

Cement Grain

All surface of Cement Particles
not available for Hyderation

Water

Entrapped Water

Cement Particle

Cement Grains
Floc

Released Water

Cement Particles Flocculate in the absence
of a dispersing agent

Fig. 5.1. Effect of surface-active agents on deflocculating of cement grains.

practice to reduce water/cement ratio for the given workability, which naturally increases the strength. Moreover, the reduction in water/cement ratio improves the durability of concrete. Sometimes the use of plasticizers is employed to reduce the cement content and heat of hydration in mass concrete.

The organic substances or combinations of organic and inorganic substances, which allow a reduction in water content for the given workability, or give a higher workability at the same water content, are termed as plasticizing admixtures. The advantages are considerable in both cases : in the former, concretes are stronger, and in the latter they are more workable.

The basic products constituting plasticizers are as follows:

(*i*) Anionic surfactants such as lignosulphonates and their modifications and derivatives, salts of sulphonates hydrocarbons.

(*ii*) Nonionic surfactants, such as polyglycol esters, acid of hydroxylated carboxylic acids and their modifications and derivatives.

(*iii*) Other products, such as carbohydrates etc.

Among these, calcium, sodium and ammonium lignosulphonates are the most used. Plasticizers are used in the amount of 0.1% to 0.4% by weight of cement. At these doses, at constant workability the reduction in mixing water is expected to be of the order of 5% to 15%. This naturally increases the strength. The increase in workability that can be expected, at the same w/c ratio, may be anything from 30 mm to 150 mm slump, depending on the dosage, initial slump of concrete, cement content and type.

A good plasticizer fluidizes the mortar or concrete in a different manner than that of the air-entraining agents. Some of the plasticizers, while improving the workability, entrains air also. As the entrainment of air reduces the mechanical strength, a good plasticizer is one which does not cause air-entrainment in concrete more than 1 or 2%.

One of the common chemicals generally used, as mentioned above is Lignosulphonic acid in the form of either its calcium or sodium salt. This material is a natural product derived from wood processing industries. Admixtures based on lignosulphonate are formulated from purified product from which the bulk of the sugars and other interfering impurities are removed to low levels. Such a product would allow adsorption into cement particles without any significant interferences with the hydration process or hydrated products. Normal water reducing admixtures may also be formulated from wholly synthetic raw materials. It is also observed that at a recommended dose, it does not affect the setting time significantly. However, at higher dosages than prescribed, it may cause excessive retardation. It must be noted that if unrefined and not properly processed lignosulphonate is used as raw material, the behaviour of plasticizer would be unpredictable. It is some times seen that this type of admixture has resulted in some increase in air-entrainment. It is advised that users should follow the instructions of well established standard manufacturers of plasticizers regarding dosage.

Action of Plasticizers

The action of plasticizers is mainly to fluidify the mix and improve the workability of concrete, mortar or grout. The mechanisms that are involved could be explained in the following way:

Dispersion. Portland cement, being in fine state of division, will have a tendency to flocculate in wet concrete. These flocculation entraps certain amount of water used in the mix and thereby all the water is not freely available to fluidify the mix.

When plasticizers are used, they get adsorbed on the cement particles. The adsorption of charged polymer on the particles of cement creates particle-to-particle repulsive forces which overcome the attractive forces. This repulsive force is called Zeta Potential, which depends on the base, solid content, quantity of plasticizer used. The overall result is that the cement particles are deflocculated and dispersed. When cement particles are deflocculated, the water trapped inside the flocs gets released and now available to fluidify the mix. Fig. 5.1 explains the mechanism.

When cement particles get flocculated there will be interparticles friction between particle to particle and floc to floc. But in the dispersed condition there is water in between the cement particle and hence the interparticle friction is reduced.

Retarding Effect. It is mentioned earlier that plasticizer gets adsorbed on the surface of cement particles and form a thin sheath. This thin sheath inhibits the surface hydration reaction between water and cement as long as sufficient plasticizer molecules are available at the particle/solution interface. The quantity of available plasticizers will progressively decrease as the polymers become entrapped in hydration products.

Many research workers explained that one or more of the following mechanisms may take place simultaneously:

- Reduction in the surface tension of water.
- Induced electrostatic repulsion between particles of cement.
- Lubricating film between cement particles.
- Dispersion of cement grains, releasing water trapped within cement flocs.
- Inhibition of the surface hydration reaction of the cement particles, leaving more water to fluidify the mix.
- Change in the morphology of the hydration products.
- Induced steric hindrance preventing particle-to-particle contact.

It may be noted that all plasticizer are to some extent set retarders, depending upon the base of plasticizers, concentration and dosage used.

Superplasticizers (High Range Water Reducers)

Superplasticizers constitute a relatively new category and improved version of plasticizer, the use of which was developed in Japan and Germany during 1960 and 1970 respectively. They are chemically different from normal plasticiszers. Use of superplasticizers permit the reduction of water to the extent upto 30 per cent without reducing workability in contrast to the possible reduction up to 15 per cent in case of plasticizers.

The use of superplasticizer is practiced for production of flowing, self levelling, self compacting and for the production of high strength and high performance concrete.

The mechanism of action of superplasticizers are more or less same as explained earlier in case of ordinary plasticizer. Only thing is that the superplasticizers are more powerful as dispersing agents and they are high range water reducers. They are called High Range Water Reducers in American literature. It is the use of superplasticizer which has made it possible to use w/c as low as 0.25 or even lower and yet to make flowing concrete to obtain strength of the order 120 Mpa or more. It is the use of superplasticizer which has made it possible to use fly ash, slag and particularly silica fume to make high performance concrete.

The use of superplasticizer in concrete is an important milestone in the advancement of concrete technology. Since their introduction in the early 1960 in Japan and in the early 1970 in Germany, it is widely used all over the world. India is catching up with the use of superplasticizer in the construction of high rise buildings, long span bridges and the recently become popular Ready Mixed Concrete Industry. Common builders and Government departments are yet to take up the use of this useful material.

Superplasticizers can produce:

● at the same w/c ratio much more workable concrete than the plain ones,

● for the same workability, it permits the use of lower w/c ratio,

● as a consequence of increased strength with lower w/c ratio, it also permits a reduction of cement content.

The superplasticizers also produce a homogeneous, cohesive concrete generally without any tendency for segregation and bleeding.

Classification of Superplasticizer. Following are a few polymers which are commonly used as base for superplasticizers.

● Sulphonated malanie-formaldehyde condensates (SMF)

● Sulphonated naphthalene-formaldehyde condensates (SNF)

● Modified lignosulphonates (MLS)

● Other types

In addition to the above, in other countries the following new generation superplasticizers are also used.

● Acrylic polymer based (AP)

● Copolymer of carboxylic acrylic acid with acrylic ester (CAE)

● Cross linked acrylic polymer (CLAP)

● Polycarboxylate ester (PC)

● Multicarboxylatethers (MCE)

● Combinations of above.

Out of the above new generation superplasticizers based on carboxylic acrylic ester (CAE) and multicarboxylatether (MCE) are discussed later.

As far as our country is concerned, at present (2000 AD), we manufacture and use the first four types of superplasticizers. The new generation superplasticizers have been tried in recent projects, but it was not found feasible for general usage on account of high cost. The first four categories of products differ from one another because of the base component or on account of different molecular weight. As a consequence each commercial product will have different action on cements. Whilst the dosage of conventional plasticizers do not exceed 0.25% by weight of cement in case of lignosulphonates, or 0.1% in case of carboxylic acids, the products of type SMF or NSF are used considerably high dosages (0.5% to 3.00%), since they do not entrain air. The modified

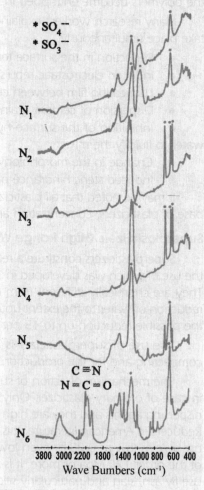

N_1 to N_5, infra-red spectrograph of a naphthalene superplasticizer; M_6, lignosulfonate superplasticizer and a mixed superplasticizer.

| Plasticizer | Superplasticizer | Acrylic polymer based new generation plasticizer |

lignosulphonate (LS) based admixtures, which have an effective fluidizing action, but at the relatively high dosages, they can produce undesirable effects, such as accelerations or delay in setting times. Moreover, they increase the air-entrainment in concrete.[5.1]

Plasticizers and superplasticizers are water based. The solid contents can vary to any extent in the products manufactured by different companies. Cost should be based on efficiencies and solid content, but not on volume or weight basis. Generally in projects cost of superplasticizers should be worked for one cubic meter of concrete. Consistency in the quality of superplasticizers supplied over a period of time can be tested and compared by "Infrared Spectrometry".

Effects of Superplasticizers on Fresh Concrete

It is to be noted that dramatic improvement in workability is not showing up when plasticizers or superplasticizers are added to very stiff or what is called zero slump concrete at nominal dosages. A mix with an initial slump of about 2 to 3 cm can only be fluidised by plasticizers or superplasticizers at nominal dosages. A high dosage is required to fluidify no slump concrete. An improvement in slump value can be obtained to the extent of 25 cm or more depending upon the initial slump of the mix, the dosage and cement content. It is often noticed that slump increases with increase in dosage. But there is no appreciable increase in slump beyond certain limit of dosage. As a matter of fact, the overdosage may sometime harm the concrete. A typical curve, showing the slump and dosage is shown in Fig. 5.2.

Compatibility of Superplasticizers and Cement

It has been noticed that all superplasticizers are not showing the same extent of improvement in fluidity with all types of cements. Some superplasticizers may show higher fluidizing effect on some type of cement than other cement. There is nothing wrong with either the superplasticizer or that of cement. The fact is that they are just not compatible to show maximum fluidizing effect. Optimum fluidizing effect at lowest dosage is an economical consideration. Giving maximum fluidizing effect for a particular superplasticizer and a cement is very complex involving many factors like composition of cement, fineness of cement etc.

Although compatibility problem looks to be very complex, it could be more or less solved by simple rough and ready field method. Incidentally this simple field test shows also the optimum dose of the superplasticizer to the cement. Following methods could be adopted.

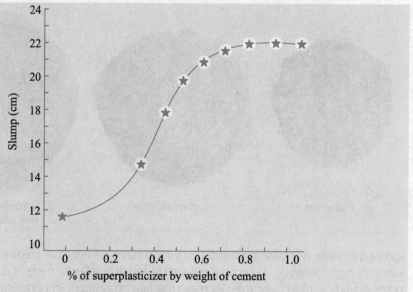

Fig. 5.2. Effect of additions of superplasticizers (Alklaryl sulphonateformaldehyde condensates) on the workability of a concrete. Cement content 300 kg/m³, w/c ratio = 0.6.

- Marsh cone test
- Mini slump test
- Flow table test.

Out of the above, Marsh cone test gives better results. In the Marsh cone test, cement slurry is made and its flowability is found out. In concrete, really come to think of it, it is the cement paste that influences flowability. Although, the quantity of aggregates, its shape and texture etc. will have some influence, it is the paste that will have greater influence. The presence of aggregate will make the test more complex and often erratic. Whereas the using of grout alone will make the test simple, consistent and indicative of the fluidifying effect of superplasticizer with a cement.

The following procedure is adopted in Marsh cone test.

Marsh cone is a conical brass vessel, which has a smooth aperture at the bottom of diameter 5 mm. The profile of the apparatus is shown in Fig. 5.3.

Take 2 kg cement, proposed to be used at the project. Take one litre of water (w/c = 0.5) and say 0.1% of plasticizer. Mix them thoroughly in a mechanical mixer (Hobart mixer is preferable) for two minutes. Hand mixing does not

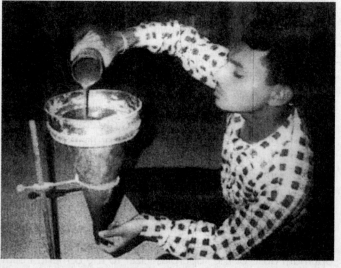

Fig. 5.3. Marsh Cone Test.

give consistent results because of unavoidable lump formation which blocks the aperture. If hand mixing is done, the slurry should be sieved through 1.18 sieve to exclude lumps. Take one litre slurry and pour it into marsh cone duly closing the aperture with a finger. Start a stop watch and simultaneously remove the finger. Find out the time taken in seconds, for complete flow out of the slurry. The time in seconds is called the "Marsh Cone Time". Repeat the test with different dosages of plasticizer. Plot a graph connecting Marsh cone time in seconds and dosages of plasticizer or superplasticizer. A typical graph is shown in Fig. 5.4. The dose at which the Marsh cone time is lowest is called the saturation point. The dose is the optimum dose for that brand of cement and plasticizer or superplasticizer for that w/c ratio.

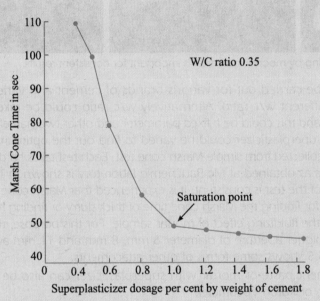

Fig. 5.4. Typical Relation between Marsh Cone Time and Dosage.

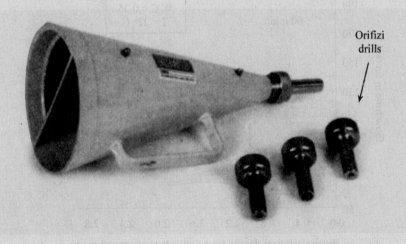

Fig. 5.5. Marsh cone viscometer with attachments, 6 mm, 8 mm and 11 mm.

Mixing by mechanical mixer is important for consistent results.

The test could be carried out for various brands of cement and various brands of superplasticizer at different w/c ratio. Alternatively w/c ratio could be taken as fixed by Concrete Mix Design and this could be a fixed parameter and other two namely the brand of cement and type of superplasticizer could be varied to find out the optimum result. Lot of useful data could be collected from simple Marsh cone test. Each test takes hardly 15 minutes. The typical test results as obtained at Mc Bauchemie laboratory is shown in Table 5.1. It is noted that the result of the test is consistent. It is experienced that Marsh cone with aperture of 5 mm is not useful for finding the Marsh cone time of thick slurry or finding retarding effect of superplasticizer or the fluidizing effect of mortar sample. For this purpose, there are other attachments having bigger aperture of diameter 6 mm, 8 mm and 11 mm available which could be used. Fig. 5.5 shows some forms of other attachments.

Viscosity of cement paste or mortar with superplasticizer can also be measured by Brookfield Viscometer, or Roton Viscometer.

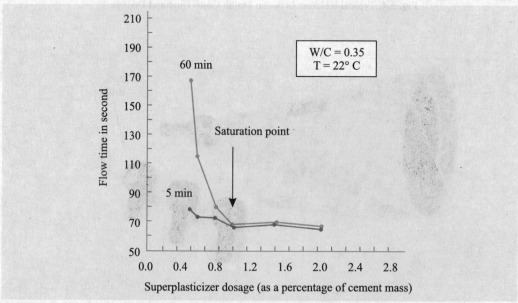

Flow time as a function of the supeplasticizer dosage

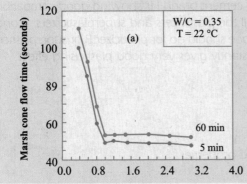

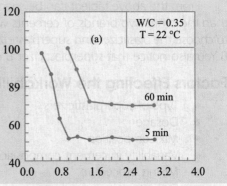

Represents the case of a fully compatible combination of cement and superplasticizer

Represents the case of incompatibility

Table. 5.1. Compatibility Study of Plasticizers and Superplasticizers with Different Cements

Cement = 2 kg.   W/C = 0.45

Sr. No.	Dosage % by wt of cement	Dosage Quantity in ml.	Type of Plasticizer	Marsh Cone Time for Cement Slurry in Seconds		
				Cement Brand I	Cement Brand II	Cement Brand III
1	0.1	2	Plasticizer A	105	110	120
2	0.1	2	Plasticizer B	72	75	103
3	0.1	2	Plasticizer C	86	88	105
4	0.5	10	Superplasticizer A	69	72	72
5	0.5	10	Superplasticizer B	59	62	65
6	0.5	10	Superplasticizer C	165	170	202
1	0.2	4	Plasticizer A	75	80	82
2	0.2	4	Plasticizer B	64	69	70
3	0.2	4	Plasticizer C	69	75	76
4	0.7	14	Superplasticizer A	63	68	66
5	0.7	14	Superplasticizer B	57	60	62
6	0.7	14	Superplasticizer C	152	156	176
1	0.3	6	Plasticizer A	75	69	70
2	0.3	6	Plasticizer B	64	65	62
3	0.3	6	Plasticizer C	69	68	65
4	0.9	18	Superplasticizer A	63	65	62
5	0.9	18	Superplasticizer B	57	55	60
6	0.9	18	Superplasticizer C	127	132	134
1	1.1	22	Superplasticizer A	58	60	60
2	1.1	22	Superplasticizer B	45	50	46
3	1.1	22	Superplasticizer C	75	83	90

From the above table it can be seen that cement brand I is showing good compatibility than the other two brands of cements with all the plasticizers and superplasticizers. If one is to choose the plasticizer and superplasticizers, one should go for plasticizer B or superplasticizer B. You also notice that superplasticizer B consistantly gives very good plasticising effect.

Factors Effecting the Workability

- Type of superplasticizers
- Dosage
- Mix composition
- Variability in cement composition and properties
- Mixing procedure
- Equipments
- Others

Type of Superplasticizers

It is a well established fact that the average molecular weight of the plasticizer is of primary importance for its efficiency as plasticizer in concrete. The higher the molecular weight, the higher is the efficiency. However, it should be noted that there is a maximum value of molecular weight beyond which efficiency is expected to decrease. It may be further noted that several intrinsic properties of the superplasticizers may influence the performance. Therefore, it is difficult to compare the efficiency of one plasticizer from the other in the absence of number of related properties of superplasticizers.

Dosage. It has been already explained while describing the Marsh cone test that the dosage of superplasticizer influences the viscosity of grout and hence the workability of

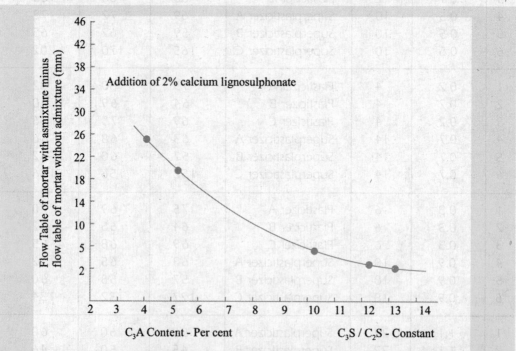

Fig. 5.6. Reduction in the workability of a cement mortar containing calcium lignosulphonate vs. per cent content of tricalcium aluminate.[5.2]

concrete. The optimum dosage can be ascertained from Marsh cone test if brand of cement, plasticizer and w/c ratio is already fixed. Simple Marsh cone test can give realistic dosage than manufacturers instructions which is general in nature. In our country generally low dosage is adopted for normal concreting operations. A dosage more than 2.5% by weight of cement is rarely used. But in other countries much higher dosages up to 4 to 5% are used in special situations. It has been reported in literatures that upto a dosage of about 3% there are no harmful effect on the hardening properties of concrete. Higher dosage is said to have affected the shrinkage and creep properties.

Mix Composition. The mix composition particularly the aggregate/cement ratio or richness of the mix, w/c ratio, and use of other supplementary cementing materials like fly ash or silica fume affects the workability. Wetter the mix better is the dispersion of cement grains and hence better workability. The size and shape of aggregate, sand grading will also have influence on the fluidifying effect.

Variability in Cement Composition. The variability in cement with respect to compound composition, in particular C_3A content, C_3S/C_2S ratio, fineness of cement, alkali content and gypsum content are responsible for the lack of compatibility with a particular type of superplasticizer and their performance in concrete. Out of the above C_3A content will have over-riding influence on the performance of superplasticizer. Fig. 5.6 shows the effect of C_3A content.

Mixing Procedure

Plasticizer must be properly and intimately mixed in concrete to bring about proper dispersion with cement particles. Therefore, hand mixing is out of question. When you use concrete mixer, generally about 80% of the total water is added to the empty drum and then materials are loaded into the drum by hopper. When you use superplasticizer, it is better to add all the water to the drum keeping about one litre of water in spare. The exact quantity of superplasticizer is diluted with that one litre of water and thrown into the drum in two or three installments over the well mixed concrete so that proper dispersion of plasticizer actually takes place in the drum. Having added the plasticizer, the concrete must be mixed for about one more minute before discharging. The practice of adding superplasticizer along with the bulk mixing water is not giving good results. Experimental result showed that adding plasticizer after three minutes of mixing has yielded better results. Fig. 5.7 shows the effect of addition of water three minutes after mixing with the water.

It has been found that all over India, electrically operated small laboratory mixer is used for conducting laboratory trials. These laboratory

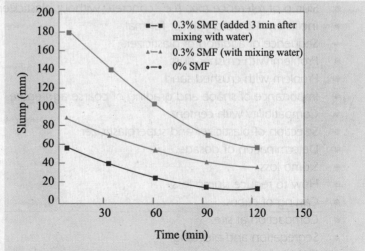

Fig. 5.7. Effect of delayed addition of sulphonated malamine formaldehyde condensate on slump and slump loss.

mixers are inefficient and they do not mix the concrete ingredients thoroughly, leave apart the efficient mixing of superplasticizers. The results obtained from the trials, using laboratory mixer, is far from realistic. In such situations the following procedure gives better consistent results.

Add all the calculated quantity of water into the drum. Then add all the quantity of cement and sand. Mix these ingredients very well. When they are well mixed, add the calculated quantity of plasticizer and thoroughly mix them together. You will notice the full action of plasticizer in fluidifying the mix. Then you add the course aggregates and mix them for another one minutes. When the mixer is not efficient as in the case of laboratory mixer, the above procedure of mixing will give good results.

Equipment. It has been discussed above that inefficient spot mixer at site or laboratory that is small mixer does not exploit the action of superplasticizer fully, often they do not even mix the concrete uniformly and properly. The fabrication of concrete mixer is not a simple job. The shape of the drum, its bottom diameter and shape, number of blades, the angle of blades, length and depth of blades, the space between drum and blade and space between the blades will have lot to do with the mixing efficiency. The manufacturers often neglect these details. Generally pan mixer show better efficiency particularly in case of small scale laboratory mixers. Such small capacity pan mixers are not generally available for trial. Some manufacturers of concrete mixers have now started fabrication and supply of pan mixers.

The mixers in the batching plant are of capacity half a cubic meter and above. They are generally of pan type. They are well designed and fabricated and as such every efficient. The mixing time is around 20 seconds. Within this short spell of 20 seconds, very intimate mixing is done. It is observed that for identical parameters concrete mixed in the batching plant gives about 20 to 30 mm more slump than trial mix carried out in laboratory using small, inefficient mixers.

Others. The slump value of a superplasticized concrete may also be affected on account of other admixtures used concurrently in concrete such as air-entraining agent, fly ash, slag or silica fume. The temperature and relative humidity also affect the result.

Site Problems in the use of Superplasticizers

Some of the practical site problems in the use of superplasticizers are listed below:
- Slump of reference mix. (*i.e.*, concrete without plasticizer)
- Inefficient laboratory mixer for trial.
- Sequence of addition of plasticizer.
- Problem with crusher dust.
- Problem with crushed sand.
- Importance of shape and grading of coarse aggregate.
- Compatibility with cement.
- Selection of plasticizer and superplasticizer.
- Determination of dosage.
- Slump loss.
- How to reduce slump loss.
- Casting of cubes.
- Compaction at site.
- Segregation and bleeding.
- Finishing.
- Removal of form work.

It is not intended to discuss each of the above points separately as some of the problems are self explanatory. The points mentioned above are discussed in general and where applicable, solution to the problems are also indicated, for general guidance.

It is mentioned earlier that very stiff zero slump concrete can not be perceptibly improved at nominal dosage. Although there is improvement in rheology of matrix with the use of superplasticizers, it does not become perceptible and measurable by slump test. If the initial concrete mix is designed in such a way as to have about 2 to 3 cm slump, then only the slump could be enhanced to a high level. High dosage of plasticizer may give good slump in case of a stiff mix. But it is uneconomical. Initial slump in the reference concrete is an important consideration.

Generally available laboratory mixers are inefficient especially when small quantity of plasticizers are used for trial mix. Use of pan mixer will give better results.

The sequence and method of addition of superplasticizer is described earlier for good results.

In the years to come for large projects one will have to go for crushed sand. In spite of the modern well designed crushers, higher quantity of dust in generally present. This dust interferes with plasticizing properties of mix and hence anticipated results are not obtainable. For the construction of Mumbai-Pune express highway, they specified only the crushed sand. The initial trials presented lot of problems with the presence of excess of crusher dust when reasonable doses of superplasticizer were used. In some sectors, some contractors had to go for combination of natural sand and crushed sand. Whereas some other contracting firm managed to use only crushed sand. Whatever it is, the dust in crushed sand affects the performance of plasticizers. Incidentally, excess of crusher dust increases drying shrinkage.

For normal strength concrete upto 30 or 40 MPa, the shape of aggregate is not of primary importance. For production of high strength concrete of the order of 50 MPa or 60 MPa, the w/c ratio become so low that shape of aggregates becomes very important and also the use of superplasticizers becomes essential for the requirement of workability, particularly when concrete is to be transported over long distance and pumped. In one situation in the construction of high rise building at Mumbai where 60 MPa concrete was used, well graded, cubical shaped aggregate, specially manufactured, could solve the problem. In one of the project sites at Delhi, where aggregates flakiness index was very high, particularly in 10 mm aggregate, the achievement of high slump was found to be difficult in spite of using high dosage of superplasticizers.

In many sites, compatibility problem with cement and plasticizer becomes primary considerations. This can be solved by simple Marsh cone test. Marsh cone test also indicates the economical dosage.

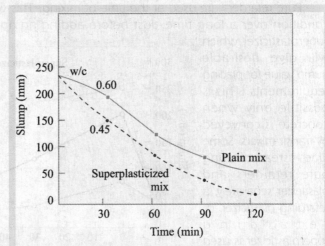

Fig. 5.8. Slump loss at 20°C for plain and superplasticized mix at the same initial slump. Superlasticizer: 0.4 per cent as dry NSF polymer by weight of cement.

Superplasticisers are costly and they operate at higher dosages. If the slump value at a point of batching and the slump value at a point of placing is known, by conducting a few field trials, it is possible to arrive at a decision whether plasticizer would be sufficient or one should go for superplasticizer. Site trials are also required to find out the dosage, the slump value and probable slump loss.

Slump Loss. One of the most important nagging site problem is the loss of slump. Slump at mixing point is not of much importance, but the slump at placing point is of primary importance. Often there is delay between mixing and placing. Achieving high slump at the mixer, only to be lost with time, before placing is a bad economy. Loss of slump is natural even with unplasticized concrete, but rate of loss slump is little more in case of superplasticized concrete. Fig. 5.8 indicates the slump loss with time.

Many users demand the slump value at mixing or batching plant and also specify the slump value after a delay of 1 or 2 or 3 hours period at placing point. It is not a correct specification. User should only specify the slump value at placing point after a delay of 1 or 2 of 3 hours. It should be left to the superplasticizer manufacturers or concrete supplier to supply concrete of slump value as demanded by user at the time of placing of concrete.

Steps for Reducing Slump Loss

The slump loss can be managed by taking any one or more of the following actions:
- Initial high slump.
- Using retarders.
- Using retarding plasticizer or superplasticizer.
- By repetitive dose.
- By dosing at final point.
- By keeping temperature low.
- By using compatible superplasticizer with cement.

When very high slump is managed at the mixing point, even if loss of slump takes place, still the residual slump will be good enough for satisfactory placing of concrete. Although this method is not a good and economical method some time this method is adopted. Fig. 5.9.

Pure retarders are used at the time of mixing. This will keep the concrete in a plastic condition over a long time. Just before adding an appropriate dose of plasticizer or superplasticizer which will give desirable slump value for placing requirements. This is possible only when concrete is conveyed by transit mixers. Some time instead of using pure retarders and plasticizer separately, a retarding plasticizer, or retarding superplasticizer is used in an appropriate dose in the initial stage itself.

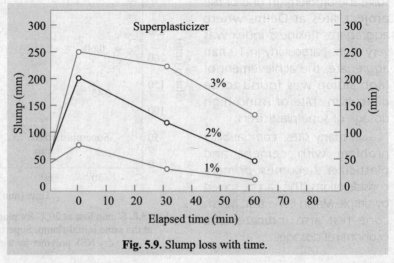

Fig. 5.9. Slump loss with time.

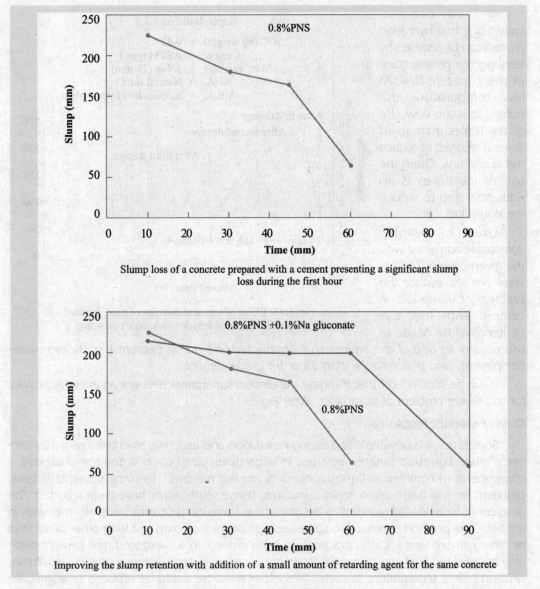

Slump loss of a concrete prepared with a cement presenting a significant slump loss during the first hour

Improving the slump retention with addition of a small amount of retarding agent for the same concrete

The retarding plasticizer or superplasticizers retains the slump for longer periods which may be sufficient for placing.

One of the common methods to combat the slump loss is to give repetitive doses at intervals and thereby boosting the slump so that required slump is maintained for long time. Figure 5.10 shows the typical repetitive method of using plasticizer. The time interval should be chosen in such a way that the concrete will have such a residual slump value which can be boosted up.

Sometimes a small dose of superplasticizer is added at the beginning and the slump is boosted up. When the concrete arrives at the pouring point, it will still have some residual slump but not good enough for placing by pump or by tremie. For pumping concrete you need a slump of around 100 mm and tremie placing the desirable slump is 150 mm. At this point an appropriate dose of superplasticizer is added to boost up the slump to required level.

It is a common knowledge that hydration process can be retarded by keeping the temperature of the concrete low. At low temperature the slump loss is also slow. Use of ice flakes instead of water is resorted to reduce the slump loss. Often the use of ice flakes is an additional step to reduce the slump loss.

Use of highly compatible admixture with the given cement or *vice-versa* will also reduce the problem of slump loss. A cement with low C_3A content will be of use in

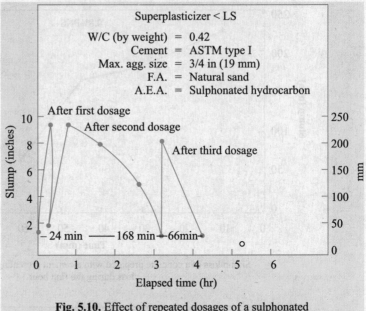

Fig. 5.10. Effect of repeated dosages of a sulphonated Naphthaline formaldehyde condensates on slump.

this regard. In one of the limited trial conducted, 43 grade cement has shown better compatibility and performance than 33 or 53 grade cement.

It will be shown later that the new generation superplasticizers are an effective answer for this severe problem of slump loss. Refer Fig. 5.14.

Other Potential Problems

Sometimes, it is possible that a strong retardation and excessive air-entrainment may take place when lignosulphonates are used in large dose, particularly when the undesirable components in commercial lignosulphonates are not removed. In some superplasticizers, problems like low fluidification, rapid slump loss, severe segregation, have been reported. The problem of incompatibility seems to be one of the common problems generally met with in the field. The practical approach to solve these problems is to cross test with other plasticizers or other cement samples, and practical solutions arrived. In a overdosed mix, cement paste may become too fluid and no longer retain the coarse or even fine aggregates in suspension, causing severe segregation. In such cases either the dose could be reduced or aggregate content, particularly the sand content may be increased.

When concrete pump and placer boom are used for placing concrete, the slump requirement is around 100 mm. Suppose 100 mm slump concrete is used for a roof slab casting, such a high slump which is undesirable for roof casting, causes problems by way of segregation and bleeding particularly in the hands of inexperienced workers. Such concrete will have to be handled with care and understanding.

Similarly, while casting cubes using highly plasticized concrete, special care and understanding of concrete is required. Compaction of cubes can not be done in the usual method of vibrating or even tamping. If the casting of the cube is done blindly without understanding the behaviour of such plastic concrete, serious segregation occurs in the cube mould. Top half of the cube mould consists only of mortar and is devoid of coarse aggregates, with the result, that such segregated concrete cubes show very low strength.

They blame the plasticizers or cement for such low strength. Often such anomalous situations have come to the notice even with major contractors.

Effect of Superplasticizers on the Properties of Hardened Concrete

Plasticizers or superplasticizers do not participate in any chemical reactions with cement or blending material used in concrete. Their actions are only physical in fluidizing the mix, made even with low water content. Their fludifying action lasts only as long as the mix is in plastic condition. Once the effect of adsorbed layer is lost, the hydration process continues normally. It can be categorically said that the use of right quality of plasticizers or superplasticizers when used in usual small dose (say up to 3% by weight of cement) there is no bad effect on the properties of hardened concrete. Only in case of bad quality lignosulphonate based plasticizer is used, it may result in air-entrainment, which reduces the strength of concrete. Since plasticizers and superplasticizers improve the workability, compactability and facilitate reduction in w/c ratio, and thereby increase the strength of concrete, it contributes to the alround improvement in the properties of hardened concrete. As a matter of fact, it is the use of superplasticizers, which is a pragmatic step to improve alround properties of hardened concrete. The use of superplasticizer has become an unavoidable material in the modern High Performance Concrete (HPC).

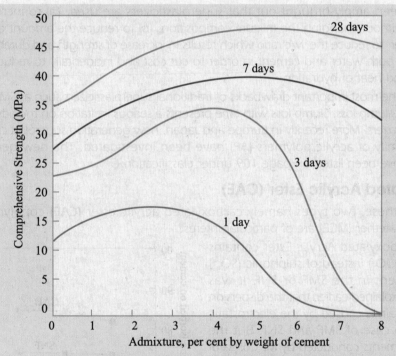

Fig. 5.11. Effect of overdose of water-reducing admixture on the comprehensive strength of concrete.

It has been mentioned earlier that all plasticizers and superplasticizers exhibit certain retarding properties. These retarding properties do not make significant difference when the dosage is normal (say upto 3%). The strength parameter is not reduced beyond one day. But when plasticizers are used in higher dose, the strength development will be greatly affected in respect of one day and even three days strength. However, seven day strength and beyond, there will not be any reduction in strength. The typical strength development of lignosulphonate type water reducing admixture is shown in Fig. 5.11.

At the same w/c ratio, naphthalene based or melamine based superplasticizers do not considerably modify the drying shrinkage of concrete. At the same consistency, they sometime reduce drying shrinkage appreciably.

The total creep is higher when concrete contains naphthalene sulphonates, at high w/c ratio (0.64). On the contrary, when w/c ratio is low, the difference in creep between samples with and without plasticizers are insignificant.

Impermeability plays a primary role on the durability of concrete and since this depends on w/c ratio, superplasticizers should exert a favourable effect. Superplasticizers, owing to the reduction in w/c ratio, reduce the penetration of chlorides and sulphate into the concrete and, therefore, improve their resistance to the de-icing effect of salt or sea water. For the same reason, the resistance to sulphate attack is also improved.

Suffice it to say that the use of plasticizer or superplasticizer, could lead to the reduction in w/c ratio, without affecting the workability and thereby concrete becomes stronger. Therefore, it will contribute to the alround improvement of hardened properties of concrete.

New Generation Superplasticizers

It has been amply brought out that superplasticizers are used, (*a*) to increase the workability without changing the mixture composition, (*b*) to reduce the amount of mixing water, in order to reduce the w/c ratio which results in increase of strength and durability, and (*c*) to reduce both water and cement in order to cut cost and incidentally to reduce creep, shrinkage, and heat of hydration.

One of the most important drawbacks of traditional superplasticizers such as SMF or SNF or MLS, is the slump loss. Slump loss with time presents a serious limitation on the advantages of superplasticizers. More recently in Europe and Japan, new generation superplasticizers – all based on family of acrylic polymers (AP) have been investigated. The new generation plasticizers have been listed on page 109 under classification

Carboxylated Acrylic Ester (CAE)

Out of these, two types namely carboxylated acrylic ester (CAE) copolymer and multicarboxylatether (MCE) are of particular interest.

The carboxylated Acrylic Ester contains carboxylic (COO⁻) instead of sulphonic (SO₃⁻) groups present in the SMF or SNF. It was thought, as explained earlier, that the dispersion of cement grain is caused by the electrostatic repulsion, in case of SMF and SNF. But the recent experiments conducted by M. Collpardi *et al* and Y.O. Tanaka *et al* did not confirm the above mechanism for the plasticizing action of the acrylic polymers. Table 5.2 indicates that AP based superplasticizers produce negligible Zeta potential change (0.3 to 5.0 mV), in contrast to SNF – based superplasticizers (23–28 mV), in aqueous suspensions of cement particles.[5.4]

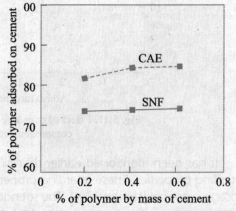

Fig. 5.12. Adsorption of CAE or SNF on cement as a function of polymer dosage (5.3).

Table 5.2. Zeta potential of cement particles in suspension with superplasticizers[5.4]

Superplasticizers	Main component	Zeta-potential (–mV)
A	AP*	5.0
B	AP	0.3
C	AP	1.0
D	AP	4.0
E	AP	4.0
F	AP	2.0
G	SNF	23.0
H	SNF	28.0

*AP = Polycarboxylate type

Figure 5.12 and Fig. 5.13 show the adsorption on cement particles and Zeta-potential measurements of CAE in comparison with SNF. In particular it is seen that adsorption of CAE is about 85% when compared to adsorption of 75% in case of SNF. Fig. 5.13 indicate that the Zeta potential of cement particle mixed with CAE appeared to be much lower than that of SNF.

It could be inferred that in case of AP-based admixtures, the increase in fluidity is not because of electrostatic repulsion associated with Zeta potential but would seem to be the higher polymer adsorption and steric hindrance effect. The new family of superplasticizers based on acrylic polymers, show the following characteristics:

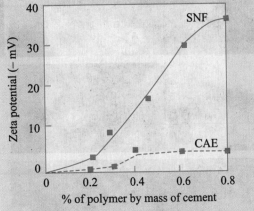

Fig. 5.13. Zeta potential of CAE or SNF cement pastes as a function of polymer dosage (3).

(a) Flowing concrete can be produced at lower w/c ratio.
(b) The effectiveness does not depend on the addition procedure (immediate or delayed).
(c) The slump loss is much reduced than the traditional sulphonated superplasticizers.

Table 5.3. Effect of method of addition of NSF or CAE superplasticizer on the slump of concrete mix[5.5]

Type	Admixture		W/C Ratio	Slump (mm)
	Dosage* (%)	Method of Addition**		
NSF	0.48	immediate	0.40	100
NSF	0.48	delayed	0.40	230
CAE	0.30	immediate	0.39	230
CAE	0.30	delayed	0.39	235

*As dry polymer by weight of cement.
** Immediate: admixture with mixing water. Delayed: admixture after 1 min of mixing.

The properties of CAE is shown in Table 5.3 and in Fig. 5.14 and Fig. 5.15 which are self explanatory about the superiority of CAE with respect to fluidifying effect, loss of slump and compressive strength. Fig. 5.16 shows the typical slump loss for various w/c ratio.

It is pointed again that increase in compressive strength is on account of the ability of CAE to reduce a higher water content for the same workability.

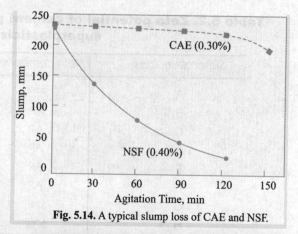

Fig. 5.14. A typical slump loss of CAE and NSF.

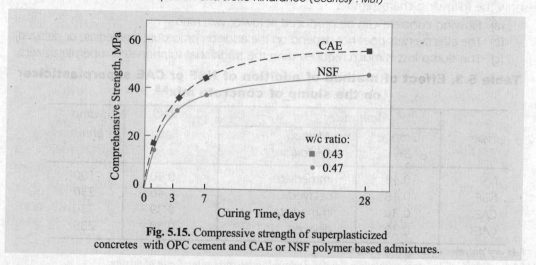

Mechanism of action of acrylic based new generation superplasticizers works on both electrostatic repulsion and steric hindrance *(Courtesy : MBT)*

Fig. 5.15. Compressive strength of superplasticized concretes with OPC cement and CAE or NSF polymer based admixtures.

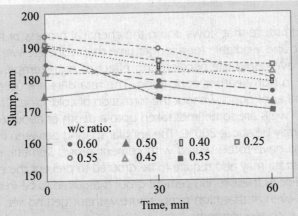

Fig. 5.16. Slump loss curves with a new bicomponent superplasticizer (8)

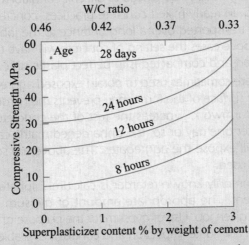

Fig. 5.17. The influence of addition of superplasticizer on the early strength
of concrete. Cement content 370 kg/m³. All concrete of same workability.
Cement: Type III (Rapid hardening)

Superplasticizers are sometime used for high early strength. The high early strength is generally obtained because of its ability to reduce the water content and, therefore w/c which develops high early strength and secondly such superplasticizers will have such a base that will not cause much retarding effect on the concrete. Fig. 5.17 shows the influence of superplasticizers on the early strength of concrete.

Multicarboxylatether

The new generation of superplasticizers which are based on poly- carboxylatether with the generic name of multicarboxylatether (MCE) is found more suitable for production of High Performance Concrete. The properties of these superplasticizers are:

- Excellent flowability at low w/c ratio
- High reduction of water
- Lower slump loss with time
- Shorter retardation time
- Very high early strength
- It works at low dosages

Retarders

A retarder is an admixture that slows down the chemical process of hydration so that concrete remains plastic and workable for a longer time than concrete without the retarder. Retarders are used to overcome the accelerating effect of high temperature on setting properties of concrete in hot weather concreting. The retarders are used in casting and consolidating large number of pours without the formation of cold joints. They are also used in grouting oil wells. Oil wells are sometimes taken upto a depth of about 6000 meter deep where the temperature may be about 200°C. The annular spacing between the steel tube and the wall of the well will have to be sealed with cement grout. Sometimes at that depth stratified or porous rockstrata may also require to be grouted to prevent the entry of gas or oil into some other strata. For all these works cement grout is required to be in mobile condition for about 3 to 4 hours, even at that high temperature without getting set. Use of retarding agent is often used for such requirements.

Sometimes concrete may have to be placed in difficult conditions and delay may occur in transporting and placing. In ready mixed concrete practices, concrete is manufactured in central batching plant and transported over a long distance to the job sites which may take considerable time. In the above cases the setting of concrete will have to be retarded, so that concrete when finally placed and compacted is in perfect plastic state.

Retarding admixtures are sometimes used to obtain exposed aggregate look in concrete. The retarder sprayed to the surface of the formwork, prevents the hardening of matrix at the interface of concrete and formwork, whereas the rest of the concrete gets hardened. On removing the formwork after one day or so, the unhardened matrix can be just washed off by a jet of water which will expose the aggregates. The above are some of the instances where a retarding agent is used.

Perhaps the most commonly known retarder is calcium sulphate. It is interground to retard the setting of cement. The appropriate amount of gypsum to be used must be determined carefully for the given job. Use of gypsum for the purpose of retarding setting time is only recommended when adequate inspection and control is available, otherwise, addition of excess amount may cause undesirable expansion and indefinite delay in the setting of concrete.

In addition to gypsum there are number of other materials found to be suitable for this purpose. They are: starches, cellulose products, sugars, acids or salts of acids. These chemicals may have variable action on different types of cement when used in different quantities. Unless experience has been had with a retarder, its use as an admixture should not be attempted without technical advice. Any mistake made in this respect may have disastrous consequences.

Common sugar is one of the most effective retarding agents used as an admixture for delaying the setting time of concrete without detrimental effect on the ultimate strength. Addition of excessive amounts will cause indefinite delay in setting. At normal temperatures addition of sugar 0.05 to 0.10 per cent have little effect on the rate of hydration, but if the quantity is increased to 0.2 per cent, hydration can be retarded to such an extent that final set may not take place for 72 hours or more. Skimmed milk powder (casein) has a retarding effect mainly due to sugar content.

Other admixtures which have been successfully used as retarding agents are Ligno sulphonic acids and their salts, hydroxylated carboxylic acids and their salts which in addition to the retarding effect also reduce the quantity of water requirement for a given workability. This also increases 28 days compressive strength by 10 to 20 per cent. Materials like mucic acid, calcium acetate and a commercial products by name "Ray lig binder" are used for set retarding purposes. These days admixtures are manufactured to combine set retarding and water reducing properties. They are usually mixtures of conventional water reducing agents plus sugars or hydroxylated carboxylic acids or their salts. Both the setting time and the rate of strength build up are effected by these materials. This is shown in Table 5.4.

Table. 5.4. Effect of retarding/water-reducing admixtures on setting time and strength build up

Admixture addition litres/50 kgs.	Setting time hrs.		W : C ratio	Compressive Strength MPa		
	Initial	Final		3 days	7 days	28 days
0	4.5	9	0.68	20	28	37
0.14	8.0	13	0.61	28	36	47
0.21	11.5	16	0.58	30	40	50
0.28	16.0	21	0.58	30	42	54

Retarding Plasticizers

It is mentioned earlier that all the plasticizers and superplasticizers by themselves show certain extent of retardation. Many a time this extent of retardation of setting time offered by admixtures will not be sufficient. Instead of adding retarders separately, retarders are mixed with plasticizers or superplasticizers at the time of commercial production. Such commercial brand is known as retarding plasticizers or retarding superplasticizers. ASTM type D is retarding plasticizers and ASTM type G is retarding superplasticizer. In the commercial formulation we have also retarding and slump retaining version.

Retarding plasticizers or superplasticizers are important category of admixtures often used in the Ready mixed concrete industry for the purposes of retaining the slump loss, during high temperature, long transportation, to avoid construction or cold joints, slip form construction and regulation of heat of hydration.

One must be careful in the selection of such ready made retarding admixtures. On account of heterogeneous nature and different molecular weight of retarders used with plasticizers, they tend to separate out. It happens when sugar solution is used as cheap retarders. When retarders like gluconate is used such separation or settlement of retarders do not happen. It is cautioned that such retarding plasticizers should always be shaken thoroughly or well stirred before use. There are cases that settlement of retarders from rest of the ingredients causing excessive retardation and failure of structures.

Accelerators

Accelerating admixtures are added to concrete to increase the rate of early strength development in concrete to
- permit earlier removal of formwork;
- reduce the required period of curing;
- advance the time that a structure can be placed in service;
- partially compensate for the retarding effect of low temperature during cold weather concreting;
- in the emergency repair work.

Table 5.5. Physical Requirements According to IS 9103 : 1999

SI No.	Requirements	Accelerating Admixture	Retarding Admixture	Water Reducing Admixture	Air-Entraining Admixture	Superplasticizing Admixture (for Water-Reduced Concrete Mix) Normal	Retarding Type	Test Ref. to IS code Clause
(1)	(2)	(3)	(4)	(5)	(6)	(7)	(8)	(9)
i.	Water content, percent of control sample, Max	—	—	95	—	80	80	7.2.5
ii.	Slump	—	—	—	—	Not more than 15 mm below that of the control mix concrete		7.2.1
iii.	Time of setting, allowable deviation from control sample hours:							7.2.3
	Intial							
	Max	−3	+3	±1	—	—	+4	
	Min	−1	+1		—	+1.5	+1	
	Final							
	Max	−2	+3	±1	—	±1.5	±3	
	Min	−1	+1		—	—	—	
iv.	Compressive strength, percent of control sample, Min							8.2.1
	1 day	—	—	—	—	140	—	
	3 days	125	90	110	90	125	125	
	7 days	100	90	110	90	125	125	
	28 days	100	90	110	90	115	115	
	6 months	90	90	100	90	100	100	
	1 year	90	90	100	90	100	100	

Table 5.5 (Continued)

(1)	(2)	(3)	(4)	(5)	(6)	(7)	(8)	(9)
v.	Flexural strength, percent of control sample, Min							8.2.2
	3 days	110	90	100	90	110	110	
	7 days	100	90	100	90	100	100	
	28 days	90	90	100	90	100	100	
vi.	Length change, percent increase over control sample, Max							8.2.3
	28 days	0.010	0.010	0.010	0.010	0.010	0.010	
	6 months	0.010	0.010	0.010	0.010	0.010	0.010	
	1 year	0.010	0.010	0.010	0.010	0.010	0.010	
vii.	Bleeding, percent increase over control sample, Max	5	5	5	5	5	5	7.2.4
viii.	Loss of workability	—	—	—	—	At 45 min the slump shall be not less than that of control mix concrete at 15 min	At 2 h, the slump shall be not less than that of control mix concrete at 15 min	7.2.1.2
ix.	Air content (%) Max, over control	—	—	—	—	1.5	1.5	

Table 5.6. Specification for various types of admixtures according to ASTM 494-82

Property	Type A, water reducing	Type B, retarding	Type C, accelerating	Type D, water reducing and retarding	Type E, water reducing and accelerating	Type F, water reducing, high range	Type G, water reducing high range and retarding
Water content, max percent of control	95	—	—	95	95	88	88
Time of setting, allowable deviation from control, min initial: at least not more than	60 earlier nor 90 later	60 later 210 later	60 earlier 210 earlier	60 later 210 later	60 earlier 210 earlier	60 earlier nor 90 later	60 later 210 later
Final: at least not more than	60 earlier nor 90 later	210 later	60 earlier	210 later	60 earlier	60 earlier nor 90 later	210 later
Compressive strength, min percent of control [a]							
1 day	—	—	—	—	—	140	125
3 days	110	90	125	110	125	125	125
7 days	110	90	100	110	110	115	115
28 days	110	90	100	110	110	110	110
6 months	100	90	90	100	100	100	100
1 year	100	90	90	100	100	100	100
Flexural strength, min percent control [a]							
3 days	100	90	110	100	110	110	110
7 days	100	90	100	100	100	100	100
28 days	100	90	90	100	100	100	100

Table 5.6 (Continued)

Length Change, max shrinkage (alternative requirements) [b]							
Percent of control	135	135	135	135	135	135	135
Increase over control	0.010	0.010	0.010	0.010	0.010	0.010	0.010
Relative durability factor, min [c]	80	80	80	80	80	80	80

[a] The compressive and flexural strength of the concrete containing the admixture under test at any test age shall be not less than 90 per cent of that attained at any previous test age. The objective of this limit is to require that the compressive and flexural strength of the concrete containing the admixture under test shall not decrease with age.

[b] Alternative requirements, percent of control limit applies when length change of control is 0.030 percent or greater; increase over control limit applies when length change of control is less than 0.030 percent.

[c] This requirement is applicable only when the admixture is to be used in air-entrained concrete which may be exposed to freezing and thawing while wet.

Table 5.7. Specification for various types of admixtures according to BS 5075: Part 1:1982.

Type of Admixture	Water reduction percent	Compaction factor	STIFFENING TIME — Time from completion of mixing to reach a resistance to penetrate* of: 0.5 MPa (70 psi)	3.5 MPa (500 psi)	COMPRESSIVE STRENGTH — percent of control mix (minimum)	Age
Accelerating	—	Not more than 0.02 below control mix	More than 1 hr.	At least 1 hr less than control mix	125	24 hr
					95	28 days
	8				—	—
Retarding	—	Not more than 0.02 below control mix	At least 1 hr longer than control mix	—	90	7 days
					95	28 days
	8				—	—
Normal-reducing	—	At least 0.03 above control mix	Within 1 hr of control mix	—	90	7 days
					90	28 days
	8	Not more than 0.02 below control mix			110	7 days
					110	28 days
Accelerating water-reducing	—	Atleast 0.03 above control mix	More than 1 hr.	Atleast 1 hr less than control mix	125	24 hrs
					90	28 days
	8	Not more than 0.02 below control mix			125	24 hrs
					110	28 days
Retarding water-reducing	—	Atleast 0.03 above control mix	Atleast 1 hr longer than control mix	—	90	7 days
					90	28 days
	8	Not more than 0.02 below control mix			110	7 days
					110	28 days

* The penetration is determined by a special brass rod of 6.175 mm in diameter.
The air content with no water reduction shall not be more than 2 per cent higher than that of the control mix, and not more than total of 3 per cent.

Table 5.8. Specification for superplasticizing admixture according to BS 5075: Part 3:1985.

Type of Admixture	Water reduction per cent	Workability	Loss of slump	STIFFENING TIME		COMPRESSIVE STRENGTH	
				Time from completion of mixing to reach a resistance to penetrate* of: 0.5 MPa (70 psi)	3.5 MPa (500 psi)	Percentage of control mix (minimum)	Age
Superplasticizing	—	Flow table: 510 to 620 mm	At 45 min not less than that of control mix at 10 to 15 min. At 4 h not more than that of control mix at 10 to 15 min.	— —	— —	90 90	7 days 28 days
Superplasticizing	16	Slump: not more than 15 mm below that of control mix	—	Within 1 hour of control mix	Within 1 hour of control mix	140 125 115	24 h 7 days 28 days
Retarding superplasticizing	—	Flow table: 510 to 620 mm	At 4 h not less than that of control mix at 10 to 15 min.	—	—	90 90	7 days 28 days
Retarding superplasticizing	16	Slump: not more than 15 mm below that of control mix	—	1 to 4 hour longer than control mix	—	125 115	7 days 28 days

* The penetration is determined by a special brass rod of 6.175 mm in diameter.
The air content with no water reduction shall not be more than 2 per cent higher than that of the control mix, and not more than total of 3 per cent.

Table 5.9. List of some of the commercial plasticizers and superplasticizers manufactured in India.

Sl.No.	Name and Address	Brand Name	Description	Function
1.	Mc-Bauchemie (Ind.) Pvt. Ltd. 201, Vardhaman Chambers Sector-17, Vashi Navi Mumbai-400703	(a) Emce Plast BV	Water reducing plasticizer	Increases workabililtty at low dosage
		(b) Emce Plast 4 BV		
		(c) Emce Plast RP	Water reducing and retarding plasticizer	-do-
		(d) Zentrament Super BV	Superplasticizer	Produces flowing pumpable concrete
		(e) Zentrament F BV	Superplasticizer	Produces high early sterngth– makes the mix flowable and pumpable
		(f) Centriplast FF 90	Superplasticizer based on melamine formaldehyde	Excellent compatibility with all cements
		(g) Zentrament T5 BV	Retarding superplasticizer	High perofrmance retarding superplasticizer–it maintains slump for longer time
		(h) Muraplast FK 61	Superplasticizer	Good plasticizing effect
		(i) MC-Erstarrungsbremse K T3	-do-	Universal retarding plasticizer
2.	Fosroc Chemicals (Ind) Ltd. Hafeeza Chamber, 2nd Floor 111/74, K.H. Road Bangalore-560027	(a) Conplast 211	Water reducing plasticizer	Increases workability
		(b) Conplast P 509	- do -	High performance plasticizer
		(c) Conplast 337	Superplasticizer	Gives high workability
		(d) Conplast 430	- do -	- do -
		(e) Conplast RP 264	Plasticizer	Retards setting time
		(f) Conplast NC	- do -	Accelerates initial setting time

Table 5.9. (Continued)

3.	Sika Qualcrete Pvt. Ltd. 24 B, Park Street Calcuta-16	(a) Plastiment BV 40	Plasticizer	Water reducing plasticizer
		(b) Sikament 300, 350, 400	- do -	- do -
		(c) Sikament FF	Superplasticizer	High range water reducer
		(d) Sikament 600	- do -	Sett retarding agents
4.	Roffe Constn. Chemicals Pvt. Ltd., 12 C, Vikas Centre S.V. Road, Santacruz (W) Mumbai-54	(a) Roff Plast 330	Plasticizer	Water reducer
		(b) Roff Super Plast 321	Superplasticizer	Gives higher early strength
		(c) Roff Super Plast 820	- do -	- do -
		(d) Roff Super Plast 840	- do -	High performance retarder

In the past one of the commonly used materials as an accelerator was calcium chloride. But, now a days it is not used. Instead, some of the soluble carbonates, silicates fluosilicates and some of the organic compounds such as triethenolamine are used. Accelerators such as fluosilicates and triethenolamine are comparatively expensive.

The recent studies have shown that calcium chloride is harmful for reinforced concrete and prestressed concrete. It may be used for plain cement concrete in comparatively high dose. The limits of chloride content in concrete is given in chapter on Durability of Concrete.

Some of the accelerators produced these days are so powerful that it is possible to make the cement set into stone hard in a matter of five minutes are less. With the availability of such powerful accelerator, the under water concreting has become easy. Similarly, the repair work that would be carried out to the waterfront structures in the region of tidal variations has become easy. The use of such powerful accelerators have facilitated, the basement waterproofing operations. In the field of prefabrication also it has become an invaluable material. As these materials could be used up to 10°C, they find an unquestionable use in cold weather concreting.

Some of the modern commercial accelerating materials are Mc-Schnell OC, Mc-Schnell SDS, Mc-Torkrethilfe BE, manufactured by Mc-Bauchemic (Ind) Pvt. Ltd. MC-Torkrethilfe BE is a material specially formulated to meet the demand for efficient and multifold properties desired for sprayed concrete and shotcreting operations. A field trial is essential to determine the dose for a given job and temperature conditions when the above materials are used.

Accelerating Plasticizers

Certain ingredients are added to accelerate the strength development of concrete to plasticizers or superplasticizers. Such accelerating superplasticizers, when added to concrete result in faster development of strength. The accelerating materials added to plasticizers or superplasticizers are triethenolamine chlorides, calcium nutrite, nitrates and flousilicates etc. The accelerating plasticizers or accelerating superplasticizers manufactured by well known companies are chloride free.

Table 5.5, Table 5.6, Table 5.7 and 5.8 shows the specification limits of IS 9103 of 1999, ASTM 494 of 1982, BS 5075 part I of 1982 and BS part 3 of 1985 respectively. Table 5.9 gives the list of some of the commercial plasticizers and superplasticizers manufactured in India.

Air-entraining Admixture

Perhaps one of the important advancements made in concrete technology was the discovery of air entrained concrete. Since 1930 there has been an ever increasing use of air entrained concrete all over the world especially, in the United States and Canada. Due to the recognition of the merits of air entrained concrete, about 85 per cent of concrete manufactured in America contains one or the other type of air entraining agent. So much so that air entraining agents have almost come to be considered a necessary 'fifth ingredient' in concrete making.

Air entrained concrete is made by mixing a small quantity of air entraining agent or by using air entraining cement. These air entraining agents incorporate millions of non-coalescing air bubbles, which will act as flexible ball bearings and will modify the properties of plastic concrete regarding workability, segregation, bleeding and finishing quality of concrete. It also modifies the properties of hardened concrete regarding its resistance to frost action and permeability.

The air voids present in concrete can be brought under two groups:

(*a*) Entrained air   (*b*) Entrapped air.

Entrained air is intentionally incorporated, minute spherical bubbles of size ranging from 5 microns to 80 microns distributed evenly in the entire mass of concrete. The entrapped air is the voids present in the concrete due to insufficient compaction. These entrapped air voids may be of any shape and size normally embracing the contour of aggregate surfaces. Their size may range from 10 to 1000 microns or more and they are not uniformly distributed throughout the concrete mass.

Air entraining agents

The following types of air entraining agents are used for making air entrained concrete.

(a) Natural wood resins

(b) Animal and vegetable fats and oils, such as tallow, olive oil and their fatty acids such as stearic and oleic acids.

(c) Various wetting agents such as alkali salts or sulphated and sulphonated organic compounds.

(d) Water soluble soaps of resin acids, and animal and vegetable fatty acids.

(e) Miscellaneous materials such as the sodium salts of petroleum sulphonic acids, hydrogen peroxide and aluminium powder, etc.

There are a number of air entraining agents available in the market. The common air entraining agents in United States are Vinsol resin, Darex, N Tair, Airalon, Orvus, Teepol, Petrosan and Cheecol. Out of these the most important air entraining agents which at one time enjoyed world-wide market are Vinsol resin and Darex.

In India, large scale use of air entrained concrete is not being practised, primarily due to the fact that frost scaling of concrete is not a serious problem in our country so far. However, the advantages of the use of air entrained concrete have been realised for the construction of multi-purpose dams. Air entrained concrete has been used in the construction of Hirakud dam, Koyna dam, Rihand dam etc. In these dams, to start with, American air entraining agents such as Vinsol resin, Darex etc. were used. Later on in 1950's certain indigenous air entraining agents were developed. They are Aerosin—HRS., Rihand A.E.A., Koynaea, Ritha powder, Hico, etc. Now modern admixture manufacturing companies are manufacturing a number of commercial air entraining agents. MC-Mischoel LP, MC-Michoel AEA, Complast AE 215, Roff AEA 330 are some of the commercial brands available in India.

Factors affecting amount of air entrainment

The manufacture of air entrained concrete is complicated by the fact that the amount of air entrainment in a mix is affected by many factors; the important ones are:

(a) The type and quantity of air entraining agent used.

(b) Water/cement ratio of the mix.

(c) Type and grading of aggregate.

(d) Mixing time.

(e) The temperature.

(f) Type of cement.

(g) Influence of compaction.

(h) Admixtures other than air entraining agent used..

Different air entraining agents produce different amounts of air entrainment, depending upon the elasticity of the film of the bubble produced, and the extent to which the surface tension is reduced. Similarly, different quantities of air entraining agents will result in different amounts of air entrainment. Water/cement ratio is one of the important factors affecting the quantity of air. At very low water/cement ratio, water films on the cement will be insufficient to produce adequate foaming action. At intermediate water/cement ratio (*viz.* 0.4 to 0.6) abundant air bubbles will be produced. But at a higher water/cement ratio although to start with, a large amount of air entrainment is produced, a large proportion of the bubbles will be lost progressively with time. The grading of aggregate has shown good influence on the quantity of air entrainment. It was established that the quantity of air increased from the lowest fineness modulus of sand to a peak at about F.M. of 2.5, and, thereafter, decreased sharply. The sand fraction of 300 and 150 microns showed a significant effect on the quantity of air entrainment. The higher quantity of these fractions resulted in more air entrainment.

The amount of air entrainment is found to increase with the mixing time upto a certain time and thereafter with prolonged mixing the air entrainment gets reduced. The temperature of concrete at the time of mixing was found to have a significant effect on the amount of air entrainment. The amount of air entrainment decreases as the temperature of concrete increases. The constituents of the cement especially the alkali content plays an important part in the entrainment of air in concrete. Similarly, the fineness of cement is also a factor.

Air content is also reduced by the process of compaction, on account of the movement of air bubbles to the surface and destruction. It is estimated that as much as 50 per cent of the entrained air may be lost after vibration for 2 1/2 minutes and as much as 80 per cent may be lost by vibration for 9 minutes. The experiments conducted at Hirakud dam indicated that an air content of 10.5 per cent after 30 sec of vibration came down to 6 per cent after 180 sec of vibration. The other admixtures used in conjunction with air entraining agents will also significantly affect the amount of air entrained. The use of fly ash in concrete will reduce the amount of air entrained. Similarly, the use of calcium chloride also has the tendency to reduce and limit air entrainment.

The Effect of Air Entrainment on the Properties of Concrete

Air entrainment will effect directly the following three properties of concrete:
(a) Increased resistance to freezing and thawing.
(b) Improvement in workability.
(c) Reduction in strength.

Incidentally air entrainment will also effect the properties of concrete in the following ways:
(a) Reduces the tendencies of segregation.
(b) Reduces the bleeding and laitance.
(c) Decreases the permeability.
(d) Increases the resistance to chemical attack.
(e) Permits reduction in sand content.
(f) Improves placeability, and early finishing.
(g) Reduces the cement content, cost, and heat of hydration.
(h) Reduces the unit weight.
(i) Permits reduction in water content.
(j) Reduces the alkali-aggregate reaction.
(k) Reduces the modulus of elasticity.

Resistance to Freezing and Thawing

The greatest advantage derived from the use of air entrained concrete is the high resistance of hardened concrete to scaling due to freezing and thawing. It is found that when ordinary concrete is subjected to a temperature below freezing point, the water contained in the pore of the concrete freezes. It is well known that the volume of ice is about 10 per cent higher than the corresponding volume of water. Hence, the ice formed in the pores of hardened concrete exerts pressure. The cumulative effect of this pressure becomes considerable, with the result that surface scaling and disruption of concrete at the weaker section takes place. Similarly, surface scaling and disruption also takes place in plain concrete when subjected to the action of salt used for deicing purpose. Similar pattern of failure of plain concrete is also noticed in concrete structures at the tidal zone and spray zone. It has been

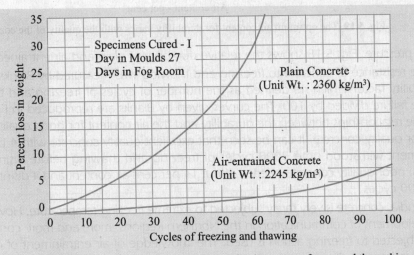

Fig. 5.18. Durability of plain and air-entrained concretes frozen and thawed in 10% CaCl₂ solution.

firmly established that air entrainment in concrete increases the resistance by about three to seven times in such situations.

Modification of pore structure is believed to be responsible for the marked improvement in resistance to frost attack. In ordinary concrete, there may exist bigger voids inter-connected by capillaries, latter being largely formed by the bleeding. But in the air entrained concrete though the total air voids are more, the voids are in the form of minute, discrete bubbles of comparatively uniform size and regular spherical shape. This air void system reduces the tendency for the formation of large crystals of ice in the concrete. Secondly, the inter-connected air voids system acts as buffer space to relieve the

Air Entrainment increses the durability of concrete in snowbound region.

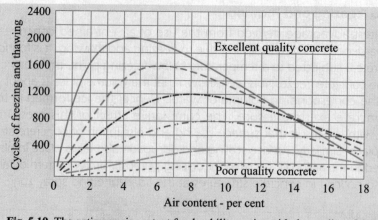

Fig. 5.19. The optimum air content for durability varies with the quality of the concrete.

internal pressure. Fig. 5.18 shows the relative durability of plain and air entrained concrete.

The resistance of concrete to freezing and thawing was measured by Blanks by means of durability factor which he defined as the number of cycles of freezing and thawing to produce failure divided by 100. The curves given by Blanks are reproduced in Fig. 5.19 to show the relationships between the durability and the air content for good quality concrete and poor quality concrete. It can be seen that excellent quality concrete with 4 per cent air entrainment withstood upto 2000 cycles of freezing and thawing before disintegration, whereas, poor quality concrete needed about 14 per cent air content and it disintegrated at about 200 cycles.

In India, concrete is very rarely subjected to extreme freezing temperature. However, with the development of communication in the Northern Regions, more and more concrete likely to be subjected to freezing action is used. The knowledge of air entrainment of concrete is required to improve the durability of concrete structures used in marine conditions. Hitherto the use of air entrainment has been practised only in the case of multi-purpose dams for the purpose of workability. And, therefore, it is necessary that Indian engineers must be educated regarding the use of air entraining agents for air entrained concrete. The use of air-entraining agent, for improvement in workability in general concrete construction is also required to be practised more and more. Air entrained mortar gives much better performance for plastering works.

Effect on workability

The entrainment of air in fresh concrete by means of air entraining agent improves workability. It was seen that the placeability of air entrained concrete having 7.5 cm slump is superior to that of non-air entrained concrete having 12.5 cm slump. This easier placeability of a lower slump should be recognised by the people concerned with concrete construction in difficult situations. Better placeability of air entrained concrete results in more homogeneous concrete with less segregation, bleeding and honeycombing. The concrete containing entrained air is more plastic and 'fatty' and can be more easily handled than ordinary concrete. The pumpability of the mix also increases enormously.

In fact, all the above qualities mentioned are closely related to workability and as such let us consider the aspect of workability.

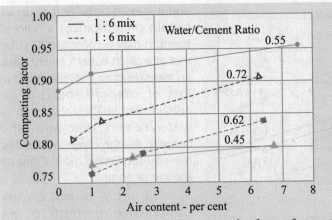

Fig. 5.20. Effect of entrained air on the compacting factor of concrete.

For adequate workability of concrete, aggregate particles must be spaced so that they can move past one another with comparative ease during mixing and placing. In non-air entrained concrete, workability can be achieved by including sufficient fine sand, cement and water to separate the particles of coarser aggregate and supply of matrix, in which movement can occur with minimum interference. By such means, spacing of the solids is increased and the dilatancy necessary for the manipulation of fresh concrete is reduced, with consequent reduction of work required.

An improvement in workability caused by air entrainment can be viewed from another angle as follows:

Proportioning of concrete mixes involves compromise between requirements for workability and requirements for strength, durability, volume stability and other properties of hardened concrete. Workability requires that the inter particle voids in the aggregates be more than filled by cement paste, whereas good quality of hardened concrete requires that these voids be just filled. It is the role of entrained air to solve this conflict. Firstly, entrained air increases the effect volume of cement paste during mixing and placing, thereby eliminating the need for extra paste to induce the workability.

Having fulfilled the requirements of workability for placing and compaction the extra air will escape or may be made to escape to achieve the desired density in the hardened concrete. As a result of compaction 1/2 to 2/3 of the air content of the fresh concrete may be driven out depending upon the duration of vibration and water/cement ratio.

The marked improvement in the workability of air entrained concrete can also be attributed to the lubricating effect of the microscopic bubbles between the fine aggregates and providing a cushioning effect between the grains of sand, thereby reducing particle interference to a minimum. In fact, they seem to introduce ball bearing upon which the particles may slide.

The effect of the percentage of air entrainment on the compacting factor for different mixes and water/cement ratios is illustrated in Fig. 5.20 which is prepared from information given by Wright. It is seen that 5 per cent air may increase the compacting factor by 0.07. A corresponding increase of the slump would be from 12 mm to 50 mm.

The increase in the workability is rather greater for wetter mixes than for drier ones, and for the leaner mixes than for the richer ones, and further it has been shown that the increase is greater for angular aggregates than for rounded ones.

Effect on strength

It can be generally stated that air entrainment in concrete reduces the compressive strength of concrete. But when the process is applied properly, taking advantage of the benefits accrued on account of air-entrainment, little or no loss of strength should take place

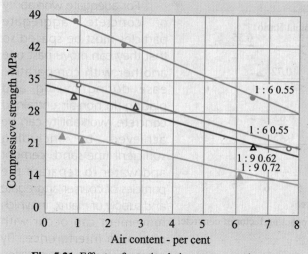

Fig. 5.21. Effects of entrained air on compressive strength.

and it is even possible that under certain circumstances a gain of strength may be possible. It is true that at a given water/cement ratio, an increase in air content results in loss of strength, but the air entrainment enables reduction of water/cement ratio and sand content, for the given workability, thereby regaining most if not all the lost strength.

The result of test on the compressive strength of air entrained concrete carried out at the Road Research Laboratory, U.K. as reported by Wright[5.7] is shown in Fig. 5.21 and in Fig. 5.22. In these tests four mixes were investigated and the air content was increased without making any other adjustments to the mix proportions. Fig. 5.21 shows the actual strength obtained. It will be seen that the strength decreases in proportion to the amount of air. In Fig. 5.22 the same results are shown expressed as a percentage of the strengths of concretes containing no air. It will be seen that a single straight line is obtained. This represents a decrease in strength of 5.5 per cent for each per cent of air entrained. A curve is also plotted showing the strength of concrete containing air voids resulting from incomplete compaction *i.e.,* entrapped air. The graph shows that the entrapped air effects the strength slightly more than the entrained air. But it must be appreciated, however, that air voids caused by

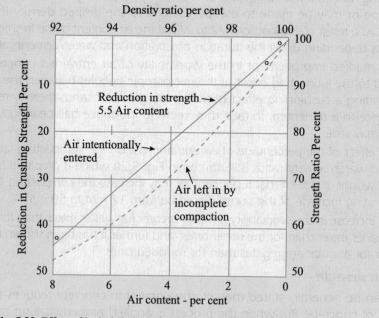

Fig. 5.22. Effect of included air on the compressive strength of concrete.[5.7]

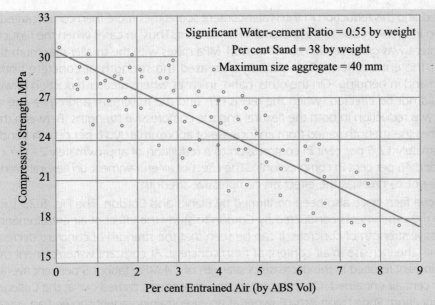

Significant Water-cement Ratio = 0.55 by weight
Per cent Sand = 38 by weight
Maximum size aggregate = 40 mm

Fig. 5.23. Concrete having the same w/c ratio and the same aggregate grading is reduced in strength approximately 1.4 MPa for each percentage increase in air content.

incomplete compaction do not provide the other advantages of entrained air such as increased durability and better workability etc.

The effect of air entrainment on strength is dependent on three factors *i.e.*, on the amount of air entrained, the richness of the mix, and on the type of air entraining agent used.

The first two factors on the strength of concrete both in compression and bending were investigated by Klieger[5.8] and the summary of the results is reproduced in Table 5.10. It can be noticed that the water content was reduced to maintain the slump constant as the air content

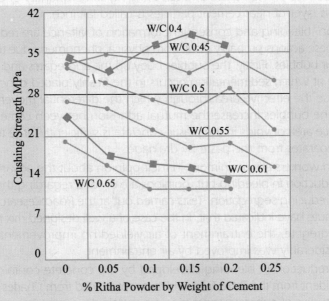

Fig. 5.24. Reduction of strength vs per cent ritha powder based experimental work carried out at college of Military Engineering, Pune.[5.9]

was increased and this reduction in the water content sometimes more than compensated for the reduction in strength due to the increase in air content. Thus, in cases when the reduction in water content was greatest such as the lean 21 MPa mixes with the smaller maximum sized aggregates, the entrainment of air actually increased the strength of concrete both in compression and in bending. On the other hand, in cases where greater reduction in water content could not be effected, when the mix is rich and the maximum aggregate size was large, there was reduction in both the flexural and the compressive strengths. Between these two extremities the strength varied from an increase of approximately 10 per cent in bending and approximately 17.5 per cent in compression to a reduction of approximately 24 per cent in bending and 46 per cent in compression[5.8]. The effect of air-entrainment on flexural strength is, therefore, not so great as the effect on compressive strength.

The above facts have also been confirmed by Blanks and Cordon. The Fig. 5.23 shows the result of the experiments conducted by Cordon to study the effect of air entrainment on the compressive strength of concrete. It can be seen that the strength of concrete decreases uniformly with the increase in air content of fresh concrete. At constant water/cement ratio, the air entrainment resulted in the decrease of strength of 1.4 MPa. (about 5 per cent average) for each per cent air entrained. On the contrary, the experiment carried out at the College of Military Engineering, Pune using Ritha Powder as an air entraining agent showed an average loss of strength of about 0.55 MPa. for each per cent air entrained. (Fig. 5.24)[5.9]

Effect on Segregation, Bleeding and Laitance

Segregation and bleeding of concrete are different manifestations of loss of homogeneity. Segregation usually implies separation of coarser aggregate from mortar or separation of cement paste from aggregates. Bleeding is the autogenous flow of mixing water within, or its emergence to the surface from freshly placed concrete, usually, as a result of sedimentation of the solids due to compaction and self weight of the solids. Bleeding results in the formation of a series of water channels some of which will extend to the surface. A layer of water will emerge at the surface of the concrete, often bringing some quantity of cement with it. The formation of this layer of neat cement particles is called laitance.

Segregation, bleeding and consequent formation of laitance are reduced greatly by air entrainment. These actions probably result from physical phenomena due to the incorporation of a system of air bubbles. Firstly, the bubbles buoy up the aggregates and cement and hence reduce the rate at which sedimentation occurs in the freshly placed concrete. Secondly, the bubbles decrease the effective area through which the differential movement of water may occur. Thirdly, the bubbles increase the mutual adhesion between cement and aggregate. Lastly, the surface area of voids in the plastic concrete is sufficiently large to retard the rate at which water separates from the paste by drainage.

All research workers are unanimous in their opinion about the advantages of entrained air regarding reduction in bleeding but, opinions are divided regarding the role played by air entrainment in reducing segregation. Tests carried out at the Road Research Laboratory, U.K., using sloping chute have indicated that, in the case of a well designed mix having only a slight tendency to segregate, the entrainment of air yielded no improvement, but a mix which segregates considerably was improved by air entrainment.

The large reduction in bleeding developed by the concrete containing air entraining admixtures is evident from the Table 5.11 which is reproduced from Charles E Wuerpel's articles on laboratory studies of concrete containing air entraining admixtures.

Table 5.10. Effect of Entrained air on Concrete Strengths[5.8]

Age at test, 28 days of moist curing, slump 50 to 75 mm

Cement content in kg/cu.m	Maximum size of aggregate mm	Average percentage change in strength for each 1 per cent of entrained air for total amounts of entrained air shown in per cent.											
		In bending						In compression					
		1	2	3	4	5	6	1	2	3	4	5	6
210	72	−1.0	−1.0	−1.3	−1.6	−1.9	−2.1	0	−1.2	−1.9	−2.6	−3.2	−3.8
	40	0	−0.5	−1.0	−1.2	−1.7	−2.1	+3.7	+1.5	−0.4	−1.8	−3.2	−4.1
	20	+2.2	+1.7	+1.5	+1.1	+0.4	0	+5.0	+3.4	+2.2	+1.7	+1.0	0
	10	+4.3	+3.6	+3.4	+2.6	+2.0	+1.7	+9.6	+7.5	+5.9	+4.4	+3.5	+2.1
	4.75	0	0	0	0	0	0	0	0	0	0	0	0
290	72	−3.8	−3.4	−3.6	−3.6	−3.7	−3.8	−7.5	−7.5	−7.5	−7.5	−7.6	−7.7
	40	−3.8	−3.8	−4.0	−4.0	−4.0	−4.0	−5.0	−5.0	−5.3	−5.5	−5.8	−6.0
	20	−2.9	−2.6	−2.7	−2.6	−2.6	−2.7	−3.3	−3.3	−3.6	−3.8	−3.8	−3.9
	10	−0.9	−0.9	−1.1	−1.3	−1.5	−1.7	0	0	−0.4	−0.8	−1.3	−2.0
	4.75	+1.0	+1.0	+0.3	−0.1	−0.4	−0.9	+3.6	+3.6	+2.4	+1.8	+1.1	+0.3
370	72	−8.6	−7.2	−6.0	−5.0	−4.1	−	−4.0	−4.3	−4.9	−5.3	−5.7	−
	40	−3.5	−3.2	−3.5	−3.7	−	−	−1.4	−2.8	−4.1	−5.0	−	−
	20	−1.4	−1.6	−1.9	−2.1	−2.2	−2.4	−2.8	−3.4	−3.3	−3.9	−4.2	−4.5
	10	−1.5	−1.5	−1.5	−1.7	−1.9	−1.9	−3.0	−2.8	−2.7	−2.6	−2.8	2.7
	4.75	−1.6	−1.6	−1.6	−1.5	−	−	−5.1	−3.7	−2.7	−1.8	−	−

Table 5.11. Effect of Admixtures on Bleeding

Air entraining admixtures	Cement factor = 240 kg/cu. m		Cement factor = 320 kg/cu. m	
	Cement A Bleeding %	Cement C Bleeding %	Cement A Bleeding %	Cement C Bleeding %
Plain Concrete	100	100	100	100
Q	52	49	42	34
R	59	56	49	49
U	25	25	19	15
V	42	33	36	30
Z	55	57	25	20

It was found that the Ritha powder proved to be an efficient air entraining agent in reducing the bleeding in cement mortar or concrete. The results of tests conducted at College of Military Engineering, Pune using Ritha powder and Vinsol resin are shown in Fig. 5.25. It can be seen that while the plain mortar bled 15 per cent of the mixing water in about 3 hours times, the mortar containing Ritha powder bled only 7 1/2 per cent of the mixing water and the mortar containing Vinsol resin bled 11 per cent of the mixing water.

Since bleeding and formation of laitance are inter-related, considerable reduction in bleeding will also automatically reduce the formation of laitance which is of considerable importance. In concrete the reduced bleeding permits early finishing of the surface reducing the waiting period for the commencement of trowelling. Reduction in bleeding also improves the wearing quality of concrete.

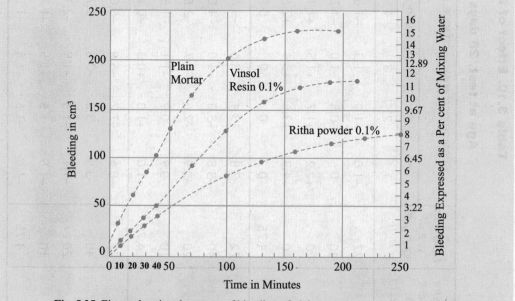

Fig. 5.25. Figure showing the extent of bleeding of plain mortar and air entrained mortar.[5.9]

Effect on Permeability

The entrainment of air does appear to have much effect on the permeability of concrete. Greater uniformity of concrete with entrained air due to its increased workability, modified pore-structure of the air entrained concrete, reduction of water channel due to reduction in bleeding, are some of the reasons for improving the permeability characteristics of air entrained concrete. Cement stored in silos built of air entrained concrete, has been found to show no caking of cement, whereas, cement stored in silos made of ordinary concrete revealed caking along the periphery of the silo. The minute disconnected air bubbles offer a better barrier to the passage of water. The reduced water/cement ratio also is one of the factors for reduced permeability.

Effect on Chemical Resistance

In view of lower permeability and absorption, the air entrained concrete will have greater resistance for chemical attack than that of normal concrete. In the Road Research Laboratory, U.K., specimens of comparable mix of ordinary and air entrained concrete have been immersed in 5 per cent solution of magnesium sulphate and the deterioration in quality has been assessed by measuring the decrease in the velocity of a ultrasonic wave through the specimen. It was found that air entrained concrete showed less deterioration than ordinary concrete.

Effect on sand, water and cement content

The minute spheroidal air bubbles act as fine aggregates and enable the reduction of fine aggregates. The reduction of fine aggregate further enables the reduction of water requirement without impairing the workability and slump. This will have to be considered in

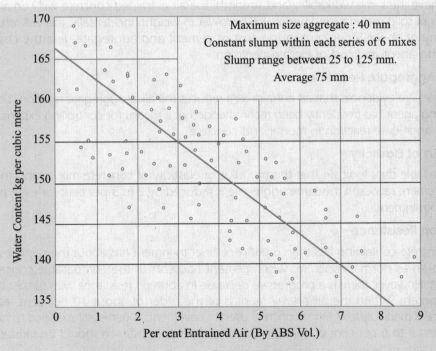

Fig. 5.26. An average reduction of 3.9 kg of water per cubic metre of concrete results from each one per cent increase in air content.[5.10]

designing an air entrained mix. On the basis of a large number of experiments it is reported that sand content by weight of total aggregate may be reduced by one per cent for each per cent increase in air entrainment upto about 8 per cent, without any appreciable change in workability or slump.

The water requirement of an average concrete mix is reduced approximately 3.5 kg/cu.m with rounded aggregate and 4.8 kg/cu.m with angular aggregates for each per cent air entraining. Fig. 5.26 shows the reduction of water for natural aggregates as given by Cordon.[5.10]

The reduction in water/cement ratio naturally effects the basic increase in strength and durability due to the non-availability of excess water for the formation of bleeding channels through the matrix of concrete. Table 5.12 shows the advantages accrued by air entrainment in concrete regarding the reduction of sand and reduction of water requirements.

Entrainment of air is particularly useful in the case of lean concrete, even from the point of view of strength. Many a time increases the strength of lean mixes. In such cases it will be possible for reducing the cement content for the given strength. Blanks and Cordon found that concrete made with 160 mm maximum size aggregate gave satisfactory strength for mass concrete work with only 106 kg cement content per cu.m. provided air was entrained. The reduction in cement content results in a lower heat of hydration in mass concrete and lower temperature rise. The decrease in temperature rise results in reduced cracking or undesirable internal stresses.

Unit Weight

The useful factor which should not be overlooked, is the reduction in density of the air entrained concrete. Comparing two mixes, one ordinary concrete and the other air entrained, which have the same workability and strength, the air entrained concrete will contain 5 per cent less of solid material, and hence will be lower in weight. Incidentally, this will result in an economy of about 5 per cent in the cost of cement and aggregate, less the cost of air entraining agent and cost of extra supervision.

Alkali-Aggregate Reaction

There are evidences that air entrainment reduces the alkali-aggregate reaction. Use of air entraining agent has frequently been recommended as a means for controlling expansion due to alklai-aggregate reaction in mortar and concrete.

Modulus of Elasticity

Available data indicate that the modulus of elasticity of concrete mix having the same water/cement ratio and the same aggregate is reduced by 2 to 3 per cent for each per cent of air entrainment.

Abrasion Resistance

Concrete containing less than 6 per cent air entrainment has about the same resistance to abrasion as normal concrete, when cement contents of the comparable concrete are constant. However, there is a progressive decrease in abrasion resistance with further increase in air content. When the air entrainment is of the order of about 10 per cent, abrasion resistance is markedly low. Since concrete used in pavements is generally specified to have not more than 3 to 6 per cent of entrained air, the abrasion resistance should be satisfactory.

Optimum Air Content in Concrete

The recommended air content in a given concrete is a function of (*a*) the purpose for which the concrete is used and its location and climatic condition (*b*) the maximum size of aggregate (*c*) the richness of the mix. Usually, the desirable air content is ranging from 3 to 6 per cent.

Lower air content is normally specified for concrete floors, in a building even in cold countries, because they are not subjected to severe weather conditions. An air content of about 4 per cent may probably be sufficient for the required workability and reduced bleeding.

For reinforced concrete of relatively high cement content, a limit of probably 3 to 4 per cent is adequate from the workability and bleeding point of view. The strength will be unduly lowered if the air content is increased.

Again, the larger the aggregate, the less is the amount of air sufficient to give desired results. For mass concrete with 160 mm maximum size aggregate, an air entrainment of about 2.5 to 3 per cent would be sufficient. But in the mass concrete if the maximum size of aggregate is smaller, a higher percentage of air entrainment is desirable.

Despite the variations, the overall limits are from 3 to 6 per cent. This range constitutes reasonable specification limits covering all conditions. There is no advantage in increasing the air content above 6 per cent even from the durability point of view. The optimum durability as measured from the resistance to freezing and thawing for good quality concrete, good resistance is achieved within 6 per cent of entrained air as can be seen from Fig. 5.19. On the other hand, air entrainment below about 3 per cent may not extend envisaged advantages of an air entrained concrete.

Measurement of Air Content in Air Entrained Concrete

The exact air content in concrete is extremely important as it affects the various properties of concrete as explained earlier. If the amount of air entrained in a mix differs widely from the design value, the properties of the concrete may be seriously affected. Too little air results in insufficient workability and too much air will result in low strength. It is, therefore, necessary that the air content should be maintained at the stipulated value. In view of the many factors affecting the air content, measurements must be done frequently throughout the progress of the work. If the air content is found to be varying beyond the specified limit, adjustment is made by altering the amount of air entraining agent.

There are mainly three methods for measuring air content of fresh concrete:

(*a*) Gravimetric Method; (*b*) Volumetric Method; (*c*) Pressure Method.

Gravimetric Method

Gravimetric method was the first to be used and it did not require any special equipment. The procedure is principally one of determining the density of fresh concrete compacted in a standard manner. This is then compared with the theoretical density of air-free concrete, calculated from the mix proportions and specific gravities of the constituent materials making the concrete. Thus if the air-free density is 2380 kg/cu.m. and the measured density is 2220 kg/cu.m., then one cu.m. of concrete will contain 2220/2380 cu.m. of solid and liquid matter and the rest being air. Therefore, the air content then is $1 - \dfrac{2220}{2380} = 0.07$ or 7%.

The gravimetric method is satisfactory for use in the laboratory but it is not well-suited for field use. It necessitates a skilled operator and an accurate balance. It also requires the

Table 5.12. Approximate sand and water content per cubic metre of plain and air-entrained concrete[5.10]

A. Natural or Rounded Coarse Aggregate

Max. size of coarse aggregate (mm)	Plain concrete		Air entrained concrete		
	Sand % of total aggregate (absolute volume)	Net water content per cu.m (kg.)	Recommended air content (%)	Sand % of total aggregate (absolute vol.)	Net water content per cu.m (kg)
12.5	51	152	6 ± 1	47	132
20	46	141	5 ± 1	42	122
25	41	136	4.5 ± 1	37	118
40	37	127	4 ± 1	34	112
50	34	120	4 ± 1	31	107
80	31	114	3.5 ± 1	28	100
160	26	100	3 ± 1	24	89

B. Manufactured Angular Coarse Aggregate

Max. size of coarse aggregate (mm)	Plain concrete		Air entrained concrete		
	Sand % of total aggregate (absolute volume)	Net water content per cu.m (kg.)	Recommended air content (%)	Sand % of total aggregate (absolute vol.)	Net water content per cu.m (kg)
12.5	55	164	6 ± 1	51	141
20	50	152	5 ± 1	46	132
25	45	147	4.5 ± 1	42	127
40	41	139	4 ± 1	38	120
50	38	132	4 ± 1	35	118
80	35	125	3.5 ± 1	32	110
160	30	112	3 ± 1	27	98

knowledge of mix proportions of concrete. Even if weigh batching is done, loss of materials, segregation and other factors may cause a sample of concrete taken in the cylinder for experiment to be different from the ideal mix. The accurate specific gravity of the materials also must be known. Without these the result will not be correct.

Volumetric Method

The volumetric method or displacement method aims at measuring directly the volume of air in the sample of fresh concrete. There are a number of modifications, but the principle is to take a sample of concrete of known volume, remove all the air and then determine the amount of water required to restore the original volume.

A vessel is partly filled with concrete, the amount of concrete being determined by weighing, or by using a vessel made in two parts, the lower one being filled completely and struck off level so that a fixed volume of concrete is obtained. Water is added to make up a given volume as indicated by a mark on the narrow neck of the second part. The air is then removed by agitation of the mixture, either by rolling or by stirring. When the removal of the air is complete, the water level is restored to its original position, by a further addition of water. The additional water required to make up the original level indicate the air content in the concrete. The air content can also be calculated by the weight of extra water.

In some variations of this method, weighing is eliminated entirely. This method requires great care and skilled operation. It is a tedious job to remove all the air, and it is difficult to know then the removal of the air is complete. The trouble caused by the formation of foam on the surface is often reduced by using some alcohol. Considerable time is consumed in rolling and stirring the sample of concrete, and generally the process must be repeated to make sure that all the air has been removed. The chief advantage of the rolling method is that it can be used with all types of aggregates and it is specially recommended for concrete containing light weight aggregate.

Pressure Method

This is perhaps the best method for finding the air content of fresh concrete because of its superiority and ease of operation. There are two different methods of measuring air by the pressure. One utilises a pressure meter that is known as the water type. The other is the Washington air meter. Both operate on the principle of Boyle's law, namely that the volume of gas at a given temperature is inversely proportional to the pressure to which it is subjected.

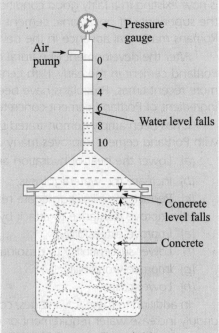

Fig. 5.27. Pressure-Type air Meter.

The Water Type Meter

The vessel is filled with concrete, compacted in a standard manner and struck off level. A cover is then clamped in position. Water is added until the level reaches "0" mark on the tube of the cover and then pressure is applied by means of a bicycle pump. The pressure is transmitted to the air entrained in the concrete, which contracts accordingly. Then the water level falls. The pressure is increased to a predetermined value as indicated by a small pressure gauge mounted on the cover. The glass gauge tube is so calibrated that the percentage of air by volume is indicated directly. The instruments are generally designed to employ a working pressure of the order of 1 kg /sq. cm. The correction may be made for the air contained in the aggregate. The apparatus is shown in Figure 5.27.

Another Model of Air Entrainment Meter.

Pozzolanic or Mineral Admixtures

The use of pozzolanic materials is as old as that of the art of concrete construction. It was recognised long time ago, that the suitable pozzolans used in appropriate amount, modify certain properties of fresh and hardened mortars and concretes. Ancient Greeks and Romans used certain finely divided siliceous materials which when mixed with lime produced strong cementing material having hydraulic properties and such cementing materials were employed in the construction of acquaducts, arch, bridges etc. One such material was consolidated volcanic ash or tuff found near Pozzuoli (Italy) near Vesuvius. This came to be designated as Pozzuolana, a general term covering similar materials of volcanic origin found in other deposits in Italy, France and Spain. Later, the term pozzolan was employed throughout Europe to designate any materials irrespective of its origin which possessed similar properties.

Specimens of concrete made by lime and volcanic ash from Mount Vesuvius were used in the construction of Caligula Wharf built in the time of Julius Caesar nearly 2000 years ago is now existing in a fairly good condition. A number of structures stand today as evidence of the superiority of pozzolanic cement over lime. They also attest the fact that Greeks and Romans made real advance in the development of cementitious materials.

After the development of natural cement during the latter part of the 18th century, the Portland cement in the early 19th century, the practice of using pozzolans declined, but in more recent times, Pozzolans have been extensively used in Europe, USA and Japan, as an ingredient of Portland cement concrete particularly for marine and hydraulic structures.

It has been amply demonstrated that the best pozzolans in optimum proportions mixed with Portland cement improves many qualities of concrete, such as:

(a) Lower the heat of hydration and thermal shrinkage;

(b) Increase the watertightness;

(c) Reduce the alkali-aggregate reaction;

(d) Improve resistance to attack by sulphate soils and sea water;

(e) Improve extensibility;

(f) Lower susceptibility to dissolution and leaching;

(g) Improve workability;

(h) Lower costs.

In addition to these advantages, contrary to the general opinion, good pozzolans will not unduly increase water requirement or drying shrinkage.

Pozzolanic Materials

Pozzolanic materials are siliceous or siliceous and aluminous materials, which in themselves possess little or no cementitious value, but will, in finely divided form and in the presence of moisture, chemically react with calcium hydroxide liberated on hydration, at ordinary temperature, to form compounds, possessing cementitious properties.

It has been shown in Chapter I that on hydration of tri-calcium silicate and di-calcium silicate, calcium hydroxide is formed as one of the products of hydration. This compound has no cementitious value and it is soluble in water and may be leached out by the percolating water. The siliceous or aluminous compound in a finely divided form react with the calcium hydroxide to form highly stable cementitious substances of complex composition involving water, calcium and silica. Generally, amorphous silicate reacts much more rapidly than the crystalline form. It is pointed out that calcium hydroxide, otherwise, a water soluble material is converted into insoluble cementitious material by the reaction of pozzolanic materials.

The reaction can be shown as

Pozzolan + Calcium Hydroxide + Water ♦ C – S – H (Gel)

This reaction is called pozzolanic reaction. The characteristic feature of pozzolanic reaction is firstly slow, with the result that heat of hydration and strength development will be accordingly slow. The reaction involves the consumption of $Ca(OH)_2$ and not production of $Ca(OH)_2$. The reduction of $Ca(OH)_2$ improves the durability of cement paste by making the paste dense and impervious.

Pozzolanic materials can be divided into two groups: natural pozzolana and artificial pozzolana.

Natural Pozzolans

- Clay and Shales
- Opalinc Cherts
- Diatomaceous Earth
- Volcanic Tuffs and Pumicites.

Artificial Pozzolans

- Fly ash
- Blast Furnace Slag
- Silica Fume
- Rice Husk ash
- Metakaoline
- Surkhi.

Other mineral admixtures, like finely ground marble, quartz, granite powder are also used. They neither exhibit the pozzolanic property nor the cementitious properties. They just act as inert filler.

Natural pozzolans such as diatomaceous earth, clay and shale, pumicites, opaline cherts etc., needs further griding and sometimes needs calcining to activate them to show pozzolanic activities. In Hirakud dam construction in Orissa, naturally occurring clay known as Talabara clay has been used as pozzolanic materials. The natural pozzolans have lost their popularity in view of the availability of more active artificial pozzolans.

Artificial Pozzolans

Fly Ash: Fly ash is finely divided residue resulting from the combustion of powdered coal and transported by the flue gases and collected by electrostatic precipitator. In U.K. it is referred as pulverised fuel ash (PFA). Fly ash is the most widely used pozzolanic material all over the world.

Fly ash was first used in large scale in the construction of Hungry Horse dam in America in the approximate amount of 30 per cent by weight of cement. Later on it was used in Canyon and Ferry dams etc. In India, Fly ash was used in Rihand dam construction replacing cement upto about 15 per cent.

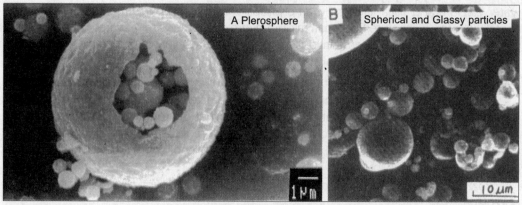

Scanning electron micrograph of Class F, Fly Ash.

In the recent time, the importance and use of fly ash in concrete has grown so much that it has almost become a common ingredient in concrete, particularly for making high strength and high performance concrete. Extensive research has been done all over the world on the benefits that could be accrued in the utilisation of fly ash as a supplementary cementitious material. High volume fly ash concrete is a subject of current interest all over the world.

The use of fly ash as concrete admixture not only extends technical advantages to the properties of concrete but also contributes to the environmental pollution control. In India alone, we produce about 75 million tons of fly ash per year, the disposal of which has become a serious environmental problem. The effective utilisation of fly ash in concrete making is, therefore, attracting serious considerations of concrete technologists and government departments.

Secondly, cement is the backbone for global infrastructural development. It was estimated that global production of cement is about 1.3 billion tons in 1996. Production of every tone of cement emits carbon dioxide to the tune of about 0.87 ton. Expressing it in another way, it can be said that 7% of the world's carbon dioxide emission is attributable to Portland cement industry. Because of the significant contribution to the environmental pollution and to the high consumption of natural resources like limestone etc., we can not go on producing more and more cement. There is a need to economise the use of cement. One of the practical solutions to economise cement is to replace cement with supplementary cementitious materials like fly ash and slag.

In India, the total production of fly ash is nearly as much as that of cement (75 million tons). But our utilisation of fly ash is only about 5% of the production. Therefore, the use of fly ash must be popularised for more than one reasons.

Rihand Irrigation Project, Uttar Pradesh - 1962

In India, fly ash was used for the first time in the construction of Rihand Irrigation Project, Uttar Pradesh in 1962, replacing cement upto about 15 per cent.

There are two ways that the fly ash can be used: one way is to intergrind certain percentage of fly ash with cement clinker at the factory to produce Portland pozzolana cement (PPC) and the second way is to use the fly ash as an admixture at the time of making concrete at the site of work. The latter method gives freedom and flexibility to the user regarding the percentage addition of fly ash.

There are about 75 thermal power plants in India. The quality of fly ash generated in different plants vary from one another to a large extent and hence they are not in a ready to use condition. To make fly ash of consistent quality, make it suitable for use in concrete, the fly ash is required to be further processed. Such processing arrangements are not available in India.

The Table 5.13 indicates the variability of Indian fly ash from different sources.[5.11]

The quality of fly ash is governed by IS 3812 - part I - 2003. The BIS specification limit for chemical requirement and physical requirement are given in Tables 5.14 and 5.15 (IS 3812–2003). High fineness, low carbon content, good reactivity are the essence of good fly ash. Since fly ash is produced by rapid cooling and solidification of molten ash, a large portion of components comprising fly ash particles are in amorphous state. The amorphous characteristics greatly contribute to the pozzolanic reaction between cement and fly ash. One of the important characteristics of fly ash is the spherical form of the particles. This shape of particle improves the flowability and reduces the water demand. The suitability of fly ash could be decided by finding the dry density of fully compacted sample.

ASTM broadly classify fly ash into two classes.

Class F: Fly ash normally produced by burning anthracite or bituminous coal, usually has less than 5% CaO. Class F fly ash has pozzolanic properties only.

Class C: Fly ash normally produced by burning lignite or sub-bituminous coal. Some class C fly ash may have CaO content in excess of 10%. In addition to pozzolanic properties, class C fly ash also possesses cementitious properties.

Fly ash, when tested in accordance with the methods of test specified in IS: 1727–1967*, shall conform to the chemical requirements given in Table 5.14.

Table 5.13. Illustrative Properties of Fly Ash from Different Sources[5.11]

Property/Source	A	B	C	D	E*
Specific gravity	1.91	2.12	2.10	2.25	2.146 to 2.429
Wet sieve analysis (Percentage retained on No. 325 BS sieve)	16.07	54.65	15.60	5.00	51.00 (Dry)
Specific surface (cm²/g Blaines)	2759	1325	2175	4016	2800 to 3250
Lime reactivity (kg/sq.cm)	86.8	56.0	40.3	79.3	56.25 to 70.31
Chemical Analysis					
Loss on ignition percentage	5.02	11.33	1.54	4.90	1–2
SiO_2	50.41	50.03	63.75	60.10	45–59
SO_3	1.71	–	–	–	Traces to 2.5
P_2O_5	0.31	–	–	–	–
Fe_2O_3	3.34	10.20	30.92	6.40	0.6–4.0
Al_2O_3	30.66	18.20	–	18.60	23.33
Ti_2	0.84	–	–	–	0.5–1.5
Mn_2O_3	0.31	–	–	–	–
CaO	3.04	6.43	2.35	6.3	5–16
MgO	0.93	3.20	0.95	3.60	1.5–5
Na_2O	3.07	–	–	–	–

Glass content: Highly variable within and between the samples but generally below 35%.

*Lignite-based

Table 5.14. Chemical Requirements (IS : 3812 – Part -1 : 2003)

Sl. No.	Characteristic	Requirement
(1)	(2)	(3)
(i)	Silicon dioxide (SiO_2) plus aluminium oxide (Al_2O_3) plus iron oxide (Fe_2O_3) per cent by mass, *Min*	70.0
(ii)	Silicon dioxide (SiO_2), per cent by mass, *Min*	35.0
(iii)	Reactive silica in perecent by mass, *Min*	20.0
(iv)	Magnesium oxide (MgO), per cent by mass, *Max*	5.0
(v)	Total sulphur as sulphur trioxide (SO_3), per cent by mass, *Max*	3.0
(vi)	Available alkalis, as sodium oxide (Na_2O), per cent by mass, *Max*	1.5
(vii)	Total chloride in present by mass, *Max*	0.05
(viii)	Loss on ignition, per cent by mass, *Max*	5.0

Note 1. Applicable only when reactive aggregates are used in concrete and are specially requested by the purchaser.

Note 2. For determination of available alkalis, IS: 4032–1968 'Method of chemical analysis of hydraulic cement' shall be referred to.

Limits regarding moisture content of fly ash shall be as agreed to between the purchaser and the supplier. All tests for the properties specified shall, however, be carried out on oven dry samples.

Table 5.15. Physical Requirements (IS : 3812 – Part -1 : 2003)

Sl. No.	Characteristic	Requirement Grade of Fly ash	
		I	II
(1)	(2)	(3)	(4)
(i)	Fineness — Specific surface in m²/kg by Blaine's permeability method, *Min*	320	250
(ii)	Lime reactivity — Average compressive strength in N/mm², *Min*	4.5	3.0
(iii)	Compressive strength at 28 days in N/mm², *Min*	Not less than 80 percent of the strength of corresponding plain cement mortar cubes	
(iv)	Soundness by autoclave test expansion of specimens, per cent, *Max*	0.8	0.8

Effect of Fly Ash on Fresh Concrete

Good fly ash with high fineness, low carbon content, highly reactive forms only a small fraction of total fly ash collected. The ESP fly ash collected in chambers I and II are generally very coarse, non spherical particles showing large ignition loss. They can be called coal ash rather than fly ash. Such fly ash (coal ash) are not suitable for use as pozzolan and they do not reduce the water demand.

Use of right quality fly ash, results in reduction of water demand for desired slump. With the reduction of unit water content, bleeding and drying shrinkage will also be reduced. Since fly ash is not

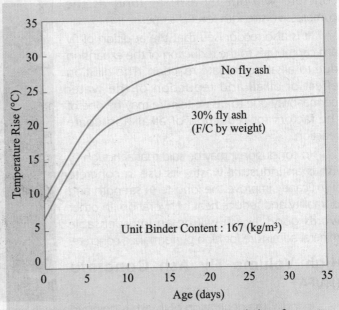

Fig. 5.28. Change in rate of the heat evolution of concrete with and without fly ash.[5.12]

highly reactive, the heat of hydration can be reduced through replacement of part of the cement with fly ash. Fig. 5.28 shows the reduction of temperature rise for 30% substitution of fly ash.[5.12]

Effects of Fly Ash on Hardened Concrete

Fly ash, when used in concrete, contributes to the strength of concrete due to its pozzolanic reactivity. However, since the pozzolanic reaction proceeds slowly, the initial strength of fly ash concrete tends to be lower than that of concrete without fly ash. Due to continued pozzolanic reactivity concrete develops greater strength at later age, which may exceed that of the concrete without fly ash. The pozzolanic reaction also contributes to making the texture of concrete dense, resulting in decrease of water permeability and gas permeability. It should be noted that since pozzolanic reaction can only proceed in the presence of water enough moisture should be available for long time. Therefore, fly ash concrete should be cured for longer period. In this sense, fly ash concrete used in under water structures such as dams will derive full benefits of attaining improved long term strength and water-tightness.

Durability of Concrete

Sufficiently cured concrete containing good quality fly ash shows dense structure which offers high resistivity to the infiltration of deleterious substances.

A point for consideration is that the pozzolanic reactivity reduces the calcium hydroxide content, which results in reduction of passivity to the steel reinforcement and at the same time the additional secondary cementitious material formed makes the paste structure dense, and thereby gives more resistance to the corrosion of reinforcement. Which one will have an overriding effect on the corrosion of reinforcement will be a point in question. Published data reports that concrete with fly ash shows similar depth of carbonation as that of concrete without fly ash, as long as the compressive strength level is same.

It is also recognised that the addition of fly ash contributes to the reduction of the expansion due to alkali-aggregate reaction. The dilution effect of alkali and reduction of the water permeability due to dense texture may be one of the factors for reduction of alkali-aggregate reaction.

In conclusion it may be said that although fly ash is an industrial waste, its use in concrete significantly improve the long term strength and durability and reduce heat of hydration. In other words good fly ash will be an indispensable mineral admixture for high performance concrete.

High Volume Fly Ash Concrete (HVFA)

In India, the generation of fly ash is going to have a quantum jump in the coming decade. It is tentatively estimated that currently (2000 AD), we

High volume Fly Ash has been used in the Barker Hall Project, University of California at Berkeley for the construction of shearwalls.

produce about 100 million tons of fly ash and out of which only about 5% is utilised, in making blended cements and in a few cases as mineral admixture. The disposal of remaining fly ash has become a serious problem. There will also be greater need to economise and to conserve the cement for more than one reasons.

One of the practical methods for conserving and economising cement and also to reduce the disposal problem of fly ash is to popularise the high volume fly ash concrete system.

High volume fly ash concrete is a concrete where in 50 to 60% fly ash is incorporated. It was first developed for mass concrete application where low heat of hydration was of primary consideration. Subsequent work has demonstrated that this type of concrete showed excellent mechanical and durability properties required for structural applications and pavement constructions. Some investigations have also shown the potential use of the high volume fly ash system for shotcreting, light weight concrete and roller compacted concrete.

In Canada, considerable work is going on the development of blended cement incorporating high volume fly ash. The use of this type of cement permits to overcome the problem of additional quality control and storage facilities at the ready-mixed concrete batching plants.

Due to very low water content of high volume fly ash concrete, the use of superplasticizer becomes necessary for obtaining workable concrete. Use of air-entraining admixtures is also concurrently used.

Most investigations on high-volume fly ash concrete were carried out at Canada Center for Mineral and Energy Technology (CANMET). The typical mix proportion used and optimised on the basis of investigations are shown below[5.13]

Table 5.16. Typical (HVFA) Mix Proportions[5.13]

	Low strength	Medium strength	High strength
Water	115 kg/m³	120 kg/m³	110 kg/m³
ASTM Type I cement	125 kg/m³	155 kg/m³	180 kg/m³
Class F fly ash	165 kg/m³	215 kg/m³	220 kg/m³
C.A.	1170 kg/m³	1195 kg/m³	1110 kg/m³
F.A.	800 kg/m³	645 kg/m³	760 kg/m³
Air-entraining Admixture	200 ml/m³	200 ml/m³	280 ml/m³
Superplasticizer	3.0 l/m³	4.5 l/m³	5.5 l/m³

Properties of (HVFA) Fresh Concrete. Most of the investigations at CANMET have been performed with flowing concrete, *i.e.*, concrete with a slump of about 180 to 220 mm. Dosage of superplasticizer may vary considerably. They have also used zero slump concrete without superplasticizer for roller-compacted concrete applications.

Bleeding and Setting Time. As the water content is low in high volume fly ash, the bleeding is very low and often negligible. Setting time is little longer than that of conventional concrete. This is because of low cement content, low rate of reaction and high content of superplasticizer. One will have to be careful in cold weather concreting in stripping the formwork.

Heat of Hydration. On account of low cement content, the heat of hydration generated is rather low. CANMET investigations have shown that the heat of hydration of HVFA was about 15 to 25°C less than that of reference concrete without fly ash. In one of the experiments, in case of a concrete block of size 3.05 x 3.05 x 3.05 meter, the maximum temperature reached was 54°C (increase of 35°C) as against a heat of hydration of 83°C (increase of 65°C) in a block of same size made out of concrete using ASTM Type I Cement only. In both the cases the weight of cementitious materials used is same.

Curing of (HVFA) Concrete

High Volume fly ash concrete is to be cured effectively and for longer duration than ordinary concrete and also normal fly ash concrete to obtain continued pozzolanic reaction so that HVFA develops desirable mechanical properties. HVFA concrete should be properly protected from premature drying by properly covering the surface.

Mechanical Properties of (HVFA) Concrete

The properties of HVFA concrete are largely dependent on characteristics of cement and fly ash. Generally the mechanical properties are good in view of low water content, lower water to cementitious ratio and dense microstructure. The typical mechanical properties of high-volume fly ash concrete as per CANMET investigation is given below in Table 5.17.

Table 5.17. Typical Mechanical Properties of Hardened High Volume Fly Ash Concrete (Medium Strength) Made at CANMET with ASTM Type I Cement.[5.13]

Compressive Strength	
1 day	8 ± 2 MPa
7 days	20 ± 4 MPa
28 days	35 ± 5 MPa
91 days	43 ± 5 MPa
365 days	55 ± 5 MPa
Flexural Strength	
14 days	4.5 ± 0.5 MPa
91 days	6.0 ± 0.5 MPa
Splitting Tensile Strength	
28 days	3.5 ± 0.5 MPa
Young's Modulus of Elasticity	
28 days	35 ± 2 GPa
91 days	38 ± 2 GPa
Drying shrinkage strain at 448 days	$500 ± 50 \times 10^{-6}$
Specific creep strain at 365 days per MPa of stress	$28 ± 4 \times 10^{-6}$

Durability of (HVFA) Concrete

Several laboratory and field investigation conducted in Canada and U.S.A. have demonstrated excellent durability of high volume fly ash concrete. It was tested for water permeability, resistance to freezing and thawing, resistance to the penetration of chloride ions, corrosion to steel reinforcement, resistance to sulphate attack, controlling alkali-aggregate expansion, carbonation and durability in marine environment. The results have shown superior quality of high volume fly ash concrete 5.13.

Use of High Volume Fly Ash

All along conventional fly ash concrete has been in use in many parts of the world for several decades. Various standards and codes have generally limited the addition of class F fly ash to 10 to 25 per cent. Laboratory and field demonstration projects during last 10–12 years have shown that concrete containing 55 to 60 per cent fly ash has excellent structural and durability characteristics, when mixed with low water to cementitious ratio and superplasticizer. Since 1985 yet another new economical, useful construction material HVFA has appeared on the construction scenario. Since then this high volume fly ash has been used in many high-rise buildings, industrial structures, water front structures, concrete roads and Roller compacted concrete dams. There is high potential for this material on account of sound economy and usefulness to absorb large quantity of under utilised otherwise harmful waste material.

Silica Fume

Silica fume, also referred to as microsilica or condensed silica fume, is another material that is used as an artificial pozzolanic admixture. It is a product resulting from reduction of high purity quartz with coal in an electric arc furnace in the manufacture of silicon or ferrosilicon alloy. Silica fume rises as an oxidised vapour. It cools, condenses and is collected in cloth bags. It is further processed to remove impurities and to control particle size. Condensed silica fume is essentially silicon dioxide (more than 90%) in noncrystalline form. Since it is an airborne material like fly ash, it has spherical shape. It is extremely fine with particle size less than 1 micron and with an average diameter of about 0.1 micron, about 100 times smaller than average cement particles. Silica fume has specific surface area of about 20,000 m^2/kg, as against 230 to 300 m^2/kg.

Silica fume as an admixture in concrete has opened up one more chapter on the advancement in concrete technology. The use of silica fume in conjunction with superplasticizer has been the backbone of modern High performance concrete. In one article published in 1998 issue of 'Concrete International' by Michael Shydlowski, President, Master Builder, Inc states "Twenty five years ago no one in the concrete construction industry could even imagine creating and placing concrete mixes that would achieve in place compressive strengths as high as 120 MPa . . . . . The structures such as Key Tower in Cleaveland with a design strength of 85 MPa, and Wacker Tower in Chicago with specified concrete strength of 85 MPa, and two Union Square in Seattle with concrete that achieved 130 MPa strength – are testaments to the benefits of silica fume technology in concrete construction".

It should be realised that silica fume by itself, do not contribute to the strength dramatically, although it does contribute to the strength property by being very fine pozzolanic material and also creating dense packing and pore filler of cement paste. Refer Fig. 5.29. Really speaking, the high strengths of high performance concrete containing silica fume are attributable, to a large degree, to the reduction in water content which becomes possible in the presence of high dose of superplasticizer and dense packing of cement paste.

Pierre-Claude Aitcin and Adam Neville in one their papers "High-Performance Concrete Demystified" states "Strengths in the range of 60 to 80 MPa were obtained without use of silica fume. Even higher strengths up to 100 MPa have been achieved, but only rarely. In our opinion there is no virtue in avoiding silica fume if it is available and economical, as its use

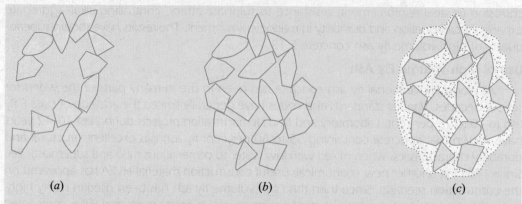

Fig. 5.29. Packing of DSP (silica fume) pastes. (*a*) flocculated ordinary cement pastes; (*b*) better packing achieved with dispersant (superplasticizer); (*c*) cement, silica fume, and superplasticizer.

simplifies the production of high performance concrete and makes it easier to achieve compressive strengths in the range of 60 to about 90 MPa. For higher strengths, the use of silica fume is essential."

Indian Scenario

Silica fume has become one of the necessary ingredients for making high strength and high performance concrete. In India, silica fume has been used very rarely. Nuclear Power Corporation was one of the first to use silica fume concrete in their Kaiga and Kota nuclear power projects.

Silica fume was also used for one of the flyovers at Mumbai where, for the first time in India 75 MPa concrete was used (1999). Silica fume is also now specified for the construction of proposed Bandra-Worli sea link project at Mumbai.

At present, India is not producing silica fume of right quality. Recently, Steel Authority of India has provided necessary facilities to produce annually about 3000 tons of silica fume at their Bhadravathi Complex. It appears that the quality of silica fume produced by them needs upgradation.

In India, however, the silica fume of international quality is marketed by Elkem Metallugy (P) Ltd., 66/67, Mahavir Centre, Sector 17, Vashi, Navi Mumbai-400 703.

Since silica fume or microsilica is an important new material, let us see this material in some detail.

- microsilica is initially produced as an ultrafine undensified powder
- at least 85% SiO_2 content
- mean particle size between 0.1 and 0.2 micron
- minimum specific surface area is 15,000 m²/kg
- spherical particle shape.

Available forms

Microsilica is available in the following forms:

- Undensified forms with bulk density of 200–300 kg/m³
- Densified forms with bulk density of 500–600 kg/m³
- Micro-pelletised forms with bulk density of 600–800 kg/m³
- Slurry forms with density 1400 kg/m³.

- Slurry is produced by mixing undensified microsilica powder and water in equal proportions by weight. Slurry is the easiest and most practical way to introduce microsilica into the concrete mix
- Surface area 15–20 m²/g
- Standard grade slurry pH value 4.7, specific gravity 1.3 to 1.4, dry content of microsilica 48 to 52%.

Pozzolanic Action

Microsilica is much more reactive than fly ash or any other natural pozzolana. The reactivity of a pozzolana can be quantified by measuring the amount of $Ca(OH)_2$ in the cement paste at different times. In one case, 15% of microsilica reduced the $Ca(OH)_2$ of two samples of cement from 24% to 12% at 90 days and from 25% to 11% in 180 days. Most research workers agree that the C – S – H formed by the reaction between microsilica and $Ca(OH)_2$ appears dense and amorphous.[5,14]

Influence on Fresh Concrete

Water demand increases in proportion to the amount of microsilica added. The increase in water demand of concrete containing microsilica will be about 1% for every 1% of cement substituted. Therefore, 20 mm maximum size aggregate concrete, containing 10% microsilica, will have an increased water content of about 20 litres/m³. Measures can be taken to avoid this increase by adjusting the aggregate grading and using superplasticizers. The addition of microsilica will lead to lower slump but more cohesive mix. The microsilica make the fresh concrete sticky in nature and hard to handle. It was also found that there was large reduction in bleeding and concrete with microsilica could be handled and transported without segregation.

It is reported that concrete containing microsilica is vulnerable to plastic shrinkage cracking and, therefore, sheet or mat curing should be considered. Microsilica concrete

Microsilica slurry   Microfiller effect

Courtesy : MC Bauchemie (India) Pvt. Ltd.

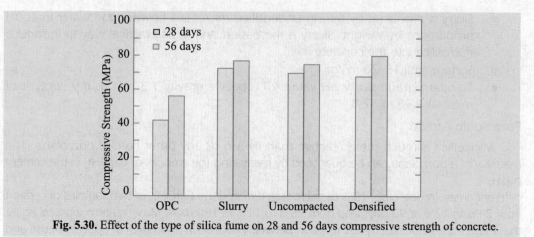

Fig. 5.30. Effect of the type of silica fume on 28 and 56 days compressive strength of concrete.

produces more heat of hydration at the initial stage of hydration. However, the total generation of heat will be less than that of reference concrete.

Influence on Hardened Concrete

Concrete containing microsilica showed outstanding characteristics in the development of strength. Fig. 5.30 shows that 60 to 80 MPa can be obtained relatively easily. It has been also found out that modulus of elasticity of microsilica concrete is less than that of concrete without microsilica at the same level of compressive strength.

As regards, the improvement in durability aspects many published reports, of this investigation carried out, indicate improvement in durability of concrete with microsilica. There are some investigations indicating contradiction, particularly with reference to resistance against frost damage.

With regard to whether or not, silica fume is effective for alkali-aggregate reaction, some research workers report that it is effective, others conclude that while it is effective, addition of silica fume in small quantities actually increases the expansion.

Mixing

By far the most popular application of microsilica is in the 50 : 50 slurry form; as it is easy to store and dispense. There are conflicting views on whether microsilica is best added in powder or slurry form. The work by Hooton among others showed that, for equivalent microsilica additions, slurry produced significantly higher compressive and tensile strengths.[5.15]

The slurry needs to be kept agitated for a few hours in a day to avoid gelling and sedimentation. Presently in India, Mc-Bauchemie (Ind) Pvt. Ltd., supply the silica fume slurry under the trade name "Centrilit Fumes".

Curing

Curing is probably the most important aspect of microsilica concrete as the material undergoes virtually zero bleeding. If the rate of evaporation from the surface is faster than the rate of migration of water from interior to the surface, plastic shrinkage takes place. In the absence of bleeding and slow movement of water from interior to the surface, early curing by way of membrane curing is essential.

Rice Husk Ash

Rice husk ash, is obtained by burning rice husk in a controlled manner without causing environmental pollution. When properly burnt it has high SiO_2 content and can be used as a concrete admixture. Rice husk ash exhibits high pozzolanic characteristics and contributes to high strength and high impermeability of concrete.

Rice husk ash (RHA) essentially consist of amorphous silica (90% SiO_2), 5% carbon, and 2% K_2O. The specific surface of RHA is between 40 – 100 m²/g.

India produces about 122 million ton of paddy every year. Each ton of paddy producers about 40 kg of RHA. There is a good potential to make use of RHA as a valuable pozzolanic material to give almost the same properties as that of microsilica.

In U.S.A., highly pozzolanic rice husk ash is patented under trade name Agrosilica and is marketed. Agrosilica exhibit superpozzolanic property when used in small quantity *i.e.*, 10% by weight of cement and it greatly enhances the workability and impermeability of concrete. It is a material of future as concrete admixtures.

Surkhi

Surkhi, was the commonest pozzolanic materials used in India. It has been used along with lime in many of our old structures, before modern Portland cement has taken its roots in India. Even after Portland cement made its appearance in the field of construction, surkhi was used as an admixture to remedy some of the shortcomings of cement concrete. Surkhi was one of the main constituents in waterproofing treatments in conjunction with lime and sometimes even with cement for extending valuable pozzolanic action to make the treatment impervious.

Surkhi is an artificial pozzolana made by powdering bricks or burnt clay balls. In some major works, for large scale production of surkhi, clay balls are specially burnt for this purpose and then powdered. By its nature, it is a very complex material differing widely in its qualities and performances. Being derived from soil, its characteristics are greatly influenced by the

BHAKRA NANGAL DAM

In Bhakra Nangal Dam scientifically made surkhi (burnt clay Pozzolana) was used about 100 tons per day at the rate of 20% Cement replacement.

constituent mineral composition of soil, degree of burning and fineness of grinding. Because of the complexity of problem there has been much confusion on account of contradictory results obtained by various research workers.

In the past, the term surkhi was used for a widely varying material with respect to composition, temperature of burning, fineness of grinding etc. Now the terminology "calcined clay Pozzolana" is used instead of the word surkhi, giving specific property and composition to this construction material. IS 1344 of 1981 covers the specification for calcined clay pozzolana for use in mortar or concrete. IS 1727 of 1967 covers the methods of test for pozzolanic materials.

Surkhi has been used as an admixture in the construction of Vanivilas Sagar dam, Krishnaraja Sagar dam, Hira Bhaskar Sagar dam, Nizamsagar, Mettur, Low Bhavani, Tungabhadra, Chambal, Kakrapara, Bhakra, and in Rana Pratap Sagar dam.

In Bhakra Nangal Project, illitic argillacious clay was calcined in an oil fired rotary kiln and the grinding operation was carried out through multichamber ball mill. Such a scientifically made surkhi was used 100 tons per day at the rate of 20% cement replacement.

In India, there are a large number of pozzolanic clay deposits of strained and impure kaolins, ferruginous or ochreous earths, altered laterites, bauxites and shales etc., available in different parts of the country, which will yield highly reactive pozzolanic materials. Central Road Research Institute, New Delhi, have conducted an all India survey of pozzolanic clay deposits.

During late 1970's and early 80's, when there was an acute shortage of cement in the country, the cement manufacturers used all kinds of calcined clay pozzolanic materials, that are not strictly conforming to the specification limits in the manufacture of PPC. This has led to the bad impression about the quality of PPC in the minds of common builders in the country. The qualities of PPC as manufactured in India today, specially by those companies who generate and use fly ash in their own plant, is of high quality. Often PPC could be considered better than OPC. Inspite of this, the users at large, as saying goes, "once bitten, twice shy", have not yet overcome their bad experience of 1980's in respect of qualities of PPC.

Presently, in view of the large scale availability of fly ash and blended cement the old practice of using surkhi and the modern calcined clay pozzolana has lost its importance.

Metakaolin

Considerable research has been done on natural pozzolans, namely on thermally activated ordinary clay and kaolinitic clay. These unpurified materials have often been called "Metakaolin". Although it showed certain amount of pozzolanic properties, they are not highly reactive. Highly reactive metakaolin is made by water processing to remove unreactive impurities to make 100% reactive pozzolan. Such a product, white or cream in colour, purified, thermally activated is called High Reactive Metakaolin (HRM).

High reactive metakaolin shows high pozzolanic reactivity and reduction in $Ca(OH)_2$ even as early as one day. It is also observed that the cement paste undergoes distinct densification. The improvement offered by this densification includes an increase in strength and decrease in permeability.

The high reactive metakaolin is having the potential to compete with silica fume.

High reactive metakaolin by trade name "Metacem" is being manufactured and marketed in India by speciality Minerals Division, Head office at Arundeep Complex, Race Course, South Baroda 390 007.

Ground Granulated Blast Furnace Slag (GGBS)

Ground granulated blast-furnace slag is a nonmetallic product consisting essentially of silicates and aluminates of calcium and other bases. The molten slag is rapidly chilled by quenching in water to form a glassy sand like granulated material. The granulated material when further ground to less than 45 micron will have specific surface of about 400 to 600 m^2/kg (Blaine).

The chemical composition of Blast Furnace Slag (BFS) is similar to that of cement clinker. Table 5.18 shows the approximate chemical composition of cement clinker, blast-furnace slag (BFS) and fly ash.

Table 5.18. Approximate Oxide Composition of Cement Clinker, BFS and Fly Ash

Sl. No.	Constituents	Percentage contents		
		Cement clinker	Blast furnace slag	Fly ash
1	CaO	60–67	30–45	1.0–3.0
2	SiO_2	17–25	30–38	35–60
3	Al_2O_3	3.0– 8.0	15–25	10–30
4	Fe_2O_3	0.5– 6.0	0.5–2.0	4–10
5	MgO	0.1– 4.0	4.0–17.0	0.2–5.0
6	MnO_2		1.0–5.0	
7	Glass		85–98	20–30
8	Specific gravity	3.15	2.9	2.1–2.6

The performance of slag largely depends on the chemical composition, glass content and fineness of grinding. The quality of slag is governed by IS 12089 of 1987. The following table shows some of the important specification limits.

Table 5.19. Specifications of BFS as per IS 12089 of 1987

(1)	Manganese oxide %	$\rightarrow$	5.5 Max
(2)	Magnesium oxide %		17.0 Max
(3)	Sulphide sulphur %		2.0 Max
(4)	Glass content %		85.0 Min
(5)	$\dfrac{CaO + MgO + 1/3\,Al_2O_3}{SiO_2 + 2/3\,Al_2O_3}$	$\geq$	1.0
	OR		
(6)	$\dfrac{CaO + MgO + Al_2O_3}{SiO_2}$	$\geq$	1.0
	where MnO in slag is more than 2.5%		
(7)	$\dfrac{CaO + C_2S + 1/2\,MgO + Al_2O_3}{SiO_2 + MnO}$	$\geq$	1.5

Table 5.20. Compositions of some of the Indian Blast Furnace Slags[5.16]

	Tisco 78	Tisco 90	Durgapur	Rourkela	Bokaro	Bhilai
SiO_2	31.66	31.50	33.00	33.50	30.50	32.50
CaO	32.25	31.50	36.00	28.50	29.50	33.50
Al_2O_3	24.00	22.50	24.00	24.50	25.00	22.50
MgO	5.92	10.00	4.00	8.00	8.50	8.00
MnO	1.25	1.25	1.40	3.00	1.00	1.00
FeO	0.80	0.85	1.00	1.00	1.00	0.80
S	0.80	0.85	0.60	0.70	0.90	0.80
Liquid Temperature	1430°C	1482°C	1457°C	1431°C	1489°C	1430°C
Hydraulic Indices	Tisco 78	Tisco 90	Durgapur	Rourkela	Bokaro	Bhilai
P	1.02	1.00	1.09	0.85	0.97	1.03
B	0.68	0.77	0.70	0.65	0.68	0.75
H	1.96	2.03	1.94	1.82	2.06	1.97
IH	1.70	1.84	1.67	1.59	1.82	1.76
I	15.89	16.00	16.00	10.00	17.75	15.00
F	1.81	1.82	1.87	1.57	1.88	1.80

Note:
$$P = CaO/SiO_2$$
$$B = (CaO + MgO)/(SiO_2 + Al_2O_3)$$
$$H = (CaO + MgO + Al_2O_3)/SiO_2$$
$$IH = (CaO + 0.56\, Al_2O_3 + 1.40\, MgO)\, SiO_2$$
$$I = 20 + CaO + Al_2O_3 + 0.5\, MgO - 2\, SiO_2$$
$$F = (CaO + 0.5S + Al_2O_3 + 0.5\, MgO)/(SiO_2 + MnO)$$

In India, we produce about 7.8 million tons of blast furnace slag. All the blast furnace slags are granulated by quenching the molten slag by high power water jet, making 100% glassy slag granules of 0.4 mm size. Indian blast furnace slag has been recently evaluated by Banerjee A.K. and the summary of the same has been reproduced in Table 5.20.

The blast furnace slag is mainly used in India for manufacturing slag cement. There are two methods for making Blast Furnace Slag Cement. In the first method blast furnace slag is interground with cement clinker alongwith gypsum. In the second method blast furnace slag is separately ground and then mixed with the cement.

Clinker is hydraulically more active than slag. It follows then that slag should be ground finer than clinker, in order to fully develop its hydraulic potential. However, since slag is much harder and difficult to grind compared to clinker, it is ground relatively coarser during the process of inter-grinding. This leads to waste of hydraulic potential of slag. Not only that the inter-grinding seriously restricts the flexibility to optimise slag level for different uses.

The hydraulic potential of both the constituents – clinker and slag can be fully exploited if they are ground separately. The level of fineness can be controlled with respect to activity, which will result in energy saving. The present trend is towards separate grinding of slag and clinker to different levels. The clinker and gypsum are generally ground to the fineness of less than 3000 cm^2/g (Blaine) and slag is ground to the level of 3000–4000 cm^2/g (Blaine) and stored separately. They are blended after weigh batching, using paddle wheel blenders, or pneumatic blenders. Pneumatic blenders give better homogeneity when compared to mechanical blenders.

Just as fly ash is used as an admixture in making concrete Ground Granulated Blast-furnace Slag popularly called GGBS is used as an admixture in making concrete. In other countries its use as an admixture is more common than its use as slag cement. Now in India, since it is available separately as ground granulated blast-furnace slag (GGBS), its use as admixture should become more common. Recently for marine outfall work at Bandra, Mumbai, GGBS has been used as an admixture to replace cement to the tune of 70%. Presently in India, with the growing popularity of RMC, the scope for using GGBS for customer's tailor made requirements should also become popular.

Performance of GGBS in Concrete

Fresh Concrete: The replacement of cement with GGBS will reduce the unit water content necessary to obtain the same slump. This reduction of unit water content will be more pronounced with increase in slag content and also on the fineness of slag. This is because of the surface configuration and particle shape of slag being different than cement particle. In addition, water used for mixing is not immediately lost, as the surface hydration of slag is slightly slower than that of cement. Fig. 5.31 and Fig. 5.32 shows the reduction in unit water content.

Reduction of bleeding is not significant with slag of 4000 cm^2/g fineness. But significant beneficial effect is observed with slag fineness of 6000 cm^2/g and above.

Hardened Concrete: Exclusive research works have shown that the use of slag leads to the enhancement of intrinsic properties of concrete in both fresh and hardened conditions. The major advantages recognised are

- Reduced heat of hydration
- Refinement of pore structures
- Reduced permeabilities to the external agencies
- Increased resistance to chemical attack.

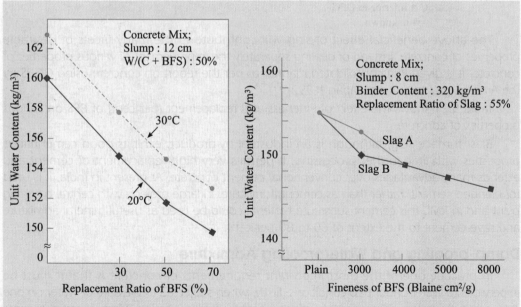

Fig. 5.31. Relationship between replacement ratio of slag and water content.[5.17]

Fig. 5.32. Relationship between fineness of BFS and unit water content.[5.18]

Table 5.21 Effect of Fineness and Replacement (per cent) of BSF on various Properties of Concrete[5.19]

Fineness (cm²/g)	2750 – 5500			5500 – 7500			7500 –		
Replacement (%)	30	50	70	30	50	70	30	50	70
Workability	B	B	B	A	A	A	A	A	A
Bleeding	B	B	C	A	A	A	A	A	A
Hydration control	A	A	A	A	A	A	A	A	A
Adiabatic temp. rise	–	–	A	–	–	A	–	–	A
Hydration-heat control	B	A	A	B	B	A	B	B	A
Early age strength	B	C	C	B	C	C	B	B	C
28 days strength	B	C	C	A	B	C	A	A	A
Long term strength	B	A	A	B	A	A	A	A	B
High strength	C	C	A	B	B	A	A	B	
Drying shrinkage	B	B	B	B	B	B	B	B	B
Freeze-thaw resistance	B	B	B	B	B	B	B	B	B
Carbonation control	–	–	C	–	–	C	–	–	C
Watertightness	B	A	A	A	A	A	A	A	A
Chloride ion resistance	B	A	A	A	A	A	A	A	A
Ability of seawater	B	A	A	B	A	A	B	A	A
Chemical resistance	B	B	A	B	B	A	B	B	A
Heat resistance	B	B	B	B	B	B	B	B	B
Availability of accelerate curing	B	B	B	B	B	B	B	B	B
Control for AAR expansion	B	A	A	B	A	A	B	A	A

Notes: A = superior to OPC (ordinary portland cement)
B = slightly better than or as well as OPC
C = inferior to OPC
– = unknown

The above beneficial effect of slag will contribute to the many facets of desirable properties of concrete. Instead of dealing separately the improvement of various properties of concrete, it is given in a consolidated manner as per the report on concrete using GGBS by the Architectural Institute of Japan (1992).[5.19]

Table 5.21 shows the effect of Fineness and replacement (per cent) of BFS on various properties of concrete.

Blast furnace slag, although is an industrial by-product, exhibits good cementitious properties with little further processing. It permits very high replacement of cement and extends many advantages over conventional cement concrete. At present in India, it is used for blended cement, rather than as cement admixture. In large projects with central batching plant and in RMC this cement substitute material could be used as useful mineral admixture and save cement to the extent of 60 to 80 per cent.

Damp-proofing and Waterproofing Admixture

In practice one of the most important requirements of concrete is that it must be impervious to water under two conditions, firstly, when subjected to pressure of water on one side, secondly, to the absorption of surface water by capillary action. Many investigators are of the opinion that the concrete, carefully designed, efficiently executed with sound materials, will be impermeable to water. However, since the usual design, placing, curing and in general the various operations involved at the site of work leave much to be desired, it is accepted that a use of a well chosen admixture may prove to be of some advantage in reducing the permeability.

It is to be noted that the use of admixture should in no case be considered as a substitute for bad materials, bad design or workmanship. In no case can an admixture be expected to compensate for cracks or large voids in concrete causing permeability.

Waterproofing admixtures may be obtained in powder, paste or liquid form and may consist of pore filling or water repellent materials. The chief materials in the pore filling class are silicate of soda, aluminium and zinc sulphates and aluminium and calcium chloride. These are chemically active pore fillers. In addition they also accelerate the setting time of concrete and thus render the concrete more impervious at early age. The chemically inactive pore filling materials are chalk, fullers earth and talc and these are usually very finely ground. Their chief action is to improve the workability and to facilitate the reduction of water for given workability and to make dense concrete which is basically impervious.

Some materials like soda, potash soaps, calcium soaps, resin, vegetable oils, fats, waxes and coal tar residues are added as water repelling materials in this group of admixtures. In some kind of waterproofing admixtures inorganic salts of fatty acids, usually calcium or ammonium stearate or oleate is added along with lime and calcium chloride. Calcium or ammonium stearate or oleate will mainly act as water repelling material, lime as pore filling material and calcium chloride accelerates the early strength development and helps in efficient curing of concrete all of which contribute towards making impervious concrete.

Some type of waterproofing admixtures may contain butyl stearate, the action of which is similar to soaps, but it does not give frothing action. Butyl stearate is superior to soap as water repellent material in concrete.

Heavy mineral oil free from fatty or vegetable oil has been proved to be effective in rendering the concrete waterproof. The use of Asphalt Cut-back oils have been tried in quantities of $2\frac{1}{2}$, 5 and 10 per cent by weight of cement. Strength and workability of the concrete was not seriously affected.

Production of concrete of low permeability depends to a great extent on successful uniform placing of the material. An agent which improves the plasticity of a given mixture without causing deleterious effects or which limits bleeding and thereby reduces the number of large voids, might also be classified as a permeability reducing admixture. Air entraining agents may also be considered under this, since they increase workability and plasticity of concrete and help to reduce water content and bleeding. An air entrained concrete has lower absorption and capillarity till such time the air content do not exceed about 6 per cent.

The aspect of damp-proofing and waterproofing of concrete is a very complex topic. It embraces the fundamentals of concrete technology. Among many other aspects, the w/c ratio used in the concrete, the compaction, curing of concrete, the admixture used to reduce the w/c ratio, the heat of hydration, the micro-cracking of concrete and many other facets influence the structure of hardened cement paste and concrete, which will have direct bearing on permeability, damp-proofing and waterproofing. This aspect is dealt in little more detail under construction chemicals later.

Gas Forming Agents

A gas forming agent is a chemical admixture such as aluminium powder. It reacts with the hydroxide produced in the hydration of cement to produce minute bubbles of hydrogen gas throughout the matrix. The extent of foam or gas produced is dependent upon the type and amount of aluminium powder, fineness and chemical composition of cement, temperature and mix proportions. Usually unpolished aluminium powder is preferred. The amount added are usually 0.005 to 0.02 per cent by weight of cement which is about one teaspoonful to a bag of cement. Larger amounts are being used for the production of light weight concrete.

The action of aluminium powder, when properly controlled causes a slight expansion in plastic concrete or mortar and this reduces or eliminates the settlement and may, accordingly, increase the bond to reinforcing bars and improve the effectiveness of grout, in filling joints. It is particularly useful for grouting under machine bases. The effect on strength depends upon whether or not the concrete is restrained from expanding. If it is restrained, the effect on strength is negligible, and if not, the loss of strength may be considerable. It is, therefore, important that the forms be tight and the grout is completely confined.

In hot weather, the action of aluminium powder may occur too quickly and beneficial action may be lost. In cold weather, the action will be slower and may not progress fast enough to produce the desired effect before the concrete has set. At normal temperature the reaction starts at the time of mixing and may continue for $1\frac{1}{2}$ to 4 hours. At temperatures above 38°C, the reaction may be completed in 30 minutes. At about 4°C the reaction may not be effective for several hours. Approximately twice as much aluminium powder is required at 4°C as at 21°C to produce the same amount of expansion.

Because very small quantity of aluminium powder is used and as it has a tendency to float on the water, the powder is generally pre-mixed with fine sand and then this mixture is added to the mixer.

Aluminium powder is also used as an admixture in the production of light weight concrete. Larger quantities of about 100 gms per bag of cement is used for this purpose. Sodium hydroxide or trisodium phosphate is sometimes added to accelerate the reaction. Sometimes an emulsifying agent may be added to stabilise the mix. By varying the proportions of aluminium powder depending upon the temperature and carefully controlling the gas formation, light weight concrete may be produced in a wide range of density. Zinc, magnesium powders and hydrogen peroxide are also used as gas forming agents.

Air-detraining agents

There have been cases where aggregates have released gas into or caused excessive air entrainment, in plastic concrete which made it necessary to use an admixture capable of dissipating the excess of air or other gas. Also it may be required to remove a part of the entrained air from concrete mixture. Compounds such as tributyl phosphate, water-insoluble alcohols and silicones have been proposed for this purpose. However, tributyl phosphate is the most widely used air-detraining agent.

Alkali-aggregate expansion inhibitors

We have already dealt with the alkali-aggregate expansion in Chapter 3. It has been seen that alkali-aggregate reaction can be reduced by the use of pozzolanic admixture. We have already dealt about the use of pozzolanic material early in this chapter. There are some evidences that air entraining admixture reduces the alkali-aggregate reaction slightly. The other admixtures that may be used to reduce the alkali-aggregate reaction are aluminium powder and lithium salts.

Workability Agents

Workability is one of the most important characteristics of concrete, specially under the following circumstances:

(a) If the concrete is to be placed around closely placed reinforcement, deep beams, thin sections etc.

(b) Where special means of placement are required such as tremie, chute or pumping methods.

(c) If the concrete is harsh because of poor aggregate characteristics or grading.

(d) For making high strength concrete when w/c ratio is very low.

In the above circumstances even the cost of achieving the workability may have to be overlooked.

Some admixtures can be used to improve workability. The materials used as workability agents are:

(a) finely divided material,

(b) plasticizers and superplasticizers,

(c) air-entraining agents

The use of finely divided admixture in appropriate quantity improves workability, reduces rate and amount of bleeding, increases the strength of lean concrete and may not increase water requirement and drying shrinkage. Common materials added as workability agents are bentonite clay, diatomaceous earth, fly ash, finely divided silica, hydrated lime and talc.

Use of plasticizers and superplasticizers are one of the most commonly adopted methods for improvement of workability in almost all the situations in concrete making practices. We have seen in good detail about the use of plasticizers and superplasticizers.

Though the chief use of air-entraining agent is to increase resistance to freezing and thawing, in our country, air-entrainment in concrete is mainly practised for improving workability. Air entraining admixtures are used as mortar and concrete plasticizers. This aspect has already been dealt with.

Grouting Agents

Grouting under different conditions or for different purposes would necessitate different qualities of grout-mixture. Sometimes grout mixtures will be required to set quickly and sometimes grout mixtures will have to be in fluid form over a long period so that they may flow into all cavities and fissures. Sometimes in grout mixtures, a little water is to be used but at the same time it should exhibit good workability to flow into the cracks and fissures. There are many admixtures which will satisfy the requirements of grout mixture. Admixtures used for grouting are:

(a) Accelerators   (b) Retarders

(c) Gas forming agents   (d) Workability agents

(e) Plasticizers.

Accelerating agents may be used in grout to hasten the set in situation where a plugging effect is desired. In such a case calcium chloride or triethanolamine can be used.

Retarders and dispersing agents may be used in a grout to aid pumpability and to effect the penetration of grout into fine cracks or seams. They include mucic acid, gypsum and a commercial brand known as RDA (Ray Lig Blinder) etc.

Gas forming admixtures can be used while grouting in completely confined areas, such as under machine bases. Aluminium powder is the most commonly used agent, which chemically reacts and forms small bubbles of hydrogen and produces expansion of the grout. This expansion eliminates settlement and shrinkage.

Plasticizers and superplasticizers in powder form is always one of the ingredients of the grout mixture for effective flowability and obtaining high strength.

Corrosion Inhibiting Agents

The problem of corrosion of reinforcing steel in concrete is universal. But it is more acute in concrete exposed to saline or brackish water or concrete exposed to industrial corrosive fumes. A patented process by Dougill was used for the North Thames Gas Board in UK, in which sodium benzoate was used as corrosion inhibiting admixture to protect the steel in reinforced concrete. In this process 2 per cent sodium benzoate is used in the mixing water or a 10 per cent benzoate cement slurry is used to paint the reinforcement or both. Sodium benzoate is also an accelerator of compressive strength.

It is found that calcium lignosulphonate decreased the rate of corrosion of steel embedded in the concrete, when the steel reinforcement in concrete is subjected to alternating or direct current.

Sodium nitrate and calcium nitrite have been found to be efficient inhibitors of corrosion of steel in autoclaved products. Two or three per cent sodium nitrate by weight of cement is said to serve the purpose. There are number of commercial admixtures available now to inhibit corrosion. Mc-Corrodur is one such admixture manufactured by Mc-Bauchimie (Ind) Pvt. Ltd. They also manufacture a two component corrosion inhibiting coating for reinforcement. This coating is used in repair system.

More about corrosion of reinforcement will be dealt under Chapter 9 on durability of concrete.

Bonding Admixture

Bonding admixtures are water emulsions of several organic materials that are mixed with cement or mortar grout for application to an old concrete surface just prior to patching with mortar or concrete. Sometimes they are mixed with the topping or patching material. Their function is to increase the bond strength between the old and new concrete. This procedure is used in patching of eroded or spalled concrete or to add relatively thin layers of resurfacing.

The commonly used bonding admixtures are made from natural rubber, synthetic rubber or from any organic polymers. The polymers include polyvinyl chloride, polyvinyl acetate etc.

Bonding admixtures fall into two general categories, namely, re-emulsifiable types and non-re-emulsifiable types. The latter is better suited for external application since it is resistant to water.

These emulsions are generally added to the mixture in proportions of 5 to 20 per cent by weight of cement. Bonding admixtures usually cause entrainment of air and a sticky consistency in a grout mixtures. They are effective only on clean and sound surfaces.

Fungicidal, Germicidal and Insecticidal Admixtures

It has been suggested that certain materials may either be ground into the cement or added as admixtures to impart fungicidal, germicidal or insecticidal properties to hardened cement pastes, mortars or concretes. These materials include polyhalogenated phenols, dieldren emulsion or copper compounds.

Colouring Agents

Pigments are often added to produce colour in the finished concrete. The requirements of suitable admixtures include (*a*) colour fastness when exposed to sunlight (*b*) chemical stability in the presence of alkalinity produced in the set cement (*c*) no adverse effect on setting time or strength development. Various metallic oxides and mineral pigments are used.

Pigments should preferably be thoroughly mixed or interground with the dry cement. They can also be mixed with dry concrete mixtures before the addition of mixing water.

RMC (India) Ltd., one of the Ready Mixed Concrete supplier markets ready mixed colour concrete for decorative pavements. Sometimes they make this colour concrete incorporating polypropelyne fibres to arrest possible cracks and craziness in the concrete floor.

Miscellaneous Admixtures

There are hundreds of commercial admixtures available in India. They effect more than one property of concrete. Sometimes they are ineffective and do not fulfil the claims of the manufacturers. It is not intended to deal in detail about these commercial admixtures. However, a few of the more important admixtures are briefly described and some of them are just named.

All these commercial admixtures can be roughly brought under two categories (*a*) Damp proofers (*b*) Surface hardeners, though there are other agents which will modify the properties like strength, setting time, workability etc.

Damp Proofers

(*a*) Accoproof: It is a white powder to be mixed with concrete at the rate of 1 kg per bag of cement for the purpose of increasing impermeability of concrete structures.

(*b*) Natson's Cement WaterProofer: As the name indicates, it is a waterproofing admixture to be admixed at the rate of 1.5 kg per bag of cement.

(*c*) Trip-L-Seal: It is a white powder, the addition of which is claimed to decrease permeability of concrete and mortars and produce rapid hardening effect.

(*d*) Cico: It is a colourless liquid which when admixed with concrete, possesses the properties of controlling setting time, promoting rapid hardening, increasing strength and rendering the concrete waterproof.

(*e*) Feb-Mix-Admix: It is a light yellow coloured liquid claimed to impart waterproofing quality to concrete and increase workability and bond.

(*f*) Cemet: It is a waterproofing admixture. The recommended dose is 3 per cent by weight of cement. It is also claimed that its use in concrete will prevent efflorescence and growth of fungi.

In addition to the above the following are some of the commercial waterproofing admixtures:

(*a*) Arzok	(*b*) Bondex
(*c*) Impermo	(*d*) Luna-Ns-1
(*e*) Sigmet	(*f*) Arconate No. 2
(*g*) Swadco No. 1	(*h*) Rela
(*i*) Wet seal	(*j*) Water lock
(*k*) Scott No. 1	(*l*) Hydrofuge
(*m*) Omson's "Watse"	

Surface Hardeners

(a) Metal Crete: Metal crete is a metallic aggregate which is tough, ductile, specially processed, size graded iron particles with or without cement dispersing agent. It is claimed that it gives greater wear resistance, corrosion resistance, non-dusting and non-slipping concrete surface.

(b) Ferrocrete No. 1: It is a surface hardener and makes the concrete surface compact, dense and homogeneous.

(c) Metal Crete Steel Patch: It is a surface hardener. When added 20 per cent by weight of cement, it is supposed to increase the compressive strength and abrasion resistance.

(d) Arconate No. 1: It is a black powder composed of iron filings. It is used as surface hardener in concrete.

In addition to the above, the other admixtures used as surface hardeners are:

(i) Ironite;   (ii) Merconite;

(iii) Meta Rock;   (iv) Purelite.

Another important admixture which has been very popular is "Lisspol N". It is a polyetheoxy surface active agent which improves workability, strength and many other important properties of concrete when used in a very small dose of $\frac{1}{2}$ oz per bag of cement.

The commercial admixtures are not dependable. It has been common experience that many a time when these admixtures are tested in a laboratory the manufacturer's or distributor's claims are not fulfilled. So it will be wrong to have much faiths in these commercial admixtures though some of them give some encouraging results.

The classification of admixtures and the various materials used are shown in Table 5.22.

Construction Chemicals

So far in this chapter we have discussed the materials that are used as admixtures to modify the properties of concrete. There are other chemicals not used as admixtures but used to enhance the performance of concrete, or used in concrete related activities in the field of construction. Such chemicals are called construction chemicals or building chemicals. The following is the list of some of the construction chemicals commonly used.

- Concrete Curing Compounds
- Polymer Bonding Agents
- Polymer Modified Mortar for Repair and Maintenance
- Mould Releasing Agents
- Installation Aids
- Floor Hardners and Dustproofers
- Non-Shrink High Strength Grout
- Surface Retarders
- Bond-aid for plastering
- Ready to use Plaster
- Guniting Aid
- Construction Chemicals for Waterproofing
  1. Integral Waterproofing Compounds
  2. Acrylic Based Polymer Coatings

Table 5.22. Classification of Admixtures[5.20]

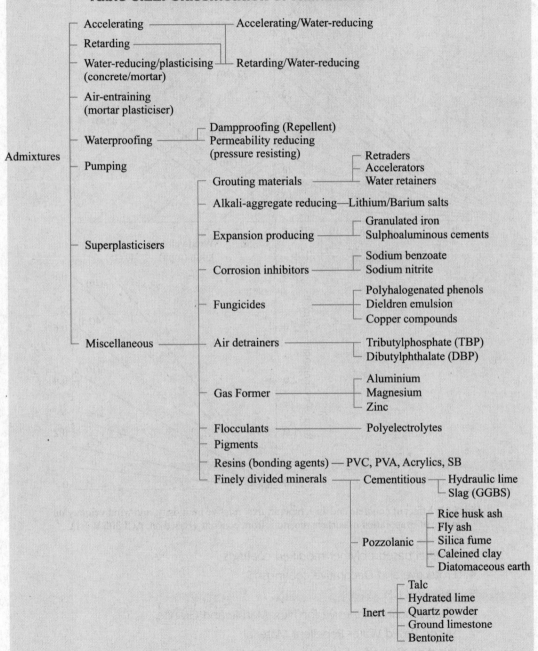

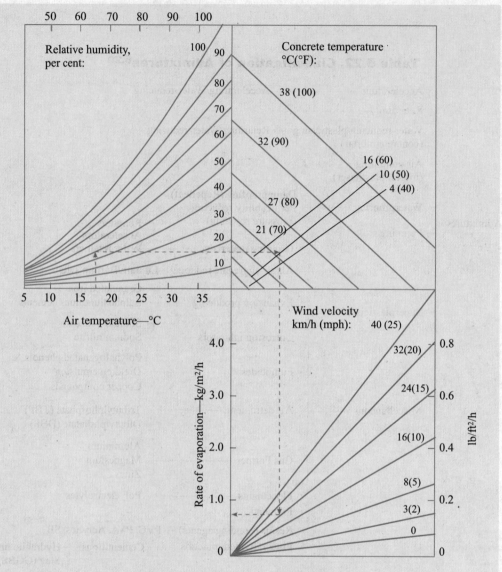

Fig. 5.33. Effect of concrete and air temperatures, relative humidsity, and wind velocity on the rate of evaporation of surface moisture from eoncrete (Based on: ACI 305.R–91).

3. Mineral based polymer modified coatings

4. Protective and Decorative coatings

5. Chemical DPC

6. Waterproofing Adhesive for Tiles, Marble and Granite

7. Silicon Based Water Repellent Material

8. Injection Grout for Cracks

9. Joint Sealants

Membrane Forming Curing Compounds

In view of insufficient curing generally carried out at site of work, the increasing importance of curing for alround good qualities of concrete, in particular, strength and durability, the need for conservation of water and common availability of curing compounds in the country, it is felt that detail information is required on this vital topic – curing of concrete by membrane forming curing compounds.

Availability of enough moisture in concrete is the essence for uninterrupted hydration process. In fresh concrete, the moisture level in concrete is much higher than the relative humidity of atmosphere. Therefore, evaporation of water takes place from the surface of concrete. To recoup the loss of water from the surface of concrete and to prevent the migration of water from the interior of concrete to surface of concrete, that is to retain adequate moisture in the concrete, certain measures are adopted. Such measures taken are generally called curing of concrete.

Drying Behaviour

Drying behaviour of concrete depends upon air temperature, relative humidity, fresh concrete temperature and wind velocity. Figure 5.33 shows drying behaviour as per Learch's investigation. The sketch is self explanatory.

Types of Curing Compounds

Liquid membrane forming curing compounds are used to retard the loss of water from concrete during the early period of setting and hardening. They are used not only for curing fresh concrete, but also for further curing of concrete after removal of form work or after initial water curing for one or two days. In the case of white pigmented curing compound it also reduces the temperature rise in concrete exposed to radiation from sun. Curing compounds are made with the following bases.

- Synthetic resin
- Wax
- Acrylic
- Chlorinated rubber.

Resin and wax based curing compounds seals the concrete surface effectively. With time their efficiency will get reduced and at about 28 days they get disintegrated and peels off. Plastering can be done after about 28 days. If plastering is required to be done earlier, the surface can be washed off with hot water. As per one set of experiments it has been revealed that the typical curing efficiency was 96% for 24 hours, 84% for 72 hours 74% for 7 days and 65% for 14 days and the average efficiency of resin and wax based membrane forming curing compound can be taken as about 80%.

Acrylic based membrane forming curing compound has the additional advantage of having better adhesion of subsequent plaster. The membrane does not get crumbled down or it need not be washed with hot water. In fact on account of inherent characteristics of acrylic emulsion the bonding for the plaster is better.

Chlorinated rubber curing compounds not only form a thin film that protects the concrete from drying out but also fill the minute pores in the surface of concrete. The surface film will wear out eventually.

Application Procedure

The curing compound is applied by brush or by spraying while the concrete is wet. In case of columns and beams the application is done after removal of formwork. On the horizontal surface, the curing compound is applied upon the complete disappearance of all bleeding water. Incase of road and Air field pavements where texturing is required, the curing compound is applied after texturing. Incase of Pune-Mumbai express highway, the pavement is cast by slip form paver. In this process concrete is finished, texturing is done and curing compound is sprayed all by mechanical means. The young concrete is covered by tents to protect green concrete from hot sun and drying winds. In the above express highway it is specified that the concrete is also water cured after one day using wet hessain cloth. Water curing over membrane curing is seemingly superfluous, but it may be helpful in keeping the temperature down.

Incase the concrete surface has dried, the surface should be sprayed with water and thoroughly wetted and made fully damp before curing compound is applied. The container of curing compound should be well stirred before use.

At present we do not have Bureau of Indian Standard Specification and Code of Practice for membrane forming curing compounds. It is under preparation. Since curing compounds are used very commonly in our country in many of the major projects, such as Sardar Sarovar dam projects, express highway projects, etc., a brief description in respect of ASTM: C 309 of 81, for "Liquid Membrane-forming Compounds for Curing concrete" and ASTM C 156 of 80 *a* for "Water Retention by concrete Curing Materials" is given below for information of users.

Scope: The specification covers liquid membrane forming compounds suitable for retarding the loss of water during the early period of hardening of concrete. The white pigmented curing compound also reduces the temperature rise in concrete exposed to radiation from sun.

The following types of compounds are included:
- clear or translucent without dye
- clear or translucent with fugitive dye
- white pigmented.

Base: The membrane forming curing compound may be
- Resin based
- Acrylic based.

General Characteristics

The clear or translucent compounds shall be colourless or light in colour. If the compound contains fugitive dye, it shall be readily distinguishable on the concrete surface for at least 4 hours after application, but shall become inconspicuous within 7 days after application, if exposed to sun light.

The white-pigmented compound shall consist of finely divided white pigment and vehicle ready mixed for immediate use as it is. The compound shall present in uniform white appearance where applied at the specified rate.

The liquid membrane forming compounds shall be of such consistency that it can be readily applied by spraying, brushing or rolling at temperature above 4°C.

The liquid membrane-forming compounds are generally applied in two coats. If need be more than two coats may be applied so that the surface is effectively sealed. The first coat shall be applied after the bleeding water, if any, is fully dried up, but the concrete surface is quite damp. Incase of formed surfaces such as columns and beams etc., the curing compound shall be applied immediately on removal of formwork.

Water Retention Test

Scope: This method covers laboratory determination of efficiency of liquid membrane forming compounds as measured by its ability to prevent moisture loss during the early period of hardening.

Apparatus

Moulds: Moulds shall be made of metal or plastic and shall be water tight. The size shall be 150 mm x 300 mm at the top, 145 mm x 295 mm at the bottom and 50 mm in height.

Curing Cabinet: A cabinet for curing the specimens at a temperature of 37°C ± 1°C and a relative humidity of 30 ± 2%.

Balances: The balance for weighing the mould and content shall have a capacity of 10 kg, sensitive to 1 gram or less. The balance used for weighing the membrane forming compound shall have a capacity of 1 kg and shall be sensitive to 0.1 gram or less.

Proportioning and Mixing Mortar

Make cement mortar of sufficient quantity required to fill the mould. The proportion of cement to standard sand is found out by making mortar of flow value of 35 ± 5 with w/c ratio of 0.40. The mould is kept on glass plate and the mortar is filled in two layers and is fully compacted. The specimen is struck off level with a straight edge. The mould together with glass plate is cleaned by means of wet clean cloth. Seal the bottom junction between mould and glass plate with paraffin wax or any other suitable material to prevent oozing of water from the junction.

Number of Specimen

A set of three or more test specimens for reference test and three or more for application of curing compound is done to constitute a test of a given curing compound.

Storage of Specimen

Immediately after moulding cleaning and sealing, place all the specimen in curing cabinet maintained at temperature 37°C ± 1°C and relative humidity of 30 ± 2%. The specimens are placed in the cabinet leaving a space of about 50 to 200 mm. Within this limit, the spacing shall be same for all the specimens. Keep all the specimens in the storage cabinet till such time, the bleeding water disappears. Apply two coats of curing compounds by means of brush. Take care to see that curing compound is applied only to the top surface and also effectively seal the junction between the mortar and mould by curing compound.

Weigh the coated specimens nearest to 1 gm. Find out the difference in weight between the coated and uncoated specimen. This gives the weight of the liquid membrane forming curing material. The weight of the curing material shall also be found out separately.

The entire operation of weighing, coating and reweighing shall not take more than 30 minutes. All the specimens are immediately placed in the storage cabinet and stipulated temperature and humidity is maintained.

Duration of Test

The specimens are kept in the curing cabinet for 72 hours after the application of curing compounds.

Corrections for Loss of Weight of Curing Compound

Take a metal pan or plate with edges raised 3 mm having an area equal to the top area of test specimen. Take the same quantity of curing material as coated to the specimen and coat the metal pan. Place the coated metal pan in the curing cabinet along with the specimen and weigh this pan at the end of the test. Use the loss in weight of the curing compound as a correction factor in calculating the curing compound added.

Calculation of Loss in Weight

At the end of the specified curing period (72 hours) weigh the mould and specimen of the uncoated and coated samples. Find out the average loss in weight of the uncoated and coated specimen and express in kg/square meter of surface. This value could be used as an indicator of efficiency of liquid membrane forming curing compound.

Test results (Water Retention)

The liquid membrane forming compound, when tested as specified above shall restrict the loss of water to not more than. 0.55 kg/m^2 of surface area in 72 hours.

There are other tests for Reflectance and Drying time (not described).

Reflectance

The white-pigmented compound, when tested, shall exhibit a daylight reflectance of not less than 60% of that of magnesium oxide.

Drying Time

The liquid membrane-forming compound, when tested shall be dry to touch in not more than 4 hours. After 12 hours the compound shall not be tacky and one should be able to walk on the coating without any foot impression left on the surface coated.

In view of the requirement of large quantity of water for curing concrete and in view of continuous, uninterrupted curing is not done at the site, particularly on vertical surfaces, sloping surfaces and difficult inaccessible places, membrane forming curing compound, though less efficient than water curing, should be made popular in our construction practices.

Emcoril and Emcoril AC are the resin based and acrylic based liquid membrane forming curing compounds manufactured by Mc Bauchemie (Ind) Pvt. Ltd.

Polymer Bonding Agents

It is one of the well known fact that there will not be perfect bond between old concrete and new concrete. Quite often new concrete or mortar is required to be laid on old concrete surface. For example, for providing an overlay on an existing pavement, in providing a screed over roof for waterproofing or repair work etc. The bonding characteristics can be greatly improved by providing a bond coat between old and new concrete surface or mixing the bonding agent with the new concrete or mortar. The use of bonding agent distinctly improves the adhesion of new concrete or mortar to old surface. The mixing of bonding agents with concrete or mortar improves the workability also at lower water cement ratio and thereby reduces the shrinkage characteristic. It also helps in water retention in concrete to reduce the risk of early drying. It further improves the water- proofing quality of the treated surface. Nafufull and Nafufill BB$_2$, Nitobond EP, Nitobond PVA, Sikadur 32, Sikadur 41, Roff Bond ERB, Roff Bond Super are some of the commercial products available as bonding agents.

Polymer Modified Mortar for Repair and Maintenance

Sometime concrete surfaces require repair. The edge of a concrete column may get chipped off; or ceiling of concrete roof may get peeled off, or a concrete floor may get pitted in course of time. Hydraulic structures often require repairing. Prefabricated members such as pipes, poles, posts and roofing elements often gets chipped off while stripping formwork, handling and transportation. In the past cement mortar was used for any kind of repair and as an universal repair materials. Cement mortar is not the right kind of material for repair. Now there are many kinds of repair materials, mostly polymer modified, available for effective repair. They adhere very firmly to the old concrete surface on account of greatly improved bond characteristics. These materials are often stronger than the parent materials. They are also admixed with some other materials which make them set and harden very rapidly. Sometime the material added eliminates the requirement for curing. Zentrifix F 82, Nafuquick, Zentrifix AS are some of the materials manufactured by Mc-Bauchemie.

Mould Releasing Agents

Wooden planks, ordinary plywood, shuttering plywood, steel plates etc., are used as shuttering materials. Concrete when set and harden adhere to the surface of the formwork and make it difficult to demould. This affects the life and quality of shuttering materials and that of concrete. At times when extra force is used to demould from the form work, concrete gets damaged. Sometime mould surface could be cement plastered surface, in which case the demoulding or stripping of concrete member becomes all the more difficult. In the past to reduce the bond between formwork and concrete, some kind of materials such as burnt engine oil, crude oil, cowdung wash, polythylene sheet etc. were used. All the above are used on account of non availability of specially made suitable and effective mould releasing materials. Now we have specially formulated mould releasing agents, separately for absorptive surfaces like timber and plywood and for non absorbent surface like steel sheet are available. Nafuplan K and Nafuplan UST are the materials manufactured by Mc-Bauchemie. Reebol Formcote, Reebol spl, Reebol Emulsion are the materials supplied by Fosroc. Separol Sika Form oil are the materials from Sika Qualcrete.

Installation Aids

Many a time we leave holes or make holes in walls, staircases, gate pillars etc., for fixing wash basin, lamp shades, hand rails or gates etc. Invariably, the holes made or kept, is larger than required. The extra space is required to be plugged subsequently. Material used in the past is cement mortar. Cement mortar takes a long time to set and harden, remain vulnerable for damage and it also shrinks. We have now specially manufactured materials which will harden to take load in a matter of 10-15 minutes and work as an ideal material from all points of view for the purpose of fixing such installations. Fig. 5.34 shows a few situations where fast curing installation aid could be used. They can also be used for fitting of antennae, fixing of pipes and sanitary appliances etc. Emfix is the name of the material manufactured by Mc-Bauchemie.

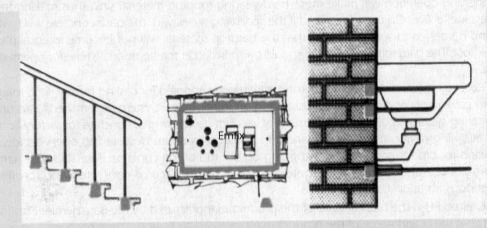

Fig. 5.34. Typical Application of Installation Aids.

Water tanks, deep pump houses, basements, pipes carrying water or sewage, sometimes develop cracks and leaks. Such leakages can be plugged by using a material called Mc-Fix ST manufactured by Mc-Bauchemie (India) Pvt. Ltd. Mc-Fix ST is a polymer modified, ready to use mortar for quick and reliable sealing and plugging of any kind of leaks. The mortar plug develops very high strength and is stone hard within about 5 to 7 minutes. Mc-Fix ST is mixed with a small quantity of water and kneaded into stiff mortar. This stiff mortar is kept pressed against the crack for 5 to 7 minutes.

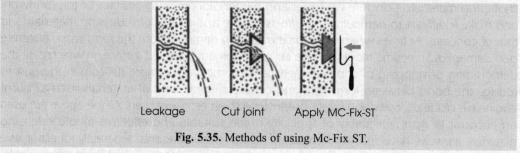

Leakage   Cut joint   Apply MC-Fix-ST

Fig. 5.35. Methods of using Mc-Fix ST.

Floor Hardeners and Dust Proofers

Floor is one of the parts of any building, particularly the industrial buildings, continuously subjected to wear and tear. The factory floor, on account of movement of materials, iron tyred trollies, vibrations caused by running machines is likely to suffer damages. Wear resistant and chemical resistant floor must be provided in the beginning itself. Replacing and repairing of old floor will interfere with the productivity and prove to be costly.

In the past, there were some materials such as Ironite, Hardonate, Metarock and other liquid floor hardeners were used to give better performance. But performances of these materials were not found to be satisfactory. Now we have modern floor toppings materials composed of corborandum or emery powders, systematically graded, mixed with processed and modified cement. This mixture when sprinkled over wet concrete floor of sufficient strength and depth is found to give an effective wear resistant, dust free, non slip floor. The quantity to be sprinkled is depending upon the degree of wear resistance required.

One difficulty is experienced in the application of wear resistant hard top material on the wet base concrete. If the sprinkling of this material is done when the base concrete is too wet, the finishing operation will make these hardwearing topping material sink, thus making the process ineffective. On the other hand if the sprinkling is delayed, the base concrete will have set and hardened to such an extent that the hardtop material will not become integral part of the floor. The hard topping material should be sprinkled at the appropriate time for optimum result.

Recently vacuum dewatering method is frequently adopted for casting factory floor, road, airfield pavements and concrete hardstanding. In India, Tremix System or Jamshedji Vaccum dewatering system is popular. Employment of vacuum dewatering of concrete for factory floor by itself will give improved performance. In addition, vacuum dewatering offers an ideal condition for broadcasting the floor topping on the top of the concrete floor slab. The hard wearing, sized and graded aggregate forms the top surface of concrete floor, to offer tremendous abrasion resistance.

Dreitop FH is the brand name of the product manufactured by Mc-Bauchemie: Nitoflor Hardtop is the brand name of the product manufactured by Fosroc. These products can also be used for existing floors with the provision of a compensating layer underscreed 25 to 30 mm thick. Use of polymer bonding agent to improve the bond between existing floor and compensating layer will improve the performance of the floor as a whole.

Abrasion and chemical resistance of industrial floor can also be improved by treating it with self-levelling epoxy coating or by screeding the floor top with epoxy mortar screeding. Nitoflor FC 140, Nitoflor TF 3000, Nitoflor TF 5000 are some of the materials manufactured by Fosroc, Sikafloor 91, Sikafloor 93, Sikafloor 81 etc., are the products from Sika and Rofflor Coat ERS, Rofloor top EFL, Rofloor top EFH are some of the Roff products. In addition to the above we have a number of epoxy flooring products such as MC-DUR 1500, MC DUR 1100, MC DUR grout etc. manufactured by MC-Bauchemie (India) Pvt. Ltd.

There are also certain materials which when applied on the concrete floor, convert the lime rich cement compounds into silicified products which gives extreme chemical and mechanical resistance and also dustproofing qualities.

Non-Shrink High Strength Grout

Grouting aspects have been touched earlier in this chapter while dealing with waterproofing of basement slab and other concrete structure showing excess of permeability. Apart from the above, grouting has become one of the most important operations in civil engineering construction. Grouting below base plate or machine foundations, grouting of foundation bolt holes in industrial structures, grouting of prestressed concrete duct, grouting in anchoring and rock bolting systems, grouting of curtain walls, grouting of fissured rocks below dam foundation, grouting the body of the newly constructed dam itself, grouting of deteriorated concrete or fire affected structures to strengthen and rehabilitate, grouting of oil wells are some of the few situations where grouting is resorted to.

The grout material should have high early and ultimate strength, free flowing at low water content, should develop good bond with set concrete, essentially it should be non-shrink in nature.

The grouting materials can be broadly classified into two categories. One is free flow grout for use in machine foundations, foundation bolts and fixing crane rails etc. The second category of grout is meant for injection grouting to fill up the small cracks which is normally done under pressure.

Emcekrete and Centicrete are the products of Mc-Bauchemie. Conbextra GP, Conbextra EP are the products of Fosroc.

Surface Retarders

Exposed aggregate finish is one kind of architectural concrete. A few years back such an architectural concrete finish was achieved by bush hammering method, or by wire brushing and water spray methods. The above old methods are not giving a good finish. Now with the availability of surface retarders, both for "face up" or "face down" application, a very pleasing exposed aggregate finish can be obtained. Often exposed aggregate finish can be given for prefabricated panels or for in-situ concrete. The beauty of exposed aggregate can be further enhanced by using different coloured aggregates.

Exposed aggregate architectural concrete by making use of Surface Retarders.

In the face down application surface retarders is brushed on the surface of moulds. This is generally done on prefab panels. After a day or so when the concrete is strong enough the panel is turned over. The concrete in the entire cross section will have hardened except the skin paste in touch with the mould. The unhardened paste is lightly brushed and washed off gently. The coarse aggregates becomes clean and fully exposed giving a pleasing architectural effect.

Incase of face up, the surface retarder is directly sprayed or brushed on the concrete surface before hydration process begins. The cement mortar on the surface does not get set where as the mortar get set below certain depth of the surface where the coarse aggregate gets fully embedded in the hardened matrix. At an appropriate time the unhardened matrix and paste at the surface can be nicely brushed and washed, exposing the coarse aggregate.

Sometime such exposed aggregate finish is given to the foot paths and walk ways on either side of roads so that the surface will become non slippery. This kind of treatments are also given in the automobile service station and parking garages. Different surface retarders are available for different sizes of coarse aggregates. The above exposed aggregate technique is also used as mechanical key for adherence of plastering. Exposed aggregate finish can be adopted for "whisper concrete" surface in express highways.

A kind of exposed aggregate finish is given to hundreds of buildings at Asiad Village Complex, New Delhi.

Bond Aid for Plastering

In the conventional system of construction, on removing the formwork, hacking is done on the surface of columns and beams and also on the ceiling of roof, to form a key between the structure and plaster. Hacking generally givers following problems:

- Uniform hacking is difficult to achieve.
- If there is delay, the structural concrete becomes so hard that hacking become difficult.
- Manual hacking is time consuming particularly at ceiling.
- Slender members particularly cantilever chajjas, louvers, sunbreakers develop structural cracks due to inconsiderate heavy hammer blows on young concrete.

To obviate the above problems liquid polymer bond aid in ready-to-use form is made use of. The surface should be clean, free from oil and grease. If washed it should be allowed to dry.

Bond aid for plastering should be applied in one coat by brushing or spraying. The plastering should be done on the principal of "wet-in-wet". That is to say that bond aid liquid should not dry when you apply plaster. A waiting period of about 60 to 90 minutes would be enough before plastering is applied.

Ready to Use Plaster

One of the common defects in buildings is cracking of plaster. A lot of care is necessary with respect to quality of sand, surface preparation, proper proportioning, consistency and bonding of plaster to base materials. In the absence of such precautions, the plaster cracks and peels off.

In India, recently Ready Mixed Plaster has been introduced by a few industries. Roofit mix is one such brand name.

Ready mixed plaster is basically a pre-mixed materials in dry form consisting of good sand and cement in different proportions for various useage. The mix also includes, such as bonding agents, water retention and workability agents like hydrated lime, air-entraining agents, fly ash and other suitable admixtures to enhance the performance of a plaster material.

It is claimed that ready to use plaster will show the following benefits.

- Consistency in quality and finish
- Less storage and mixing area
- Lower material consumption
- Crack-free plaster
- No curing
- Better adhesion and workability
- Minimal wastage.

Roofit Ready to use Plaster is available in 40 kg bag and in many different grades for using in internal or external plaster, mortar for brick or block work, and as a screed material for tiling works.

Guniting Aid. Guniting and shortcreting have become popular methods of application of mortar or concrete in new constructions or repair techniques. To overcome the problems associated with sprayed concrete, we have now guniting aid in powder form or liquid form to accelerate the setting and hardening, to seal water seepage in tunnelling operations, to improve bonding, to reduce wastage of material by rebounding and to obtain many more advantage in sprayed concrete. Mc-Torkrethifle B.E. is the product of Mc-Bauchemie (India) Pvt. Ltd. and Conplast Spray Set is the Fosroc product for the above purpose.

Construction Chemicals for Waterproofing

Inspite of many fold advancement made in Concrete Technology and the ability to produce high quality concrete, it has not been possible to really make waterproof structures. The problem of waterproofing of roofs, walls, bathrooms, toilets, kitchens, basements, swimming pools, and water tanks etc. have not been much reduced. There are number of materials and methods available in the country for waterproofing purposes. But most of them fail due to one or the other reasons. Waterproofing has remained as an unsolved complex problem. A successful waterproofing not only depends upon the quality and durability of material but also the workmanship, environment and type of structures. Leaving all other aspects, the material part is only discussed below.

It should be remembered that the use of plasticizers, superplasticizers, air-entraining agents, puzolanic materials and other workability agents, help in reducing the permeability of concrete by reducing the requirement of mixing water and hence they can also be regarded as waterproof material. In addition, there are other materials and chemicals available for waterproofing concrete structures.

These materials can be grouped as follows

- Integral waterproofing compounds
- Acrylic Based Polymer Coatings
- Mineral Based Polymer Modified Coatings
- Chemical DPC for Rising Dampness
- Waterproofing Adhesive for tiles, Marble and Granite
- Silicon Based Water Repellent material
- Injection grout for cracks
- Protective and Decorative Coatings
- Joint Sealants

Integral Waterproofing Compounds

This topic has been partly covered on page 166.

The integral waterproofing compounds have been in use for the last 4 – 5 decades. They were used as admixtures to make concrete waterproof. These conventional waterproofing admixtures are either porefillers, or workability agents or water repellents, and as such they are useful to a limited extent. For example, root slabs undergo thermal expansion and subsequent contraction. With the result concrete slabs develop minute cracks in the body of concrete. Concrete slab also develop minute cracks on account of long term drying shrinkage. In both the above cases, integral waterproofing compound will not be of much use. Only in situations where concrete is continuously in wet or in damp condition, integral water proofing will be of some use. The classical integral waterproofing compounds are Cico, Pudlo, Impermo, Accoproof etc.

There are new brands of integral waterproofing compounds such as Mc-special DM, Dichtament DM, Putz-Dichtament from MC Bauchemie and conplast prolapin 421 IC, conplast prolapin I – P etc. from Fosroc chemicals are useful in making concrete more workable and homogeneous. They also help in reducing w/c ratio, which properties extend better waterproffing quality. The modern integral waterproofing compounds are a shade better than the old products. The performance requirements of integral waterproofing of compound are covered in IS 2645 of 1975.

Acrylic Based Polymer Coatings

One of the important reasons why a roof slab leaks, even if you take all the care in making good concrete, well compacted and well cured is that the roof is subjected to variations of temperature between day and night or season to season. Variation of temperature causes micro cracks in concrete and these micro cracks propagate with time and make the cracks grow wider and wider which leads to leaking of roof. The increase in long term drying shrinkage with age, is also another factor contributing to the leakage of roof or other concrete members.

Structural inadequacy, or failure to adhere to the proper detailing of reinforcement, or the unequal settlement etc are some of the additional reasons for development of cracks in concrete members.

In such situations a membrane forming waterproofing materials are ideal. The membrane should be tough, water resistant, solar reflective, elastic, elastomeric and durable. They allow the movement of the concrete members, but keep the qualities of the membrane intact.

One such material available today is Roofex 2000, material manufactured by MC-Bauchemie (Ind) Pvt. Ltd. The surface is cleaned, a priming coat and dust binder is applied over which Roofex 2000 is applied by means of brush or spray in two coats, right angles to each other. In applying this material manufacturers instructions should be strictly followed.

Any cracks in the plaster of parapet wall or vertical surface can be treated with this material. Generally this material is available in white colour but it can be made to order in any other colour for aesthetic requirements.

The Indian standard is being formulated for the use of such membrane forming waterproof coatings.

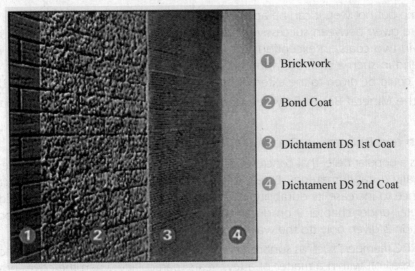

① Brickwork

② Bond Coat

③ Dichtament DS 1st Coat

④ Dichtament DS 2nd Coat

Waterproofing by Mineral Based Polymer Modified Coatings.

Mineral Based Polymer Modified Coatings

Waterproofing of concrete, brick masonry and cement bound surfaces can be achieved by a specially made slurry coatings. Slurry consists of specially processed hydraulically setting powder component and a liquid polymer component. These two materials when mixed in a specified manner forms a brushable slurry. Two coats of this slurry when applied on roof surface or on any other vertical surface in basement, water tank or sunken portion of bathroom etc. forms a long lasting waterproofing coat. This coating requires curing for a week or so. The coating so formed is elastic and abrasion resistant to some extent. To make it long lasting the coatings may be protected by mortar screeding or tiles. The trade name of the above material is Dichtament DS, manufactured by MC-Bauchemic (India) Pvt. Ltd. The Brush Bond of Fosroc Coy and another material called xypex are also available in the market.

The materials described above although exhibit good waterproofing qualities the coating is not very elastic. Its performance in sunken portion of bathroom and such other areas where the concrete is not subjected variation in temperature, will be good. But it may not perform well on roof slab for not being flexible to the required extent, to cope up with the thermal movement of roof slab.

There is a modified version of Dichtament DS called Dichtament DS – flex. It is formulated in such a way that higher amount of polymer component is added to make it flexible to take care of possible small cracks in roof slab or such other situations.

A further modified version of the above has been made to give a better waterproofing and abrasion resistance to the treatment. The modified version will make the coating tough, more elastic and better waterproofing. This modified version of waterproofing system is specially applicable to terrace gardens, parking places, basements, swimming pools, sanitary areas etc. This coating also gives protection to chlorides, sulphates and carbonation attack on bridges and also protect underground structures. The trade name is Zentrifix Elastic, manufactured by MC-Bauchemie (India) Pvt. ltd.

The above is one of the best waterproofing treatments when application is done strictly as per manufacturers instructions. Being flexible and having good crack bridging quality, it is an ideal material for prefabricated roof construction. Before applying the surface should be made damp but not wet. It can be applied by trowel or brush in two coats. A gap of about 3–4 hrs are given between successive coats. Though a standard thickness of 2–3 mm are achieved in two coats, in exceptional situation a maximum thickness of 4 mm could be allowed and in such a case the application should be done in three coats. A three coat treatment could be given to the external face of masonry wall in basement construction.

For the Mineral Based Polymer Modified Coatings the BIS specification is under preparation.

Protective and Decorative Coatings

It was a popular belief that concrete structures do not require protection and the concrete is a naturally durable material. Lately it is realised that concrete needs protection and maintenance to increase its durability in hostile conditions. This aspect will be covered in greater detail under chapter 9 on durability of concrete. However, under the above topic consideration is given only tto the waterproofing quality.

This RCC members such as sunbreakers, louvers, facia, facades, sun shades and chajjas, crack and spall off within a matter of a few years, particularly when the cover provided to these thin and delicate members are inadequate. Water seeps into these members and corrodes the reinforcement in no time. Corrosion is also accelerated by carbonation. To enhance the durability of such thin members and to make them waterproof, acrylic based waterproof, carbonation resistant coating is given. Incidentally it will present aesthetic and decorative look. A number of such protective, waterproof decorative paints, based on acrylic polymer and selected mineral filler are available in market. Emcecolour-Flex is one such paint manufactured by MC Bauchemie and Dekgaurd S is the product of Fosroc chemicals. Generally they are white but could be produced in any colour in the factory.

Chemical DPC

Often old buildings are not provided with damp-proof course. The water from the ground rises by capillary action. This rising water brings with it the dissolved salts and chemicals which result in peeling of plaster affecting the durability of structure, and also make

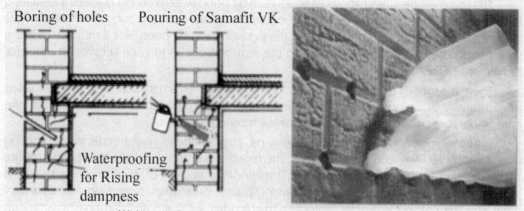

Boring of holes   Pouring of Samafit VK

Waterproofing for Rising dampness

Water proofing for Risingdampness — Intrucing new DPC

buildings unhygenic. Attempts were made to cut the wall thickness in stages and introduce new DPC, but this method was found to be not only cumbersome but also ineffective. Now we have materials that can be injected into the wall at appropriate level to seal the capillaries and thereby to stop the upward movement of water. The system involves a two component material called Samafit VK_1 and Samafit VK_2 manufactured by MC Bauchemie (Ind) Pvt. Ltd.

Above the ground level and below the plinth level, holes are drilled in a particular system. Samafit VK_1 is injected into this hole till absorption stops. After another 1/2 to 1 hour's time the other fluid namely Samafit VK_2 is similarly introduced. These two liquids react with each other to form a kind of jelly like substance which block the capillary cavities in the brickwall and stops the capillary rise of water. In this way rising dampness in buildings, where damp proof course is not provided earlier, can be stopped.

Waterproofing Adhesives for Tiles, Marble and Granite

The normal practice followed for fixing glazed tiles in bathroom, lavatory, kitchen, and other places is the use of stiff neat cement paste. The existing practice, though somewhat satisfactory in the indoor conditions from the point of fixity, such practice is unsatisfactory when used in outdoor conditions and also from the point of view of waterproofing quality. The

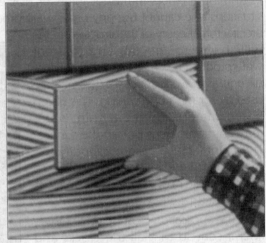

cement paste applied at the back of tiles do not often flow towards the edges of the tiles and as such water enter at the edges, particularly when white cement applied as joint filler become ineffective. In large number of cases it is seen that paintings and plaster gets affected behind these glazed tiles supposedly applied to prevent moisture movement from wet areas.

Cement paste is not the right material for fixing the glazed tiles. There are, polymer based, hydraulically setting, ready to use, waterproof tile adhesive available in the market. They offer many advantages over the conventional method of tile fixing such as better bond and adhesion, strengths, faster work, good waterproofing quality to

Waterproofing Adhesives for Tiles, Marble and Granite.

the wall. They are also suitable for exterior and overhead surfaces. No curing of tile surface becomes necessary. If the wall and plastered surface is done to good plumb, a screeding of only 1 – 2 mm thickness of this modern material will be sufficient to fix the tiles in which case, the adoption of this material will also become economical. The modern tile adhesive material offers special advantages for fixing glazed tiles in swimming pools both on floor and at side walls. It provides one more barrier for the purpose of waterproofing.

Many a time, the glazed tiles fixed on the kitchen platform or bathroom floor gets dirty or damaged. It requires to be replaced. Normal practice is to chip off the old tile, screed cement paste or mortar and then lay the new tiles. With modern tile adhesive, it is not necessary to remove the old tile. Tile adhesive can be screeded on the existing tiles and new tiles are laid over the old tiles. The bonding quality is such that good adherence takes place tile over tile. This saves considerable cost and time and the operation becomes simple.

Marble and granite are increasingly used for cladding wall surfaces both internally and externally. Marble and granite have become the most common treatment for external cladding of prestigious buildings. They are used in the form of tiles or large panels. In the past for fixing thin marble and granite tiles cement paste was used and for fixing large slabs and panels, epoxy and dowel pins were used. Now there are specially made ready to use high strength polymer bonding materials available which can be used with confidence both for internal and external use. Requirement of dowels are eliminated in most of the cases except for cladding of large panels at very high level for extra safety. Marble and granite can even be fixed on boards, inclined surface underside of beams and in ceilings by the use of this new powerful adhesives.

Zentrival PL for fixing glazed tiles and ceramic tiles and Zentrival HS for marble, granite and stones are the materials manufactured by Mc-Bauchemie (India) Pvt. Ltd., Nitobond EP, Nitobond PVA, Nitotile SP are some of the products manufactured by Fosroc.

Silicon Based Water Repellant Materials

Sometimes, in buildings brick works are not plastered. Bricks are exposed as they are. If good quality, well burnt bricks are not used in such constructions, the absorptive bricks permits the movement of moisture inside. Old heritage buildings built in stone masonry may suffer from minute cracks in mortar joints or plastered surface may develop craziness. In such situations one cannot use any other waterproofing treatment which will spoil the intended architectural beauty of the structures. One will have to go for transparent waterproofing treatment. For this purpose silicon based water repellant materials are used by spraying or brushing. This silicon based material forms a thin water repellant transparent film on the surface. The manufacturers slightly modify this material to make it little flexible to accommodate minor building movements due to thermal effect.

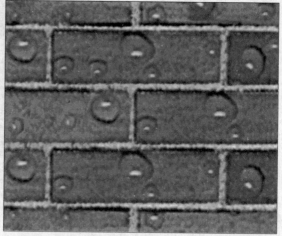

The application must be done in one liberal coat so that all the cracks and crevices are effectively sealed. Brick surface absorbs this material making the surface water repellant. Sometimes bricks or blocks are immersed in such materials before using for greater water repellant qualities.

Waterproofing by Silicon Based Water Repellant Material.

This type of waterproofing materials are used in many monumental stone buildings and old palaces so that original look of the stone masonry is maintained, while making the masonry waterproof.

The treatment though effective, is not found to be long lasting on account of the movement of building components and the lack of required flexibility of the film. The treatment may have to be repeated at closer intervals, say once in 3–4 years. As it is not a costly material, one can afford to repeat the treatment.

This material is covered in IS 12027 of 1987. NISIWA SH is the brand name of one such material manufactured by MC-Bauchemie (Ind) Pvt. Ltd.

Injection Grout for Cracks

Injection grouting is one of the powerful methods commonly adopted for stopping leakages in dams, basements, swimming pools, construction joints and even in the leaking roofs. A few years back, cement was used for grouting purposes. Cement is not an ideal material for grouting, as it shrinks while setting and hardening. Non-shrink or expansive cementing material is the appropriate material. We have quite a few materials available in the market for filling up cracks and crevices in concrete structures to make them waterproof or for repair and rehabilitation of structures. The grouts are produced with selected water repellant, silicifying chemical compounds and inert fillers to achieve varied characteristics like water impermeability, non shrinkage, free flowability etc. They are suitable for gravity grouting as well as pressure grouting. Grouting of concrete structure is one of the powerful methods for strengthening and waterproofing of unhealthy structures. Centicrete is the trade name of one of the materials manufactured by MC-Bauchemie. Conbex 100 is the material marketed by Fosroc chemicals.

Joint Sealants

Joints in buildings, bridges, roads and airfield pavements are inescapable. They may be expansion joints, construction joints or dummy joints. Such joints must be effectively sealed to facilitate movement of structure, to provide waterproofing quality or to improve the riding qualities. While providing large openings and windows in buildings there exists gap between wall and window frames, through which water flows inside. Such gaps in the window should also be effectively sealed. The gaps resulting in installation of sanitary appliances are also required to be sealed. There were no effective materials in Indian market hitherto. Now we have modern materials like Polysulphide sealants and gun applied Silicone Rubber sealants, Sanitary sealant and Acrylic sealants. Nitoseal 215 (1) of Fosroc, Sikalastic, Sika-SII A, Sikacryl GP of Sika Qiualcrete and sani seal of Roff are some of the materials available in the market for the purpose of sealing the joints.

Concrete Repair System

It was once thought that concrete structures are durable and lasts almost forever. But now it is realised that concrete is not as durable as it was thought to be. It was also the earlier

STAGES OF REPAIR WORK

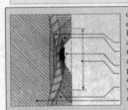

diagrammatic view of need for and limits to exposure of reinforcement steel :
Reinforcement steel, unsound concrete and areas over corroded reinforcement are removed concrete broken out.
area of reinforcement steel to be treated with a protective coat.
carbonated concrete (solid, over non corroded steel, is not removed).
non carbonted concrete (solid).

Corrosion inhibitor and bond coat
Zentrifix KMH
Corrosion protection and bond coat to be mixed only with water prior to application in 2 coats

Surface Preparation
Hammer testing the concrete surface for cavities and chiselling of all losse partions to expose sound core concrete and expose rusted reinforcement.

Concrete Replacement
Zentrifix GSE/GM2/ KA50
Hydraulically setting coarse reair mortar
Zentrifix Elastic/F92
Flexible fine repair mortar

Cleaning Procedure
Clean rusted reinforcement and expose concrete surface by sandblasting, mechancial devices or any other established method.

Surface protection
EmceColor-flex/ Betonflair W/Bentonflair CT
Anti carbonation, crack bridging coating to be applied in two coats.

belief that concrete needs no protection. It was discussed earlier that concrete needs to be maintained and protected. Another wrong notion that prevailed was that concrete cannot be repaired. Now there are materials and methods for effective repair of damaged concrete structures which is discussed below.

Concrete is constantly under attack of environmental pollution, moisture ingress, penetration of chlorides and sulphates and other deleterious chemicals. The durability of concrete is then affected. Of all forces of degradation, carbonation is believed to be one of the potent causes of deterioration of concrete. This aspect is going to be discussed in detail under chapter 9 – durability of concrete.

Concrete repair has become a major subject all over the world. In India, a few newly constructed major bridges have come for repair. In places like Mumbai, innumerable buildings require repair. Many government departments have constituted their own separate "Repair Boards" to deal only with repair. Water tanks are one type of structures often come to repair prematurely.

In the past, there was no effective method of repairing cracked, spalled and deteriorated concrete. They were left as such for eventual failure. In the recent past, guniting was practised for repair of concrete. Guniting has not proved to be an effective method of repair. But now very effective concrete repair system is available. The repair system can take care of the concrete cancer and increase the longevity of the structure. The repair material used are stronger than the parent material. The efficient bond coat, effective carbonation resistant fine mortar, corrosion inhibiting primer, protective coating make the system very effective. Where reinforcement is corroded more than 50%, extra bars may be provided before repair mortar is applied. The whole repair process becomes a bit costly but often repair is inevitable and the higher cost has to be endured

Mc-Bauchemie (India) Pvt. Ltd. have a series of repair materials and well designed repair system. The Figure shows the repair process which is self explanatory.

REFERENCES

5.1   Murata, et.al., Development in the use of superplasticizers, ACI Publication, SP 68-1981.

5.2   Massaza F. and Testalin M., Latest development in the use of Admixtures for Cement and Concrete, Cemento, 77 No. 2-1980.

5.3   Collepardi M., The World of Chemical Admixtures in Concrete, Processing of the Congress, Our World in Concrete and Structures, Singapore 1993.

5.4   Sakai E and Daiman M, Dispersion Mechanism of Alite Stabilised by Superplasticizers Containing Polyethylene oxide Graft Chains - 1997.

5.5. Collepardi M et.al., Zero Slump Loss Superplasticized Concrete, Proceedings of the Congress, Our World in Concrete and Structures, Singapore, Singapore - 1993.

5.6   Fakuda M et.al., Slump Control and Properties of Concrete with a new superplasticizer, Proceedings of International RILEM Symposium on Admixtures for Concrete - Omprovement of Properties, Barcelona, Spain - May 1990.

5.7   Wright PJF, Entrained Air in Concrete, Proceedings of Institution of Civil Engineers, London - May 1953.

5.8   Klieger P, Studies on the Effect of Entrained Air on the Strength and Durability of Concrete made with Various Maximum size of Aggregates, Proceedings of the Highway Research Board, Vol 31 - 1952.

5.9 Shetty M.S., Use of Ritha Powder as an Air-Entraining Agent, Indian Concrete Journal, March 1972.

5.10 Cordon W.A., Entrained Air—A Factor in the Design of Concrete Mixes, ACI Journal, Jan 1948.

5.11 Chatterjee A.K., Availability and use of Pozzolonic and Cementitious Solid Wastes in India, Concrete Technology for Sustainable Development in the Twenty-first Century, organised by CANMET/ACI, Hyderabad, Feb. 1999.

5.12 Efrent R.J., Bureau of Reclamation, Experiences with Fly ash and other Pozzolans in Concrete, Proceedings 3rd International Ash Utilisation Symposium - 1973.

5.13 Malhotra and A. Bilodean, High Volume Fly-ash System, The Concrete for Sustainable Development, Concrete Technology for Sustainable Development in the Twenty-First Century, Organised by CANMET/ACI, Hyderabad, Feb. 1999.

5.14 Micro Silica in Concrete, Technical Report Ni. 41, Report of a Concrete Society Working Party - 1993.

5.15 Hooton R.G., Some Aspects of Durability with Condensed Silica Fume in Pastes, Mortars and Concretes, Proceedings of an International Workshop on Condensed Silica Fume in Concrete, Montreal, May 1987.

5.16 Banerjee A.K., Evaluation of Indian Blast Furnace Salg for Cement, Iron and Steel Review, July 1997.

5.17 Takano et.al., Slump Loss of Concrete Made with GGBS, Symposium on the Use of GGBS, Japan Socciety of Civil Engineers - 1987.

5.18 Endo H. et.al., Effects of the Use of GGBS on Mix Proportion and Strength of Concrete, Symposium on the use of GGBS, Japan Society of Civil Engineers - 1987.

5.19 Architectural Institute of Japan, State-of-the-Art Report on Concrete Using GGBS - 1992.

5.20 Rixom H.R., Concrete Admixtures—Use and Applications, Cement Admixtures Association - 1977.

Concrete Pump and Placing Boom at Work in a Major Construction Site.

- Workability
- Segregation
- Bleeding
- Setting Time of Concrete
- Process of Manufacture of Concrete
- Choosing the Correct Pump
- General Points on Using Vibrators
- Further Instructions on use of Vibrators
- Curing of Concrete
- Finishing

6

Fresh Concrete

Fresh concrete or plastic concrete is a freshly mixed material which can be moulded into any shape. The relative quantities of cement, aggregates and water mixed together, control the properties of concrete in the wet state as well as in the hardened state. It is worthwhile looking back at what we have discussed in Chapters I and III regarding quantity of water before we discuss its role in fresh concrete in this chapter.

In Chapter I, we have discussed the role of water and the quantity of water required for chemical combination with cement and to occupy the gel pores. We have seen that the theoretical water/cement ratio required for these two purposes is about 0.38. Use of water/cement ratio more than this, will result in capillary cavities; and less than this, will result in incomplete hydration and also lack of space in the system for the development of gel.

In Chapter III, we have discussed that while making mortar for concrete, the quantity of water used will get altered at site either due to the presence of free surface moisture in the aggregates or due to the absorption characteristics of dry and porous aggregates. The water/cement ratio to be actually adopted at site is required to be adjusted keeping the above in mind.

In this chapter one more aspect for deciding the water/cement ratio will be introduced *i.e.,* the water/cement ratio required from the point of view of workability of concrete.

Workability

A theoretical water/cement ratio calculated from the considerations discussed above is not going to give an ideal situation for maximum strength. Hundred per cent compaction of concrete is an important parameter for contributing to the maximum strength. Lack of compaction will result in air voids whose demaging effect on strength and durability is equally or more predominant than the presence of capillary cavities.

Harsh concrete

unworkable

Medium workability

generally workable

Highly workable concrete

Degree of workability

To enable the concrete to be fully compacted with given efforts, normally a higher water/cement ratio than that calculated by theoretical considerations may be required. That is to say the function of water is also to lubricate the concrete so that the concrete can be compacted with specified effort forthcoming at the site of work. The lubrication required for handling concrete without segregation, for placing without loss of homogeneity, for compacting with the amount of efforts forth-coming and to finish it sufficiently easily, the presence of a certain quantity of water is of vital importance.

The quality of concrete satisfying the above requirements is termed as workable concrete. The word "workability" or workable concrete signifies much wider and deeper meaning than the other terminology "consistency" often used loosely for workability. Consistency is a general term to indicate the degree of fluidity or the degree of mobility. A concrete which has high consistency and which is more mobile, need not be of right workability for a particular job. Every job requires a particular workability. A concrete which is considered workable for mass concrete foundation is not workable for concrete to be used in roof construction, or even in roof construction, concrete considered workable when vibrator is used, is not workable when concrete is to be compacted by hand. Similarly a concrete considered workable when used in thick section is not workable when required to be used in thin sections. Therefore, the word workability assumes full significance of the type of work, thickness of section, extent of reinforcement and mode of compaction.

For a concrete technologist, a comprehensive knowledge of workability is required to design a mix. Workability is a parameter, a mix designer is required to specify in the mix design process, with full understanding of the type of work, distance of transport, loss of slump, method of placing, and many other parameters involved. Assumption of right workability with proper understanding backed by experience will make the concreting operation economical and durable.

Many research workers tried to define the word workability. But as it signifies much wider properties and qualities of concrete, and does not project any one particular meaning, it eludes all precise definitions. Road Research laboratory, U.K., who have extensively studied the field of compaction and workability, defined workability as "the property of concrete which determines the amount of useful internal work necessary to produce full compaction." Another definition which envelopes a wider meaning is that, it is defined as the "ease with which concrete can be compacted hundred per cent having regard to mode of compaction and place of deposition." Without dwelling much on the merits and demerits of various definitions of workability, having explained the importance and full meaning of the term workability, we shall see the factors affecting workability.

Factors Affecting Workability

Workable concrete is the one which exhibits very little internal friction between particle and particle or which overcomes the frictional resistance offered by the formwork surface or reinforcement contained in the concrete with just the amount of compacting efforts forthcoming. The factors helping concrete to have more lubricating effect to reduce internal friction for helping easy compaction are given below:

(a) Water Content
(b) Mix Proportions
(c) Size of Aggregates
(d) Shape of Aggregates
(e) Surface Texture of Aggregate
(f) Grading of Aggregate
(g) Use of Admixtures.

(a) Water Content: Water content in a given volume of concrete, will have significant influences on the workability. The higher the water content per cubic meter of concrete, the higher will be the fluidity of concrete, which is one of the important factors affecting workability. At the work site, supervisors who are not well versed with the practice of making good concrete, resort to adding more water for increasing workability. This practice is often resorted to because this is one of the easiest corrective measures that can be taken at site. It should be noted that from the desirability point of view, increase of water content is the last recourse to be taken for improving the workability even in the case of uncontrolled concrete. For controlled concrete one cannot arbitrarily increase the water content. In case, all other steps to improve workability fail, only as last recourse the addition of more water can be considered. More water can be added, provided a correspondingly higher quantity of cement is also added to keep the water/cement ratio constant, so that the strength remains the same.

(b) Mix Proportions: Aggregate/cement ratio is an important factor influencing workability. The higher the aggregate/cement ratio, the leaner is the concrete. In lean concrete, less quantity of paste is available for providing lubrication, per unit surface area of aggregate and hence the mobility of aggregate is restrained. On the other hand, in case of rich concrete with lower aggregate/cement ratio, more paste is available to make the mix cohesive and fatty to give better workability.

(c) Size of Aggregate: The bigger the size of the aggregate, the less is the surface area and hence less amount of water is required for wetting the surface and less matrix or paste is required for lubricating the surface to reduce internal friction. For a given quantity of water and paste, bigger size of aggregates will give higher workability. The above, of course will be true within certain limits.

(d) Shape of Aggregates: The shape of aggregates influences workability in good measure. Angular, elongated or flaky aggregate makes the concrete very harsh when compared to rounded aggregates or cubical shaped aggregates. Contribution to better workability of rounded aggregate will come from the fact that for the given volume or weight it will have less surface area and less voids than angular or flaky aggregate. Not only that, being round in shape, the frictional resistance is also greatly reduced. This explains the reason why river sand and gravel provide greater workability to concrete than crushed sand and aggregate.

The importance of shape of the aggregate will be of great significance in the case of present day high strength and high performance concrete when we use very low w/c in the order of about 0.25. We have already talked about that in the years to come natural sand will be exhausted or costly. One has to go for manufactured sand. Shape of crushed sand as available today is unsuitable but the modern crushers are designed to yield well shaped and well graded aggregates.

(e) Surface Texture: The influence of surface texture on workability is again due to the fact that the total surface area of rough textured aggregate is more than the surface area of smooth rounded aggregate of same volume. From the earlier discussions it can be inferred that rough textured aggregate will show poor workability and smooth or glassy textured aggregate will give better workability. A reduction of inter particle frictional resistance offered by smooth aggregates also contributes to higher workability.

(f) Grading of Aggregates: This is one of the factors which will have maximum influence on workability. A well graded aggregate is the one which has least amount of voids in a given volume. Other factors being constant, when the total voids are less, excess paste is available to give better lubricating effect. With excess amount of paste, the mixture becomes cohesive and fatty which prevents segregation of particles. Aggregate particles will slide past each other with the least amount of compacting efforts. The better the grading, the less is the void content and higher the workability. The above is true for the given amount of paste volume.

(g) Use of Admixtures: Of all the factors mentioned above, the most import factor which affects the workability is the use of admixtures. In Chapter 5, it is amply described that the plasticizers and superplasticizers greatly improve the workability many folds. It is to be noted that initial slump of concrete mix or what is called the slump of reference mix should be about 2 to 3 cm to enhance the slump many fold at a minimum doze. One should manupulate other factors to obtain initial slump of 2 to 3 cm in the reference mix. Without initial slump of 2 – 3 cm, the workability can be increased to higher level but it requires higher dosage – hence uneconomical.

Use of air-entraining agent being surface-active, reduces the internal friction between the particles. They also act as artificial fine aggregates of very smooth surface. It can be viewed that air bubbles act as a sort of ball bearing between the particles to slide past each other and give easy mobility to the particles. Similarly, the fine glassy pozzolanic materials, inspite of increasing the surface area, offer better lubricating effects for giving better workability.

Measurement of Workability

It is discussed earlier that workability of concrete is a complex property. Just as it eludes all precise definition, it also eludes precise measurements. Numerous attempts have been made by many research workers to quantitatively measure this important and vital property of concrete. But none of these methods are satisfactory for precisely measuring or expressing this property to bring out its full meaning. Some of the tests, measure the parameters very close to workability and provide useful information. The following tests are commonly employed to measure workability.

(a) Slump Test   (b) Compacting Factor Test

(c) Flow Test   (d) Kelly Ball Test

(e) Vee Bee Consistometer Test.

Slump Test

Slump test is the most commonly used method of measuring consistency of concrete which can be employed either in laboratory or at site of work. It is not a suitable method for very wet or very dry concrete. It does not measure all factors contributing to workability, nor is it always representative of the placability of the concrete. However, it is used conveniently as a control test and gives an indication of the uniformity of concrete from batch to batch. Repeated batches of the same mix, brought to the same slump, will have the same water content and water cement ratio, provided the weights of aggregate, cement and admixtures are uniform and aggregate grading is within acceptable limits. Additional information on workability and quality of concrete can be obtained by observing the manner in which concrete slumps. Quality of concrete can also be further assessed by giving a few tappings or blows by tamping rod to the base plate. The deformation shows the characteristics of concrete with respect to tendency for segregation.

The appartus for conducting the slump test essentially consists of a metallic mould in the form of a frustum of a cone having the internal dimensions as under:

Bottom diameter	:	20 cm
Top diameter	:	10 cm
Height	:	30 cm

The thickness of the metallic sheet for the mould should not be thinner than 1.6 mm. Sometimes the mould is provided with suitable guides for lifting vertically up. For tamping the concrete, a steel tamping rod 16 mm dia, 0.6 meter along with bullet end is used. Fig. 6.1, shows the details of the slump cone appartus. The internal surface of the mould is thoroughly cleaned and freed from superfluous moisture and adherence of any old set concrete before commencing the test. The mould is placed on a smooth, horizontal, rigid and non-absorbant surface The mould is then filled in four layers, each approximately 1/4 of the height of the mould. Each layer is tamped 25 times by the tamping rod taking

Slump Test Apparatus

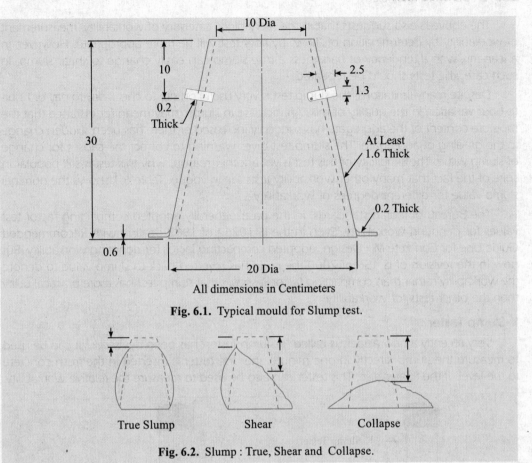

Fig. 6.1. Typical mould for Slump test.

True Slump   Shear   Collapse

Fig. 6.2. Slump : True, Shear and Collapse.

care to distribute the strokes evenly over the cross section. After the top layer has been rodded, the concrete is struck off level with a trowel and tamping rod. The mould is removed from the concrete immediately by raising it slowly and carefully in a vertical direction. This allows the concrete to subside. This subsidence is referred as SLUMP of concrete. The difference in level between the height of the mould and that of the highest point of the subsided concrete is measured. This difference in height in mm. is taken as Slump of Concrete. ASTM measure the centre of the slumped concrete as the difference in height. ASTM also specifies 3 layers.

The pattern of slump is shown in Fig. 6.2. It indicates the characteristic of concrete in addition to the slump value. If the concrete slumps evenly it is called true slamp. If one half of the cone slides down, it is called shear slump. In case of a shear slump, the slump value is measured as the difference in height between the height of the mould and the average value of the subsidence. Shear slump also indicates that the concrete is non-cohesive and shows the characteristic of segregation.

It is seen that the slump test gives fairly good consistent results for a plastic-mix. This test is not sensitive for a stiff-mix. In case of dry-mix, no variation can be detected between mixes of different workability. In the case of rich mixes, the value is often satisfactory, their slump being sensitive to variations in workability. IS 456 of 2000 suggests that in the "very low" category of workability where strict control is necessary, for example, pavement quality concrete, (PQC) measurement of workability by determination of compacting factor will be more appropriate than slump and a value of 0.75 to 0.80 compacting factor is suggested.

The above IS also suggests that in the "very high" category of workability, measurement of workability by determination of "flow" by flow test will be more appropriate. However, in a lean-mix with a tendency of harshness a true slump can easily change to shear slump. In such case, the tests should be repeated.

Despite many limitations, the slump test is very useful on site to check day-to-day or hour-to-hour variation in the quality of mix. An increase in slump, may mean for instance that the moisture content of the aggregate has suddenly increased or there has been sudden change in the grading of aggregate. The slump test gives warning to correct the causes for change of slump value. The simplicity of this test is yet another reason, why this test is still popular in spite of the fact that many other workability tests are in vogue. Table 6.1 shows the nominal slump value for different degrees of workability.

The Bureau of Indian standards, in the past, generally adopted compacting factor test values for denoting workability. Even in the IS 10262 of 1982 dealing with Recommended Guide Line for Concrete Mix Design, adopted compacting factor for denoting workability. But now in the revision of IS 456 of 2000 the code has reverted back to slump value to denote the workability rather than compacting factor. It shows that slump test has more practical utility than the other tests for workability.

K-Slump Tester

Very recently a new appartus called "K-Slump Tester" has been devised.[6.1] It can be used to measure the slump directly in one minute after the tester is inserted in the fresh concrete to the level of the floater disc. This tester can also be used to measure the relative workability.

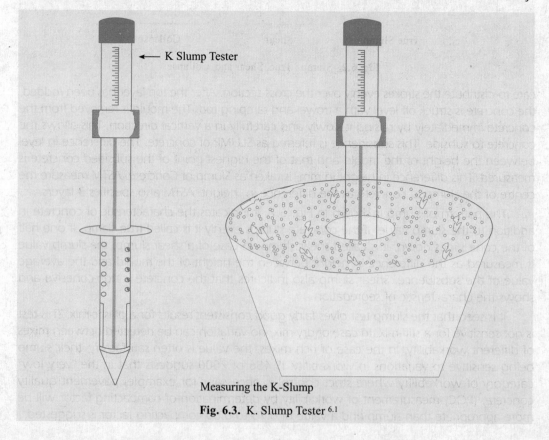

Measuring the K-Slump

Fig. 6.3. K. Slump Tester [6.1]

The appartus comprises of the following four principal parts:-

1. A chrome plated steel tube with external and internal diameters of 1.9 and 1.6 cm respectively. The tube is 25 cm long and its lower part is used to make the test. The length of this part is 15.5 cm which includes the solid cone that facilitates inserting the tube into the concrete. Two types of openings are provided in this part: 4 rectangular slots 5.1 cm long and 0.8 cm wide and 22 round holes 0.64 cm in diameter; all these openings are distributed uniformly in the lower part as shown in Figure 6.3.

K-Slump Tester

Table 6.1. Workability, Slump and Compacting Factor of Concretes with 20 mm or 40 mm Maximum Size of Aggregate

Degree of workability	Slump mm	Compacting factor		Use for which concrete is suitable
		Small appartus	Large appartus	
Very Low compacting factor is suitable	–	0.78	0.80	Roads vibrated by power-operated machines. At the more workable end of this group, concrete may be compacted in certain cases with hand-operated machines.
Low	25–75	0.85	0.87	Roads vibrated by hand-operated machines. At the more workable end of this group, concrete may be manually compacted in roads using aggregate of rounded or irregular shape. Mass concrete foundations without vibration or lightly reinforced sections with vibration.
Medium	50–100	0.92	0.935	At the less workable end of this group, manually compacted flat slabs using crushed aggregates. Normal reinforced concrete manually compacted and heavily reinforced sections with vibration
High	100–150	0.95	0.96	For sections with congested reinforcement. Not normally suitable for vibration. For pumping and tremie placing
Very High	–	–	–	Flow table test is more suitable.

2. A disc floater 6 cm in diameter and 0.24 cm in thickness which divides the tube into two parts: the upper part serves as a handle and the lower one is for testing as already mentioned. The disc serves also to prevent the tester from sinking into the concrete beyond the preselected level.

3. A hollow plastic rod 1.3 cm in diameter and 25 cm long which contains a graduated scale in centimeters. This rod can move freely inside the tube and can be used to measure the height of mortar that flows into the tube and stays there. The rod is plugged at each end with a plastic cap to prevent concrete or any other material from seeping inside.

4. An aluminium cap 3 cm diameter and 2.25 cm long which has a little hole and a screw that can be used to set and adjust the reference zero of the apparatus. There is also in the upper part of the tube, a small pin which is used to support the measuring rod at the beginning of the test. The total weight of the appartus is 226 g.

The following procedure is used:

(a) Wet the tester with water and shake off the excess.

(b) Raise the measuring rod, tilt slightly and let it rest on the pin located inside the tester.

(c) Insert the tester on the levelled surface of concrete vertically down until the disc floater rests at the surface of the concrete. Do not rotate while inserting or removing the tester.

(d) After 60 seconds, lower the measuring rod slowly until it rests on the surface of the concrete that has entered the tube and read the K-Slump directly on the scale of the measuring rod.

(e) Raise the measuring rod again and let it rest on its pin.

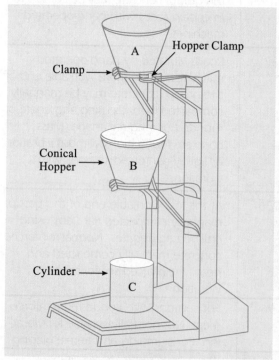

Fig. 6.4. Compacting Factor Apparatus

Compacting Factor Apparatus

(f) Remove the tester from the concrete vertically up and again lower the measuring rod slowly till it touches the surface of the concrete retained in the tube and read workability (W) directly on the scale of the measuring rod.

Remarks

In the concrete industry, the slump test is still the most widely used test to control the consistency of concrete mixtures, even though there are some questions about its significance and its effectiveness. Many agree that the test is awkward and is not in keeping with the strides that the industry has made since 1913 when the slump cone was first introduced. Several apparatus have been proposed to replace or supplement the slump cone, but in general they have proved to be rich in theory and poor in practice. Their use is still limited mainly to research work in laboratories.

The K-slump apparatus is very simple, practical, and economical to use, both in the field and the laboratory. It has proven, with over 450 tests, that it has a good correlation with the slump cone.

The K-slump tester can be used to measure slump in one minute in cylinders, pails, buckets, wheel-barrows, slabs or any other desired location where the fresh concrete is placed. A workability index can be determined by the tester.

Compacting Factor Test

The compacting factor test is designed primarily for use in the laboratory but it can also be used in the field. It is more precise and sensitive than the slump test and is particularly useful for concrete mixes of very low workability as are normally used when concrete is to be compacted by vibration. Such dry concrete are insensitive to slump test. The diagram of the apparatus is shown in Figure 6.4. The essential dimensions of the hoppers and mould and the distance between them are shown in Table 6.2.

The compacting factor test has been developed at the Road Research Laboratory U.K. and it is claimed that it is one of the most efficient tests for measuring the workability of concrete. This test works on the principle of determining the degree of compaction achieved by a standard amount of work done by allowing the concrete to fall through a standard height. The degree of compaction, called the compacting factor is measured by the density ratio *i.e.*, the ratio of the density actually achieved in the test to density of same concrete fully compacted.

Table 6.2. Essential Dimension of the Compacting Factor Appartus for use with Aggregate not exceeding 40 mm Nominal Max. Size

Upper Hopper, A	Dimension cm
Top internal diameter	25.4
Bottom internal diameter	12.7
Internal height	27.9
Lower hopper, B	
Top internal diameter	22.9
Bottom internal diameter	12.7
Internal height	22.9

Cylinder, C	
Internal diameter	15.2
Internal height	30.5
Distance between bottom of upper hopper and top of lower hopper	20.3
Distance between bottom of lower hopper and top of cylinder	20.3

The sample of concrete to be tested is placed in the upper hopper up to the brim. The trap-door is opened so that the concrete falls into the lower hopper. Then the trap-door of the lower hopper is opened and the concrete is allowed to fall into the cylinder. In the case of a dry-mix, it is likely that the concrete may not fall on opening the trap-door. In such a case, a slight poking by a rod may be required to set the concrete in motion. The excess concrete remaining above the top level of the cylinder is then cut off with the help of plane blades supplied with the apparatus. The outside of the cylinder is wiped clean. The concrete is filled up exactly upto the top level of the cylinder. It is weighed to the nearest 10 grams. This weight is known as "Weight of partially compacted concrete". The cylinder is emptied and then refilled with the concrete from the same sample in layers approximately 5 cm deep. The layers are heavily rammed or preferably vibrated so as to obtain full compaction. The top surface of the fully compacted concrete is then carefully struck off level with the top of the cylinder and weighed to the nearest 10 gm. This weight is known as "Weight of fully compacted concrete".

$$\text{The Compacting Factor} = \frac{\text{Weight of partially compacted concrete}}{\text{Weight of fully compacted concrete}}$$

The weight of fully compacted concrete can also be calculated by knowing the proportion of materials, their respective specific gravities, and the volume of the cylinder. It is seen from experience, that it makes very little difference in compacting factor value, whether the weight of fully compacted concrete is calculated theoretically or found out actually after 100 per cent compaction.

It can be realised that the compacting factor test measures the inherent characteristics of the concrete which relates very close to the workability requirements of concrete and as such it is one of the good tests to depict the workability of concrete.

Flow Test

This is a laboratory test, which gives an indication of the quality of concrete with respect to consistency, cohesiveness and the proneness to segregation. In this test, a standard mass of concrete is subjected to jolting. The spread or the flow of the concrete is measured and this flow is related to workability.

Fig. 6.5 shows the details of apparatus used. It can be seen that the apparatus consists of flow table, about 76 cm. in diameter over which concentric circles are marked. A mould made from smooth metal casting in the form of a frustum of a cone is used with the following internal dimensions. The base is 25 cm. in diameter, upper surface 17 cm. in diameter, and height of the cone is 12 cm.

The table top is cleaned of all gritty material and is wetted. The mould is kept on the centre of the table, firmly held and is filled in two layers. Each layer is rodded 25 times with a tamping rod 1.6 cm in diameter and 61 cm long rounded at the lower tamping end. After

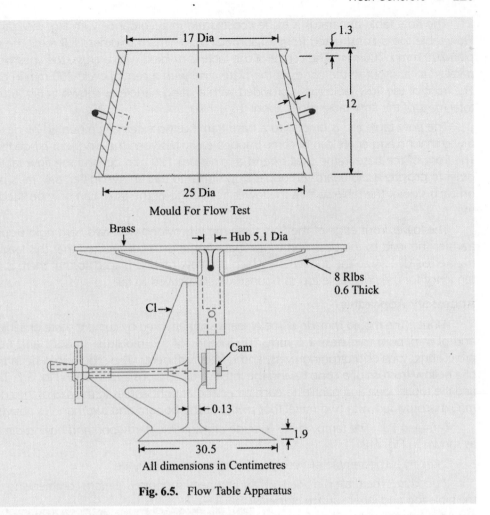

Mould For Flow Test

Fig. 6.5. Flow Table Apparatus

All dimensions in Centimetres

the top layer is rodded evenly, the excess of concrete which has overflowed the mould is removed. The mould is lifted vertically upward and the concrete stands on its own without support. The table is then raised and dropped 12.5 mm 15 times in about 15 seconds. The diameter of the spread concrete is measured in about 6 directions to the nearest 5 mm and the average spread is noted. The flow of concrete is the percentage increase in the average diameter of the spread concrete over the base diameter of the mould

$$\text{Flow, per cent} = \frac{\text{Spread diameter in cm} - 25}{25} \times 100$$

The value could range anything from 0 to 150 per cent.

A close look at the pattern of spread of concrete can also give a good indication of the characteristics of concrete such as tendency for segregation.

Flow Table Apparatus

The BIS has recently introduced another new equipment for measuring flow value of concrete. This new flow table test is in the line with BS 1881 part 105 of 1984 and DIN 1048 part I. The apparatus and method of testing is described below.

The flow table apparatus is to be constructed in accordance with Fig. 6.6. (a) and (b) Flow table top is constructed from a flat metal of minimum thickness 1.5 mm. The top is in plan 700 mm x 700 mm. The centre of the table is marked with a cross, the lines which run paralled to and out to the edges of the plate, and with a central circle 200 mm in diameter. The front of the flow table top is provided with a lifting handle as shown in Fig. 6.6 (b) The total mass of the flow table top is about 16 ± 1 kg.

The flow table top is hinged to a base frame using externally mounted hinges in such a way that no aggregate can become trapped easily between the hinges or hinged surfaces. The front of the base frame shall extend a minimum 120 mm beyond the flow table top in order to provide a top board. An upper stop similar to that shown in Fig. 6.6. (a) is provided on each side of the table so that the lower front edge of the table can only be lifted 40 ± 1 mm.

The lower front edge of the flow table top is provided with two hard rigid stops which transfer the load to the base frame. The base frame is so constructed that this load is then transferred directly to the surface on which the flow table is placed so that there is minimal tendency for the flow table top to bounce when allowed to fall.

Accessory Apparatus

Mould: The mould is made of metal readily not attacked by cement paste or liable to rust and of minimum thickness 1.5 mm. The interior of the mould is smooth and free from projections, such as protruding rivets, and is free from dents. The mould shall be in the form of a hollow frustum of a cone having the internal dimensions as shown in Fig. 6.7. The base and the top is open and parallel to each other and at right angles to the axis of the cone. The mould is provided with two metal foot pieces at the bottom and two handles above them.

Tamping Bar: The tamping bar is made of a suitable hardwood and having dimensions as shown in Fig. 6.8.

Sampling: The sample of freshly mixed concrete is obtained.

Procedure: The table is made level and properly supported. Before commencing the test, the table-top and inner surface of the mould is wiped with a damp cloth. The slump cone is placed centrally on the table. The slump cone is filled with concrete in two equal layers, each layer tamped lightly 10 times with the wooden tamping bar. After filling the mould, the concrete is struck off flush with the upper edge of the slump cone and the free area of the table-top cleaned off.

Half a minute after striking off the concrete, the cone is slowly raised vertically by the handles. After this, the table-top raised by the handle and allowed to fall 15 times in 15 seconds. The concrete spreads itself out. The diameter of the concrete spread shall

Flow Table Apparatus

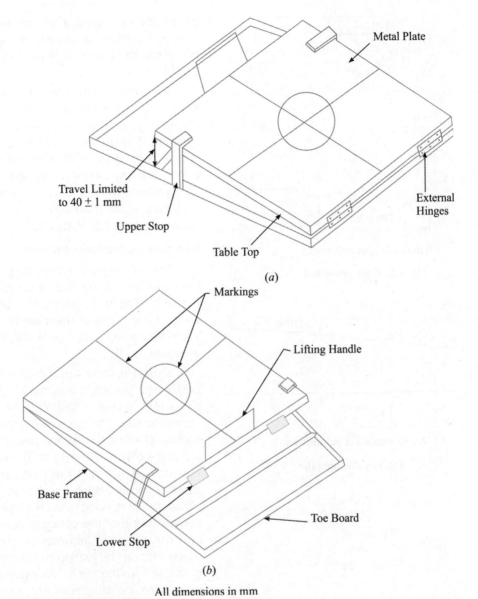

Metal Plate

Travel Limited
to 40 ± 1 mm

External
Hinges

Upper Stop

Table Top

(*a*)

Markings

Lifting Handle

Base Frame

Toe Board

Lower Stop

(*b*)

All dimensions in mm

Fig. 6.6. Flow Table Appartus (as per IS 9103 of 1999)

then be measured in two directions, parallel to the table edges. The arithmetic mean of the two diameters shall be the measurement of flow in millimeters.

Kelly Ball Test

This is a simple field test consisting of the measurement of the indentation made by 15 cm diameter metal hemisphere weighing 13.6 kg. when freely placed on fresh concrete. The test has been devised by Kelly and hence known as Kelly Ball Test. This has not been covered by Indian Standards Specification. The advantages of this test is that it can be performed on the concrete placed in site and it is claimed that this test can be performed faster with a greater precision than slump test. The disadvantages are that it requires a large sample of concrete and it cannot be used when the concrete is placed in thin section. The minimum

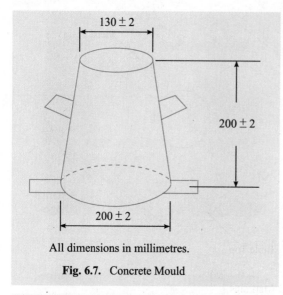

130 ± 2

200 ± 2

200 ± 2

All dimensions in millimetres.

Fig. 6.7. Concrete Mould

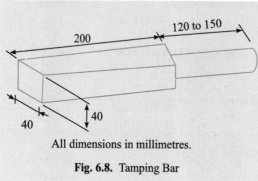

200

120 to 150

40

40

All dimensions in millimetres.

Fig. 6.8. Tamping Bar

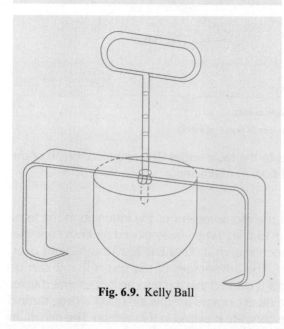

Fig. 6.9. Kelly Ball

depth of concrete must be at least 20 cm and the minimum distance from the centre of the ball to nearest edge of the concrete 23 cm.

The surface of the concrete is struck off level, avoiding excess working, the ball is lowered gradually on the surface of the concrete. The depth of penetration is read immediately on the stem to the nearest 6 mm. The test can be performed in about 15 seconds and it gives much more consistent results than Slump Test. Fig. 6.9. shows the Kelly Ball apparatus.

Vee Bee Consistometer Test

This is a good laboratory test to measure indirectly the workability of concrete. This test consists of a vibrating table, a metal pot, a sheet metal cone, a standard iron rod. The apparatus is shown in Figure. 6.10.

Slump test as described earlier is performed, placing the slump cone inside the sheet metal cylindrical pot of the consistometer. The glass disc attached to the swivel arm is turned and placed on the top of the concrete in the pot. The electrical vibrator is then switched on and simultaneously a stop watch started. The vibration is continued till such a time as the conical shape of the concrete disappears and the concrete assumes a cylindrical shape. This can be judged by observing the glass disc from the top for disappearance of transparency. Immediately when the concrete fully assumes a cylindrical shape, the stop watch is switched off. The time required for the shape of concrete to change from slump cone shape to cylindrical shape in seconds is known as Vee Bee Degree. This method is very suitable for very dry concrete whose slump value cannot be measured by Slump Test, but the vibration is too vigorous for concrete with a slump greater than about 50 mm.

Segregation

Segregation can be defined as the separation of the constituent materials of concrete. A good concrete is one in which all the ingredients are properly distributed to make a homogeneous mixture. If a sample of concrete exhibits a tendency for separation of say, coarse aggregate from the rest of the ingredients, then, that sample is said to be showing the tendency for segregation. Such concrete is not only going to be weak; lack of homogeneity is also going to induce all undesirable properties in the hardened concrete.

There are considerable differences in the sizes and specific gravities of the constituent ingredients of concrete. Therefore, it is natural that the materials show a tendency to fall apart. Segregation may be of three types — firstly, the coarse aggregate separating out or settling down from the rest of the matrix, secondly, the paste or matrix

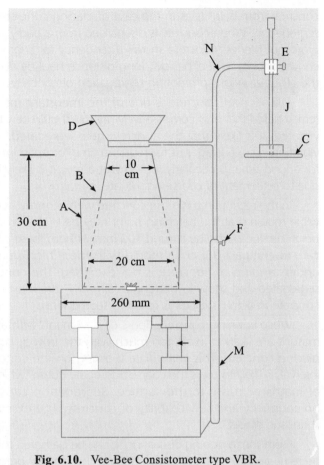

Fig. 6.10. Vee-Bee Consistometer type VBR.

Vee-Bee Consistometer

separating away from coarse aggregate and thirdly, water separating out from the rest of the material being a material of lowest specific gravity.

A well made concrete, taking into consideration various parameters such as grading, size, shape and surface texture of aggregate with optimum quantity of waters makes a cohesive mix. Such concrete will not exhibit any tendency for segregation. The cohesive and fatty characteristics of matrix do not allow the aggregate to fall apart, at the same time, the matrix itself is sufficiently contained by the aggregate. Similarly, water also does not find it easy to move out freely from the rest of the ingredients.

The conditions favourable for segregation are, as can be seen from the above para, the badly proportioned mix where sufficient matrix is not there to bind and contain the aggregates. Insufficiently mixed concrete with excess water content shows a higher tendency for segregation. Dropping of concrete from heights as in the case of placing concrete in column concreting will result in segregation. When concrete is discharged from a badly designed mixer, or from a mixer with worn out blades, concrete shows a tendency for segregation. Conveyance of concrete by conveyor belts, wheel barrow, long distance haul by dumper, long lift by skip and hoist are the other situations promoting segregation of concrete.

Vibration of concrete is one of the important methods of compaction. It should be remembered that only comparatively dry mix should be vibrated. It too wet a mix is excessively vibrated, it is likely that the concrete gets segregated. It should also be remembered that vibration is continued just for required time for optimim results. If the vibration is continued for a long time, particularly, in too wet a mix, it is likely to result in segregation of concrete due to settlement of coarse aggregate in matrix.

In the recent time we use concrete with very high slump particularly in RMC. The slump value required at the batching point may be in the order of 150 mm and at the pumping point the slump may be around 100 mm. At both these points cubes are cast. One has to take care to compact the cube mould with these high slump concrete. If sufficient care and understanding of concrete is not exercised, the concrete in the cube mould may get segregated and show low strength. Similarly care must be taken in the compaction of such concrete in actual structures to avoid segregation.

While finishing concrete floors or pavement, with a view to achieve a smooth surface, masons are likely to work too much with the trowel, float or tamping rule immediately on placing concrete. This immediate working on the concrete on placing, without any time interval, is likely to press the coarse aggregate down, which results in the movement of excess of matrix or paste to the surface. Segragation caused on this account, impairs the homogeneity and serviceability of concrete. The excess mortar at the top causes plastic shrinkage cracks.

From the foregoing discussion, it can be gathered that the tendency for segregation can be remedied by correctly proportioning the mix, by proper handling, transporting, placing, compacting and finishing. At any stage, if segregation is observed, remixing for a short time would make the concrete again homogeneous. As mentioned earlier, a cohesive mix would reduce the tendency for segregation. For this reason, use of certain workability agents and pozzolanic materials greatly help in reducing segregation. The use of air-entraining agent appreciably reduces segregation.

Segregation is difficult to measure quantitatively, but it can be easily observed at the time of concreting operation. The pattern of subsidence of concrete in slump test or the pattern of spread in the flow test gives a fair idea of the quality of concrete with respect to segregation.

Bleeding

Bleeding is sometimes referred as water gain. It is a particular form of segregation, in which some of the water from the concrete comes out to the surface of the concrete, being of the lowest specific gravity among all the ingredients of concrete. Bleeding is predominantly observed in a highly wet mix, badly proportioned and insufficiently mixed concrete. In thin members like roof slab or road slabs and when concrete is placed in sunny weather show excessive bleeding.

Due to bleeding, water comes up and accumulates at the surface. Sometimes, along with this water, certain quantity of cement also comes to the surface. When the surface is worked up with the trowel and floats, the aggregate goes down and the cement and water come up to the top surface. This formation of cement paste at the surface is known as "Laitance".

In such a case, the top surface of slabs and pavements will not have good wearing quality. This laitance formed on roads produces dust in summer and mud in rainy season. Owing to the fact that the top surface has a higher content of water and is also devoid of aggregate matter; it also develops higher shrinkage cracks. If laitance is formed on a particular lift, a plane of weakness would form and the bond with the next lift would be poor. This could be avoided by removing the laitance fully before the next lift is poured.

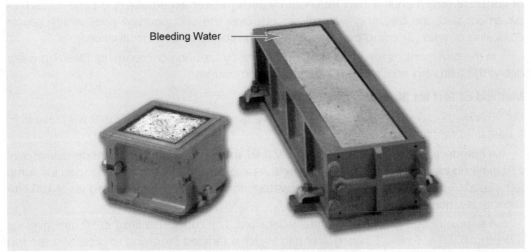

Bleeding Water ————

Example of external bleeding

Water while traversing from bottom to top, makes continuous channels. If the water cement ratio used is more than 0.7, the bleeding channels will remain continuous and unsegmented by the development of gel. This continuous bleeding channels are often responsible for causing permeability of the concrete structures.

While the mixing water is in the process of coming up, it may be intercepted by aggregates. The bleeding water is likely to accumulate below the aggregate. This accumulation of water creates water voids and reduces the bond between the aggregates and the paste. The above aspect is more pronounced in the case of flaky aggregate. Similarly, the water that accumulates below the reinforcing bars, particularly below the cranked bars, reduces the bond between the reinforcement and the concrete. The poor bond between the aggregate and the paste or the reinforcement and the paste due to bleeding can be remedied by revibration of concrete. The formation of laitance and the consequent bad effect can be reduced by delayed finishing operations.

Bleeding rate increases with time up to about one hour or so and thereafter the rate decreases but continues more or less till the final setting time of cement.

Bleeding is an inherent phenomenon in concrete. All the same, it can be reduced by proper proportioning and uniform and complete mixing. Use of finely divided pozzolanic materials reduces bleeding by creating a longer path for the water to traverse. It has been already discussed that the use of air-entraining agent is very effective in reducing the bleeding. It is also reported that the bleeding can be reduced by the use of finer cement or cement with low alkali content. Rich mixes are less susceptible to bleeding than lean mixes.

The bleeding is not completely harmful if the rate of evaporation of water from the surface is equal to the rate of bleeding. Removal of water, after it had played its role in providing workability, from the body of concrete by way of bleeding will do good to the concrete. Early bleeding when the concrete mass is fully plastic, may not cause much harm, because concrete being in a fully plastic condition at that stage, will get subsided and compacted. It is the delayed bleeding, when the concrete has lost its plasticity, that causes undue harm to the concrete. Controlled revibration may be adopted to overcome the bad effect of bleeding.

Bleeding presents a very serious problem when Slip Form Paver is used for construction of concrete pavements. If two much of bleeding water accumulates on the surface of pavement slab, the bleeding water flows out over the unsupported sides which causes collapsing of sides. Bleeding becomes a major consideration in such situations.

In the pavement construction finishing is done by texturing or brooming. Bleeding water delays the texturing and application of curing compounds.

Method of Test for Bleeding of Concrete

This method covers determination of relative quantity of mixing water that will bleed from a sample of freshly mixed concrete.

A cylindrical container of approximately 0.01 m³ capacity, having an inside diameter of 250 mm and inside height of 280 mm is used. A tamping bar similar to the one used for slump test is used. A pepette for drawing off free water from the surface, a graduated jar of 100 cm³ capacity is required for test.

A sample of freshly mixed concrete is obtained. The concrete is filled in 50 mm layer for a depth of 250 ± 3 mm (5 layers) and each layer is tamped by giving strokes, and the top surface is made smooth by trowelling.

The test specimen is weighed and the weight of the concrete is noted. Knowing the total water content in 1 m³ of concrete quantity of water in the cylindrical container is also calculated.

The cylindrical container is kept in a level surface free from vibration at a temperature of 27°C ± 2°C. it is covered with a lid. Water accumulated at the top is drawn by means of pipette at 10 minutes interval for the first 40 minutes and at 30 minutes interval subsequently till bleeding ceases. To facilitate collection of bleeding water the container may be slightly tilted. All the bleeding water collected in a jar.

$$\text{Bleeding water percentage} = \frac{\text{Total quantity of bleeding water}}{\text{Total quantity of water in the sample of concrete}} \times 100$$

Setting Time of Concrete

We have discussed about the setting time of cement in Chapter 2. Setting time of cement is found out by a standard vicat apparatus in laboratory conditions. Setting time, both initial and final indicate the quality of cement.

Setting time of concrete differs widely from setting time of cement. Setting time of concrete does not coincide with the setting time of cement with which the concrete is made. The setting time of concrete depends upon the w/c ratio, temperature conditions, type of cement, use of mineral admixture, use of plasticizers–in particular retarding plasticizer. The setting parameter of concrete is more of practical significance for site engineers than setting time of cement. When retarding plasticizers are used, the increase in setting time, the duration upto which concrete remains in plastic condition is of special interest.

The setting time of concrete is found by pentrometer test. This method of test is covered by IS 8142 of 1976 and ASTM C – 403. The procedure given below may also be applied to prepared mortar and grouts.

The apparatus consist of a container which should have minimum lateral dimension of 150 mm and minimum depth of 150 mm.

There are six penetration needles with bearing areas of 645, 323, 161, 65, 32 and 16 mm². Each needle stem is scribed circumferentially at a distance of 25 mm from the bearing area.

A device is provided to measure the force required to cause penetration of the needle.

The test procedure involves the collection of representative sample of concrete in sufficient quantity and sieve it through 4.75 mm sieve and the resulting mortar is filled in the container. Compact the mortar by rodding, tapping, rocking or by vibrating. Level the surface and keep it covered to prevent the loss of moisture. Remove bleeding water, if any, by means of pipette. Insert a needle of appropriate size, depending upon the degree of setting of the mortar in the following manner.

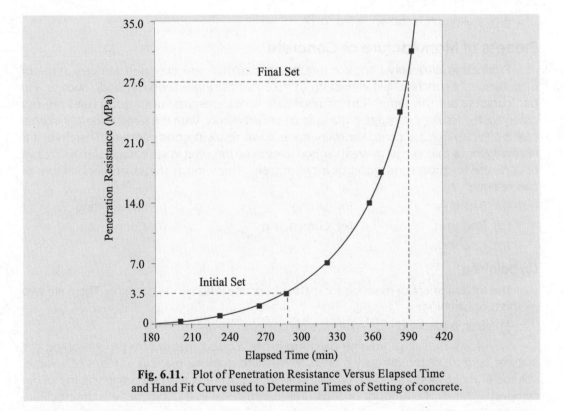

Fig. 6.11. Plot of Penetration Resistance Versus Elapsed Time and Hand Fit Curve used to Determine Times of Setting of concrete.

Bring the bearing surface of needle in contact with the mortar surface. Gradually and uniformly apply a vertical force downwards on the apparatus until the needle penetrates to a depth of 25 ± 1.5 mm, as indicated by the scribe mark. The time taken to penetrate 25 mm depth could be about 10 seconds. Record the force required to produce 25 mm penetration and the time of inserting from the time water is added to cement. Calculate the penetration resistance by dividing the recorded force by the bearing area of the needle. This is the penetration resistance. For the subsequent penetration avoid the area where the mortar has been disturbed. The clear distance should be two times the diameter of the bearing area. Needle is inserted at least 25 mm away from the wall of container.

Plot a graph of penetration resistance as ordinate and elapsed time as abscissa. Not less than six penetration resistance determination is made. Continue the tests until one penetration resistance of at least 27.6 MPa is reached. Connect the various point by a smooth curve.

Needle with different bearing area

From penetration resistance equal to 3.5 MPa, draw a horizontal line. The point of intersection of this with the smooth curve, is read on the *x*-axis which gives the initial setting time. Similarly a horizontal line is drawn from the penetration resistance of 27.6 MPa and point it cuts the smooth curve is read on the *x*-axis which gives the final set.

A typical graph is shown in Fig. 6.11

Process of Manufacture of Concrete

Production of quality concrete requires meticulous care exercised at every stage of manufacture of concrete. It is interesting to note that the ingredients of good concrete and bad concrete are the same. If meticulous care is not exercised, and good rules are not observed, the resultant concrete is going to be of bad quality. With the same material if intense care is taken to exercise control at every stage, it will result in good concrete. Therefore, it is necessary for us to know what are the good rules to be followed in each stage of manufacture of concrete for producing good quality concrete. The various stages of manufacture of concrete are:

(*a*) Batching   (*b*) Mixing   (*c*) Transporting

(*d*) Placing   (*e*) Compacting   (*f*) Curing

(*g*) Finishing.

(*a*) Batching

The measurement of materials for making concrete is known as batching. There are two methods of batching:

(*i*) Volume batching   (*ii*) Weigh batching

(*i*) Volume batching: Volume batching is not a good method for proportioning the material because of the difficulty it offers to measure granular material in terms of volume. Volume of moist sand in a loose condition weighs much less than the same volume of dry compacted sand. The amount of solid granular material in a cubic metre is an indefinite quantity. Because of this, for quality concrete material have to be measured by weight only. However, for unimportant concrete or for any small job, concrete may be batched by volume.

Cement is always measured by weight. It is never measured in volume. Generally, for each batch mix, one bag of cement is used. The volume of one bag of cement is taken as thirty five (35) litres. Gauge boxes are used for measuring the fine and coarse aggregates. The typical sketch of a guage box is shown in Figure 6.12. The volume of the box is made equal to the volume of one bag of cement *i.e.*, 35 litres or multiple thereof. The gauge boxes are

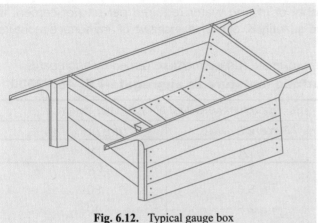

Fig. 6.12. Typical gauge box

made comparatively deeper with narrow surface rather than shallow with wider surface to facilitate easy estimation of top level. Sometimes bottomless gauge-boxes are used. This should be avoided. Correction to the effect of bulking should be made to cater for bulking of fine aggregate, when the fine aggregate is moist and volume batching is adopted.

Gauge boxes are generally called farmas. They can be made of timber or steel plates. Often in India volume batching is adopted even for large concreting operations. In a major site it is recommended to have the following gauge boxes at site to cater for change in Mix Design or bulking of sand. The volume of each gauge box is clearly marked with paint on the external surface.

Table 6.3. Volume of Various gauge boxes

Item	Width cm	Height cm	Depth cm	Volume litres	Quantity number
A	33.3	30	20	20	1
B	33.3	30	25	25	2
C	33.3	30	30	30	2
D	33.3	30	35	35	2
E	33.3	30	40	40	2
F	33.3	30	45	45	2
G	33.3	30	50	50	1

The batch volume for some of the commonly used mixes is shown in Table 6.4.

Table 6.4 Batch volume of materials for various mixes

	Cement kg.	Sand, litres	Coarse aggregate, litres
1 : 1 : 2 (M 200)	50	35	70
1 : 1 1/2 : 3 (M 200)	50	52.5	105
1 : 2 : 3	50	70	105
1 : 2 : 4 (M 150)	50	70	140
1 : 2 1/2 : 5	50	87.5	175
1 : 3 : 6 (M 100)	50	105	210

Water is measured either in kg. or litres as may be convenient. In this case, the two units are same, as the density of water is one kg. per litre. The quantity of water required is a product of water/cement ratio and the weight of cement; for a example, if the water/cement ratio of 0.5 is specified, the quantity of mixing water required per bag of cement is 0.5 x 50.00 = 25 kg. or 25 litres. The quantity is, of coarse, inclusive of any surface moisture present in the aggregate.

The following table gives the approximate surface moisture carried by aggregates

Table 6.5. Approximate Surface moisture in aggregate–I.S. 456-2000

Aggregates	Approximate Quantity of surface water	
	Percent by Mass	Litre per m³
(1)	(2)	(3)
Very wet sand	7.5	120
Moderately wet sand	5.0	80
Moist sand	2.5	40
Moist gravel or crushed rock	1.25 – 2.5	20 – 40

(ii) Weigh Batching: Strictly speaking, weigh batching is the correct method of measuring the materials. For important concrete, invariably, weigh batching system should be adopted. Use of weight system in batching, facilitates accuracy, flexibility and simplicity. Different types of weigh batchers are available, The particular type to be used, depends upon the nature of the job. Large weigh batching plants have automatic weighing equipment. The use of this automatic equipment for batching is one of sophistication and requires qualified and experienced engineers. In this, further complication will come to adjust water content to cater for the moisture content in the aggregate. In smaller works, the weighing arrangement consists of two weighing buckets, each connected through a system of levers to spring-loaded

dials which indicate the load. The weighing buckets are mounted on a central spindle about which they rotate. Thus one can be loaded while the other is being discharged into the mixer skip. A simple spring balance or the common platform weighing machines also can be used for small jobs.

On large work sites, the weigh bucket type of weighing equipments are used. This fed from a large overhead storage hopper and it discharges by gravity, straight into the mixer. The weighing is done through a lever-arm system and two interlinked beams and jockey weights. The required quantity of say, coarse aggregate is weighed,

Weigh Batcher

having only the lower beam in operation. After balancing, by turning the smaller lever, to the left of the beam, the two beams are interlinked and the fine aggregate is added until they both balance. The final balance is indicated by the pointer on the scale to the right of the beams. Discharge is through the swivel gate at the bottom.

Automatic batching plants are available in small or large capacity. In this, the operator has only to press one or two buttons to put into motion the weighing of all the different materials, the flow of each being cut off when the correct weight is reached. In their most advanced forms, automatic plants are electrically operated on a punched card system. This type of plant is particularly only suitable for the production of ready-mixed concrete in which very frequent changes in mix proportion have to be made to meet the varying requirements of different customers.

In some of the recent automatic weigh batching equipments, recorders are fitted which record graphically the weight of each material, delivered to each batch. They are meant to record, and check the actual and designed proportions.

Aggregate weighing machines require regular attention if they are to maintain their accuracy. Check calibrations should always be made by adding weights in the hopper equal to the full weight of the aggregate in the batch. The error found is adjusted from time to time.

In small jobs, cement is often not weighed; it is added in bags assuming the weight of the bag as 50 kg. In reality, though the cement bag is made of 50 kg. at the factory, due to transporation, handling at a number of places, it loses some cement, particularly, when jute bags are used. In fact, the weight of a cement bag at the site is considerably less. Sometimes, the loss of weight becomes more than 5 kg. This is one of the sources of error in volume batching and also in weigh batching, when the cement is not actually weighed. But in important major concreting jobs, cement is also actually weighed and the exact proportion as designed is maintained.

Measurement of Water: When weigh batching is adopted, the measurement of water must be done accurately. Addition of water by graduated bucket in terms of litres will not be accurate enough for the reason of spillage of water etc. It is usual to have the water measured in a horizontal tank or vertical tank fitted to the mixer. These tanks are filled up after every batch. The filling is so designed to have a control to admit any desired quantity of water. Sometimes, water-meters are fitted in the main water supply to the mixer from which the exact quantity of water can be let into the mixer.

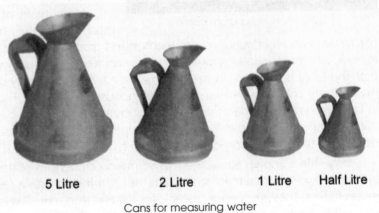

5 Litre   **2 Litre**   **1 Litre**   **Half Litre**

Cans for measuring water

In modern batching plants sophisticated automatic microprocessor controlled weigh batching arrangements, not only accurately measures the constituent materials, but also the moisture content of aggregates. Moisture content is automatically measured by sensor probes and corrective action is taken to deduct that much quantity of water contained in sand from the total quantity of water. A number of such sophisticated batching plants are working in our country. for the last 4 – 5 years.

Mixing

Thorough mixing of the materials is essential for the production of uniform concrete. The mixing should ensure that the mass becomes homogeneous, uniform in colour and consistency. There are two methods adopted for mixing concrete:

(*i*) Hand mixing   (*ii*)Machine mixing

Hand Mixing: Hand mixing is practised for small scale unimportant concrete works. As the mixing cannot be thorough and efficient, it is desirable to add 10 per cent more cement to cater for the inferior concrete produced by this method.

Hand mixing should be done over an impervious concrete or brick floor of sufficiently large size to take one bag of cement. Spread out the measured quantity of coarse aggregate and fine aggregate in alternate layers. Pour the cement on the top of it, and mix them dry by shovel, turning the mixture over and over again until uniformity of colour is achieved. This uniform mixture is spread out in thickness of about 20 cm. Water is taken in a water-can fitted with a rose-head and sprinkled over the mixture and simultaneously turned over. This operation is continued till such time a good uniform, homogeneous concrete is obtained. It is of particular importance to see that the water is not poured but it is only sprinkled. Water in small quantity should be added towards the end of the mixing to get the just required consistency. At that stage, even a small quantity of water makes difference.

Laboratory tilting drum mixer

Machine Mixing: Mixing of concrete is almost invariably carried out by machine, for reinforced concrete work and for medium or large scale mass concrete work. Machine mixing is not only efficient, but also economical, when the quantity of concrete to be produced is large.

Many types of mixers are available for mixing concrete. They can be classified as batch-mixers and continuous mixers. Batch mixers produce concrete, batch by batch with time interval, whereas continuous mixers produce concrete continuously without stoppage till such time the plant is working. In this, materials are fed continuously by screw feeders and the materials are continuously mixed and continuously discharged. This type of mixers are used in large works such as dams. In normal concrete work, it is the batch mixers that are used. Batch mixer may be of pan type or drum type. The drum type may be further classified as tilting, non-tilting, reversing or forced action type.

Very little is known about the relative mixing efficiencies of the various types of mixers, but some evidences are there to suggest that pan mixers with a revolving star of blades are more efficient. They are specially suitable for stiff and lean mixes, which present difficulties with most other types of mixers, mainly due to sticking of mortar in the drum. The shape of the drum, the angle and size of blades, the angle at which the drum is held, affect the efficiency of mixer. It is seen that tilting drum to some extent is more efficient than non-tilting drum. In non-tilting drum for discharging concrete, a chute is introduced into the drum by operating a lever. The concrete which is being mixed in the drum, falls into the inclined chute and gets discharged out. It is seen that a little more of segregation takes place, when a non-tilting mixer is used. It is observed in practice that, generally, in any type of mixer, even after thorough mixing in the drum, while it is discharged, more of coarse aggregate comes out first and at the end matrix gets discharged. It is necessary that a little bit of re-mixing is essential, after discharged from mixer, on the platform to off-set the effect of segregation caused while concrete is discharged from the mixer.

As per I.S. 1791–1985, concrete mixers are designated by a number representing its nominal mixed batch capacity in litres. The following are the standardized sizes of three types:

a. Tilting: 85 T, 100 T, 140 T, 200 T

b. Non-Tilting: 200 NT, 280 NT, 375 NT, 500 NT, 1000 NT

c. Reversing: 200 R, 280 R, 375 R, 500 R and 1000 R

The letters T, NT, R denote tilting, non-tilting and reversing respectively. Fig 6.13 illustrates diagrammatically the type of mixers.

Normally, a batch of concrete is made with ingredients corresponding to 50 kg cement. If one has a choice for indenting a mixer, one should ask for such a capacity mixer that should hold all the materials for one bag of cement. This of course, depends on the proportion of the mix. For example, for 1 : 2 : 4 mix, the ideal mixer is of 200 litres capacity, whereas if the ratio is 1 : 3 : 6, the requirement will be of 280 litres capacity to facilitate one bag mix. Mixer of 200 litres capacity is insufficient for 1 : 3 : 6 mix and also mixer of 280 litres is too big, hence uneconomical for 1 : 2 : 4 concrete.

Pan / paddle mixer   Concrete mixer with hydraulic hopper 10/7

To get better efficiency, the sequence of charging the loading skip is as under:

Firstly, about half the quantity of coarse aggregate is placed in the skip over which about half the quantity of fine aggregate is poured. On that, the full quantity of cement *i.e.*, one bag is poured over which the remaining portion of coarse aggregate and fine aggregate is deposited in sequence. This prevents spilling of cement, while discharging into the drum and also this prevents the blowing away of cement in windy weather.

Before the loaded skip is discharged to the drum, about 25 per cent of the total quantity of water required for mixing, is introduced into the mixer drum to wet the drum and to prevent any cement sticking to the blades or at the bottom of the drum. Immediately, on discharging the dry material into the drum, the remaining 75 per cent of water is added to the drum. If the mixer has got an arrangement for independent feeding of water, it is desirable that the remaining 75 per cent of water is admitted simultaneously along with the other materials. The time is counted from the moment all the materials, particularly, the complete quantity of water is fed into the drum.

When plasticizer or superplasticizer

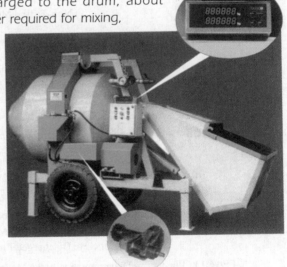

Reversible drum concrete mixer / mini batching plant

Concrete high-speed mixer in a batching plant.

is used, the usual procedure could be adopted except that about one litre of water is held back. Calculated quantity of plasticizer or superplasticizer is mixed with that one litre of water and the same is added to the mixer drum after about one minute of mixing. It is desirable that concrete is mixed little longer (say 1/2 minute more) so that the plasticizing effect is fully achieved by proper dispersion.

When plasticizers are used, generally one has to do number of trials in the laboratory for arriving at proper dosage and required slump. Small scale laboratory mixers are inefficient and do not mix the ingredients properly. Plasticizer in small quantity do not get properly dispersed with cement particles. To improve the situations, the following sequence may be adopted.

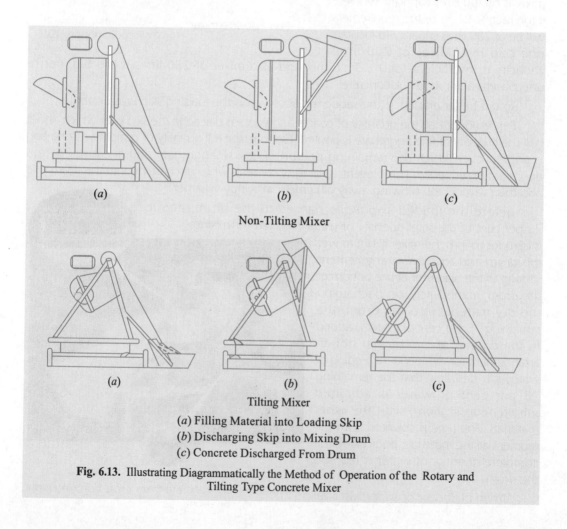

(a)   (b)   (c)

Non-Tilting Mixer

(a)   (b)   (c)

Tilting Mixer

(*a*) Filling Material into Loading Skip
(*b*) Discharging Skip into Mixing Drum
(*c*) Concrete Discharged From Drum

Fig. 6.13. Illustrating Diagrammatically the Method of Operation of the Rotary and Tilting Type Concrete Mixer

Firstly, add all the water except about half a litre. Add cement and then add sand. Make an intimate mortar mix. Dilute calculated quantity of plasticizer with the remaining half a litre of water and pour it into the drum. Rotate the drum for another half a minute, so that plasticizer gets well mixed with cement mortar and then add both the fractions (20 mm and 10 mm) of coarse aggregate. This procedure is found to give better and consistent results.

Mixing Time: Concrete mixers are generally designed to run at a speed of 15 to 20 revolutions per minute. For proper mixing, it is seen that about 25 to 30 revolutions are required in a well designed mixer. In the site, the normal tendency is to speed up the outturn of concrete by reducing the mixing time. This results in poor quality of concrete. On the other

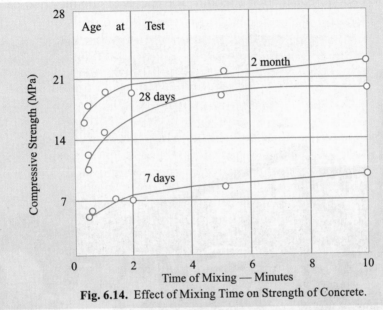

Fig. 6.14. Effect of Mixing Time on Strength of Concrete.

hand, if the concrete is mixed for a comparatively longer time, it is uneconomical from the point of view of rate of production of concrete and fuel consumption. Therefore, it is of importance to mix the concrete for such a duration which will accrue optimum benefit.

It is seen from the experiments that the quality of concrete in terms of compressive strength will increase with the increase in the time of mixing, but for mixing time beyond two minutes, the improvement in compressive strength is not very significant. Fig. 6.14. shows the effect of mixing time on strength of concrete.

Concrete mixer is not a simple apparatus. Lot of considerations have gone as input in the design of the mixer drum. The shape of drum, the number of blades, inclination of blades with respect to drum surface, the length of blades, the depth of blades, the space between the drum and the blades, the space between metal strips of blades and speed of rotation etc., are important to give uniform mixing quality and optimum time of mixing.

Generally mixing time is related to the capacity of mixer. The mixing time varies between 1° to 2° minutes. Bigger the capacity of the drum more is the mixing time. However, modern high speed pan mixer used in RMC, mixes the concrete in about 15 to 30 secs. One cubic meter capacity high speed Pan Mixer takes only about 2 minutes for batching and mixing. The batching plant takes about 12 minutes to load a transit mixer of 6 m³ capacity.

Sometimes, at a site of work concrete may not be discharged from the drum and concrete may be kept rotating in the drum for long time, as for instance when some quarrel or dispute takes place with the workers, or when unanticipated repair or modification is required to be done on the formwork and reinforcement. Long-time mixing of concrete will generally result in increase of compressive strength of concrete within limits. Due to mixing over long periods, the effective water/cement ratio gets reduced, owing to the absorption of water by aggregate and evaporation. It is also possible that the increase in strength may be due to the improvement in workability on account of excess of fines, resulting from the abrasion and attrition of coarse aggregate in the mix, and from the coarse aggregates themselves becoming rounded. The above may not be true in all conditions and in all cases. Sometimes, the evaporation of water and formation of excess fines may reduce the workability and hence bring about reduction in strength. The excess of fine may also cause greater shrinkage.

Modern ready mixed concrete plant.

In case of long haul involved in delivering ready-mixed concrete to the site of work, concrete is mixed intermittently to reduce the bad effect of continuous mixing. A pertinent point to note in this connection is that when the concrete is mixed or agitated from time to time with a short interval, the normal rule of initial setting time is not becoming applicable. The concrete that is kept in agitation, does not exactly follow the setting time rule as applicable to concrete kept in an unagitated and quiescent condition.

Retempering of Concrete

Often long hauls are involved in the following situation-delivery of concrete from central mixing plant, in road construction, in constructing lengthy tunnels, in transportation of concrete by manual labour in hilly terrain. Loss of workability and undue stiffening of concrete may take place at the time of placing on actual work site. Engineers at site, many a time, reject the concrete partially set and unduly stiffened due to the time elapsed between mixing and placing. Mixed concrete is a costly material and it can not be wasted without any regard to cost. It is required to see whether such a stiffened concrete could be used on work without undue harm. The process of remixing of concrete, if necessary, with addition of just the required quantity of water is known as "Retempering of Concrete". Sometimes, a small quantity of extra cement is also added while retempering. Many specifications do not permit retempering. I.S. 457 – 1957 did not permit retempering of partially hardened concrete or mortar requiring renewed mixing, with or without addition of cement, aggregate or water. However, many research workers are of the view that retempering with the addition of a small quantity of water may be permitted to obtain the desired slump provided the designed water/cement ratio is not exceeded. They caution that the production of concrete of excessive slump or adding water in excess of designed water cement ratio to compensate for slump loss resulting from delays in delivery or placing should be prohibited. It is seen from the investigations, retempering of concrete which is too wet a mix, at a delay of about one hour or so showed an increase in compressive strength of 2 to 15 per cent. Retempering at further delay resulted in loss of strength. However, this loss of strength is smaller than would be expected from the consideration of the total water/cement ratio i.e., the initial water cement ratio plus water added for retempering to bring the mix back into the initial degree of workability.

Maintenance of Mixer

Concrete mixers are often used continuously without stopping for several hours for continuous mixing and placing. It is of utmost importance that a mixer should not stop in between concreting operation. For this reason, concrete mixer must be kept well maintained. Mixer is placed at the site on a firm and levelled platform. The drum and blades must be kept absolutely clean at the end of concreting operation. The drum must be kept in the tilting position or kept covered when not in use to prevent the collection of rain water. The skip is operated carefully and it must rest on proper cushion such as sand bags.

Transporting Concrete

Concrete can be transported by a variety of methods and equipments. The precaution to be taken while transporting concrete is that the homogeneity obtained at the time of mixing should be maintained while being transported to the final place of deposition. The methods adopted for transportation of concrete are:

(a) Mortar Pan
(b) Wheel Barrow, Hand Cart
(c) Crane, Bucket and Rope way
(d) Truck Mixer and Dumpers
(e) Belt Conveyors
(f) Chute
(g) Skip and Hoist
(h) Tansit Mixer
(i) Pump and Pipe Line
(j) Helicoptor.

Mortar Pan: Use of mortar pan for transporation of concrete is one of the common methods adopted in this country. It is labour intensive. In this case, concrete is carried in small quantities. While this method nullifies the segregation to some extent, particularly in thick members, it suffers from the disadvantage that this method exposes greater surface area of concrete for drying conditions. This results in

Tough Rider for transporting concrete.

Truck mixer and dumper for transporting stiff concrete

greater loss of water, particularly, in hot weather concreting and under conditions of low humidity. It is to be noted that the mortar pans must be wetted to start with and it must be kept clean during the entire operation of concreting. Mortar pan method of conveyance of concrete can be adopted for concreting at the ground level, below or above the ground level without much difficulties.

Wheel Barrow: Wheel barrows are normally used for transporting concrete to be placed at ground level. This method is employed for hauling concrete for comparatively longer distance as in the case of concrete road construction. If concrete is conveyed by wheel barrow over a long distance, on rough ground, it is likely that the concrete gets segregated due to vibration. The coarse aggregates settle down to the bottom and matrix moves to the top surface. To avoid this situation, sometimes, wheel barrows are provided with pneumatic wheel to reduce vibration. A wooden plank road is also provided to reduce vibration and hence segregation.

Crane, Bucket and Rope Way: A crane and bucket is one of the right equipment for transporting concrete above ground level. Crane can handle concrete in high rise construction projects and are becoming a familiar sites in big cities. Cranes are fast and versatile to move concrete horizontally as well as vertically along the boom and allows the placement of concrete at the exact point. Cranes carry skips or buckets containing concrete. Skips have discharge door at the bottom, whereas buckets are tilted for emptying. For a medium scale job the bucket capacity may be 0.5 m³.

Rope way and bucket of various sizes are used for transporting concrete to a place, where simple method of transporting concrete is found not feasible. For the concrete works in a valley or the construction work of a pier in the river or for dam construction, this method of transporting by rope way and bucket is adopted. The mixing of concrete is done on the bank or abutment at a convenient place and the bucket is brought by a pulley or some other arrangement. It is filled up and then taken away to any point that is required. The vertical movement of the bucket is also controlled by another set of pullies. Sometimes, cable and car arrangement is also made for controlling the movement of the bucket. This is one of the methods generally adopted for concreting dam work or bridge work. Since the size of the bucket is considerably large and concrete is not exposed to sun and wind there would not be much change in the state of concrete or workability.

For discharging the concrete, the bucket may be tilted or sometimes, the concrete is made to discharge with the help of a hinged bottom. Discharge of concrete may also be through a gate system operated by compressed air. The operation of controlling the gate may be done manually or mechanically. It should be practised that concrete is discharged from the smallest height possible and should not be made to freely fall from great height.

Truck Mixer and Dumpers: For large concrete works particularly for concrete to be placed at ground level, trucks and dumpers or ordinary open steel-body tipping lorries can be used. As they can travel to any part of the work, they have much advantage over the jubilee wagons, which require rail tracks. Dumpers are of usually 2 to 3 cubic metre capacity, whereas the capacity of truck may be 4 cubic metre or more. Before loading with the concrete, the inside of the body should be just wetted with water. Tarpaulins or other covers may be provided to cover the wet concrete during transit to prevent evaporation. When the haul is long, it is advisable to use agitators which prevent segregation and stiffening. The agitators help the mixing process at a slow speed.

For road construction using Slip Form Paver large quantity of concrete is required to be supplied continuously. A number of dumpers of 6 m³ capacity are employed to supply concrete. Small dumper called Tough Riders are used for factory floor construction.

Belt Conveyors: Belt conveyors have very limited applications in concrete construction. The principal objection is the tendency of the concrete to segregate on steep inclines, at transfer points or change of direction, and at the points where the belt passes over the rollers. Another disadvantage is that the concrete is exposed over long stretches which causes drying and stiffening particularly, in hot, dry and windy weather. Segregation also takes place due to the vibration of rubber belt. It is necessary that the concrete should be remixed at the end of delivery before placing on the final position.

Modern Belt Conveyors can have adjustable reach, travelling diverter and variable speed both forward and reverse. Conveyors can place large volumes of concrete quickly where access is limited. There are portable belt conveyors used for short distances or lifts. The end discharge arrangements must be such as to prevent segregation and remove all the mortar on the return of belt. In adverse weather conditions (hot and windy) long reaches of belt must be covered.

Chute: Chutes are generally provided for transporting concrete from ground level to a lower level. The sections of chute should be made of or lined with metal and all runs shall have approximately the same slope, not flatter than 1 vertical to 2 1/2 horizontal. The lay-out is made in such a way that the concrete will slide evenly in a compact mass without any separation or segregation. The required consistency of the concrete should not be changed in order to facilitate chuting. If it becomes necessary to change the consistency the concrete mix will be completely redesigned.

Transporting and placing concrete by chute.

This is not a good method of transporting concrete. However, it is adopted, when movement of labour cannot be allowed due to lack of space or for fear of disturbance to reinforcement or other arrangements already incorporated. (Electrical conduits or switch boards etc.,).

Skip and Hoist: This is one of the widely adopted methods for transporting concrete vertically up for multistorey building construction. Employing mortar pan with the staging and human ladder for transporting

Tower Hoist and Winch, for lifting concrete to higher level.

concrete is not normally possible for more than 3 or 4 storeyed building constructions. For laying concrete in taller structures, chain hoist or platform hoist or skip hoist is adopted.

At the ground level, mixer directly feeds the skip and the skip travels up over rails upto the level where concrete is required. At that point, the skip discharges the concrete automatically or on manual operation. The quality of concrete *i.e.* the freedom from segregation will depend upon the extent of travel and rolling over the rails. If the concrete has travelled a considerable height, it is necessary that concrete on discharge is required to be turned over before being placed finally.

Transit Mixer, a popular mathod of transporting concrete over a long distance.

Transit Mixer

Transit mixer is one of the most popular equipments for transporting concrete over a long distance particularly in Ready Mixed Concrete plant (RMC). In India, today (2000 AD) there are about 35 RMC plants and a number of central batching plants are working. It is a fair estimate that there are over 600 transit mixers in operation in India. They are truck mounted having a capacity of 4 to 7 m³. There are two variations. In one, mixed concrete is transported to the site by keeping it agitated all along at a speed varying between 2 to 6 revolutions per minute. In the other category, the concrete is batched at the central batching plant and mixing is done in the truck mixer either in transit or immediately prior to discharging the concrete at site. Transit-mixing permits longer haul and is less vulnerable in case of delay. The truck mixer the speed of rotating of drum is between 4–16 revolution per minute. A limit of 300 revolutions for both agitating and mixing is laid down by ASTM C 94 or alternatively, the concretes must be placed within $1\frac{1}{2}$ of mixing. In case of transit mixing, water need not be added till such time the mixing is commenced. BS 5328 – 1991, restrict the time of 2 hours during which, cement and moist sand are allowed to remain in contact. But the above restrictions are to be on the safe side. Exceeding these limit is not going to be harmful if the mix remains sufficiently workable for full compaction.

With the development of twin fin process mixer, the transit mixers have become more efficient in mixing. In these mixers, in addition to the outer spirals, have two opposed inner spirals. The outer spirals convey the mix materials towards the bottom of the drum, while the opposed mixing spirals push the mix towards the feed opening. The repeated counter current mixing process is taking place within the mixer drum.

Sometimes a small concrete pump is also mounted on the truck carrying transit mixer. This pump, pumps the concrete discharged from transit mixer. Currently we have placer boom also as part of the truck carrying transit mixer and concrete pump and with their help concrete is transported, pumped and placed into the formwork of a structure easily.

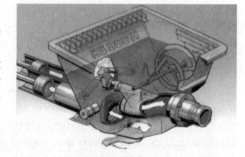

Pumping arrangements

As per estimate made by CM Doordi, the cost of transportation of concrete by transit mixer varies between Rs 160 to 180 per cubic metre.[6.2]

Pumps and Pipeline

Pumping of concrete is universally accepted as one of the main methods of concrete transportation and placing. Adoption of pumping is increasing throughout the world as pumps become more reliable and also the concrete mixes that enable the concrete to be pumped are also better understood.

Development of Concrete Pump: The first patent for a concrete pump was taken in USA in the year 1913 [6.3]. By about 1930 several countries developed and manufactured concrete pump with sliding plate valves. By about 1950s and 1960s concrete pumping became widely used method in Germany. Forty per cent of their concrete was placed by pumping. The keen rivalry between the leading German manufacturers, namely, Schwing, Putzmeister and Elba, has boosted the development of concrete pump and in particular the valve design which is

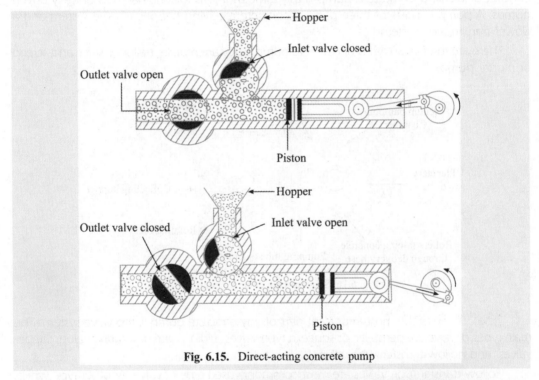

Fig. 6.15. Direct-acting concrete pump

the most important part of the whole system.

Concrete Pumps: The modern concrete pump is a sophisticated, reliable and robust machine. In the past a simple two-stroke mechanical pump consisted of a receiving hopper, an inlet and an outlet valve, a piston and a cylinder. The pump was powered by a diesel engine. The

Pump and pipeline

pumping action starts with the suction stroke drawing concrete into the cylinder as the piston moves backwards. During this operation the outlet value is closed. On the forward stroke, the inlet valve closes and the outlet valve opens to allow concrete to be pushed into the delivery pipe. Fig. 6.15 illustrates the principle.

The modern concrete pump still operates on the same principles but with lot of improvements and refinements in the whole operations. During 1963, squeeze type pump was developed in U.S.A. In this concrete placed in a collecting hopper is fed by rotating blades into a flexible pipe connected to the pumping chamber, which is under a vacuum of about 600 mm of mercury. The vacuum ensures that, except when being squeezed by roller, the pipe shape remains cylindrical and thus permits a continuous flow of concrete. Two rotating rollers progressively squeeze the flexible pipes and thus move the concrete into the delivery pipe. Fig. 6.16. shows the action of squeeze pump.

The hydraulic piston pump is the most widely used modern pump. Specification differ but concept of working of modern pump is the same as it was for original mechanically driven pumps. A pump consists of three parts, a concrete receiving happer, a valve system and a power transmission system.

There are three main types of concrete pump. They are mobile, trailor or static and screed or mortar pump.

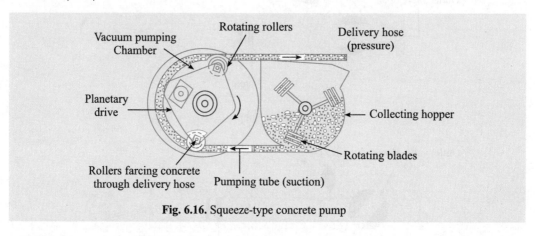

Fig. 6.16. Squeeze-type concrete pump

Types of valve: The most important part of any concrete pump is the valve system. The main types of valve are peristaltic or squeeze type valves, sliding gate or rotating value, flapper valves, and hollow transfer tube valves.

Hollow transfer tube valves are most commonly used type of valve. Another type which is used extensively is the Rock Valve. The S valve used by Putzmeister is another example of a transfer tube value.

Pipelines and couplings: It is not enough to have an efficient pump. It is equally important to have correct diameter of pipeline with adequate wall thickness for a given operating pressure and well designed coupling system for trouble free operation. A poor pipeline can easily cause blockages arising from leakage of grout. Pushing of abrasive material at high pressure, through pipeline inevitably creates a great deal of wear. Continuous handling, frequent securing and releasing of couplings creates wear at joints. All these must be maintained well for trouble free function and safety.

It is important to choose the correct diameter and wall thickness of the pipeline to match the pump and required placing rate. Generally almost all pumped concrete is conveyed through 125 mm pipeline. There are exceptions. For long, horizontal distance involving high pumping pressures, a large diameter pipe would be more suitable on account of less resistance to flow. For pumping concrete to heights, on account of the fact that gravity and the weight of concrete in the line, a smallest possible diameter of pipelines should be used.

As a guide, a pump with an output of 30 m³/h and with not more than 200 m of pipeline one may suggest 100 mm diameter, but for length in excess of 500 meter, a 150 mm diameter could be considered.

Diameter of pipeline has also bearing on the size of aggregate. General rule is that the pipe diameter should be between 3 to 4 times the largest size of aggregate. For example if maximum size of aggregate in concrete is 40 mm, the diameter of pipe could be between 120 mm to 160 mm. But use of 125 mm pipe can be considered suitable.

The individual pipe sections with lengths of 1m, 2m or 3 m are connected by means of various types of quick-locking couplings. For change in pipe line directions bends of different degrees (90 deg., 60 deg., 45 deg., 30 deg. and 15 deg.) are available. The bends have a radius of 1 m. But bends with radius of r = 250 mm are used in placing booms.

Laying the Pipeline: A carefully laid pipeline is the prerequisite for trouble free pumping operation. Time, money and trouble are saved at sites if the installation of concrete pump and the laying of pipelines are thoroughly planned and carried out with care. Leaky pipes and coupling points often results in plugs and impede the pushing of concrete on account of escape of air or water. Pipelines must be well anchored when bends are introduced.

Particular care must be taken when laying vertical line. It is difficult to dismantle individual pipe. Therefore, install only such pipes which are in good condition. Pumps should not be kept very close to the vertical pipe. There must be some starting distance. This could be about 10 to 15% of the vertical distance.

Capabilities of Concrete Pump: Concrete has been pumped to a height over 400 m and a horizontal distance of over 2000 m. This requires selected high pressure pump and special attention to concrete mix design. It is reported that in February, 1985, a record for vertical concrete pumping of 432 m was achieved at the Estangento sallente power station in the Spanish Pyrenees. A Putzmeister stationary high pressure pump with an S-transfer tube valve was used. This pump had a theoretical output of 120 m³/h, 180 mm delivery cylinder and an effective concrete pressure of over 200 bar, 630 meter of 125 mm diameter high pressure pipeline was used.

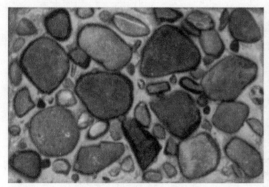

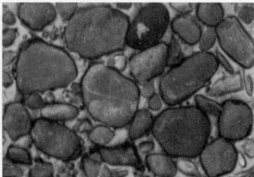

Well pumpable concrete   Badly pumpable concrete

For the above work, concrete mix consisted of 506 kg 12 – 25 mm granite aggregate, 362 kg 5 – 12 mm granite aggregate, 655 kg 0 – 5 mm granite sand, 0 – 3 mm river sand, 211 kg cement, 90 kg fly ash and 183 litre water.

Pumpable Concrete : A concrete which can be pushed through a pipeline is called a pumpable concrete. It is made in such a manner that its friction at the inner wall of the pipeline does not become very high and that it does not wedge while flowing through the pipeline. A clear understanding of what happens to concrete when it is pumped through pipeline is fundamental to any study of concrete pumping. Pumpable concrete emerging from a pipeline flows in the form of a plug which is separated from the pipe wall by a thin lubricating layer consisting of cement paste. The water in the paste is hydraulically linked with the interparticle water layer in the plug. Fig. 6.17 shows the concrete flow under pressure.

For continuous plug movement, the pressure generated by the flow resistance must not be greater than the pump pressure rating. However, if the concrete is too saturated at higher w/c ratio, the concrete at certain pump pressures may be such that water is forced out of the

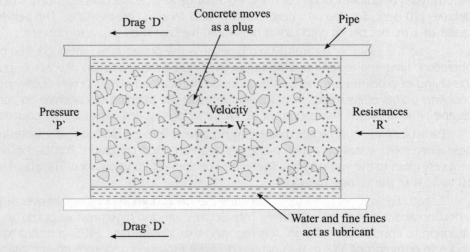

Fig. 6.17. Representation of concrete flow under pressure

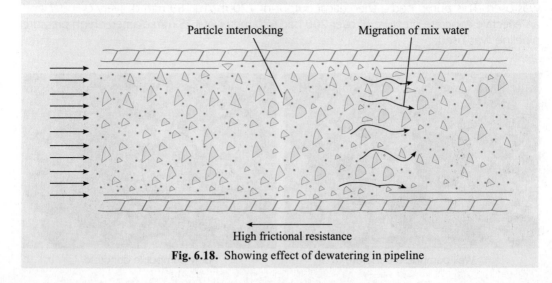

Fig. 6.18. Showing effect of dewatering in pipeline

mix, creating an increase in flow resistance and a possible blockage. Fig. 6.18 illustrates such a condition. In other words, a very stiff concrete is not pumpable and also a concrete with high w/c ratio is also not pumpable. It is interesting to note that if a concrete is pumpable, it is implied that it is a good concrete.

Design Considerations for Pumpable Concrete : The mix is proportioned in such a way that it is able to bind all the constituent materials together under pressure from the pump and thereby avoiding segregation and bleeding. The mix must also facilitate the radial movement of sufficient grout to maintain the lubricating film initially placed on the pipeline wall. The mix should also be able to deform while flowing through bends. To achieve this, the proportion of fines *i.e.,* cement and fine particles below 0.25 mm size (particles below 300 microns Appx.) is of prime importance. The quantities of fine particles between 350 to 400 kg/m³ are considered necessary for pumpable concrete. The above quantities are not only found necessary for maintaining the lubricating film, but it is important for quality and workability and to cover individual grains.

There are two main reasons why blockages occur and that the plug of concrete will not move:

- Water is being forced out of the mix creating bleeding and blockage by jamming, or
- There is too much frictional resistance due to the nature of the ingredients of the mix.

Fig. 6.19. shows the relationship between cement content and aggregate void content and excessive frictional resistance on segregation and bleeding.

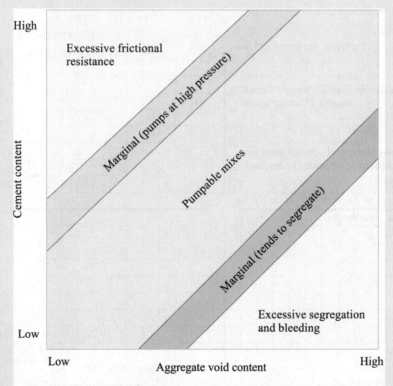

Fig. 6.19. Relationship between cement content, aggregate void content and excessive friction on segregation and bleeding

While it is important to maintain good grading and low void content, it is not always possible to design pumpable mix around ideal aggregate. Naturally occurring aggregate as well as crushed aggregates are suitable for pumpable mix, but it is essential to be aware of grading, void content and uniformity. The slump of pumpable concrete is kept at 75 mm to collapse range and the diameter of the pipeline is at least 3 – 4 times the maximum size of aggregate.

Mix Design process of pumpable concrete will be further dealt in Chapter 11under "Concrete Mix Design."

Choosing the Correct Pump

For choosing the correct pump one must know the following factors

- Length of horizontal pipe
- Length of vertical pipe
- Number of bends
- Diameter of pipeline
- Length of flexible hose
- Changes in line diameter
- Slump of Concrete.

Fig. 6.20 hows the line pressure and pumping rate as functions of line diameter, pumping distance and slump. Making use of this nomograph one can find the rated capacity of the pump. This rated capacity should be modified to actual capacity required.

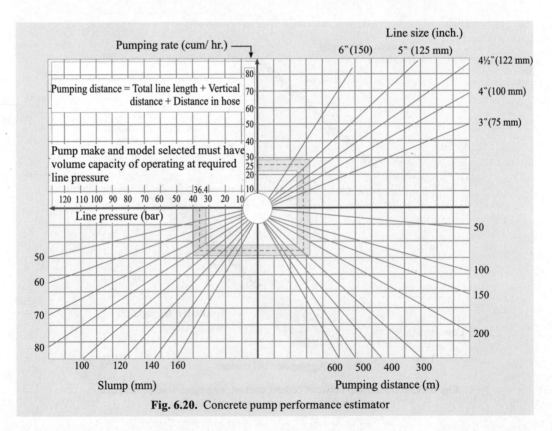

Fig. 6.20. Concrete pump performance estimator

Pressure in the pipe can be estimated using the following guidelines.

- Start up pressure required by pump = 20 bars
- Every 20 m horizontal pipeline = 1.0 bar
- Every 4 m Vertical pipeline = 1.0 bar
- Every 90° bend = 1.0 bar
- Every 45° bend = 0.5 bar
- Every pipe coupling = 0.1 bar
- Every 5 m end hose = 2.0 bar
- Safety factor = 10% extra

Example No. 1. If a trailer mounted pump kept 40 m away from the building and if it is required to pump concrete 100 m vertically, calculate pressure in the pipeline.

- Start up pressure 20 bars
- Vertical length of pipeline = 100 m

$$\therefore \text{Pressure} = \frac{100}{4} \qquad 25 \text{ bars}$$

- Horizontal length = 40 m

$$\therefore \text{Pressure} = \frac{40}{20} \qquad 2 \text{ bars}$$

- Couplings 60 Nos
  Pressure = 60 x 0.1   6 bars
- 90° bends 2 nos
  Pressure = 2 x 1   2 bars
- End Hose 5 m
  Pressure = 1 x 2   2 bars

Total Pressure	57 bars
Add 10% as safety factor	6
∴ Total Pressure	63 bars

Example No. 2. A concrete pump is placed 45 m from a building of height 50 m. The placing boom projects 4 m extra height over the building and it can reach a vertical height of another 25 m with four 90° bends and three 30° bends. The average out put required is 30 m³/h. The diameter of pipeline is 125 mm. The slump of concrete is 70 mm.

First find out the theoretical length of pipeline

The length of pipeline = 45 m + 50 m = 95 m

There are four 90° bends and three 30° bends making a total of $4 \times 90 + 3 \times 30 = 360° + 90° = 450°$.

Assuming that the bends have a radius of 1 m, 30° is equivalent to 1 m, and, therefore,

450° is equivalent to $\dfrac{450}{30} = 15$ m

The vertical reach of placing is 25 m, and the bends in the placing boom are assumed to be equivalent to 10 m.

Therefore, the theoretical length of pipeline is 95 + 15 + 25 + 10 = 145 m.

The height to which the concrete has to be pumped is 50 + 4 = 54 m

The static pressure due to vertical pumping is, therefore, 54 x 0.25 = 14 bar

Using the above data *i.e.*, corrected output, pipeline diameter, theoretical length of pipeline and slump, it is possible to arrive at the line pressure using nomograph Fig. 6.21.

On the nomograph Fig 6.21 locate 40 m³/h output. (30 m³ x 4/3 = theoretical output = 40 m³/h). Move across to the right to cut pipeline diameter (125 mm). Then move downwards to meet the theoretical length of pipeline (145 m). Now move to left to intersect the slump line (70 mm). Then move vertically up to meet the pumping pressure line. The reading at this point is shown as 35 bar (Appnox). To this should be added the static pressure of 14 bar, giving a total of 49 bar. The pump chosen, therefore, should have a rated maximum pressure of a figure in excess of 49 bar. The manufacturers will provide their recommended percentage to be added which is normally between 20 and 30%. in this case, the pump required would, therefore, have a line pressure capacity of between 60 and 70 bars.

Common Problems in Pumping Concrete: The most common problem in pumping concrete is blockage. If concrete fails to emerge at the end of pipeline, if pump is mechanically sound, it would mean that there is blockage somewhere in the system. This will be indicated by an increase in the pressure shown on the pressure gauge. Most blockages occur at tapered sections at the pump end.

Blockages take place generally due to the unsuitability of concrete mix, pipeline and joint deficiencies and operator's error or careless use of hose end.

It has been already discussed regarding the quality of pumpable concrete. A concrete of right consistency which forms a concrete plug surrounded by lubricating slurry formed inside

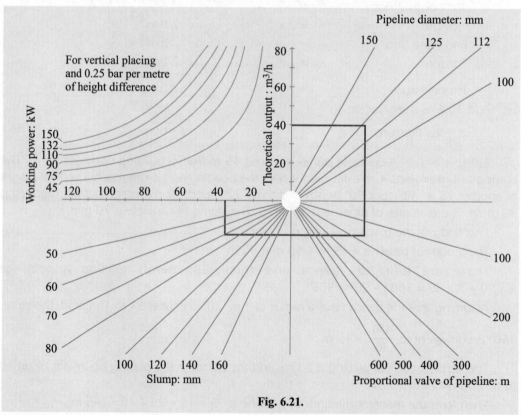

Fig. 6.21.

the wall of pipeline with right amount of water, well proportioned, homogeneously mixed concrete can only be pumped. It can be rightly said that a pumpable concrete is a good concrete.

Sometimes, high temperature, use of admixtures, particularly, accelerating admixtures and use of high grade cement may cause blockages. Chances of blockage are more if continuous pumping is not done.

A pipeline which is not well cleaned after the previous operation, uncleaned, worn-out hoses, too many and too sharp bends, use of worn out joints are also other reasons for blockages.

Operators must realise and use sufficient quantity of lubricating grout to cover the complete length of pipeline before pumping of concrete. The hose must be well lubricated. Extreme care should be taken in handling the flexible rubber end hose. Careless bending can cause blockages.

Clearing Blockages: A minor blockage may be cleared by forward and reverse pumping. Excess pressure should not be blindly exerted. If may make the problem worse.

Sometime shortening the pipeline will reduce pressure and on restarting pumping the blockage gets cleared off.

Tapping the pipeline with hammer and observing the sound one can often locate a blockage.

Blockage could be cleared by rodding or by using sponge ball pushed by compressed air or water at high pressure.

Placing Concrete

It is not enough that a concrete mix correctly designed, batched, mixed and transported, it is of utmost importance that the concrete must be placed in systematic manner to yield optimum results. The precautions to be taken and methods adopted while placing concrete in the under-mentioned situations, will be discussed.

Paving concrete by slip-forming to get sinusoidal profile for linking with the adjacent slab.

Courtesy : Wirtgen

(a) Placing concrete within earth mould.
   (example: Foundation concrete for a wall or column).

(b) Placing concrete within large earth mould or timber plank formwork.
   (example: Road slab and Airfield slab).

(c) Placing concrete in layers within timber or steel shutters.
   (example: Mass concrete in dam construction or construction of concrete abutment or pier).

(d) Placing concrete within usual from work.
   (example: Columns, beams and floors).

(e) Placing concrete under water.

Concrete is invariably laid as foundation bed below the walls or columns. Before placing the concrete in the foundation, all the loose earth must be removed from the bed. Any root of trees passing through the foundation must be cut, charred or tarred effectively to prevent its further growth and piercing the concrete at a later date. The surface of the earth, if dry, must be just made damp so that the earth does not absorb water from concrete. On the other hand if the foundation bed is too wet and rain-soaked, the water and slush must be removed completely to expose firm bed before placing concrete. If there is any seepage of water taking place into the foundation trench, effective method for diverting the flow of water must be adopted before concrete is placed in the trench or pit.

Mould with floating suspension for simultaneous castig of parapetwall.

For the construction of road slabs, airfield slabs and ground floor slabs in buildings, concrete is placed in bays. The ground surface on which the concrete is placed must be free from loose earth, pool of water and other organic matters like grass, roots, leaves etc. The earth must be properly compacted and made sufficiently damp to prevent the absorption of water from concrete. If this is not done, the bottom portion of concrete is likely to become weak. Sometimes, to prevent absorption of moisture from concrete, by the large surface of earth, in case of thin road slabs, use of polyethylene film is used in between concrete and ground. Concrete is laid in alternative bays giving enough scope for the concrete to undergo sufficient shrinkage. Provisions for contraction joints and dummy joints are given. It must be remembered that the concrete must be dumped and not poured. It is also to be ensured that concrete must be placed in just required thickness. The practice of placing concrete in a heap at one place and then dragging it should be avoided.

When concrete is laid in great thickness, as in the case of concrete raft for a high rise building or in the construction of concrete pier or abutment or in the construction of mass concrete dam, concrete is placed in layers. The thickness of layers depends upon the mode of compaction. In reinforced concrete, it is a good practice to place concrete in layers of about 15 to 30 cm thick and in mass concrete, the thickness of layer may vary anything between 35 to 45 cm. Several such layers may be placed in succession to form one lift, provided they follow one another quickly enough to avoid cold joints. The thickness of layer is limited by the method of compaction and size and frequency of vibrator used.

Before placing the concrete, the surface of the previous lift is cleaned thoroughly with water jet and scrubbing by wire brush. In case of dam, even sand blasting is also adopted. The old surface is sometimes hacked and made rough by removing all the laitance and loose material. The surface is wetted. Sometimes, a neat cement slurry or a very thin layer of rich mortar with fine sand is dashed against the old surface, and then the fresh concrete is placed.

The whole operation must be progressed and arranged in such a way that, cold joints are avoided as far as possible. When concrete is laid in layers, it is better to leave the top of the layer rough, so that the succeeding layer can have a good bond with the previous layer. Where the concrete is subjected to horizontal thrust, bond bars, bond rails or bond stones are provided to obtain a good bond between the successive layers. Of course, such arrangements are required for placing mass concrete in layers, but not for reinforced concrete.

Certain good rules should be observed while placing concrete within the formwork, as in the case of beams and columns. Firstly, it must be checked that the reinforcement is correctly tied, placed and is having appropriate cover. The joints between planks, plywoods or sheets must be properly and effectively plugged so that matrix will not escape when the concrete is vibrated. The inside of the formwork should be applied with mould releasing agents for easy stripping. Such purpose made mould releasing agents are separately available for steel or timber shuttering. The reinforcement should be clean and free from oil. Where reinforcement is placed in a congested manner, the concrete must be placed very carefully, in small quantity at a time so that it does not block the entry of subsequent concrete. The above situation often takes place in heavily reinforced concrete columns with close lateral ties, at the junction of column and beam and in deep beams. Generally, difficulties are experienced for placing concrete in the column. Often concrete is required to be poured from a greater height. When the concrete is poured from a height, against reinforcement and lateral ties, it is likely to segregate or block the space to prevent further entry of concrete. To avoid this,

Placing concrete by pump and placing boom.

concrete is directed by tremie, drop chute or by any other means to direct the concrete within the reinforcement and ties. Sometimes, when the formwork is too narrow, or reinforcement is too congested to allow the use of tremie or drop chute, a small opening in one of the sides is made and the concrete is introduced from this opening instead of pouring from the top. It is advisable that care must be taken at the stage of detailing of reinforcement for the difficulty in pouring concrete. In long span bridges the depth of prestressed concrete girders may be of the order of even 4 – 5 meters involving congested reinforcement. In such situations planning for placing concrete in one operation requires serious considerations on the part of designer.

Form work: Form work shall be designed and constructed so as to remain sufficiently rigid during placing and compaction of concrete. The joints are plugged to prevent the loss of slurry from concrete.

Stripping Time: Formwork should not be removed until the concrete has developed a strength of at least twice the stress to which concrete may be subjected at the time of removal of formwork. In special circumstances the strength development of concrete can be assessed by placing companion cubes near the structure and curing the same in the manner simulating curing conditions of structures. In normal circumstances, where ambient temperature does not fall below 15°C and where ordinary Portland cement is used and adequate curing is done, following striking period can be considered sufficient as per IS 456 of 2000.

Table 6.6. Stripping Time of Formwork

Sr. No.	Type of Formwork	Minimum period before striking formwork
1.	Vertical formwork to columns walls and beams	16 – 24 hours
2.	Soffit formwork to slabs (props to be refixed immediately after removal of formwork)	3 days
3.	Soffit formwork to beams (Props to be refixed immediately after removal of formwork)	7 days
4.	Props to slab	
	spanning up to 4.5 m	7 days
	spanning over 4.5 m	14 days
5.	Props to beam and arches	
	Spanning up to 6 m	14 days
	Spanning over 6 m	21 days

Note: For other cements and lower temperature, the stripping time recommended above may be suitably modified.

Underwater Concreting

Concrete is often required to be placed underwater or in a trench filled with the bentonite slurry. In such cases, use of bottom dump bucket or tremie pipe is made use of. In the bottom dump bucket concrete is taken through the water in a water-tight box or bucket and on reaching the final place of deposition the bottom is made to open by some mechanism and the whole concrete is dumped slowly. This method will not give a satisfactory result as certain amount of washing away of cement is bound to occur.

In some situations, dry or semi-dry mixture of cement, fine and coarse aggregate are filled in cement bags and such bagged concrete is deposited on the bed below the water. This method also does not give satisfactory concrete, as the concrete mass will be full of voids interspersed with the putricible gunny bags. The satisfactory method of placing concrete under water is by the use of tremie pipe.

The word "tremie" is derived from the french word hopper.

A tremie pipe is a pipe having a diameter of about 20 cm capable of easy coupling for increase or decrease of length. A funnel is fitted to the top end to facilitate pouring of concrete. The bottom end is closed with a plug or thick polyethylene sheet or such other material and taken below the water and made to rest at the point where the concrete is going to be placed. Since the end is blocked, no water will have entered the pipe. The concrete having a very high slump of about 15 to 20 cm is poured into the funnel. When the whole length of pipe is filled up with the concrete, the tremie pipe is lifted up and a slight jerk is given by a winch and pully arrangement. When the pipe is raised and given a jerk, due to the weight of concrete, the bottom plug falls and the concrete gets discharged. Particular care must be taken at this stage to see that the end of the tremie pipe remains inside the concrete, so that no water enters into the pipe from the bottom. In other words, the tremie pipe remains plugged at the lower end by concrete. Again concrete is poured over the funnel and when the whole length of the tremie pipe is filled with concrete, the pipe is again slightly lifted and given slight jerk. Care is taken all the time to keep the lower end of the tremie pipe well embedded in the wet concrete. The concrete in the tremie pipe gets discharged. In this way, concrete work is progressed without stopping till the concrete level comes above the water level.

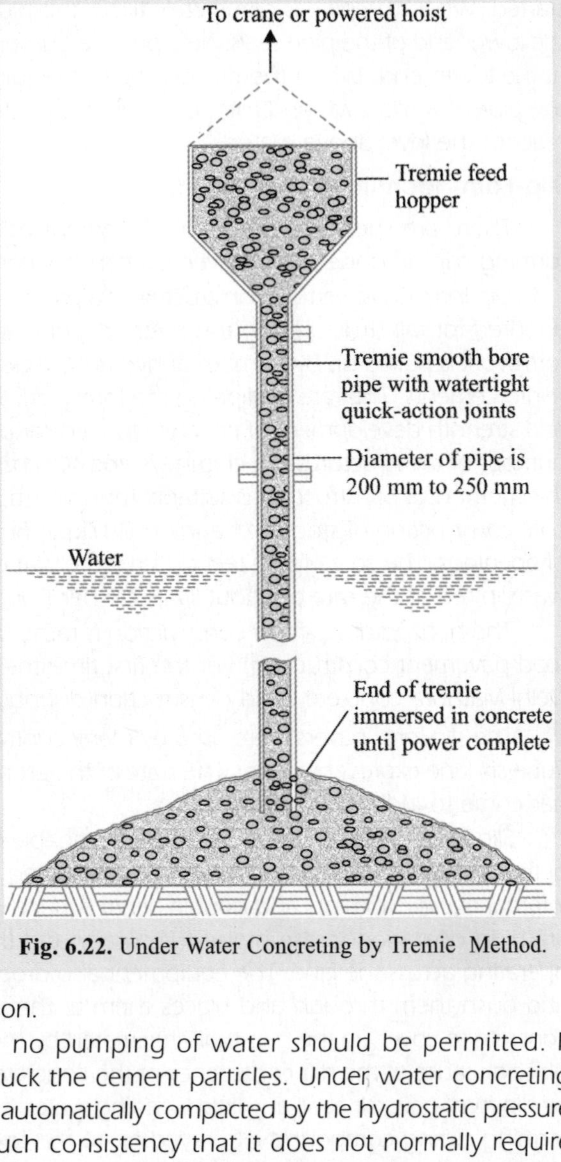

Fig. 6.22 shows the underwater concreting by tremie.

This method if executed properly, has the advantage that the concrete does not get affected by water except the top layer. The top layer is scrubbed or cut off to remove the affected concrete at the end of the whole operation.

Fig. 6.22. Under Water Concreting by Tremie Method.

During the course of concreting, no pumping of water should be permitted. If simultaneous pumping is done, it may suck the cement particles. Under water concreting need not be compacted, as concrete gets automatically compacted by the hydrostatic pressure of water. Secondly, the concrete is of such consistency that it does not normally require compaction. One of the disadvantages of under water concreting in this method is that a high water/cement ratio is required for high consistency which reduces the strength of concrete. But at present, with the use of superplasticizer, it is not a constraint. A concrete with as low a w/c ratio as 0.3 or even less can be placed by tremie method.

Another method, not so commonly employed to place concrete below water is the grouting process of prepacked aggregate. Coarse aggregate is dumped to assume full dimension of the concrete mass. Cement mortar grout is injected through pipes, which extend up to the bottom of the aggregate bed. The pipes are slowly withdrawn, as the grouting progresses. The grout forces the water out from the interstices and occupies the space. For plugging the well foundation this method is often adopted.

Concrete also can be placed under water by the use of pipes and concrete pumps. The pipeline is plugged at one end and lowered until it rests at the bottom. Pumping is then started. When the pipe is completely filled, the plug is forced out, the concrete surrounding the lower end of the pipe seals the pipe. The pumping is done against the pressure of the plug at the lower end. When the pumping effort required is too great to overcome the pressure, the pipe is withdrawn and the operation is repeated. This process is repeated until concrete reaches the level above water.

Slip-Form Technique

There are special methods of placement of concrete using slip-form technique. Slip-forming can be done both for vertical construction or horizontal construction.

Slip-forming of vertical construction is a proven method of concrete construction generally adopted for tall structures. In this method, concrete is continuously placed, compacted and formwork is pulled up by number of hydraulic Jacks, giving reaction, against jack rods or main reinforcements. The rate of slipping the formwork will vary depending upon the temperature and strength development of concrete to withstand without the support of formwork. In India number of tall structures like chimneys and silos have been built by this technique. Although this method of construction is suitable for uniform shapped structures it was adopted for the core construction of stock exchange building at Bombay having irregular shape and number of openings. The core of 380 feet tall structure was completed in about 38 days. The formwork was slipped at the rate of about 12.5 cm per hour.

The horizontal slip-form construction is rather a new technique in India. It is adopted for road pavement construction. For the first time the slip-form paving method was adopted in Delhi-Mathura concrete Road construction during mid 1990's.

The slip-form pavers were used by many contracting firms in the construction of Mumbai-Pune six lane express highway. The state-of the art method of slip form pavement construction has come to India in a big way.

Slip-form paver is a major equipment, capable of spreading the concrete dumped in front of the machine by tippers or dumpers, compacting the concrete through number of powerful internal needle vibrators and double beam surface vibrators. The paver carries out the smooth finishing operation to the highest accuracy and then texture the surface with nylon brush operating across the lane. The equipment also drops the tie bar at the predetermined interval and push them through and places them at the predetermined depth and recompact the concrete to cover up the gap that are created by the dowel bars. Generally no bleeding takes place because of the stiff consistency of the concrete (2 cm slump) that is designed for placing by slip-form paver. If at all any little bleeding water is there, upon its disappearance, membrane forming curing compound is sprayed on to the textured surface of concrete.

All the above operations are continuously carried out and the slip-form paver crawls continuously on tracked wheel, guided by laser control. Proper alignment to cater for straight line, or curve of any degree with calculated super elevation, or upward or downward gradients are controlled by laser application. Computerised laser control is the backbone of this state-of- the art slip-form paver equipment. The speed of construction *i.e.,* the speed of continuous movement of paver is around 1 meter per minute and in a day of 16 hours working, this equipment can complete about one km of one lane road of width 3.75 m and depth 35 cm.

In the Mumbai-Pune express highway construction, they have used two types of paving equipments namely wirtgen SP 500 and CMI.

They are used for lane by lane construction. Whereas in Europe and the other advanced countries, slip-form pavers capable of completing two or three lanes in one operation are used.

Placing high quality concrete by slip-form technique for a width of 8.5 m.

To feed such a paver, large quantity of concrete of uniform quality is required. In India today, the capacity of batching is a limitation. In Europe continuous batching plants which can supply consistent quality of concrete at a rate of 150 to 250 m³/hr are available. This rate will make it possible to supply extra wide slip-form paver. Sophistication in road construction has just started in India. With the experience gained, we will be able to produce large quantities of manufactured fine and coarse aggregate of right quality needed for high rate of production of concrete to meet the requirement of multi lane slip-form paver.

Compaction of Concrete

Compaction of concrete is the process adopted for expelling the entrapped air from the concrete. In the process of mixing, transporting and placing of concrete air is likely to get entrapped in the concrete. The lower the workability, higher is the amount of air entrapped. In other words, stiff concrete mix has high percentage of entrapped air and, therefore , would need higher compacting efforts than high workable mixes.

If this air is not removed fully, the concrete loses strength considerably. Fig. 6.23 shows the relationship between loss of strength and air voids left due to lack of compaction. It can be seen from the figure that 5 per cent voids reduce the strength of cocrete by about 30 per cent and 10 per cent voids redduce the strength by over 50 per cent. Therefore, it is imperative that 100 per cent compaction of concrete is one of the most important aim to be kept in mind in good concrete-making practices.

It must be borne in mind that 100 per cent compaction is important not only from the point of view of strength, but also from the point of durability. In recent time, durability becomes more important than strength.

Insufficient compaction increases the permeability of concrete resulting in easy entry for aggressive chemicals in solutin, which attack concrete and reinforcement to reduce the durability of concrete. Therefore, 100 per cent compaction of concrete is of paramount importance.

In order to achieve full compaction and maximum density, with reasonable compacting efforts available at site, it is necessary to use a mix with adequate workability. It is also of common knowledge that the mix should not be too wet for easy compaction which also reduces the strength of concrete. For maximum strength, driest possible concrete should be compacted 100 per cent. The overall economy demands 100 per cent compaction with a reasonable compacting efforts available in the field.

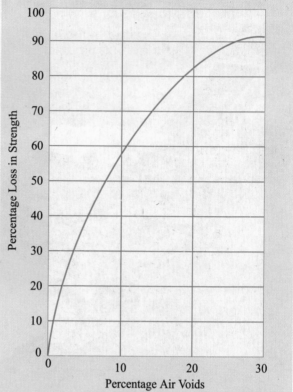

Fig. 6.23. Relationship between loss of strength and air-void space

The following methods are adopted for compacting the concrete:

(a) *Hand Compaction*
    (*i*) Rodding   (*ii*) Ramming   (*iii*) Tamping

(b) *Compaction by Vibration*
    (*i*) Internal vibrator (Needle vibrator)
    (*ii*) Formwork vibrator (External vibrator)
    (*iii*) Table vibrator
    (*iv*) Platform vibrator
    (*v*) Surface vibrator (Screed vibrator)
    (*vi*) Vibratory Roller.

(c) Compaction by Pressure and Jolting

(d) Compaction by Spinning.

Hand Compaction: Hand compaction of concrete is adopted in case of unimportant concrete work of small magnitude. Sometimes, this method is also applied in such situation, where a large quantity of reinforcement is used, which cannot be normally compacted by mechanical means. Hand compaction consists of rodding, ramming or tamping. When hand compaction is adopted, the consistency of concrete is maintained at a higher level. The thickness of the layer of concrete is limited to about 15 to 20 cm. Rodding is nothing but poking the concrete with about 2 metre long, 16 mm diameter rod to pack the concrete between the reinforcement and sharp corners and edges. Rodding is done continuously over the complete area to effectively pack the concrete and drive away entrapped air. Sometimes, instead of iron rod, bamboos or cane is also used for rodding purpose.

Ramming should be done with care. Light ramming can be permitted in unreinforced foundation concrete or in ground floor construction. Ramming should not be permitted in case of reinforced concrete or in the upper floor construction, where concrete is placed in the formwork supported on struts. If ramming is adopted in the above case the position of the reinforcement may be disturbed or the formwork may fail, particularly, if steel rammer is used.

Tamping is one of the usual methods adopted in compacting roof or floor slab or road pavements where the thickness of concrete is comparatively less and the surface to be finished smooth and level. Tamping consists of beating the top surface by wooden cross beam of section about 10 x 10 cm. Since the tamping bar is sufficiently long it not only compacts, but also levels the top surface across the entire width.

Compaction by Vibration: It is pointed out that the compaction by hand, if properly carried out on concrete with sufficient workability, gives satisfactory results, but the strength of the hand compacted concrete will be necessarily low because of higher water cement ratio required for full compaction. Where high strength is required, it is necessary that stiff concrete,

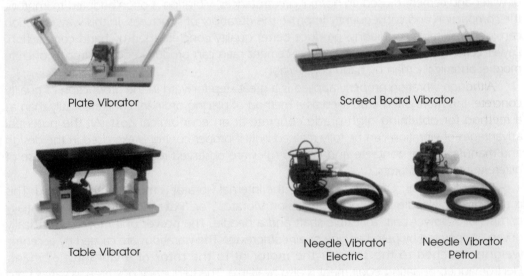

Plate Vibrator	Screed Board Vibrator
Table Vibrator	Needle Vibrator Electric — Needle Vibrator Petrol

with low water/cement ratio be used. To compact such concrete, mechanically operated vibratory equipment, must be used. The vibrated concrete with low water/cement ratio will have many advantages over the hand compacted concrete with higher water/cement ratio.

The modern high frequency vibrators make it possible to place economically concrete which is impracticable to place by hand. A concrete with about 4 cm slump can be placed and compacted fully in a closely spaced reinforced concrete work, whereas, for hand compaction, much higher consistency say about 12 cm slump may be required. The action of vibration is to set the particles of fresh concrete in motion, reducing the friction between them and affecting a temporary liquefaction of concrete which enables easy settlement.

While vibration itself does not affect the strength of concrete which is controlled by the water/cement ratio, it permits the use of less water. Concrete of higher strength and better quality can, therefore, be made with a given cement factor with less mixing water. Where only

Double Beam Screed Board Vibrator

a given strength is required, it can be obtained with leaner mixes than possible with hand compaction, making the process economical. Vibration, therefore, permits improvement in the quality of concrete and in economy.

Compaction of concrete by vibration has almost completely revolutionised the concept of concrete technology, making possible the use of low slump stiff mixes for production of high quality concrete with required strength and impermeability. The use of vibration may be essential for the production of good concrete where the congestion of the reinforcement or the inaccessibility of the concrete in the formwork is such that hand compaction methods are not practicable. Vibration may also be necessary if the available aggregates are of such poor shape and texture which would produce a concrete of poor workability unless large amount of water and cement is used. In normal circumstances, vibration is often adopted to improve the compaction and consequently improve the durability of structures. In this way, vibration can, under suitable conditions, produce better quality concrete than by hand compaction. Lower cement content and lower water-cement ratio can produce equally strong concrete more economically than by hand compaction.

Although vibration properly applied is a great step forward in the production of quality concrete, it is more often employed as a method of placing ordinary concrete easily than as a method for obtaining high grade concrete at an economical cost. All the potential advantages of vibration can be fully realised only if proper control is exercised in the design and manufacture of concrete and certain rules are observed regarding the proper use of different types of vibrators.

Internal Vibrator: Of all the vibrators, the internal vibrator is most commonly used. This is also called, "Needle Vibrator", "Immersion Vibrator", or "Poker Vibrator". This essentially consists of a power unit, a flexible shaft and a needle. The power unit may be electrically driven or operated by petrol engine or air compressor. The vibrations are caused by eccentric weights attached to the shaft or the motor or to the rotor of a vibrating element. Electromagnet, pulsating equipment is also available. The frequency of vibration varies upto 12,000 cycles of vibration per minute. The needle diameter varies from 20 mm to 75 mm and its length varies from 25 cm to 90 cm. The bigger needle is used in the construction of mass concrete dam. Sometimes, arrangements are available such that the needle can be replaced by a blade of approximately the same length. This blade facilitates vibration of members, where, due to the congested reinforcement, the needle would not go in, but this blade can effectively vibrate. They are portable and can be shifted from place to place very easily during concreting operation. They can also be used in difficult positions and situations.

Formwork Vibrator (External Vibrator): Formwork vibrators are used for concreting columns, thin walls or in the casting of precast units. The machine is clamped on to the external wall surface of the formwork. The vibration is given to the formwork so that the concrete in the vicinity of the shutter gets vibrated. This method of vibrating concrete is particularly useful and adopted where reinforcement, lateral ties and spacers interfere too much with the internal vibrator. Use of formwork vibrator will produce a good finish to the concrete surface. Since the vibration is given to the concrete indirectly through the formwork, they consume more power and the efficiency of external vibrator is lower than the efficiency of internal vibrator.

Table Vibrator: This is the special case of formwork vibrator, where the vibrator is clamped to the table. or table is mounted on springs which are vibrated transferring the vibration to the table. They are commonly used for vibrating concrete cubes. Any article kept on the table gets vibrated. This is adopted mostly in the laboratories and in making small but precise prefabricated R.C.C. members.

Vibrating Table

Platform Vibrator: Platform vibrator is nothing but a table vibrator, but it is larger in size. This is used in the manufacture of large prefabricated concrete elements such as electric poles, railway sleepers, prefabricated roofing elements etc. Sometimes, the platform vibrator is also coupled with jerking or shock giving arrangements such that a thorugh compaction is given to the concrete.

Surface Vibrator: Surface vibrators are sometimes knows as, "Screed Board Vibrators". A small vibrator placed on the screed board gives an effective method of compacting and levelling of thin concrete members, such as floor slabs, roof slabs and road surface. Mostly, floor slabs and roof slabs are

Vibrating Table

so thin that internal vibrator or any other type of vibrator cannot be easily employed. In such cases, the surface vibrator can be effectively used. In general, surface vibrators are not effective beyond about 15 cm. In the modern construction practices like vaccum dewatering technique, or slip-form paving technique, the use of screed board vibrator are common feature. In the above situations double beam screed board vibrators are often used.

Compaction by Pressure and Jolting: This is one of the effective methods of compacting very dry concrete. This method is often used for compacting hollow blocks, cavity blocks and solid concrete blocks. The stiff concrete is vibrated, pressed and also given jolts. With the combined action of the jolts vibrations and pressure, the stiff concrete gets compacted to a dense form to give good strength and volume stability. By employing great pressure, a concrete of very low water cement ratio can be compacted to yield very high strength.

Compaction by Spinning: Spinning is one of the recent methods of compaction of concrete. This method of compaction is adopted for the fabrication of concrete pipes. The plastic concrete when spun at a very high speed, gets well compacted by centrifugal force. Patented products such a "Hume Pipes", "spun pipes" are compacted by spinning process.

Vibratory Roller: One of the recent developments of compacting very dry and lean concrete is the use of Vibratory Roller. Such concrete is known as Roller Compacted Concrete. This method of concrete construction originated from Japan and spread to USA and other countries mainly for the construction of dams and pavements. Heavy roller which vibrates while rolling is used for the compaction of dry lean concrete. Such roller compacted concrete of grade M 10 has been successfully used as base course, 15 cm thick, for the Delhi-Mathura highway and Mumbai-Pune express highways.

General Points on Using Vibrators

Vibrators may be powered by any of the following units:

(a) Electric motors either driving the vibrator through flexible shaft or situated in the head of the vibrator.

(b) Internal combustion engine driving the vibrator needle through flexible shaft, and

(c) Compressed-air motor situated near the head of the vibrator.

Where reliable supplies of electricity is available the electric motor is generally the most satisfactory and economical power unit. The speed is relatively constant, and the cables supplying current are light and easily handled.

Small portable petrol engines are sometimes used for vibrating concrete. They are more easily put out of action by site conditions. They are not so reliable as the electric or compressed-air motors. They should be located conveniently near the work to be vibrated and should be properly secured to their base.

Compressed-air motors are generally quite suitable but pneumatic vibrators are sometimes difficult to manipulate where the compressor cannot be placed adjacent to the work such as on high scaffoldings or at depths below ground level due to the heavy weight of air hoses.

Compressed-air vibrators give trouble especially in cold weather, by freezing at exhaust unless alcohol is trickled into the air line or dry air is used. Glycol type antifreeze agents tend to cause gumming of the vibrator valves. There is also a tendency for moisture to collect in the motor, hence care should be taken to remove the possible damage.

The speed of both the petrol and compressed-air motors tend to vary giving rise to variation in the compacting effect of the vibrator.

Further Instructions on use of Vibrators

Care shall be taken that the vibrating head does not come into contact with hard objects like hardened concrete, steel and wood, as otherwise the impact may damage the bearings. The prime mover should as far as possible, be started only when head is raised or resting on soft support. Similar precautions shall be observed while introducing or withdrawing the vibrator in the concrete to be consolidated. When the space for introduction is narrow, the vibrator should be switched on only after the vibrator head has been introduced into the concrete. Unnecessary sharp bends in the flexible shaft drive shall be avoided.

Vibrators conforming to the requirements of IS 2505-1963 (i.e., Specification for concrete vibrators, immersion type) shall be used. The size and characteristics of the vibrator suitable for a particular job vary with the concrete mix design, quality and workability of concrete, placing conditions, size and shape of the member and shall be selected depending upon various requirements. Guidance regarding selection of a suitable vibrator may be obtained from Table 6.7.

Correct design of concrete mix and an effective control in the manufacture of concrete, right from the selection of constituent materials through its correct proportioning to its placing, are essential to obtain maximum benefits of vibration. For best results, the concrete to be vibrated shall be of the stiffest possible consistency, generally within a range of 0.75 to 0.85 compacting factor, provided the fine mortar in concrete shows at least a greasy wet appearance when the vibrator is slowly withdrawn from the concrete and the material closes over the space occupied by the vibrator needle leaving no pronounced hole. The vibration of concrete of very high workability will not increase its strength; it may on the contrary, cause segregation. Formation of a watery grout on the surface of the concrete due to vibration is an indication that the concrete is too softly made and unsuitable for vibration; a close textured layer of viscous grout may, however, be allowed.

For vibrated concrete, the formwork shall be stronger than is necessary for hand compacted concrete and greater care is exercised in its assembly. It must be designed to take up increased pressure of concrete and pressure variations caused in the neighbourhood of the vibrating head which may result in the excessive local stress on the formwork. More exact details on the possible pressures are not available and much depends upon experience, judgement and the character of work. The joints of the formwork shall be made and maintained tight and close enough to prevent the squeezing out of grout or sucking in of air during vibration. Absence of this precaution may cause honey-combing in the surface of concrete, impairing the appearance and sometimes weakening the structure.

The amount of mortar leakage or the permissible gap between sheathing boards will depend on the desired final appearance of the work but normally gaps larger than 1.5 mm between the boards should not be permitted. Sometimes even narrower joints may be objectionable from the point of view of their effect on the surface appearance of certain structures. The number of joints should be made as few as possible by making the shutter sections large. Applications of mould releasing agents on the formwork, to prevent the adhesion on concrete should be very thin as otherwise they may mix with the concrete under the effect of vibration, and cause air entrainment and blow holes on the concrete surface.

The vibrator may be used vertically, horizontally or at an angle depending upon the nature of the job. But needle vibrators should be immersed in beams and other thick sections, vertically at regular intervals. The concrete to be vibrated shall be placed in position in level layers of suitable thickness not greater than the effective length of the vibrator needle.

The concrete at the surface must be distributed as horizontally as possible, since the concrete flows in slopes while being vibrated and may segregate. The vibration shall, therefore, not be done in the neighbourhood of slopes. The internal vibrator should not be used to spread the concrete from the filling as this can cause considerable segregation of concrete. It is advisable to deposit concrete well in advance of the point of vibration. This prevents the concrete from subsiding non-uniformly and thus prevents the formation of incipient plastic cracks. When the concrete is being continuously deposited to an uniform depth along a member, vibrator shall not be operated too near the free end of the advancing concrete, usually not within 120 cm of it. Every effort must be made to keep the surface of the previously placed layer of concrete alive so that the succeeding layer can be bonded with it by the vibration process. However, if due to unforeseen circumstances the concrete has hardened in the underlying layer to such an extent that it cannot be penetrated by the vibrator but is still fresh (just after initial set) unimposed bond can be achieved between the top and underlying layers by systematically and thoroughly vibrating the new concrete into contact with old.

Height of Concrete Layer

Concrete is placed in thin layers consistent with the method being used to place and vibrate the concrete. Usually concrete shall be placed in a thickness not more than 60 cm and on initial placing in thickness not more than 15 cm. The suprimposed load increasing with the height of the layer will favour the action of the vibrator, but as it is also the path of air forced upwards, it may trap air rising up by vibration. Very deep layers (say more than 60 cm) should, therefore, be avoided although the height of layer can also be one metre provided the vibrator used is sufficiently powerful, as in dams.

Depth of Immersion of Vibrator

To be fully effective, the active part of the vibrator shall be completely immersed in the concrete. Its compacting action can be usually assisted by maintaining a head of concrete above the active part of the vibrator, the primary object of which is to press down upon and confine the concrete in the zone of influence of the vibrator. The vibrator head shall be dipped through the filling which is to be consolidated to a further depth of 10 to 20 cm in the lower layer which has already been consolidated so that there is a good combination of various layers and the grout in the lower layer is distributed in the new filling.

Spacing and Number of Insertion Positions

The points of insertion of the vibrator in the concrete shall be so spaced that the range of action overlap to some extent and the freshly filled concrete is sufficiently compacted everywhere. The range of action varies with the characteristics of the vibrator and the composition and workability of concrete. The range of action and the degree of compaction can be recognized from the rising air bubbles and the formation of a thin shining film around the vibrating head. With concrete of workability of 0.78 to 0.85 compacting factor, the vibrator shall generally be operated at points 35 to 90 cm apart. The specified spacing between the dipping positions shall be maintained uniformly throughout the surface of concrete so that the concrete is uniformly vibrated.

Speed of Insertion and Withdrawal of the Vibrating Head

The vibrating head shall be regularly and uniformly inserted in the concrete so that it penetrates of its own accord and shall be withdrawn quite slowly whilst still running so as to allow redistribution of concrete in its wake and allow the concrete to flow back into the hole behind the vibrator. The rate of withdrawal is determined by the rate at which the compaction in the active zone is completed. Usually a speed of 3 cm/s gives sufficient consolidation without undue strain on the operator. Further concrete is added as the vibrators are

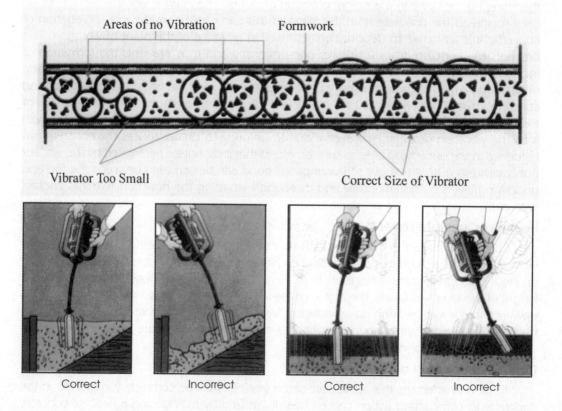

Areas of no Vibration Formwork

Vibrator Too Small Correct Size of Vibrator

Correct   Incorrect   Correct   Incorrect

withdrawn so as to maintain the head of the concrete until the lift of the concrete is completed.

Duration of Vibration

New filling shall be vibrated while the concrete is plastic, preferably within one hour. The duration of vibration in each position of insertion is dependent upon the height of the layer, the size and characteristics of the vibrator and the workability of the concrete mix. It is better to insert the vibrating head at a number of places than to leave it for a long time in one place, as in the latter case, there is a tendency for formation of mortar pocket at the point of insertion of the vibrator.

The vibrator head shall be kept in one position till the concrete within its influence is completely consolidated which will be indicated by formation of circular shaped cement grout on the surface of concrete, appearance of flattened glistening surface and cessation of the rise of entrapped air. Vibration shall be continued until the coarse aggregate particles have blended into the surface but have not disappeared.

The time required to effect complete consolidation is readily judged by the experienced vibrator operator through the feel of the vibrator, resumption of frequency of vibration after the short period of dropping off of frequency when the vibrator is first inserted. Doubt about the adequacy of vibration should always be resolved by further vibration; well proportioned concrete of the correct consistency is not readily susceptible to over-vibration.

Vibrating Concrete at Junctions with Hardened Concrete

In cases where concrete has to be joined with rock or hardened concrete, defects can occur owing to the layers nearest to the hardened concrete not being sufficiently vibrated. In such cases the procedure given below should be adopted:

The hardened concrete surface should be prepared by hacking or roughening and removing laitance, greasy matter and loose particles. The cleaned surface shall be wetted. A cement sand grout of proportion 1:1 and of creamy consistency is then applied to the wet surface of the old concrete, and the fresh concrete vibrated against it.

Vibrating the Reinforced Concrete

The reinforcement should be designed to leave sufficient space for the vibrating head. Where possible, the reinforcement may be grouped so that the width of groups of bars does not exceed 25 cm and a space of 7.5 cm exists between the groups of bars to allow the vibrator to pass freely; the space between the bars in any group may be reduced to two-thirds of the nominal size of coarse aggregate.

When the reinforcements lie very close to each other, greater care is taken in vibrating so that no pockets or collections of grout are formed. Except where some of the concrete has already set and provided that the reinforcement is adequately supported and secured, the vibrator may be pressed against the reinforcement.

Vibrating near the Formwork

For obtaining a smooth close textured external surface, the concrete should have a sufficient content of matrix. The vibrator head shall not be brought very near the formwork as this may cause formation of water whirls (stagnations), especially if the concrete containing too little of fine aggregate. On the other hand, a close textured surface may not be obtained, if the positions of insertion are too far away from the formwork. The most suitable distance of the vibrator from the formwork is 10 to 20 cm. With the vibration done at the correct depth

Table 6. 7. Characteristics and Applications of Immersion Vibrators

Sr. No.	Characteristics of Vibrator				Application
	Length of the Vibrating Needle	Diameter of the Vibrating Needle	Recommended frequency of vibration under no Load State, Min Vibration	* Recommended vibration Acceleration (operation in Air), Min	
	mm	mm	VPM	g⁺	
(1)	(2)	(3)	(4)	(5)	(6)
(i)	up to 350	up to 35	9000	30 to 50	Plastic, workable concrete in very thin members and confined places and for fabrication of laboratory test specimens. Suitable as an auxiliary to larger vibrators in prestressed work, where many cables and ducts cause congestion in the forms.
(ii)	250 to 500	Over 35 up to 60	9000	Over 30 up to 60	Plastic, workable concrete in thin walls, columns, beams, precast piles, light bridge decks, and along construction joints.
(iii)	250 to 700	Over 60 up to 75	7000	Over 60 up to 75	Plastic, workable concrete in general construction, such as walls, columns. beams, precast piles, heavy floors, bridge deck and roof slabs. Auxiliary vibration adjacent to forms mass concrete and pavements.

Table 6.7   (Contd.)

(1)	(2)	(3)	(4)	(5)	(6)
(iv)	300 to 450	Over 75 up to 90	7000	Over 75 up to 90	Mass and structural concrete deposited in increments up to 2 m^3 in heavy construction in relatively open forms, in power houses, heavy bridge piers and foundations and for auxiliary vibration in foundations and for auxiliary vibration in dam construction near forms and around embedded items and reinforcing steel.
(v)	200 to 475	Over 90	6000	Over 90	Mass concrete containing 15 cm. aggregate deposited in increments up to 8 m^3, in gravity dams, large piers, massive walls, etc. Two or more vibrators will be required to operate simultaneously to melt down and consolidate increments of concrete of 4 m^3 or greater volume deposited at one time in the forms.

* Value of acceleration measured in concrete should not be less then 75 per cent of the values given above.

† Acceleration due to gravity.

and with sufficient grout rising up at the formwork, the outside surface will generally have a close textured appearance. In the positions of formwork difficult to reach and in concrete walls less than 30 cm thick it is preferable to use vibrators of small size which can be brought to the required place and which will not excessively strain the formwork.

Vibrating High Walls and Columns

While designing the formwork, reinforcement, as well as the division of layers for high walls and columns, it should be kept in mind that with the usual driving shaft lengths it is not possible to penetrate the vibrating head more than three metres in the formwork. In the case of higher walls and columns it is recommended to introduce the shaft driven vibrating needle through a side opening into the formwork. For use with high walls and columns, the flexible driving shaft can be brought to a length of six to eight metres or even more by using adopter pieces. The motor-in-head type vibrators are more useful for the purpose in cases where a very long current cable can be used for sinking the vibrator to a greater depth.

Over-Vibration

There is a possibility of over-vibration while trying to achieve thorough vibration, but it is exceedingly unlikely in well proportioned mixes containing normal weight aggregates. Generally, with properly designed mixes, extended vibration will be only a waste of effort without any particular harm to the concrete.

However, where the concrete is too workable for the conditions of placing, or where the quantity of mortar is excess of the volume of voids in the coarse aggregate, or where the grading of the aggregate is unsatisfactory, over-vibration will encourage segregation, causing migration of the lighter and smaller constituents of the mix to the surface, thereby producing layer of mortar or laitance on the surface, and leakage of mortar through the defective joints in the formwork. This may produce concrete with poor resistance to abrasion and attack by various agencies, such as frost, or may result in planes of weakness where successive lifts are being placed. If over vibration occurs, it will be immediately evident to an experienced vibrator operator or supervisor by a frothy appearance due to the accumulation of many small air bubbles and the settlement of coarse aggregates beneath the surface. These results are more liable to occur when the concrete is too wet and the proper correction will be to reduce the workability (not the vibration), until the evidence of over-vibration disappears during the amount of vibration judged necessary to consolidate the concrete and to eliminate air-bubble blemishes.

Output of Immersion Vibrator

Output of compacted concrete may be taken as 3 to 5 cubic metre per hour depending upon the consistency of the mix for a light type of vibrator, having a centrifugal force of about 200 kg. The out-turn will be as much as 12 to 25 cubic metre per hour for a heavy type of vibrator having a centrifugal force of 450 kg.

Re-vibration

Re-vibration is delayed vibration of concrete that has already been placed and compacted. It may occur while placing successive layers of concrete, when vibrations in the upper layer of fresh concrete are transmitted to the underlaying layer which has partially hardened or may be done intentionally to achieve certain advantages.

Except in the case of exposed concrete and provided the concrete becomes plastic under vibration, re-vibration is not harmful and may be beneficial. By repeated vibration over a long period (repetition of vibration earliest after one hour from the time of initial vibration), the quality of concrete can be improved because it rearranges the aggregate particles and eliminates entrapped water from under the aggragae and reinforcing steel, with the consequence of full contact between mortar and coarse aggregate or between steel and mortar and thus produces stronger and watertight concrete. Plastic shrinkage cracks as well as other disturbances like hollow space below the reinforcement bars and below the coarse aggregate, can thereby be closed again provided the concrete becomes soft again when the vibrator head in introduced. Re-vibration of concrete results in improved compressive and bond strength, reduction of honey-comb, release of water trapped under horizontal reinforcing bars and removal of air and water pockets.

Re-vibration is most effective at the lapse of maximum time after the initial vibration, provided the concrete is sufficiently plastic to allow the vibrator to sink of its own weight into the concrete and make it momentarily plastic.

Vibration of Lightweight Concrete

In general, principles and recommended practices for consolidation of concrete of normal weight hold good for concrete made with light weight aggregate, provided certain precautions are observed.

There is always a tendency for light weight pieces of aggregate to rise to the surface of fresh concrete, particularly under the action of over-vibration; and a fairly stiff mix, with the minimum amount of vibration necessary to consolidate the concrete in the forms without honey-comb is the best insurance against undesirable segregation. The rise of lightweight coarse aggregate particles to the surface, caused by over-vibration resulting from too wet a mix makes finishing difficult if not impossible.

Curing of Concrete

We have discussed in Chapter I the hydration aspect of cement. Concrete derives its strength by the hydration of cement particles. The hydration of cement is not a momentary action but a process continuing for long time. Of cource, the rate of hydration is fast to start with, but countinues over a very long time at a decreasing rate. The quantity of the product of hydration and consequently the amount of gel formed depends upon the extent of hydration. It has been mentioned earlier that cement requires a water/cement ratio about 0.23 for hydration and a water/cement ratio of 0.15 for filling the voids in the gel pores. In other words, a water/cement ratio of about 0.38 would be required to hydrate all the particles of cement and also to occupy the space in the gel pores. Theoretically, for a concrete made and contained in a sealed container a water cement ratio of 0.38 would satisfy the requirement of

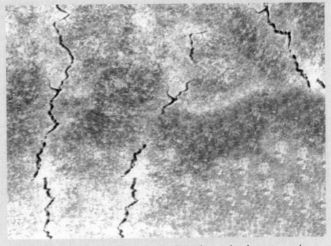

Fig.6.24. Cracks on concrete surface due to inadequate curing.

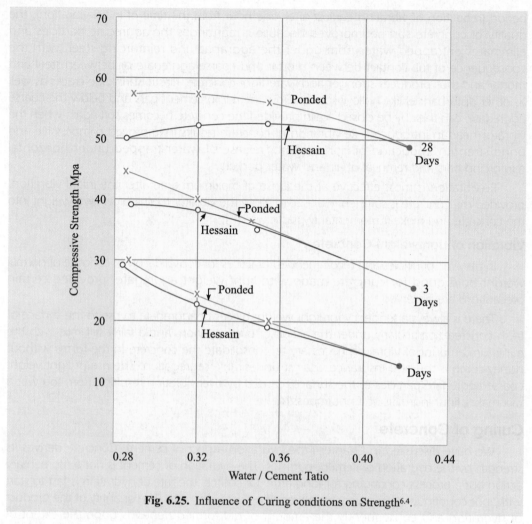

Fig. 6.25. Influence of Curing conditions on Strength[6.4].

water for hydration and at the same time no capillary vavities would be left. However, it is seen that practically a water/cement ratio of 0.5 will be required for complete hydration in a sealed container for keeping up the desirable relative humidity level.

In the field and in actual work, it is a different story. Even though a higher water/cement ratio is used, since the concrete is open to atmosphere, the water used in the concrete evaporates and the water available in the concrete will not be sufficient for effective hydration to take place particularly in the top layer. Fig. 5.33 on page 173, Chapter 5, shows the drying behaviour of concrete. If the hydration is to continue unbated, extra water must be added to replenish the loss of water on account of absorption and evaporation. Alternatively, some measures must be taken by way of provision of impervious covering or application of curing compounds to prevent the loss of water from the surface of the concrete. Therefore, the curing can be considered as creation of a favourable environment during the early period for uninterrupted hydration. The desirable conditions are, a suitable temperature and ample moisture.

Curing can also be described as keeping the concrete moist and warm enough so that the hydration of cement can continue. More elaborately, it can be described as the process of maintaining a satisfactory moisture content and a favourable temperature in concrete during the period immediately following placement, so that hydration of cement may continue until the desired properties are developed to a sufficient degree to meet the requirement of service.

Curing is being given a place of increasing importance as the demand for high quality concrete is increasing. It has been recognized that the quality of concrete shows all round improvement with efficient uninterrupted curing. If curing is neglected in the early period of hydration, the quality of concrete will experience a sort of irreparable loss. An efficient curing in the early period of hydration can be compared to a good and wholesome feeding given to a new born baby.

A concrete laid in the afternoon of a hot summer day in a dry climatic region, is apt to dry out quickly. The surface layer of concrete exposed to acute drying condition, with the combined effect of hot sun and drying wind is likely to be made up of poorly hydrated cement with inferior gel structure which does not give the desirable bond and strength characteristics. In addition, the top surface, particularly that of road or floor pavement is also subjected to a large magnitude of plastic shrinkage stresses. The dried concrete naturally being weak, cannot withstand these stresses with the result that innumerable cracks develop at the surface Fig. 6.24, shows plastic shrinkage cracks on concrete surface due to quick drying and inadequate early curing. The top surface of such hardened concrete on account of poor gel structure, suffers from lack of wearing quality and abrasion resistance. Therefore, such surfaces create mud in the rainy season and dust in summer.

The quick surface drying of concrete results in the movement of moisture from the interior to the surface. This steep moisture gradient cause high internal stresses which are also responsible for internal micro cracks in the semi-plastic concrete.

Concrete, while hydrating, releases high heat of hydration. This heat is harmful from the point of view of volume stability. If the heat generated is removed by some means, the adverse effect due to the generation of heat can be reduced. This can be done by a thorough water curing. Fig. 6.25, shows the influence of curing by ponding and wet covering.[6.4]

Curing Methods

Curing methods may be divided broadly into four categories:

(a) Water curing   (b) Membrane curing   (c) Application of heat   (d) Miscellaneous

Water Curing

This is by far the best method of curing as it satisfies all the requirements of curing, namely, promotion of hydration, elimination of shrinkage and absorption of the heat of hydration. It is pointed out that even if the membrane method is adopted, it is desirable that a certain extent of water curing is done before the concrete is covered with membranes. Water curing can be done in the following ways:

(a) Immersion   (b) Ponding

(c) Spraying or Fogging   (d) Wet covering

The precast concrete items are normally immersed in curing tanks for a certain duration. Pavement slabs, roof slab etc. are covered under water by making small ponds. Vertical retaining wall or plastered surfaces or concrete columns etc. are cured by spraying water. In some cases, wet coverings such as wet gunny bags, hessian cloth, jute matting, straw etc., are wrapped to vertical surface for keeping the concrete wet. For horizontal surfaces saw dust, earth or sand are used as wet covering to keep the concrete in wet condition for a longer time so that the concrete is not unduly dried to prevent hydration.

Membrane Curing

Sometimes, concrete works are carried out in places where there is acute shortage of water. The lavish application of water for water curing is not possible for reasons of economy. It has been pointed out earlier that curing does not mean only application of water, it means also creation of conditions for promotion of uninterrupted and progressive hydration. It is also pointed out that the quantity of water, normally mixed for making concrete is more than sufficient to hydrate the cement, provided this water is not allowed to go out from the body of concrete. For this reason, concrete could be covered with membrane

Membrane curing by spraying.

which will effectively seal off the evaporation of water from concrete. It is found that the application of membrane or a sealing compound, after a short spell of water curing for one or two days is sometimes beneficial.

Sometimes, concrete is placed in some inaccessible, difficult or far off places. The curing of such concrete cannot be properly supervised. The curing is entirely left to the workmen, who do not quite understand the importance of regular uninterrupted curing. In such cases, it is much safer to adopt membrane curing rather than to leave the responsibility of curing to workers.

Large number of sealing compounds have been developed in recent years. The idea is to obtain a continuous seal over the concrete surface by means of a firm impervious film to prevent moisture in concrete from escaping by evaporation. Sometimes, such films have been used at the interface of the ground and concrete to prevent the absorption of water by the ground from the concrete. Some of the materials, that can be used for this purpose are bituminous compounds, polyethylene or polyester film, waterproof paper, rubber compounds etc.

Bituminous compound being black in colour, absorbs heat when it is applied on the top surface of the concrete. This results in the increase of temperature in the body of concrete which is undesirable. For this purpose, other modified materials which are not black in colour are in use. Such compounds are known as "Clear Compounds". It is also suggested that a lime wash may be given over the black coating to prevent heat absorption.

Membrane curing is a good method of maintaining a satisfactory state of wetness in the body of concrete to promote continuous hydration when original water/cement ratio used is not less than 0.5. To achieve best results, membrane is applied after one or two days' of actual wet curing. Since no replenishing of water is done after the membrane has been applied it should be ensured that the membrane is of good quality and it is applied effectively. Two or three coats may be required for effective sealing of the surface to prevent the evaporation of water.

Curing vertical surface by wet covering.

Enough has been written in Chapter 5 on the modern curing compounds that are available today. Increase in volume of construction, shortage of water and need for conservation of water, increase in cost of labour and availability of effective curing compounds have encouraged the use of curing compounds in concrete construction. Curing compound is an obvious choice for curing canal lining, sloping roofs and textured surface of concrete pavements.

It is seen that there are some fear and apprehension in the mind of builders and contractors regarding the use of membrane forming curing compounds. No doubt that curing compounds are not as efficient and as ideal as water curing. The efficiency of curing compounds can be at best be 80% of water curing. But this 80% curing is done in a foolproof manner. Although water curing is ideal in theory, it is often done intermittently and hence, in reality the envisaged advantage is not there, in which case membrane curing may give better results.

For further details refer Chapter 5 where more information about curing compounds. Method for determining the efficiency of curing compounds etc., are given.

When waterproofing paper or polyethylene film are used as membrane, care must be taken to see that these are not punctured anywhere and also see whether adequate laping is given at the junction and this lap is effectively sealed.

Application of heat

The development of strength of concrete is a function of not only time but also that of temperature. When concrete is subjected to higher temperature it accelerates the hydration process resulting in faster development of strength. Concrete cannot be subjected to dry heat to accelerate the hydration process as the presence of moisture is also an essential requisite. Therefore, subjecting the concrete to higher temperature and maintaining the required wetness can be achieved by subjecting the concrete to steam curing.

A faster attainment of strength will contribute to many other advantages mentioned below.

(*a*) Concrete is vulnerable to damage only for short time.

(*b*) Concrete member can be handled very quickly.

(*c*) Less space will be sufficient in the casting yerd.

(*d*) A smaller curing tank will be sufficient.

(*e*) A higher outturn is possible for a given capital outlay.

(*f*) The work can be put on to service at a much early time,

(*g*) A fewer number of formwork will be sufficient or alternatively with the given number of formwork more outturn will be achieved.

(*h*) Prestressing bed can be released early for further casting.

From the above mentioned advantages it can be seen that steam curing will give not only economical advantages, but also technical advantages in the matter of prefabrication of concrete elements.

The exposure of concrete to higher temperature is done in the following manner:

(a) Steam curing at ordinary pressure.

(b) Steam curing at high pressure.

(c) Curing by Infra-red radiation.

(d) Electrical curing.

Steam curing at ordinary pressure

This method of curing is often adopted for pefabricated concrete elements. Application of steam curing to *in situ* construction will be a little difficult task. However, at some places it has been tried for *in situ* construction by forming a steam jacket with the help of tarpaulin or thick polyethylene sheets. But this method of application of steam for *in situ* work is found to be wasteful and the intended rate of development of strength and benefit is not really achieved.

Beam under steam curing.

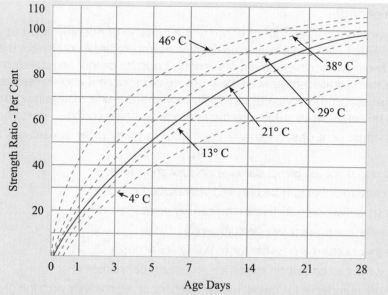

Fig. 6.26. Ratio of strength of concrete cured at different temperatures to the 28 day strength of concrete cured at 21°C (W/C Ratio = 0.50, the specimens were cast sealed, and cured at the indicated temperature).[6.5]

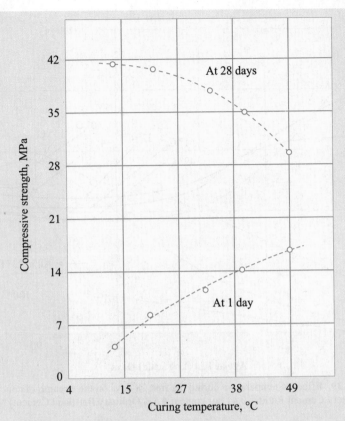

Fig. 6.27. One-day strength increases with increasing curing temperature but 28-day strength decreases with increasing curing temperature.[6.6]

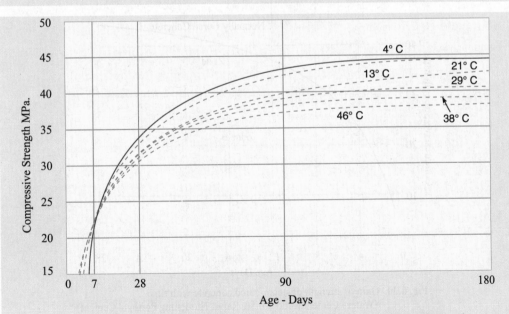

Fig. 6.28.. Effect of tempreture during the first two hours after casting on the development of strength (all specimens sealed and after 2 hours cured at 21° C.[6.5]

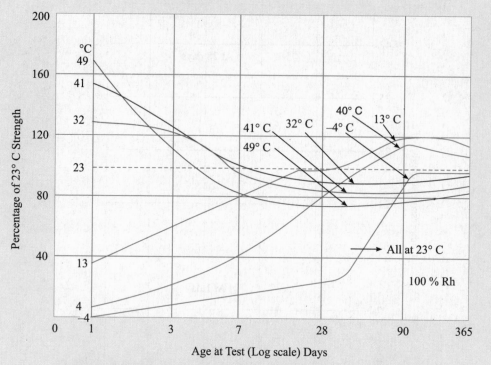

Fig. 6.29. Effect of temperature during the first 28 days on the strength of concrete Water / Cement Ratio = 0.41, air content 4.5% Ordinary Portiland Cement).[6.7]

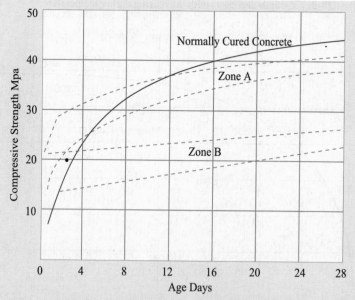

Fig. 6.30. Gain of strength of steam-cured concrete with time (Water / Cement Ratio = 0.50, Rapid-Hardening Portland Cement).

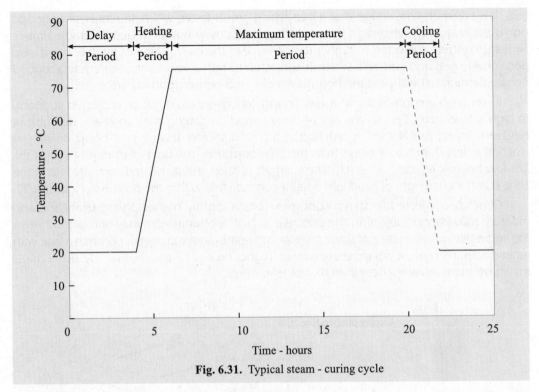

Fig. 6.31. Typical steam - curing cycle

Steam curing at ordinary pressure is applied mostly on prefabricated elements stored in a chamber. The chamber should be big enough to hold a day's production. The door is closed and steam is applied. The steam may be applied either continuously or intermittently. An accelerated hydration takes place at this higher temperature and the concrete products attain the 28 days strength of normal concrete in about 3 days.

In large prefabricated factories they have tunnel curing arrangements. The tunnel of sufficient length and size is maintained at different temperature starting from a low temperature in the beginning of the tunnel to a maximum temperature of about 90°C at the end of the tunnel. The concrete products mounted on trollies move in a very slow speed subjecting the concrete products progressively to higher and higher temperature. Alternatively, the trollies are kept stationarily at different zones for some period and finally come out of tunnel.

The influence of curing temperature on strength of concrete is shown in Fig. 6.26 and 6.28.[6.5]

It is interesting to note that concrete subjected to higher temperature at the early period of hydration is found to lose some of the strength gained at a later age. Such concrete is said to undergo "Retrogression of Strength". Figure 6.29 shows the effect of temperature on strength of concrete. It can be seen from Figure 6.29 that the concrete subjected to higher temperature at early age, no doubt attains higher strength at a shorter duration, but suffers considerable retrogression of strength. Fig. 6.29 . On the contrary, concrete cured at a comparatively lower temperature takes longer time to develop strength but the strength attained will not be lost at later ages. The phenomenon of retrogression of strength explains that faster hydration will result in the formation of poor quality gels with porous open structure, whereas the gel formed slowly but steadily at lower temperature are of good quality which are compact and dense in nature. This aspect can be compared to the growth of wood cells. It is common knowledge that a tree which grows faster, will yield timber of poor and non-durable quality, whereas a tree, which grows slowly will yield good durable timber. Similarly, concrete subjected to higher temperature in the early period of hydration will yield poor quality gels and concrete which is subjected to rather low temperature (say about 13 degree Centigrade) will yield the best quality gel, and hence good concrete.

It has been emphasized that a very young concrete should not be subjected suddenly to high temperature. Certain amount of delay period on casting the concrete is desirable. It has been found that if 49°C is reached in a period shorter than 2 to 3 hours or 99°C is reached in less than 6 to 7 hours from the time of mixing, the gain of strength beyond the first few hours is effected adversely. The strength of such rapidly heated concrete falls in the zone B and the strength of gradually heated concrete falls within the zone A in Figure. 6.30.

Concrete subjected to steam curing exhibits a slightly higher drying shrinkage and moisture movement. Subjecting the concrete to higher temperature may also slightly effect the aggregate quality in case of some artificial aggregate. Steam curing of concrete made with rapid hardening cement will generate a much higher heat of hydration. Similarly, richer mixes may have more adverse effect than that of lean mixes.

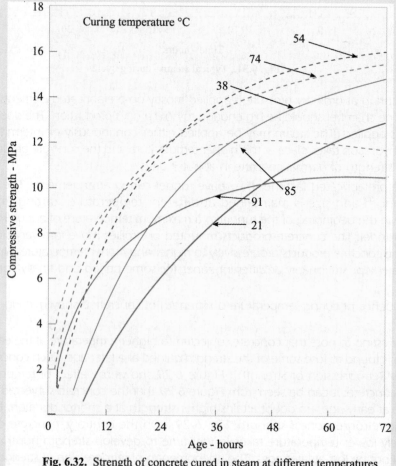

Fig. 6.32. Strength of concrete cured in steam at different temperatures
(water / cement ratio = 0.50; steam curing applied immediately after casting)[6.8]

In India, steam curing is often adopted for precast elements, specially prestressed concrete sleepers. Concrete sleepers are being introduced on the entire Indian Railway. For rapid development of strength, they use special type of cement namely IRST 40 and also subject the sleepers to steam curing.

Large number of bridges are being built for infrastructural development in India. There are requirements for casting of innumerable precast prestressed girders. These girders are steam cured for faster development of strength which has many other associated advantages.

A steam-curving cycle consists of:

- an initial delay prior to steaming,
- a period for increasing the temperature,
- a period for retaining the temperature,
- a period for decreasing the temperature.

A typical steam curing cycle at ordinary pressure is shown Fig. 6.31 and typical strength of steam cured concrete at different temperature in shown in Fig. 6.32.

High Pressure Steam Curing

In the steam curing at atmospheric pressure, the temperature of the steam is naturally below 100°C. The steam will get converted into water, thus it can be called in a way, as hot water curing. This is done in an open atmosphere.

The high pressure steam curing is something different from ordinary steam curing, in that the curing is carried out in a closed chamber. The superheated steam at high pressure and high temperature is applied on the concrete. This process is also called "Autoclaving". The autoclaving process is practised in curing precast concrete products in the factory, particularly, for the lightweight concrete products. In India, this high pressure steam curing is practised in the manufacture of cellular concrete products, such as Siporex, Celcrete etc. The following advantages are derived from high pressure steam curing process:

(a) High pressure steam cured concrete develops in one day, or less the strength as much as the 28 days' strength of normally cured concrete. The strength developed does not show retrogression.

(b) High pressure steam cured concrete exhibits higher resistance to sulphate attack, freezing and thawing action and chemical action. It also shows less efflorescence.

(c) High pressure steam cured concrete exhibits lower drying shrinkage, and moisture movement.

In high pressure steam curing, concrete is subjected to a maximum temperature of about 175°C which corresponds to a steam pressure of about 8.5 kg/sq.cm.

When the concrete is to be subjected to high pressure steam curing, it is invariably made by admixing with 20 to 30 per cent of pozzolanic material such as crushed stone dust. In case of normal curing, the liberation of $Ca(OH)_2$ is a slow process. Therefore, when pozzolanic materials are added, the pozzolanic reactivity also will be a slow process. But in case of high pressure steam curing a good amount of $Ca(OH)_2$ will be liberated in a very short time and reaction between $Ca(OH)_2$ and pozzolanic material takes place in an accelerated manner. A good amount of technical advantage is achieved by admixing the concrete with pozzolanic material.

High pressure steam curing exhibits higher strength and durability particularly in the case of cement containing a proportionately higher amount of C_3S. A sample of cement containing higher proportion of C_2S is not benefited to the same extent, as it produces lower amount of $Ca(OH)_2$

It is also observed that improvement in durability is more for the concrete made with higher water/cement ratio, than for the concrete made with low water/cement ratio.

Owing to the combination of $Ca(OH)_2$ with siliceous material within a matter of 24 hours in the case of high steam curing, concrete becomes impervious and hence durable. The fact is that the concrete in the absence of free Calcium Hydroxide becomes dense and less permeable, and also accounts for higher chemical resistance and higher strength.

The higher rate of development of strength is attributed to the higher temperature to which a concrete is subjected. Earlier it is brought out that if the concrete is subjected to very high temperature, particularly in the early period of hydration, most of the strength gained will be lost because of the formation of poor quality gel. The above is true for steam cured concrete at atmospheric pressure. The high pressure steam cured concrete does not exhibit retrogression of strength. The possible explanation is that in the case of high pressure steam curing, the quality and uniformity of pore structure formed is different. At high temperature the amorphous calcium silicates are probably converted to crystalline forms. Probably due to high pressure the frame work of the gel will become more compact and dense. This perhaps explains why the retrogression of strength does not take place in the case of high pressure steam curing.

In ordinarily cured concrete, the specific surface of the gel is estimated to be about two million sq cm per gram of cement, whereas in the case of high pressure steam cured concrete, the specific surface of gel is in the order of seventy thousand sq cm per gram. In other words, the gels are about 20 times coarser than ordinarily cured concrete. It is common knowledge, that finer material shrinks more than coarser material. Therefore, ordinary concrete made up of finer gels shrinks more than high pressure steam cured concrete made up of coarser gel. In quantitative terms, the high pressure steam cured concrete undergoes shrinkage of 1/3 to 1/6 of that of concrete cured at normal temperature. When pozzolanic material is added to the mix, the shrinkage is found to be higher, but still it shrinks only about 1/2 of the shrinkage of normally cured concrete.

Due to the absence of free calcium hydroxide no efflorescence is seen in case of high pressure steam cured concrete.

Due to the formation of coarser gel, the bond strength of concrete to the reinforcement is reduced by about 30 per cent to 50 per cent when compared with ordinary moist-cured concrete. High pressure steam cured concrete is rather brittle and whitish in colour. On the whole, high pressure steam curing produces good quality dense and durable concrete:

The concrete products as moulded with only a couple of hours delay period is subjected to maximum temperature over a period of 3 to 5 hours. This is followed by about 5 to 8 hours at this temperature. Pressure and temperature is realeased in about one hour. The detail steaming cycle depends on the plant, quality of material thickness of member etc. The length of delay period before subjecting to high pressure steam curing does not materially affect the quality of high pressure steam cured concrete.

Curing by Infra-red Radiation

Curing of concrete by Infra-red Radiation has been practised in very cold climatic regions in Russia. It is claimed that much more rapid gain of strength can be obtained than with steam curing and that rapid initial temperature does not cause a decrease in the ultimate strength as in the case of steam curing at ordinary pressure. The system is very often adopted for the curing of hollow concrete products. The normal operative temperature is kept at about 90°C.

Electrical Curing

Another method of curing concrete, which is applicable mostly to very cold climatic regions is the use of electricity. This method is not likely to find much application in ordinary climate owing to economic reasons.

Concrete can be cured electrically by passing an alternating current (Electrolysis trouble will be encountered if direct current is used) through the concrete itself between two electrodes either buried in or applied to the surface of the concrete. Care must be taken to prevent the moisture from going out leaving the concrete completely dry. As this method is not likely to be adopted in this country, for a long time to come, this aspect is not discussed in detail.

Miscellaneous Methods of Curing

Calcium chloride is used either as a surface coating or as an admixture. It has been used satisfactorily as a curing medium. Both these methods are based on the fact that calcium chloride being a salt, shows affinity for moisture. The salt, not only absorbs moisture from atmosphere but also retains it at the surface. This moisture held at the surface prevents the mixing water from evaporation and thereby keeps the concrete wet for a long time to promote hydration.

Formwork prevents escaping of moisture from the concrete, particularly, in the case of beams and columns. Keeping the formwork intact and sealing the joint with wax or any other sealing compound prevents the evaporation of moisture from the concrete. This procedure of promoting hydration, can be considered as one of the miscellaneous methods of curing.

When to Start Curing and how Long to Cure

Many a time an engineer at site wonders, how early he should start curing by way of application of water. This problem arises, particularly, in case of hot weather concreting. In an arid region, concrete placed as a road slab or roof slab gets dried up in a very short time, say within 2 hours. Often questions are asked whether water can be poured over the above concrete within two hours to prevent the drying. The associated problem is, if water is applied within say two hours, whether it will interfere with the water/cement ratio and cause harmful effects. In other words, question is how early water can be applied over concrete surface so that uninterrupted and continued hydration takes place, without causing interference with the water/cement ratio. The answer is that first of all, concrete should not be allowed to dry fast in any situation. Concrete that are liable to quick drying is required to be covered with wet gunny bag or wet hessian cloth properly squeezed, so that the water does not drip and at the same time, does not allow the concrete to dry. This condition should be maintained for 24 hours or at least till the final setting time of cement at which duration the concrete will have assumed the final volume. Even if water is poured, after this time, it is not going to interfere with the water/cement ratio. However, the best practice is to keep the concrete under the wet gunny bag for 24 hours and then commence water curing by way of ponding or spraying. Of course, when curing compound is used immediately after bleeding water, if any, dries up, the question of when to start water curing does not arise at all.

There is a wrong notion with common builders that commencement of curing should be done only on the following day after concreting. Even on the next day they make arrangements and build bunds with mud or lean mortar to retain water. This further delays the curing. Such practice is followed for concrete road construction by municipal corporations also. It is a bad practice. It is difficult to set time frame how early water curing can be started. It depends on, prevailing temperature, humidity, wind velocity, type of cement, fineness of cement, w/c used and size of member etc. The point to observe is that, the top surface of concrete should not be allowed to dry. Enough moisture must be present to promote hydration. To satisfy the above conditions any practical steps can be undertaken, including the application of fine spray or fogging without disturbing surface finish. Such measures may be taken as early as two hours after casting. It is pointed out that early curing is important for 53 grade cement.

Incidentally, it is seen that test cubes cast at site are allowed to dry without covering the top with wet covering. They are allowed to dry in the hot sun. Such cubes develop cracks and show low strength when crushed. It is usual that they complain about poor quality of cement or concrete.

Regarding how long to cure, it is again difficult to set a limit. Since all the desirable properties of concrete are improved by curing, the curing period should be as long as practical. For general guidance, concrete must be cured till it attains about 70% of specified strength. At lower temperature curing period must be increased.

Since the rate of hydration is influenced by cement composition and fineness, the curing period should be prolonged for concretes made with cements of slow strength gain characteristics. Pozzolanic cement or concrete admixed with pozzolanic material is required to be cured for longer duration. Mass concrete, heavy footings, large piers, abutments, should be cured for at least 2 weeks.

Finishing of road pavement

To assertain the period of curing or stripping of formwork, cubes or beams are cast and kept adjacent to the structure they represent and cured by the same method. The strength of these cubes or beams at different intervals of time would give better idea about the strength development of structures. The above method does not truly indicate the strength development of massive girder subjected to steam curing because of size difference of cubes and girders.

Finishing

Finishing operation is the last operation in making concrete. Finishing in real sence does not apply to all concrete operations. For a beam concreting, finishing may not be applicable, whereas for the concrete road pavement, airfield pavement or for the flooring of a domestic building, careful finishing is of great importance. Concrete is often dubbed as a drab material, incapable of offering pleasant architectural appearance and finish. This shortcoming of concrete is being rectified and concretes these days are made to exhibit pleasant surface finishes. Particularly, many types of prefabricated concrete panels used as floor slab or wall unit are made in such a way as to give very attractive architectural affect. Even concrete claddings are made to give attractive look.

In recent years there has been a growing tendency to develop and use various surface treatments which permit concrete structures to proudly proclaim its nature instead of covering itself with an expensive veneer. The property of concrete to reproduce form markings such as board mark finishes, use of linings or special types of formworks, special techniques for the application of applied finishes have been encouraged. Surface finishes may be grouped as under:

(a) Formwork Finishes   (b) Surface Treatment
(c) Applied Finishes.

Formwork Finishes

Concrete obeys the shape of formwork *i.e.,* centering work. By judiciously assembling the formwork either in plane surface or in undulated fashion or having the joints in a particular "V" shaped manner to get regular fins or groves, a pleasing surface finish can be given to concrete. The architect's imaginations can be fully exploited to give many varieties of look to the concrete surface. The use of small battens can give a good look to the concrete surface.

A pre-fabricated wall unit cast between steel formwork having very smooth surface using right proportioning of materials can give such a nice surface which can never be obtained by the best masons. Similarly, the prefabricated floor units can have such a fine finish at the ceiling which cannot be obtained by the best masons with the best efforts. These days with the cost of labour going up, attention is naturally directed to the self-finishing of the concrete surface,

Mechanical trowel for finishing factory floor.
Sometimes surface hardener is sprinkled and finished.

particularly, for floor slabs, by the use of good formwork material such as steel sheets or shuttering type plywood.

Surface Treatment

This is one of the widely used methods for surface finishing. The concrete pavement slab is required to be plane but rough to exhibit skid resistance, so is the air-field pavements and road slabs. Concrete having been brought to the plane level surface, is raked lightly or broomed or textured or scratched to make the surface rough.

A domestic floor slab is required to be smooth, wear resisting and crack-free. The technique of finishing the concrete floor requires very careful considerations. The proportioning of the mix must be appropriate without excess or deficient of matrix. Water/cement ratio should be such that it provides the just required consistency to facilitate spreading and good levelling, yet to give no bleeding. Surface must be finished at the same rate as the placing of concrete. Particular care must be taken to the extent and time of trowelling. Use of wooden float is better to start with but at the end steel trowel may be used. In all the operation, care must be taken to see that no laitance is formed and no excessive mortar or water accumulates on the surface of the floor, which reduces the wear resistance of the floor. The excess of mortar at the surface causes craziness due to increased shrinkage. Achieving a good surface finish to a concrete floor requires considerable experience and devotion on the part of the mason. A hurried completion of surface operation will make a poor surface.

Often concrete is placed at a much faster rate than the speed of finish by the masons with the result that concrete dries up and mason is not able to bring the concrete to a good level. He resorts to applying extra rich mortar to bring the floor surface to good level. This practice of applying rich mortar spcecially made to the surface is not desirable. This practice, firstly reduces the bond. Secondly, reduces the strength and wear resistance than the homogeneous concrete. Thirdly, mortar shrinks more than that of concrete. Therefore, application of a thick layer of mortar over set concrete is objectionable. It is a good practice to the finish the floor with the matrix that comes to the top of the concrete due to the compaction of concrete and by working with mason's tamping rule. In case the above is not possible, use of extra mortar may be permitted to avoid very poor surface finish. But it is necessary to observe the following precautions:

Exposed aggregate finish

(a) The mortar composition be the same as that of concrete.

(b) It should be applied as thin a layer as possible before the base concrete is hardened, and rubbed smooth.

(c) Sprinkling of dry cement in good quantity is not a good practice, however a small quantity may be permitted to reduce the bad effect of bleeding, taking care to see that it does not make the top layer too rich.

Exposed Aggregate-Finish: This is one of the methods of giving good look to the concrete surface. The beauty can be further enhanced by the use of coloured pebbles or quartz. One or two days after casting, the matrix is removed by washing the surface with water or by slight brushing and washing. One face of the aggregate particles will adhere to the matrix and the other face gets exposed. This exposed surface will give a pleasing look. Sometimes, retarding agent is applied to the formwork surface. The matrix at the surface being in contact with the retarding agent, does not get hardened, whereas rest of the portion gets hardened. On washing or light brushing, the unhardened matrix gets washed out, exposing the aggregate.

Applied finish work done at CME

Sometimes use of hydrochloric acid solution made up of one part of acid to six parts of water is used for washing the concrete surface to expose the aggregate. The acid attacks the cement and enables it to be brushed off. Care must be taken that the workman should use rubber-gloves and on completion of washing by the acid, the surface should be treated with alkaline solution to neutralise any remaining acid. This method of using acid should not be applied for concrete made with limestone aggregate.

Bush Hammering: A Bush Hammer is a tool with a series of pyramidal teeth on its face. They may be hand operated or pneumatically or electrically operated. Hand tools are suitable for small jobs but power operated equipment is used for large surface.

Bush Hammer gives rapid blows to the concrete surface and not only removes the outer cement film but also breaks some of the exposed aggregate giving a bright, colourful and attractive surface. Very pleasant effects may be obtained by carefully arranging large aggregates at the surface and later removing the matrix by bush hammer.

Concrete should be at least three weaks old, before it is bush hammered. Otherwise, there is a danger of whole pieces of aggregates being dislodged. The quality of concrete which is to be treated this way by bush hammering must be of high quality and good workmanship.

Applied Finish: The term applied finish is used to denote the application of rendering to the exteriors of concrete structures. The concrete surface is cleaned and roughned and kept wet for sufficiently long time. Over this a mortar of proportion of about 1:3 is applied. This mortar rendering can be given any required pleasant finish, such as cement stippling either fine or coarse, combed finish, keying, renderings etc.

Sometimes this rendering applied on wall is pressed with sponge. The sponge absorbs cement and water exposes sand particles. The sponge is washed and again rubbed against the surface. With the repetition of this process, the surface gets a finish, known as "Sand Facing".

A wet plastic mix of three parts of cement, , one part of lime, six parts of sand and 4 parts of about 5 mm size peagravel aggregate is thrown against wall surface by means of a scoop or plasterer's trowel. This finish is known as "Rough Cast Finish".

Upon a 10 mm thick coat of one part of cement, one part of lime and five parts of sand, while it is still plastic, is thrown about 6 mm size selected well-washed pebbles. This kind of finish is known as "Pebble Dash".

The latest method of finish given to the concrete surface is known as "Fair Crete" finish. This rendering can be given to the concrete *in situ* or better still to the concrete panels. Such panels are used as cladding to the concrete structures.

Fair crete is nothing but a highly air-entrained mortar (air-entrainment is to be extent of 25 per cent) mixed with chopped jute fibre. This mortar is spread and pressed by a mould having different designs. The impression of the mould is translated into the mortar. Air entrained mortar being foamy in nature takes the impression of the mould. A wide variety of designs and murals can be translated to the air entrained mortar surface. The jute fibre increases the tensile strength of the fair crete.

Miscellaneous Finishes: Non-slip Finish: Surface of ramps, railway platforms, surroundings of swimming pools etc., are required to posses a highly nonslip texture. To obtain this quality, an abrasive grit is sprinkled over the surface during the floating operations. The surface is lightly floated just to embed the abrasive grit at the surface. Sometimes, epoxy screed is also given to the surface over which silica sand is sprinkled while the epoxy is still wet.

Coloured Finish: Principal materials used for colouring concrete are:

(a) Pigment admixtures   (b) Chemical stains
(c) Paints   (d) White cement   (e) Coloured concrete.

Pigment admixtures may be added integrally to the topping mix, blended with the dry cement, or pigments may be dusted on to the topping immediately on application of screed. Of all the methods, mixing integrally with the mortar is the best method, next to using coloured cements. Sometimes, certain chemicals are used to give desirable colour to the concrete surface. Similarly, cement based paints or other colour paints are also used.

White cement is used in different ways to give different look to the concrete. White and coloured cements have been used as toppings in factory floor finish.

Recently RMC (India), a Ready Mix Concrete supplying company, have started supplying Ready Mixed coloured concrete in various colours. They incorporate certain percentage of fibres in this concrete to take care of shrinkage cracks and to impart other desirable properties to the concrete.. Such coloured concrete can be used indoors or outdoor application as a substitute to ordinary concrete.

Wear Resistant Floor Finish: A wear resisting quality of a concrete floor surface can be improved by using solutions of certain chemicals known as "Liquid Harderners". They include, fluosilicates of magnesium and zinc, sodium silicate, gums and waxes. When the compounds penetrate the pores in the topping, they form crystalline or gummy deposits and thus tend to make the floor less pervious and reduce dusting either by acting as plastic binders or making the surface harder.

Sometimes, iron filing and iron chips are mixed with the toppings and the floor is made in a normal manner. The rusting of the iron filings and chips increases in volume and thereby makes the concrete dense giving the floor better wear resistance. They are known as "Ironite floor toppings". Fibre reinforced concrete also has demonstrated a better wear-resistance quality in case of road and airfield slabs. We have already discussed about Wear Resistant floor finish in Chapter 5 under construction chemicals. Attention is drawn to the present day availability and application Epoxy Paint, Epoxy mortar, self levelling Epoxy screed etc., for the use of Wear Resistant floor and decorative floor finish. They are widely used in modern construction.

Requirement of a good finish: A good concrete floor should have a surface which is durable, non-absorptive, suitable texture, free from cracks, crazing and other defects. In other words, the floor should satisfactorily withstand wear from traffic. It should be sufficiently impervious to passage of water, oils or other liquids. It should possess a texture in keeping with the required appearance, should be easy to clean and be safe against slipping. It should structurally be sound and must act in unison with sub-floor.

Grinding and Polishing: Floors when properly constructed using materials of good quality, are dustless, dense, easily cleaned and attractive in appearance. When grinding is specified, it should be started after the surface has hardened sufficiently to prevent dislodgement of aggregate particles and should be continued until the coarse aggregates are exposed. The machine used should be of approved type with stones that cut freely and rapidly. The floor is kept wet during the grinding process and the cuttings are removed by spraying and flushing with water. After the surface is ground, air holes, pits and the other blemishes are filled with a thin grout composed of one part of fine carborundum grit and one part of portland cement. This grout is spread over the floor and worked into the pits with the straight edge after which it is rubbed into the floor with a grinding machine. When the fillings are hardened for seven days, the floor is given final grinding.

Craziness: While we are discussing about the surface finish it will be pertinent to discuss the craziness *i.e.*, the development of fine shallow hair cracks on concrete surface.

The surface appearance of concrete is often spoilt by a fairly close pattern of hair cracks which may appear within the first year, occasionally after longer periods. The cracks do not penetrate deep into the concrete and do not indicate any structural weakness. They are most obvious immediately after the surface of the concrete has dried when wetted they become prominent. It is not possible to state any precautions which will definitely prevent craziness but its occurrence can be minimised. Craziness is due to drying shrinkage or carbonation or due to differential shrinkage between the surface of the concrete and the main body of the concrete. This differential shrinkage is accentuated if the skin is richer than the parent concrete. It is known that drying shrinkage is greatest when the concrete dries up fast after casting. The first

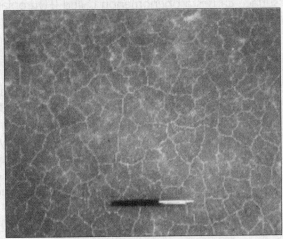
Craziness in the surface of concrete.

precaution to take, therefore, is very careful curing so that the initial drying period is extended over as long a time as possible so that the shrinkage of the outer skin is kept in conformity with the shrinkage of the main body of the concrete. Steep moisture gradients between the surface and the interior of the concrete must be avoided if possible. Cracking will not occur if the concrete is sufficiently strong to resist the tensile forces caused by differential shrinkage but it does not appear possible to prevent crazing by making a very strong concrete.

The object must therefore be to minimise shrinkage of the surface skin and this is best achieved by adequate curing and by taking measures to prevent shrinkage by avoiding too rich surface. The following precautions will help greatly:

(*a*) Trowelling the surface as little as possible and in particular avoiding the use of a steel float.

(*b*) Avoiding the use of rich facing mixes, say, not richer than 1:3.

(*c*) Use of as low a water-cement ratio as possible consistent with adequate compaction.

(*d*) Avoiding grouting processes or rubbing the surface with neat cement paste.

(*e*) Over vibration which results in bringing too much slurry to the top or side. (adjacent to formwork).

Crazing may also be due to carbonation and thermal effects. A cement-rich skin is liable to expand and contract more with difference in temperature than the interior of the concrete. The wetting and drying process is, however, a far more potent factor for causing craziness. The most important causes of crazing are thermal stresses and long term drying shrinkage.

Whisper Concrete Finish : One of the disadvantages of Concrete Roads is that they produce lot of noise when vehicles travel at high speed, due to friction between tyres and hard road surface. In Europe the noise level has become intolerable to the people living by the side of roads where about a lakh of vehicles move at a speed of about 120 km per hour. Belgium was the first country to take measure to reduce noise pollution.

It may be recalled that, texturing or brooming is done as a surface finish for the new road pavement construction to provide skid resistance. Over the time, the texturing gets worn out and the surnace becomes smooth. When it rains, the pool of water on the smooth concrete surface causes a phenomenon called "Hydroplaning" when vehicle move at high speed, which results in loss of control and skidding.

Concrete roads needs roughening and resurfacing after some years of use. This is done by regrooving. Regrooving is nothing but cutting and creating grooves about 2 mm deep across the vehicular movement. This is a costly and laborious practice. Instead, Belgium authorities tried exposed aggregate finish. On the smoothened road surface, they overlaid 40–50 mm of concrete, having a maximum size of 6–8 mm coarse aggregate. The surface of new concrete, while still green, was sprayed with a retarder consisting of glucose, water and alcohol. It was immediately covered by polyethylene sheet. After about 8–36, hours, the polyethylene sheet is removed and the road surface was swept and washed with stiff rotating bristle brushes. The top unset cement mortar to a depth of about 1.5 to 2 mm is removed exposing the aggregate, making the surface rough enough for safe high speed vehicular movement.

When vehicles moved at high speed on such exposed aggregate surface it was found to every ones surprise that noise level was much reduced than normal concrete surface. In fact, it was found that noise level was lower than the case of black-topped road pavement. Further trials were conducted and it was confirmed that exposed aggregate finish provides not only skid resistance but also reduces the noise. The Belgian authorities called it as "whisper" concrete.

Mostly in many continental countries where concrete pavements are popular, they provide 40–50 mm layer of whisper concrete. They found that there is very little difference in cost between regrooving and providing whisper concrete. It was also seen that providing a white topping, that is, providing concrete pavement over bituninous pavement, adoption of whisper concrete gave good economy.

In U.K., they took up the use of whisper concrete pavement during 1995, and has given good guide lines for adoption of whisper concrete.

Some of the important guidelines are:

● Under standard highway conditions, a concrete road should consist of cement bound sub-base, between 150–200 mm thick. On top of this, there should be 200 mm of continuously reinforced concrete pavement (CRCP) followed by 50 mm of whisper concrete surfacing.

● Normally 8 mm size coarse aggregate should be used for whisper concrete layer. Not more than 3% of these should be oversize and 10% undersize.

● The flakiness index should be less than 25%.

● Coarse aggregate should form around 60% of whisper concrete. Sand should be very fine.

● Spray retarder consisting of glucose, water and alcohol. They cover the surface with polyethylene sheet.

● After 8 to 36 hours, remove the polyethylene sheet and brush the surface with mechanically rotating stiff bristle to remove cement mortar from the top 1.5 mm.

As far as India is concerned, whisper concrete is not going to be a necessity for some years to come.

REFERENCES

6.1 Nasser KW, *New and simple tester for slump of concrete ACI Journal*, October 1976.

6.2 Dordi C.M., Equipment for Transporting and Placing Eoncrete, Seminar on Concrete Plant and Equipment, Ahmedabad, Nov. 1995.

6.3 cooke T.H., Concrete Pumping and Spraying, A Practical Guide, Thomas Telford, London.

6.4 Klieger P, *Early High Strength Concrete for Prestressing, world conference on prestressed concrete* July 1957.

6.5 Price W.H., *Factors Influencing Concrete strength, ACI Journal* Feb. 1951.

6.6 Verbick et.al., Structure and Physical Properties of Cement Pastes, Proceedings, Fifth International Symposium on the Chemistry of Cement, The Cement Association of Japan, Tokyo, 1968.

6.7 Klier P, *Effect of Mixing and Curing Temperature on concrete strength ACI Journal* June 1958.

6.8 U.S. Bureau of Reclamation, Concrete Manual, 8th Edition, Denver, Colarado, 1975.

Testing Equipments for Finding Strength of Concrete

CHAPTER

Strength of Concrete

General

The compressive strength of concrete is one of the most important and useful properties of concrete. In most structural applications concrete is employed primarily to resist compressive stresses. In those cases where strength in tension or in shear is of primary importance, the compressive strength is frequently used as a measure of these properties. Therefore, the concrete making properties of various ingredients of mix are usually measured in terms of the compressive strength. Compressive strength is also used as a qualitative measure for other properties of hardened concrete. No exact quantitative relationship between compressive strength and flexural strength, tensile strength, modulus of elasticity, wear resistance, fire resistance, or permeability have been established nor are they likely to be. However, approximate or statistical relationships, in some cases, have been established and these give much useful information to engineers. It should be emphasised that compressive strength gives only an approximate value of these properties and that other tests specifically designed to determine these properties should be useful if more precise results are required. For instance, the indicated compressive strength increases as the specimen size decreases, whereas the modulus of elasticity decreases. The modulus of elasticity in this case does not follow the compressive strength. The other case where the compressive strength does no indicate the useful property of concrete is when the concrete is subjected to freezing and thawing. Concrete containing about 6 per cent of entrained air which is relatively weaker in strength is found to be more durable than dense and strong concrete.

The compressive strength of concrete is generally determined by testing cubes or cylinders made in laboratory or field or cores drilled from hardened concrete at site or from the non-destructive testing of the specimen or actual structures. The testing of hardened concrete is discussed in the subsequent chapter.

Strength of concrete is its resistance to rupture. It may be measured in a number of ways, such as, strength in compression, in tension, in shear or in flexure. All these indicate strength with reference to a particular method of testing. When concrete fails under a compressive load the failure is essentially a mixture of crushing and shear failure. The mechanics of failure is a complex phenomena. It can be assumed that the concrete in resisting failure, generates both cohesion and internal friction. The cohesion and internal friction developed by concrete in resisting failure is related to more or less a single parameter *i.e.*, w/c ratio.

The modern version of original water/cement ratio rule can be given as follows:

For a given cement and acceptable aggregates, the strength that may be developed by workable, properly placed mixture of cement, aggregate and water (under the same mixing, curing and testing conditions) is influenced by:

(*a*) Ratio of cement to mixing water;

(*b*) Ratio of cement to aggregate;

(*c*) Grading, surface texture, shape, strength and stiffness of aggregate particles;

(*d*) Maximum size of aggregate.

In the above it can be further inferred that water/cement ratio primarily affects the strength, whereas other factors indirectly affect the strength of concrete by affecting the water/cement ratio.

Water/Cement Ratio

Strength of concrete primarily depends upon the strength of cement paste. It has been shown in Chapter I that the strength of cement paste depends upon the dilution of paste or in other words, the strength of paste increases with cement content and decreases with air and water content. In 1918 Abrams presented his classic law in the form:

$$S = \frac{A}{B^x}$$

where x =water/cement ratio by volume and for 28 days results the constants A and B are 14,000 lbs/sq. in. and 7 respectively.[7.1]

Abrams water/cement ratio law states that the strength of concrete is only dependent upon water/cement ratio provided the mix is workable. In the past many theories have been propounded by many research workers. Some of them held valid for some time and then underwent some changes while others did not stand the test of time and hence slowly disappeared. But Abrams' water/cement ratio law stood the test of time and is held valid even today as a fundamental truth in concrete-making practices. No doubt some modifications have been suggested but the truth of the statement could not be challenged.

Strictly speaking, it was Feret who formulated in as early as 1897, a general rule defining the strength of the concrete paste and concrete in terms of volume fractions of the constituents by the equation:

$$S = K \left(\frac{c}{c+e+a} \right)^2$$

where   S = Strength of concrete
c, e and   a = volume of cement, water and air respectively and
        K = a constant.

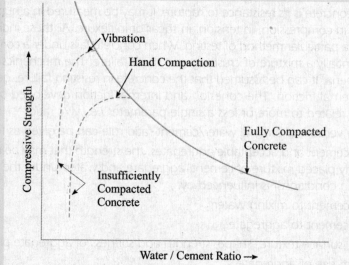

Fig. 7.1. The relation between strength and water/cement ratio of concrete.

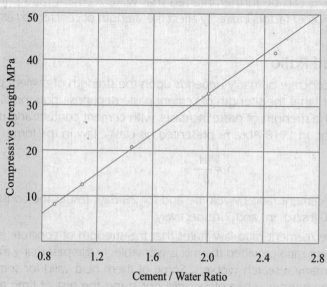

Fig. 7.2. The relation between strength and cement / water ratio.

In this expression the volume of air is also included because it is not only the water/cement ratio but also the degree of compaction, which indirectly means the volume of air filled voids in the concrete is taken into account in estimating the strength of concrete. The relation between the water/cement ratio and strength of concrete is shown in Fig. 7.1. It can be seen that lower water/cement ratio could be used when the concrete is vibrated to achieve higher strength, whereas comparatively higher water/cement ratio is required when concrete is hand-compacted. In both cases when the water/cement ratio is below the practical limit the strength of the concrete falls rapidly due to introduction of air voids.

The graph showing the relationship between the strength and water/cement ratio is approximately hyperbolic in shape. Sometimes it is difficult to interpolate the intermediate value. From geometry it can be deduced that if the graphs is drawn between the strength and the cement/water ratio an approximately linear relationship will be obtained. This linear relationship is more convenient to use than water/cement ratio curve for interpolation. Fig. 7.2 shows the relationship between compressive strength and cement/water ratio.

Gel/Space Ratio

Many research workers commented on the validity of water/cement ratio law as propounded by Duff Abrams. They have forwarded a few of the limitations of the water/cement ratio law and argued that Abrams water/cement ratio law can only be called a rule and not a law because Abrams' statement does not include many qualifications necessary for its validity to call it a law. Some of the limitations are that the strength at any water/cement ratio depends on the degree of hydration of cement and its chemical and physical properties, the temperature at which the hydration takes place, the air content in case of air entrained concrete, the change in the effective water/cement ratio and the formation of fissures and cracks due to bleeding or shrinkage.

Instead of relating the strength to water/cement ratio, the strength can be more correctly related to the solid products of hydration of cement to the space available for formation of this product. Powers and Brownyard have established the relationship between the strength and gel/space ratio.[7.2] This ratio is defined as the ratio of the volume of the hydrated cement paste to the sum of volumes of the hydrated cement and of the capillary pores.

Power's experiment showed that the strength of concrete bears a specific relationship with the gel/space ratio. He found the relationship to be $240\,x^3$, where x is the gel/space ratio and 240 represents the intrinsic strength of the gel in MPa for the type of cement and specimen used.[7.3] The strength calculated by Power's expression holds good for an ideal case. Fig. 7.3 shows the relationship between strength and gel/space ratio. It is pointed out that the relationship between the strength and water/cement ratio will hold

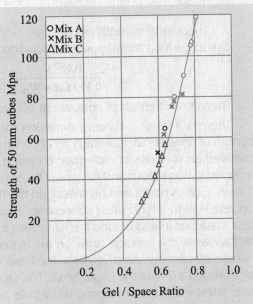

Fig. 7.3. Relation between the compressive strength of mortar and gel/space ratio

good primarily for 28 days strength for fully compacted concrete, whereas, the relationship between the strength and gel/space ratio is independent of age. Gel/space ratio can be calculated at any age and for any fraction of hydration of cement. The following examples show how to calculate the gel/space ratio.

Calculation of gel/space ratio for complete hydration

Let $\qquad$ C = weight of cement in gm.

V_C = specific volume of cement = 0.319 ml/gm.

W_O = volume of mixing water in ml.

Assuming that 1 ml. of cement on hydration will produce 2.06 ml of gel,

Volume of gel = C x 0.319 x 2.06

Space available = C x 0.319 + W_O

∴ $\qquad$ Gel/Space ratio = $x = \dfrac{\text{Volume of gel}}{\text{Space available}} = \dfrac{0.657\,C}{0.319\,C + W_O}$

Calculation of gel/space ratio for partial hydration

Let $\quad$ α = Fraction of cement that has hydrated

Volume of gel = C x α x 0.319 x 2.06

Total space available C V_C α + W_O

∴ $\qquad$ Gel/space ratio = $x = \dfrac{2.06 \times 0.319 \times C\alpha}{0.319\,C\alpha + W_O}$.

Example: Calculate the gel/space ratio and the theoretical strength of a sample of concrete made with 500 gm. of cement with 0.5 water/cement ratio, on full hydration and at 60 per cent hydration.

Gel/space ratio on full hydration $\qquad = \dfrac{0.657\,C}{0.319\,C + W_O} = 0.802$ say 0.8

∴ Theoretical strength of concrete $= 240 \times (0.8)^3 = 123$ MPa

Gel/space ratio for 60 percent hydration.

$$x = \frac{0.657\,C}{0.319\,C\alpha + W_O} = \frac{0.657 \times 500 \times 0.6}{0.319 \times 500 \times 0.6 + 250} = \frac{197.1}{345.7} = 0.57$$

Theoretical strength of concrete at 60 per cent hydration = 240 x (0.57)³ = 44.4 MPa

There is a lot of difference between the theoretical strength of concrete and actual strength of concrete. Actual strength of concrete is much lower than the theoretical strength estimated on the basis of molecular cohesion and surface energy of a solid assumed to be perfectly homogeneous and flawless. The actual reduction of strength is due to the presence of flaws. Griffith postulated his theory on the flaws in concrete. He explains that the flaws in concrete lead to a high stress concentrations in the material under load, so that a very high stress is reached in and around the flaws with the result that the material gets fractured around this flaw while the average stress on the material, taking the cross section of the material as a whole, remains comparatively low. The flaws vary in size. The high stress concentration takes place around a few of the larger flaws. This situation leads to failure of the material at a much lower stress intensity considering the whole process. Presence of bigger flaws brings down the actual strength to a much lower value than the theoretical strength.

Cement paste in concrete contains many discontinuities such as voids, fissures, bleeding channels, rupture of bond due to drying shrinkage and temperature stresses etc. It has been difficult to explain how exactly these various flaws contribute to the reduction in actual strength of concrete. However, Griffith's theory which explains the failure of concrete has been accepted to satisfactorily explain the failure of brittle materials such as concrete.

Gain of Strength with Age

The concrete develops strength with continued hydration. The rate of gain of strength is faster to start with and the rate gets reduced with age. It is customary to assume the 28 days strength as the full strength of concrete. Actually concrete develops strength beyond 28 days also. Earlier codes have not been permitting to consider this increase of strength beyond 28 days for design purposes. The increase in strength beyond 28 days used to get immersed with the factor of safety. With better understanding of the material, progressive designers have been trying to reduce the factor of safety and make the structure more economical. In this direction, the increase in strength beyond 28 days is taken into consideration in design of structures. Some of the more progressive codes have been permitting this practice. Table 7.1 gives the age factors for permissible compressive stress in concrete, as per British Code.

Table 7.1. Age Factors for Permissible Compressive Stress in Concrete as per British Code

Minimum age of member when full design load is applied, months	Age factor for low-strength concrete	Additional strength for high strength concrete MPa
1	1.00	0
2	1.10	4.2
3	1.16	5.5
6	1.20	7.7
12	1.24	10.2

Earlier IS code 456 of 1978 considered age factor and allowed the increase in design stress in the lower columns in multistorey buildings. Earlier only one type of cement *i.e.*, cement governed by IS- 269 of 1976 was used in which case there was appreciable increase in strength after 28 days. After gradation of OPC the present day cements particularly 53 grade cements, being ground finer, the increase in strength after 28 days is nominal. Most of the strength developments in respect of well cured concrete will have taken place by 28 days. Therefore, allowing age factor is not generally found necessary. Therefore, in IS 456 of 2000, the clause is revised.

Bandra Worli Sea Link Project - an artist's impression.
In this 8 lane bridge 60 MPa concrete is going to be used.
Courtesy : Hindustan Construction Company.

The clause states "There is normally a gain of strength beyond 28 days. The quantum of increase depends upon the grade and type of cement, curing and environmental conditions etc. The design should be based on 28 days characteristic strength of concrete unless there is an evidence to justify a higher strength for a particular structure due to age"

The table number 7.2 gives the grades of concrete as per IS-456 of 2000

Table 7.2. Grades of Concrete as per IS - 456 of 2000

Group	Grade Designation	Specified characterstic compressive strength of 150 mm cube at 28 days in N/mm²
Ordinary Concrete	M 10	10
	M 15	15
	M 20	20
Standard Concrete	M 25	25
	M 30	30
	M 35	35
	M 40	40
	M 45	45
	M 50	50
	M 55	55
High Strength Concrete	M 60	60
	M 65	65
	M 70	70
	M 75	75
	M 80	80

Permissible stresses in concrete is given in Table. 7.3 and 7.4. (IS 456 of 2000)

Table 7.3. Permissible stresses in Concrete
All values in N/mm² (IS 456 of 2000)

Grade of concrete	Permissible stress in compression		Permissible stress in Bond (average) for Plain Bars in tension
	Bending	Direct	
M 10	3.0	2.5	—
M 15	5.0	4.0	0.6
M 20	7.0	5.0	0.8
M 25	8.5	6.0	0.9
M 30	10.0	8.0	1.0
M 35	11.5	9.0	1.1
M 40	13.0	10.0	1.2
M 45	14.5	11.0	1.3
M 50	16.0	12.0	1.4

Note: The bond stress may be increased by 25 per cent for bars in compression.

Table 7.4. Permissible shear stress in concrete as per IS 456 of 2000

$\dfrac{100 \times As}{bd}$ (1)	*Permissible shear stress in concrete N/mm²* *Grades of concrete*					
	M 15 (2)	*M 20* (3)	*M 25* (4)	*M 30* (5)	*M 35* (6)	*M 40 and above* (7)
≤ 0.15	0.18	0.18	0.19	0.20	0.20	0.20
0.25	0.22	0.22	0.23	0.23	0.23	0.23
0.50	0.29	0.30	0.31	0.31	0.31	0.32
0.75	0.34	0.35	0.36	0.37	0.37	0.38
1.00	0.37	0.39	0.40	0.41	0.42	0.42
1.25	0.40	0.42	0.44	0.45	0.45	0.46
1.50	0.42	0.45	0.46	0.48	0.49	0.49
1.75	0.44	0.47	0.49	0.50	0.52	0.52
2.00	0.44	0.49	0.51	0.53	0.54	0.55
2.25	0.44	0.51	0.53	0.55	0.56	0.57
2.50	0.44	0.51	0.55	0.57	0.58	0.60
2.75	0.44	0.51	0.56	0.58	0.60	0.62
3.00 and Above	0.44	0.51	0.57	0.60	0.62	0.63

Many a time it may be necessary to estimate the strength of concrete at an early age. One may not be able to wait for 28 days. Many research workers have attempted to estimate the strength of concrete at 1, 3 or 7 days and correlate it to 28 days strength. The relationship between the strength of concrete at a lower age and 28 days depends upon many factors such as compound composition of cement, fineness of grinding and temperature of curing etc. Furthermore mixes with low water/cement ratio gains strength, expressed as a percentage of long term strength, more rapidly than that of concrete with higher water/cement ratio. This is presumably because the cement particles are held at a closer interval in case of low water/cement ratio than that of higher water/cement ratio, in which case there is a much better possibility for the formation of continuous system of gel which gives more strength. Many research workers have forwarded certain relationships between 7

Bandra Worli Sea Link Project under construction with high performance concrete.
Courtesy : Hindustan Construction Company.

days strength and 28 days strength. In Germany the relation between 28 days strength, σ_{28} and the 7 days strength, σ_7 is taken to lie between,

$$\sigma_{28} = 1.4\,\sigma_7 + 150 \quad \text{and} \quad \sigma_{28} = 1.7\,\sigma_7 + 850$$

σ being expressed in pounds/sq. inch.

Another relation suggested is of the type

$$f_{28} = K_2(f_7)^{K_1}$$

where, f_7 and f_{28} are the strengths at 7 and 28 days respectively and K_1 and K_2 are the coefficients, which is different for different cements and curing conditions.

The value of K_1 ranges from 0.3 to 0.8 and that of K_2 from 3 to 6.

The strength of concrete is generally estimated at 28 days by crushing field test cubes or cylinders made from the representative concrete used for the structure. Often it is questioned about the utility of ascertaining 28 days strength by which time considerable amount of concrete will have been placed and the works may have progressed. It is then rather too late for remedial measures, if the result of the test cube at 28 days is too low. On the other hand, the structure will be uneconomical if the result of the test cube is too high.

It is, therefore, of tremendous advantage to be able to predict 28 days strength within a few hours of casting the concrete so that we have a good idea about the strength of concrete, so that satisfactory remedial measures could be taken immediately before it is too late. There are many methods for predicting the 28 days strength, within a short period of casting. Out of these the method suggested by Prof. King is found to have good field correlations.

Accelerated Curing test

In the acclerated curing test the standard cubes are cast, they are covered with top plate and the joints are sealed with special grease to prevent drying. Within 30 minutes of adding water, the cubes having sealed effectively, are placed in an air-tight oven which is then switched on. The oven temperature is brought to 93°C in about one hour time. It is kept at this temperature for 5 hours. At the end of this period the cubes are removed from oven, stripped, cooled, and tested. The time allowed for this operation is 30 minutes.

The strength of concrete is determined within 7 hours of casting and this acclerated strength shows good relationship with 7 and 28 days strengths of normally cured concrete. Fig. 7.4 shows relationship between acclereated strength and normally cured concrete strength at 7 and 28 days.

One of the main factors that affects the rate of gain of strength is the fineness of cement. It has been estimated that particles of cement over 40 micron in size contribute to the compressive strength of concrete only over long periods, while those particles smaller than 25 to 30 micron contribute to the 28 days strength, those particles smaller than 20 to 25 micron contribute to the 7 days strength, and particles smaller than 5 to 7 micron contribute to the 1 or 2 days strength.

Relative gain of strength with the time of concretes made with different water/cement ratio using ordinary Portland cement is shown in Fig. 7.5.

Maturity Concept of Concrete

While dealing with curing and strength development, we have so far considered only the time aspect. It has been pointed out earlier that it is not only the time but also the temperature during the early period of hydration that influence the rate of gain of strength of concrete. Since the strength development of concrete depends on both time and temperature it can be said that strength is a function of summation of product of time and temperature. This summation is called maturity of concrete.

$$\text{Maturity} = \Sigma \text{ (time x temperature)}$$

The temperature is reckoned from an origin lying between −12 and −10°C. It was experimentally found that the hydration of concrete continues to take place upto about −11°C. Therefore, −11°C is taken as a datum line for computing maturity.

Maturity is measured in degree centigrade hours (°C hrs) or degree centigrade days (°C days). Fig. 7.6. shows that the strength plotted against the logarithm of maturity gives a straight line.

A sample of concrete cured at 18°C for 28 days is taken as fully matured concrete. Its maturity would be equal to

$$28 \times 24 \times [18 - (-11)] = 19488°C \text{ h.}$$

However, in standard calculations the maturity of fully cured concrete is taken as 19,800°Ch.. (The discrepancy is because of the origin or the datum is not exactly being −11 C as used in calculation).

If the period is broken into smaller intervals and if the corresponding temperature is recorded for each interval of time, the summation of the product of time and temperature will

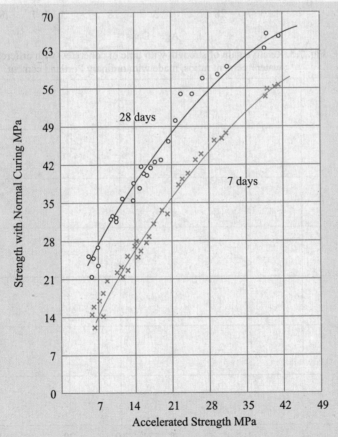

Fig. 7.4. The relation between strength determined by Kings accelerated curing test and the 7 and 28-days strength of concrete moist-cured at 20°C.[7.4]

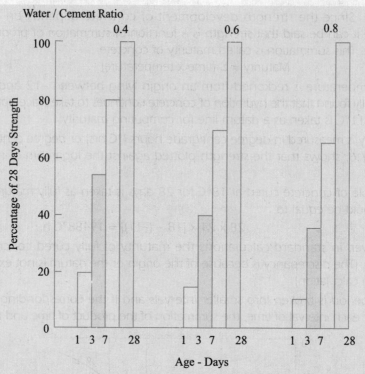

Fig. 7.5. Relative gain of strength with time of concretes with different water / cement ratios, made with ordinary Portland cement.

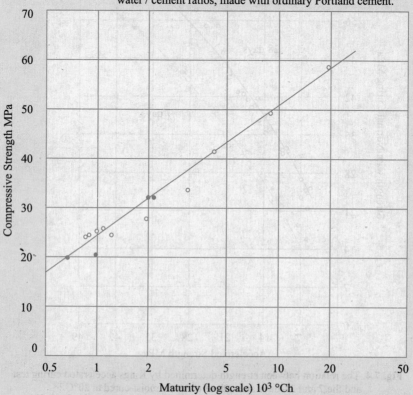

Fig. 7.6. Relation between Logarithm of Maturity and Strength.

give an accurate picture of the maturity of concrete. In the absence of such detailed temperature history with respect to the time interval, the maturity figure can be arrived at by multiplying duration in hours by the average temperature at which the concrete is cured. Of course, the maturity calculated as above will be less accurate.

Maturity concept is useful for estimating the strength of concrete at any other maturity as a percentage of strength of concrete of known maturity. In other words, if we know the strength of concrete at full maturity (19,800°Ch), we can calculate the percentage strength of identical concrete at any other maturity by using the following equation given by Plowman.

Strength at any maturity as a percentage of strength at maturity of

$$19,800°\text{Ch.} = A + B\log_{10}\frac{(\text{maturity})}{10^3}$$

The values of coefficients, A and B depend on the strength level of concrete. The values are given in Table 7.5

Table 7.5. Plowman's Coefficients for Maturity Equation[7.5]

Strength after 28 days at 18°C (Maturity of 19,800°Ch): MPa	Coefficient	
	A	B
Less than 17.5	10	68
17.5 – 35.0	21	61
35.0 – 52.5	32	54
52.5 – 70.0	42	46.5

The values of A and B are plotted against the cube strength at the maturity of 19,800° Ch. A straight line relationship will be obtained indicating that they are directly proportional to the strength. Plowman divided the strength into 4 zones as shown in Table 7.5 and has assigned the values of A and B for each zone. It is to be noted that the maturity equation holds good for the initial temperature of concrete less than about 38°C. Fig. 7.7 gives the value of constant A and B when strength and temperature are expressed in lbs/sq inch and °F respectively.

The following examples illustrate the theory:

Example 1: The strength of a sample of fully matured concrete is found to be 40.00 MPa find the strength of identical concrete at the age of 7 days when cured at an average temperature during day time at 20°C, and night time at 10°C.

Maturity of concrete at the age of 7 days

$$= \Sigma \,(\text{time} \times \text{Temperature})$$
$$= 7 \times 12 \times [20 - (-11)] + 7 \times 12 \times [10 - (-11)]$$
$$= 7 \times 12 \times 31 + 7 \times 12 \times 21$$
$$= 4368°\text{Ch.}$$

The strength range of this concrete falls in Zone III for which the constant A is 32 and B is 54.

$$\therefore \text{ the percentage strength of concrete at maturity of } 4368°\text{Ch.} = A + B\log_{10}\frac{(4368)}{1000}$$

$$= 32 + 54 \times \log_{10}(4.368) = 32 + 54 \times 0.6403 = 66.5$$

$\therefore$ The strength at 7 days = 40.0 x $\dfrac{66.5}{100}$ = 26.5 MPa

Example 2: Laboratory experiments conducted at (Pune) on a particular mix showed a strength of 32.5 MPa for fully matured concrete. Find whether formwork can be removed for an identical concrete placed at Srinagar at the age 15 days when the average temperature is 5°C if the concrete is likely to be subjected to a stripping stress of 25.0 MPa.

Strength of fully matured concrete = 32.5 MPa. Maturity of identical concrete at 15 days when cured at a temperature of 5°C = 15 x 24 x [5 − (− 11)]

$$= 15 \times 24 \times 16 = 5760°\text{Ch}.$$

This concrete falls in Zone No. II for which the value of constants are

$$A = 21 \quad \text{and} \quad B = 61.$$

Percentage of strength = $A + B \log_{10} \dfrac{(\text{Maturity})}{1000}$ = $21 + 61 \log_{10} \left(\dfrac{(5760)}{1000}\right)$

$$= 21 + 61 \times \text{Log}_{10}\ 5.760$$
$$= 21 + 61 \times 0.7604 = 67.38$$

$\therefore$ The strength of concrete at 15 days = 32.5 x $\dfrac{67.38}{100}$ = 21.9 MPa.

Since the strength of concrete is less than the stress to which it is likely to be subjected while stripping the formwork, the concrete may fail. Therefore, the formwork cannot be removed at 15 days time.

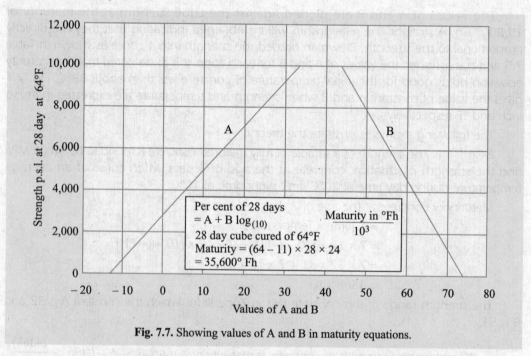

Fig. 7.7. Showing values of A and B in maturity equations.

If the strength at a given maturity is known, then the number of days required to reach the same strength at any other temperature can also be calculated from,

$$\frac{M}{24[t-(-11)]}$$

where, M = Maturity for the given strength, and t the alternative temperature in centigrade.

In the above example for reaching the same strength, number of days required,

$$= \frac{M}{24[t-(-11)]} = \frac{19800}{24[5-(11)]} = \frac{19800}{24 \times 16} = 52 \text{ days.}$$

This is to say that the concrete cured at 5°C would take about 52 days to achieve full maturity.

Effect of Maximum size of Aggregate on Strength

At one time it was thought that the use of larger size aggregate leads to higher strength. This was due to the fact that the larger the aggregate the lower is the total surface area and, therefore, the lower is the requirement of water for the given workability. For this reason, a lower water/cement ratio can be used which will result in higher strength.

However, later it was found that the use of larger size aggregate did not contribute to higher strength as expected from the theoretical considerations due to the following reasons.

The larger maximum size aggregate gives lower surface area for developments of gel bonds which is responsible for the lower strength of the concrete. Secondly bigger aggregate size causes a more heterogeneity in the concrete which will prevent the uniform distribution of load when stressed.

When large size aggregate is used, due to internal bleeding, the transition zone will become much weaker due to the development of microcracks which result in lower compressive strength.

Generally, high strength concrete or rich concrete is adversely affected by the use of large size aggregate. But in lean mixes or weaker concrete the influence of size of the aggregate gets reduced. It is interesting to note that in lean mixes larger aggregate gives highest strength while in rich mixes it is the smaller aggregate which yields higher strength. Fig. 7.8. shows the influence of maximum size of aggregate on compressive strength of concrete.[7.6] Fig. 7.9. depicts the influence of size of aggregate on compressive strength of concrete for different w/c ratio.

Relation Between Compressive and Tensile Strength

In reinforced concrete construction the strength of the concrete in compression is only taken into consideration. The tensile strength of concrete is generally not taken into consideration. But the design of concrete pavement slabs is often based on the flexural strength of concrete. Therefore, it is necessary to assess the flexural strength of concrete either from the compressive strength or independently.

As measurements and control of compressive strength in field are easier and more convenient, it has been customary to find out the compressive strength for different conditions and to correlate this compressive strength to flexural strength. Having established a satisfactory relationship between flexural and compressive strength, pavement, can be designed for a specified flexural strength value, or this value could be used in any other situations when required.

It is seen that strength of concrete in compression and tension (both direct tension and flexural tension) are closely related, but the relationship is not of the type of direct

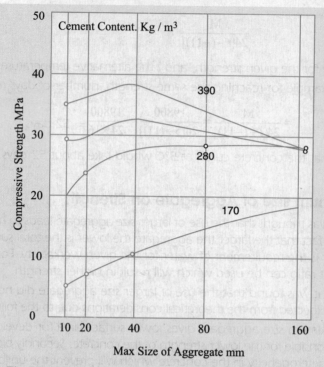

Fig. 7.8. Influence of maximum size of aggregate on 28-day compressive strength of concrete of different richness[7.6]

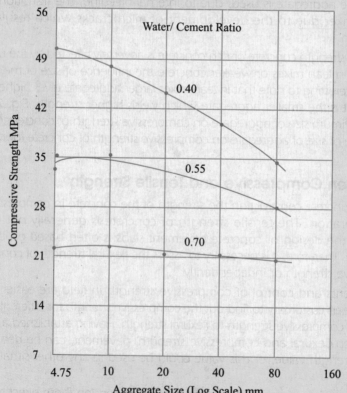

Fig. 7.9. The influence of maximum size of aggregate on compressive strength of concrete.[7.6]

proportionality. The ratio of the two strengths depends on general level of strength of concrete. In other words, for higher compressive strength concrete shows higher tensile strength, but the rate of increase of tensile strength is of decreasing order.

The type of coarse aggregate influences this relationship. Crushed aggregate gives relatively higher flexural strength than compressive strength. This is attributed to the improved bond strength between cement paste and aggregate particles. The tensile strength of concrete, as compared to its compressive strength, is more sensitive to improper curing. This may be due to the inferior quality of gel formation as a result of improper curing and also due to the fact that improperly cured concrete may suffer from more shrinkage cracks.

The use of pozzolanic material increases the tensile strength of concrete.

From the extensive study, carried out at Central Road Research Laboratory (CRRI) the following statistical relationship between tensile strength and compressive strength were established.

(i) $y = 15.3x - 9.00$ for 20 mm maximum size aggregate.

(ii) $y = 14.1x - 10.4$ for 20 mm maximum size natural gravel.

(iii) $y = 9.9x - 0.55$ for 40 mm maximum size crushed aggregate.

(iv) $y = 9.8x - 2.52$ for 40 mm maximum size natural gravel. Where y is the compressive strength of concrete MPa and x is the flexural strength of concrete MPa.

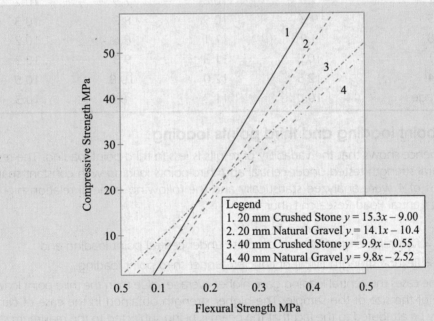

Fig. 7.10. Statistical relation between flexural and compressive strength of concrete with different types and sizes of aggregate.[7.7]

Subjecting all the data to statistical treatment the following general relationship has been established at CRRI between flexural and compressive strength of concrete:

$$y = 11x - 3.4$$

Fig. 7.10 shows the relationships between compressive strength and flexural strength of concrete for various aggregates.

The flexural strength of concrete was found to be 8 to 11 per cent of the compressive stength of the concrete for higher ranges of concrete strength (greater than 25 MPa) and 9 to 12.8 per cent for lower ranges of concrete strength (less than 25 MPa) as shown in Table 7.6.

The flexural to compressive strength ratio was higher with aggregate of 40 mm maximum size than with those of 20 mm maximum size. In general the ratio was found to be slightly higher in the case of natural gravel as compared to crushed stone.

Flexural strength of concrete is usually found by testing plain concrete beams. Two methods of loading of the beam specimen for finding out flexural strength are practised:

Table 7.6. Flexural Strength Expressed as Percentages of Compressive Strength of Concrete using Gravel and Crushed Stone Aggregate[7.7]

Compressive Strength MPa	Flexural Strength as Percentage of Compressive Strength per cent			
	Gravel Aggregate with Maximum size		Crushed Stone Aggregate with Maximum Size	
	20 mm	*40 mm*	*20 mm*	*40 mm*
49	8.7	-	7.7	-
42	9.0	10.8	7.9	10.2
35	9.3	10.9	8.2	10.3
28	9.9	11.1	8.6	10.2
21	10.8	11.3	9.3	10.3
14	12.5	12.0	10.8	10.5
Average	10.0	11.2	8.8	10.3

Central point loading and third points loading

Experience shows that the variability of results is less in third-point loading. The results of the flexural strength tested under central and third-points loading with constant span to depth ratios of 4 were analyzed statistically and the following general relationship was obtained at Central Road Research Laboratory.

$$x_1 = x_2 + 0.72$$

where, x_1 = flaxural strength (MPa) of concrete under central point loading and

x_2 = flexural strength (MPa) of concrete under third point loading.

In all the cases the central loading gave higher average value than the third-point loading irrespective of the size of the sample. The higher strength obtained in the case of central loading may be attributed to the fact that the beam is being subjected to the maximum stress at a pre-determined location not necessarily the weakest. In the standard methods for finding the flexural strength of concrete, the span to depth ratio of the specimen is kept at 4. If the span to depth ratio is increased or decreased, the flexural strength was found to alter. A change in this ratio by one induced 3 per cent and 2.5 per cent change in strength when tested by third-point and central point loading respectively. With the increase in span to depth ratio the flexural strength decreased.

The rate of stress application was found to influence the flexural strength of concrete to a very significant extent. The strength increased upto about 25 per cent with increase in stressing rate compared to the standard rate of 0.7 MPa per minute. The increase was found more with the leaner mixes.

There are number of empirical relationships connecting tensile strength and compressive strength of concrete. One of the common relationships is shown below.

$$\text{Tensile Strength} = K \text{ (Compressive Strength)}^n$$

where, value of K varies from 6.2 for gravels to 10.4 for crushed rock (average value is 8.3) and value of n may vary from 1/2 to 3/4

Further data obtained at the Laboratories of Portland Cement Association giving the relationship between compressive and tensile strength of concrete is shown in Table 7.7.

Table 7.7. Relation Between Compressive and Tensile Strength of Concrete[7.8]

Compressive Strength of Cylinders	Strength Ratio		
	Modulus of repture* to compressive strength	Direct tensile strength to compressive strength	Direct tensile strength to modulus of rupture
MPa			
7	0.23	0.11	0.48
14	0.19	0.10	0.53
21	0.16	0.09	0.57
28	0.15	0.09	0.59
35	0.14	0.08	0.59
42	0.13	0.08	0.60
49	0.12	0.07	0.61
56	0.12	0.07	0.62
63	0.11	0.07	0.63

*Determined under third-point loading.

The Indian Standard IS = 456 of 2000 gives the following relationship between the compressive strength and flexural strength

$$\text{Flexural Strength} = 0.7 \sqrt{f_{ck}}$$

where f_{ck} is the characteristic compressive strength of concrete in N/mm²

Bond Strength

We can consider the bond strength from two different angles; one is the bond strength between paste and steel reinforcement and the other is the bond strength between paste and aggregate. Firstly, let us consider the bond strength between paste and steel reinforcement.

Bond strength between paste and steel reinforcement is of considerable importance. A perfect bond, existing between concrete and steel reinforcement is one of the fundamental assumptions of reinforced concrete. Bond strength arises primarily from the friction and adhesion between concrete and steel. The roughness of the steel surface is also one of the factors affecting bond strength. The bond strength of concrete is a function of compressive strength and is approximately proportional to the compressive strength upto about 20 MPa. For higher strength, increase in bond strength becomes progressively smaller. Table 7.3 gives the value of bond strength corresponding to the compressive strength. The bond strength, is also a function of specific surface of gel. Cement which consists of a higher percentage of C_2S will give higher specific surface of gel, thereby giving higher bond strength. On the other hand, concrete containing more C_3S or the concrete cured at higher temperature results in smaller specific surface of gel which gives a lower bond strength. It has been already pointed out that high pressure steam cured concrete produces gel whose specific surface is about 1/20 of the specific surface of the gel produced by normal curing. Therefore, bond strength of high pressure steam cured concrete is correspondingly lower.

Aggregate-Cement Bond Strengths

Concrete can be regarded as a chain in which aggregates are the links bonded together by cement paste. Just as the strength of a chain as a whole is depending upon the strength of welding of the individual links, the strength of concrete as a whole is depending upon the strength (bond strength) of the hydrated hardened cement paste (hcp). By and large the strength of hcp is depending upon w/c ratio which determines the quality, continuity, density, porosity of the products of hydration in particular the C-S-H gel. Stronger the gel bond stronger is the concrete. Aggregates generally being much stronger than the paste (gel bond), its strength is not of consequence in normal strength concrete. The strength of aggregate is of consideration in high strength concrete and light weight concrete.

The explanation that the strength of Concrete is limited by strength of the paste, will hold good when we consider concrete as two phase material. If we take a closer look into the structure of the concrete, a third phase comes into consideration *i.e.,* inter-face between the paste and aggregate known as Transition Zone. In the ultimate analysis it is the integrity of the transition zone that influences the strength of concrete.

As we have seen earlier, bleeding takes place in fresh concrete. The bleeding water in the process of coming up gets intercepted by aggregates, particularly large size flaky and elongated aggregate and gets accumulated at the inter-face between paste and aggregates. The extra water remaining at the inter-face, results in poor paste structure and poor gel bond at the transition zone.

The paste shrinks while hardening. The magnitude of shrinkage is higher with higher water content, in which case, a higher shrinkage takes place at the transition zone which results in greater shrinkage cracks at the transition zone.

In case of shrinkage taking place on account of heat of

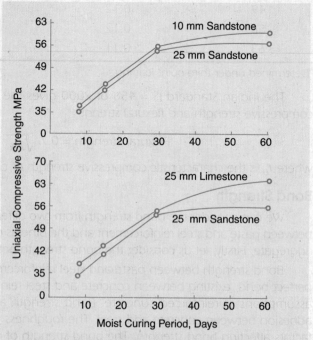

Fig. 7.11. Influence of the aggregate size and mineralogy on compressive strength of concrete.

hydration, the weak gel structure at the transition zone also suffers a higher degree of shrinkage. The same situation will take place if the concrete is subjected to heat or cold during the service life.

It can be deduced that there are considerable microcracks or what you call "faults", exists in the transition zone even before the concrete structures are subjected to any load or stress. When subjected to some stress, the existing micro cracks in transition zone propagate much faster with tiny jumps and develop bigger cracks than rest of the body of concrete and structure fails much earlier than the general strength of concrete. Therefore, the transition zone is the weakest link of the chain. It is the strength limiting phase in concrete.

Point to note is that we have to come back to the basics. It is the w/c ratio that again influences the quality of transition zone in low and medium strength concrete. The w/c ratio is not exerting the same influence on high strength concrete *ie.,* for very low w/c ratio. It has been seen that for w/c less than 0.3, disproportionately high increase in compressive strength can be achieved for very small reduction in w/c. This phenomenon is attributed mainly to a significant improvement in the strength of transition zone at very low w/c ratio.

Aggregate characteristics other than strength, such as size, shape, surface texture and grading are known to affect the strength of concrete. The increase in strength is generally attributed to indirect change in w/c ratio. Recent studies have shown that the above characteristics of aggregates have independent influence on the strength properties of concrete other than through w/c ratio by improving the quality of transition zone.

J.J Flyover at Mumbai where high strength, high performance concrete 75 MPa was used for the first time in India (2002).

Courtesy : Gammon India

There are number of published literatures which indicate that under identical conditions, calcareous aggregates give higher strength than siliceous aggregates. The result of studies conducted at university of California is shown in Fig. 7.11.

The strength of concrete embraces so many aspects that it is difficult to describe all the factors that influences the strength of concrete. The entire book on concrete technology, in a way is dealing with the strength properties of concrete. In this book, the various aspects on strength properties of concrete is described in various chapters.

High Strength Concrete

Concrete is generally classified as Normal Strength Concrete (NSC), High Strength Concrete (HSC) and Ultra High Strength Concrete (UHSC). There are no clear cut boundary for the above classification. Indian Standard Recommended Methods of Mix Design denotes the boundary at 35 MPa between NSC and HSC. They did not talk about UHSC. But elsewhere in the international forum, about thirty years ago, the high strength lable was applied to concrete having strength above 40 MPa. More recently, the threshold rose to 50 to 60 MPa. In the world scenario, however, in the last 15 years, concrete of very high strength entered the field of construction, in particular construction of high-rise buildings and long span bridges. Concrete strengths of 90 to 120 MPa are occasionally used. Table 7.8 shows the kind of high strength produced in RMC plant.

The advent of Prestressed Concrete Technology Techniques has given impetus for making concrete of higher strength. In India, there are cases of using high strength concrete for prestressed concrete bridges. The first prestressed concrete bridge was built in 1949 for the Assam Rail Link at Siliguri. In fifty's a number of pretressed concrete structures were built using concrete of strength from 35 MPa to 45 MPa. But strength of concrete more than 35 MPa was not commonly used in general construction practices. Probably concrete of strength more than 35 MPa was used in large scale in Konkan Railway project during early 90's and concretisation of Mumbai Muncipal Corporation Roads. It is only during 90's use of high strength concrete has taken its due place in Indian construction scenario. Of late concrete of strength

Vidya Sagar Setu at Kolkata where longest cable stayed bridge (in India) was built using high strength concrete.

varying from 45 MPa to 60 MPa has been used in high rise buildings at Mumbai, Delhi and other Metropolitan cities. Similarly high strength concrete was employed in bridges and flyovers. Presently (year 2000) in India, concrete of strength 75 MPa is being used for the first time in one of the flyovers at Mumbai. Other notable example of using high strength concrete in India is in the construction of containment Dome at Kaiga Power Project. They have used High performance concrete of strength 60 MPa with silica fume as one of the constituents.

Ready Mixed Concrete has taken its roots in India now. The manufacture of high strength concrete will grow to find its due place in concrete construction for all the obvious benefits. In the modern batching plants high strength concrete is produced in a mechanical manner. Of course, one has to take care about mix proportioning, shape of aggregates, use of supplementary cementitious materials, silica fume and superplasticizers. With the modern equipments, understanding of the role of the constituent materials, production of high strength concrete has become a routine matter.

There are special methods of making high strength concrete. They are given below.

(a) Seeding   (b) Revibration   (c) High speed slurry mixing;

(d) Use of admixtures   (e) Inhibition of cracks   (f) Sulphur impregnation;

(*g*) Use of cementitious aggregates.

Seeding: This involves adding a small percentage of finely ground, fully hydrated Portland cement to the fresh concrete mix. The mechanism by which this is supposed to aid strength development is difficult to explain. This method may not hold much promise.

Revibration: Concrete undergoes plastic shrinkage. Mixing water creates continuous capillary channels, bleeding, and water accumulates at some selected places. All these reduce the strength of concrete. Controlled revibration removes all these defects and increases the strength of concrete.

High Speed slurry mixing: This process involves the advance preparation of cement-water mixture which is then blended with aggregate to produce concrete. Higher compressive strength obtained is attributed to more efficient hydration of cement particles and water achieved in the vigorous blending of cement paste.

Use of Admixtures: Use of water reducing agents are known to produce increased compressive strengths.

Inhibition of cracks: Concrete fails by the formation and propagation of cracks. If the propagation of cracks is inhibited, the strength will be higher. Replacement of 2– 3% of fine aggregate by polythene or polystyrene "lenticules" 0.025 mm thick and 3 to 4 mm in diameter results in higher strength. They appear to act as crack arresters without necessitating extra water for workability. Concrete cubes made in this way have yielded strength upto 105 MPa.

Sulphur Impregnation: Satisfactory high strength concrete have been produced by impregnating low strength porous concrete by sulphur. The process consists of moist curing the fresh concrete specimens for 24 hours, drying them at 120°C for 24 hours, immersing the specimen in molten sulphur under vacuum for 2 hours and then releasing the vacuum and soaking them for an additional ° hour for further infiltration of sulphur. The sulphur-infiltrated concrete has given strength upto 58 MPa.

Use of Cementitious aggregates: It has been found that use of cementitious aggregates has yielded high strength. Cement fondu is kind of clinker. This glassy clinker when finely ground results in a kind of cement. When coarsely crushed, it makes a kind of aggregate known as ALAG. Using Alag as aggregate, strength upto 125 MPa has been obtained with water/cement ratio 0.32.

Ultra High Strength Concrete

As technology advances, it is but natural that concrete technologists are directing their attention beyond high strength concrete to ultra high strength concrete. The following techniques are used for producing ultra high strength concrete.

(*a*) Compaction by pressure (*b*) Helical binding;

(*c*) Polymerisation in concrete (*d*) Reactive powder concrete.

Compaction by Pressure: It has been pointed out earlier that cement paste derives strength due to the combined effect of friction and bond. In ceramic material, grain size and porosity would be the most important parameters affecting friction and bond and hence the strength. It has been attempted to reduce grain size and porosity by the application of tremendous pressure at room temperature and also at higher temperature.

Unusually high strength have been generated in materials by employing "hot pressing" techniques and intermediate ranges of strengths have been achieved by applying high pressure at room temperature to Portland cement pastes. Strengths as high as 680 MPa (compressive), 66 MPa (indirect tensile) have been obtained by subjecting cement pastes to 357 MPa pressure under a temperature of 250°C. The water/cement ratio used was 0.093. It was also seen that hot pressed materials are volume stable. The micro structure of such materials are very compact, consisting of intergrowth of dense hydrated cement gel surrounding residual unhydrated cement grain cores. The lowest porosity of the materials measured was approximately 1.8%.

Table 7.8. Composition of Experimental Concretes Produced in a Ready-mix Plant[7.9] (In U.S.A.)

Concrete type	Reference	Silica fume	Fly ash	Slag + silica fume		
W/(c + m)		0.30	0.30	0.30	0.3	0.25
Water kg/m³		127	128	129	131	128
Cement						
ASTM Type II	kg/m³	450	425	365	228	168
Silica fume	kg/m³	-	45	-	45	54
Fly ash	kg/m³	-	-	95	-	-
Slag	kg/m³	-	-	-	183	320
Dolomite limestone		1100	1110	1115	110	1100
Coarse aggregate	kg/m³					
Fine aggregate	kg/m³	815	810	810	800	730
Superplasticizer*	L/m³	15.3	14	13	12	13
Slump after 45 minutes (mm)		110	180	170	220	210
Strength at 28 day (MPa)		99	110	90	105	114
Strength at 91 day (MPa)		109	118	111	121	126
Strength at 1 year (MPa)		119	127	125	127	137

*Sodium salt of a naphthalin sulphonate

Helical Binding: This is an indirect method of achieving ultra high strength in concrete. High tensile steel wire binding externally over the concrete cylinder results in good strength.

Polymer Concrete: Impregnation of monomer into the pores of hardened concrete and then getting it polymerised by irradiation or thermal catalytic process, results in the development of very high strength. This method of making ultra high strength concrete holds much promise. This aspect has been discussed in detail in Chapter 12 under special concrete.

Reactive Powder Concrete: High strength Concrete with strength of 100 – 120 MPa have been used for the construction of structural members. Concrete with 250 to 300 MPa are also used for non-structural applications such as flooring, safes and storage of nuclear wastes.

For structural uses, high ductility is required along with high-strength. Reactive powder concrete (RPC) has been developed to have a strength from 200 to 800 MPa with required ductility.

Concrete is a heterogeneous material and strength obtained by cement paste is not fully retained when sand and aggregates are added. The Reactive Power concrete is made by replacing the convential sand and aggregate by ground quartz less than 300 micron size, silica fume, synthesized precipitated silica, steel fibres about 1 cm in length and 180 micron in diameter.

The typical composition and mechanical property of the RPC of 200 MPa strength and 800 MPa strength are shown in Table. 7.9. and Table. 7.10 respectively.

Table No.7.9. Typical Composition of Reactive Powder Concrete 200 [7.10]

1	Portland Cement-Type V	955 kg/m^3
2	Fine Sand (150-400 micron)	1051 kg/m^3
3	Silica Fume (18 m^2/gram)	229 kg/m^3
4	Precipitated Silica (35 m^2/g)	10 kg/m^3
5	Superplasticizer (Polyacrylate)	13 kg/m^3
6	Steel fibres	191 kg/m^3
7	Total water	153 kg/m^3
8	Compressive Strength (Cylinder)	170 - 230 MPa
9	Flexural strength	25–60 MPa
10	Young's Modulus	54 - 60 GPa

Table 7.10. Typical Composition of Reactive Powder Concrete 800 [7.10]

1	Portland Cement-Type V	1000 kg/m^3
2	Fine Sand (150 - 400 microns)	500 kg/m^3
3	Ground quartz (4 microns)	390 kg/m^3
4	Silica fume (18 m^2/gram)	230 kg/m^3
5	Superplasticizer (Polyacrylate)	18 kg/m^3
6	Steel fibres (length 3 mm and dia. 180 μ)	630 kg/m^3
7	Total water	180 kg/m^3
8	Compressive Strength (cylinder)	490- 680 MPa
9	Flexural Strength	45 - 102 MPa
10	Young's Modulus	65 - 75 GPa

High-Performance concrete

Recently a new term "High performance concrete" is used for concrete mixture which possess high workability, high strength, high modulus of elasticity, high density, high dimensional stability, low permeability and resistance to chemical attack.

There is a little controversy between the terms high-strength and high-performance concrete. High-performance concrete is also, a high-strength concrete but it has a few more attributes specifically designed as mentioned above. It is, therefore, logical to describe by the more widely embracing term "High Performance Concrete" (HPC).

It may be recalled that in normal concrete, relatively low strength and elastic modulus are the result of high heterogeneous nature of structure of the material, particularly the porous and weak transition zone, which exists at the cement paste-aggregate interface. By densification and strengthening of the transition zone, many desirable properties can be improved many fold. This aspect has been already discussed in detail. A substantial reduction of quantity of mixing water is the fundamental step for making HPC. Reduction of w/c ratio will result in high strength concrete. But reduction in w/c ratio to less than 0.3 will greatly improve the qualities of transition zone to give inherent qualities expected in HPC.

To improve the qualities of transition zone, use of silica fume is also found to be necessary. Silica fumes becomes a necessary ingredient for strength above to 80 MPa. The best quality fly ash and GGBS may be used for other nominal benefits. Inspite of the fact that these pozzolanic materials increase the water demand, their benefits will out weigh the disadvantages. The crux of whole problem lies in using very low w/c ratio, consistant with high workability at the time of placing and compacting. Neville opines that the lowest w/c ratio that could be used is 0.22.[7.9]

Adopting w/c ratio in the range of 0.25 to 0.3 and getting a high slump is possible only with the use of superplasticizer. Therefore, use of appropriate superplasticizer is a key material in making HPC. The associated problem is the selection of superplasticizer and that of cement so that they are compatible and retain the slump and rheological properties for a sufficiently long time till concrete is placed and compacted.

Aggregates for HPC

In normal strength concrete, the strengths of aggregate by itself plays a minor role. Any aggregate available at the site could be used with little modification of their grading. The situation is rather different with HPC, where the bond between aggregate and hydrated cement paste is so strong that it results in significant transfer of stress across the transition zone. At the same time, the strength of the cement paste phase, on account very low w/c ratio is

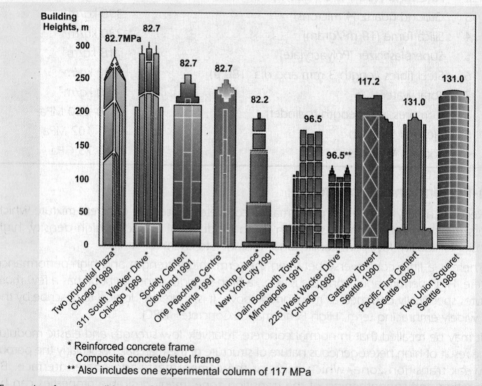

Example of some well-known Structures where HPC was used. Strength of concrete is shown on the top of each building.

so high that sometimes it is higher than the strength of aggregate particles. Observation of fractured surface in HPC has shown that they pass through the coarse aggregate particles as often as, if not more often than, through the cement paste itself. Indeed in many instances, the strength of aggregate particles has been found to be the factor that limits the compressive strength of HPC.

On the basis of practical experience it is seen that for concrete strength up to 100 MPa, maximum size of 20 mm aggregate could be used. However, for concrete in excess of 100 MPa, the maximum size of coarse aggregate should be limited to 10 to 12 mm.

Table 7.11. Typical HPC mixtures used in some important buildings in USA and other countries.

Mixture Number		1	2	3	4	5
Water	kg/m³	195	165	135	145	130
Cement	kg/m³	505	451	500	315	513
Fly ash	kg/m³	60	-	-	-	-
Slag	kg/m³	-	-	-	137	-
Silica fume	kg/m³	-	-	30	36	43
Coarse aggregates	kg/m³	1030	1030	1100	1130	1080
Fine aggregate	kg/m³	630	745	700	745	685
Water reducer	ml/m³	975	-	-	900	-
Retarder	L/m³	-	4.5	1.8	-	-
Superplasticizer	L/m³	-	11.25	14	5.9	15.7
W/(c + m)		0.35	0.37	0.27	0.31	0.25
Strength at 28 day	(MPa)	65	80	93	83	119
Strength at 91 day	(MPa)	79	87	107	93	145

1- Water Tower Place, Chicago 1975

2- Joigny Bridge, France 1989

3- La Laurentienne Building, Montreal (1984)

4- Scotia Plaza, Toronto (1987)

5- Two Union square, Seattle (1988)

Regarding the shape of the aggregate, crushed aggregate can be used, but utmost care should be taken to see that aggregates are cubic in shape, with minimum amount of flaky or elongated particles. The latter would effect not only the strength but also adversely affect the workability. In one site in Mumbai even for 60 MPa concrete they had to go for well processed and well graded cubic shaped, coarse aggregate from the point of view of workability. For HPC shape and size of the aggregate becomes an important parameter. Table No. 7.11. gives the composition and stength of HPC that are used in some important buildings in USA and other countries.

In India, it is reported, that HPC of the strength 60 MPa was used for the first time for the construction of containment dome at Kaiga and Rajasthan Atomic Power Projects.

REFERENCES

7.1 Kenneth Newman, *The structural and properties of concrete –an Introducting review, International concrete on the structure of concrete,* Sept. 1965.

7.2 T.C. Powers and T.L. Brownyard, *Studies of the Physical properties of hardened Portland Cement paste, Journal of Americal Concrete Institute,* Oct 1946 to April 1947. (Nine parts).

7.3 Powers T.C. *The physical structure and Engineering properties of concrete, Portland Cement Association Research department Bulletin,* July 1958.

7.4 King JUH, *Further Notes on the Acclereated Test for the concrete, chartered civil Engineer,* May 1957.

7.5 Plowman J.M., *Maturity and strength of concrete, Magazene of concrete Research,* March 1956.

7.6 Cordon W.A. et al, *Variables in concrete aggregates and portland cement paste which influence the strength of concrete, ACI Journal,* Aug. 1963.

7.7 Ghosh, R.K., et al, *Flexural strength of Concrete–its variations, relationship with compressive strength and use in concrete mix design,* Proc. IRC Road Research Bulletin, No. 16 of 1972.

7.8 Price W.H., *Factors Influencing concrete strength, ACI Journal,* Feb. 1951.

7.9 Aitcin P.C. and Neville A., *High Performance Concrete Demgstified,* Concrete International, Jan. 1993.

7.10 Richard P. and Chegrezy M.H., *Reactive Powder Concretes with High Ductility and 200 – 800 MPa Compressive Strengths, Proceedings of V.M. Malhotra Symposium, Sp-144, ACI, 1994.*

Length Comparator with specimen in place

CHAPTER

Elasticity, Creep and Shrinkage

Elastic Properties of Concrete

In the theory of reinforced concrete, it is assumed that concrete is elastic, isotropic, homogenous and that it conforms to Hooke's law. Actually none of these assumptions are strictly true and concrete is not a prefectly elastic material. Concrete deforms when load is applied but this deformation does not follow any simple set rule. The deformation depends upon the magnitude of the load, the rate at which the load is applied and the elapsed time after which the observation is made. In other words, the rheological behaviour of concrete *i.e.*, the response of concrete to applied load is quite complex.

The knowledge of rheological properties of concrete is necessary to calculate deflection of structures, and design of concrete members with respect to their section, quantity of steel and stress analysis. When reinforced concrete is designed by elastic theory it is assumed that a perfect bond exists between concrete and steel. The stress in steel is "*m*" times the stress in concrete where "*m*" is the ratio between modulus of elasticity of steel and concrete, known as modular ratio. The accuracy of design will naturally be dependent upon the value of the modulus of elasticity of concrete, because the modulus of elasticity of steel is more or less a definite quantity.

It is to be further noted that concrete exhibits very peculiar rheological behaviour because of its being a heterogeneous, multi-phase material whose behaviour is influenced by the elastic properties and morphology of gel structures. The modulus of elasticity of concrete being so important and at the same time so complicated, we shall see this aspect in little more detail.

The modulus of elasticity is determined by subjecting a cube or cylinder specimen to uniaxial compression and measuring the

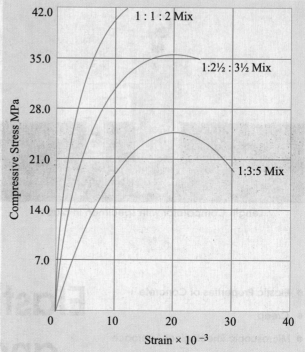

Fig. 8.1. Stress / strain curves for different mixes.

deformations by means of dial gauges fixed between certain gauge length. Dial gauge reading divided by gauge length will give the strain and load applied divided by area of cross-section will give the stress. A series of readings are taken and the stress-strain relationship is established.

The modulus of elasticity can also be determined by subjecting a concrete beam to bending and then using the formulae for deflection and substituting other parameters. The modulus of elasticity so found out from actual loading is called static modulus of elasticity. It is seen that even under short term loading concrete does not behave as an elastic material. However, up to about 10-15% of the ultimate strength of concrete, the stress-strain graph is not very much curved and hence can give more accurate value. For higher stresses the stress-strain relationship will be greatly curved and as such it will be inaccurate. Figure 8.1 shows stress-strain relationship for various concrete mixes.

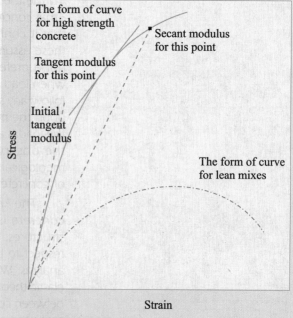

Fig. 8.2. The different modulus of elasticity.

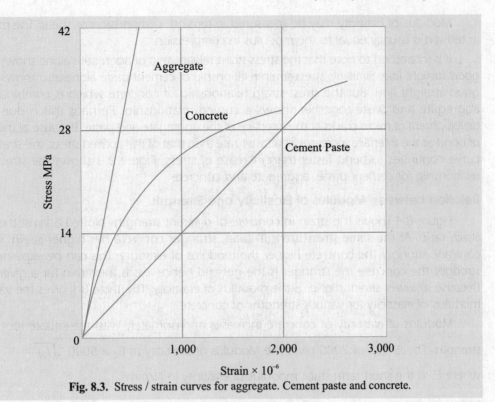

Fig. 8.3. Stress / strain curves for aggregate. Cement paste and concrete.

In view of the peculiar and complex behaviour of stress-strain relationship, the modulus of elasticity of concrete is defined in somewhat arbitrary manner. The modulus of elasticity of concrete is designated in various ways and they have been illustrated on the stress-strain curve in Figure 8.2. The term Young's modulus of elasticity can strictly be applied only to the straight part of stress-strain curve. In the case of concrete, since no part of the graph is straight, the modulus of elasticity is found out with reference to the tangent drawn to the curve at the origin. The modulus found from this tangent is referred as initial tangent modulus. This gives satisfactory results only at low stress value. For higher stress value it gives a misleading picture.

Tangent can also be drawn at any other point on the stress-strain curve. The modulus of elasticity calculated with reference to this tangent is then called tangent modulus. The tangent modulus also does not give a realistic value of modulus of elasticity for the stress level much above or much below the point at which the tangent is drawn. The value of modulus of elasticity will be satisfactory only for stress level in the vicinity of the point considered.

A line can be drawn connecting a specified point on the stress-strain curve to the origin of the curve. If the modulus of elasticity is calculated with reference to the slope of this line, the modulus of elasticity is referred as secant modulus. If the modulus of elasticity is found out with reference to the chord drawn between two specified points on the stress-strain curve then such value of the modulus of elasticity is known as chord modulus.

The modulus of elasticity most commonly used in practice is secant modulus. There is no standard method of determining the secant modulus. Sometime it is measured at stresses ranging from 3 to 14 MPa and sometime the secant is drawn to point representing a stress level of 15, 25, 33, or 50 per cent of ultimate strength. Since the value of secant modulus decreases with increase in stress, the stress at which the secant modulus has been found out should always be stated.

Modulus of elasticity may be measured in tension, compression or shear. The modulus in tension is usually equal to the modulus in compression.

It is interesting to note that the stress-strain relationship of aggregate alone shows a fairly good straight line. Similarly, stress-strain relationship of cement paste alone also shows a fairly good straight line. But the stress-strain relationship of concrete which is combination of aggregate and paste together shows a curved relationship. Perhaps this is due to the development of micro cracks at the interface of the aggregate and paste. Because of the failure of bond at the interface increases at a faster rate than that of the applied stress, the stress-strain curve continues to bend faster than increase of stress. Figure 8.3 shows the stress-strain relationship for cement paste, aggregate and concrete.

Relation between Modulus of Elasticity and Strength

Figure 8.4 shows the strain in concrete of different strengths plotted against the stress-strain ratio. At the same stress-strength ratio, stronger concrete has higher strain. On the contrary, stronger the concrete higher the modulus of elasticity. This can be explained that stronger the concrete the stronger is the gel and hence less is the strain for a given load. Because of lower strain, higher is the modulus of elasticity. The Table 8.1 gives the values of modulus of elasticity for various strengths of concrete.

Modulus of elasticity of concrete increases approximately with the square root of the strength. The IS 456 of 2000 gives the Modulus of elasticity as $E_C = 5000 \sqrt{f_{ck}}$

where E_C is the short term static modulus of elasticity in N/mm^2.

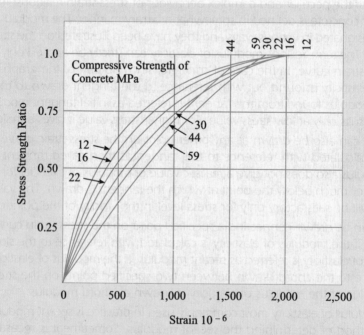

Fig. 8.4. Relation between stress / strength ratio and strain
for concretes of different strengths.

Table 8.1. Modulus of Elasticity of Concrete of Different strengths

Average compressive strength of works cubes MPa	Modulus of Elasticity GPa
21	21.4
28	28.5
35	32.1
42	35.7
56	42.9
70	46.4

Actual measured values may differ by ± 20 per cent from the values obtained from the above expression.

Factors Affecting Modulus of Elasticity

As explained earlier, one of the important factors affecting the modulus of elasticity of concrete is the strength of concrete. This can be represented in many ways such as the relationship between ratio of mix or water/cement ratio. The modulus of elasticity also depends upon the state of wetness of concrete when other conditions being the same. Wet concrete will show higher modulus of elasticity than dry concrete. This is in contrast to the strength property that dry concrete has higher strength than wet concrete. The possible reason is that wet concrete being saturated with water, experiences less strain for a given stress and, therefore, gives higher modulus of elasticity, whereas dry concrete shows higher strain for given stress on account of less gel water and inter-crystal adsorbed water. Figure 8.5 shows the influence of moisture content on the modulus of elasticity.

Figure 8.5 also shows the relationship between the modulus of elasticity, mix proportions and age of concrete. It can be seen that richer mixes show higher modulus of elasticity. Similarly older the concrete which again is supposed to have become stronger shows higher

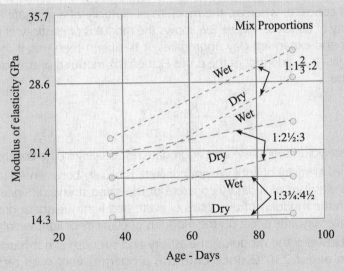

Fig. 8.5. Influence of moisture condition at test on the secant modulus of elasticity at 5.7 MPa of concretes at different ages.

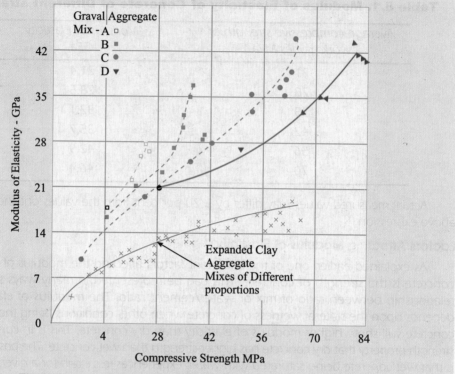

Fig. 8.6. Static modulus of elasticity of concretes made with gravel aggregate and expanded clay aggregate, and tested at different ages up to one year.

modulus of elasticity, thereby confirming that the stronger the concrete higher is the modulus of elasticity.

The quality and quantity of aggregate will have a significant effect on the modulus of elasticity. It is to be remembered that the strength of aggregate will not have significant effect on the strength of concrete, whereas, the modulus of elasticity of aggregate influences the modulus of elasticity of concrete. Figure 8.6 shows the modulus of elasticity of concrete with gravel aggregates and expanded clay aggregates. It has been seen that if the modulus of elasticity of aggregate is E_a and that of the paste E_p then the modulus of elasticity of concrete E is found out to be

$$\frac{1}{E} = \frac{V_p}{E_p} + \frac{V_a}{E_a}$$

where V_p and V_a are volume of paste and aggregate respectively in the concrete.

The modulus of elasticity of light weight concrete is usually between 40 to 80 per cent of the modulus of elasticity of ordinary concrete of the same strength. Since there is little difference between the modulus of elasticities of paste and light weight aggregate the mix proportions will have very little effect on the modulus of elasticity of light weight concrete.[8.1]

The relation between the modulus of elasticity and strength is not much effected by temperature upto about 230°C since both the properties vary with temperature in approximately the same manner. Steam-curved concrete shows a slightly lower modulus than water-curved concrete of the same strength.

Experiments have shown that the modulus in tension does not appear to differ much from modulus in compression. As the experimental set-up presents some difficulties, only limited work has been done to determine the modulus of elasticity in tension.

Since the principal use of reinforced concrete is in flexural members, considerable amount of work has been conducted to find out the modulus of elasticity in flexure on specimens of beam. The approach was to load the beam, measure deflection caused by known loads and to calculate the modulus of elasticity from well-known beam deflection formulae. It has been seen that the stress-strain curves in flexure agreed well with the stress-strain curve obtained in companion cylinders concentrically loaded in compression.

Dynamic Modulus of Elasticity

It has been explained earlier that the stress-strain relationship of concrete exhibits complexity particularly due to the peculiar behaviour of gel structure and the manner in which the water is held in hardened concrete. The value of E is found out by actual loading of concrete *i.e.*, the static modulus of elasticity does not truly represent the elastic behaviour of concrete due to the phenomenon of creep. The elastic modulus of elasticity will get affected more seriously at higher stresses when the effect of creep is more pronounced.

Attempts have been made to find out the modulus of elasticity from the data obtained by non-destructive testing of concrete. The modulus of elasticity can be determined by subjecting the concrete member to longitudinal vibration at their natural frequency. This method involves the determination of either resonant frequency through a specimen of concrete or pulse velocity travelling through the concrete. (More detail on this aspect is given under the chapter ('Testing of concrete'). By making use of the above parameters modulus of elasticity can be calculated from the following relationship.

$$E_d = Kn^2L^2\rho$$

where E_d is the dynamic modulus of elasticity; K is a constant, n is the resonant frequency; L is the length of specimen; and ρ is the density of concrete.

If L is measured in millimetres and ρ in kg/m³

then $$E_d = 4 \times 10^{-15}\, n^2L^2\rho \text{ GPa}$$

The value of E found out in this method by the velocity of sound or frequency of sound is referred as dynamic modulus of elasticity, in contrast to the value of E found out by actual loading of the specimen and from stress-strain relationship which is known as static modulus of elasticity.

The value of dynamic modulus of elasticity computed from ultrasonic pulse velocity method is somewhat higher than those determined by static method. This is because the modulus of elasticity as determined by dynamic modulus is unaffected by creep. The creep also does not

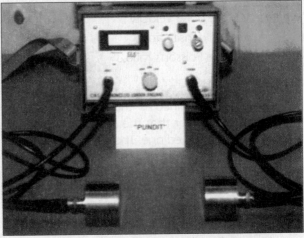

Ultra Sonic Pulse Velocity Equipment is used for finding dynamic modulus of elasticity.

significantly effect the initial tangent modulus in the static method. Therefore, the value of dynamic modulus and the value of initial tangent modulus are found to be more or less agree with each other. Approximate relationship between the two modulai expressed in GN/m² is given by

$$E_c = 1.25\ E_d - 19$$

where E_c and E_d are the static and dynamic modulus of elasticity.

The relationship does not apply to light weight concrete or for very rich concrete with cement content more than 500 kg/m³. For light weight concrete the relationship can be as follows

$$E_c = 1.04\ E_d - 4.1$$

Poisson's Ratio

Sometimes in design and analysis of structures, the knowledge of poisson's ratio is required. Poisson's ratio is the ratio between lateral strain to the longitudinal strain. It is generally denoted by the letter μ. For normal concrete the value of poisson's ratio lies in the range of 0.15 to 0.20 when actually determined from strain measurements.

As an alternative method, poisson's ratio can be determined from ultrasonic pulse velocity method and by finding out the fundamental resonant frequency of longitudinal vibration of concrete beam. The poisson's ratio μ can be calculated from the following equation.

$$\left(\frac{V^2}{2nL}\right)^2 = \frac{1-\mu}{(1+\mu)(1-2\mu)}$$

where V is the pulse velocity (mm/s),

n is the resonant frequency (Hz) and L is the length of the beam (in mm). The value of the poisson's ratio found out dynamically is little higher than the value of static method. The value ranges from 0.2 to 0.24.

Dynamic modulus of elasticity can also be found out from the following equation.

$$E_d = \rho V^2 \frac{(1+\mu)(1-2\mu)}{(1-\mu)}$$

where V is the pulse velocity

ρ is the density and

μ is the Poisson's ratio

Creep

Creep can be defined as "the time-dependent" part of the strain resulting from stress. We have discussed earlier that the stress-strain relationship of concrete is not a straight line relationship but a curved one. The degree of curvature of the stress-strain relationship depends upon many factors amongst which the intensity of stress and time for which the load is acting are of significant interest. Therefore, it clearly shows that the relation between stress and strain for concrete is a function of time. The gradual increase in strain, without increase in stress, with the time is due to creep. From this explanation creep can also be defined as the increase in strain under sustained stress.

All materials undergo creep under some conditions of loading to a greater or smaller extent. But concrete creeps significantly at all stresses and for a long time. Furthermore, creep of concrete is approximately linear function of stress upto 30 to 40 per cent of its strength. The order of magnitude of creep of concrete is much greater than that of other crystalline material except for metals in the final stage of yielding prior to failure. Therefore, creep in concrete is considered to be an isolated rheological phenomenon and this is associated with the gel structure of cement paste. Cement paste plays a dominant role in the deformation of concrete. The aggregates, depending upon the type and proportions modify the deformation characteristics to a greater or lesser extent. Therefore, it is logical initially to examine the structure of cement paste and how it influences creep behaviour and then to consider how the presence of aggregate modifies the creep behaviour.

Cement paste essentially consists of unhydrated cement grains surrounded by the product of hydration mostly in the form of gel. These gels are interpenetrated by gel pores and interspersed by capillary cavities. The process of hydration generates more and more of gel and subsequently there will be reduction of unhydrated cement and capillary cavities. In young concrete, gel pores are filled with gel water and capillary cavities may or may not be filled with water. The movement of water held in gel and paste structure takes place under the influence of internal and external water vapour pressure. The movement of water may also take place due to the sustained load on concrete.

The formation of gel and the state of existence of water are the significant factors on the deformative characteristics of concrete. The gel provides the rigidity both by the formation of chemical bonds and by the surface force of attraction while the water can be existing in three categories namely combined water, gel water and capillary water.

It is interesting to find how such a conglomeration of very fine colloidal particles with enclosed water-filled viods behave under the action of external forces. One of the explanations given to the mechanics of creeps is based on the theory that the colloidal particles slide against each other to re-adjust their position displacing the water held in gel pores and capillary cavities. This flow of gel and the consequent displacement of water is responsible for complex deformation behaviour and creep of concrete.

Creep takes place only under stress. Under sustained stress, with time, the gel, the adsorbed water layer, the water held in the gel pores and capillary pores yields, flows and readjust themselves, which behaviour is termed as creep in concrete.

Rheological Representation of Creep

Analysis of the mechanical behaviour of a material like hardened cement paste which exhibits both elastic and inelastic components of deformation under load, can be expressed in rheological terms. The rheological approach illustrates the mechanical behaviour of an ideal elastic, viscous and plastic components.

Macroscopic Rheological Approach

At the macroscopic level, the structure of cement paste can be represented as a continuous solid phase containing saturated voids having a wide ranges of sizes. Figure 8.7 (a) shows macroscopic representation of deformational behaviour of hardened cement paste. This model can show the time-dependent volume changes, as long as the isotropic stresses are applied through the solid phase and the drainage of the liquid can take place.[8.2]

The corresponding rheological model consists of a spring device representing the elastic mass around a central viscous dash-pot representing the confined liquid. Refer Figure 8.7 (b). With the help of this model it is possible to have an idea about the deformational behaviour of cement paste.

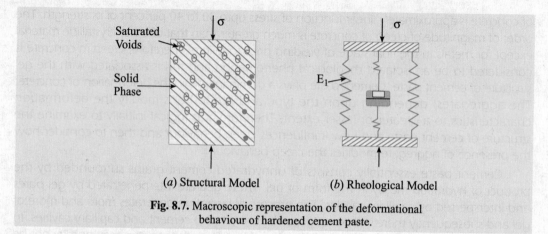

Fig. 8.7. Macroscopic representation of the deformational behaviour of hardened cement paste.

Microscopic Rheological Approach

At the microscopic level, the structure of cement of gel can be represented as an anisotropic crystal clusters randomly oriented in a solid matrix (Figure 8.8). The application of a macroscopic shear stress to the anisotropic system results in an irrecoverable volumetric contraction of the spaces in some of the clusters [Figure 8.8 (a)] and a separation in other clusters [Figure 8.8 (b)]. Only. a fraction of the elements is subjected to pure shear [Figure 8.8 (c)]. On removal of the load there is a visco-elastic recovery, but due to some deviatory stress component, certain local irrecoverable volume changes will remain. Figure 8.9 shows the further submicroscopic models. They represented metastable crystalline gel consisting of two sheet like crystals separated by a layer of water. Three basically different mechanisms of deformation are possible. They are compressive stresses normal to contact layer [Figure 8.9 (a)] tensile stresses normal to the contact layer [Figure 8.9 (b)] sheer stresses parallel to the contant layer [Figure 8.9 (c)]

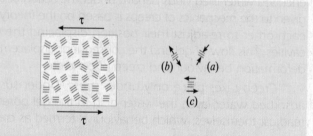

Fig. 8.8. Microscopic model representing the deformational behaviour of anisotropic crystal clusters under deviatory stress.

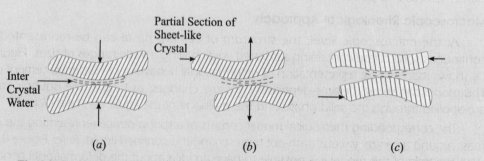

Fig. 8.9. Sub-microscopic models representing the three basic intercrystal mechanical states.

In mechanism (*a*), the liquid is compressed and squeezed out laterally. This is accompanied by a reduction of the intercrystalline space. The rate of liquid movement is slow and will decrease with narrowing of space which tends towards a limit equal to a monomolecular compressed water layer (about 3 Å). This squeezing away of liquid against strong frictional forces is the principal cause of the time dependent, irrecoverable changes in the cement gel.

In mechanism (*b*), visco-elastic elongation may be expected, at a faster rate than in the case of compression. This elongation is restrained, however, by the solid matrix and delayed, although complete recovery may be expected long after unloading.

In mechanism (*c*), the shear stress results in the water layers.[8.3]

Under the complex systems of applied loading, below the elastic limit of the material, various combinations of these basic mechanisms of deformation may be expected. On the basis of the available experimental evidence, it may be assumed that the long term deformation mechanism in cement gel is that involving narrowing of the intercrystalline spaces. This is reflected in the slow and decreasing rate of time-dependent of deformation, as well as in the irrecoverable component of the deformations which increase with loading time.

The time dependent deformation behaviour of loaded and unloaded hardened cement paste shows a distinct similarity between creep (and its recovery) and shrinkage (and swelling). All these processes are governed by movement or migration of the various types of water held. It can be further explained as follows:

Application of uniaxial compression which is the most usual type of loading, results in as instantaneous elastic response of both solid and liquid systems. The external load is distributed between these two phases. Under sustained load, the compressed liquid begins to diffuse and migrate from high to lower stressed areas. Under uniform pressure, migration takes place outwards from the body. This mechanism is accompanied by a transfer of load from the liquid phase to the surrounding solid, so that stress acting on the solid matrix increases gradually, resulting in an increased elastic deformation.

There is reason to believe that, after several days under sustained load, the pressure on the capillary water gradually disappears, being transferred to the surrounding gel. Similarly, the pressure on the gel pore water disappears after some weeks. The pressure on the inter and intracrystalline adsorbed water continues to act during the entire period of loading, although the magnitude decreases gradually. It can be said that the ultimate deformation of the hardened cement paste, in fact, is the elastic response of its solid matrix, which behaves as if the spaces within it (which are filled with unstable gel) were quite empty.

Hydration under Sustained Load

Under sustained load the cement paste continues to undergo creep deformation. If the member is subjected to a drying condition this member will also undergo continuous shrinkage. The migration of liquid from the gel pore due to creep may promote the shrinkage to small extent. It can be viewed that the creep, the shrinkage and the slip deformations at the discontinuities cause deformations and micro cracks. It should be remembered that the process of hydration is also simultaneously progressing due to which more gel is formed which will naturally heal-up the microcracks produced by the creep and shrinkage. This healing up micro cracks by the delayed hydration process is also responsible for increasing the irrecoverable component of the deformation.

Increased rigidity and strength development with age are additional contribution of hydration to time dependent deformation. Moreover, it is likely that, with continuing hydration the growth of the solid phase at the expense of the liquid phase gradually changes the parameter governing the extent and rate of the total creep.

Concrete structures in practice are subjected to loading and drying. At the same time certain amount of delayed hydration also takes place. Under such a complex situation, the structure creeps, undergoes drying shrinkage, experiences micro cracks and also due to progressive hydration, heals up the micro cracks that are formed due to any reason.

Measurement of Creep

Creep is usually determined by measuring the change with time in the strain of specimen subjected to constant stress and stored under appropriate condition. A typical testing device is shown in Figure 8.10. The spring ensures that the load is sensibly constant in spite of the fact that the specimen contracts with time. Under such conditions, creep continues for a very long time, but the rate of creep decreases with time.

Under compressive stress, the creep measurement is associated with shrinkage of concrete. It is necessary to keep companion unloaded specimens to eliminate the effect of shrinkage and other autogenous volume change. While this correction is qualitatively correct and yields usable results, some research workers maintained that shrinkage and creep are not independent and are of the opinion that the two effects are not additive as assumed in the test.

It is generally assumed that the creep continues to assume a limiting value after an infinite time under load. It is estimated that 26

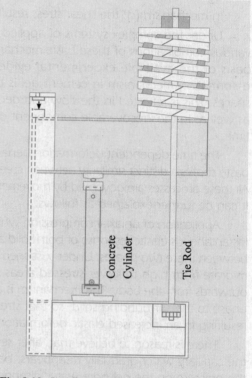

Fig. 8.10. Loading device for the measurement of creep under a constant stress.

per cent of the 20 year creep occurs in 2 weeks. 55 per cent of 20 year creep occurs in 3 months and 76 per cent of 20 year creep occurs in one year.

If creep after one year is taken as unity, then the average value of creep at later ages are:

$\qquad$ 1.14 after 2 years
$\qquad$ 1.20 after 5 years
$\qquad$ 1.26 after 10 years
$\qquad$ 1.33 after 20 years and
$\qquad$ 1.36 after 30 years

There are many expressions to give the magnitude of ultimate creep in concrete member. Ross suggested the relation between specific creep (creep strain per unit stress) 'c' and time under load 't' in the form[8.4]

$$c = \frac{t}{a + bt}$$

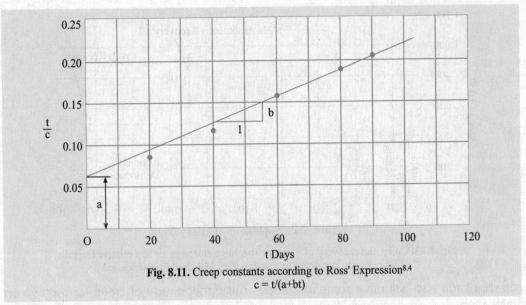

Fig. 8.11. Creep constants according to Ross' Expression[8.4]

$$c = t/(a+bt)$$

where '*a*' and '*b*' are constants. If a graph is drawn with *t* in the *x*-axis and t/c in the *y*-axis it shows a straight line of slope *b* and the intercept on the $\dfrac{t}{c}$ is equal to *a*.

Then the constant can be easily found out. Refer Figure 8.11. The ultimate crep at infinite time will be $\dfrac{1}{b}$ from the above expression. It is interesting to observe that when $t = a/b$,

$c = \dfrac{1}{2}\, b.$ *i.e.,* one half of the ultimate creep is realised at time $t = a/b.$

As indicated earlier if a loaded concrete member is kept in atmoshpere subjected to shrinkage, the member will undergo deformation from 3 different causes: namely elastic deformation, drying shrinkage and creep deformation. Figure 8.12 shows the time dependent deformation in concrete subjected to sustained load. In order to estimate the magnitude of creep in a member subjected to drying, a companion specimen is always placed at the same temperature and humidity condition and the shrinkage of the unloaded specimen is found and this magnitude of deformation is subtracted from the total deformation of the loaded member. Knowing the instantaneous elastic deformation, the creep deformation can be calculated. In this, for simplicity sake it is assumed that the shrinkage of concrete does not effect the creep in addition to the load. In fact it is to be noted that in addition to the load,

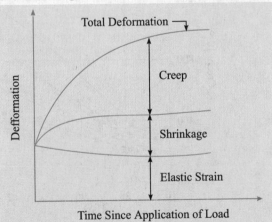

Fig. 8.12. Time-dependent deformations in concrete subjected to a sustained load.

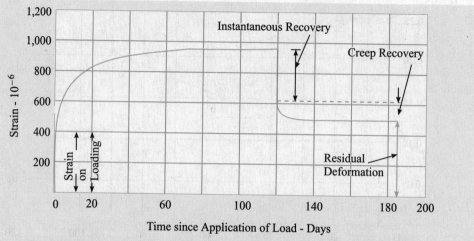

Fig. 8.13. Creep and recovery of a mortar specimen stored in air at a relative humidity of 95 per cent, subjected to a stress of 15 MPa and then unloaded.

the shrinkage also will have some influence on the magnitude of creep, and creep on shrinkage.

If a member is loaded and if this load is sustained for some length of time and then removed, the specimen instantaneously recovers the elastic strain. The magnitude of instantaneous recovery of the elastic strain is something less than that of the magnitude of the elastic strain on loading. With time, certain amount of creep strain is also recovered. It is estimated that about 15 per cent of creep is only recoverable. The member will have certain amount of residual strain. This shows that the creep is not a simply reversible phenomenon. Figure 8.13 shows the pattern of strain of a loaded specimen and the recovery of strain on unloading after some time.

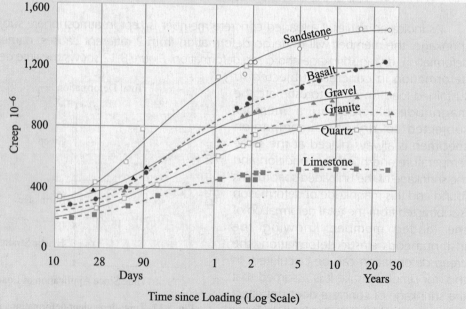

Fig. 8.14. Creep of concretes of fixed proportions but made with different aggregates, loaded at the age of 28 days, and stored in air at 21°C and a relative humidity of 50 per cent.

Factors Affecting Creep

Influence of Aggregate: Aggregate undergoes very little creep. It is really the paste which is responsible for the creep. However, the aggregate influences the creep of concrete through a restraining effect on the magnitude of creep. The paste which is creeping under load is restrained by aggregate which do not creep. The stronger the aggregate the more is the restraining effect and hence the less is the magnitude of creep. Figure 8.14 shows the effect of the quality of aggregate on the magnitude of creep.

The grading, the shape, the maximum size of aggregate have been suggested as factors affecting creep. But it is later shown that the effect of aggregate and their properties mentioned above *per se* do not effect the creep , but indirectly they affect the creep from the point of view of total aggregate content in the concrete. The modulus of elasticity of aggregate is one of the important factors influencing creep. It can be easily imagined that the higher the modulus of elasticity the less is the creep. Light weight aggregate shows substantially higher creep than normal weight aggregate. Persuambly this is because of lower modulus of elasticity.

Influence of Mix Proportions: The amount of paste content and its quality is one of the most important factors influencing creep. A poorer paste structure undergoes higher creep. Therefore, it can be said that creep increases with increase in water/cement ratio. In other words, it can also be said that creep is inversely proportional to the strength of concrete. Broadly speaking, all other factors which are affecting the water/cement ratio is also affecting the creep. The following table shows the creep of concretes of different strength.

Table 8.2. Creep of Concrete of Different Strength

Compressive strength at the time of application of load MPa	Ultimate specific creep 10^{-6} per MPa	Ultimate creep at stress-strength ratio of 30 per cent 10^{-6}
14	999	933
28	114	1067
42	78	1100
56	57	1067

Figure 8.15. hows the specific creep as a function of water/cement ratio.

Influence of Age: Age at which a concrete members is loaded will have a predominant effect on the magnitude of creep. This can be easily understood from the fact that the quality of gel improves with time. Such gel creeps less, whereas a young gel under load being not so stronger creeps more. What is said above is not a very accurate statement because of the fact that the moisture content of the concrete being different at different age, also influences the magnitude of creep.

Effects of Creep: The magnitude of creep is dependent on many factors, the main factors being time and leval of stress. In reinforced concrete beams, creep increases the deflection with time and may be a critical consideration in design.

In reinforced concrete columns, creep property of concrete is useful. Under load immediately elastic deformation takes place. Concrete creeps and deforms. It can not deform independent of steel reinforcement. There will be gradual transfer of stress from concrete to steel. The extra load in the steel is required to be shared by concrete and this situation results

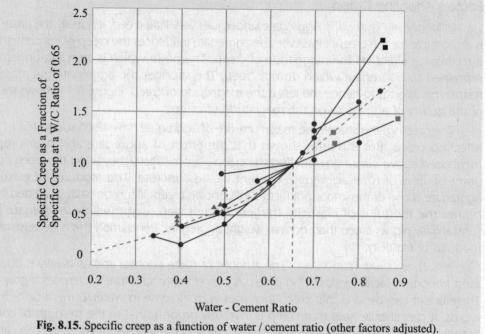

Fig. 8.15. Specific creep as a function of water / cement ratio (other factors adjusted).

in employment and development of full strength of both the materials. However, in eccentrically loaded columns, creep increases the deflection and can load to buckling.

In case of statically indeterminate structures and column and beam junctions creep may relieve the stress concentration induced by shrinkage, temperatures changes or movement of support. Creep property of concrete will be useful in all concrete structures to reduce the internal stresses due to non-uniform load or restrained shrinkage.

In mass concrete structures such as dams, on account of differential temperature conditions at the interior and surface, creep is harmful and by itself may be a cause of cracking in the interior of dams. Therefore, all precautions and steps must be taken to see that increase in temperature does not take place in the interior of mass concrete structure.

Loss of prestress due to creep of concrete in prestressed concrete structure is well known and provision is made for the loss of prestress in the design of such structures.

Shrinkage

It has been indicated in the earlier chapter that concrete is subjected to changes in volume either autogenous or induced. Volume change is one of the most detrimental properties of concrete, which affects the long-term strength and durability. To the practical engineer, the aspect of volume change in concrete is important from the point of view that it causes unsightly cracks in concrete. We have discussed elsewhere the effect of volume change due to thermal properties of aggregate and concrete, due to alkali/aggregate reaction, due to sulphate action etc. Presently we shall discuss the volume change on account of inherenet properties of concrete "shrinkage".

One of the most objectionable defects in concrete is the presence of cracks, particularly in floors and pavements. One of the important factors that contribute to the cracks in floors and pavements is that due to shrinkage. It is difficult to make concrete which does not shrink and crack. It is only a question of magnitude. Now the question is how to reduce the shrinkage and shrinkage cracks in concrete structures. As shrinkage is an inherent property of concrete it demands greater understanding of the various properties of concrete, which influence its shrinkage characteristics. It is only when the mechanism of all kinds of shrinkage and the factors affecting the shrinkage are understood, an engineer will be in a better position to control and limit the shrinkage in the body of concrete.

The term shrinkage is loosely used to describe the various aspects of volume changes in concrete due to loss of moisture at different stages due to different reasons. To understand this aspect more closely, shrinkage can be classified in the following way:

(*a*) Plastic Shrinkage;   (*b*) Drying Shrinkage;

(*c*) Autogeneous Shrinkage;   (*d*) Carbonation Shrinkage.

Plastic Shrinkage

Shrinkage of this type manifests itself soon after the concrete is placed in the forms while the concrete is still in the plastic state. Loss of water by evaporation from the surface of concrete or by the absorption by aggregate or subgrade, is believed to be the reasons of plastic shrinkage. The loss of water results in the reduction of volume. The aggregate particles or the reinforcement comes in the way of subsidence due to which cracks may appear at the surface or internally around the aggregate or reinforcement.

In case of floors and pavements where the surface area exposed to drying is large as compared to depth, when this large surface is exposed to hot sun and drying wind, the surface of concrete dries very fast which results in plastic shrinkage.

Sometimes even if the concrete is not subjected to severe drying, but poorly made with a high water/cement ratio, large quantity of water bleeds and accumulates at the surface.

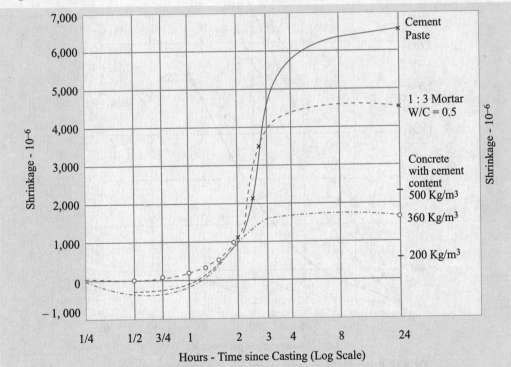

Fig. 8.16. The influence of cement content of the mix on early shrinkage in air at 20°C and 50 per cent relative humidity with wind velocity of 1.0 m/s.[8.5]

When this water at the surface dries out, the surface concrete collapses causing cracks.

Plastic concrete is sometimes subjected to unintended vibration or yielding of formwork support which again causes plastic shrinkage cracks as the concrete at this stage has not developed enough strength. From the above it can

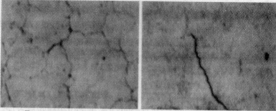

Typical Plastic Shrinkage cracks due to rapid evaporation of water from hot sun and drying wind.

be inferred that high water/cement ratio, badly proportioned concrete, rapid drying, greater bleeding, unintended vibration etc., are some of the reasons for plastic shrinkage. It can also be further added that richer concrete undergoes greater plastic shrinkage. Figure 8.16 shows the influence of cement content on plastic shrinkage.[8.5]

Plastic shrinkage can be reduced mainly by preventing the rapid loss of water from surface. This can be done by covering the surface with polyethylene sheeting immediately on finishing operation; by monomolecular coatings by fog spray that keeps the surface moist; or by working at night. An effective method of removing plastic shrinkage cracks is to revibrate the concrete in a controlled manner. Use of small quantity of aluminium power is also suggested to offset the effect of plastic shrinkage. Similarly, expansive cement or shrinkage

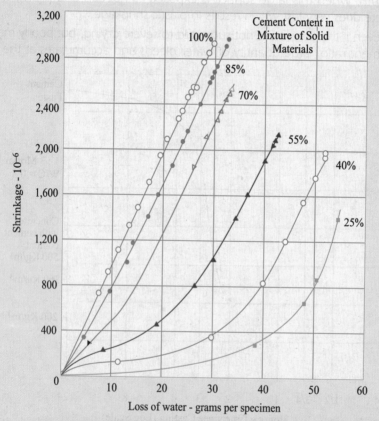

Fig. 8.17. Relation between shrinkage and loss of water from specimens of Cement–pulverised silica pastes cured for 7 days at 21°C and then dried.[8.6]

compensating cement also can be used for controlling the shrinkage during the setting of concrete. The principal property of such cement is that the expansion induced in the plastic concrete will almost offset the normal shrinkage due to loss of moisture. Under correct usage, the distance between the joints can sometimes be tripled without increasing the level of shrinkage cracking. Further, use of unneeded high slump concrete, over sanded mix, higher air entraining should be discouraged in order to reduce the higher plastic shrinkage.

Drying Shrinkage

Just as the hydration of cement is an ever lasting process, the drying shrinkage is also an ever lasting process when

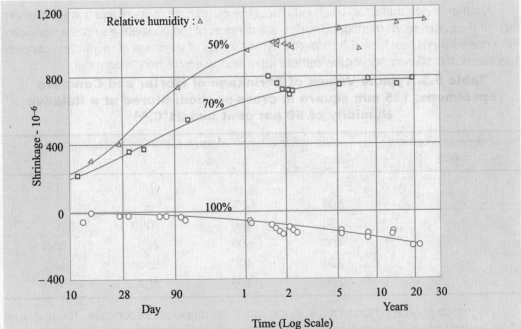

Fig. 8.18. Typical apparatus for drying shrinkage and moisture movement tests.

Fig. 8.19. Relation between shrinkage and time for concrete stored at different relative humidities.[8.3]

concrete is subjected to drying conditions. The drying shrinkage of concrete is analogous to the mechanism of drying of timber specimen. The loss of free water contained in hardened concrete, does not result in any appreciable dimension change. It is the loss of water held in gel pores that causes the change in the volume. Figure 8.17 shows the relationship between loss of moisture and shrinkage. Under drying conditions, the gel water is lost progressively over a long time, as long as the concrete is kept in drying conditions. It is theoretically estimated that the total linear change due to long time drying shrinkage could be of the order of $10,000 \times 10^{-6}$. But values upto $4,000 \times 10^{-6}$ have been actually observed. Figure 8.18 shows the typical apparatus for measuring shrinkage.

Cement paste shrinks more than mortar and mortar shrinks more than concrete. Concrete made with smaller size aggregate shrinks more than concrete made with bigger size aggregate. The magnitude of drying shrinkage is also a function of the fineness of gel. The finer the gel the more is the shrinkage. It has been pointed out earlier that the high pressure steam cured concrete with low specific surface of gel, shrinks much less than that of normally cured cement gel.

Factors Affecting Shrinkage

One of the most important factors that affects shrinkage is the drying condition or in other words, the relative humidity of the atmoshphere at which the concrete specimen is kept. If the concrete is placed in 100 per cent relative humidity for any length of time, there will not be any shrinkage, instead there will be a slight swelling. The typical relationship between shrinkage and time for which concrete is stored at different relative humidities is shown in Figure 8.19. The graph shows that the magnitude of shrinkage increases with time and also with the reduction of relative humidity. The rate of shrinkage decreases rapidly with time. It is observed that 14 to 34 per cent of the 20 year shrinkage occurs in 2 weeks, 40 to 80 per cent of the 20 year shrinkage occurs in 3 months and 66 to 85 per cent of the 20 year shrinkage occurs in one year.

Another important factor which influences the magnitude of shrinkage is water/cement ratio of the concrete. As mentioned earlier, the richness of the concrete also has a significant influence on shrinkage. Table 8.3 shows the typical values of shrinkage of mortar and concrete specimens, for different aggregate/cement ratio, and water/cement ratio.

Table 8.3. Typical Values of Shrinkage of Mortar and Concrete Specimens, 125 mm square in cross-section; Stored at a Relative Humidity of 50 per cent and 21°C.[8.8]

Aggregate/cement ratio	Shrinkage after six months (10^{-6}) for water/cement ratio of			
	0.4	0.5	0.6	0.7
3	800	1200	–	–
4	550	850	1,050	
5	400	600	750	850
6	300	400	550	650
7	200	300	400	500

Aggregate plays an important role in the shrinkage properties of concrete. The quantum of an aggregate, its size, and its modulus of elasticity influence the magnitude of drying

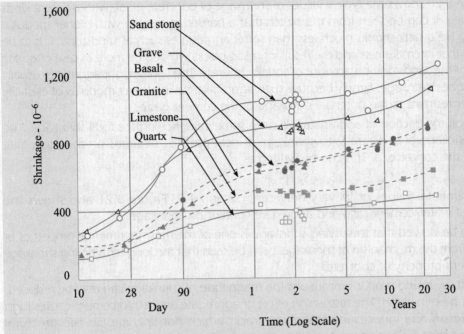

Fig. 8.20. Shrinkage of concretes of fixed mix proportions but made with different aggregates and stored in air at 21°C and a relative humidity of 50 percent.

shrinkage. The grading of aggregate by itself may not directly make any significant influence. But since it affects the quantum of paste and water/cement ratio, it definitely influences the drying shrinkage indirectly. The aggregate particles restrain the shrinkage of the paste. The harder aggregate does not shrink in unison with the shrinking of the paste whereby it results in higher shrinkage stresses, but low magnitude of total shrinkage. But a softer aggregate yields to the shrinkage stresses of the paste and thereby experiences lower magnitude of shrinkage stresses within the body, but greater magnitude of total shrinkage.

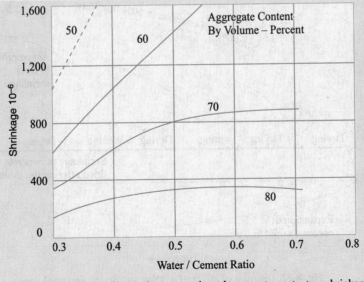

Fig. 8.21. Influence of water / cement ratio and aggregate content on shrinkage.[8.7]

Figure 8.20 shows the typical values of shrinkage of concrete made with different kinds of aggregate. It can be seen from the sketch that a harder aggregate with higher modulus of elasticity like quartz shrinks much less than softer aggregates such as sandstone. It is to be also noted that internal stress and the resultant micro cracks will also be more in case of quartz than that of the sandstone on account of shrinkage stress. The light-weight aggregate usually leads to higher shrinkage, largely because such aggregate having lower modulus of elasticity offers lesser restraint to the potential shrinkage of the cement paste.

The volume fraction of aggregate will have some influence on the total shrinkage. The ratio of shrinkage of concrete S_c to shrinkage of neat paste S_p depends on the aggregate content in the concrete, a. This can be written as

$$S_c = S_p \, (1-a)^n$$

Experimental values of 'n' vary between 1.2 and 1.7. Figure 8.21 also shows the influence of water/cement ratio and aggregate content on shrinkage.

It is to be viewed that the drying shrinkage is one of the most detrimental properties of concrete. From the mechanism of shrinkage it can be seen that the long term drying shrinkage is an inherent property of concrete.

At best, by taking proper precautions the magnitude of shrinkage can only be reduced, but cannot be eliminated. The restraining effect of aggregate and reinforcement causes high internal stresses and induces internal micro cracks which not only impairs the structural integrity and strength but also reduces the durability of concrete. Another aspect to be seen with respect to the drying shrinkage is that moisture loss takes place at the surface of the member, which may not be compensated in the same rate by the movement of moisture from interior to the surface. As a result, moisture gradient is set up in a concrete specimen. The moisture gradient induces differential stresses, which again induces cracks.

As the drying takes place at the surface of the concrete, the magnitude of shrinkage varies considerably with the size and thickness of the specimen. Investigations have been carried out to find out the influence of the size of specimen on shrinkage. It is observed that

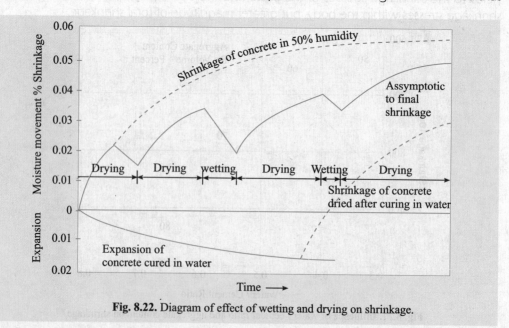

Fig. 8.22. Diagram of effect of wetting and drying on shrinkage.

shrinkage decreases with an increase in the size of the specimen. But above some value, the size effect is no longer apparent.

It is pertinent at this point to bring out that the concrete or cement product undergoes long term drying shrinkage in varying magnitude depending upon the various factors mentioned in the proceeding paragraphs. The effect of this shrinkage is to cause cracks in the concrete. Ordinary Portland cement does not show good extensibility (the property to withstand greater, volume change without being cracked). In this respect low heat cement or Portland pozzolana cement will have higher extensibility. It may not be out of place to point out that addition of a certain quantity of lime will improve the extensibility of ordinary cement concrete. The superiority of lime mortar for internal plaster over cement mortar is from the point of view of the superior extensibility of lime mortar over cement mortar by about 7 times. A continuous surface, like plaster on the wall, undergoes tremendous change in volume, and as such cement mortar having low extensibility, is not able to withstand the volume change without cracking, where lime mortar or gauged mortar having higher extensibility gives better performance.

Moisture Movement

Concrete shrinks when allowed to dry in air at a lower relative humidity and it swells when kept at 100 per cent relative humidity or when placed in water. Just as drying shrinkage is an ever continuing process, swelling, when continuously placed in water is also an ever continuing process. If a concrete sample subjected to drying condition, at some stage, is subjected to wetting condition, it starts swelling. It is interesting to note that all the initial drying shrinkage is not recovered even after prolonged storage in water which shows that the phenomenon of drying shrinkage is not a fully reversible one. For the usual range of concrete, the irreversible part of shrinkage, represents between 0.3 and 0.6 of the drying shrinkage, the lower value being more common. Just as the drying shrinkage is due to loss of adsorbed water around gel particles, swelling is due to the adsorption of water by the cement gel. The water molecules act against the cohesive force and tend to force the gel particles further apart as a result of which swelling takes place. In addition, the ingress of water decreases the surface tension of the gel.

The property of swelling when placed in wet condition, and shrinking when placed in drying condition is referred as moisture movement in concrete. Figure 8.22 shows the typical moisture movement of 1:1 cement mortar mix, stored alternatively in water and dried in air to 50 per cent relative humidity. The moisture movement in concrete induces alternatively compressive stress and tensile stress which may cause fatigue in concrete which reduces the durability of concrete owing to reversal of stresses.

Autogeneous Shrinkage

In a conservative system i.e. where no moisture movement to or from the paste is permitted, when temperature is constant some shrinkage may occur. The shrinkage of such a conservative system is known as a autogeneous shrinkage.

Autogeneous shrinkage is of minor importance and is not applicable in practice to many situations except that of mass of concrete in the interior of a concrete dam. The magnitude of autogeneous shrinkage is in the order of about 100×10^{-6}.

Carbonation Shrinkage

Carbonation shrinkage is a phenomenon very recently recognised. Carbon dioxide present in the atmoshphere reacts in the presence of water with hydrated cement. Calcium hydroxide [Ca(OH)$_2$] gets converted to calcium carbonate and also some other cement compounds are decomposed. Such a complete decomposition of calcium compound in hydrated cement is chemically possible even at the low pressure of carbon dioxide in normal atmoshphere. Carbonation penetrates beyond the exposed surface of concrete only very slowly.

The rate of penetration of carbon dioxide depends also on the moisture content of the concrete and the relative humidity of the ambient medium. Carbonation is accompanied by an increase in weight of the concrete and by shrinkage. Carbonation shrinkage is probably caused by the dissolution of crystals of calcium hydroxide and deposition of calcium carbonate in its place. As the new product is less in volume than the product replaced, shrinkage takes place.

Carbonation of concrete also results in increased strength and reduced permeability, possibly because water released by carbonation promotes the process of hydration and also calcium carbonate reduces the voids within the cement paste. As the magnitude of carbonation shrinkage is very small when compared to long term drying shrinkage, this aspect is not of much significance. But carbonation reduces the alkalinity of concrete which gives a protective coating to the reinforcement against rusting. If depth of carbonation reaches upto steel reinforcements, the steel becomes liable for corrosion.

REFERENCES

8.1   Shideler J.J., *Light weight concrete for structural use, ACI Journal*, Oct 1957.

8.2   Ori Ishai, *The Time—dependent Deformational Behaviour of Cement Paste, Mortar and Concrete, International conference on structure of concrete*, Sept 1965.

8.3   Troxell G.C. etal, *Long-time creep and shrinkage Tests of plain and Reinforced concrete Proceedings* ASTM V 58, 1958.

8.4   Ross A.D., *Concrete creep Data, The structural Engineer*, 1937.

8.5   L'Hermite, *Volume Changes of Concrete,* Proceedings, 4th International Symposium on the Chemistry of Cement, Washington D.C. 1960.

8.6   Powers T.C., *Causes and Control of Colume Change,* Journal of Portland Cement Association, Research and Development Laboratories No. 1, Jan 1959.

8.7   Odman STA, *Effects of Variation in Volume, Surface Area Exposed to Drying and Composition of Concrete on Shrinkage*, RILEM/CEMBREAU, International Colloguium of the Shrinkage of Hydrulic Concretes, Madrid 1968.

8.8   Lea F.M., *The Chemistry of Cement and Concrete*, 1956.

An architect's rendering of the Hindu Temple built at Kauai Island, Hawaii. A massive concrete foundation was laid to last for at least one thousand years. They have used high volume fly ash concrete replacing OPC by 57%.

Courtesy : P.K. Mehta

9
CHAPTER

Durability of Concrete

General

For a long time, concrete was considered to be very durable material requiring a little or no maintenance. The assumption is largely true, except when it is subjected to highly aggressive environments. We build concrete structures in highly polluted urban and industrial areas, aggressive marine environments, harmful sub-soil water in coastal area and many other hostile conditions where other materials of construction are found to be non-durable. Since the use of concrete in recent years, have spread to highly harsh and hostile conditions, the earlier impression that concrete is a very durable material is being threatened, particularly on account of premature failures of number of structures in the recent past.

In the past, only strength of concrete was considered in the concrete mix design procedure assuming strength of concrete is an all pervading factor for all other desirable properties of concrete including durability. For the first time, this pious opinion was proved wrong in late 1930's when

Hoover Dam, USA (1931-36).
A symbolic structure for Sustainable Development with ever 1000 years of predicted life

they found that series of failures of concrete pavements have taken place due to frost attack. Although compressive strength is a measure of durability to a great extent it is not entirely true that the strong concrete is always a durable concrete. For example, while it is structurally possible to build a jetty pier in marine conditions with 20 MPa concrete, environmental condition can lead this structure to a disastrous consequences. In addition to strength of concrete another factor, environmental condition or what we generally call exposure condition has become an important consideration for durability.

Concrete durability is a subject of major concern in many countries. Number of international seminars are held on concrete durability and numerous papers written on failures of concrete structures are discussed and state-of-the-art reports are written and disseminated , regularly.

In the recent revision of IS 456 of 2000, one of the major points discussed, deliberated and revised is the durability aspects of concrete, in line with codes of practices of other countries, who have better experiences in dealing with durability of concrete structures.

One of the main reasons for deterioration of concrete in the past, is that too much emphasis is placed on concrete compressive strength. As a matter of fact, advancement in concrete technology has been generally on the strength of concrete. It is now recognised that strength of concrete alone is not sufficient, the degree of harshness of the environmental condition to which concrete is exposed over its entire life is equally important. Therefore, both strength and durability have to be considered explicitly at the design stage. It is interesting to consider yet another view point regarding strength and durability relationship.

Strength and Durability Relationship

In the previous paragraphs, we have been discussing all the time that although the strength of concrete has direct relationship with durability it does not hold gold in all situations.

This aspect needs little more discussions.

Generally, construction industry needs faster development of strength in concrete so that the projects can be completed in time or before time. This demand is catered by high early strength cement, use of very low W/C ratio through the use of increased cement content and reduced water content. The above steps result in higher thermal shrinkage, drying shrinkage, modulus of elasticity and lower creep coefficients. With higher quantity of cement content, the concrete exhibits greater cracking tendencies because of increased thermal and drying shrinkage. As the creep coefficient is low in such concrete, there will not be much scope for relaxation of stresses. Therefore, high early strength concretes are more prone to cracking than moderate or low strength concrete. Of course, the structural cracks in high strength concrete can be controlled by use of sufficient steel reinforcements. But this practice does not help the concrete durability, as provision of more steel reinforcement, will only results in conversion of the bigger cracks into smaller cracks. All the same even this smaller cracks are sufficient to allow oxygen, carbon dioxide, and moisture get into the concrete to affect the long term durability of concrete.

Field experience have also corroborated that high early strength concrete are more cracks-prone. According to a recent report, the cracks in pier caps have been attributed to the use of high cement content in concrete. Contractors apparently thought that a higher than the desired strength would speed up the construction time, and therefore used high cement content.

Similarly, report submitted by National Cooperative Highway Research Programme (NCHRP) of USA during 1995, based on their survey, showed that more than, 100000 concrete bridge decks in USA showed full depth transverse cracks even before structures were less than one month old. The reasons given are that combination of thermal shrinkage and drying shrinkage caused most of the cracks. It is to be noted that deck concrete is made of high strength concrete. These concretes have a high elastic modulus at an early age. Therefore, they develop high stresses for a given temperature change or amount of drying shrinkage. The most important point is that such concrete creeps little to relieve the stresses.

A point for consideration is that, the high early strength concrete made with modern Portland cement which are finer in nature, containing higher sulphates and alkalis, when used 400 kg/m^3 or more, are prone to cracking. Therefore if long-term service life is the goal, a proper balance between a too high and a too low cement content must be considered. This is where the use of mineral admixtures comes in handy.

We discussed in the above paragraphs, that the present day practice is to use high early strength concrete for early completion of projects. We have also seen that high early strength concrete made by using very low W/C ratio of the order of 0.30 or less by using low water content and high cement content is prone to micro cracking which affects the long term durability.

It is interesting to see that the above point of view is not fully convincing when seen from many other considerations.

Firstly, the high early strength concrete has high cement content and low water content. On account of low water content, only surface hydration of cement particle would have taken place leaving considerable amount of unhydrated core of cement grains. This unhydrated core of cement grains has strength in reserve. When micro cracks have developed, the unhydrated core gets hydrated, getting moisture through micro cracks. The hydration products so generated seal the cracks and restore the integrity of concrete for long term durability.

Secondly, as per Aiticin, the quality of products of hydration (gel) formed in the case of low W/C ratio is superior to the quality of gel formed in the case of high W/C ratio. [9.1]

Again as per Aiticin, in low W/C ratio concrete (high early strength concrete) the weak transition zone between aggregate and hydrated cement paste does not exist at all. Unhydrated cement particles are also available in such low W/C ratio concrete for any eventual healing of micro cracks.

Thirdly, the micro structure of concrete with very low W/C ratio, is much stronger and less permeable. The interconnected network of capillaries are so fine that water cannot flow any more through them. It is reported that when tested for chloride ion permeability, it showed 10-50 times slower penetration than low strength concrete.

It is difficult to conclude whether the micro cracks developed in high early strength concrete reduces the long term durability or the delayed hydration of unhydrated core of cement grains would heal up the micro cracks and thereby improve long term durability along with the better quality of product of hydration, higher strength, reduced permeability, in case of low W/C ratio concrete. It is a subject for research.

Volume Change in Concrete

It will not be wrong to attribute the lack of durability to the reason of volume change in concrete. Volume change in concrete is caused by many factors. As a matter of fact, probing into the factors causing volume change in concrete will lead to an interesting study of concrete technology. The various causes that are responsible for volume change, fully expose the various factors affecting durability which encompasses wide spectrum of concrete technology.

If one takes a close look, one comes to know that, the entire hydration process is nothing but an internal volume change, the effect of heat of hydration, the pozzolamic action, the sulphate action, the carbonation, moisture movement, all types of shrinkages, the effect of chlorides, rusting of steel reinforcement and host of other aspects come under the preview of volume change in concrete.

It can also be viewed that it is the permeability that leads to volume change. The volume change results in cracks. It is the cracks that promotes more permeability and thus it becomes a cyclic action, till such time that concrete undergoes deterioration, degradation, disruption and eventual failure.

Definition of Durability

The durability of cement concrete is defined as its ability to resist weathering action, chemical attack, abrasion, or any other process of deterioration. Durable concrete will retain its original form, quality, and serviceability when exposed to its environment.

Significance of Durability

When designing a concrete mix or designing a concrete structure, the exposure condition at which the concrete is supposed to withstand is to be assessed in the beginning with good judgement. In case of foundations, the soil characteristics are also required to be investigated. The environmental pollution is increasing day by day particularly in urban areas and industrial atmospheres. It is reported that in industrially developed countries over 40 per cent of total resources of the building industries are spent on repairs and maintenance. In India, the money that is spent on repair of buildings is also considerable. Every government department and municipal bodies have their own "Repair Boards" to deal with repairs of buildings. It is a sad state of affairs that we do not give enough attention to durability aspects even when we carry out repairs.

We carry out repairs job in a casual manner using only ordinary cement mortar practised decades back. Today, special repair materials and techniques are available. The use of such materials make the repair job more effective and durable. This aspects have been covered in chapter 5.

Another point for consideration is that, presently, the use of concrete has been extended to more hostile environments, having already used up all good, favourable sites. Even the good materials such as aggregate, sand are becoming short supply. No doubt that the cement production is modernised, but sometimes the second grade raw materials such as limestones containing excess of chloride is being used for pressing economical reasons. Earlier specifications of portland cement permitted a maximum chloride content of 0.05 per cent. Recently, maximum permissible chloride content in cement has been increased to 0.1 per cent. This high permissible chloride content in cement demands much stricter durability considerations in other aspects of concrete making practices to keep the total chloride content in concrete within the permissible limits. In other words, considerations for durability of modern concrete constructions assume much more importance, than hitherto practised.

Impact of W/C Ratio on Durability

In the preceding pages we have discussed that volume change results in cracks and cracks are responsible for disintegration of concrete. We may add now that permeability is the contributory factor for volume change and higher W/C ratio is the fundamental cause of higher permeability. Therefore, use of higher W/C ratio — permeability — volume change — cracks — disintegration — failure of concrete is a cyclic process in concrete. Therefore, for a durable concrete, use of lowest possible W/C ratio is the fundamental requirement to produce dense and impermeable concrete.

There is a tremendous change in the micro structure of concrete made with high W/C ratio and low W/C ratio. With low W/C ratio the permeability decreases to such a level that these concretes are impervious to water. This does not mean that they do not contain interconnected network of capillaries, but these capillaries are so fine that water cannot flow any more through them. When such concretes are tested for chloride ions permeability test, it is found that chloride ions diffuse such concretes at a rate 10 — 50 times slower than that of high W/C ratio concrete.

It has been proved beyond doubt that low W/C ratio concrete are less sensitive to carbonation, external chemical attack and other detrimental effects that causes lack of durability of concrete. It has been reported that it become impossible to corrode unprotected steel reinforcement in accelerated corrosion test of a concrete with very low W/C ratio. From this it could be inferred that the best way to protect reinforcing steel against corrosion is to use low W/C and adequate cover, rather than using higher W/C ratio and then protecting the steel by epoxy coating.

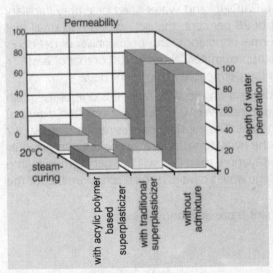

Degree of Permeability

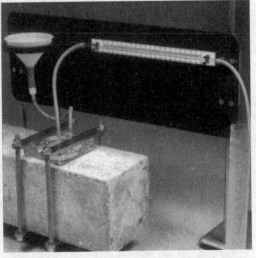

Cap and Initial Surface Absorption Test (ISAT)

It is easy to preach on paper the virtues of using low W/C ratio for all-round durability of concrete. But in actual practice for many years it has been found almost impossible to reduce the W/C ratio below 0.4. This situation has changed for the last fifteen years in India with the practice of using superplasticizers. The advent and use of superplasticizers have revolutionised the art and science of making durable concrete by drastically reducing the W/C ratio of concrete. The modern superplasticizers are so efficient that it is now possible to make flowing concrete with a W/C as low as 0.25 or even as low as 0.20. This technological breakthrough, in conjunction with the use of silica fume and other secondary cementitious materials, has made it possible to develop a new family of high-strength concrete which is generally referred as high-performance concrete—a concrete which is very durable.

In most of these new low W/C ratio concretes, as explained earlier, there is not enough water available to fully hydrate all the cement particles. The water available can only hydrate the surface of cement particles and there exist plenty of unhydrated particles which can play an important role as they constitute strength in reserve. If for any reasons, structural or environmental, concrete gets cracked, the unhydrated cement particles begin hydrating as soon as water or moisture starts penetrating through cracks. This is to say that unhydrated cement particles offer self healing potential to improve durability of concrete.

Permeability

We have discussed that W/C ratio is the fundamental point for concrete durability. Another important point for consideration is the permeability of concrete. When we talk about durability of concrete, generally we start discussion from the permeability of concrete as it has much wider and direct repercussion on durability than that of W/C ratio. For example, micro-cracks at transition zone is a consideration for permeability whereas W/C ratio may not get involved directly. It may be mentioned that microcracks in the initial stage are so small that they may not increase the permeability. But propagation of microcracks with time due to drying shrinkage, thermal shrinkage and externally applied load will increase the permeability of the system.

Permeability of Cement Paste

The cement paste consists of C-S-H gel, $Ca(OH)_2$ and water filled or empty capillary cavities. Although gel is porous to the extent of 28 per cent, the gel pores are so small that hardly any water can pass through under normal conditions. The permeability of gel pores is estimated to be about 7×10^{-16} m/s. That is approximately about 1/100 of that of paste.[9.2] Therefore, the gel pores do not contribute to the permeability of cement paste.

The extent and size of capillary cavities depend on the W/C ratio. It is one of the main factors contributing to the permeability of paste. At lower W/C ratio, not only the extent of capillary cavities is less but the diameter is also small. The capillary cavities resulting at low W/C ratio, will get filled up within a few days by the hydration products of cement. Only unduly large cavities resulting from higher W/C ratio (say more than 0.7) will not get filled up by the products of hydration, and will remain as unsegmented cavities, which is responsible for the permeability of paste.

Table 9.1 shows the permeability of cement paste at various ages

Table 9.1. Reduction in Permeability of Cement Paste (W/C Ratio = 0.7) with Progress of Hydration. [9.3]

Age days	Coefficient of Permeability Km/s
fresh	2×10^{-6}
5 days	4×10^{-10}
6 days	1×10^{-10}
8 days	4×10^{-11}
13 days	5×10^{-12}
24 days	1×10^{-12}
ultimate	6×10^{-13} (calculated)

It is very interesting to see that the permeability of cement paste with very low W/C ratio can be compared to the permeability of dense rocks. Table 9.2 shows the comparison between permeabilities of rocks and cement paste.

Table 9.2. Comparison Between Permeabilities of Rocks and Cement Pastes [9.2]

Type of Rocks	Coefficient of Permeability m/s	Water/cement ratio of mature paste of the same permeability
1. Dense trap	2.47×10^{-14}	0.38
2. Quartz cliorite	8.24×10^{-14}	0.42
3. Marble	2.39×10^{-13}	0.48
4. Marble	5.77×10^{-12}	0.66
5. Granite	5.35×10^{-11}	0.70
6. Sandstone	1.23×10^{-10}	0.71
7. Granite	1.56×10^{-10}	0.71

From Table 9.2 it is seen that the cement paste even with high W/C ratio of 0.70 is quite impervious as that of granite with coefficient of permeability of 5.35×10^{-11} m/s. This value of coefficient of permeability is so small, that physically no water will permeate through in any perceptible manner. However in actual practice, it is noticed that mortar and concrete exhibit appreciable permeability much higher than the values shown in the table 9.2. This is definitely not because of the permeability of aggregates in mortar or concrete. The aggregate used in mortar or concrete is as impermeable as that of paste as can be seen in Table 9.2. The higher permeability of mortar or concrete in actual structures is due to the following reasons.

(a) Formation of microcracks developed due to long term drying shrinkage and thermal stresses.

(b) The large microcracks generated with time in the transition zones.

(c) Cracks generated through higher structural stresses.

(d) Due to volume change and cracks produced on account of various minor reasons.

(e) Existence of entrapped air due to insufficient compaction.

Fig. 9.1 shows the relation between permeability and capillary porosity of cement paste

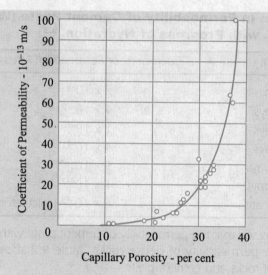

Fig. 9.1. Relation between permeability and capillary porosity of cement paste [9.2]

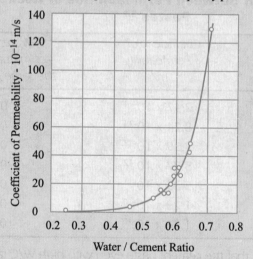

Fig. 9.2. Relation between permeability and water/cement ratio for mature cement pastes (93 per cent of cement hydrated) [9.3]

Fig. 9.2 shows the relation between permeability and water/cement ratio for mature cement paste (93 per cent of cement hydrated)

From Fig. 9.2 it can be seen that coefficient of permeability increases more than 100 times from W/C ratio of 0.4 to 0.7. Therefore, many code of practices fix the maximum W/C ratio at 0.4 so that the ingress of aggressive chemicals is restricted. The restriction of W/C ratio is also imposed in liquid retaining structures.

Permeability of Concrete

Theoretically, the introduction of aggregate of low permeability into cement paste, it is expected to reduce the permeability of the system because the aggregate particles intercept the channels of flows and make it take a circuitous route. Compared to neat cement paste, concrete with the same W/C ratio and degree of maturity, should give a lower coefficient of permeability. But in practice, it is seen from test data it is not the case. The introduction of aggregate, particularly larger size of aggregates increase the permeability considerably.

The explanation lies in the development of microcracks that are produced in the transition zone. Opinion differs in this regard about the size of microcracks that are generated at the transition zone. However, the drying shrinkage, thermal shrinkage and externally applied load may cause cracks in weak transition zone at the young age. It is reported that the size of the cracks in transition zone is much bigger than most of the capillary cavities present in cement paste.

Table 9.3 shows the typical observed values of permeability of concrete used in some of the dams in the United States.

In-situ Water Permeability of Concrete

The use of pozzolanic materials in optimum proportion reduces the permeability of concrete. This is evidently due to the conversion of calcium hydroxide, otherwise soluble and leachable, into cementitious product.

Though air-entrainment, makes the concrete porous, when used up to 6%, makes the concrete more impervious, contrary to general belief.

Table 9.3. Typical values of Permeability of concrete used in Dams

Cement Content kg/m³	Water/Cement Ratio	Permeability 10^{-12} m/s
156	0.69	8
151	0.74	24
138	0.75	35
223	0.46	28

High pressure steam cured concrete in conjunction with crushed silica decreases the permeability. This is due to the formation of coarser C-S-H gel, lower drying shrinkage and accelerated conversion of $Ca(OH)_2$ into cementitious products.

Interaction Between Permeability, Volume Change and Cracking

In the preceding pages we have discussed about permeability, volume change and cracking of concrete are responsible for lack of durability of concrete and concrete structures. It is difficult to pin point which of these are primarily responsible for affecting durability. Permeability of concrete is often referred as the root cause for lack of durability. But it can be seen that volume change that takes place in an otherwise impervious concrete due to heat of hydration or internal manifestation can crack the concrete affecting durability. Microcracks in transition zone even in initially impermeable concrete, can start the cycle of deterioration process in concrete. Therefore, these three factors, one follows the other two, like day follows the night, are responsible for affecting durability of concrete and concrete structures.

Table 9.4. Types and Causes of Concrete Cracks[9.4]

	1. Primary Classification	2. Secondary Classification	3. Cause	4. Example or Contributing Condition	5. Remedy
	Prehardening → Constructional Movement	Subgrade	Settlement of subgrade	Moisture changes in Subgrade or lack of compaction of subgrade	Control of subgrading
	Prehardening → Constructional Movement	Formwork	Movement of formwork	Swelling of wood or pressure of wet concrete	Construction of adequate forms
	Prehardening → Setting Shrinkage	Settlement Shrinkage	Reinforcement or formwork obstructions; Settlement of concrete during setting	Settlement of around obstruction mix too fluid	Dense mixes with low water content & adequate compaction of low lifts
	Prehardening → Setting Shrinkage	Plastic shrinkage	Chemical reactions	Cracks occur soon after placing and under moist conditions	Remedy not clear but refloating eliminates cracks
	Prehardening → Setting Shrinkage	Drying shrinkage	Rapid drying while setting occurs	Cracking of exposed surfaces due to high wind, low humidity or temperature differential	Proper protection

Table 9.5. Other Properties, Types and Causes of Concrete Cracking[9.4]

After hardening

1. Primary Classification	2. Secondary Classification	3. Cause	4. Example or Contributing Condition	5. Remedy
Drying Shrinkage		Loss of water	Cracking of building slabs and walls	Dense mixes with low cement and water content; adequate curing
Chemical action	Concrete	Reactive aggregates	Expansion of internal mass resulting in cracking of external skin	Low alkali cement and non-reactive aggregates
Chemical action	Steel	Corrosion of reinforcement		Thick and dense layer of protective concrete
Temperature	Internal	Differential expansions and contraction	Heat of hydration of cement; aggregates of abnormal thermal expansion	Low-heat cement and control of temperature rise; aggregates of normal thermal expansion
Temperature	External	Climatic changes	Large slabs or walls without adequate joints	Adequate expansion contraction joints
Temperature	External	Frost and ice action	Spalling of surface	Air entrainment and sound concrete
Structural failure		Excessive Tensile stresses due to loads	Building settlement, excessive loads, vibration, earthquakes, and insufficient reinforcement	Correct design of structure

Table 9.6. Various Types and Causes of Cracks in Concrete

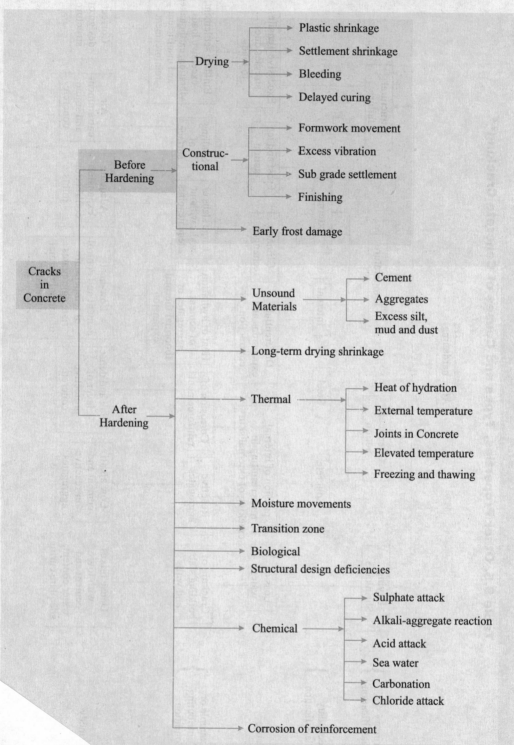

In discussing durability of concrete, one can go through permeability route, or volume change route or cracks route. By following any one of the above routes, it is possible to discuss the entire aspects of durability of concrete. Therefore, we shall follow the "cracks in concrete" route to discuss and describe the various factors that affect the durability of concrete.

Factors Contributing to Cracks in Concrete

Mercer L.B,[9.4] in his paper on classification of concrete cracks has given two tables to explain the types and causes of concrete cracks Refer Table 9.4 and Table 9.5.

But in our discussion, we shall follow the Table 9.6 step by step and describe the cracks in concrete which affect durability of concrete.

Plastic Shrinkage Cracks

Water from fresh concrete can be lost by evaporation, absorption by subgrade, formwork and in hydration process. When the loss of water from surface of concrete is faster than the migration of water from interior to the surface, the surface dries up. This creates moisture gradient which results in surface cracking while concrete is still in plastic condition. The magnitude of plastic shrinkage and plastic shrinkage cracks are depending upon ambient temperature, relative humidity and wind velocity. In other words, it depends upon the rate of evaporation of water from the surface of concrete.

Rate of evaporation in excess of 1 kg/m^2 per hour is considered critical (refer Fig. 5.33). In such a situation, the following measures could be taken to reduce or eliminate plastic shrinkage cracks.

- Moisten the subgrade and formworks.
- Erect temporary wind breakers to reduce the wind velocity over concrete.
- Erect temporary roof to protect green concrete from hot sun.
- Reduce the time between placing and finishing. If there is delay cover the concrete with polythylene sheets.
- Minimise evaporation by covering concrete with burlap, fog spray and curing compound.

Fig. 9.3 shows the typical plastic shrinkage cracks. It is seen that cracks are parallel to one another and are spaced 0.3 to 1.0 meter apart. They can be deep and the width varying from 0.1 to 3.0 mm.

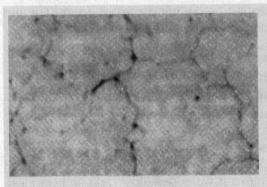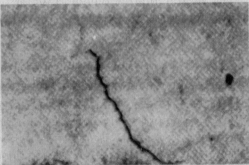

Fig. 9.3. Typical plastic shrinkage cracks.[9.5]

Plastic shrinkage cracks are very common in hot weather conditions in pavements floor and roof slab concrete.

Once they are formed it is difficult to rectify. In case of prefabricated units, they can be healed by controlled revibration, if the concrete is in plastic condition. In roof and floor slab it is difficult to repair. However, sometimes, a thick slurry is poured over the cracks and well worked by trowel after striking each side of the cracks to seal the same. The best way is to take all precautions to prevent evaporation of water from the wet concrete, finish it fast, and cure it as early as feasible.

In Mumbai - Pune express highway, the fresh concrete is protected by 100 meter long low tent erected on wheel to brake the wind and also to protect the green concrete from hot sun. In addition, curing compound is sprayed immediately after finishing operations.

Plastic shrinkage cracks, if care is not taken, will affect the durability of concrete in many ways.

Settlement Cracks

Plastic concrete when vibrated or otherwise settles. If the concrete is free to settle uniformly, then there is no cracks. If there is any obstruction to uniform settlement by way of reinforcement or larger piece of aggregate, then it creates some voids or cracks. This is called settlement cracks. This generally happens in a deep beam.

Concrete should be poured in layers and each layer should be properly compacted. Building up of large quantity of concrete over a beam should be avoided.

Sometimes, the settlement cracks and voids are so severe it needs grouting operators to seal them off. Revibration, if possible is an effective step. Otherwise, they effect the structural integrity of the beam or any other member and badly affects, the durability.

Bleeding

Water being the lightest ingredient of all the other materials in concrete, bleeding, *i.e.*, the upward movement of water when concrete settle downwards, is natural in concrete.

The bleeding water, in certain situations emerge at the surface and in some other situations may not come up to the surface. But bleeding does take place.

The bleeding water gets trapped by flat or flaky pieces of aggregates and also by reinforcement and gets accumulated below such aggregates and reinforcement. This is known as internal bleeding. In addition to internal bleeding, the water may further emerge out and accumulate on the top surface of concrete.

Firstly the internal bleeding water trapped below flat pieces of aggregate and reinforcement affect the bond between hardened cement paste, (hcp) and aggregate or reinforcement on account of local higher W/C ratio. The interface is easily prone to microcracking due to shrinkage stresses caused on dissipation of heat of hydration and drying shrinkage. The interface becomes a weak link in concrete. On loading, the micro cracks propagate further, making the concrete susceptible to degradation by environmental agencies.

The bleeding water, emerged at the top surface of concrete, when evaporates make the top surface porous, having very little abrasion resistances. Often, masons float the concrete when bleeding water is still standing on the surface. Too much working of the top surface presses the coarse aggregate down and brings up fine particles of cement and water. Such top surface made up of too fine materials with excess water develops cracks and craziness, affecting durability of concrete.

Delayed Curing

Fundamental requirement for good concrete is to maintain uninterrupted hydration, especially at early age, when the hydration process is faster. If young concrete dries up fast due to hot sun, drying winds and lower relative humidity, the top surface of concrete is devoid of enough water for continuous hydration process. This results in, as described earlier, formation of plastic shrinkage cracks, poorly formed hydration products and all other deformities in the structures of hydrated cement paste.

Modern high grade cements, being finely ground, with higher C_3S content needs early curing particularly in hot weather conditions. Structural members which are thin with large surface to volume ratio, such as sunbreakers, chajja etc., needs early curing .

The common builders in India have wrong notion that curing is to be done only on the following day of concreting. They are insensitive to the cry of drying and thirsty concrete for water or keeping it in required state of wetness. Delayed curing or interruption in continuous curing or not curing for required period are common bad practices followed in most of the construction site in India. Delayed or interrupted curing or not curing for required period can be compared to an ill fed babies or poorly fed human beings during growing years. Such persons are vulnerable to all kinds of diseases and sure to die prematurely. Similarly, insufficient curing is one of the major causes for lack of strength and durability of concrete structures.

Constructional Effects

In many construction sites, properly designed standard formworks are not used. Formworks are made in an adhoc manner. Such formworks may fail to maintain their rigidity and firmness when wet concrete is placed and vibrated. Sinking, bending, settlement or lack of rigidity of formwork may cause cracks or deformation in plastic concrete, after compaction, which may go unnoticed.

It is well known that excess vibration causes segregation which affects the uniformity of concrete mix. These days high consistency concrete is used either for pumping requirements or on account of using superplasticizers. Care must be taken to vibrate such high slump concrete, otherwise, segregation is sure to take place. Segregated concrete matrix, devoid of coarse aggregate, shrinks more than homogeneous concrete and exhibits high shrinkage cracks.

Recently, in one of the major construction sites in Mumbai-Pune express highway, in a road over bridge prestressed concrete girder, 2 to 3 cm thick matrix emerged next to the shuttering plate on account of careless over vibration. On removal of formwork, due to delayed or inefficient curing visible cracks and craziness appeared in such places only. The contractor, much against advice, chipped off such cracked mortar and replastered. This action is sure to reduce the durability of such important prestressed concrete girder.

Finishing becomes an important operation in situations where abrasion resistance is an important factor, such as roads and airfield pavements, factory floor, dock yard, warehouse floor etc. Ideally, cement paste must be contained by fine aggregate and matrix must be contained by coarse aggregates. Such a uniform mixture, devoid of excess paste on the surface will suffer from almost no shrinkage and exhibit good abrasion resistance. The stiffness of concrete at the time of trowelling, extent of trowelling and method of trowelling will all become important to improve the abrasion resistance and durability of concrete surface.

Early Frost Damage

At low temperature, the rate of hydration is slow. The hydration process stops at about $-10°C$. Till such low temperature hydration process though slow, continues. Freshly mixed concrete must not be exposed to freezing condition to protect the same from disruptive action of ice lens. Ice lens will assume 9 per cent more volume than the equivalent water volume. The cumulative effect of increased volume disrupts the integrity of fresh concrete. Once frozen, it is difficult to bring back the integrity of concrete subsequently. It is reported that significant ultimate strength reductions up to about 50 per cent, can occur if concrete is frozen within a few hours after placement or before it attains a compressive strength of 3.5 MPa.

Pure water freezes at 0°C. The water in fresh concrete is not pure, but it is a solution of various salts and as such it does not freeze at 0°C, but at lower than 0°C. It must also be understood that, as long as the temperature is more than −10°C, the hydration process continues and concrete gets heated due to heat of hydration. The temperature inside concrete is also influenced by formwork material, reinforcements exposed to outside weather, and thickness of member. Therefore, it is difficult to forecast whether the concrete has undergone freezing or not.

When concrete has attained a strength of 3.5 MPa, some quantity of water may have been consumed in the hydration process as bound water and certain amount of water may have been imbibed in gel pores. The gel pores are so fine that no ice could be formed in it. Partially filled capillary water, even if it is frozen no appreciable damage will have taken place to seriously disrupt the concrete. It is only saturated and fully filled capillary water, when no hydration has taken place, if frozen, will cause disruption of concrete and affect the longterm durability.

Unsound Materials

Cement or aggregate is considered unsound when they cause unacceptable extent of volume change in hardened concrete or mortar which causes cracks and affects durability.

In cement, if the raw materials contain more lime that can combine with other acidic oxides, or if the raw materials are not properly burnt to the required temperature for the lime to get fully combined with other oxides, cement becomes unsound. Similarly, the presence of MgO which reacts with water in the similar manner as CaO, can also cause unsoundness.

We all know that gypsum is added in appropriate quantity depending upon the C_3A content to prevent flash setting. By chance if gypsum is added in excess quantity, it can cause unsoundness in cement by way of slow expansion in hardened concrete.

Aggregates containing certain materials such as shale, clay lumps, coal, iron pyrites etc. show unsoundness later when concrete undergoes wetting and drying or freezing and thawing. Moisture absorption is often used as a rough index for unsoundness. But there are standard tests for unsoundness of coarse aggregates.

Now a days, crushed sand is being used more often in large works and this practice will grow. Unless proper care is taken crushed sand is likely to contain considerable amount of dust. The excess dust (very fine particle less than 75 micron) is harmful from many points of view and more important being that it causes cracks in concrete.

In many parts of our country, good natural fine aggregate is not available. Often they contain unacceptable amount of organic and inorganic fine particles referred as silt. Excess silt in sand interfere with setting time, shrinkage and bond strength. The ultimate effect is the reduction in tensile strength and shrinkage cracks. One of the contributory causes of cracks and craziness in plaster is the presence of excessive silt and mud in natural sand.

Shrinkage

Shrinkage of concrete is one of the important factors contributing to lack of durability of concrete. Shrinkage is mainly responsible for causing cracks of larger magnitude or minor microcracks. The aspect of cracking in concrete is very complex, involving many factors such as magnitude of shrinkage, degree of retraint, extensibility of concrete, extent of stress relaxation by creep and at what age the shrinkage is appearing etc. Fig. 9.4 shows the influence of shrinkage and creep relaxation on concrete cracking. From Fig. 9.4 it can be seen that the cracking does not take place at the predicted point, but the cracking is delayed because of stress relaxation due to creep. Cracks can be avoided only if the stress induced by shrinkage strain, after relaxation by creep, is at all time less than the tensile strength of concrete. The above situation is not happening in most of the cases and as such generally shrinkage causes cracks in concrete.

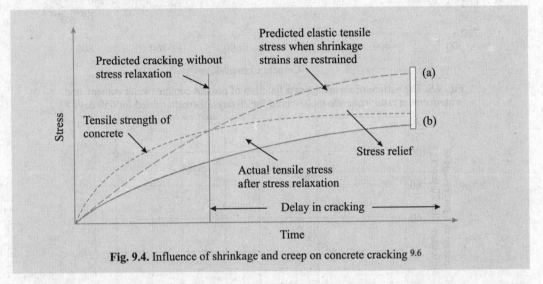

Fig. 9.4. Influence of shrinkage and creep on concrete cracking [9.6]

When we discuss about the shrinkage of concrete, there are mainly three aspects of shrinkage which are required to be considered.

Firstly, the drying shrinkage, secondly the thermal shrinkage related to heat of hydration and subsequent cooling, and thirdly thermal shrinkage in connection with concrete subjected to variation of ambient temperature. First let us consider the long-term drying shrinkage, which is referred as drying shrinkage.

Drying Shrinkage

Drying shrinkage in concrete is an inherent property of concrete. This aspect has been dealt in greater detail in chapter 8. The shrinkage is one of the fundamental reasons for initial induction of micro cracks in concrete. The mechanism involved are too complex. Generally the pattern of shrinkage is a function of cement content, water content and W/C ratio. In practical terms at a constant W/C ratio, shrinkage increases with an increase in cement content. But at a given, workability, which approximately means a constant water content, shrinkage is unaffected by the increase in cement content, or shrinkage even decreases because of lower W/C ratio. At lower W/C ratio concrete is stronger to resist shrinkage. But it should not be forgotten that stronger concrete, creeps less, there is less stress relaxation and therefore more microcracks. Fig. 9.5 shows the pattern of shrinkage connecting cement content, W/C ratio and water content.

The drying shrinkage takes place over long period if concrete is subjected to lower relative humidity. Fig. 9.6 shows the range of shrinkage vs time. It is seen that shrinkage increases with time but at a decreasing rate.

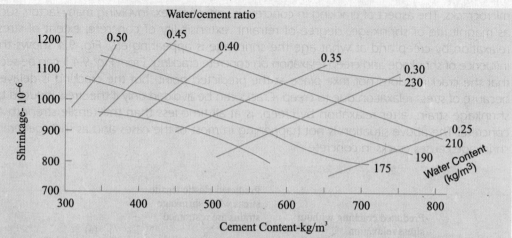

Fig. 9.5. The pattern of shrinkage as a function of cement content, water content, and water/cement ratio; concrete moist-cured for 28 days, thereafter dried for 450 days [9.7]

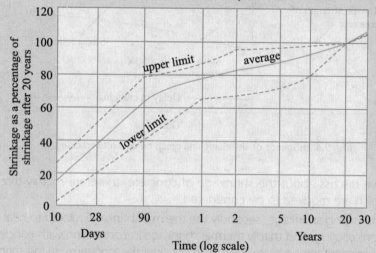

Fig. 9.6. Range of shrinkage-time-curves for different concretes stored at relative humidities of 50 and 70 per cent [9.8]

According to ACI 209 R–92 the development of shrinkage with time is given by the following equation :

$$S_t = \frac{t}{35+t} \times S_{ult.}$$

when S_t = shrinkage after t days since the end of 7 days moist curing

$S_{ult.}$ = ultimate shrinkage, and

t = time in days since the end of moist curing.

Although the above equation is subject to considerable variability, this equation can be used to estimate ultimate shrinkage of a wide range of moist cured concrete. It can be seen that 50 per cent of ultimate shrinkage is expected to occur after 35 days of drying. For steam cured concrete, the value of 35 in the denominator is replaced by 55, and time t is reckoned from the end of steam curing, generally 1 to 3 days.

The IS 456 of 2000, makes the following statement: In the absence of test data, the approximate value of the total shrinkage strain for design may be taken as 0.0003.

In addition to drying shrinkage, which takes place throughout the mass, may be in different magnitude, across the cross-section, there is another type of shrinkage known as carbonation shrinkage which occurs near surface zone of concrete where CO_2 can react with

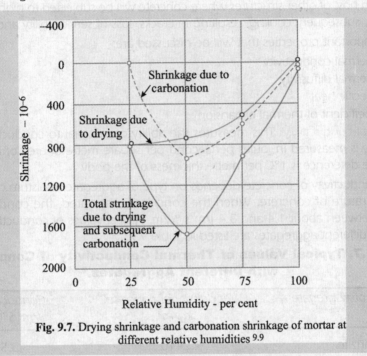

Fig. 9.7. Drying shrinkage and carbonation shrinkage of mortar at different relative humidities [9.9]

$Ca(OH)_2$ to form $CaCO_3$. Carbonation of concrete has serious repercussion on concrete durability which we shall deal separately. For the time being we shall deal with the total shrinkage due to drying and subsequent carbonation. Fig. 9.7 shows the drying shrinkage and carbonation shrinkage of mortar at different relative humidities. It can be noticed that carbonation shrinkage is nearly nil at less than 25 percent relative humidity because of lack of water in the pores to produce carbonic acid. The carbonation shrinkage is also nearly nil at 100 per cent relative humidity because the diffusion of CO_2 is not taking place on account of pores filled with water. It can also be noted that at 100 per cent relative humidity even drying shrinkage is also not there. Possibly there is a slight swelling.

It is mentioned earlier that 50 per cent of shrinkage will have taken place in about 35 days or considerable amount of shrinkage will have taken place near the surface even earlier. At such an early age, the concrete will not have attained good strength to resist shrinkage stress and therefore the concrete is much more vulnerable to cracking inspite of stress relaxation by high creep at low strength.

Thermal Shrinkage

We shall now discuss the aspects of shrinkage associated with heat of hydration. Before we go into the aspect of thermal shrinkage it is necessary at this stage to go into the thermal properties of concrete to understand the behaviour of concrete to heating and cooling. The study of thermal properties of concrete is an important aspect while dealing with the durability of concrete.

Concrete is a material used in all climatic regions for all kinds of structures. Knowledge of thermal expansion is required in long span bridge girders, high rise buildings subjected to variation of temperatures, in calculating thermal strains in chimneys, blast furnace and pressure vessels, in dealing with pavements and construction joints, in dealing with design of concrete dams and in host of other structures where concrete will be subjected to higher temperatures such as fire, subsequent cooling, resulting in cracks, loss of serviceability and durability.

The important properties that will be discussed are:

- Thermal conductivity
- Thermal diffusivity
- Specific heat
- Coefficient of thermal expansion

Thermal conductivity: This measures the ability of material to conduct heat. Thermal conductivity is measured in joules per second per square metre of area of body when the temperature deference is 1°C per metre thickness of the body.

The conductivity of concrete depends on type of aggregate, moisture content, density, and temperature of concrete. When the concrete is saturated, the conductivity ranges generally between about 1.4 and 3.4 j/m²s °c/m. Typical values of conductivity of concrete made with different aggregates are listed in Table 9.7.

Table 9.7. Typical Values of Thermal Conductivity of Concrete Made with Different Aggregates.[9.11]

Type of Aggregate	Wet density of concrete kg/m³	Conductivity J/m² S°C/m
Quartzite	2440	3.5
Dolomite	2500	3.3
Limestone	2450	3.2
Sandstone	2400	2.9
Granite	2420	2.6
Basalt	2520	2.0
Baryte	3040	2.0
Expanded shale	1590	0.80

Table 9.8 shows the values of conductivity recommended by Loudon and Stacey [9.10]

Thermal diffusivity: Diffusivity represents the rate at which temperature changes within the concrete mass. Diffusivity is simply related to the conductivity by the following equation.

$$\text{Diffusivity} = \frac{\text{Conductivity}}{CP}$$

where C is the specific heat, and P is the density of concrete.

The range of diffusivity of concrete is between 0.002 to 0.006 m²/h

Table 9.8

Values of Conductivity Recommended by Loudon and Stacey.[9.10]

Conductivity, $Jm/m^2s°C/m$

Unit weight	For concrete protected from weather				For concrete exposed to weather			
	Aerated concrete	Light weight concrete with foamed slag	Light weight concrete with expanded clay or sintered fly ash	Normal weight aggregate concrete	Aerated concrete	Light weight concrete with foamed slag	Light weight concrete with expanded clay or sintered fly ash	Normal weight aggregate concrete
kg/m³								
320	0.109	0.087	0.130		0.123	0.100	0.145	
480	0.145	0.116	0.173		0.166	0.130	0.187	
640	0.203	0.159	0.230		0.223	0.173	0.260	
800	0.260	0.203	0.303		0.273	0.230	0.332	
960	0.315	0.260	0.376		0.360	0.289	0.433	
1120	0.389	0.315	0.462		0.433	0.360	0.519	
1280	0.476	0.389	0.562		0.533	0.433	0.635	
1440		0.462	0.678					
1600		0.549	0.794	0.706				0.808
1760		0.649	0.952	0.838				0.952
1920				1.056				1.194
2080				1.315				1.488
2240				1.696				1.904
2400				2.267				2.561

Specific heat. It is defined as the quantity of heat required to raise the temperature of a unit mass of a material by one degree centigrade. The common range of values for concrete is between 840 and 1170 j/kg per °C

Coefficient of thermal expansion

Coefficient of thermal expansion is defined as the change in unit length per degree change of temperature. In concrete it depends upon the mix proportions. The coefficient of thermal expansion of hydrated cement paste varies between 11×10^{-6} and 20×10^{-6} per °C. Coefficient of thermal expansion of aggregates vary between 5×10^{-6} and 12×10^{-6} per °C. Limestones and Gabbros will have low values and Gravel and Quartzite will have high values of coefficient of thermal expansion. Therefore the kind of aggregate and content of aggregate influences the coefficient of thermal expansion of concrete.

It has been discussed earlier while dealing with the properties of aggregate in chapter 3, that too much of thermal incompatibility between aggregate and paste, causes differential expansion and contraction resulting in rupture of bond at the interface of paste and aggregate. Coefficient of thermal expansion of 1:6 concrete made with different aggregates is given in Table 9.9

Table 9.9. Coefficient of Expansion of 1:6 Concretes Made with Different Aggregates[9.12]

Type of aggregate	Linear coefficient of thermal expansion		
	Air-cured concrete 10^{-6} per °C	Water-cured concrete 10^{-6} per °C	Air cured and wetted concrete 10^{-6} per °C
Gravel	13.1	12.2	11.7
Granite	9.5	8.6	7.7
Quartzite	12.8	12.2	11.7
Dolerite	9.5	8.5	7.9
Sandstone	11.7	10.1	8.6
Limestone	7.4	6.1	5.9
Portland stone	7.4	6.1	6.5
Blast furnace slag	10.6	9.2	8.8
Foamed slag	12.1	9.2	8.5

The values of the coefficient of thermal expansion of concrete, so far discussed applies to concrete subjected to a temperature less than about 65°C. It has been seen that the concrete subjected to higher temperatures show somewhat different values, presumably because of the lower moisture content in the concrete. The importance of the values of coefficient of thermal expansion becomes necessary at higher temperature when dealing with concrete subjected fire or higher temperatures. Table 9.10 shows the values of the coefficient of thermal expansion at conditions of higher temperatures.

Having seen a few aspects of properties of concrete which have bearing on expansion and contraction on heating and cooling, let us revert back to thermal shrinkage associated with heat of hydration.

A large quantity of heat, up to about 500 j/g (120 cal/g) could be liberated in the hydration of cement. Since the thermal conductivity of concrete is low, a very high

Table 9.10

Coefficient of Thermal Expansion of Concrete at High Temperature[9.13]

Curing condition	Water/ cement ratio	Cement content Kg/m³	Aggregate	Linear coefficient of thermal expansion at the age of 28 days below 260°C 10^{-6} per °C	28 days Above 430°C 10^{-6} per °C	90 days below 260°C 10^{-6} per °C	90 days above 430°C 10^{-6} per °C
	0.4	435		7.6	20.3	6.5	11.2
Moist	0.6	310	Calcareous	12.8	20.5	8.4	22.5
	0.8	245	Gravel	11.0	21.1	16.7	32.8
Air	0.4	435		7.7	18.9	12.2	20.7
50 per cent	0.6	310	Calcareous	7.7	21.1	8.8	20.2
relative humidity	0.8	245	Gravel	9.6	20.7	11.7	21.6
Moist air	0.68	355	Expanded	6.1	7.5	—	—
	0.68	3.55	Shale	4.7	9.7	5.0	8.8

temperature could be generated in the interior of a large mass of concrete. At the same time, the exterior of the concrete mass loses heat with the result a steep temperature gradient may get established. During subsequent cooling of the interior, serious cracking may take place.

The rate of evolution of heat as well as total heat generated depend on the compound composition of cement. C_3S and C_3A produces large amount of heat in a short time. The fineness of cement also influences the rate of heat development. The faster rate of heat development is more harmful than the total heat of hydration which develops slowly. Therefore for mass concrete and hydraulic structures they use cement with low C_3S and C_3A. It is also advantages to use low cement content and blended cement. Blended cement with high pozzolanic material content gives out the heat rather slowly because of slow pozzolanic reaction, during which time certain quantity of heat gets dissipated, virtually reducing temperature difference between interior and exterior.

Mass Concrete

Mass concrete is a concrete having considerable dimensions that may get affected by thermal behaviour of concrete. Concrete dam is one such example of mass concrete. In the design of dam, strength of concrete is of less importance. The primary considerations are given to the aspect of how to reduce the heat of hydration, or if certain amount of heat is generated, how to absorb such heat so that the heat inside the body of concrete is minimised so that it does not cause any detrimental effect by way of cracks in concrete.

Now a days, there are many structural elements which are of sizeable dimensions, such as bridge piers, deep beams, massive columns, thick foundation concrete etc. The pouring of concrete in such massive sections need understanding of thermal behaviour mainly with respect to heat of hydration of concrete. Fig. 9.8 and Fig. 9.9 show the typical pattern of temperature change which causes external and internal cracking of large concrete mass. Fitz Gibbon from his research work has shown that temperature deference of more than 20°C between surface and interior causes cracks, assuming the coefficient of thermal expansion of

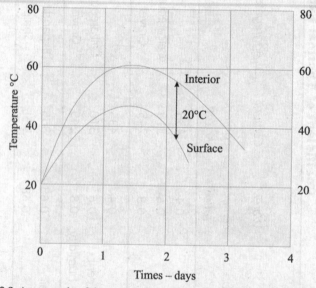

Fig. 9.8. An example of the pattern of temperature change which causes external cracking of large concrete mass. The critical 20 °C temperature difference occurs during cooling. 9.14

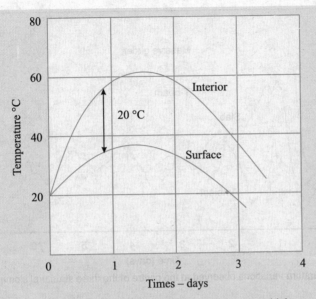

Fig. 9.9. An example of the pattern of temperature change which causes internal cracking of a large concrete mass. The critical 20 °C temperature difference occurs during heating but the cracks open only when the interior has cooled through a greater temperature range than the exterior [9.14]

concrete as 10×10^{-6} per °C. A deference of 20°C, the differential strain would come to 200×10^{-6}. This amount of strain is considered as a realistic tensile strain at cracking.

Aitcin and Raid cites a case where a 1.1 m square column made of reinforced concrete with ASTM type I cement content of 500 kg/m³ and a silica fume content of 30 kg/m³, showed a rise in temperature of 45°C above the ambient temperature, after 30 hours of placing.[9.15] Therefore, there is a need for controlling the heat of hydration in concrete and also not allowing the surface of the concrete to cool rapidly. If the surface is insulated, the difference in temperature between interior and exterior is reduced which improves the cracking behaviour. The retention of the formwork and its insulating properties may be made use of to reduce the difference in temperatures between interior and surface,.

In reinforced mass concrete structures also cracking will develop, if the difference in temperature between the interior and the exterior is large. However, appropriate detailing of the reinforcement could be made to control the width and spacing of cracks. Fitz Gibbon estimated that the temperature rise under adiabatic condition is 12°C per 100 kg of cement per cubic metre of concrete, regardless of the type of cement used, for cement contents between 300 to 600 kg/m³. The above fact shows the importance of using blended cement in mass concrete and use of high volume fly ash in concrete constructions for crack free durable concrete.

Thermal Expansion and Shrinkage

Now let us see the effect of expansion and contraction of concrete subjected to ambient increase or decrease of temperature and their effect on concrete cracking.

Earlier we have discussed about the increase and decrease of temperature in concrete due to heat of hydration. The thermal changes due to heat of hydration will only be important for first few days in normal structures but may last for longer time in large mass concrete.

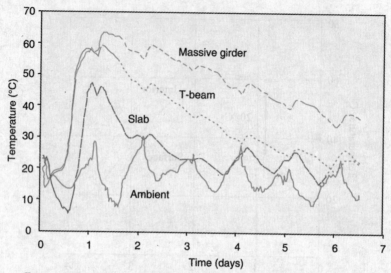

Temperature variations observed at the centre of the three structural elements

Under the above sub heading we are going to discuss about the concrete members, subjected to external temperatures, such as roof slabs, road or airfields pavements, bridge decks and other members. They are subjected to diurnal or seasonal changes of temperature. In India, in certain states or cities, the change of ambient temperature in day and night could be as high as 30°C and the change in temperature of actual concrete surface is much higher than 30°C. The seasonal variation could be as large as 40°C. In other countries, in the middle east it is of still higher ranges.

The change in diurnal or seasonal temperatures mentioned above makes the concrete expand and contract. Since the structures are not free to expand and contract on account of restraint at support in case of roof slabs and sub grade reaction in case of pavements, a considerable tensile stress more than the tensile strength is generated resulting in cracks in concrete.

It is usual that the diurnal variation of temperature in a place like Pune is 20°C or more, (In many other cities, in India too the variation could be as high as 30°C or more). We can have an idea of the tensile strain or the tensile stress that could develop in concrete, from the following calculations.

Assume the characteristic compressive strength of concrete = 25 MPa

$$\text{Modulus of Elasticity} = 5000 \times \sqrt{f_{ck}} \ \text{N/mm}^2$$

$$= 2.5 \times 10^4 \ \text{N/mm}^2$$

$$\text{Flexural strength} = 0.7 \times \sqrt{f_{ck}} \ \text{N/mm}^2$$

$$= 3.5 \ \text{N/mm}^2$$

Assume the coefficient of thermal expansion of concrete

$$= 10 \times 10^{-6} \ \text{per °C}$$

Assume the diurnal variation of temperature is 20°C

∴ The thermal shrinkage strain $= 20 \times 10 \times 10^{-6}$

$$= 200 \times 10^{-6}$$

It has been seen from experimental work by Lowe that concrete cracks at a differential strain of 200×10^{-6}. A strain which is more than 200×10^{-6} will cause a very high degree of microcracking in concrete. Further,

$$\text{Modulus of elasticity} = \frac{\text{stress}}{\text{strain}}$$

$$2.5 \times 10^4 = \frac{\text{stress}}{200 \times 10^{-6}}$$

$$\text{Tensile stress} = 2.5 \times 10^4 \times 200 \times 10^{-6}$$
$$= 5.0 \text{ N/mm}^2$$

Tensile strength of concrete = 3.5 N/mm^2. Therefore a tensile stress of 5.0 N/mm^2 is sure to cause microcracks in concrete. The tensile stress will be much higher in case of stronger concrete with higher modulus of elasticity and higher degree of variation of temperature. No doubt concrete of higher compressive strength will have higher tensile strength to withstand the higher tensile stress. But due to lower value of creep of such concrete, a smaller extent of stress relaxation takes place and as such, the stronger concrete will crack more than weaker concrete, from this consideration. However, as written earlier, cracking of concrete is a complex matter.

Extensibility

From the above examples and explanation the magnitude of the shrinkage strain is only one of the factors contributing to the cracking of concrete. The following are the other factors influencing the cracking of concrete.

- *Modulus of elasticity:* The lower the modulus of elasticity, the lower will be the amount of induced elastic tensile stress for a given magnitude of shrinkage.
- *Creep:* The higher the creep, the higher is the extent of stress relaxation and hence lower is the net tensile stress.
- *Tensile strength:* Higher the compressive strength, the higher will be the tensile strength, and therefore the lower is the risk that tensile stress will exceed the tensile strength.

The combination of factors that are desirable to reduce the advent of cracking in concrete can be described by a single term called extensibility. Concrete is said to have a higher degree of extensibility when it can be subjected to large deformations without cracking. Obviously, for a minimum cracking, the concrete should undergo not only less shrinkage but also should have high degree of extensibility (*i.e.,* low elastic modulus, high creep, and high tensile strength). In general, as said earlier, high strength concretes may be more prone to cracking on account of greater thermal shrinkage (higher cement content) and lower stress relaxation (lower creep). On the other hand, low-strength concretes tend to crack less, because of lower thermal shrinkage (lower cement content) and higher stress relaxation (higher creep).

Incidentally, lime mortar has 5 – 7 times more extensibility than cement mortar. Therefore, lime mortar used as plaster, cracks less than cement mortar plaster.

In the foregoing paragraphs we have described about the cracks produced in concrete by virtue of variation in the ambient temperature. Sometimes it is possible that combined effect of shrinkage caused by heat of hydration, long-term drying shrinkage and shrinkage on account of variation in ambient temperature, may cause such a high total shrinkage, which may virtually cause considerable cracking of concrete members, particularly in roof slabs and concrete pavements.

It is seen that roof slab may not leak for a few years. But due to long-term drying shrinkage increasing with age and cyclic expansion and contraction due to variation of external temperatures, the roof slab is likely to leak, after some years. The leakage causes corrosion of reinforcements and affect the durability. Therefore however good is the quality of concrete in roof slab water-proofing treatment is necessary to stop leakage and to increase the durability of structures.

Similarly, to improve the functional efficiency and to increase the durability of concrete pavements well-planned and designed joints must be provided in the construction of road, airfield pavements and industrial floors.

Joints in Concrete

Industrial floors and concrete pavements are constructed generally in alternate bays to allow for the incidental early shrinkage of concrete. A time interval as much as practicable is given between the adjacent bays to provide scope for the maximum possible shrinkage. In case of roof slab of large dimension and in other special cases, expansion joints are provided to cater for the expansion and contraction. In pavements proper joints are provided to direct the possible cracks arising out of expansion and out of thermal expansion and contraction, due to variation in temperature and also due to long-term drying shrinkage.

Joints can be broadly classified into four categories:
- Construction joints
- Expansion joints
- Contraction joints
- Isolation joints

Construction Joints

Construction joints are the temporary joints left between subsequent concreting operations. The position of the construction joints should be pre-planned before concreting is started. Till such position and location, concrete must be poured in one operation. The joints must be made at such places that the concrete is less vulnerable to maximum bending moment and maximum shear force. In walls and columns construction, joints should be horizontal and arranged at such a level to coincide with the general architectural features. In columns, the concrete should be filled to the level, preferably, a few inches below the junction of beams. Joints in beams and slabs should be formed at the point of minimum shear. It is also not desirable to have the construction joints at the point of maximum bending moment, therefore the joints may be made at the extreme position of the middle third.

The procedure for joining the new concrete to the old concrete at the place of construction joint has been described under placing of concrete. Construction joint should be properly masked when finishing the structure. Badly made and unmasked construction joint will give an ugly appearance to the concrete construction. The groove may be incorporated at the joint to make a feature and to hide the joint. Refer Fig. 9.10.

Expansion Joints

Concrete is subjected to volume change due to many reasons. Provision must be made to cater for the volume change by way of joint to relieve the stresses produced. Expansion is a function of length. In case of a small building, the magnitude of expansion is not much

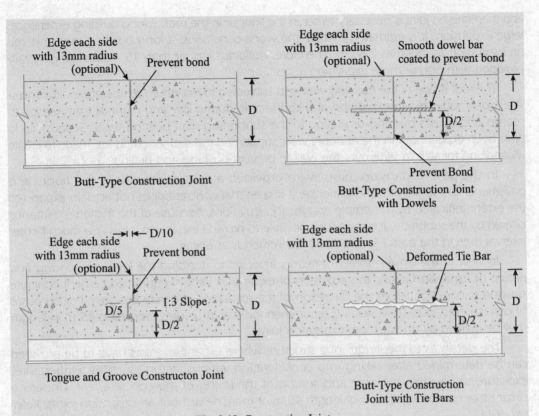

Fig. 9.10. Construction Joints

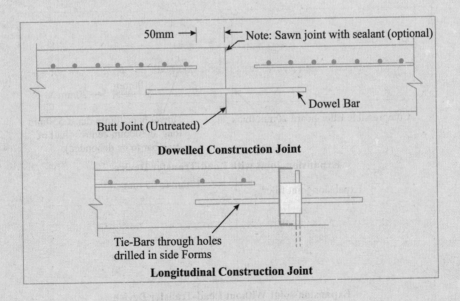

Fig. 9.10 Constuction Joints

and therefore no joint is necessary either in the floor or in the roof. A long building experiences large expansion. It is estimated that for the worst conditions, a long building may undergo an expansion as much as 2.5 cm. Therefore, buildings longer than 45 metres are generally provided with one or more expansion joints.

The roof is one of the building elements subjected to maximum temperature differences. The roof is subjected to expansion and contraction during day and night or from season to season and causes pushing or pulling to the supporting load bearing walls. Serious cracks have been experienced in the masonry walls supporting the slab. Attempts are made to create a condition for slab to slide over the wall to prevent pushing and pulling.

In the past, expansion joints were provided at closer intervals in the floors and pavements. These days from experience, it is seen that concrete does not actually expand to the extent indicated by the simple analytical calculations, because of the frictional resistance offered by the subgrade. It is therefore, possible to provide expansion joints at a much farther interval than in the past. I.S. 456-2000 recommends as under:

In view of the large number of factors involved in deciding the location, spacing and nature of expansion joints, the provision of expansion joint in reinforced cement concrete structures should be left to the discretion of the reinforced concrete designer. For purposes of general guidance, however, it is recommended that structures exceeding 45 m in length shall be divided by one or more expansion joints.

The details as to the length of a structure where expansion joints have to be provided can be determined after taking into consideration various factors, such as temperature, exposure to weather, the time and season of the laying of the concrete, etc. Under no circumstances shall a structure of length 45 m or more be without an expansion joints. Refer Fig. 9.11.

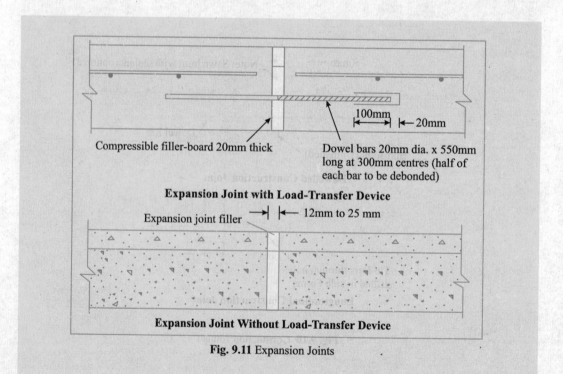

Compressible filler-board 20mm thick

Dowel bars 20mm dia. x 550mm long at 300mm centres (half of each bar to be debonded)

100mm   20mm

Expansion Joint with Load-Transfer Device

Expansion joint filler   12mm to 25 mm

Expansion Joint Without Load-Transfer Device

Fig. 9.11 Expansion Joints

Contraction Joints

Concrete undergoes plastic shrinkage and drying shrinkage as a result of which concrete shrinks. When shrinkage is restrained, stresses are developed which result in the formation of cracks. To avoid these cracks, contraction joints are provided. Normally, the interval at which these joints are provided will vary from 5 to 10 metres. Contraction joints are sometimes called dummy joints or control joints. Contraction joints will not be necessary if sufficient reinforcement is provided to take up the shrinkage stresses. Contraction joints are generally provided in unreinforced floors and pavements.

.Contraction joints are made at the time of laying concrete by embedding a timber batton or plank of sufficient depth and required thickness. This is subsequently removed when the concrete is hardened. Sometimes, steel plates of sufficient thickness and width are beaten

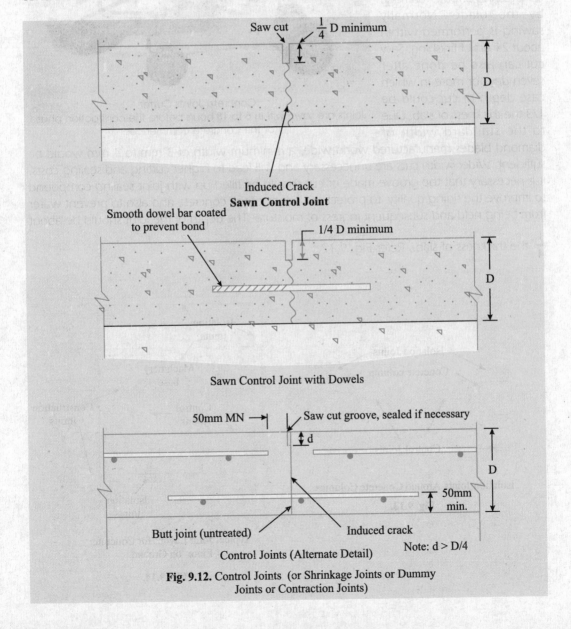

Fig. 9.12. Control Joints (or Shrinkage Joints or Dummy
Joints or Contraction Joints)

down into the fresh concrete and then removed when the concrete is hardened. Thirdly, the contraction joint of stipulated width and depth is cut by employing a joint sawing machine. Sawing the joint is a very common practice in the recent time. Sawing is done as soon as the concrete is strong enough to resist tearing or other damage by the blade. Normally sawing is performed within about 24 hrs of finishing. Saw cut can also be done after seven days or more in which case depth of cut could be 1/3 the thickness of slab. Due to the standard width of

Concrete Joints Cutter
Joints are sawn within 6 to 18 hours before the contraction phase of the concrete commences.

diamond blades manufactured world wide, a minimum width of 3 mm to 4 mm would be sufficient. Wider width cuts are unnecessary and will lead to higher cutting and sealing costs. It is necessary that the groove made or cut should be filled up with joint sealing compound to improve the riding quality, to protect the edges of the concrete and also to prevent water from being held and subsequent ingress of moisture. The depth of the joint should be about $\frac{1}{4}$ the thickness of slab., Refer Fig. 9.12.

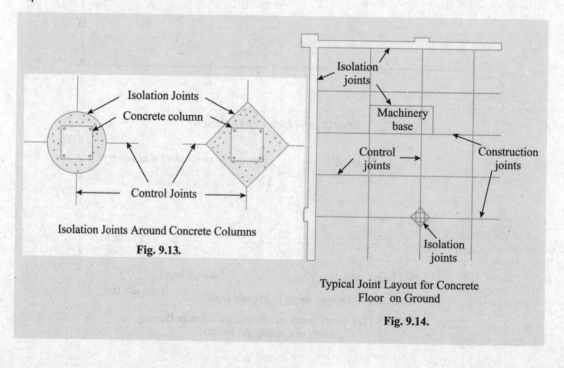

Isolation Joints Around Concrete Columns

Fig. 9.13.

Typical Joint Layout for Concrete Floor on Ground

Fig. 9.14.

Spacing of Contraction Joints

Contraction joints are generally spaced 4.5 to 5.0 m intervals in unreinforced slabs. The spacing could be increased approximately upto 15 m in reinforced slabs depending upon the amount of reinforcement. The IRC stipulations on contraction joint spacing, with and without reinforcement, are given in table below:

Slab thickness (cm)	Air-cured concrete Joints spacing (m)	Weight of reinforcement for reinforced slabs (kg/m²)
a. Unreinforced Slabs		
10	4.5	-
15	4.5	-
20	4.5	-
b. Reinforced slabs		
10	7.5	2.2
15	13.0	2.7
20	14.0	3.8
25 and above	17.0	5.5

Spacing of Contraction Joints

The spacing of expansion joints, has been a matter of discussion because of varied practices and ranges from 20 meters to a few hundred meters. Recommended expansion joint spacing for Indian temperature conditions are given in table below:

Period of construction	Degree of roughness of sub grade / sub base	Maximum expansion joint spacing (m) Slab thickness		
		20 cm	30 cm	40 cm
Winter	Smooth	50	50	60
(Oct – March)	Rough	140	140	140
Summer	Smooth	90	90	120
(April – Sept)	Rough	140	140	140

In residential flooring the conventional contraction joint is omitted by casting the slab in alternate bays, to allow for the complete plastic shrinkage and also for maximum extent of drying shrinkage. It is usual to place glass-strip or aluminium strip in between the bays to create discontinuity between adjacent bays to prevent the development of continuous cracks.

Isolation Joints: This joint, as the name indicates is provided where the concrete floor meets the permanent structural elements such as walls, columns, foundation blocks, machine foundations etc. Since the movements associated with these structural elements are different from those of the concrete floor, an isolation joints are provided between them. It is provided to full depth of the concrete floor. The width (the gap) of such joint is kept about 10 to 12 mm. To avoid ingress of moisture or other undesirable materials, these joints are filled with a resilient materials and topped with joint fillings compounds. Refer fig. 9.13. Typical joint layout for concrete floor on ground is shown in fig. 9.14

Concrete Subjected to High Temperature

Fire Resistance

Concrete, though not a refractory material, is incombustible and has good fire-resistant properties. Fire resistance of concrete structure is determined by three main factors—the capacity of the concrete itself to withstand heat and the subsequent action of water without losing strength unduly, without cracking or spalling; the conductivity of the concrete to heat; and coefficient of thermal expansion of concrete. In the case of reinforced concrete, the fire resistance is not only dependent upon the type of concrete but also on the thickness of cover to reinforcement, The fire introduces high temperature gradients and as a result of it, the surface layers tend to separate and spall off from the cooler interior. The heating of reinforcement aggravates the expansion both laterally and longitudinally of the reinforcement bars resulting in loss of bond and loss of strength of reinforcement.

The effect of increase in temperature on the strength of concrete is not much upto a temperature of about 250°C but above 300°C, definite loss of strength takes place. Hydrated hardened concrete contains a considerable proportion of free calcium hydroxide which loses its water above 400°C leaving calcium oxide. If this calcium oxide gets wetted or is exposed to moist air, rehydrates to calcium hydroxide accompanied by an expansion in volume. This expansion disrupts the concrete. Portland blast furnace slag cement is found to be more resistant to the action of fire in this regard.

In mortar and concrete, the aggregates undergo a progressive expansion on heating while the hydrated products of the set cement, beyond the point of maximum expansion, shrinks. These two opposing actions progressively weaken and crack the concrete. The various aggregates used differ considerably in their behaviour on heating. Quartz, the principal mineral in sand, granites and gravels expands steadily upto about 573°C. At this temperature it undergoes a sudden expansion of 0.85%. This expansion has a disruptive action on the stability of concrete. The fire resisting properties of concrete is least, if quartz is the predominant mineral in the aggregate.

The best fire resistant aggregates, amongst the igneous rocks are, the basalts and dolerites. Limestone expands steadily until temperature of about 900°C and then begins to

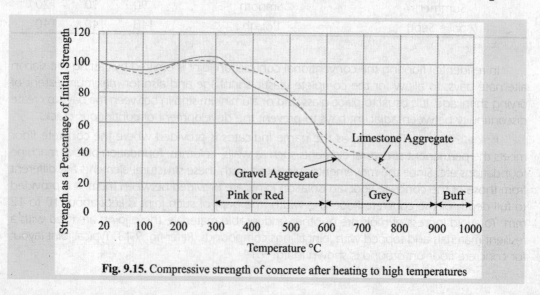

Fig. 9.15. Compressive strength of concrete after heating to high temperatures

contract owing to decomposition with liberation of carbon dioxide. Since the decomposition takes place only at a very high temperature of 900°C, it has been found that dense limestone is considered as a good fire resistant aggregate. Perhaps the best fire resistant aggregate is blast furnace slag aggregate. Broken bricks also form a good aggregate in respect of fire resistance. The long series of tests indicated that even the best fire resistant concretes have been found to fail if concrete is exposed for a considerable period to a temperature exceeding 900°C, while serious reduction in strength occurs at a temperature of about 600°C. Concrete does not show appreciable loss of strength upto a temperature of about 300°C. The loss of strength may be about 50% or more at about 500°C. Figures 9.15 and 9.16 show the effect of different temperatures on the strength of concrete and Fig. 9.17 shows the influence of temperature on the relative modulus of elasticity.

Freezing and Thawing

The lack of durability of concrete on account of freezing and thawing action of frost is not of great importance to Indian conditions. But it is of greatest considerations in most part of the world. However, certain regions in India, experience sub-zero temperatures in winter.

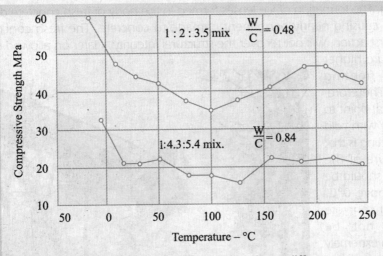

Fig. 9.16. Compressive strength of concrete after heating to different temperatures

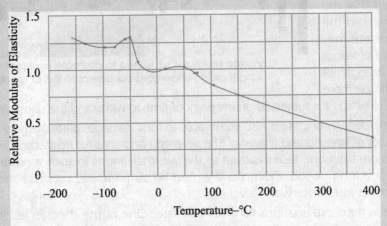

Fig. 9.17. Influence of temperature on Modulus of Elasticity of concrete

The concrete structures particularly, the one which are exposed to atmosphere are subjected to cycles of freezing and thawing and as such suffer from the damaging action of frost. The frost action is one of the most powerful weathering action on the durability of concrete. In the extreme conditions, the life span of concrete can be reduced to just a couple of years. The damage from freezing and thawing is most common and as such it is one of the extensively studied field on weathering of concrete in the United States of America, Russia and Northern European countries.

Though the durability of concrete is affected by alternative wetting and drying, heating and cooling, penetration and deposition of salt and other aggressive chemicals, leaching of calcium hydroxide, action of certain acids, alkali-aggregate reaction, mechanical wear and tear, abrasion and cavitation, one of the very important factors affecting the durability of concrete in the cold countries, is the action of frost. Therefore the aspect of frost resistance is of much importance and has been studied for more than 70 years.

It is very well known that fresh concrete should not be subjected to freezing temperature. Fresh concrete contains a considerable quantity of free water; if this free water is subjected to freezing temperature discrete ice lenses are formed. Water expands about 9% in volume during freezing. The formation of ice lenses formed in the body of fresh concrete disrupt the fresh concrete causing nearly permanent damage to concrete. The fresh concrete once subjected to forst action, will not recover the structural integrity, if later on allowed to harden at a temperature higher than the freezing temperature. Therefore, the fundamental point to note in dealing with cold weather concreting is that the temperature of the fresh concrete should be maintained above 0°C. The hardening concrete also should not be subjected to an extremely low temperature. It has been estimated that the freezing of water in the hardened concrete may exert a pressure of about 14 MPa. The strength of concrete should be more

Concrete structures subjected to alternate cycles of freezing and thawing undergoes considerable loss of durability.

than the stress to which it is subjected at any point of time to withstand the damaging action.

The fully hardened concrete is also vulnerable to forst damage, particularly to the effect of alternate cycles of freezing and thawing. The severest conditions for frost action arise when concrete has more than one face exposed to the weather and is in such a position that it remains wet for a long period. Examples are road kerbs, parapets, concrete members in hydraulic structures just above water level etc.

There are various explanations for frost damage. One of the theories attributes the damage directly to the empty space available being insufficient to accommodate the additional solid produced when the free water held in concrete freezes. The damage is related to the degree of saturation.

Another theory attributes the failure to the production of pressure due to the growth of ice lenses parallel to the surface of the concrete owing to the migration of water from capillaries where the freezing point is depressed. This is similar to the theory of forst heaving in soils. Yet another theory explains the failure to generation of water pressure within the capillary cavities as the ice crystals grow. This hydraulic pressure can only be delivered by flow of water in other spaces, since the ice formed on the surface seals the exterior and the pressure generated forces the water through the fine capillaries. The local pressure so generated eventually exceeds the tensile strength of the concrete and causes breakdown. In all these theories, the permeability, rate of absorption and degree of saturation of the concrete are all important factors. Freezing starts at the surface in the largest cavities and gradually extends to smaller cavities. Water contained in the gel pores are too small to get frozen till the temperature goes below—78°C. In practice no ice is formed in the gel pores. The resistance of concrete to frost action depends on the strength of the paste, water/cement ratio, type of aggregate used, age of concrete, duration and extent to which the concrete is subjected to freezing action. More than all these one of the main factors is the degree of saturation of concrete.

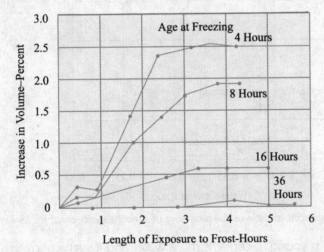

Fig. 9.18. Increase in volume of concrete during prolonged freezing as a function of age when freezing starts [9.16]

Figure 9.18 indicates the increase in volume to the length of exposure at the different ages and figure 9.19 shows the increase in volume with the number of cycles of freezing at different ages. The fully dry concrete is totally unaffected by frost action, but this is a theoretical statement; because when freezing takes place, naturally, the concrete becomes wet subsequently and loses durability. Figure 9.20 illustrates the influence of water/cement ratio on the frost resistance of concrete. The fine air bubbles entrained in the body of the concrete will act as a buffer to relieve the pressure created while freezing. The part of the water while getting frozen, runs into neighbouring air voids which are partially or fully empty. This relieves the pressure. Figure 9.20 shows the superiority of air entrained concrete with respect to freezing action.

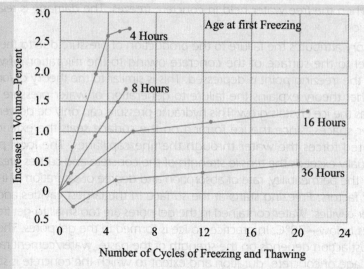

Fig. 9.19. Increase in volume of concrete subjected to freezing and thawing as a function of age at whch first freezing starts

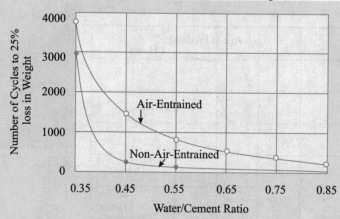

9.20. Influence of water/cement ratio on the resistance of concrete moist-cured for 28 days [9.16]

When the concrete is young, it contains more water and if such concrete is subjected to a low temperature greater quantity of water gets frozen and the total disruptive force is of a high order; whereas concrete at later ages contains less moisture and the freezing of such concrete will exert less total pressure. This is shown in Fig. 9.18

The frost damage can be assessed in several ways. Assessment of loss of weight of a sample of concrete subjected to a certain number of cycles of freezing and thawing is one of the methods. Measuring the change in the ultrasonic pulse-velocity or the change in the dynamic modulus of elasticity of specimen is another method. The resistance of the concrete to freezing and thawing is also measured by the durability factor. Blanks defined the durability factor as the "Number of cycles of freezing and thawing to produce failure divided by one hundred". ASTM method of calculating the durability factor is to continue freezing and thawing for 300 cycles or until the dynamic modulus of elasticity is reduced to 60% of its original value, whichever occurs first.

$$\text{The durability factor} = \frac{\text{Number of cycles at the end of test} \times \text{Percentage of original modulus}}{300}$$

There are no established criteria for acceptance or rejection of concrete in terms of the durability factor. Its value is primarily for comparison of different concretes, preferably when only one variable is changed. However, some guidance in interpretation can be obtained from the following.

A factor smaller than 40 indicates that the concrete is unsatisfactory with respect to resistance to freezing and thawing. 40 to 60 is the range for doubtful performance. Above 60, the concrete is probably satisfactory and value around 100 is considered satisfactory.

Deicing Effect of Salts

Deicing chemicals used for snow and ice clearance can cause and aggravate surface scaling. Studies have shown that formation of salt crystals in concrete may contribute to concrete scaling and deterioration layer by layer.

In cold regions in the winter, sodium chloride or calcium chloride is used for de-icing snow clearance on concrete roads. The repeated use of salts causes surface scaling of concrete roads. This has been attributed to the physical action of salt and not the chemical action. The use of air-entrainment makes the concrete road more resistance to surface scaling on account of salt action.

Moisture Movement

We discussed the topic moisture movement in chapter 8. We may recall that concrete shrinks when allowed to dry in air at low relative humidity and it swells when placed in water. Concrete members in outdoor conditions such as pavements, bridge decks, transmission poles, water tanks, swimming pools etc are subjected to alternate wetting and drying conditions and therefore undergoes expansion and shrinkage.

The exposure of concrete to repetitive expansion and shrinkage or repetitive compressive stress and tensile stress which may cause fatigue in concrete and affect the durability of concrete.

It is a common experience that swimming pools which are kept dry for some times for repairs or such other reasons, develops cracks and leaks.

Transition Zone

We have dealt with the topic transition zone in some detail under the topic of strength in chapter 7. Now, when we are dealing with cracks and durability of concrete, it is necessary to touch upon this as it is of fundamental nature in inducing micro cracks due to very many reasons. Micro cracks in transition zone is a strength limiting factor. Concrete is a brittle material which develops microcracks even before any load is applied.

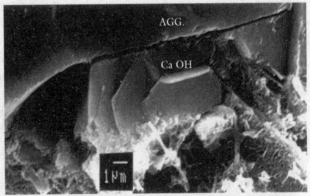

Transition zone between aggregate and hydrated cement paste.

On account of the dissimilar material, lack of bond, higher W/C ratio, and bleeding water, the transition zone becomes the weakest link in concrete mass. Under load, microcracks propagate further starting from largest microcracks. At a stress level of 70 per cent of the ultimate strength, the mortar matrix develops small cracks. With increasing stress level, the matrix cracks gradually and spreads throughout the mass. The microcracks in the transition zone at the interface with steel reinforcement becomes more permeable and admits air and water to promote corrosion of steel reinforcement. Incidentally these microcracks increases the depth of carbonation also .

Generally speaking, the microcracking at the transition zone is a general feature of concrete which is fundamentally responsible for reducing the long term durability of concrete.

Biological Process

It is a common site that in many buildings plants grow and the roots slowly penetrate into concrete or small cracks in concrete and converts it into bigger cracks with further growth. Even small plants such as lichen, algae and mass growing on concrete surface attract moisture and encourage physical and chemical process to deteriorate the concrete. Besides, humic acid produced by micro-growth reacts with cement.

In tropical countries, the concrete sewers carrying sewage, produce hydrogen sulphide (H_2S) due to anerobic decomposition of sulphur compounds. Hydrogen sulphide gets oxidised by aerobic bacteria producing sulphuric acid. The sulphuric acid attack the concrete above the liquid level on the crown portion of concrete sewer. In this way progressive deterioration of concrete takes place.

Marine borers and marine plants also contribute to the deterioration of concrete. Sometimes in tropical conditions algae, fungi and bacteria use atmospheric nitrogen to form nitric acid which attack concrete.

Structural Design Difficiencies

Sometimes inadequate provision of main steel reinforcement, or inadequate provision for temperature reinforcement, or wrong spacing of bars, or absence of corner reinforcement may cause unacceptable cracks in concrete. One of the most common occurrence is the displacement of top bars in cantilever thin chajjas, by the movement of concreting gang, causes cracks at the junction point of cantilever chajja.

Innumerable examples can be cited such as conjestion of reinforcement and difficulties in proper compacting concrete, particularly at the column and beam junctions, deep beams, the negative reinforcement over T and L beams, should be taken care. In the absence of such care concrete is sure to crack.

In certain structures the ultimate creep deformation must be considered, otherwise more than the permissible deflection due to excess creep and unacceptable width of cracks will affect durability.

The permissible width of crack depends upon the functions of the structural members and on the exposure conditions of the concrete. Reis et al suggest the following permissible crack widths.[9.17]

Interior members	0.35 mm
Exterior members under normal exposure conditions	0.25 mm
Exterior members exposed to aggressive environment	0.15 mm

Chemical Action

When we are dealing with the durability of concrete, chemical attack which results in volume change, cracking of concrete and the consequent deterioration of concrete becomes an important part of discussion.

Under chemical attack, we shall discuss about sulphate attack, alkali-aggregate reaction, carbonation, deicing effect of salt, acid attack and effect of sea water.

Sulphate Attack

Most soils contain some sulphate in the form of calcium, sodium, potassium and magnesium. They occur in soil or ground water. Because of solubility of calcium sulphate is low, ground waters contain more of other sulphates and less of calcium sulphate. Ammonium sulphate is frequently present in agricultural soil and water from the use of fertilizers or from sewage and industrial effluents. Decay of organic matters in marshy land, shallow lakes often leads to the formation of H_2S, which can be transformed into sulphuric acid by bacterial action. Water used in concrete cooling towers can also be a potential source of sulphate attack on concrete. Therefore sulphate attack is a common occurrence in natural or industrial situations.

Solid sulphates do not attack the concrete severely but when the chemicals are in solution, they find entry into porous concrete and react with the hydrated cement products. Of all the sulphates, magnesium sulphate causes maximum damage to concrete. A characteristic whitish appearance is the indication of sulphate attack.

The term sulphate attack denote an increase in the volume of cement paste in concrete or mortar due to the chemical action between the products of hydration of cement and solution containing sulphates. In the hardened concrete, calcium aluminate hydrate (C-A-H) can react with sulphate salt from outside. The product of reaction is calcium sulphoaluminate, forming within the framework of hydrated cement paste. Because of the increase in volume of the solid phase which can go up to 227 per cent, a gradual disintegration of concrete takes place.

The reactions of the various sulphates with hardened cement paste is shown below

Let us take the example of Sodium Sulphate attacking $Ca(OH)_2$

$Ca(OH)_2 + Na_2SO_4 . 10H_2O \longrightarrow CaSO_4 . 2H_2O + 2NaOH + 8H_2O.$

The reaction with calcium aluminate hydrate is as follows

$2(3CaO . Al_2O_3 . 12H_2O) + 3(Na_2SO_4 . 10H_2O)$

$$\longrightarrow 3CaO . Al_2O_3 . 3CaSO_4 . 31H_2O + 2Al(OH)_3 + 6NaOH + 17 H_2O$$

Calcium sulphate attacks only calcium aluminate hydrate producing calcium sulpho aluminate ($3CaO . Al_2O_3 . 3CaSO_4 . 32H_2O$) known as ettringite. Molecules of water may be 32 or 31.

On the other hand magnesium sulphate has a more far reaching action than other sulphates because it reacts not only with calcium hydroxide and hydrated calcium aluminates like other sulphates but also decomposes the hydrated calcium silicates completely and makes it a friable mass.

The rate of sulphate attack increases with the increase in the strength of solution. A saturated solution of magnesium sulphate can cause serious damage to concrete with higher water cement ratio in a short time. However, if the concrete is made with low water cement ratio, the concrete can withstand the action of magnesium sulphate for 2 or 3 years. The concentration of sulphates is expressed as the number of parts by weight of SO_3 per million parts. 1000 PPM is considered moderately severe and 2000 PPM is considered very severe, especially if $MgSO_4$ is the predominant constituent.

Another factor influencing the rate of attack is the speed in which the sulphate gone into the reaction is replenished. For this it can be seen that when the concrete is subjected to the pressure of sulphate bearing water on one side the rate of attack is highest. Similarly, alternate wetting and drying due to tidal variation or spraying leads to rapid attack.

Methods of Controlling Sulphate Attack

Having studied the mechanism of sulphate attack on concrete it will be easy for us to deal with the methods for controlling the sulphate attack.

(a) Use of Sulphate Resisting Cement

The most efficient method of resisting the sulphate attack is to use cement with the low C_3A content. This has been discussed in detail earlier in chapter I. In general, it has been found that a C_3A content of 7% gives a rough division between cements of good and poor performance in sulphate waters.

(b) Quality Concrete

A well designed, placed and compacted concrete which is dense and impermeable exhibits a higher resistance to sulphate attack. Similarly, a concrete with low water/cement ratio also demonstrates a higher resistance to sulphate attack.

(c) Use of air-entrainment

Use of air-entrainment to the extent of about 6% (six per cent) has beneficial effect on the sulphate resisting qualities of concrete. The beneficial effect is possibly due to reduction of segregation, improvement in workability, reduction in bleeding and in general better impermeability of concrete.

(d) Use of pozzolana

Incorporation of or replacing a part of cement by a pozzolanic material reduces the sulphate attack. Admixing of pozzolana converts the leachable calcium hydroxide into insoluble non-leachable cementitious product. This pozzolanic action is responsible for impermeability of concrete. Secondly, the removal of calcium hydroxide reduces the susceptibility of concrete to attack by magnesium sulphate.

(e) High Pressure Steam Curing

High pressure steam curing improve the resistance of concrete to sulphate attack. This improvement is due to the change of C_3AH_6 into a less reactive phase and also to the removal or reduction of calcium hydroxide by the reaction of silica which is invariably mixed when high pressure steam curing method is adopted.

(f) Use of High Alumina Cement

The cause of great resistance shown by high alumina cement to the action of sulphate is still not fully understood. However, it is attributed in part to the absence of any free calcium hydroxide in the set cement, in contrast to Portland cement. High alumina cement contains approximately 40% alumina, a compound very susceptible to sulphate attack, when in normal portland cement. But this percentage of alumina present in high alumina cement behaves in a different way. The primary cause of resistance is attributed to formation of protective films which inhibit the penetration or diffusion of sulphate ions into the interior. It should be remembered that high alumina cement may not show higher resistance to sulphate attack at higher temperature.

A comprehensive study of concrete exposed to natural sulphate soils and to pure sulphate solution in the laboratory for periods ranging upto 25 years, was reported by Miller and Manson. The conclusions derived from this extensive study is given below.

(a) There was a definite correlation between the sulphate resistance of Portland cement and the amount of tricalcium aluminate (C_3A) it contained. High resistance was found for Portland cements containing not more than 5.5 per cent C_3A.

(b) There was no indication that the finer grinding of the cements had any influence on sulphate resistance.

(c) The resistance of seven Portland-pozzolana cements varied over nearly as wide a range as was observed for the 122 Portland cements.

(d) Four calcium aluminate cements (Cement Fondu or similar-non Portland cement) consistently showed a very high resistance to the sulphate bearing water. There was however, some indication that these cements are not completely stable at temperatures above 21 to 38°C.

(e) Specimens cured in steam at temperatures of 100°C and especially at 176°C were highly resistant. The degree of improvement was greatest for those cements originally not highly resistant, that is, those with relatively high C_3A.

(f) Few of the 40 admixtures tried gave markedly improved resistance; many had no effect and some were deleterious. The most effective were linseed, soyabean, and tung oils.

A large scale study of resistance of concrete to sulphate soils formed a part of the long-time study of cement performance in concrete. This was carried out by the Portland Cement Association (USA) under the general supervision of an Advisory committee. About 1000 concrete beams of size 15 x 13 x 86 cm were embedded horizontally to half their 15 cm depth in soils containing about 10 per cent soluble sulphates. For half of the specimens the sulphate was principally sodium sulphate. For the other half, 2/3 number of specimen it was sodium sulphate and 1/3 magnesium sulphate. The soil in each basin was alternately made wet and dry. The prevailing temperature was above 0°C.

Twenty-seven different Portland cements including all five ASTM type, were used in three concrete mixtures containing cement 223, 307, 390 kg/m³.

A report of results to 20 years was published in 1965. With respect to sulphate attack, the following conclusions were drawn. [9.18]

(a) The resistance of concrete to attack by solutions of sulphate salts increases with reduction of C_3A content in the cement. At 6 years, a C_3A content of 7% as calculated without correction for minor oxides provided a good separation between cements of good and poor sulphates resistance. After 20 years, it was concluded that a C_3A content of 5.5 per cent as corrected for minor oxides and about 3.5 per cent as determined by X-ray analysis, were fairly good values for separating superior and poor resistance in the richest mix. It is interesting to note that the 10 year report (1953) observed that beams in the soil containing $MgSO_4$ as well Na_2SO_4 were less attacked than those in the soil containing mainly Na_2SO_4. This result is contrary to expectations based on some studies conducted with concretes and mortars continually immersed in sulphate solutions. It was tentatively ascribed to differences in the nature of the salt deposit on the beams resulting from evaporation.

Table 9.11. Requirements for Concrete Exposed to Sulphate Attack. As per IS 456 : 2000

Sl.	Class	Concentration of Sulphates, Expressed as SO_3			Type of Cement	Dense, Fully compacted Concrete. Made with 20 mm Nominal Maximum Size Aggregates Complying with IS 383	
		In Soil		In Ground Water		Minimum Cement Content kg/m³	Maximum Free Water/ Cement Ratio
		Total SO_3 Percent	SO_3 in 2 : 1 Water: Soil Extract g/l	g/l			
(1)	(2)	(3)	(4)	(5)	(6)	(7)	(8)
(i)	1	Traces (< 0.2)	Less than 1.0	Less than 0.3	Ordinary Portland cement or Portland slag cement or Portland pozzolana cement	280	0.55
(ii)	2	0.2 to 0.5	1.0 to 1.9	0.3 to 1.2	Ordinary Portland cement or Portland slag cement or Portland pozzolana cement	330	0.50
					Supersulphated cement or sulphate resisting Portland cement	310	0.50
(iii)	3	0.5 to 1.0	1.9 to 3.1	1.2 to 2.5	Supersulphated cement or sulphate resisting Portland cement	330	0.50
					Portland pozzolana cement or Portland slag cement	350	0.45

Table 9.11. (Contd.)

(iv)	4	1.0 to 2.0	2.5 to 5.0	3.1 to 5.0	Supersulphated or sulphate resisting Portland cement	370	0.45
(v)	5	More than 2.0	Morethan 5.0	More than 5.0	Sulphate resisting Portland cement or supersulphated cement with protective coating.	400	0.40

Notes

1. Cement content given in this table is irrespective of grades of cement.

2. Use of supersulphated cement is generally restricted where the prevailing temperature is above 40°C.

3. Supersulphated cement gives an acceptable life provided that the concrete is dense and prepared with a water-cement ratio of 0.4 or less, in mineral acids, down to pH 3.5.

4. The cement contents given in col 7 of this table are the minimum recommended. For SO_3 contents near the upper limit of any class, cement contents above these minimum are advised.

5. For severe conditions, such as thin sections under hydrostatic pressure on one side only and sections partly immersed, considerations should be given to a further reduction of water-cement ratio.

6. Portland slag cement conforming to IS 455 with slag content more than 50 percent exhibits better sulphate resisting properties.

7. Where chloride is encountered along with sulphates in soil or ground water, ordinary Portland cement with C_3A content from 5 to 8 percent shall be desirable to be used in concrete, instead of sulphate resisting cement. Alternatively, Portland slag cement conforming to IS 455 having more than 50 percent slag or a blend of ordinary Portland cement and slag may be used provided sufficient information is available on performance of such blended cements in these conditions.

(b) Air entrainment improved the performance of almost all of the specimens exposed to alternate drying and soaking in sulphate soils.

(c) Influence of cement content of concrete (and accompanying change in water-cement ratio) was highly significant. For the richest mix, attack was slow, at 6 years little difference in resistance between cements could be seen. For the intermediate and lean mixes, the attack was more rapid, and important differences related to cement composition, especially C_3A content, were clearly evident at that time.

Where hardened Portland cement concrete is exposed to soil or ground water containing sulphate compounds, it is necessary to limit the permeability of the concrete. It is also recommended that with the higher sulphate concentration it is necessary to use cement with higher resistance to sulphates, higher cement content and lower water/cement ratio. IS 456 of 2000 gives the recommendations for the type of cement, maximum free W/C ratio and minimum cement content, which are required at different sulphate concentrations in near-neutral ground water having pH of 6 to 9. Table 9.11 shows the requirements for concrete exposed to sulphate attack. For very high sulphate concentrations class 5 in the table 9.11, some form of lining such as polyethylene or polychloroprene sheet, or surface coating based on asphalt, chlorinated rubber, expoxy, or polyurethene materials should be used to prevent access by the sulphate solution. IS 456 of 2000 also stipulates the sulphates in concrete in the following way.

Sulphates are present in most cements and in some aggregates: excessive amount of water-soluble sulphate from these or other mix constituents can cause expansion and disruption of concrete. To prevent this, the total water-soluble sulphate content of the concrete mix, expressed as SO_3, should not exceed 4 per cent by mass of the cement in the mix. The sulphate content should be calculated as the total from the various constituents of the mix.

The 4 per cent limit does not apply to concrete made with supersulphated cement complying with IS 6909.

Alkali-Aggregate Reaction

Detailed discussion has been done on alkali-aggregate reaction in chapter 3 under aggregate and testing of aggregates. Alkali-aggregate reaction (AAR) is basically a chemical reaction between the hydroxyl ions in the pore water within concrete and certain types of rock minerals which sometimes occur as part of aggregates. Since reactive silica in the aggregate is involved in this chemical reaction it is often called alkali-silica reaction (ASR). Since the first paper published by Stantan during 1940's on this subject, a considerable studies have been made and now it is recognised as one of the major causes of cracking of concrete. Primarily the reaction produces what is called alkali-silica gel of unlimited swelling type under favourable conditions of moisture and temperature,

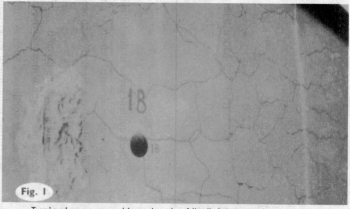

Fig. 1

Typical map cracking due to Alkali-Aggregate reaction

in voids and cracks and further it causes disruption and pattern cracking. The crack width can range from 0.1 mm to as much as 10 mm.

What was seen as a rare case in 1940's have been recognised now as one of the general occurrence in present day concrete to a greater or smaller magnitude. Aggregates used in large concrete construction should be suitably tested to detect tendency for alkali-aggregate reaction.

In the construction of nuclear power project at Kaiga initially they did not investigate the quality of aggregate. Later on they suspected the aggregate and as a remedial measure, they went in for low alkali cement having alkali content of less than 0.4.

As the concrete technologists are now more conscious about AAR, the cement manufactures are more careful about alkali content (K_2O and Na_2O) or what is called soda equivalent. This is calculated as the actual Na_2O content plus 0.658 times the K_2O content of the clinker. It should be less than 0.6 per cent by mass of cement. Alkali content of 0.6 could be considered as a threshold point of high alkali cement.

It is to be pointed out that alkali-silica reaction takes place only at high concentrations of OH^-, that is at high pH value in the pore water. The pH of the pore water depends on the alkali content of cement. Heigh alkali cement may

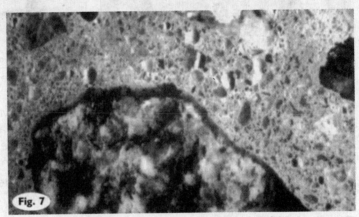

Dark reaction rim on aggregate border

lead to a pH of about 13.5 to 13.9 and low alkali cement results in a pH of about 12.7 to 13.1. An increase in pH of 1.0 represents a ten fold increase in hydrogen ion concentration. Therefore low alkali cement which produces low pH value in the pore water is safe against potentially reactive aggregate.

Alkalis not only comes from cement but also comes from sand containing sodium chloride, admixtures, mixing water, sea water penetration, fly ash, blast furnace slag and deicing salt getting into concrete. Alkalis from all these sources must be included in finding the total alkalis. British standard 5328 : part 1 : 1091 specifies a maximum of 3.0 kg of alkalis (expressed as soda equivalent) in 1 m^3 of concrete in case of alkali reactive aggregates are used.

Acid Attack

Concrete is not fully resistant to acids. Most acid solutions will slowly or rapidly disintegrate portland cement concrete depending upon the type and concentration of acid. Certain acids, such as oxalic acid and phosphoric acids are harmless. The most vulnerable part of the cement hydrate is $Ca(OH)_2$, but C-S-H gel can also be attacked. Silicious aggregates are more resistant than calcareous aggregates.

Concrete can be attacked by liquids with pH value less than 6.5. But the attack is severe only at a pH value below 5.5. At a pH value below 4.5, the attack is very severe. As the attack

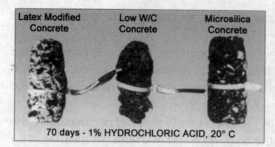

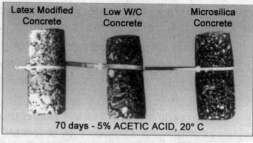

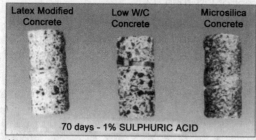

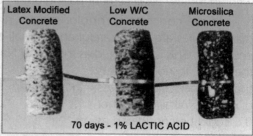

Relative acids resistance of concrete
Courtesy : P.K. Mehta

proceeds, all the cement compounds are eventually broken down and leached away, together with any carbonate aggregate material. With the sulphuric acid attack, calcium sulphate formed can proceed to react with calcium aluminate phase in cement to form calcium sulphoaluminate, which on crystallisation can cause expansion and disruption of concrete.

If acids or salt solutions are able to reach the reinforcing steel through cracks or porosity of concrete, corrosion can occur which will cause cracking.

Concrete in Sea Water

Large number of concrete structures are exposed to sea water either directly or indirectly. For several reasons, effect of sea water on concrete deserves special attention. The coastal and offshore structures are exposed to simultaneous action of a number of physical and chemical deterioration process. The concrete in sea water is subjected to chloride induced corrosion of steel, freezing and thawing, salt weathering, abrasion by sand held in water and other floating bodies.

Sea water generally contains 3.5 per cent of salt by weight. The ionic concentration of Na^+ and Cl^- are the highest, typically 11,000 and 20,000 mg/litre respectively. It also contains Mg^{2+} and SO_4^{2-}, typically 1400 and 2700 mg/litre respectively. The PH of sea water varies between 7.5 and 8.4. The average value is 8.2. Sea water also contains some amount of CO_2.

We have already seen earlier in this chapter that magnesium sulphate reacts with free calcium hydroxide in set Portland cement to form calcium sulphate, at the same time precipitating magnesium hydroxide. $MgSO_4$ also reacts with the hydrated calcium aluminate to form calcium sulpho aluminate. These have often been assumed to be the actions primarily responsible for the chemical attack of concrete by sea water.

It is commonly observed that deterioration of concrete in sea water is often not characterised by the expansion found in concrete exposed to sulphate action, but takes more the form of erosion or loss of constituents from the parent mass without exhibiting undue expansion. It is inferred that the presence of chlorides in sea water may have retarded the swelling of concrete in sulphate solution. It is also found that concrete will have lost some part of lime content due to leaching. Both calcium hydroxide and calcium sulphate are considerably more soluble in sea water and this, will result in increased leaching action. To put it briefly, concrete undergoes several reactions concurrently when subjected to sea water. A concrete of not too massive dimensions exposed to sea water is more likely to show the effects of leaching than expansion, whereas massive structures like dock walls etc. may show the effects of expansion also. The rate of chemical attack is increased in temperate zones.

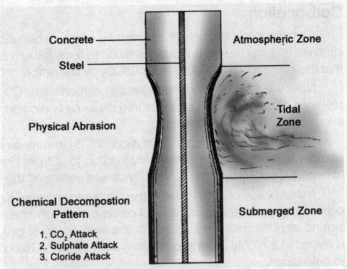

Diagrammatic representation of deterioration of concrete exposed to seawater.
Courtesy : P.K. Mehta

Experience has shown that most severe attack of sea water on concrete occurs just above the level of high water. The portion between low and high water marks is less affected and the parts below the water level which are continuously remain immersed are least affected. The crystallisation of salt in the portion of concrete above high water level is responsible for disruption of concrete. In place of cold climatic region, the freezing of water in pores at the spray level of concrete is responsible for causing lack of durability in concrete. Freezing of water may also take place between the tidal variation level.

It is to be admitted that concrete is not 100% impervious. The water that permeates into the concrete causes corrosion of steel. The product of corrosion being of higher volume than the material they replace, exert pressure which results in lack of durability to reinforced concrete. It is also seen that the lack off durability is more in case of reinforced concrete than the identical plain concrete.

Sea water holds certain quantity of sand and silt particularly in the shallow end. The velocity of wave action causes abrasion of concrete. The impact and the mechanical force of wave action also contributes to the lack of durability of concrete.

From the foregoing discussion it will be easy to formulate steps to improve the durability of concrete in sea water. Apart from the right type of cement with low C_3A content, the other factor to be considered is the use of rich concrete with low water/cement ratio. The rich concrete with low water/cement ratio mainly makes the concrete impervious to the attack of sea water, and also having very little capillary pores does not hold water, to cause expansion either by freezing or by crystallisation of salt. Provision of adequate cover is another desirable step for increasing durability of reinforced concrete. Use of pozzolanic material is yet another desirable step that could be taken to improve durability against sea water. A good compaction, well made construction joints etc. are other points helping the durability of concrete in sea water. Whenever possible, high pressure steam-cured prefabricated concrete elements should be used for better durability.

Carbonation

Carbonation of concrete is a process by which carbon dioxide from the air penetrates into concrete and reacts with calcium hydroxide to form calcium carbonates. We have seen earlier that the conversion of $Ca(OH)_2$ into $CaCO_3$ by the action of CO_2 results in a small shrinkage.

Now we shall see another aspect of carbonation. CO_2 by itself is not reactive. In the presence of moisture, CO_2 changes into dilute carbonic acid which attacks the concrete and also reduces alkalinity of concrete.

Air contains CO_2. The concentration of CO_2 in rural air may be about 0.03 per cent by volume. In large cities the content may go up to 0.3 per cent or exceptionally it may go up to even 1.0 per cent. In the tunnel, if not well ventilated the intensity may be much heigher.

The pH value of pore water in the hardened concrete is generally between 12.5 to 13.5 depending upon the alkali content of cement. The high alkalinity forms a thin passivating layer around steel reinforcement and protect it from action of oxygen and water. As long as steel is placed in a highly alkaline condition, it is not going to corrode. Such condition is known as passivation.

In actual practice CO_2 present in atmosphere in smaller or greater concentration, permeates into concrete and carbonates the concrete and reduces the alkalinity of concrete. The pH value of pore water in the hardened cement paste which was around 13 will be reduced to around 9.0. When all the $Ca(OH)_2$ has become carbonated, the pH value will reduce upto about 8.3.[9.19] In such a low pH value, the protective layer gets destroyed and the steel is exposed to corrosion.

The carbonation of concrete is one of the main reasons for corrosion of reinforcement. Of course, oxygen and moisture are the other components required for corrosion of embedded steel.

Rate of Carbonation: The rate of carbonation depends on the following factors.

- The level of pore water *i.e.*, relative humidity.
- Grade of concrete
- Permeability of concrete
- Whether the concrete is protected or not
- depth of cover
- Time

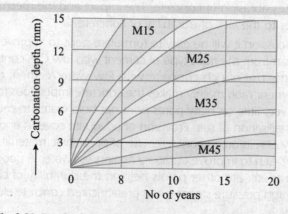

Fig. 9.21. Depth of carbonation with respect to strength (grade) of concrete

It is interesting to know that if pore is filled with water the diffusion of CO_2 is very slow. But whatever CO_2 is diffused into the concrete, is readily formed into dilute carbonic acid reduces the alkalinity.

On the other hand if the pores are rather dry, that is at low relative humidity the CO_2 remains in gaseous form and does not react with hydrated cement. The moisture penetration from external source is necessary to carbonate the concrete.

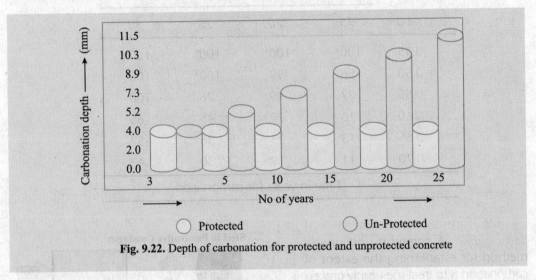

Fig. 9.22. Depth of carbonation for protected and unprotected concrete

Table 9.12. Depth of carbonation with age and grade of concrete.

Age-years	Depth of Carbonation (mm)	
	M 20	*M 40*
2	5.0	0.5
5	8.0	1.0
10	12.0	2.0
50	25.0	4.0

The highest rate of carbonation occurs at a relative humidity of between 50 and 70 per cent

The rate of carbonation depth will be slower in case of stronger concrete for the obvious reason that stronger concrete is much denser with lower W/C ratio. It again indicates that the permeability of the concrete, particularly that of skin concrete is much less at lower W/C and as such the diffusion of CO_2 does not take place faster, as in the case of more permeable concrete with higher W/C ratio. Fig. 9.21 and table 9.12 show the depth of carbonation in various grades of concretes.

It is now well recognised that concrete needs protection for longer durability. Protective coating is required to be given for long span bridge girders, flyovers, industrial structures and chimneys. The fig. 9.22 shows carbonation depth of protected and unprotected concrete.

Depth of cover plays an important role in protecting the steel from carbonation. The table

9.13 shows relationships between W/C, depth of cover and time in years for carbonation depth to reach the reinforcement.

Table 9.13. Approximate relations between W/C, depth of cover and time in years for carbonation depth to reach the reinforcement.

W/C	Depth of cover (mm)			
ratio	15	20	25	30
0.45	100⁺	100⁺	100⁺	100⁺
0.50	56	99	100⁺	100⁺
0.55	27	49	76	100
0.60	16	29	45	65
0.65	13	23	36	52
0.70	11	19	30	43

Time in years for carbonation

Measurement of depth of carbonation: A common and simple method for establishing the extent of carbonation is to treat the freshly broken surface of concrete with a solution of phenophthalein in diluted alcohol. If the Ca(OH) is unaffected by CO_2 the colour turns out to be pink. If the concrete is carbonated it will remain uncloured. It should be noted that the pink colour indicates that enough $Ca(OH)_2$ is present but it may have been carbonated to a lesser extent. The colour pink will show even up to a pH value of about 9.5.

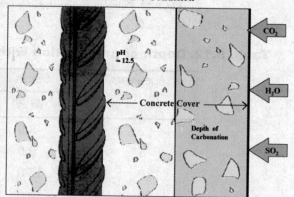

Steel in Passivative Condition

Concrete is under continuous attack by aggressive environmental agencies. Good concrete and suffecient cover is the answer for durability.

Chloride Attack

Chloride attack is one of the most important aspects for consideration when we deal with the durability of concrete. Chloride attack is particularly important because it primarily causes corrosion of reinforcement. Statistics have indicated that over 40 per cent of failure of structures is due to corrosion of reinforcement.

We have already discussed that due to the high alkality of concrete a protective oxide film is present on the surface of steel reinforcement. The protective passivity layer can be lost due to carbonation. This protective layer also can be lost due to the presence of chloride in the presence of water and oxygen. In reality the action of chloride in inducing corrosion of reinforcement is more serious than any other reasons. One may recall that sulphates attack the concrete whereas the chloride attacks steel reinforcements.

Measurement of Depth of Carbonation

Concrete is unaffected by CO_2

Concrete is carbonated

Pink colour indicates that $Ca(OH)_2$ is unaffected by carbonation. The uncoloured portion indicates that concrete is carbonated.

Chloride enters the concrete from cement, water, aggregate and sometimes from admixtures. The present day admixtures are generally contain negligible quantity of chloride or what they call chloride free. Chloride can enter the concrete by diffusion from environment. The Bureau of Indian Standard earlier specified the maximum chloride content in cement as 0.05 per cent. But it is now increased the allowable chloride content in cement to 0.1 per cent. IS 456 of 2000 limits the chloride content as (cl) in the concrete at the time of placing is shown in Table 9.14.

Table 9.14. Limits of Chloride Content of Concrete (IS 456 of 2000)

Sl. No	Type or Use of Concrete	Maximum Total acid soluble chloride Content. Expressed as kg/m^3 of concrete
1.	Concrete containing metal and steam cured at elevated temperature and prestressed concrete	0.4
2.	Reinforced concrete or plain concrete containing embedded metal	0.6
3.	Concrete not containing embedded metal or any material requiring protection from chloride	3.0

The amount of chloride required for initiating corrosion is partly dependent on the pH value of the pore water in concrete. At a pH value less than 11.5 corrosion may occur without the presence of chloride. At pH value greater than 11.5 a good amount of chloride is required.

Limiting values of chloride contents, above which corrosion may be imminent, for various values of pH are indicated in table 9.15. The total chloride in concrete is present partly as insoluble chlorialuminates and partly in soluble form. It is the soluble chloride, which is responsible for corrosion of reinforcement.

Table 9.15. Limiting Chloride Content Corresponding to pH of concrete[9.20]

pH	Chloride content g/litre	ppm
13.5	6.7400	6740
13.0	2.1300	2130
12.5	0.6720	672
12.0	0.2130	213
11.5	0.0670	67
11.0	0.0213	21
10.0	0.0021	2
9.02	0.0002	0.2

Chloride Permeability Based on Charge Passed

(As per ASTM C 1202)

Chloride Permealility	Charges passed (Coulombs)	Type of Concrete
High	≤ 4000	High water-cement ratio, ≤ 0.6
Moderate	2000 to 4000	Moderate W/C ratio (0.4 to 0.5)
Low	1000 to 2000	Water-cement ratio ≤ 0.4
Very Low	100 to 1000	Latex modified concrete
Negligible	≤ 100	Polymer Impregnated concrete

Corrosion of Steel (Chloride induced)

Corrosion of steel in concrete is an electrochemical process. When there is a difference in electrical potential along the steel reinforcement in concrete, an electrochemical cell is set up. In the steel, one part becomes anode and other part becomes cathode connected by electrolyte in the form of pore water in the hardened cement paste. The positively charged ferrous ions Fe^{++} at the anode pass into solution while the negatively charged free electrons e^- pass through the steel into cathode where they are absorbed by the constituents of the electrolyte and combine with water and oxygen to form hydroxyl ions $(OH)^-$. These travel

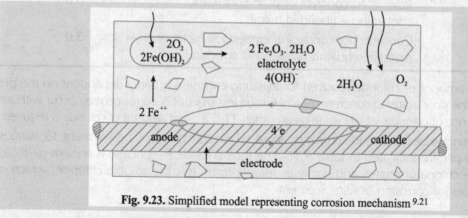

Fig. 9.23. Simplified model representing corrosion mechanism [9.21]

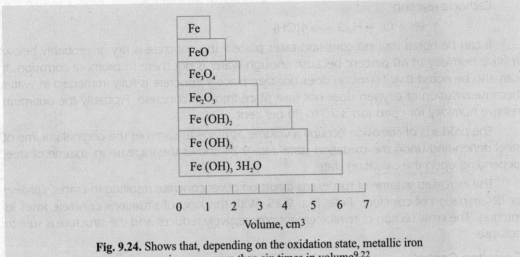

Fig. 9.24. Shows that, depending on the oxidation state, metallic iron can increase more than six times in volume[9.22]

through the electrolyte and combine with the ferrous ions to form ferric hydroxide which is converted by further oxidation to rust. Refer Fig. 9.23.

The reactions are discribed below

Anodic reactions

$$Fe \longrightarrow Fe^{++} + 2e^-$$

$$Fe^{++} + 2(OH)^- \longrightarrow Fe(OH)_2 \quad \text{(Ferrous hydroxide)}$$

$$4\,Fe(OH)_2 + 2H_2O + O_2 \longrightarrow 4Fe(OH)_3 \quad \text{(Ferric oxide)}$$

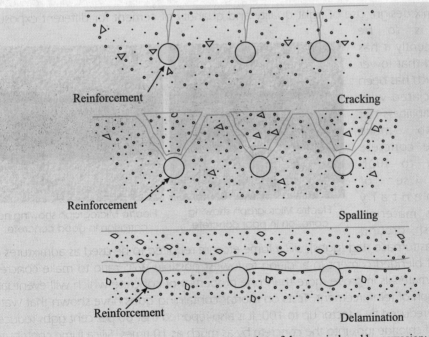

Fig. 9.25. Diagrammatic representation of damage induced by corrosion: cracking, spalling, and delamination

Cathodic reaction

$$4e^- + O_2 + H_2O \longrightarrow 4(OH)^-$$

It can be noted that no corrosion takes place if the concrete is dry or probably below relative humidity of 60 percent because enough water is not there to promote corrosion. It can also be noted that corrosion does not take place if concrete is fully immersed in water because diffusion of oxygen does not take place into the concrete. Probably the optimum relative humidity for corrosion is 70 to 80 per cent.

The products of corrosion occupy a volume as many as six times the original volume of steel depending upon the oxidation state. Fig. 9.24 shows the increase in volume of steel depending upon the oxidation state.

The increased volume of rust exerts thrust on cover concrete resulting in cracks, spalling or delamination of concrete. Refer Fig. 9.25. With this kind of situations concrete loses its integrity. The cross section of reinforcement progressively reduces and the structure is sure to collapse.

Corrosion Control

From the literature survey and case studies it has been reported that 40% of failure of structures is on account of corrosion of embedded steel reinforcement in concrete. Therefore corrosion control of steel reinforcement is a subject of paramount importance.

First and foremost for corrosion control is the good quality of concrete through good construction practices. It is a very vast subject touches the fundamentals of choosing constituent material and good rules to be followed during various stages of production of concrete. In particular the use of lowest possible water/cement ratio having regard to workability. In view of the general availability of superplasticizers, it should be used to cut down the W/C ratio to make dense concrete.

Proper mix design, use of right quality and quantity of cement for different exposure conditions is to be adopted. Recently it has been realised that lower W/C ratio which has been always associated with lower permeability is not enough to make impermeable concrete contributing to high durability. Use of supplementary cementitious materials such as fly ash, ground

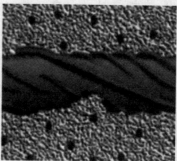

Electro Micrograph showing corrosion in poor concrete

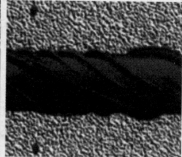

Electro Micrograph showing no corrosion in good concrete

granulated blastfurnace slag (ggbs), silica fume etc. are required to be used as admixtures or in the form of blended cement in addition to lowest possible W/C ratio to make concrete dense. These materials improve more than one properties of concrete which will eventually reduce corrosion of reinforcement. Tests on mortar containing ggbs have shown that water permeability is reduced by a factor up to 100. It is also reported that 60 per cent ggbs reduced the diffusion of chloride ions into the concrete by as much as 10 times. Silica fume contributes to the all-round improvements in the quality of concrete which are responsible for reducing

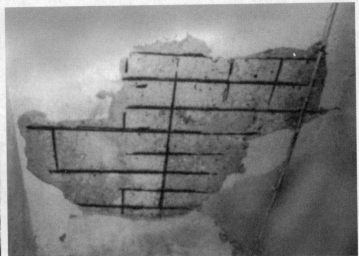

Crack formed due to bursting pressure on account of rusting of reinforcements

Example of delamination of concrete cover

corrosion of steel reinforcement. The improvement in the microstructure of hydrated cement paste is ultimately responsible for protecting the steel reinforcement from corrosion.

In short it can be said that if we make good concrete with low permeability and improved microstructure, it will be durable by itself and also it can take care of the reinforcement contained in it to a great extent. It is always not possible to make such ideal concrete, particularly, in view of the complex environmental and exposure conditions. Further, the inherent long term drying shrinkage and microcracks in concrete, the problems become more serious. This demands certain other measures to control the corrosion of steel reinforcement. They are listed and briefly explained.

- Metallurgical methods
- Corrosion inhibitors
- Coatings to reinforcement
- Cathodic protection
- Coatings to concrete
- Design and detailing

Metallurgical Methods: Steel can be made more corrosion resistant by altering its structure through metallurgical processes. Different methods such as rapid quenching of the hot bars by series of water jets, or by keeping the hot steel bars for a short time in a water bath, and by such other process the mechanical properties and corrosion resistance property of steel can be improved. There are many situations where stainless steel reinforcements are used for long term durability of concrete structures.

Corrosion inhibitors: Corrosion can be prevented or delayed by chemical method by using certain corrosion inhibiting chemicals such as nitrites, phosphates, benzoates etc. Of the available materials, the most widely used admixture is based on calcium nitrite. It is added to the concrete during mixing of concrete. The typical dosage is of the order of 10-30 litres per m^3 of concrete depending on chloride levels in concrete.

As mentioned earlier, in the high pH of concrete, the steel is protected by a passivating layer of ferric oxide on the surface of steel. However, the passivating layer also contain some

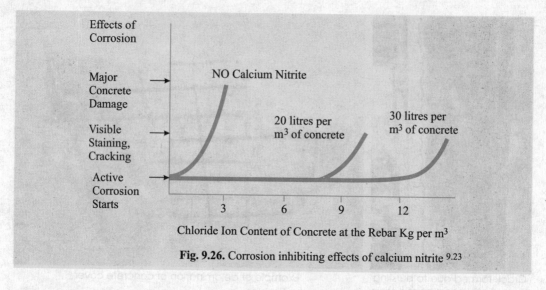

Fig. 9.26. Corrosion inhibiting effects of calcium nitrite [9.23]

ferrous oxide which can initiate corrosion when the chloride ions reach the steel. The nitrite ions present in the corrosion inhibiting admixture will oxidise the ferrous oxide to ferric oxide, thus stabalising the passivating layer even in the presence of chlorides. The concentration of nitrite must by sufficient to cope up with the continuing ingress of chloride ions.

Calcium nitrite corrosion inhibitor comes in a liquid from containing about 30 per cent calcium nitrite solids by weight. The more corrosion inhibitor is added, the longer the onset of corrosion will be delayed. Since most structures in a chloride environment reach a level of about 7 kg of chloride iron per m^3 during their service life, use of less than 18 litres/m^3 of calcium nitrite solution is not recommended.

Fig. 9.26 shows that without an inhibitor the reinforcing steel starts to corrode when the chloride content at the rebar reaches a threshold level of 0.7 kg/m^3. Although the corrosion process starts when the threshold level is reacted, it may take several years for staining, cracking and spalling to become apparent and several more years before deterioration occurs. Adding calcium nitrite increases this corrosion threshold. When you add 20 litres/m^3, corrosion will not begin until over 7.7 kg/m^3 of chloride is present in the concrete at the rebar.

Coatings to reinforcement: The object of coating to steel bar is to provide a durable barrier to aggressive materials,

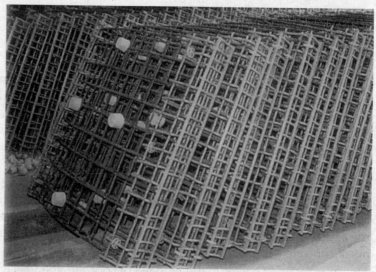

Reinforcement cage, partly coated with fusion bonded epoxy, for precast segment.

such as chlorides. The coatings should be robust to withstand fabrication of reinforcement cage, and pouring of concrete and compaction by vibrating needle.

Simple cement slurry coating is a cheap method for temporary protection against rusting of reinforcement in storage.

Central Electro Chemical Research Institute, (CECRI) Karaikudi have suggested a method for prevention of corrosion in steel reinforcement in concrete. The steps involved in this process are

Derusting: The reinforcements are cleaned with a derusting solution. This is followed without delay by cleaning the rods with wet waste cloth and cleaning powder. The rods are then rinsed in running water and air dried.

Phosphating: Phosphate jelly is applied to the bars with fine brush. The jelly is left for 45-60 minutes and then removed by wet cloth. An inhibitor solution is then brushed over the phosphated surface.

Cement coating: A slurry is made by mixing the inhibitor solution with portland cement and applied on the bar. A sealing solution is brushed after the rods are air cured. The sealing solution has an insite curing effect. The second coat of slurry is then applied and the bars are air dried.

Sealing: Two coats of sealing solution are applied to the bars in order to seal the micro-pores of the cement coat and to make it impermeable to corrosive salts.

The above is a patent method evolved by CECRI and license is given to certain agencies. Somehow or other this method has not become very popular. Some experienced consultants and engineers are doubting the efficacy of this method.

Fusion Bonded Epoxy Coating: It is one of the effective methods of coating rebars. The fusion bonded epoxy coating is a specialised job carried out in a factory and not at site of work. Plants are designed to coat the straight bars in a continuous process. Initially the bar is shot blasted to remove all mill scale and to give the kind of surface finish required. This ensures an adequate bond between epoxy and steel. The bar is then heated to a carefully controlled temperature, before passing through a spray booth. Electrostatically charged epoxy powder particles are deposited evenly on the surface of the bar. It looks, greenish in colour. The coating thickness may vary from 130 to 300 microns.

Although epoxy coated bars have an excellent protection to corrosion in aggressive environment, there are a few limitations.

Galvanising process adopted for corrosion resistance.

After the treatment, cutting and bending may injure the steel which needs certain site treatment. The site treatment is likely to be inefficient. The presence of any defect in the treated body can induce severe localised corrosion which defeat the very purpose. The bars can not be welded. The epoxy is not resistant to ultraviolet rays of sun. The bars should not be exposed to sun for long duration before use.

The coating may get damaged during vibration of concrete. The treatment is very costly: Nearly as costly as that of steel. All the same, this method of protection to the steel is being given to all the flyovers and other structures at Mumbai.

Galvanised reinforcement: Galvanising of reinforcement consists of dipping the steel bars in molten zinc. This results in a coating of zinc bonded to the surface of steel. The zinc surface reacts with calcium hydroxide in the concrete to form a passive layer and prevents corrosion

Cathodic Protection: Cathodic protection is one of the effective, well known, and extensively used methods for prevention of corrosion in concrete structures in more advanced countries. Due to high cost and long term monitoring required for this method, it is not very much used in India.

The cathodic protection comprises of application of impressed current to an electrode laid on the concrete above steel reinforcement. This electrode serves as anode and the steel reinforcement which is connected to the negative terminal of a DC source acts as a cathode. In this process the external anode is subjected to corrode and the cathodic reinforcement is protected against corrosion and hence the name "Cathodic protection".

In this process the negative chloride ions which are responsible for the damage of the passivating film, are drawn away from the vicinity of steel towards the anode where they are oxidised to form chlorine gas. The environment around the steel reinforcement reverts back to alkaline condition which protects the steel.

The other recent development in corrosion control methods are Realkalisation and Desalination.

The realkalisation process allows to make the concrete alkaline again and passivate the reinforcing steel by electrochemical method. This brings back the lost alkalinity of concrete to sufficiently high level to reform and maintain the passive layer on the steel.

In the desalination process the chloride ions are removed from the concrete, particularly from the vicinity of the steel reinforcement by certain electrical method to restablish the passive layer on the steel.[9.25]

Coatings to Concrete: In the past it was believed that concrete by itself is a durable material which needs no protection or maintenance. This belief is no more hold good particularly on account of environmental pollution, industrial fumes and contamination of ground water. In addition to the coating of reinforcement by appropriate material, a

Biggest world map was drawn on cooling tower in Germany using Emce Colour - flex for protection of concrete subjected to aggressive acidic environment.

Courtesy : MC Bauchemie (India) Pvt. Ltd.

surface coating to the concrete member is given to increase the durability further. The coatings serve the dual purpose of protection and decoration. Fig. 9.22 shows the reduction in depth of carbonation of the protected concrete.

Giving protective coatings to major concrete structures such as bridges, flyovers, industrial buildings and chimneys have become a common specification in India as in other countries. Four km long bridge on national highway at Cochin was recently coated with Emceecolor Flex, a material manufactured by MC-Bauchemie (Ind) Pvt. Ltd. Almost all the flyovers at Mumbai are being coated for additional durability.

Acrylic based protective cum decorative coating is given to J.J Flyover at Bombay (shown above) and to many other bridges and flyovers in India, particularly in coastal regions.
Courtesy : MC Bauchemie (India) Pvt. Ltd.

Bridge piers and girders are of considerable dimensions. Freshly made concrete members contain plenty of water in the pore structures. It takes long time to dry. Such freshly made concrete structures should not be coated with epoxy or other materials which will seal off and prevent the internal moisture from going out in consonance with atmospheric conditions. The moisture trapped inside the concrete can do untold harm to the durability of concrete in addition to damaging the protective coating itself. For better durability, the concrete should be able to "breathe" i.e, water vapour should be able to migrate from inside to outside and from outside to inside. But water as it is, should not be able to enter from outside to inside. The protective coating given to the concrete should be of the above characteristics.

Therefore, it is pointed out that the expoxy coating which does not allow the concrete to breathe should not be used for coating concrete members.

Instead, the protective coating should be based on acrylics which retains the breathing property of concrete, while protecting the concrete from other harmful environmental agencies, in particular entry of water and carbonation.

In addition, epoxy based coating material is not resistant to ultra violet rays when exposed to sunlight and also it is not flexible. Whereas the coating material based on acrylic polymer is resistant to ultra violet rays of sun and is flexible.

Coating is not only required for bridges, flyovers and industrial structures, it is also required for very thin members like fins, facade, sunbreakers and other delicate concrete structures where specified amount of cover can not be given. Therefore, acrylic based protective cum decorative coatings can be given for additional durability of such concrete members.

Design and Detailing

The structural designer should take all precautions in designing and detailing, with respect to spacing between bars for the concrete to flow between reinforcements, to facilitate vibration of concrete, to give proper cover to the steel reinforcements, to restrict the crack width etc.

Nominal Cover to Reinforcement: The nominal cover is applicable to all steel reinforcement including links.

For longitudinal reinforcing bars in a column, nominal cover in any case not less than 40 mm or less than the diameter of the bar. In the case of columns of minimum dimension of 200 mm or under, whose reinforcing bars do not exceed 12 mm, a nominal cover of 25 mm may be used.

Typical cover blocks for reinforcement. The one in the extreme right is used in the Delhi Metro works.

For footings a minimum over should be 50 mm. Minimum values of nominal cover to all reinforcement including links is to be provided having taken into account the specified period of fire resistance up to 4 hrs.

Table 9.16. Nominal cover to meet the Durability Requirements as per IS 456 of 2000.

Exposure	Nominal Concrete cover in mm not less than
Mild	20
Moderate	30
Severe	45
Very Severe	50
Extreme	75

Notes: (1) For main reinforcement up to 12 mm diameter bar for mild exposures, the nominal cover may be reduced by 5 mm.

(2) Unless specified otherwise, actual concrete cover should not deviate from the required nominal cover by + 10 mm or 0 mm.

The quality of concrete in the cover region is likely to be of poor quality because of wall-effect. The packing of coarse aggregate is looser at the vicinity of formwork. There is always an increase of paste and less of aggregate in these areas. For long time, this wall-effect phenomenon was not considered as very important from durability point of view because concretes of low slump have been used. But, of late, concretes of slump higher than 200 mm are often used. This high slump concrete increases the risk of segregation and phase separation.

In such cases, addition of colloidal agent., also known as anti-washout, or anti-bleeding admixture could be used to eliminate phase separation problems.

Another method of improving the quality of skin concrete or what is sometimes called covercrete is to adopt permeable formwork technique. This technique is something like vacuum dewatering technique where extra unwanted water is removed by vacuum process. In the case of permeable formwork water from skin portion of concrete is removed by polypropylene fabrics fixed to plywood backing which contain drain holds. Thus, the formwork acts as a filter, through which air and bleed water escape. The permeable formwork lowers the W/C ratio in the concrete up to a depth of 20 mm, making the surface zone resistant against carbonation and diffusion of chloride ions.

Crack Width

IS 456 of 2000 specifies crack width as follows. The surface width of the cracks should not, in general, exceed 0.3 mm in members where cracking is not harmful and does not have any serious adverse effect upon the preservation of reinforcing steel nor upon the durability of structures. In members cracking of the tensile zone is harmful either because they are exposed to the effects of

Crack Detection Microscope   Digital Crack Measuring Gauge

the weather or continuously exposed to moisture or in contact with soil or ground water, an upper limit of 0.2 mm is suggested for the maximum width of cracks. For aggressive environment such as severe category of exposure conditions, the surface width of cracks should not in general exceed 0.1 mm

Some specifications limit the crack widths at points near the main reinforcements instead of at the surface. FIP (International Prestressing Federation) recommend the maximum crack width at the main reinforcement to be 0.004 times the nominal cover. If the nominal cover is 50 mm the crack width at the surface comes to 0.004 x 50 = 0.2 mm.

Crack widths at the surface play an important role in the durability of concrete structures. The structural designer should understand and give serious considerations while designing the structures.

If we take a survey of what we have dealt so far in this chapter we come to know that durability of concrete structures get effected by the development of cracks in concrete due to different reasons as described in table 9.6

Before we conclude the discussion on durability of concrete a few more additional information that affects the durability of concrete, which are not directly related to the cracks in concrete, but will have considerable bearing on durability is dealt in subsequent pages.

Deterioration of Concrete by Abrasion, Erosion and Cavitation

Concrete used in certain situations is required to exhibit good abrasion and erosion properties. Abrasion refers to wearing away of the surface by friction. Erosion refers to the same action by fluids. The cavitation refers to the damage due to non-linear flow of water at velocities more than 12 metres per second. The concrete used in the roads, floors and pavements and the concrete used in the hydraulic structures should exhibit resistance against abrasion, erosion and cavitation.

The resistance against these is closely connected with the compressive strength of concrete. The more the compressive strength the higher is the resistance to abrasion. Hardness of aggregate, particularly the coarse aggregate is important to abrasion resistance. Although for concrete of strength of 56 MPa and above, the effect of aggregate hardness is not so important.

The shape and surface texture of aggregate also plays an important part in the abrasion resistance of concrete. A smooth rounded aggregate, when subjected to lateral load, may get dislodged due to lack of bond and interlocking effect of the aggregate. Once the aggregate is dislodged and removed, the paste does not withstand the abrasion action. Rough and angular aggregate with better bond and interlocking effect stands up well against abrasion. If the aggregates are firmly embedded in the matrix, the wearing out of the surface will be uniform without pitting. A placing of homogeneous unsegregated concrete will also exhibit better abrasion resistance. In closed conduits or in a sheet of water flowing over a weir, vapour bubbles are formed in running water whenever the pressure at a point in the water is reduced to its vapour pressure at the existing temperature. Vapour bubbles flow downstream with the water and when they enter a region of higher pressure, they collapse with great impact. The formation of vapour bubbles and their subsequent collapse is called cavitation. The energy given up on their collapse causes "cavitation damage". At higher velocities, the forces of cavitation may be strong enough to damage the concrete surface in a very serious manner.

The method adopted for avoiding cavitation, apart from careful designing of the structure, making smooth surface free from irregularities is other effective step. The concrete should be of high strength, well cured and finished smooth. Epoxy screeding and polymer application to the surface is said to be effective against cavitation.

Effects of Some Materials on Durability

Action of mineral oils

Mineral such as petrol, and petroleum distillates in general, do not attack hardened concrete though they seriously affect hardening process of fresh concrete. Creosotes which contain phenols may have some effects on concretes. Lubricating oils which are entirely of mineral origin do not attack concrete. As a matter of fact, often concrete tanks are used as a storage tanks for mineral oils. To reduce permeability, rich concrete is used and also some kind of surface treatment such a four coats of sodium silicate is applied.

Action of Organic Acids

There are a number of organic acids which sometimes come into contact with concrete and cause deleterious effect on it. Acetic acid, lactic acid and butyric acid attack concrete with severity depending upon concentration and temperature. Fresh milk has so little lactic acid that it does not harm concrete. Formic acid is corrosive to concrete. Tannic acid and phenols are only mildly corrosive. Oleic, stearic acids occurring in various oils and fats, though insoluble in water have some corrosive action on concrete.

Vegetables and Animal Oils and Fats

Many vegetable oils contain small amounts of free fatty essence and produce a slow deterioration of concrete surfaces. Most fresh animal oils contain little acid but rancid animal oils contain considerably more acid and therefore are corrosive. Some fish oils are said to be more corrosive than other animal oils. Laboratory tests show that Portland cements concrete are rapidly attacked by cotton-seed oils.

Action of Sugar on Concrete

Sugar is a powerful retarding agent, but its action on hardened concrete is not of much consequence, though it may gradually corrode the concrete. Concrete tanks have been used for the storage of molasses with satisfactory results. It should be noted that concrete tanks should be well cured for at least 28 days before being charged with syrups and molasses. It is also recommended that the surface of concrete tanks may be treated with sodium silicate solution or tar or asphalt.

Action of Sewage

Domestic sewage has not got detrimental effect on good concrete. As such, concrete pipes are used for conveying sewage; also concrete is used for constructing sewage treatment plants. Hydrogen sulphide gas which may be evolved from septic sewage in sewer or sludge digestion tank, though by itself is not harmful, may promote the formation of sulphuric acid which can attack the concrete surface above the liquid level. Concrete sewers running full are not attacked.

If the sewage contains more than 150 ppm of soluble sulphate salts (as SO_4), sulphate attack may take place. Domestic sewage rarely contains this amount of sulphate salts but discharge of certain industrial wastes into sewer could increase the concentration of sulphate salts.

Concrete pipes to carry sewage should be of low permeability to minimise penetration of liquid. This could be done by rich concrete, low water cement ratio and good compaction to increase the durability of the sewer. It should be seen that formation of sulphuric acid is avoided by keeping sufficient quantity of flow, proper ventilation of sewer and by avoiding the stagnation or septicity of sewage.

Surface Treatments of Concrete

There are large varieties of materials, which are applied to surface of concrete either to waterproof the surface or to render it resistant to attack of chemical agencies. Sometimes, they are added to give a quick hardening effect so that concrete is made stronger within a short period to enable it to withstand destructive forces. Some of the materials used for surface treatments are listed below:

(a) Aqueous solution of sodium silicate.

(b) Magnesium or zinc silico fluoride.

(c) Drying oils such as linseed or tung oil.

(d) Chlorinated rubber paints.

(e) Neoprene paints.

(f) Epoxy paints or coal tar epoxy paints.

(g) Silicon fluoride (SiF_4) treatment.

Concrete surface can be hardened and rendered more resistant to abrasion, or less liable to create dust, by suitable treatment. The surface of the hardened and air-dry concrete may be treated with a solution of sodium silicate, aluminium, or zinc sulphate, or silicofluorides, or with drying oil like linseed oil or tung oil; alternatively a proportion of carborundum or fused alumina, or one of the finely divided iron-ammonium chloride preparations, may be incorporated in the surface layer of the concrete while placing.

Carborundum, fused alumina, and finely divided iron are effective in rendering a concrete surface less slippery and more-resistant to abrasion, but they are not very effective in rendering the surface less dusty. Treatment with a solution of sodium silicate hardens a concrete surface and also renders it less dusty. Treatment with the sulphate solutions and slilicoflouride is also effective.

Tung oil and linseed oil are applied to concrete surface either neat, hot or thinned with turpentine or white spirits. The treatment gives a hard surface and freedom from dust. Floor paints also have a reasonable durability if the conditions of wear are not heavy. Oil paints with a tung-oil medium, or bituminous paints, can be used, but paints containing synthetic resins particularly polyurethanes or epoxyesters, or chlorinated rubber have a greater resistance to wear. None of these surface treatments are effective on a weak or friable concrete surface.

Treatment with the Sodium Silicate and Silicofluoride only affords protection against mild conditions of attack either by aqueous solutions or organic liquids. Drying oils can exert a protective influence for some years against dilute aqueous solutions of aggressive soils. The surface coatings by chlorinated rubber paints, neoprene paints, epoxy paints etc. are found to be effective in protecting concrete against aqueous solutions of salts and dilute acids. Epoxy paints or synthetic resin lacquers specially prepared for the treatment of concrete surfaces have given good protection.

The above materials have often been applied for protecting concrete surfaces from abrasion, erosion and general deteriorating action of concrete piles, jetty piers and other hydraulic structures. A treatment by bitumen and coal tar has been found to give protection against insects and borers. Some plastic materials, rubber, latex glass fibre coatings, PVC linings have also been given to concrete in certain situations for increasing durability.

One of the important surface treatment adopted to increase the durability of concrete is what is known as 'Ocrate Process'. In this, concrete member is impregnated with Silico fluoride under pressure. This method has been adopted to increase the durability of precast concrete piles and pipes carrying sewage.

Lastly, one of the recent application to improve the durability of concrete is the technique of polymer impregnation. Polymer application to the concrete surface, improves the durability of concrete manifold. Though, this process is at present very costly, there is to doubt that the technique of polymer application to concrete will have a bright future.

Before we end this chapter, it is pertinent to bring out a few tables on exposure conditions which have serious bearing on durability of concrete. As per IS 456 of 2000, the general environment to which the concrete will be exposed during its working life is classified into five levels of severity, that is, mild, moderate, severe, very severe and extreme. This is described in Table 9.17

Table 9.17. Environmental Exposure Conditions (IS 456 of 2000)

Environment	Exposure Conditions
Mild	Concrete surfaces protected against weather or aggressive conditions except those situated in coastal areas
Moderate	Concrete surfaces sheltered from severe rain or freezing whilst wet Concrete exposed to condensation and rain. Concrete continuously under water. Concrete in contact or buried under non-aggressive soil/

	ground water.	
Severe	Concrete surfaces exposed to severe rain, alternate wetting and drying or occasional freezing whilst wet or severe condensation. Concrete Completely immersed in Sea water.	
Very Severe	Concrete surfaces exposed to sea water spray, corrosive fumes or severe freezing conditions whilst wet. Concrete in contact or buried under aggressive subsoil/ground water. Concrete exposed to coastal environment	
Extreme	Surface of members in tidal zone, members in dired contact with liquid/solid aggressive chemicals	

It is stressed time and again that the free W/C ratio is very important factor in governing the durability of concrete. It should always be the lowest value. Appropriate values for minimum cement content, the maximum free W/C ratio and the minimum grade of concrete are given in Table 9.18. as given in IS 456 of 2000, for different exposure conditions.

The minimum cement content and maximum W/C ratio apply to 20 mm nominal maximum size aggregate. For other sizes of aggregate, they should be changed as per Table 9.19.

Maximum Cement Content: Cement content not including fly ash and ground granulated blast furnace slag in excess of 450 kg/m³ should not be used unless special consideration has been given in design to the increased risk of cracking due to drying shrinkage in thin sections, or to early thermal cracking and to the increased risk of damage due to alkali silica reaction.

Table 9.18. Minimum Cement Content, Maximum W/C Ratio and Minimum Grade of Concrete for Different Exposures with Normal Weight Aggregates of 20 mm Nominal Maximum size. IS 456 : 2000

Sl. No.	Exposure	Plain Concrete			Reinforced Concrete		
		Minimum cement contents kg/m³	Maximum Free W/C ratio	Minimum Grade of concrete	Minimum Cement Content kg/m³	Maximum Free W/C ratio	Minimum Grade of Concrete
1.	Mild	220	0.60	–	300	0.55	M 20
2.	Moderate	240	0.60	M 15	300	0.50	M 25
3.	Severe	250	0.50	M 20	320	0.45	M 30
4.	Very Severe	260	0.45	M 20	340	0.45	M 35
5.	Extreme	280	0.40	M 25	360	0.40	M 40

Notes: (1) Cement content prescribed in this table is irrespective of the grade of cement and it is inclusive of all supplementary cementitious materials. The additions of all supplementary cementitious materials may be taken into account in the concrete composition with respect to the cement content and W/C ratio if the suitability is established and as long as the maximum amounts taken into account do not exceed the limit prescribed in relevant codes.

(2) Minimum grade for plain concrete under mild exposure condition is not specified.

Table 9.19. Adjustments to Minimum Cement Contents for Aggregates other than 20 mm Nominal Maximum Size as per IS 456-2000

Sl. No.	Nominal Maximum Aggregate Size mm	Adjustment to Minimum cement contents in table 9.18. kg/m³
1.	10	+ 40
2.	20	0
3.	40	− 30

The above two tables *i.e.*, Table No. 9.18 and Table No. 9.19 are important from the points of concrete mix design by IS method. With the introduction of revised by IS 456 of 2000, the IS 10262 of 1982 for concrete mix design has become in-operational. However, when the I.S. mix design method is revised the above two tables forms back bone of the concrete mix design.

For general imformation and also to carry out the concrete mix design as per British method (DOE method), Table 9.20 and Table 9.21 are also given.

Table 9.20. Requirements of BS 8110: Part I: 1985 to Ensure Durability Under Specified Exposure Conditions of Reinforced and Prestressed Concrete Made with Normal Weight Aggregate.

Condition of exposure	Nominal Cover of Concrete in mm				
Mild	25	20	20	20	20
Moderate	–	35	30	25	20
Severe	–	–	40	30	25
Very Severe	–	–	50	40	30
Extreme	–	–	–	60	50
Maximum Water/ Cementitious material ratio	0.65	0.60	0.55	0.50	0.45
Minimum content of cementitious Material in kg/m³	275	300	325	350	400
Minimum grade MPa	30	35	40	45	50

Note: (1) Grade is characteristic cube strength

(2) This table applies when maximum size of aggregate is 20 mm. When it is 10 mm and 14 mm respectively, the content of cementitious material should be increased by 40 kg/m³ and 20 kg/m³. Conversely for maximum size of aggregate of 40 mm, the content of cementitious material can be reduced by 30 kg/m³. Prestressed concrete must contain at least 300 kg/m³ of cementitious material.

(3) For exposure to freezing and thawing, air-entrainment should be used.

Table 9.21. Requirements of BS 8110: Part 1-1985 to Ensure Durability under Specified Conditions of Exposure of Plain Concrete.

Environment	Exposure Condition	Maximum free water/cementitious material ratio	Minimum Content of cementitious material kg/m³ for nominal maximum size of aggregate				Minimum grade MPa
			40 mm	20 mm	14 mm	10 mm	
Mild	Concrete surfaces protected against weather or aggressive condition.	0.80	150	180	200	220	20
Moderate	Concrete surfaces sheltered from severe rain whilst wet. Concrete surfaces subject to condensation. Concrete continuously under water. Concrete in contact with non-aggressive soil.	0.65	245	275	295	315	30
Severe	Concrete surfaces exposed to severe rain, alternating wetting and drying or occasional freezing or severe condensation.	0.60	270	300	320	340	35
Very Severe	Concrete surfaces exposed to sea water spray de-icing salts (directly or indirectly), corrosive fumes or severe freezing conditions whilst wet.	0.55	295	325	345	365	35
Extreme	Concrete surfaces exposed to abrasive action, e.g., sea water carrying solids or flowing water with pH ≤ 4.5 or machinery or vehicles.	0.50	320	350	370	390	45

Note:
(1) Cementitious materials is inclusive of slag or fly ash.
(2) Grade of concrete is the characteristic cube strength
(3) For very severe conditions only air-entrained concrete to be used.

Concluding Remarks on Durability

Strength and durability are the two important properties of concrete. They are like two legs of a human body. In India with the availability of good cement since about 1985, good strength can be obtained if reasonable care is taken. But, samething can not be said with regard to durability, because of the rapid deterioration in environmental conditions and the use of concrete has spread to much more hostile regions than ever before.

Concrete is a very loyal and dependable construction material. It should not be abused to the limit as it is done today. It should be used with understanding, love and care.

All that is written in this chapter is a scientific exposition at macro and micro-level of durability problem. It will give an indepth knowledge and better understanding for making good standard concrete for our infrastructural development which we have just started. The information contained in this chapter may be little difficult for the consumption of our common builders who are involved with about 80 per cent of total concrete made in our country.

What is relevant to him in respect of durability is what is written in the chapters from 1 to 6. These chapters deal with the good concrete construction practices for making durable concrete. They are to be considered as introductory part of chapter 9 *i.e.*, on durability.

It may not be out of place to emphasize that we, civil engineers, common builders, site engineers, teachers, concrete technologists and all others who are involved in making concrete, have a lot of responsibilities for making durable concrete for which our country spends about 25 per cent of nation's annual budget. Which other section of our society has more responsibility than we–friends of concrete.

AIM SHOULD BE TO MAKE OUR CONCRETE AS DURABLE AS THESE MONUMENTS!

REFERENCES

9.1 P.C. Aitcin-Durable concrete current Practice and future trends Proceedings of Mohan Malhotra Symposium, ACI, SP 144.

9.2 T.C. Powers-structure and Physical Properties of Hardened Cement Paste-journal of American ceramic Society 1958.

9.3 T.C. Powers et. al. – Permeability of Portland Cement Paste, journal of ACI Nov 1954.

9.4 Mercer L.B-Classification of concrete cracks, Common Wealth Engineers, Vol. 34 sept. 1944

9.5 Hot Weather Concreting, ACI 305 R-1977 revised 1982 ACI Committee Report.

9.6 J.W. Kelly-Cracks in Concrete-the Causes and Cures, Concrete Construction 9-1964

9.7 M Shoya-Drying Shrinkage and Moisture Loss of Superplasticiser Admixed Concrete of Low W/C ratio-Transaction of Japan Concrete Institute-1997.

9.8 Troxell et.al. –Long Time Creep and Shrinkage Tests of Plain and Reinforced Concrete, Proceedings of ASTM-1958.

9.9 G.J. Verbeek-Carboration of Hydrated Portland Cement, ASTM sp. Tech. Publication No 205-1958.

9.10 Lauden Stacey E.F. –Thermal and Acoustic Properties of Light Weight Concrete, Structural Concrete (London) March-April 1966.

9.11 J.M. Scanlon and J.E. Mcdonald Thermal Properties of Concrete and Concrete Making-ASTM sp.Tech. Publication No 169C-1994

9.12 The Thermal Expansion of Concrete-Technical Paper No 7, ITMSO London 1951.

9.13 Some Physical Properties of Concrete at High Temperature ACI Journal April 1958.

9.14 ME Fitz Gibbon-Large Pours-2, Heat Generation and Control Concrete-10 No 12 London Dec. 1976.

9.15 Curring Temperature and Very High Strength Concrete-Concrete International 10, No 10, 1988.

9.16 Tests of Resistance of Concrete to Early Frost Action, RILEM Symposium on Winter Concreting-1956.

9.17 Causes and Control of Cracking in Concrete Reinforced with High Strength Steel Bars-A Review of Research-University of Illinois Engineering Experiment Station Bulletin no 479 (1965)

9.18 Long Time Study of Cement Performance in Concrete, 20 years Report, Research Dept. Bulletin 175. Portland Cement Association 1965.

9.19 V.G. Papadakis et.al. Effect of Composition and Environmental Factors and Cement-Lime Mortar Coating on Concrete Carbonation-Material and Structures-25 No 149 (1992)

9.20 Durability of Concrete Structures ICI Technical Monograph-2000.

9.21 P.A.M. Basheer-An Introduction Model for Causes of Deterioration and Permeability of Concrete Proceedings of Mohan Malhotra Symposium-1994.

9.22 Beton-Bogen, Aalberg Cement Company-Aalberg, Denmark 1981.

9.23 Arthur-L. Walitt - Calcium Nitrite Offers Long-term Corrosion Prevention W.R. Grace and Co., Construction Department Division.

9.24 Plain and Reinforced Concrete-Code of Practice, IS 456 of 2000 (Fourth Revision)

9.25 M.N. Ramesh, Modern Techniques of Corrosion Control in Reinforced Concrete. ICI Seminar on concrete for Coastal Area Feb. 2000.

9.26 A.M. Neville and J.J. Brooks Concrete Technology, Longman Group Ltd. 1987.

9.27 A.M. Neville, Properties of Concrete Fourth Edition 1996.

9.28 Steven H Kosmatka and William C. Panarese, Design and Control of Concrete Mixes, Portland Cement Association, Thirteenth Edition 1994.

9.29 P. Kumar Mehta, Paulo J.M. Monteiro, Concrete Microstructure, Properties, and Materials, Indian Edition. 1997.

Concrete testing and Diagnosing Kit

10

Testing of Hardened Concrete

Testing of hardened concrete plays an important role in controlling and confirming the quality of cement concrete works. Systematic testing of raw materials, fresh concrete and hardened concrete are inseparable part of any quality control programme for concrete, which helps to achieve higher efficiency of the material used and greater assurance of the performance of the concrete with regard to both strength and durability. The test methods should be simple, direct and convenient to apply.

One of the purposes of testing hardened concrete is to confirm that the concrete used at site has developed the required strength. As the hardening of the concrete takes time, one will not come to know, the actual strength of concrete for some time. This is an inherent disadvantage in conventional test. But, if strength of concrete is to be known at an early period, accelerated strength test can be carried out to predict 28 days strength. But mostly when correct materials are used and careful steps are taken at every stage of the work, concretes normally give the required strength. The tests also have a deterring effect on those responsible for construction work. The results of the test on hardened concrete, even if they are known late, helps to reveal the quality of concrete and enable adjustments to be made in the production of further concretes. Tests are made by casting cubes or cylinder from the representative concrete or cores cut from the actual concrete. It is to be remembered that standard compression test specimens give a measure of the potential strength of the concrete, and not of the strength of the concrete in structure. Knowledge of the strength of concrete in structure can not be directly obtained from tests on separately made specimens.

Compression Test

Compression test is the most common test conducted on hardened concrete, partly because it is an easy test to perform, and partly because most of the desirable characteristic properties of concrete are qualitatively related to its compressive strength.

Cube beam and cylinder moulding

The compression test is carried out on specimens cubical or cylindrical in shape. Prism is also sometimes used, but it is not common in our country. Sometimes, the compression strength of concrete is determined using parts of a beam tested in flexure. The end parts of beam are left intact after failure in flexure and, because the beam is usually of square cross section, this part of the beam could be used to find out the compressive strength.

The cube specimen is of the size 15 x 15 x 15 cm. If the largest nominal size of the aggregate does not exceed 20 mm, 10 cm size cubes may also be used as an alternative. Cylindrical test specimens have a length equal to twice the diameter. They are 15 cm in diameter and 30 cm long. Smaller test specimens may be used but a ratio of the diameter of the specimen to maximum size of aggregate, not less than 3 to 1 is maintained.

Moulds

Metal moulds, preferably steel or cast iron, thick enough to prevent distortion are required. They are made in such a manner as to facilitate the removal of the moulded specimen without damage and are so machined that, when it is assembled ready for use, the dimensions and internal faces are required to be accurate within the following limits.

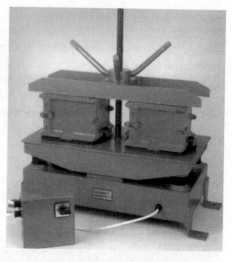

Vibrating table for cubes

The height of the mould and the distance between the opposite faces are of the specified size ± 0.2 mm. The angle between adjacent internal faces and between internal faces and top and bottom planes of the mould is required to be 90° ± 0.5°. The interior faces of the mould, are plane surfaces with a permissible variation of 0.03 mm. Each mould is provided with a metal base plate having a plane surface. The base plate is of such dimensions as to support the mould during the filling without leakage and it is preferably attached to the mould by springs or screws. The parts of the mould, when assembled, are positively and rigidly held together, and suitable methods of ensuring this, both during the filling and on subsequent handling of the filled mould, are required to be provided.

In assembling the mould for use, the joints between the sections of the mould are thinly coated with mould oil and a similar coating of mould oil is applied between the contact surface of the bottom of the mould and the base plate in order to ensure that no water escapes during the filling. The interior surfaces of the assembled mould is also required to be thinly coated with mould oil to prevent adhesion of concrete.

The cylindrical mould is required to be of metal which shall be not less than 3 mm thick. Each mould is capable of being opened longitudinally to facilitate removal of the specimen and is provided with means of keeping it closed while in use. Care should be taken so that the ends are not departed from a plane surface, perpendicular to the axis of the mould, by more than 0.05 mm. When assembled ready for use the mean internal diameter of the mould should be 15.0 cm ± 0.2 mm. and in no direction the internal diameter be less than 14.95 cm. or more than 15.05 cm. The height maintained is 30.0 cm ± 0.1 mm. Each mould is provided with a metal base plate, and with a capping plate of glass or orther suitable material. The base plate and the capping plate are required to be at least 6.5 mm thick and such that they do not depart from a plane surface by more than 0.02 mm. The base plate supports the mould during filling without leakage and is rigidly attached to the mould. The mould and base plate are coated with a thin film of mould oil before use, in order to prevent adhesion of concrete.

A steel bar 16 mm in diameter, 0.6 m long and bullet pointed at the lower end serves as a tamping bar.

Compacting

The test cube specimens are made as soon as practicable after mixing and in such a way as to produce full compaction of the concrete with neither segregation nor excessive laitance. The concrete is filled into the mould in layers approximately 5 cm deep. In placing each

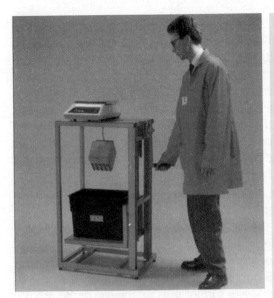

Buoyancy Balance

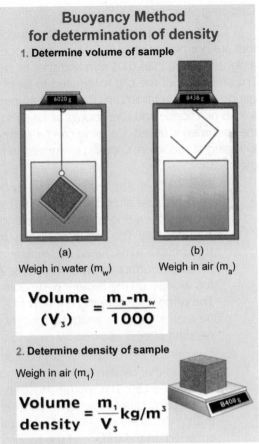

Buoyancy Method for determination of density

1. Determine volume of sample

(a)
Weigh in water (m_w)

(b)
Weigh in air (m_a)

$$\text{Volume}\ (V_3) = \frac{m_a - m_w}{1000}$$

2. Determine density of sample

Weigh in air (m_1)

$$\text{Volume density} = \frac{m_1}{V_3}\,kg/m^3$$

scoopful of concrete, the scoop is required to be moved around the top edge of the mould as the concrete slides from it, in order to ensure a symmetrical distribution of the concrete within the mould. Each layer is compacted either by hand or by vibration. After the top layer has been compacted the surface of the concrete is brought to the finished level with the top of the mould, using a trowel. The top is covered with a glass or metal plate to prevent evaporation.

Compacting by Hand

When compacting by hand, the standard tamping bar is used and the strokes of the bar are distributed in a uniform manner over the cross-section of the mould. The number of strokes per layer required to produce the specified conditions vary according to the type of concrete. For cubical specimens, in no case should the concrete be subject to less than 35 strokes per layer for 15 cm or 25 strokes per layer for 10 cm cubes. For cylindrical specimens, the number of strokes are not less than thirty per layer. The strokes penetrate into the underlying layer and the bottom layer is rodded throughout its depth. Where voids are left by the tamping bar, the sides of the mould are tapped to close the voids.

Compacting by Vibration

When compacting by vibration, each layer is vibrated by means of an electric or pneumatic hammer or vibrator or by means of a suitable vibrating table until the specified condition is attained. The mode and quantum of vibration of the laboratory specimen shall be as nearly the same as those adopted in actual concreting operations. Care must be taken while compacting high slump concrete which are generally placed by pumping. If care its not taken severe segregation takes place in the mould, which results in low strength when cubes are crushed. The cube crushing strength does not represent the strength of the concrete.

Capping Specimens

Capping is applicable to cylindrical specimen. The ends of all cylindrical test specimens that are not plane within 0.05 mm are capped. The capped surfaces are not departed from a plane by more than 0.05 mm and shall be nearly at right angles to the axis of the specimens. The planeness of the cap is required to be checked by means of a straight edge and feeler gauge, making a minimum of three measurements on different diameters. Caps are made as thin as practicable and care should be taken so that flaw or fracture does not take place, when the specimen is tested. Capping can be done on completion of casting or a few hours prior to testing of specimen. Capping is required to be carried out according to one of the following methods:

(a) *Neat Cement:* The test cylinders may be capped with a thin layer of stiff, neat Portland cement paste after the concrete has set in the moulds: Capping is done after about 4 hours of casting so that concrete in the cylinder undergoes plastic shrinkage and subsides fully. The cap is formed by means of a glass plate not less than 6.5 mm in thickness or a machined metal plate not less than 13 mm in thickness and having a minimum surface dimension at least 25 mm larger than the diameter of the mould. It is worked on the cement paste until its lower surface rests on the top of the mould. The cement for capping is mixed to a stiff paste for about 2 to 4 hours before it is to be used in order to avoid the tendency of the cap to shrink. Adhesion of paste to the capping plate is avoided by coating the plate with a thin coat of oil or grease.

(b) *Cement Mortar:* On completion of casting cylinder, a mortar is gauged using cement similar to that used in the concrete and sand which passes IS Sieve 300 but is retained on IS Sieve 150. The mortar should have a water/cement ratio not higher than that of the concrete of which the specimen is made, and should be of a stiff consistency. If an excessively wet mix of concrete is being tested, any free water which has collected on the surface of the specimen should be removed with a sponge, blotting paper or other suitable absorbant material before the cap is formed. The mortar is then applied firmly and compacted with a trowel to a slightly convex surface above the edge of the mould, after which the capping plate is pressed down on the cap with a rotary motion until it makes complete contact with the rim of the mould. The plate should be left in position until the specimen is removed from the mould.

(c) *Sulphur:* Just prior to testing, the cylindrical specimens are capped with a sulphur mixture consisting of 1 part of sulphur to 2 or 3 parts of inert filler, such as fire-clay. The specimens are securely held in a special jig so that the caps formed have a true plane surface. Care has to be taken to ensure that the sulphur compound is not over-heated as it will not then develop the required compressive strength. Sulphur caps are allowed to harden for at least 2 hours before applying the load.

Compression testing machine

(d) Hard Plaster: Just prior to testing, specimens are capped with hard plaster having a compressive strength of at least 42 MPa cm in an hour. Such plasters are generally available as proprietary material. The caps can be formed by means of a glass plate not less than 13 mm in thickness, having a minimum surface dimension at lest 25 mm larger than the diameter of the mould. The glass plate is lightly coated with oil to avoid sticking. Ordinary plaster of paris will not serve the purpose of capping material due to its low compressive strength.

Curing

The test specimens are stored in place free from vibration, in moist air of at least 90% relative humidity and at a temperature of 27° ± 2°C for 24 hours ± $1/2$ hour from the time of addition of water to the dry ingredients. After this period, the specimens are marked and removed from the moulds and unless required for test within 24 hours, immediately submerged in clean fresh water or saturated lime solution and kept there until taken out just prior to test. The water or solution in which the specimens are submerged, are renewed every seven days and are maintained at a temperature of 27° ± 2°C. The specimens are not to be allowed to become dry at any time until they have been tested.

Making and Curing Compression Test Specimen in the Field

The test specimens are stored on the site at a place free from vibration, under damp matting, sacks or other similar material for 24 hours ± $1/2$ hour from the time of addition of water to the other ingredients. The temperature of the place of storage should be within the range of 22° to 32°C. After the period of 24 hours, they should be marked for later identification removed from the moulds and unless required for testing within 24 hours, stored in clean water at a temperature of 24° to 30°C until they are transported to the testing laboratory. They should be sent to the testing laboratory well packed in damp sand, damp sacks, or other suitable material so as to arrive there in a damp condition not less than 24 hours before the time of test. On arrival at the testing laboratory, the specimens are stored in water at a temperature of 27° ± 2°C until the time of test. Records of the daily maximum and minimum temperature should be kept both during the period the specimens remain on the site and in the laboratory particularly in cold weather regions.

Failure of Compression Specimen

Compression test develops a rather more complex system of stresses. Due to compression load, the cube or cylinder undergoes lateral expansion owing to the Poisson's ratio effect. The steel platens do not undergo lateral expansion to the some extent that of concrete, with the result that steel restrains the expansion tendency of concrete in the lateral direction. This induces a tangential force between the end surfaces of the concrete specimen and the adjacent steel platens of the testing machine. It has been found that the lateral strain in the steel platens is only 0.4 of the lateral strain in the concrete. Due to ths the platen restrains the lateral expansion of the concrete in the parts of the specimen near its end. The degree of restraint exercised depends on the friction actually developed. When the friction is eliminated by applying grease, graphite or paraffin wax to the bearing surfaces the specimen exhibits a larger lateral expansion and eventually splits along its full length.

With friction acting *i.e.*, under normal conditions of test, the elements within the specimen is subjected to a shearing stress as well as compression. The magnitude of the shear stress decreases and the lateral expansion increases in distance from the platen. As a result of the restraint, in a specimen tested to destruction there is a relatively undamaged cone of

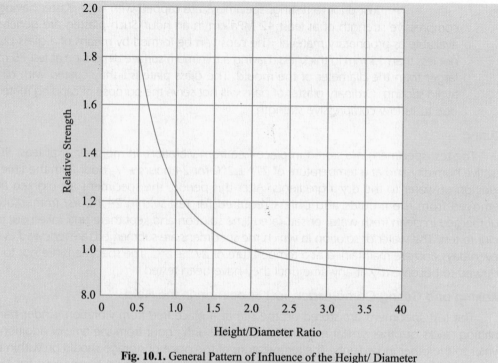

Fig. 10.1. General Pattern of Influence of the Height/ Diameter
ratio on the apparent strength of a cylinder.

height equal to $\dfrac{\sqrt{3}}{2}$ *d* (where *d* is the lateral dimension of the specimen).[10.1] But if the
specimen is longer than about 1.7 *d*, a part it of will be free from the restraining effect of the
platen. Specimens whose length is less than 1.5 *d*, show a considerably higher strength than
those with a greater length. (See Fig. 10.1).

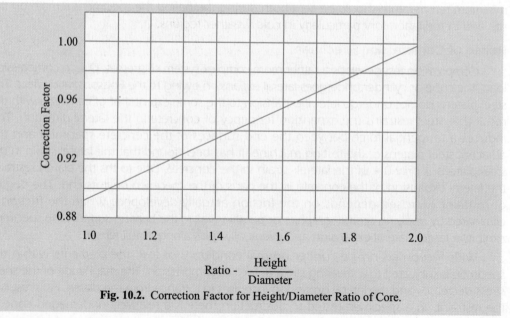

Fig. 10.2. Correction Factor for Height/Diameter Ratio of Core.

Effect of the Height/Diameter Ratio on Strength

Normally, height of the cylinder "*h*" is made twice the diameter "*d*", but sometimes, particularly, when the core is cut from the road pavements or airfield pavements or foundations concrete, it is not possible to keep the heigh/diameter ratio of 2:1. The diameter of the core depends upon the cutting tool, and the height of the core will depend upon the thickness of the concrete member. If the cut length of the core is too long. It can be trimmed to *h/d* ratio of 2 before testing. But with too short a core, it is necessary to estimate the strength of the same concrete, as if it had been determined on a specimen with *h/d* ratio equal to 2.

Fig. 10.2 shows the correction factor for height/diameter ratio of a core (IS 516.1959).

Murdock and Kesler[10.2] found that correlation factor is not a constant one but depends on the strength level of concrete. High strength concrete is less affected than the low strength concrete. Figure 10.3 shows the influence of *h/d* ratio on the strength of cylinder for different strength levels.

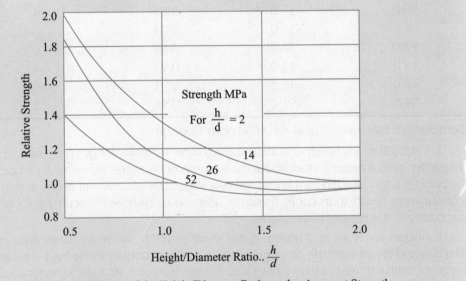

Fig. 10.3. Influence of the Height/Diameter Ratio on the Apparent Strength
of a Cylinder for Different Strength Levels.

Figure 10.1 shows the general pattern of influence of *h/d* ratio on the strength of cylinder.

It is interesting to note that the restraining effect of the platens of the testing machine extends over the entire height of the cube but leaves unaffected a part of test cylinder because of greater height. It is, therefore, the strength of the cube made from identical concrete will be different from the strength of the cylinder. Normally strength of the cylinder is taken as 0.8 times the strength of the cube, but experiments have shown that there is no unique relationship between the strength of cube and strength of cylinder. It was seen that the strength relation varies with the level of the strength of concrete. For higher strength, the difference between the strength of cube and cylinder is becoming narrow. For 100 MPa concrete the ratio may become nearly 1.00. Table 10.1 shows the strength pattern of cubes and cylinders.

Table 10.1. Strength of Cubes and Cylinders

Compressive Strength		Ratio of strengths cylinder/ cube	Difference of strength (cube-cylinders)
Cube MPa	Cylinder MPa		MPa
9.0	7.0	0.77	2
16.0	12.0	0.77	4
20.0	16.0	0.76	4
25.0	20.0	0.81	5
28.0	25.0	0.87	3
30.0	27.0	0.91	3
30.0	28.0	3.91	2
36.0	32.0	3.89	4
37.0	35.0	0.94	2
43.0	37.0	0.87	6
45.0	42.0	0.92	3
49.0	45.0	0.91	4
54.0	51.0	0.96	3

Comparison between Cube and Cylinder Strength

It is difficult to say whether cube test gives more realistic strength properties of concrete or cylinder gives a better picture about the strength of concrete. However, it can be said that the cylinder is less affected by the end restrains caused by platens and hence it seems to give more uniform results than cube. Therefore, the use of cylinder is becoming more popular, particularly in the research laboratories.

Cylinders are cast and tested in the same position, whereas cubes are cast in one direction and tested from the other direction. In actual structures in the field, the casting and loading is similar to that of the cylinder and not like the cube. As such, cylinder simulates the condition of the actual structural member in the field in respect of direction of load.

The points in favour of the cube specimen are that the shape of the cube resembles the shape of the structural members often met with on the ground. The cube does not require capping, whereas cylinder requires capping. The capping material used in case cylinder may influence to some extent the strength of the cylinder.

The Flexural Strength of Concrete

Concrete as we know is relatively strong in compression and weak in tension. In reinforced concrete members, little dependence is placed on the tensile strength of concrete since steel reinforcing bars are provided to resist all tensile forces. However, tensile stresses are likely to develop in concrete due to drying shrinkage, rusting of steel reinforcement, temperature gradients and many other reasons. Therefore, the knowledge of tensile strength of concrete is of importance.

A concrete road slab is called upon to resist tensile stresses from two principal sources— wheel loads and volume change in the concrete. Wheel loads may cause high tensile stresses due to bending, when there is an inadequate subgrade support. Volume changes, resulting from changes in temperature and moisture, may produce tensile stresses, due to warping and due to the movement of the slab along the subgrade.

Stresses due to volume changes alone may be high. The longitudinal tensile stress in the bottom of the pavement, caused by restraint and temperature warping, frequently amounts to as much as 2.5 MPa at certain periods of the year and the corresponding stress in the transverse direction is approximately 0.9 MPa. These stresses are additive to those produced by wheel loads on unsupported portions of the slab.

Determination of Tensile Strength

Direct measurement of tensile strength of concrete is difficult. Neither specimens nor testing apparatus have been designed which assure uniform distribution of the "pull" applied

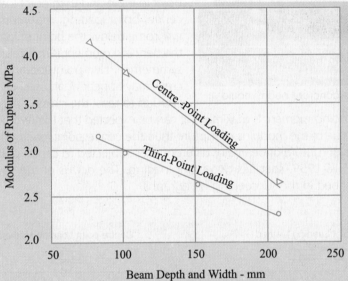

Fig. 10.4. Modulus of Beams of Reputure of Different Sizes Subjected to Centre-point and Third-point Loading[10.3]

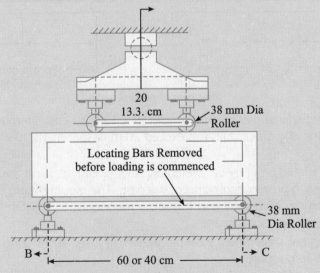

Fig. 10.5. Arrangement for Loading of Flexural Test Specimen

Flexural testing of concrete beam mould

to the concrete. While a number of investigations involving the direct measurement of tensile strength have been made, beam tests are found to be dependable to measure flexural strength property of concrete.

The value of the modulus of rupture (extreme fibre stress in bending) depends on the dimension of the beam and manner of loading. The systems of loading used in finding out the flexural tension are central point loading and third point loading. In the central point loading, maximum fibre stress will come below the point of loading where the bending moment is maximum. In case of symmetrical two point loading, the critical crack may appear at any section, not strong enough to resist the stress within the middle third, where the bending moment is maximum. It can be expected that the two point loading will yield a lower value of the modulus of rupture than the centre point loading. Figure 10.4 shows the modulus of rupture of beams of different sizes subjected to centre point and third point loading. I.S. 516-1959, specifies two point loading. The details of the specimen and procedure are described in the succeeding paragraphs.

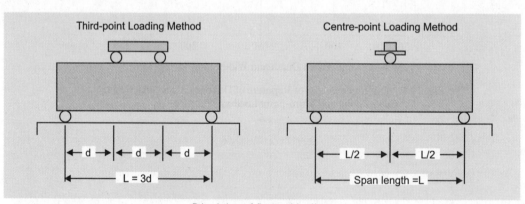

Principles of flexural testing

The standard size of the specimens are 15 x 15 x 70 cm. Alternatively, if the largest nominal size of the aggregate does not exceed 20 mm, specimens 10 x 10 x 50 cm may be used.

The mould should be of metal, preferably steel or cast iron and the metal should be of sufficient thickness to prevent spreading or warping. The mould should be constructed with the longer dimension horizontal and in such a manner as to facilitate the removal of the moulded specimens without damage.

The tamping bar should be a steel bar weighing 2 kg, 40 cm long and should have a ramming face 25 mm square.

The testing machine may be of any reliable type of sufficient capacity for the tests and capable of applying the load at the rate specified. The permissible errors should not be greater that ± 0.5 per cent of the applied load where a high degree of accuracy is required and not greater than ± 1.5 per cent of the applied load for commercial type of use. The bed of the testing machine should be provided with two steel rollers, 38 mm in diameter, on which the specimen is to be supported, and these rollers should be so mounted that the distance from centre to centre is 60 mm for 15 cm specimen or 40 cm for 10.0 cm specimens. The load is applied through two similar rollers mounted at the third points of the supporting span, that is, spaced at 20 or 13.3 cm centre to centre. The load is divided equally between the two loading rollers, and all rollers are mounted in such a manner that the load is applied axially and without subjecting specimen to any torsional stresses or restrains. The loading set up is shown in Fig. 10.5.

Procedure

Test specimens are stored in water at a temperature of 24° to 30°C for 48 hours before testing. They are tested immediately on removal from the water whilst they are still in a wet condition. The dimensions of each specimen should be noted before testing. No preparation of the surfaces is required.

Placing the Specimen in the Testing Machine

The bearing surfaces of the supporting and loading rollers are wiped clean, and any loose sand or other material removed from the surfaces of the specimen where they are to make contact with the rollers. The specimen is then placed in the machine in such a manner that the load is applied to the uppermost surface as cast in the mould, along two lines spaced 20.0 or 13.3 cm apart. The axis of the specimen is carefully aligned with the axis of the loading device. No packing is used between the bearing surfaces of the specimen and the rollers. The load is applied without shock and increasing continuously at a rate such that the extreme fibre stress increases at approximately 0.7 kg/sq cm/min that is, at a rate of loading of 400 kg/min for the 15.0 cm specimens and at a rate of 180 kg/min for the 10.0 cm specimens. The load is increased until the specimen fails, and the maximum load applied to the specimen during the test is recorded. The appearance of the fractured faces of concrete and any unusual features in the type of failure is noted.

The flexural strength of the specimen is expressed as the modulus of rupture f_b which if 'a' equals the distance between the line of fracture and the nearer support, measured on the centre line of the tensile side of the specimen, in cm, is calculated to the nearest 0.05 MPa as follows:

$$f_b = \frac{P \times l}{b \times d^2}$$

When 'a' is greater than 20.0 cm for 15.0 cm specimen or greater than 13.3 cm for a 10.0 cm specimen, or

$$f_b = \frac{3p \times a}{b \times d^2}$$

when 'a' is less than 20.0 cm but greater than 17.0 cm for 15.0 specimen, or less than 13.3 cm but greater than 11.0 cm for a 10.0 cm specimen where

b = measured width in cm of the specimen,

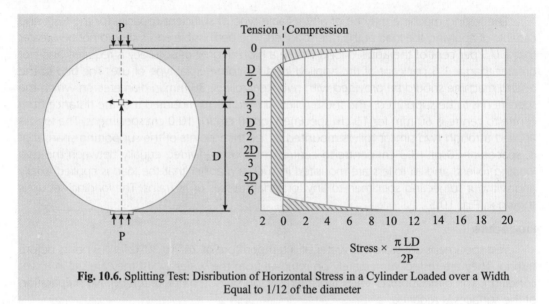

Fig. 10.6. Splitting Test: Disribution of Horizontal Stress in a Cylinder Loaded over a Width Equal to 1/12 of the diameter

d = measured depth in cm of the specimen at the point of failure,

l = length in cm of the span on which the specimen was supported, and

p = maximum load in kg applied to the specimen.

If '*a*' is less than 17.0 cm for a 15.0 cm specimen, or less than 11.0 cm for a 10.0 cm specimen, the results of the test be discarded.

As mentioned earlier, it is difficult to measure the tensile strength of concrete directly. Of late some methods have been used with the help of epoxy bonded end pieces to facilitate direct pulling. Attempts have also been made to find out direct tensile strength of concrete by making briquette of figure 8 shape for direct pulling but this method was presenting some difficulty with grip and introduction of secondary stresses while being pulled.

Whatever may be the methods adopted for finding out the ultimate direct tensile strength, it is almost impossible to apply truly axial load. There is

Splitting tensile test

always some eccentricity present. The stresses are changed due to eccentricity of loading. These may introduce major error on the stresses developed regardless of specimen size and shape.

The third problem is the stresses induced due to the grips. There is a tendency for the specimen to break near the ends. This problem is always overcome by reducing the section of the central portion of the test specimen. The method in which steel plates are glued with the epoxies to the ends of test specimen, eliminates stresses due to griping, but offers no solution for the eccentricity problem.

All direct tension test methods require expensive universal testing machine. This explains why these tests are not used on a routine basis and are not yet standardised.

Indirect Tension Test Methods

Cylinder Splitting Tension Test. This is also sometimes referred as, "Brazilian Test". This test was developed in Brazil in 1943. At about the same time this was also independently developed in Japan.

The test is carried out by placing a cylindrical specimen horizontally between the loading surfaces of a compression testing machine and the load is applied until failure of the cylinder, along the vertical diameter. Figure 10.6 shows the test specimen and the stress pattern in the cylinder respectively.

When the load is applied along the generatrix, an element on the vertical diameter of the cylinder is subjected to a vertical compressive stress of

$$\frac{2P}{pLD} \left[\frac{D^2}{r(D-r)} - 1 \right]$$

and a horizontal stress of

$$\frac{2P}{pLD}$$

where, P is the compressive load on the cylinder

L is the length of cylinder

D is its diameter

and r and $(D - r)$ are the distances of the elements from the two loads respectively.

The loading condition produces a high compressive stress immediately below the two generators to which the load is applied. But the larger portion corresponding to depth is subjected to a uniform tensile stress acting horizontally. It is estimated that the compressive stress is acting for about 1/6 depth and the remaining 5/6 depth is subjected to tension.

In order to reduce the magnitude of the high compression stresses near the points of application of the load, narrow packing strips of suitable material such as plywood are placed between the specimen and loading platens of the testing machine. The packing strips should be soft enough to allow distribution of load over a reasonable area, yet narrow and thin enough to prevent large contact area. Normally, a plywood strip of 25 mm wide, 3 mm thick and 30 cm long is used.

The main advantage of this method is that the same type of specimen and the same testing machine as are used for the compression test can be employed for this test. That is why this test is gaining popularity. The splitting test is simple to perform and gives more uniform results than other tension tests. Strength determined in the splitting test is believed to be closer to the true tensile strength of concrete, than the modulus of rupture. Splitting strength gives about 5 to 12% higher value than the direct tensile strength.

Ring Tension Test [10.17]

Another test for finding out the tensile strength of concrete is known as "Ring Tension Test". Briefly in this method, a hydrostatic pressure is applied radially against the inside periphery of 15 cm diameter, 4 mm thick and 4 mm high concrete ring specimen. The resulting tensile stress developed in the specimen are determined from the equations of the stress analysis of thick walled cylinders, as given below:

$$f_t = \frac{P_i r_i^2}{r_0^2 - r_i^2}\left(1 - \frac{r_0^2}{r^2}\right)$$

where, f_t = Tensile strength

p_i = Applied hydrostatic pressure

r_i = Internal radius

r_0 = External radius

r = Radius at point of failure

Advantages of Ring Tension Test

The nature of the load application in this test is such that no clamping and misalignment stresses are introduced in the test specimen, a condition difficult to avoid in direct tests.

The entire volume of the ring is subjected to tensile stresses with the uniformly distributed maximum stress occurring along the entire periphery of the ring. This is never achieved in the flexural tests and even in the cylinder splitting test a compressive load acting on a diametral plane creates a uniform tensile stress over that plane only.

The magnitude of the radial compressive stress is quite small when compared with the tangential stress. This is a definite advantage over the splitting tension test in which the minimum compressive stresses occurring at the centre line of the splitting plane is about three times the corresponding tensile stress.

Limitations of Ring Tension Test

The drawbacks of this test are that here also, the derivation of equations used for the stress analysis is based upon Hook's Law of linear stress-strain proportionality. The ring tensile strengths obtained appear to be somewhat higher than the true tensile strength of concrete, the magnitude of the exact difference has yet to be firmly established.

Double Punch Test [10.16]

Yet another test to find out the indirect tensile strength of concrete is known as "Double Punch Test". In this test, a concrete cylinder is placed vertically between the loading plates of the compression test machine and compressed by the steel punches located concentrically on the top and bottom surfaces of the cylinder.

An ideal failure mechanism will consist of many simple tension cracks in radial direction and two cone shaped rupture surfaces directly under the loads. Two cone shapes move towards each other as a rigid body and displace the surrounding material horizontally sideways. The formulae for calculating the tensile strength has been calculated on the basis of limit analysis. The relation is :

$$f_t = \frac{Q}{(1.20\,bH - a^2)}$$

where, a = radius of punch

b = radius of cylinder

H = height of the cylinder

Q = load at failure

Factors influencing the strength results

It has already been pointed out that shape and size of specimen affects the strength results. If the strength of the 15 cm size cube is taken as standard, then the strength of 10 cm cube should be reduced by 10%. Strength of the cylinder of size 15 cm diameter and 30 cm long is taken as 0.8 of the strength of 15 cm cube. Where cubes larger than 15 cm are adopted, generally no modification to the strength is necessary unless otherwise specified.

The planeness of the end condition of specimen and capping material used for the cylinder affects the strength. The employment of lubricating material at the bearing surface of the sample affect the strength of concrete.

The effect of height to diameter ratio has already been discussed.

The rate of application of load has a considerable affect on the apparent strength of concrete; the lower the rate of application of load, the lower will be the recorded strength. The reason for this is probably the effect of creep. If the load is applied slowly, or in the application of load, if there is some time-lag, the specimen will undergo certain amount of creep which will increase the strain. The enhanced strain due to creep will be responsible for failure of the sample, at a lower value of stress applied. The Figure 10.7 shows the influence of rate of application of load on the compressive strength of concrete.

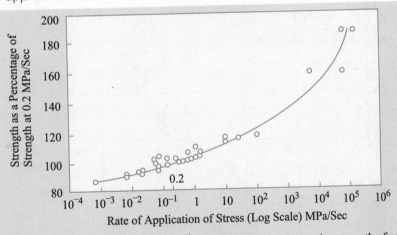

Fig. 10.7. Influence of the rate of application of load on the compressive strength of concrete [10.4]

The state of moisture content of the specimen influences the observed strength to a great extent. If two cubes made from identical concrete, one is wet and another is dry, if tested at the same age, the dry cube gives higher strength than the wet cube. It is quite probable that the dry cube may have undergone drying shrinkage which will have ultimately caused some amount of drying shrinkage cracks and bond failures. From this simple reason it must give an impression that dry cube must give a lower value, but on the contrary the result is the other way. The probable explanation is that due to wetting, some sort of dilation of cement gel will take place by the adsorbed water. The forces of cohesion of the solid particles are then decreased. Perhaps the decrease of strength on account of reduction of cohesion owing to the adsorbed water may be more than that of the loss of strength due to rupture of gel bonds on account of drying shrinkage.

To have a standard condition for test specimens, it is usual to test a specimen immediately on removal from the curing water tank. This condition has the advantage of being better reproducible than a dry condition which includes greatly varying degrees of dryness.

It was earlier pointed out that contrary to expectations, the wet concrete exhibits higher modulus of elasticity. Strength and modulus of elasticity do not go hand in hand in the case of wet concrete.

Test Cores

The test specimen, cube or cylinder is made from the representative sample of concrete used for a particular member, the strength of which we are interested. As the member can not be in fact tested, we test the parallel concrete by making cubes or cylinders. It is to be understood that the strength of the cube specimen cannot be same as that of the member because of the differences with respect to the degree of compaction, curing standard, uniformity of concrete, evaporation, loss of mixing water etc. At best the result of cube or cylinder can give only a rough estimate of the real strength of the member.

To arrive at a better picture of the strength of the actual member, attempts are made to cut cores from the parent concrete and test the cores for strength. Perhaps this will give a better picture about the strength of actual concrete in the member.

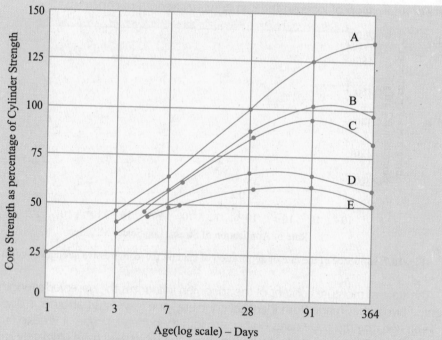

Fig. 10.8. Development with time of strength of concrete cores made with Type 1 cement expressed as a percentage of 28-day strength of standard cylinder (38 MPa : (*A*) standard cylinder; (*B*) well-cured slab, core tested dry (*C*) well-cured slab, core tested wet; (*D*) poorly cured slab, core tested dry; (*E*) poorly cured slab, core tested wet [10.5]

Core can be drilled at the suspected part of the structure or to detect segregation or honey combing or to check the bond at construction joint or to verify the thickness of pavement.

The disadvantages are that while cutting the core, the structural integrity of the concrete across the full cross-section may be affected to some extent and secondly that the diameter to height ratio may be other than that of the standard cylinder. Capping of both ends will be required which will again introduce some differences in the strength. Existence of reinforcement will also present difficulty in cutting a clean core.

The cores cut to determine the strength of concrete of the actual structure may also indicate segregation and honey combing of concrete. In some cases, the beam specimens are also sawn from the road and airfield slabs for finding flexural strength. In practice, it is seen that the strength of the core is found to be less than that of the strength of standard cylinders. Apart from other reasons, it is mainly because site curing is invariably inferior to curing under standard moist condition.

Strength of Cores

The reduction in strength of cores appear to be greater in stronger concrete. The reduction in the strength can be as high as 15 per cent for 40 MPa concrete. Generally, a reduction of 5 to 7 per cent is considered reasonable. It has been reported by many investigators that in situ concrete gains very little strength after 28 days. Tests on high strength concrete show that, although the strength of cores increase with age, the core strength, even up to the age of 1 year, remains lower than the strength of standard 28 day cylinders. Fig. 10.8 and Table. 10. 2 illustrates the above statements.

Table 10.2. Development of strength of Cores with Age

Age days	Strength MPa		Core strength as a proportion of strength of
	Standard cylinders	Cores.	28-day standard cylinder
7	66.0	57.9	0.72
28	80.4	58.5	0.73
56	86.0	61.2	0.76
180	97.9	70.6	0.88
365	101.3	75.4	0.94

Non-Destructive Testing Methods

Non-destructive methods have been in use for about four decades. In this period, the development has taken place to such an extent that it is now considered as a powerful method for evaluating existing concrete structures with regard to their strength and durability apart form assessment and control of quality of hardened concrete. In certain cases, the investigation of crack depth, microcracks, and progressive deterioration are also studied by this method.

Though non-destructive testing methods are relatively simple to perform, the analysis and interpretation of test results are not so easy. Therefore, special knowledge is required to analyses the hardened properties of concrete. In the non-destructive methods of testing, the specimen are not loaded to failure and as such the strength inferred or estimated cannot be expected to yield absolute values of strength. These methods, therefore, attempt to measure some other properties of concrete from which an estimate of its strength, durability and elastic

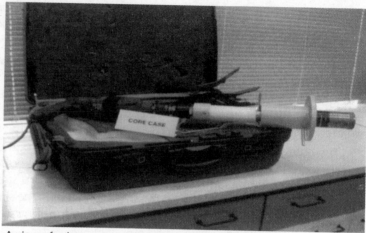

A view of rotary core cutting drill with necessary arrangement, ready to extract 50 mm dia core.

parameters are obtained. Some such properties of concrete are hardness, resistance to penetration of projectiles, rebound number, resonant frequency and ability to allow ultrasonic pulse velocity to propagate through it. The electrical properties of concrete, its ability to absorb, scatter and transmit X-rays and Gamma-rays, its response to nuclear activation and its acoustic emission allow us to estimate its moisture content, density, thickness and its cement content. Based upon the above, various non-destructive methods of testing concrete have been developed:

1. Surface hardness tests: These are of indentation type, include the Williams testing pistol and impact hammers, and are used only for estimation of concrete strength.

2. Rebound test: The rebound hammer test measures the elastic rebound of concrete and is primarily used for estimation of concrete strength and for comparative investigations.

3. Penetration and Pull out techniques: These include the use of the Simbi hammer, Spit pins, the Windsor probe, and the pullout test. These measure the penetration and pullout resistance of concrete and are used for strength estimations, but they can also be used for comparative studies.

4. Dynamic or vibration tests: These include resonant frequency and mechanical sonic and ultrasonic pulse velocity methods. These are used to evaluate durability and uniformity of concrete and to estimate its strength and elastic properties.

5. Combined methods: The combined methods involving ultrasonic pulse velocity and rebound hammer have been used to estimate strength of concrete.

6. Radioactive and nuclear methods: These include the X-ray and Gamma-ray penetration tests for measurement of density and thickness of concrete. Also, the neutron scattering and neutron activation methods are used for moisture and cement content determination.

7. Magnetic and electrical methods: The magnetic methods are primarily concerned with determining cover of reinforcement in concrete, whereas the electrical methods, including microwave absorption techniques, have been used to measure moisture content and thickness of concrete.

8. Acoustic emission techniques: These have been used to study the initiation and growth of cracks in concrete.

9. Surfaces Hardness Methods: The fact that concrete hardens with increase in age, the measure of hardness of surface may indicate the strength of concrete. Various methods and equipments are devised to measure hardness of concrete surface. William testing pistol, Frank spring hammer, and Einbeck pendulum hammer are some of the devices for measuring surface hardness.

Schmidt's Rebound Hammer

Schmidt's rebound hammer developed in 1948 is one of the commonly adopted equipments for measuring the surface hardness. The sectional view of the hammer is shown in Figure 10.9.

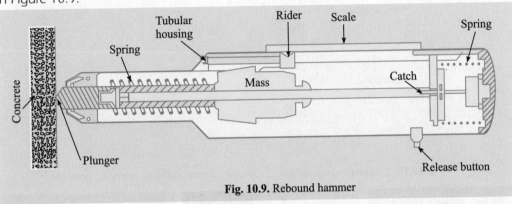

Fig. 10.9. Rebound hammer

It consist of a spring control hammer that slides on a plunger within a tubular housing. When the plunger is pressed against the surface of the concrete, the mass rebound from the plunger. It retracts against the force of the spring. The hammer impacts against the concrete and the spring control mass rebounds, taking the rider with it along the guide scale. By pushing a button, the rider can be held in position to allow the reading to be taken. The distance travelled by the mass, is called the rebound number. It is indicated by the rider moving along a graduated scale.

Each hammer varies considerably in performance and needs calibration for use on concrete made with the aggregates from specific source. The test can be conducted horizontally, vertically—upwards or onwards or at any intermediate angle. At each angle the rebound number will be different for the same concrete and will require separate calibration or correction chart. Fig.10.11 shows the typical relationship between compressive strength and rebound number with hammer horizontal and vertical on a dry or wet surface of concrete.

Limitation: Although, rebound hammer provides a quick inexpensive means of checking uniformity of concrete, it has serious limitations and these must be recognised. The results are affected by:

(a) Smoothness of surface under test.

(b) Size, shape and rigidity of the specimen.

(c) Age of specimen.

(d) Surface and internal moisture condition of the concrete.

(e) Type of coarse aggregate.

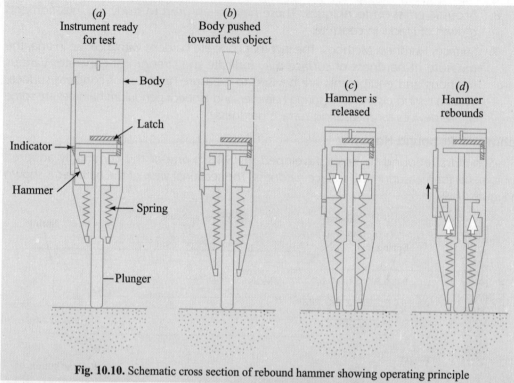

(a)
Instrument ready
for test

(b)
Body pushed
toward test object

(c)
Hammer is
released

(d)
Hammer
rebounds

←— Body

Latch

Indicator —→

Hammer

Spring

—Plunger

Fig. 10.10. Schematic cross section of rebound hammer showing operating principle

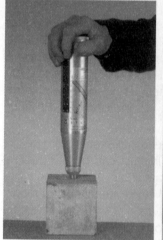

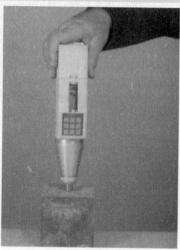

Concrete test hammer,
normal

Concrete test hammer,
digital

Testing anvil

(f) Type of cement.

(g) Type of mould.

(h) Carbonation of concrete surface.

Rebound Number and Strength of Concrete

Investigations have shown that there is a general correlation between compressive strength of concrete and rebound number; however, there is a wide degree of disagreement

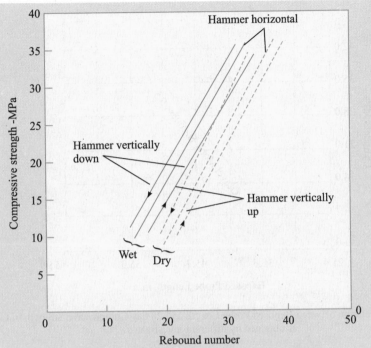

Fig. 10.11. Relationship between compressive strength and Rebound number
with Hammer horizontal and vertical on a Dry and a
Wet Surface of Concrete.

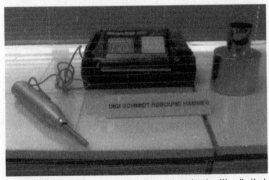

A view of Rebound Hammer connected with digital
recording monitor and Test Anvil for calibration.

among various research workers regarding the accuracy of estimation of strength from rebound readings. The variation of strength of a properly calibrated hammer may lie between ±15% and ±20%.

The relationship between flexural strength and rebound number is found to be similar to those obtained for compressive strength, except that the scatter of the results is greater. Fig. 10.11 shows the relationship between compressive strength of concrete cylinders and rebound numbers.[10.6]

During 1965 and 1967 an international survey on the use of the Schmidt rebound hammer was carried out by RILEM. Majority of those who spoke were against the use of Schmidt rebound hammer in acceptance testing. The consensus was that, "the Schmidt rebound hammer is useful to very useful in checking uniformity of concrete and comparing one concrete against another but it can only be used as a rough indication of concrete strength in absolute terms".

Penetration Techniques

The measurement of hardness by probing techniques was first reported during 1954. Two techniques were used. In one case, a hammer known as, "Simbi" was used to perforate

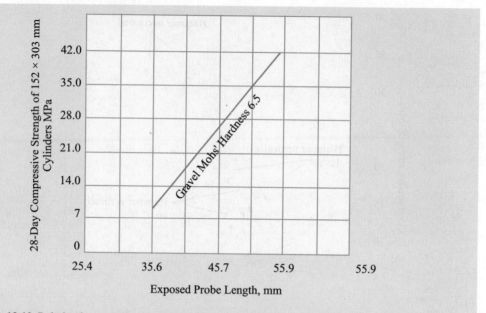

Fig. 10.12. Relation between Exposed Probe Length and 28 day Compressive Strength of Concrete as obtained by different investigators. 10.7

concrete and the depth of borehole was correlated to compressive strength of concrete cubes. In the other technique, the probing of concrete was achieved by blasting with spit pins and the depth of penetration of the pins was correlated with compressive strength of concrete.

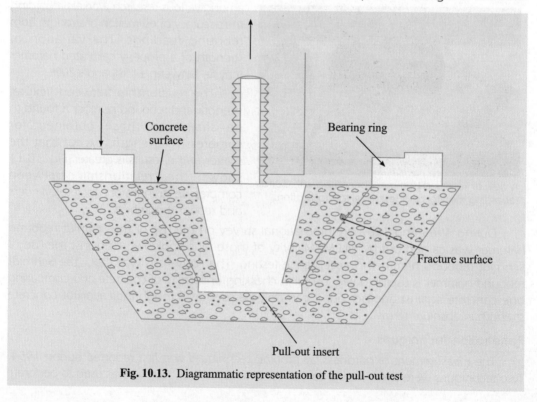

Fig. 10.13. Diagrammatic representation of the pull-out test

The accuracy of this test was found to be ±25%. However, it is further seen that, "Simbi" and spit pins were more effected by the arrangement of coarse aggregate, than the tests using rebound hammers.

During 1964 and 1966, a technique known as the "Windsor Probe" was advanced for testing concrete in the laboratory and *in situ*. The windsor probe is a hardness tester of the surface of the concrete. It is an equipment consisting of a powder activated gun, hardened alloy probes, loaded cartridges, and depth gauge for measuring penetration of probes. The probe is driven into the concrete by firing of a precision powder charge cartridges. The exposed length is measured by calibrated depth gauge and this is correlated to the strength of concrete cylinders. Fig. 10.12 shows the relationship between exposed probe length and 28 day-compressive strength.[10.7]

The windsor probe test cannot be really considered as a non-destructive testing, as it makes a hole and damages the structure. It can only be considered non-destructive to the extent that concrete can be tested *in situ* and structural members. In case of big structures like pavements or retaining walls etc., the structure need not be discarded.

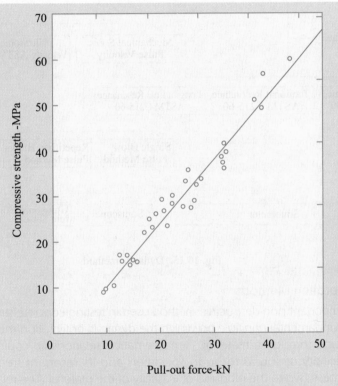

Fig. 10.14. Relation between compressive strength of cores and pull-out force for actual structures [10.8]

The Windsor probe test is basically a hardness tester and, like other hardness testers, should not be expected to yield accurate absolute values of strength of concrete in a structure. However, like the "Schmidt rebound hammer", the probe test provides a good method for determining the relative strength of concrete in the same structure or relative strength in different structures without extensive calibration with specific concrete.

Pullout test

A pullout test measures the force required to pull out from the concrete a specially shaped rod whose enlarged end has been cast into that concrete. The stronger the concrete, the more is the force required to pullout. The ideal way to use pullout test in the field would be to incorporate assemblies in the structure. These standard specimens could then be pulled out at any point of time. The force required denotes the strength of concrete. Another way to use pullout test in the field would be to cast one or two large blocks of concrete incorporating pullout assemblies. Pullout test could then be performed to assess the strength of concrete. Figure 10.14 shows the relationship between compressive strength and pullout strength [10.8]

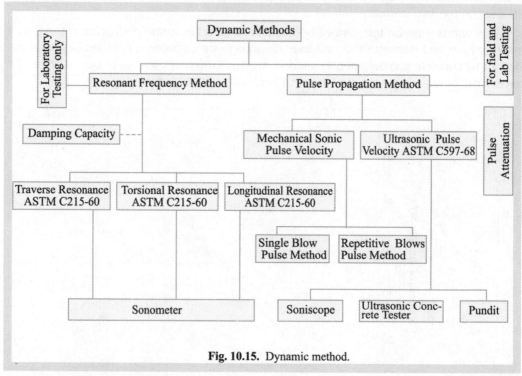

Fig. 10.15. Dynamic method.

Dynamic or Vibration Methods

This is the important non-destructive method used in testing concrete strength and other properties. The fundamental principle on which the dynamic or vibration methods are based is velocity of sound through a material. A mathematical relationship could be established between the velocity of sound through specimen and its resonant frequency and the relationships of these two to the modulus of elasticity of the material. The relationships which are derived for solid mediums considered to be homogeneous, isotropic and perfectly elastic, but they may be applied to heterogeneous materials like concrete.

The velocity of sound in a solid can be measured by determining the resonant frequency of specimen or by recording the time of travel of short pulses of vibration passing through the samples. In non-destructive testing of concrete, either resonance method or pulse velocity techniques could be adopted. Figure 10.15 shows dynamic methods of testing concrete.

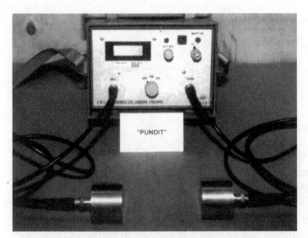

Ultrasonic Pulse Velocity Test Equipment

Resonant Frequency Method

This method is based upon the determination of the fundamental resonant frequency of vibration of a specimen.

The resonance is indicated by the point of maximum amplitude for the various driving frequencies generated. The equipment used for this is usually known as 'Sonometer". Resonant frequency methods are mostly used in the laboratory. Figure 10.16 shows schematic diagram of a typical apparatus.

Usefulness of Resonant Frequency Method

These tests can normally be carried out only on small sized specimens in a laboratory rather than on structural members in the field. The possibility of vibrating structural members at resonance is neither practical nor desirable. The size of specimens in these tests is usually limited to 150 x 300 mm cylinders or 75 x 75 x 300 mm prisms.

The equations for the calculation of dynamic modulus involve "shape factor" corrections. This necessarily limits the shape of the specimens to cylindrical or prismatical types. Any deviation from the standard shapes can render the application of shape factor corrections rather complex.

Notwithstanding the above limitations, the resonance tests do provide an excellent means for studying the deterioration of concrete specimens subjected to repeated cycles of freezing and thawing and to deterioration due to acidic and alkali attack. The use of resonance tests in the determination of damage by fire has also been reported.

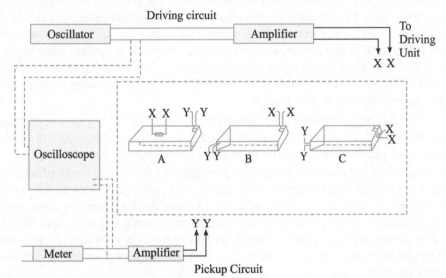

Fig. 10.16. Schematic Diagram of a Typical Apparatus showing Driver and Pickup positions for the three types of vibration. A.Transverse. Resonance. B.Torsional resonance C.Longitudinal Resonance

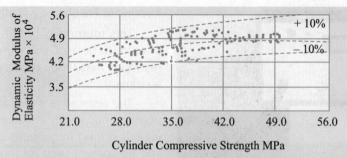

Fig. 10.17. Relationship between Dynamic Modulus of Elasticity and Compressive Strength of Concrete.[10.9]

The resonant frequency test results are often used to calculate dynamic Young's modulus of elasticity of concrete but the values obtained are somewhat higher than those obtained with standard static tests carried out at lower rates of loading. The use of dynamic Young's modulus in design calculations is not recommended.

Various investigators have published correlations between the strength of concrete and its dynamic modulus of elasticity. (Figure 10.17). The indiscriminate use of such correlations to predict compressive and/or flexural strength of concrete is strongly discouraged unless similar relationships have been established in the laboratory for the particular concrete under investigation.

Pulse Velocity Method

This can be sub-divided into two parts:

(a) Mechanical sonic pulse velocity method, which involves measurement of the time of travel of longitudinal or compressional waves generated by a single impact hammer blow or repeated blows.

(b) Ultrasonic Pulse Velocity Method, which involves measurement of the time of travel of electronically generated mechanical pulses through the concrete.

Out of these two, the ultrasonic pulse method has gained considerable popularity all over the world. When mechanical impulses are applied to a solid mass, three different kinds of waves are generated. These are generally known as longitudinal waves, shear waves and surface waves. These three waves travel at different speeds. The longitudinal or compressional waves travel about twice as fast as the other two types. The shear or transverse waves are not so fast, the surface waves are the slowest.

The pulses can be generated either by hammer blows or by the use of an electroacoustic transducer. Electroacoustic transducers are preferred as they provide better control on the type and frequency of pulses generated. The instrument used is called "Soniscope".

Ultrasonic pulse velocity method consists of measuring the time of travel of an ultrasonic pulse, passing through the concrete to be tested. The pulse generator circuit consists of electronic circuit for generating pulses and a transducer for transforming these electronic pulses into mechanical energy having vibration frequencies in the range of 15 to 50 kHz. The time of travel between initial onset and the reception of the pulse is measured electronically. The path length between transducer divided by the time of travel gives the average velocity of wave propagation.

Recently, battery operated fully portable digitised units have become available in U.K. One such unit is called "PUNDIT" (Protable Ultrasonic Non-destructive Digital-Indicating Tester.). It only weights 3 kgs.[10.10]

Techniques of Measuring Pulse Velocity through Concrete

There are three ways of measuring pulse velocity through concrete. They are:

(a) Direct transmission.

(b) Indirect transmission.

(c) Surface transmission.

Figure 10.18 shows the methods of measuring.

Factors Affecting the Measurement of Pulse Velocity

The measurement of pulse velocity is affected by a number of factors regardless of the properties of concrete.

1. Smoothness of contact surface under test: It is important to maintain good acoustical contact between the surface of concrete and the face of each transducer. Generally this does not pose any problem because in normal testing sufficient cast surfaces are available for good contact. However, when it is necessary to hold the transducer against an unmoulded surface, for example, the top surface of a test cylinder, it is desirable to smoothen the surface by the use of a carborundum stone and the transducers should be held tightly against the concrete

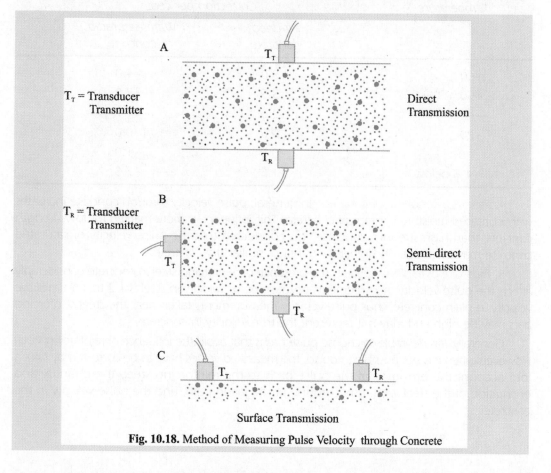

Fig. 10.18. Method of Measuring Pulse Velocity through Concrete

surface. In addition, the use of a coupling medium such as a thin film of oil, soap, jelly, or kaolin glycerol paste should be used.

2. Influence of path length on pulse velocity: As concrete is inherently heterogeneous, it is essential that path length be sufficiently long so as to avoid any errors introduced due to its heterogeneity. In field work, this does not pose any difficulty because pulse velocity measurements are generally carried out on thick structural concrete members, where the path lengths may be anywhere from 300 mm in the case of columns to 23 m in mass gravity dams. However, in the laboratory where generally small specimens are used, the path length can affect the pulse velocity readings.

3. Temperature of concrete: It has been reported that variations of the ambient temperature between 5° C and 30° C do not significantly affect the pulse velocity measurements in concrete. At temperatures between 30° C and 60°C, there is up to 5% reduction in pulse velocity. This is probably due to the initiation of microcracking in concrete. At below freezing temperature, the free water freezes within concrete thus resulting in an increase in pulse velocity. At 4° C, an increase of up to 7.5% in the pulse velocity through water-saturated concrete has been reported. The detailed corrections to pulse velocity measurements due to change in temperature are given in Table 10.3.

Table 10.3. Corrections to Pulse Velocity Measurements due to changes in Temperature

Temperature	Correction per cent	
°C	Air-dried concrete	Water-saturated concrete
+60	+5.0	+4.0
+50	+3.5	+2.8
+40	+2.0	+1.7
+20	0.0	0.0
0	−0.5	−1.0
−4 & below	−1.5	−7.5

4. Moisture condition of concrete: In general, pulse velocity through concrete increases with increased moisture content of concrete. This influence is more marked for low-strength concrete than high strength concrete. It is considered that the pulse velocity of saturated concrete may be about 2% higher than that of similar dry concrete.

5. Presence of reinforcing steel: The presence of reinforcing steel in concrete considerably affects the pulse velocity measurements because pulse velocity in steel is 1.2 to 1.9 times the velocity in plain concrete, thus pulse velocity measurements taken near the steel reinforcing bars may be high and may not represent the true velocity in concrete.

Generally, it is desirable to choose pulse paths that avoid the influence of reinforcing steel. However, when it is not possible to do so, the measured values have to be corrected by taking into account the proximity of the pulse path to the reinforcing steel, the quantity and orientation of the steel with respect to the propagation path, and the pulse velocity in the concrete.

When the axis of reinforcing bars is perpendicular to the direction of propagation and the quantity of reinforcement is small, the influence of the reinforcement on the pulse velocity is generally small. The correction factors are of the order of 1– 4% depending upon the quality of the surrounding concrete the higher the quality of concrete, the smaller the correcting factor.

When the axis of the reinforcing bars is parallel to the direction of propagation of the pulse, the influence of reinforcement cannot be avoided easily. The pulse velocity measurements can be corrected but correction factors are of approximate nature only, and in case of two-way reinforcement it is almost impossible to make any reliable corrections.

Accuracy of Measurement. It is generally agreed that the ultrasonic concrete tester measures the transit time through small specimens with an accuracy of 0.1 microseconds; for the specimens of the same length, the accuracy of measurement for the soniscope and the PUNDIT is of the order of 0.5 microseconds. Thus, the former instrument is ideally suited for controlled laboratory studies, whereas the latter are best suited for field investigations where the path lengths are longer.

Applications

The pulse velocity methods have been used to evaluate concrete structures and attempts have been made to correlate the pulse velocity with strength and other properties of concrete. The various applications of the pulse velocity methods are described below:

Establishing uniformity of concrete: For establishing the uniformity of concrete, the ultrasonic concrete tester is an ideal tool for laboratory specimens, whereas the soniscope and PUNDIT provide an excellent means for both laboratory and field studies.

Establishing acceptance criteria: Generally, high pulse velocity reading in concrete are indicative of concrete of good quality. Table 10.4 gives the pulse velocity ratings, as given by Leslie and Cheesman.

Table 10.4. Suggested Pulse Velocity for Concrete[10.11]

Pulse velocity (m/s)					General conditions
4575	...	...	...	...	Excellent
3660—4575	...	...	...	...	Good
3050—3660	...	...	...	...	Questionable
2135—3050	...	...	...	...	Poor
2135	...	...	...	...	Very poor

Table 10.5. Velocity Criterion for Concrete Quality Grading (As per IS : 13311-Part I)

SL. No.	Pulse velocity by cross-probing, km/sec.	Concrete quality greading
1.	Above 4.5	Excellent
2.	3.5 to 4.5	Good
3.	3.0 to 3.5	Medium
4.	Below 3.0	Doubtful

Table 10.6. Velocity Criterion for Concrete Quality Grading by Surface Probing (As per NCBM)

SL. No.	Pulse velocity by surface probing, km/sec.	Concrete quality grading
1.	Above 3.5	Excellent
2.	3.0 to 3.5	Good
3.	2.5 to 3.0	Medium
4.	Below 2.5	Poor

Determination of pulse modulus of elasticity: Theoretically, the values of the pulse modulus of elasticity calculated from the readings obtained with the soniscope or the ultrasonic concrete tester should be the same as those obtained with resonant frequency techniques. However, this has not been found to be so.

For this reason and also because the modulus of elasticity depends upon density and Poisson's ratio, most researchers have attempted to use pulse velocity itself as a criterion of the quality of concrete without attempting to calculate moduli therefrom. If it is desired to compute modulus of elasticity from the pulse velocity, the formulae given under Chapter 8 should be used.

Estimation of strength of concrete: Various researchers have attempted to correlate compressive and flexural strength of concrete with pulse velocity. Fig 10.19 show relationship between pulse velocity and compressive strength for various aggregate/cement ratio. [10.12]

Determination of setting characteristics of concrete: The determination of the rate of setting of concrete by means of the soniscope has been widely used.

Studies on durability of concrete: Durability of concrete under freeze-thaw action and the aggressive environments such as sulphate attack and acidic waters, have been studied by various investigators using the pulse velocity technique to assess damage.

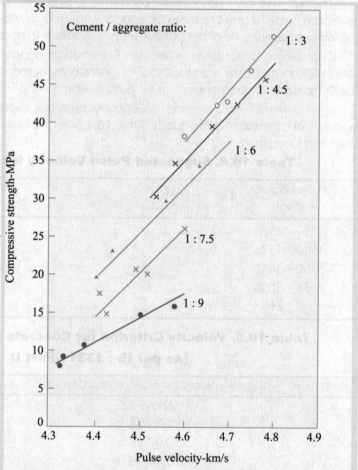

Fig. 10.19. Relation between Compressive Strength and ultrasonic pulse velocity of concrete cubes of different mix proportions

Pulse velocity techniques have been successfully used for the measurement and detection of cracks. The basic principle of crack detection is that, if the crack is of appreciable width and considerable depth, perpendicular to the test path, no signal will be received at the receiving transducer. If the depth of the crack is small, compared to the distance between the transducers, the pulse will pass around the end of the crack and the signal is received at the transducer. However, in doing so, it would have travelled a distance longer than the straight line path upon which pulse velocity computations are made. The difference in the pulse velocity is then used to estimate the path length and hence crack depth. Figure 10.20 shows the principle involved in measurements of crack depth.

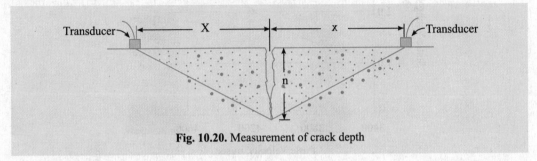

Fig. 10.20. Measurement of crack depth

Measurement of deterioration of concrete due to fire exposure: Pulse velocity techniques have been used to estimate the deterioration due to fire. In one of the experiments, prisms of the size 88 x 102 x 406 mm have been exposed to fire for 1 hour at temperatures ranging from 100° to 1000°C. After the exposure, the specimens were removed from the furnace and allowed to cool to room temperature. Pulse velocity was then measured using the ultrasonic concrete tester, following this, the prisms were tested in flexure. The per cent loss in pulse

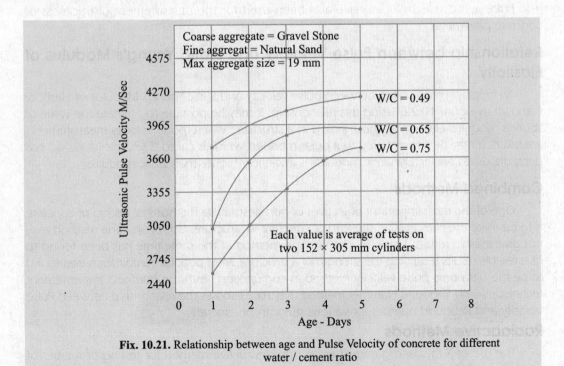

Fix. 10.21. Relationship between age and Pulse Velocity of concrete for different water / cement ratio

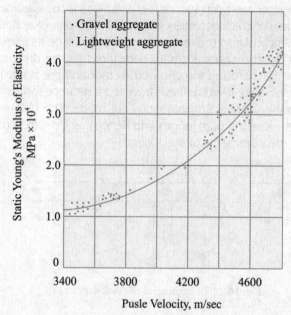

Fig. 10.22. Relationship between Ultrasonic Pulse Velocity and Static Young's Modulus of Elasticity[10.13]

velocity followed very closely the per cent loss in flexural strength of test prisms after fire exposure.

Determination of the time of removal of form work can be sometimes assessed by measuring the pulse velocity. Figure 10.21 shows the relationship between age and pulse velocity for different water/cement ratio.

Pulse velocity techniques have also been used for the measurement of thickness of concrete pavements.

Relationship between Pulse Velocity and Static Young's Modulus of Elasticity

An empirical relationship between pulse velocity and Static Young's Modulus of elasticity is shown in Figure 10.22. Using this relationship, it may be possible to estimate the value of Young's modulus elasticity at those points in a structure, where pulse velocity measurements are taken. It may be remembered that pulse modulus which is called "Dynamic Modulus" has been discussed earlier. Dynamic modulus is invariably higher than static modulus.

Combined Methods

One of the most important objectives of non-destructive methods of testing of concrete is to estimate the compressive strength of concrete in structure. Use of any one method may not give reliable results. Using more than one method at the same time has been found to give reliable results regarding the strength of a structure. Most popular combination was found to be the ultrasonic pulse velocity method in conjunction with the hardness measurement techniques, and Rebound Hammer method. Fig.10.23 shows the relationship between Pulse Velocity and Rebound number for various strength of concrete.

Radioactive Methods

The use of X-rays and gamma-rays as non-destructive method for testing properties of concrete is relatively new. X-ray and gamma-rays both components of the high energy region

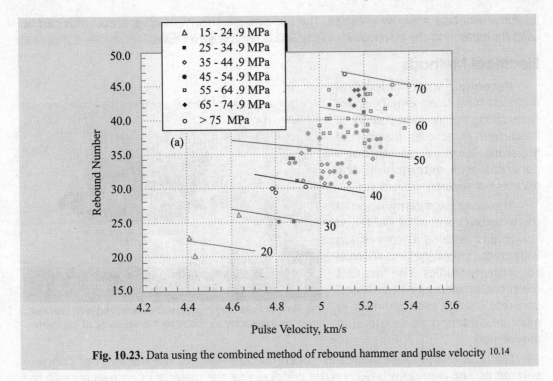

Fig. 10.23. Data using the combined method of rebound hammer and pulse velocity [10.14]

on the electromagnetic spectrum penerate concrete but undergo attenuation in the process. The degree of attenuation depends on the kind of matter traversed, its thickness, and the wavelength of the radiation. The intensity of the incident gamma-rays and the emerging gamma-rays after passing through the specimens are measured. These two values are made use of for calculating the density of structural concrete members.

Gamma-rays transmission method has been used to measure the thickness of concrete slabs of known density. Gamma radiation source of known intensity is made to pass and penetrate through the concrete. The intensity at the other face is measured. From this thickness of the concrete is calculated.

Nuclear Methods

Use of nuclear methods for non-destructive measurement of some properties of concrete is of recent origin. Two principal techniques have been reported, namely neutron scattering methods for determining the moisture content of concrete and neutron activation analysis for the determination of cement content. These methods are not suitable for finding out the strength of concrete.

Magnetic Methods

Battery operated magnetic devices that can measure the depth of reinforcement cover in concrete and detect the position of

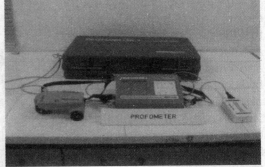

A view of Profometer with attached Scanner to locate the reinforcements and to determine spacing, diameter and concrete cover.

reinforcement bars are now available. The apparatus is known as cover meter. This can be used for measuring the cover given in the lightly reinforced sections.

Electrical Methods

Recently some electrical methods have been employed for determining the moisture content of hardened concrete, tracing of moisture permeation through concrete and determining the thickness of concrete pavements.

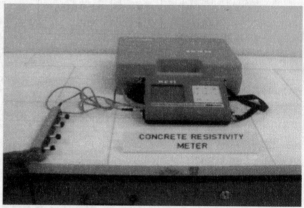

The accurate determination of the moisture content of hardened concrete is required in connection with creep, shrinkage and thermal conductivity studies. The fact that dielectric properties of hardened concrete change with changes in moisture content is made use of in this method.

A view of Resistivity meter well connected with Wenner four probe, ready to measure the resistivity of concrete.

Electrical resistivity methods have been used to find out the thickness of concrete pavements. The method is based on the principle that the material offers resistance to the passage of an electric current. A concrete pavement has a resistivity characteristic that is different from that of the underlying subgrade layers. A change in the slope of the resistivity verses depth curve is used to estimate the depth of concrete pavement.

Tests on Composition of Hardened Concrete

Sometimes the dispute regarding the quality of work may arise between contractor and department and this dispute may be submitted to arbitration. In such cases, it will be necessary that the composition of the hardened cement concrete may be required to be ascertained by chemical analysis.

Determination of Cement Content

The method of finding out the cement content is based on the fact that the silicates in Portland cement are much more readily decomposed and made soluble in dilute hydrochloric acid than the solubility of silica contained in the aggregates. Similarly, the lime contained in cement is much more soluble than lime content in aggregates, with the exception of lime stone aggregates.

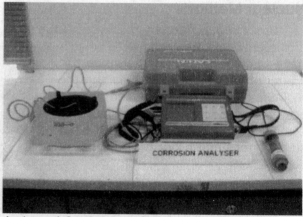

The procedure is to crush a representative sample of the concrete

A view of Corrosion Analyser for half-cell potential measurement with the help of copper/copper sulphate reference electrode.

and dehydrate it at a temperature of 550°C for 3 hours. A small portion of the sample is taken and treated with 1:3 hydrochloric acid. The quantity of silica is determined by standard chemical methods.

The filtrate from the silica determination contains soluble calcium oxide from the aggregate and the cement, and further calculations depend on whether or not the aggregate is largely siliceous. If the original aggregate is available its solubility should be tested.

From the contents of soluble silica and calcium oxide the cement content in the original volume of the sample can be calculated, using A.S.T.M. Standard method C 85-66. These results are reliable and can be used to check the cement content of different parts of a structure, *e.g.*, when it is desired to establish whether or not segregation has taken place. The accuracy of the test is, however, lowest for mixes with low cement contents, and, it is often in this type of mix that the exact value of cement content is required. Furthermore, the test depends on the knowledge of the chemical composition of aggregate, which may not be available for testing. When large amounts of both soluble silica and calcium oxide are liberated from the aggregate, the method is not reliable.

More complex techniques are prescribed by B.S. 1881 : Part 6 : 1971 but it should be noted that chemical tests are rather, expensive and are used only in resolving disputes, and not as a means of control of the quality of concrete.

Determination of the Original Water/Cement Ratio

A method of estimating the water/cement ratio that existed at the time of placing of a concrete mix, now hardened, has been developed by Brown. In essence, this involves determining the volume of the capillary pores and the weight of cement and combined water.

A sample of concrete is oven-dried at 105°C and the air is removed from the pores under vacuum. The pores are then refilled with carbon tetrachloride, whose weight is measured, and hence the weight of the water which originally occupied the pores can be calculated. Since the voids formed through air entrainment are discontinuous they remain filled with air when the vacuum is applied and no water is absorbed in them. The result of the test is thus unaffected by entrained air.

The sample is now broken up, the carbon tetrachloride having been allowed to evaporate, and the aggregate is separated out and weighed. The loss on ignition and the CO_2 content of the remaining fine material are determined, and from these two quantities the weight of combined water can be calculated.

The sum of the combined water and the pore water gives the original mixing water. The quantity of anhydrous cement can also be determined either in conjunction with this test or by the method described earlier and hence the water/cement ratio of the mix can be calculated within about 0.02 of the true value. The technique has been developed into a standard method of B.S. 1881 : Part 6 : 1971.

Physical Method

Polivka 10.15 has successfully used a "Point-count" method on a sawn and varnished surface of a dried concrete specimen to determine its cement content, total aggregate content, and fine/coarse aggregate ratio. The basis of the method is the fact that the relative volumes of the constituents of a heterogeneous solid are directly proportional to their relative areas in a plane section, and also to the intercepts of these areas along a random line. Furthermore, the frequency with which a constituent occurs at a given number of equally spaced points along a random line is a direct measure of the relative volume of that constituent in the solid. Thus point-count by means of a stereo-microscope can rapidly give the volumetric proportions of a hardened concrete specimen.

The aggregate and the voids (containing air or evaporable water) can be identified, the remainder being assumed to be hydrated cement. In order to convert the quantity of the latter to the volume of unhydrated cement, we have to know the specific gravity of dry cement and the non-evaporable water content of hydrated cement.

The test determines the cement content of the concrete within 10 per cent but the original water content or voids ratio cannot be estimated since no distinction is made in the test between air and water voids.

Accelerated Curing Test

Concrete is usually tested at the age of 7 days and 28 days. Concrete mixes are designed usually for 28 days strength and sometimes for 7 days strength. One will come to know whether the concrete has attained specified strength or not, at the end of 28 days or 7 days. At the work site, normally, concrete is placed daily. In some situations, concrete is poured daily, over the previoulsy laid concrete, as in the case of columns, retaining walls etc. The progress of laying concrete cannot be held up for 28 days or even 7 days until the strength is ascertained. When the concrete strength is known, after 28 days and if it happens to be inferior concrete, not satisfying the required strength, the engineer will be put to an embarrassing situation. Sometimes, it may so happen, that the upper lift may satisfy the strength requirement but the lower one may fail to satisfy the strength requirement. Some of the suggestions given to overcome such situations are devaluation of work, dismantling of all the works, redesigning and reducing the load of the structure above the level of such weak concrete, grouting of concrete etc. It can be said that none of the above suggestions are satisfactory.

Perhaps, finding out the strength of concrete in 8 hours time and correlating it to 28 days strength is the best method to overcome such situations. If one comes to know, in about 8 hours time, the 28 days strength, if the concrete does not satisfy, steps could be taken without any legal complication by replacing the faulty concrete. The problem is only to find out the 28 days strength, reliably in about 8 hours.

Many research workers worked in this directions to depict 28 days strength within a short period. Out of all the procedures, accelerated curing test developed by Prof. King is considered to be more accurate and easy for adoption.

In this test, standard concrete cubes are made. These cube moulds are covered both on top and bottom by cover plates and sealed with the grease at the contact surface, to prevent escaping of moisture from concrete. Cubes are placed in an airtight oven within 30 minutes of the addition of water and then switched on. The temperature is brought on to 93°C in about an hour. The cubes are kept at this temperature for a period of 5 hours. Then the cubes are stripped off and allowed to cool within half an hour. The total time spent is 7 hours. At the end of 7 hours the cube is crushed. Seven days or 28 days strength of the concrete is deduced from the standard curve established giving the relationship between King's accelerated curing test results and 7 and 28 days strength. The relationship is shown in Figure 7.4. [10.18]

REFERENCES

10.1   Neville A.M., *The Failure of Concrete Compression Test Specimens, Civil Engineering* July, 1957.

10.2   Murdock J.U. and Kesler C.L., *Effect on Length to Diameter Ratio of Specimen on the Apparent Compressive Strength of Concrete ASTM Bulletin,* April 1957.

10.3   Wright PJF, *The Effect of the Method of Test on the Flexural Strength of Concrete, Magazine of Concrete Research,* Vol 4 No. II.

10.4   Mehenry D and Shideler JJ, *Review of Data on effect of Speed in Mechanical Testing of Concrete, A.S.T.M. special Technical Publication* No. 185, 1956.

10.5   R.D. Gaynor, One look at concrete compressive Strength, *NRMCA Publication No. 147 of* Nov. 1974.

10.6   Willetts C.H. Investigation of the Schmidt concrete Test Hammer, *Miscellaneous Paper No. 6-627, U.S. Army Engineer Waterways Experiment Station,* June 1958.

10.7   Arni H.T. Impact and Penetration Tests of Portland Cement Concrete, *Highway Research Record* No. 378 of 1972.

10.8   U.Bellander, *Strength in Concrete Structures,* CBI Report, Sweedish Cement and Concrete Research Institute 1978.

10.9   Sharma M.R. and Gupta B.L., *Sonic Modulus is Related Strength and static Modulus of high strength Concrete, The Indian Concrete Journal,* April 1960.

10.10 Pundit Manual, CNS *Instrument Limited, 61-63 Holmes Road London. N.W. 5.*

10.11 Leslie J.R. and Cheesman W.J., *An Ultrasonic Method of Studying Deterioration and Cracking in Concrete Structures ACI Journal,* Sept. 1949.

10.12 Jones R, *Non Destructive Testing of Concrete, Cambridge University Press London* 1962.

10.13 Elvery R.H. and Forrester J.A., *Non-Destructive Testing of Concrete, Progress in Construction, Science and Technology,* 1971.

10.14 N.J. Cario, *Non Destructive Testing of Concrete: History and Challenges.* Proceedings of Mohan Malhotra Symposium, ACI SP 144–1994.

10.15 Polivka M. and Kelly J.W, *A Physical Method for Determining the Composition of Hardened Concrete A.S.T.M. Sp. Technical Publication* 205 1958.

10.16 Chen W.F., *Double Punch Test for Tensile Strength of Concrete, Proc ACI No. 12 Vol-67,* Dec. 1970.

10.17 Malhotra V.M., *Problems Associated with Determining the Tensile Strength of Concrete, Transactions of the Engineering Institute of Canada,* Vol 10 July 1967.

10.18 King JUH, *Further notes on Accelerated Test for Concrete,* Chartered Civil Engineer, May 1957.

Ready Mixed Concrete Plant to follow up the Good Concrete Mix Design

11

C H A P T E R

Concrete Mix Design

General

One of the ultimate aims of studying the various properties of the materials of concrete, plastic concrete and hardened concrete, is to enable a concrete technologist to design a concrete mix for a particular strength and durability. The design of concrete mix is not a simple task on account of the widely varying properties of the constituent materials, the conditions that prevail at the site of work, in particular the exposure condition, and the conditions that are demanded for a particular work for which the mix is designed. Design of concrete mix requires complete knowledge of the various properties of these constituent materials, the implications in case of change on these conditions at the site, the impact of the properties of plastic concrete on the hardened concrete and the complicated inter-relationship between the variables. All these make the task of mix design more complex and difficult. Design of concrete mix needs not only the knowledge of material properties and properties of concrete in plastic condition, it also needs wider knowledge and experience of concreting. Even then the proportion of the materials of concrete found out at the laboratory requires modification and readjustments to suit the field conditions.

With better understanding of the properties, the concrete is becoming more and more an exact material than in the past. The structural designer stipulates certain minimum strength; and the concrete technologist designs the concrete mix with the knowledge of the materials, site exposure conditions and standard of supervision available at the site of work to achieve this minimum strength and durability. Further, the site engineer is required to make the concrete at site, closely following the parameters suggested by the mix designer to achieve the minimum strength specified by the structural engineer. In some cases the site engineer may be required to slightly modify the mix proportions given by the mix designer. He also makes cubes or cylinders sufficient in numbers and test them to confirm the achievements with respect to the minimum specified strength. Mix designer, earlier, may have made trial cubes with representative materials to arrive at the value of standard deviation or coefficient of variation to be used in the mix design.

Mix design can be defined as the process of selecting suitable ingredients of concrete and determining their relative proportions with the object of producing concrete of certain minimum strength and durability as economically as possible. The purpose of designing as can be seen from the above definitions is two-fold. The first object is to achieve the stipulated minimum strength and durability. The second object is to make the concrete in the most economical manner. Cost wise all concretes depend primarily on two factors; namely cost of material and cost of labour. Labour cost, by way of formworks, batching, mixing, transporting, and curing is nearly same for good concrete and bad concrete. Therefore attention is mainly directed to the cost of materials. Since the cost of cement is many times more than the cost of other ingredients, attention is mainly directed to the use of as little cement as possible consistent with strength and durability.

Concept of Mix Design

It will be worthwhile to recall at this stage the relationships between aggregate and paste which are the two essential ingredients of concrete. Workability of the mass is provided by the lubricating effect of the paste and is influenced by the amount and dilution of paste. The strength of concrete is limited by the strength of paste, since mineral aggregates with rare exceptions, are far stronger than the paste compound. Essentially the permeability of concrete is governed by the quality and continuity of the paste, since little water flows through aggregate either under pressure or by capillarity. Further, the predominant contribution to drying shrinkage of concretes is that of paste.

Since the properties of concrete are governed to a considerable extent by the quality of paste, it is helpful to consider more closely the structure of the paste. The fresh paste is a suspension, not a solution of cement in water.

The more dilute the paste, the greater the spacing between cement particles, and thus the weaker will be the ultimate paste structure. The other conditions being equal, for workable mixes, the strength of concrete varies as an inverse function of the water/cement ratio. Since the quantity of water required also depends upon the amount of paste, it is important that as little paste as possible should be used and hence the importance of grading.

Variables in Proportioning

With the given materials, the four variable factors to be considered in connection with specifying a concrete mix are:

(a) Water-Cement ratio

(b) Cement content or cement-aggregate ratio

(c) Gradation of the aggregates

(d) Consistency.

In general all four of these inter-related variables cannot be chosen or manipulated arbitrarily. Usually two or three factors are specified, and the others are adjusted to give minimum workability and economy. Water/cement ratio expresses the dilution of the paste-cement content varies directly with the amount of paste. Gradation of aggregate is controlled by varying the amount of given fine and coarse aggregate. Consistency is established by practical requirements of placing. In brief, the effort in proportioning is to use a minimum amount of paste (and therefore cement) that will lubricate the mass while fresh and after hardening will bind the aggregate particles together and fill the space between them. Any excess of paste involves greater cost, greater drying shrinkage, greater susceptibility to percolation of water and therefore attack by aggressive waters and weathering action. This is achieved by minimising the voids by good gradation.

Various Methods of Proportioning

(a) Arbitrary proportion

(b) Fineness modulus method

(c) Maximum density method

(d) Surface area method

(e) Indian Road Congress, IRC 44 method

(f) High strength concrete mix design

(g) Mix design based on flexural strength

(h) Road note No. 4 (Grading Curve method)

(i) ACI Committee 211 method

(j) DOE method

(k) Mix design for pumpable concrete

(l) Indian standard Recommended method IS 10262-82

Out of the above methods, some of them are not very widely used these days because of some defficulties or drawbacks in the procedures for arriving at the satisfactory proportions. The ACI Committee 211 method, the DOE method and Indian standard recommended methods are commonly used. Since concrete is very commonly placed by pumping these days method of mix design of pumpable concrete has become important. Therefore, only the more popular and currently used methods are described.

Before we deal with some of the important methods of concrete mix design, it is necessary to get acquainted with statistical quality control methods, which are common to all the methods of mix design.

Statistical Quality Control of Concrete

Concrete like most other construction processes, have certain amount of variability both in materials as well as in constructional methods. This results in variation of strength from batch to batch and also within the batch. It becomes very difficult to assess the strength of the final product. It is not possible to have a large number of destructive tests for evaluating the strength of the end products and as such we have to resort to sample tests. It will be very costly to have very rigid criteria to reject the structure on the basis of a single or a few standard samples. The basis of acceptance of a sample is that a reasonable control of concrete work can be provided, by ensuring that the probability of test result falling below the design strength is not more than a specified tolerance level.

The aim of quality control is to limit the variability as much as practicable. Statistical quality control method provides a scientific approach to the concrete designer to understand the realistic variability of the materials so as to lay down design specifications with proper tolerance to cater for unavoidable variations. The acceptance criteria are based on statistical evaluation of the test result of samples taken at random during execution. By devising a proper sampling plan it is possible to ensure a certain quality at a specified risk. Thus the method provides a scientific basis of acceptance which is not only realistic but also restrictive as required by the design requirements for the concrete construction.

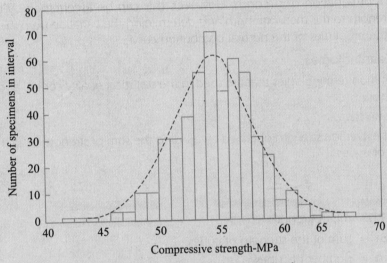

Fig. 11.1. A histogram of strength values

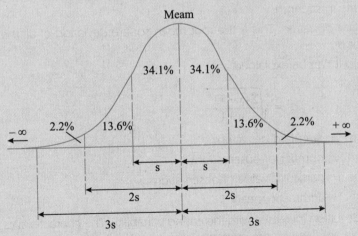

Fig. 11.2. Normal distribution curve; percentage of specimens in intervals of one standard deviation shown

The quality of concrete will be of immense value for large contracts where the specifications insist on certain minimum requirements. The efforts put in will be more than repaid by the resulting savings in the overall concreting operations.

The compressive strength test cubes from random sampling of a mix, exhibit variations, which are inherent in the various operations involved in the making and testing of concrete. If a number of cube test results are plotted on histogram, the results are found so follow a bell shaped curve known as "Normal Distribution Curve". The results are said to follow a normal distribution curve if they are equally spaced about the mean value and if the largest number of the cubes have a strength closer to the mean value, and very few number of results with much greater or less value than the mean value. However, some divergence from the smooth curve can be expected, particularly if the number of results available is relatively small. Fig 11.1 and Fig 11.2 show the histogram and the normal distribution curve respectively.

The arithmetic mean or the average value of the number of test result gives no indication of the extent of variation of strength. However, this can be ascertained by relating the individual strength to the mean strength and determining the variation from the mean with the help of the properties of the normal distribution curve.

Common Terminologies

The common terminologies that are used in the statistical quality control of concrete are explained below.

(a) Mean strength:

This is the average strength obtained by dividing the sum of strength of all the cubes by the number of cubes.

$$\bar{x} = \frac{\Sigma x}{n}$$

where $\bar{x}$ = mean strength

Σx = sum of the strength of cubes

n = number of cubes.

(b) Variance: This is the measure of variability or difference between any single observed data from the mean strength.

(c) Standard deviation: This is the root mean square deviation of all the results. This is denoted by s or σ.

Numerically it can be explained as,

$$\sigma = \sqrt{\frac{\Sigma(x - \bar{x})^2}{n - 1}}$$

where σ = Standard deviation,

n = number of observations

x = particular value of observations

$\bar{x}$ = arithmetic mean.

Standard deviation increases with increasing variability. The characteristics of the normal distribution curve are fixed by the average value and the standard deviation. The spread of the curve along the horizontal scale is governed by the standard deviation, while the position of the curve along the vertical scale is fixed by the mean value.

(d) *Coefficient of variation:* It is an alternative method of expressing the variation of results. It is a non-dimensional measure of variation obtained by dividing the standard deviation by the arithmetic mean and is expressed as:

$$v = \frac{\Sigma}{\bar{x}} \times 100$$

where v = coefficient of variation.

Calculation of Standard Deviation and Coefficient of Variation

Table 11.1 gives the typical method of calculating the standard deviation and coefficient of variation for a set of cubes cast and tested. Table 11.2 gives the value of typical standard deviation for different conditions.

Relationship between Average Design Strength and Specified Minimum Strength

In the design of concrete mixes, the average design strength to be aimed at should be appreciably higher than the minimum strength stipulated by the structural designer. The value of average design strength to be aimed at will depend upon the quality control exercised at the time of making concrete.

Table 11.1. Example of Calculation of Standard Deviation

Sample Number	Crushing Strength (x) MPa	Average strength $\bar{x} = \dfrac{\Sigma x}{n}$	Deviation $(x - \bar{x})$	Square of Deviation $(x - \bar{x})^2$
1	43		+ 2.8	7.84
2	48		+ 7.8	60.84
3	40		− 0.2	0.04
4	38		− 2.2	4.84
5	36		− 4.2	16.64
6	39		− 1.2	1.44
7	42		+ 1.8	3.24
8	45		+ 4.8	23.04
9	37		− 3.2	10.24
10	35	40.2	− 5.2	27.04
11	39		− 1.2	1.44
12	41		+ 0.8	0.64
13	49		+ 8.8	77.44
14	46		+ 5.8	33.64
15	36		− 4.2	16.64
16	38		− 2.2	4.84
17	32		− 8.2	67.24
18	39		− 1.2	1.44
19	41		+ 0.8	0.64
20	40		− 0.2	0.04
	Total 804			Total 359.20

$$\text{Average strength} = \frac{804}{20} = 40.2$$

$$\text{Standard deviation} = \sqrt{\frac{359.20}{N-1}}$$

$$= \frac{359.2}{19} = 4.34 \text{ MPa}$$

$$\text{Coefficient of Variation} = \frac{\text{Standard deviation}}{\text{Average strength}} \times 100$$

$$= \frac{4.34}{40.20} \times 100 = 10.80\%$$

Table 11.2. Typical values of the Standard Deviation for Different Conditions of Placing and Mixing Control

Placing and Mixing condition	Degree of control	Standard Deviation MPa
Dried aggregates, completely accurate grading, exact water/cement ratio, controlled temperature curing.	Laboratory Precision	1.3
Weigh-batching of all materials, control of aggregate grading, 3 sizes of aggregate plus sand, control of water added to allow for moisture content of aggregates, allowance for weight of aggregate & sand displaced by water, continual supervision.	Excellent	2.8
Weigh-batching of all materials, strict control of aggregate grading, control of water added to allow for moisture content of aggregates, continual supervision.	High	3.5
Weigh-batching of all materials, control of aggregate grading, control of water added, frequent supervision.	Very good	4.2
Weighing of all materials, water content controlled by inspection of mix, periodic check of workability, use of two sizes of aggregate (fine & coarse) only, intermittent supervision.	Good	5.7
Volume batching of all aggregates allowing for bulking of sand, weigh batching of cement, water content controlled by inspection of mix, intermittent supervision.	Fair	6.5
Volume batching of all materials, use of all in aggregate, little or no supervision.	Poor Uncontrolled	7.0 8.5

The value of standard deviation or coefficient of variation could be used to determine the average design strength of the mixes.

The following relationship can be used if standard deviation is made use of:

$$S_{av} = S_{min} + K\sigma$$

where S_{av} = Average design strength

S_{min} = Minimum strength

σ = Standard deviation

K = Himsworth constant

Refer table 11.3. If 1% result is allowed to fall below the minimum, the value of K is taken as 2.33). If 5% of result is allowed to fall below the minimum, the value of K is taken as 1.64 but it is generally taken as 1.65.

If coefficient of variation is used,

$$S_{av} = \frac{S_{min}}{1 - \dfrac{Kv}{100}}$$

where v = Coefficient of variation and other notations have the same significance.

The use of either the standard deviation or the coefficient of variation is based on the following argument. If control was perfect, so that the materials and all operations involved in making concrete including sampling and testing were uniform, then every result would be the same and would correspond to the mean value. It is impossible for each operation to be perfect. The more uniform the operations the closer will be the result to the mean value and hence the lower will be the value of the standard deviation.

Table 11.3. Value for the Factor K Himsworth Constants[11.1]

Percentage of results allowed to fall below the minimum			Value K
0.1	...	...	3.09
0.6	...	...	2.50
1.0	...	...	2.33
2.5	...	...	1.96
6.6	...	...	1.50
16.00	...	...	1.00

It follows that if the same degree of control is exercised on the concrete with the mean strength of 15 MPa, the standard deviation will be same as for concrete with mean strength 45 MPa. Therefore, the concrete quality can be changed by standard deviation. In fact, site experience shows that it is more difficult to achieve consistent results with high strength concrete and the standard deviation is greater for high strength concrete than for concretes of medium or low strength.

It has been suggested that the standard deviation is proportional to the value of mean strength. In other words,

$$\frac{\text{Standard deviation}}{\text{Mean strength}} = \text{a constant}$$

This, of course, is the coefficient of variation. With a constant coefficient of variation the standard deviation increases with strength and is larger for higher strength.

There are some arguments as to whether the standard deviation or the coefficient of variation is correct parameter to apply. Murdock and Errntroy have shown that the coefficient of variation more nearly represents a particular standard of control at relatively low strengths, while the standard deviation more nearly represents the standard at high strength.[11.2] Indian standard method and most of the mix design methods adopt standard deviation parameter.

American Concrete Institute Method of Mix Design[11.3]

This method of proportioning was first published in 1944 by ACI committee 613. In 1954 the method was revised to include, among other modifications, the use of entrained air. In 1970, the method of mix design became the responsibility of ACI committee 211. ACI committee 211 have further updated the method (ACI–211.1) of 1991. Almost all of the major multipurpose concrete dams in India built during 1950 have been designed by using then prevalent ACI Committee method of mix design.

We shall now deal with the latest ACI Committee 211.1 of 1991 method. It has the advantages of simplicity in that it applies equally well, and with more or less identical procedure to rounded or angular aggregate, to regular or light weight aggregates and to air-entrained or non-air-entrained concretes. The ACI Committee mix design method assume certain basic facts which have been substantiated by field experiments or large works. They are:

(a) The method makes use of the established fact, that over a considerable range of practical proportions, fresh concrete of given slump and containing a reasonably well graded aggregate of given maximum size will have practically a constant total water content regardless of variations in water/cement ratio and cement content, which are necessarily interrelated.

(b) It makes use of the relation that the optimum dry rodded volume of coarse aggregate per unit volume of concrete depends on its maximum size and the fineness modulus of the fine aggregate as indicated in Table 11.4 regardless of shape of particles. The effect of angularity is reflected in the void content, thus angular coarse aggregates require more mortar than rounded coarse aggregate.

(c) Irrespective of the methods of compaction, even after complete compaction is done, a definite percentage of air remains which is inversely proportional to the maximum size of the aggregate.

The following is the procedure of mix design in this method:

(a) Data to be collected :

(i) Fineness modulus of selected F.A.

(ii) Unit weight of dry rodded coarse aggregate.

(iii) Sp. gravity of coarse and fine aggregates in SSD condition

(iv) Absorption characteristics of both coarse and fine aggregates.

(v) Specific gravity of cement.

Table 11.4. Dry Bulk Volume of Coarse Aggregate per Unit Volume of Concrete as given by ACI 211.1—91

Maximum Size of Aggregate	Bulk volume of dry rodded coarse aggregate per unit volume of concrete for fineness modulus of sand of			
F.M.	2.40	2.60	2.80	3.00
10	0.50	0.48	0.46	0.44
12.5	0.59	0.57	0.55	0.53
20	0.66	0.64	0.62	0.60
25	0.71	0.69	0.67	0.65
40	0.75	0.73	0.71	0.69
50	0.78	0.76	0.74	0.72
70	0.82	0.80	0.78	0.76
150	0.87	0.85	0.83	0.81

Note: The values given will produce a mix that is suitable for reinforced concrete construction. For less workable concrete the values may be increased by about 10 percent. For more workable concrete such as pumpable concrete the values may be reduced by up to 10 per cent.

(b) From the minimum strength specified, estimate the average design strength either by using standard deviation or by using coefficient of variation.

(c) Find the water/cement ratio from the strength point of view from Table 11.5. Find also the water/cement ratio from durability point of view from Table 11.6. Adopt lower value out of strength consideration and durability consideration.

Table 11.5. Relation between water/cement ratio and average compressive strength of concrete, according to ACI 211.1–91

Average compressive strength at 28 days	Effective water/cement ratio (by mass)	
	Non-air	Air-entrained
MPa	entrained concrete	concrete
45	0.38	–
40	0.43	–
35	0.48	0.40
30	0.55	0.46
25	0.62	0.53
20	0.70	0.61
15	0.80	0.71

Note: Measured on standard cylinders. The values given are for a maximum size of aggregate of 20 o 25 mm and for ordinary portland cement and for recommended percent of air entrainment shown in Table 11.8.

Table 11.6. Requirements of ACI 318-89 for W/C ratio and Strength for Special Exposure Conditions

Exposure Condition	Maximum W/C ratio, normal density aggregate concrete	Minimum design strength, low density aggregate concrete MPa
I. Concrete Intended to be Watertight		
(a) Exposed to fresh water	0.5	25
(b) exposed to brackish or sea water	0.45	30
II Concrete exposed to freezing and thawing in a moist condition:		
(a) kerbs, gutters, gaurd rails or thin sections	0.45	30
(b) other elements	0.50	25
(c) in presense of de-icing chemicals	0.45	30
III. For corrosion protection of reinforced concrete exposed to de-icing salts, brackish water, sea water or spray from these sources	0.40	33

(d) Decide maximum size of aggregate to be used. Generally for RCC work 20 mm and prestressed concrete 10 mm size are used.

(e) Decide workability in terms of slump for the type of job in hand. General guidance can be taken from table 11.7.

Table 11.7. Recommended Values of Slump for Various Types of Construction as given by ACI 211.1-91

Type of Construction	Range of Slump mm
Reinforced foundation walls and footings	20–80
Plain footings, caissons and substructure walls	20–80
Beams and reinforced walls	20–100
Building columns	20–100
Pavements and slabs	20–80
Mass Concrete	20–80

Note: The upper limit of slump may be increased by 20 mm for compaction by hand.

Table 11.8. Approximate requirements for mixing water and air content for different workabilities and nominal maximum size of Aggregates according to ACI 211.1-91

Workability or Air content	Water Content, Kg/m³ of concrete for indicated maximum aggregate size							
	10 mm	12.5 mm	20mm	25 mm	40 mm	50 mm	70 mm	150 mm
Non-air-entrained concrete								
Slump 30–50 mm	205	200	185	180	160	155	145	125
80–100 mm	225	215	200	195	175	170	160	140
150–180 mm	240	230	210	205	185	180	170	–
Approximate entrapped air content per cent	3	2.5	2	1.5	1	0.5	0.3	0.2
Air-entrained Concrete								
Slump 30–50 mm	180	175	165	160	145	140	135	120
80–100 mm	200	190	180	175	160	155	150	135
150–180 mm	215	205	190	185	170	165	160	–
Recommended average total air content percent								
Mild exposure	4.5	4.0	3.5	3.0	2.5	2.0	1.5	1.0
Moderate exposure	6.0	5.5	5.0	4.5	4.5	4.0	3.5	3.0
Extreme exposure	7.5	7.0	6.0	6.0	5.5	5.0	4.5	4.0

Table 11.9. First estimate of density (unit weight) of fresh concrete as given by ACI 211.1-91

Maximum size of aggregate mm	First estimate of density (unit weight) of fresh concrete	
	Non-air-entrained kg/m³	Air-entrained kg/m³
10	2285	2190
12.5	2315	2235
20	2355	2280
25	2375	2315
40	2420	2355
50	2445	2375
70	2465	2400
150	2505	2435

(f) The total water in kg/m³ of concrete is read from table 11.8 entering the table with the selected slump and selected maximum size of aggregate. Table 11.8 also gives the approximate amount of accidentally entrapped air in non-air-entrained concrete.

(g) Cement content is computed by dividing the total water content by the water/cement ratio.

(h) From table 11.4 the bulk volume of dry rodded coarse aggregate per unit volume of concrete is selected, for the particular maximum size of coarse aggregate and fineness modulus of fine aggregate.

(j) The weight of C.A. per cubic meter of concrete is calculated by multiplying the bulk volume with bulk density.

(k) The solid volume of coarse aggregate in one cubic meter of concrete is calculated by knowing the specific gravity of C.A.

(l) Similarly the solid volume of cement, water and volume of air is calculated in one cubic meter of concrete.

(m) The solid volume of sand is computed by subtracting from the total volume of concrete the solid volume of cement, coarse aggregate, water and entrapped air.

(n) Wight of fine aggregate is calculated by multiplying the solid volume of fine aggregate by specific gravity of F.A.

Table 11.10. Required increase in strength (mean strength) for specified design strength (specified characteristic strength) when no tests records are available, according to ACI 318–89

Specified design Strength MPa	Required increase in strength MPa
less than 21	7
21 to 35	8.5
35 or more	10.0

Example: ACI Committee 211.1-91 method

Design a concrete mix for construction of an elevated water tank. The specified design strength of concrete (characteristic strength) is 30 MPa at 28 days measured on standard cylinders. Standard deviation can be taken as 4 MPa. The specific gravity of FA and C.A. are 2.65 and 2.7 respectively. The dry rodded bulk density of C.A. is 1600 kg/m3, and fineness modulus of FA is 2.80. Ordinary Portland cement (Type I) will be used. A slump of 50 mm is necessary. C.A. is found to be absorptive to the extent of 1% and free surface moisture in sand is found to be 2 per cent. Assume any other essential data.

(a) Assuming 5 per cent of results are allowed to fall below specified design strength,

The mean strength, $\quad f_m = f_{min} + ks$

$$= 30 + 1.64 \times 4$$

$$= 36.56$$

say 36.5 MPa

(b) Since OPC is used, from table 11.5, the estimated w/c ratio is 0.47.

This w/c ratio from strength point of view is to be checked against maximum w/c ratio given for special exposure condition given in Table 11.6 and minimum of the two is to be adopted.

From exposure condition Table11.6, the maximum w/c ratio is 0.50

Therefore, adopt w/c ratio of 0.47

(c) From Table 11.8, for a slump of 50 mm, 20 mm maximum size of aggregate, for non-air-entrained concrete,

the mixing water content is 185 kg/m³ of concrete. Also the approximate entrapped air content is 2 per cent.

The required cement content $\quad = \dfrac{185}{0.47}$

$$= 394 \text{ kg/m}^3$$

(d) From Table 11.4, for 20 mm coarse aggregate, for fineness modulus of 2.80, the dry rodded bulk volume of C.A. is 0.62 per unit volume of concrete.

(e) Therefore the weight of C.A. $\quad = 0.62 \times 1600$

$$= 992 \text{ kg/m}^3$$

(f) From Table 11.9, the first estimate of density of fresh concrete for 20 mm maximum size of aggregate and for non-air-entrained concrete = 2355 kg/m³

(g) The weight of all the known ingredient of concrete

weight of water $\quad = 185$ kg/m³

weight of cement $\quad = 394$ kg.m³

weight of C.A. $= 992$ kg/m³

weight of F.A. $= 2355 - (185 + 394 + 992)$

$$= 784 \text{ kg/m}^3$$

(h) Alternatively the weight of F.A. can also be found out by absolute volume method which is more accurate, as follows.

Tabulate the absolute volume of all the known ingredients

Item number	Ingredients	Weight kg/m³	Absolute volume cm³
1.	Cement	394	$\frac{394}{3.15} \times 10^3 = 125 \times 10^3$
2.	Water	185	$\frac{185}{1} \times 10^3 = 185 \times 10^3$
3.	Coarse Aggregate	992	$\frac{992}{2.7} \times 10^3 = 367 \times 10^3$
4.	Air		$\frac{2}{100} \times 10^6 = 20 \times 10^3$

Total absolute volume $= 697 \times 10^3$ cm³

Therefore absolute volume of F.A.

$$= (1000 - 697) \times 10^3$$
$$= 303 \times 10^3$$
Weight of FA $= 303 \times 2.65$
$$= 803 \text{ kg/m}^3$$
Adopt F.A. $= 803$ kg/m³.

(*i*) Estimated quantities of materials per cubic meter of concrete are

Cement $= 394$ kg

F.A $= 803$ kg

C.A $= 992$ kg

Water $= 185$ kg

Density of fresh concrete 2374 kg/m³ as against 2355 read from Table 11.9

(*j*) Proportions

C	:	F.A	:	C.A	:	water
394	:	803	:	992	:	185
1	:	2.04	:	2.52	:	0.47

Weight of materials for one bag mix in kg = 50 : 102 : 126 : 23.5

The above quantities is on the basis that both F.A and C.A are in saturated and surface dry condition (SSD conditions).

(*k*) The proportions are required to be adjusted for the field conditions. FA has surface moisture of 2 per cent

∴ Total free surface moisture in FA $= \frac{2}{100} \times 803 = 16.06$ kg/m³

Weight of F.A in field condition $= 803 + 16.06 = 819.06$ kg/m³

say 819 kg/m³

C.A absorbs 1% water

∴ Quantity of water absorbed by C.A. $= \dfrac{1}{100}$ x 992 = 9.92 kg/m^3

∴ Weight of C.A in field condition

= 992 – 9.92

= 982.08 kg/m^3

say 982.0 kg/m^3

With regard to water, 16.06 kg of water is contributed by F.A and 9.92 kg of water is absorbed by C.A.

Therefore 16.06 – 9.92 = 6.14 kg of extra water is contributed by aggregates. This quantity of water is deducted from Total water

i.e., 185.00 – 6.14 = 178.86 kg/m^3

say 179 kg/m^3

(*l*) Quantities of materials to be used in field duly corrected for free surface moisture in F.A and absorption characteristic of C.A

Cement = 394 kg/m^3

F.A. = 819 kg/m^3

C.A. = 982 kg/m^3

Water = 179 kg/m^3

Field density of fresh concrete = 2374 kg/m^3

(*m*) Field proportion as worked out above may not give the final answer. A trial mix is then made to study the properties of such a concrete in respect of workability, cohesiveness, finishing quality, yield and 28 days compressive strength. The mix may need grading improvement, by way of change in proportion between various fractions of C.A. or change in prportion between FA and CA. If feasible, change in the shape of C.A particularly 10 mm fraction would greatly improve the situation. If F.A and C.A are having different specific gravities, any change in their earlier calculated proportion, may affect the yield of concrete.

If all the avenues do not improve the qualities of the concrete designed for the work in hand, then only, one must resort to increase in water content. If water content is increased, corresponding increase in cement content is also made so that W/C ratio remains same.

When both water and cement is increased, it will affect the yield of concrete. Therefore to keep the yield constant, both the quantities of F.A and C.A is required to be reduced correspondingly. All these needs a number of trials before one arrives at the final proportions. The mix designer must have sufficient experience, understanding and feel of concrete.

Road Note No. 4 Method

This method of designing concrete mix proportions is mainly based on the extensive laboratory and field experiments carried out by the Road Research Laboratory, U.K. It was first published in Road Note No 4 during 1950. They have established relationship between various properties of concrete and variable parameters. A series of standard grading curves have been established to give grading limits for all-in aggregates graded down from 20 mm and 40 mm. The grading curve as established and made use of in the mix design is shown in Fig. 3.4 and 3.5 in Chapter 3. The procedure of mix design by Road Note No 4 is also called Grading Curve Method.

This method of mix design was popular and was widely used up to 1970's all over the world. Most of our concrete roads and air field pavements where designed by this method.

The Building Research Establishment of Department of Environment (DOE) U.K. has evolved another method called DOE method to replace the earlier Road Note No 4 method.

DOE Method of Concrete Mix Design[11.4]

The DOE method was first published in 1975 and then revised in 1988. While Road Note No 4 or Grading Curve Method was specifically developed for concrete pavements, the DOE method is applicable to concrete for most purposes, including roads. The method can be used for concrete containing fly ash (in U.K. it is called pulverized fuel ash, PFA) or GGBFS.

Since DOE method presently is the standard British method of concrete mix design, the procedure involved in this method is described instead of out dated Road Note No 4 method.

The following are the steps involved in DOE method.

Step 1: Find the target mean strength from the specified characteristic strength

Target mean strength = specified characteristic strength + Standard deviation x risk factor.

(risk factor is on the assumption that 5 percent of results are allowed to fall less than the specified characteristic strength).

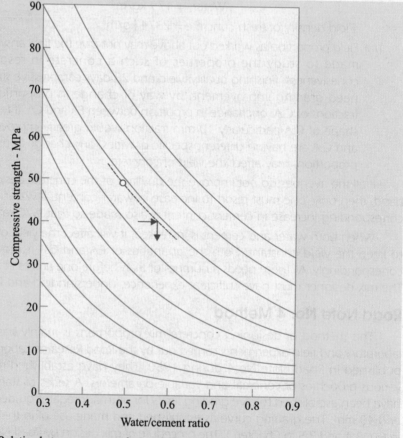

Fig. 11.3. Relation between compressive strength and free water/cement ratio for use in the British mix design method.
(Building Research Establishment, Crown copyright)

Step 2: Calculate the water/cement ratio. This is done in a rather round about method, using

Table 11.11 and Fig. 11.3.

Table 11.11 gives the approximate compressive strength of concretes made with a free w/c ratio of 0.50.

Using this table find out the 28 days strength for the approximate type of cement and types of C.A.

Mark a point on the "Y" axis in Fig. 11.3 equal to the compressive strength read form Table 11.11

Table 11.11. Approximate Compressive Strength of Concrete Made with a free Water/Cement Ratio of 0.50. According to the 1988 British Method

Type of Cement	Type of C.A	Compressive Strength at the age (cube) of days MPa			
		3	7	28	91
Ordinary Portland cement (Type I)	uncrushed	22	30	42	49
Sulphate Resisting Cement (Type V)	Crushed	27	36	49	56
Rapid-Hardening Portland Cement (Type III)	Uncrushed	29	37	48	54
	Crushed	34	43	55	61

which is at a W/C ratio of 0.50. Through this intersection point, draw a parallel dotted curve nearest to the intersection point. Using this new curve, we read off the W/C ratio as against target mean strength.

As an example, referring to Table 11.11 for sulphate resisting cement, crushed aggregate, approximate compressive strength, with a free W/C ratio of 0.5 at 28 days is 49 MPa. In Fig. 11.3 intersection point of 49 MPa and W/C ratio of 0.50 is marked. A parallel dotted curve is drawn to the neighboring curve. Water/Cement ratio is read off on this new dotted curve for any target mean strength. This Water/Cement ratio must be compared to the W/C requirement for durability (refer Table 9.20 or Table 9.21 given under chapter 9 on durability, depending upon whether it is RCC or plain concrete.

Step 3: Next decide water content for the required workability, expressed in terms of slump or Vebe time, taking into consideration the size of aggregate and its type from Table 11.12.

Table 11.12. Approximate Free Water Contents Required to Give Various Levels of Workability According to 1988 British method

Aggregate		Water Content kg/m³ for:			
Max-size mm	Type	Slump 0–10 Vebe > 12 seconds	10–30 6–12	30–60 3–6	60–180 0–3
10	Uncrushed	150	180	205	225
	Crushed	180	205	230	250
20	Uncrushed	135	160	180	195
	crushed	170	190	210	225
40	Uncrushed	115	140	160	175
	crushed	155	175	190	205

Table 11.13. Reduction in the free water contents of Table 11.12 when using fly ash

Percentage of Fly ash in Cementitious material	Slump mm Vebe seconds	Reduction in Water content kg/m³			
		0–10 > 12	10–30 6–12	30–60 3–6	60–180 0–3
10		5	5	5	10
20		10	10	10	15
30		15	15	20	20
40		20	20	25	25
50		25	25	30	30

Step 4: Find the cement content knowing the water/cement ratio and water content. Cement content is calculated simply deviding the water content by W/C ratio. The cement content so calculated should be compared with the minimum cement content specified from the durability consideration as given in Table 9.20 or Table 9.21 and higher of the two should be adopted. Sometime maximum cement content is also specified. The calculated cement content must be less than the specified maximum cement content.

Step 5: Next find out the total aggregate content. This requires an estimate of the wet density of the fully compacted concrete. This can be found out from Fig. 11.4 for approximate water content and specific gravity of aggregate. If sp. gr. is unknown, the value of 2.6 for uncrushed aggregate and 2.7 for crushed aggregate can be assumed. The aggregate content is obtained by subtracting the weight of cement and water content from weight of fresh concrete.

Step 6: Then, proportion of fine aggregate is determined in the total aggregate using Fig. 11.5. Fig. 11.5(a) is for 10 mm size, 11.5(b) is for 20 mm size and Fig. 11.5(c) is for 40 mm size coarse aggregate. The parameters involved in Fig. 11.5 are maximum size of coarse aggregate, the level of workability, the water/cement ratio, and the percentage of fines

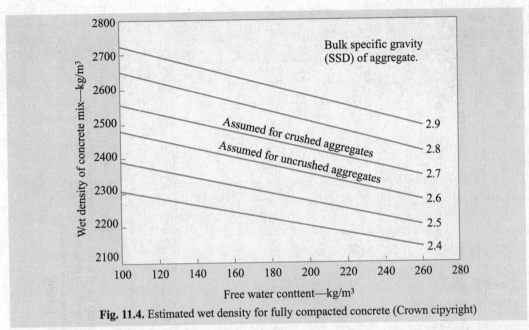

Fig. 11.4. Estimated wet density for fully compacted concrete (Crown cipyright)

passing 600 µ seive. Once the proportion of F.A. is obtained, multiplying by the weight of total aggregate gives the weight of fine aggregate. Then the weight of the C.A. can be found out. Course aggregate can be further devided into different fractions depending on the shape of aggregate. As a general guidance the figures given in Table 11.14 can be used.

Table 11.14. Proportion of Coarse Aggregate Fractions According to the 1988 British method

Total C.A	5–10 mm	10–20 mm	20–40 mm
100	33	67	–
100	18	27	55

The proportion so worked out should be tried in a trial mix and confirmed about its suitability for the given concrete structure.

Table 11.13 gives the reduction of free water contents from the figures given in Table 11.12 when fly ash is used in the mix.

Example—DOE Method

Design a concrete mix for a reinforced concrete work which will be exposed to the moderate condition. The concrete is to be designed for a mean compressive strength of 30 MPa at the age of 28 days. A requirement off 25 mm cover is prescribed. Maximum size of aggregate is 20 mm uncrushed aggregate will be used. Sieve analysis shows that 50% passes through 600 µ seive. The bulk specific gravity of aggregate is found to be 2.65

First step is to find out the target mean strength. In the above problem the target mean strength is directly given as 30 MPa at 28 days (cube strength)

Second step is to find out the water/cement ratio for 30 MPa concrete.

For this we have to refer to Table 11.11. Refering to Table 11.11, for OPC, uncrushed aggregate, for W/C ratio of 0.5, 28 days compressive strength is 42 MPa. In Fig. 11.3 find an

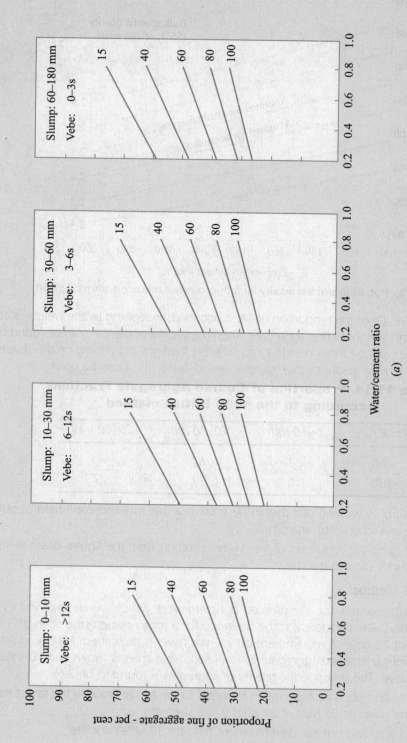

Fig. 11.5. Recommended percentage of fine aggregate in total aggregate as a function of free water/cement ratio for various values of workability and maximum size of aggregate: (*a*) 10 mm, (*b*) 20 mm, and (*c*) 40 mm Numbers on each graph are the percentage of fines passing a 600 μm sieve. (Building Research Establishment, Crown copyright)

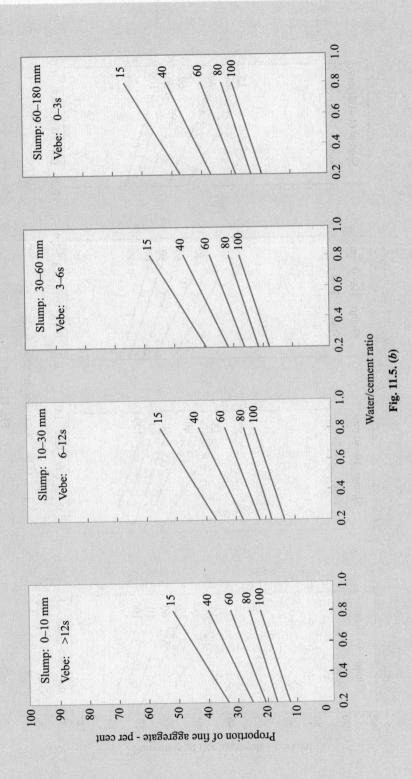

Fig. 11.5. (b)

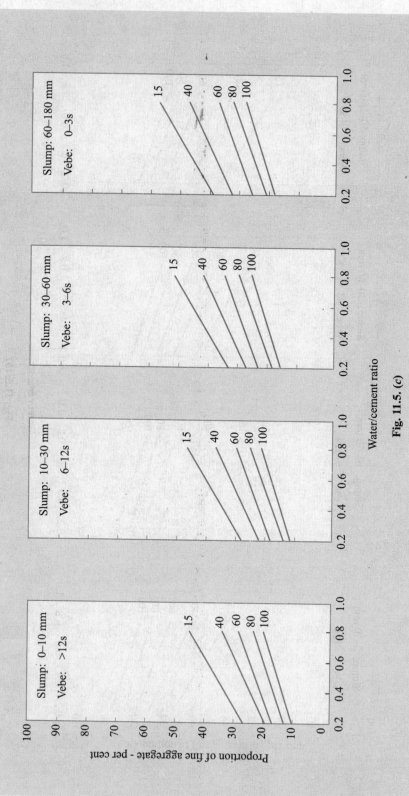

Fig. 11.5. (c)

intersection point for 42 MPa and 0.5 W/C ratio. Draw a dotted line curve parallel to the neighbouring curve. From this curve read off the W/C ratio for a target mean strength of 30 MPa.

The Water/cement ratio is = 0.62

Check this W/C ratio from durability consideration from Table 9.20. The maximum W/C ratio permitted is 0.50. Adopt lower of the two

Therefore adopt W/C ratio of 0.50

Next decide the water content for slump of 75 mm (assumed) 20 mm uncrushed aggregate from Table 11.12.

The water content is 195 kg/m³

With W/C of 0.5 and water content of 195 kg/m³, the cement content works out to

$$\frac{195}{0.5} = 390 \text{ kg/m}^3$$

Check this cement content with that of durability requirements given in Table 9.20. Minimum cement content from durability point of view is 350 kg/m³. Adopt greater of the two.

Therefore adopt cement content = 390 kg/m³

Next, find out the density of fresh concrete from Fig. 11.4 for water content of 195 kg/m³,

20 mm uncrushed aggregate of sp.gr. 2.65

The wet density = 2400 kg/m³

Next, find the weight of total aggregate

2400 – (195 +390) = 1815 kg/m³

Next, find the percentage of fine aggregate from Fig. 11.5(b)

For 20 mm aggregate size, W/C ratio of 0.50,

Slump of 75 mm, for 50% fines passing through 600 μ sieve, the percentage of

    F.A. = 40 percent

 Weight of F A. = $1815 \times \dfrac{40}{100}$ = 726 kg/m³

∴ Weight of C.A. = 1815 – 726

       = 1089 kg/m³

Estimated quantities in kg/m³

    Cement = 390

     F.A. = 726

     C.A. = 1089

    Water = 195

   Wet density   2400

The above quantities are required to be adjusted for the field moisture content and absorption characteristics of aggregates

Lastly trial mixes are made to arrive at the correct quality of concrete.

Concrete Mix Design Procedure for Concrete with Fly Ash by DOE Method

Use of fly ash is gaining popularity in India as in other countries. Therefore one has to be acquainted with the procedure of concrete mix containing fly ash. The following example of Mix Design containing fly ash illustrates the procedures.

Example of Mix Design with Fly ash with DOE method

Design a concrete mix for a chracteristic strength of 25 MPa. (The target mean strength can be taken as 33 MPa). Crushed aggregates are used. The grading of F.A shows that 40% passes through 600 μ seive. Placing condition requires a slump range of 30–60 mm. The concrete is to be used in a moderate exposure condition. The cover to reinforcement adopted is 25 mm. The sp. gr. of F.A. is 2.6 and that of C.A is 2.7. It is proposed to use 30 percent fly ash.

In the case of mixes containing fly ash, DOE method gives the cement content as

$$C = \frac{(100 - p)W}{(100 - 0.7p)\left\{\dfrac{W}{C + 0.3F}\right\}}$$

fly ash content, $F = \dfrac{pC}{100 - p}$

where $p = \dfrac{100F}{C + F}$

i.e., p is the percentage of fly ash in the total cementitious material.

W is the free water content

$\dfrac{W}{C + 0.3F}$ is the free water/cementitious ratio for design strength in Fig. 11.3. The free water/cementitious material ratio W/C + F should then be compared with the specified value.

The free water/cement ratio to be used in Fig. 11.3 is $\dfrac{W}{C + 0.3F}$

From Table 11.11, Compressive strength of ordinary cement with fly ash mix with a free $\dfrac{W}{C + 0.3F}$ ratio of 0.5 is 49 MPa. For target mean strength of 33 MPa, Fig. 11.3 gives a free $\dfrac{W}{C + 0.3F}$ ratio of 0.65. (This value is not to be compared with the maximum permissible value of those given in table 9.20, but is used only for strength purposes)

Referring to Table 11.12.

For slump of 60 mm, for maxim size aggregate of 20 mm, in case of crushed aggregate, the approximate water content is 210 kg/m³

Since 30 per cent of fly ash is used, referring to Table 11.13, This water content is to be reduced by 20 kg/m³

∴   The water content = 210 – 20

= 190 kg/m³

Then cement content $= \dfrac{(100-30)190}{(100-0.7\times30)(0.65)}$

$= 259 \text{ kg/m}^3$

and the fly ash content $F = \dfrac{pC}{100-p}$

$= \dfrac{30\times259}{100-30} = 111.0 \text{ kg/m}^3$

Hence the total cementitious material content is $259 + 111.0 \text{ kg/m}^3 = 370 \text{ kg/m}^3$

The free water/cementitious material ratio is $\dfrac{190}{370} = 0.51$

Referring to Table 9.20.

For moderate exposure condition, and concrete cover of 25 mm, the maximum free water/cementitious material ratio is 0.50 and minimum cement content is 350 kg/m³

Referring to Table 9.20 cement content satisfies the durability requirement. But water/cementitious material ratio does not satisfy the durability requirement. Therefore adopt Water/cementitious material ratio of 0.50, instead of 0.51.

Then water content $= 370 \times 0.5$

$= 185 \text{ l/m}^3$

From Fig. 11.4, for water content of 185 l/m³, average specific gravity of 2.65 of aggregates, the wet density of concrete comes to 2415 kg/m³

Hence the total weight of aggregates

$= 2415 - (259 + 111 + 185)$

$= 1860 \text{ kg/m}^3$

From Fig. 11.5(*b*)

For free water/cementitious material ratio of 0.50, and for F.A, 40% passing through 600 μ seive, and for slump of 30–60 mm the proportion of F.A is = 38%

$\therefore$ Weight of F.A $= \dfrac{38}{100} \times 1860$

$= 707 \text{ kg/m}^3$

Weight of C.A $= 1860 - 707$

$= 1153 \text{ kg/m}^3$

Estimated quantities of materials in kg per m³ on the basis of SSD condition

Cement $= 259.00$

Fly ash $= 111.00$

Fine aggregate $= 707.00$

Coarse aggregate   = 1153.00

Water   =   185.00

Total   = 2415 kg/m³

The above weights of F.A, C.A are to be adjusted depending upon the free moisture content and absorption characteristics of aggregates. The corresponding correction is also to be made in the quantity of actual water added. and also consequent changes in the quantities of aggregates.

Then trial mixes are made to see that the concrete satisfies all the requirements in plastic conditions and strength at 28 days. If not, minor adjustment is made in the quantities of materials worked out.

Alternatively Superplasticizers in appropriate dose could be used for getting required workability.

Note: Referring to Table 9.20. The minimum grade of concrete is to be 45 MPa. This, aspect has not been satisfied. If this condition is to be satisfied, the whole problem is to be reviewed and reworked out.

Fig. 11.6. Degree of workability

Mix Design for Pumpable Concrete[11.5]

A concrete which can be pushed through a pipe line is called a pumpable concrete. It is proportioned in such a manner that its friction at the inner wall of the pipeline does not become so high to prevent its movement at the pressure applied by the pump. A pumpable concrete is no special concrete. It is a standardised good concrete with certain content of fines to offer lubrication at the inner wall of pipe line.

The pumpable concrete has:

(a) a minimum content of FINES (cement + fine aggregate particle smaller than 0.25 mm size) of approximately 400 kg/m³ for maximum size of 32 mm C.A. In case of very angular, flaky aggregates this quantity is to be increased by approximately 10%.

(b) a minimum cement content of approximately 240 kg/m³ for maximum size of 32 mm

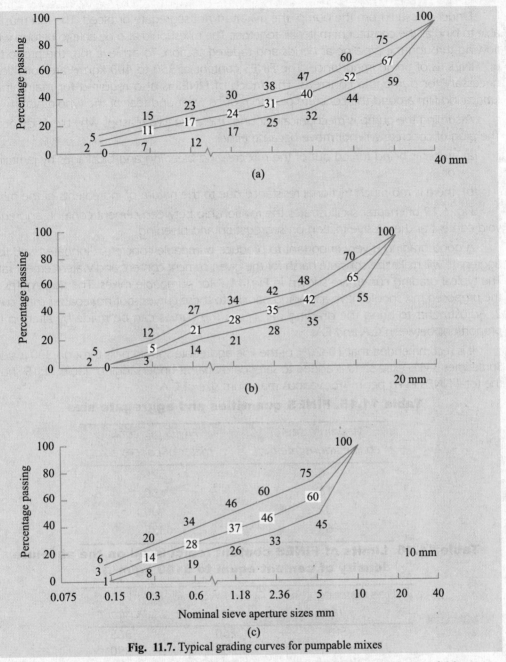

Fig. 11.7. Typical grading curves for pumpable mixes

C.A. It must be increased by 10% in case of maximum size aggregate of 16 mm.

(c) a water/cement ratio of 0.42 to 0.65

(d) a slump of 75 mm to 150 mm or a consistency determinable by means of the flow table spread in the range of k_2 and k_3 (refer Fig. 11.6)

(e) a grading of aggregate typically as shown in Fig. 11.7 is to be used.

A clear understanding of what happens to concrete when it is pumped through a pipeline is fundamental to any study of concrete pumping and when designing a pumpable concrete mix.

Under pressure from the pump, the mix must not segregate or bleed. The mix must be able to bind all the constituent materials together. The mix should also be able to deform while flowing through the pipeline at bends and tapered section. To achieve this, the proportion of "FINES" is of prime importance. The FINES content of 350 to 400 kg/m³ are considered necessary for pumpable concrete. This much of FINES is also required for maintaining lubricating film around the concrete plug to reduce wear and tear of the whole system.

Assuming the pump is mechanically sound, there are two reasons why blockage occur. The plug of concrete will not move because either

(a) water is being forced out of the mix creating bleeding and blockages by jamming, or

(b) there is too much frictional resistance due to the nature of ingredients of the mix.

Fig. 6.19 of chapter six illustrates the relationship between cement content, aggregate void content and excessive friction on segregation and bleeding.

A good grading is very important to produce pumpable concrete. Elongated and flaky aggregate will make the concrete harsh for the given cement content and water/cement ratio. The typical grading curves are shown in Fig. 11.7 for pumpable mixes. The aggregates for the proposed mix should have a grading parallel to these curves, but not coarser than curve 2. Adjustments to bring the grading parallel to the curves can be made by altering the proportions between C.A and F.A.

It is recommended that 10–20% of the fine aggregate should pass through 300 μ sieve. Sometimes 3–4% extra sand is added to safeguard against undersanding. Table 11.15 shows the total FINES in kg per m³ for various maximum size of C.A.

Table 11.15. FINES quantities and aggregate size

Maximum size of coarse aggregate mm	FINES per cubic meter of concrete kg
8	525
16	450
32	400
63	325

Table 11.16. Limits of FINES content (calculated on the absolute density of cement equal to 3100 kg/m³.)

Free water content l/m³	FINE solids kg/m³	
	Minimum	Maximum
150	260	365
160	280	390
170	295	415
180	315	440
190	330	465
200	350	490
210	365	515
220	385	540
230	400	565
240	420	590

Table 11.17. Mix Proportions on SSD basis for 75–100 mm slump

Material	Quantity in kg
Fine Aggregate	880
Coarse Aggregate	930
OPC	310
Water	190
Total	2310

Table 11.18. Absolute density of materials

Material	Density kg/m³
OPC	3100
F.A	2650
C.A	2550

Table 11.19. Aggregate Gradings (for mix proportions in Table 11.17)

Sieve Size mm	Percentage passing Coarse Agg.	Fine Agg.
20	100	
14	60	
10	37	100
5	6	94
2.4	1	84
1.2		70
0.6		53
0.3		18
0.15		5

Table 11.20. Calculation of all-in aggregate grading, based on F.A content of 880 kg and C.A content of 930 kg/m³ and as per grading given in Table 11.19.

Sieve Size mm	Percentage Passing C.A	F.A	Combined grading
20	51.5	48.5	100
14	31.0	48.5	79.5
10	19.0	48.5	67.5
5	3.0	45.5	48.5
2.4	0.5	41.0	41.5
1.2	–	34.0	34.0
0.6		25.5	25.5
0.3		9.0	9.0
0.15		2.5	2.5

Example: Basic design calculations for a pumpable concrete mix

The following steps will illustrate the procedure.

(a) While Fig. 11.7 shows the typical grading limits, Fig. 11.8 shows the more acceptable grading limits for pumpable concrete using 20 mm maximum size aggregates. The grading pattern should fall within the curve envelope of Fig. 11.8. If necessary the proportions of fine and coarse aggregate can be readjusted.

(b) The limits of the FINES content should be as given in Table 11.16

(c) Mix proportions on SSD basis, for 75 to 100 mm slump, are given in Table 11.17.

(d) The mix proportions given in Table 11.17 is based on the gradings of aggregate as given in Table 11.19.

(e) The absolute density of material used is given in Table 11.18.

(f) The calculation of grading of combined aggregate on the basis of proportions given in Table 11.17 is given in Table 11.20. These combined grading figures should fall within the limits indicated in Fig. 11.8.

(g) The FINES content should then be worked out.

cement content = 310 kg (From Table 11.17)

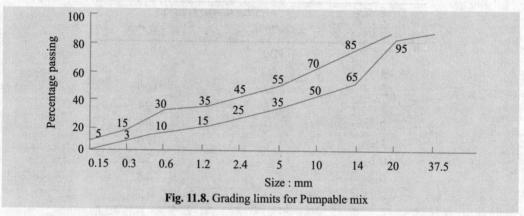

Fig. 11.8. Grading limits for Pumpable mix

Fine aggregate grading shows that 18% passing through 0.3 mm sieve and 5% passing through 0.15 mm by interpolation probable percentage passing through 0.25 mm sieve $= 15\%$

$\therefore$ Fine particles in sand $= \dfrac{15}{100} \times 880 = 132$ kg/m^3

$\therefore$ Total FINES $= 310 + 132$

$= 442$ kg/m^3

Referring to Table 11.16 for 190 l/m^3 of water content, the range of FINES is 330 to 465 kg/m^3

$\therefore$ FINES of 442 kg/m^3 is considered suitable.

Note. Crushed aggregate can be obtained in wide range of single sized particles from which required gradings can be readily produced. These aggregates usually require higher sand contents to achieve the required void content. Crushed fine aggregates contain lot of dust that passing the 150 m sieve and care must be taken to avoid excess of dust which could cause high pipe line friction and blockages.

Indian Standard Recommended Method of Concrete Mix Design (IS 10262 – 1982)

The Bureau of Indian Standards, recommended a set of procedure for design of concrete mix mainly based on the work done in national laboratories. The mix design procedures are covered in IS 10262–82. The methods given can be applied for both medium strength and high strength concrete.

Before we proceed with describing this method step by step, the following short comings in this method are pointed out. Some of them have arisen in view of the revision of IS 456–2000. The procedures of concrete mix design needs revision and at this point of time (2000 AD) a committee has been formed to look into the matter of Mix Design.

(i)   The strength of cement as available in the country today has greatly improved since 1982. The 28-day strength of A, B, C, D, E, F, category of cement is to be reviewed.

(ii) The graph connecting, different strength of cements and W/C is to be reestablished.

(iii) The graph connecting 28-day compressive strength of concrete and W/C ratio is to be extended up to 80 MPa, if this graph is to cater for high strength concrete.

(iv) As per the revision of IS 456–2000, the degree of workability is expressed in terms of slump instead of compacting factor. This results in change of values in estimating approximate sand and water contents for normal concrete up to 35 MPa and high strength concrete above 35 MPa. The Table giving adjustment of values in water content and sand percentage for other than standard conditions, requires appropriate changes and modifications.

(v)   In view of the above and other changes made in the revision of IS 456–2000, the mix design procedure as recommended in IS 10262–82 is required to be modified to the extent considered necessary and examples of mix design is worked out

However, in the absence of revision of Indian Standard on method of Mix Design, the existing method i.e., IS 10262 of 1982 is described below step by step. Wherever it is possible, the new information given in IS 456 of 2000 have been incorporated and the procedure is modified to that extent.

(a)   Target mean strength for mix design: The target mean compressive $(\bar{f}_{ck})$ strength at 28 days is given by

$$\bar{f}_{ck} = f_{ck} + tS$$

where f_{ck} = characteristic compressive strength at 28 days.

S is the standard deviation. The value of the standard deviation has to be worked out from the trials conducted in the laboratory or field. An example has been worked out in Table 11.1. In the absence of such trials, the value of standard deviation can be adopted from Table 11.22, to facilitate initial mix design. As soon as enough test results become available, standard deviation should be worked out and the mix design is modified accordingly.

t = a statistical value depending on expected proportion of low results (risk factor). According to IS: 456–2000 and IS: 1343–'80, the characteristic strength is defined as that value below which not more than 5 per cent results are expected to fall, in which case the above equation reduces to—

$$\bar{f}_{ck} = f_{ck} + 1.65\ S \qquad \text{(Refer Table 11.21)}$$

Table 11.21. Values of Tolerance Factor (*t*) (Risk Factor)

Tolerance level. No of Samples	1 in 10	1 in 15	1 in 20	1 in 40	1 in 100
10	1.37	1.65	1.81	2.23	2.76
20	1.32	1.58	1.72	2.09	2.53
30	1.31	1.54	1.70	2.04	2.46
Infinite	1.28	1.50	1.64	1.96	2.33

Note: Under conditions of major concreting Job, where large number of samples are tested, it would be appropriate to adopt a tolerance factor corresponding to infinite number of samples.

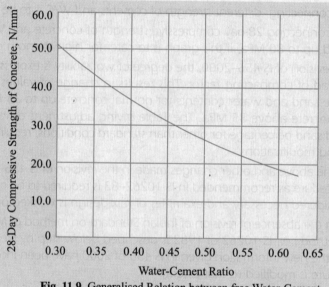

Fig. 11.9. Generalised Relation between free Water-Cement Ratio and Compressive strength of concrete

(b)   Selection of Water/Cement ratio

Various parameters like types of cement, aggregate, maximum size of aggregate, surface texture of aggregate etc. are influencing the strength of concrete, when water/cement ratio remain constant, hence it is desirable to establish a relation between concrete strength and free water cement ratio with materials and condition to be used actually at site. In absence of such relationship, the free water/cement ratio corresponding to the target strength may be determined from the relationship shown in Fig. 11.9.

Table 11.22. Assumed standard Deviation as per IS 456 of 2000

Grade of Concrete	Assumed standard Deviation N/mm^2
M 10	
M 15	3.5

M 20	
M 25	
M 30	4.00
M 35	
M 40	5.00
M 45	
M 50	

Note: The above values correspond to the site control having proper storage of cement, weigh batching of all materials, controlled addition of water; regular checking of all materials, aggregate gradings and moisture content; and periodical checking of workability and strength. Where there is deviation from the above, the values given in the above table shall be increased by 1 N/mm²

One of the good features of IS 10262 of 1982 method of mix design is that it incorporates the strength of cement in the mix design procedure. By incorporating the strength of cement, it is possible to effect economy in concrete mix.

If the 28 days strength of cement is known, use of Fig. 11.10 may be made for more accurate estimation of water cement ratio. However, this will need at least 28 days for testing the strength of cement, thereby delaying the whole process by 28 days. Accelerated strength test may be adopted to cut down the delay.

In view of the improvements in the quality and strength of Indian cement since 1982 the graph given in Fig. 11.11 will give a more realistic picture of water-cement ratio.

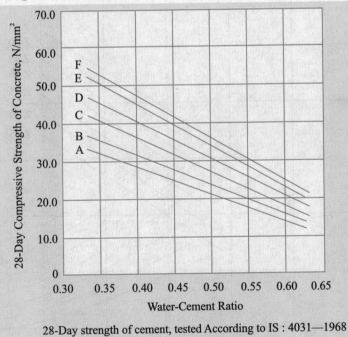

28-Day strength of cement, tested According to IS : 4031—1968

A = 31.9–36.8 N/mm²
B = 36.8–41.7 N/mm²
C = 41.7–46.6 N/mm²

D = 46.6–51.5 N/mm²
E = 51.5–56.4 N/mm²
F = 56.4–61.3 N/mm²

Fig. 11.10. Relation between free Water-Cement Ratio and Concrete Strength for different cement strengths.

The graph given in Fig. 11.11 is not a part of IS recommended method of mix design. But the author recommends the use of Fig. 11.11 for better results. This graph is taken from practice in Germany.

The free water-cement ratio thus selected as mentioned above, should be checked against the limiting water-cement ratio for the durability requirement (Table 9.18 and the lower of the two values should be adopted.

(c) *Estimation of Entrapped Air.* The air content is estimated from Table 11.23 for the normal maximum size of aggregate used.

Table 11.23. Approximate Entrapped Air Content

Maximum Size of Aggregate (mm)	Entrapped Air, as % of Volume of Concrete
10	3.0
20	2.0
40	1.0

(d) *Selection of Water Content and Fine to Total Aggregate ratio*

The water content and percentage of sand in total aggregate by absolute volume are determined from Table 11.24 and 11.25 for medium (below grade M 35) and high strength

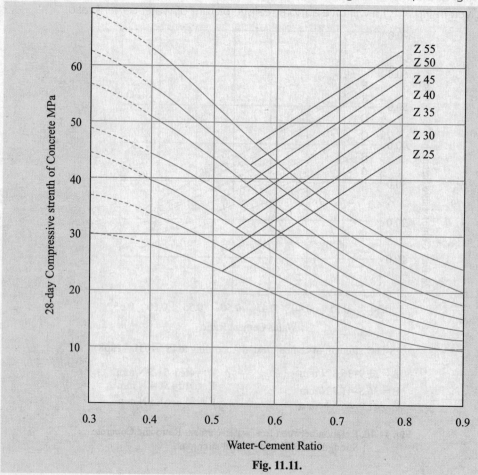

Fig. 11.11.

(above grade M 35) concrete respectively. Both Table 11.24 and Table 11.25 are based on the following conditions.

(*a*) Crushed (Angular) coarse aggregate, conforming to IS: 383—'70.

(*b*) Fine aggregate consisting of natural sand conforming to grading zone II of Table of IS: 383—'70.

(*c*) Workability corresponds to compacting factor of 0.80 (Slump 30 mm approximately)

Water cement ratio in case of Table 11.24 is 0.6 0 (by mass) whereas the same for Table 11.25 is 0.35 (by mass). For any departure from above mentioned conditions, corrections have to be applied as per Table 11.26, for water content and percent sand in total aggregate by absolute volume, determined from table 11.24 or table 11.25.

Note: Refer Table 6.1 for relation between compacting factor and slump.

Table 11.24. Approximate Sand and Water Contents Per Cubic Metre of Concrete W/C = 0.60, Workability = 0.80 C.F.
(Slump 30 mm approximately)
(Applicable for concrete upto grade M 35)

Maximum Size of Aggregate (mm)	Water Content including Surface Water, Per Cubic Metre of Concrete (kg)	Sand as per cent of Total Aggregate by Absolute volume
10	200	40
20	186	35
40	165	30

Table 11.25. Approximate Sand and Water Contents Per Cubic Metre of Concrete W/C = 0.35, Workability = 0.80 C.F.
(Applicable for above grade M 35)

Maximum Size of Aggregate	Water Content including Surface Water Per Cubic Metre of Concrete (kg)	Sand as per cent of Total Aggregate by Absolute Volume
10	200	28
20	180	25

Table 11.26. Adjustment of Values in Water Content and Sand Percentage for Other Conditions

Change in Conditions Stipulated for Tables	Adjustment Required in	
	Water Content	% Sand in Total Aggregate
For sand conforming to grading Zone I, Zone III or Zone IV of Table 4, IS: 383–1979	0	+ 1.5% for Zone I − 1.5 % for Zone III − 3% for Zone IV
Increase or decrease in the value of compacting factor by 0.1	± 3%	0
Each 0.05 increase or decrease in water-cement ratio	0	± 1%
For rounded aggregate	− 15 kg	− 7%

(e) Calculation of Cement Content. The cement content per unit volume of concrete may be calculated from free water-cement ratio and the quantity of water per unit volume of concrete (cement by mass = Water content/Water cement ratio).

The cement content so calculated shall be checked against the minimum cement content for the requirement of drurability Table 9.18 and the greater of the two values to be adopted.

(f) Calculation of aggregate content. Aggregate content can be determined from the following equations:

$$V = \left[W + \frac{C}{S_e} + \frac{1}{P} \frac{f_a}{S_{fa}} \right] \frac{1}{1000} \qquad \qquad \dots (1)$$

$$C_a = \frac{1-P}{P} \times f_a \times \frac{S_{ca}}{S_{fa}} \qquad \qquad \dots (2)$$

where

V = absolute volume of fresh concrete, which is equal to gross volume (m³) minus the volume of entrapped air,

W = Mass of water (kg) per m³ of concrete

C = Mass of cement (kg) per m³ of concrete

S_c = Specific gravity of cement

P = Ratio of FA to total aggregate by absolute volume

f_a, C_a = Total masses of FA and CA (kg) per m³ of concrete respectively and

S_{fa}, S_{ca} = Specific gravities of saturated, surface dry fine aggregate and coarse aggregate respectively.

(g) Actual quantities required for mix. It may be mentioned that above mix proportion has been arrived at on the assumption that aggregates are saturated and surface dry. For any deviation from this condition *i.e.,* when aggregate are moist or air dry or bone dry, correction has to be applied on quantity of mixing water as well to the aggregate.

(h) The calculated mix proportions shall be checked by means of trial batches. Quantities of material for each trial shall be enough for at least three 150 mm size cubes and concrete required to carry out workability test according to IS: 1199–'59.

Trial mix number 1 should be checked for workability and freedom from segregation and bleeding and its finishing property.

If the measured workability is different from that assumed in the calculation, a change in the water content has to done from table 11.26 and the whole mix design has to be recalculated keeping W/C ratio constant. A minor adjustment in the aggregate quantity may be made to improve the finishing quality or freedom from segregation and bleeding. This will comprise trial mix number 2. Now water/cement ratio is changed by ± 10 per cent of pre-selected value and mix proportions are recalculated. These will form trial mix numbers 3 and 4. Testing for trial mix numbers 2, 3, 4 are done simultaneously. These tests normally provide sufficient information, including the relationship between compressive strength and water cement ratio, from which the mix proportions for field trials may be arrived at.

Illustrative Example of Concrete Mix Design (Grade M 20)

(a) Design stipulations

(i)	Characteristic compressive strength required in the field at 28 days.	20 MPa
(ii)	Maximum size of aggregate	20 mm (angular)
(iii)	Degree of workability	0.90 compacting factor
(iv)	Degree of quality control	Good
(v)	Type of Exposure	Mild

(b) Test data for Materials

(i)	Specific gravity of cement	3.15
(ii)	Compressive strength of cement at 7 days	Satisfies the requirement of IS: 269–1989
(iii)	1. Specific gravity of coarse aggregates	2.60
	2. Specific gravity of fine aggregates	2.60
(iv)	Water absorption:	
	1. Coarse aggregate	0.50%
	2. Fine aggregate	1.0%
(v)	Free (surface) moisture:	
	1. Coarse aggregate	Nil
	2. Fine aggregate	2.0%
(vi)	Sieve analysis is shown below:	

1. Coarse aggregate

Sieve size (mm)	Analysis of Coarse aggregate fractions (% passing)		Percentage of different Fractions			Remark
	I	II	I 60%	II 40%	Combined 100%	
20	100	100	60	40	10	Conforming
10	0	71.20	0	28.5	28.5	to Table 2, IS: 383—
4.75		9.40	–	3.7	3.7	1970
2.36	–	–	–	–	–	

2. Fine aggregate

Sieve sizes	Fine aggregate (% passing)	Remarks
4.75 mm	100	
2.36 mm	100	
1.18 mm	93	Conforming to grading
600 micron	60	Zone III of Table 4
300 micron	12	IS: 385–1970
150 micron	2	

(c) Target mean strength of concrete

The target mean strength for specified characteristic cube strength is

$20 + 1.65 \times 4 = 26.6$ MPa   (refer Table 11.21 and Table 11.22 for values of t and s)

(d) Selection of water-cement ratio

From Fig. 11.10 the water-cement ratio required for the target mean strength of 26.6 MPa is 0.50. This is lower than the maximum value of 0.55 prescribed for 'Mild' exposure. (refer Table 9.18) adopt W/C ratio of 0.50.

(e) Selection of water and sand content

From Table 11.24, for 20 mm maximum size aggregate, sand conforming to grading Zone II, water content per cubic metre of concrete = 186 kg and sand content as percentage of total aggregate by absolute volume = 35 per cent.

For change in value in water-cement ratio, compacting factor, for sand belonging to Zone III, following adjustment is required.

Change in Condition (See Table 11.26)	Per cent adjustment required Water content	Sand in total aggregate
For decrease in water-cement ratio by (0.60–0.50) that is 0.10.	0	– 2.0
For increase in compacting factor (0.9–0.8), that is 0.10	+ 3	0
For sand conforming to Zone III of Table 4, IS: 383–1970	0	– 1.5
Total	+ 3	– 3.5

Therefore, required sand content as percentage of total aggregate by absolute volume

$$= 35 - 3.5 = 31.5\%$$

Required water content $= 186 + 5.58 = 191.6$ $1/m^3$

(f) Determination of cement content

Water-cement ratio = 0.50

water = 191.6 litre

∴   cement $= \dfrac{191.6}{0.50} = 383$ kg/m^3

This cement content is adequate for 'mild' exposure condition. (refer Table 9.18)

(g) Determination of coarse and fine aggregate contents

From Table 11.23, for the specified maximum size of aggregate of 20 mm, the amount of entrapped air in the wet concrete is 2 per cent. Taking this into account and applying equations. 1 and 2 given on page 494.

$$0.98 = \left[191.6 + \frac{383}{3.15} + \frac{1}{0.315} \times \frac{f_a}{2.60}\right] \frac{1}{1000}$$

$f_a = 546$ kg/m^3, and

$$C_a = \frac{1-0315}{0.315} \times 546 \times \frac{2.6}{2.6} = 1188 \text{ kg/m}^3$$

$f_a = 546 \text{ kg/m}^3$, and

$C_a = 1188 \text{ kg/m}^3$.

The mix proportion then becomes:

Water	Cement	Fine aggregate	Coarse Aggregate
191.6	383 kg	546 kg	1188 kg
0.50 :	1 :	1.425	: 3.10

(h) Actual quantities required for the mix per bag of cement

The mix is 0.50 : 1 : 1.425 : 3.10. For 50 kg of cement, the quantity of materials are worked out as below:

(i) Cement = 50 kg

(ii) Sand = 71.0 kg

(iii) Coarse aggregate = 155 kg $\begin{vmatrix} \text{Fraction I} & = 60\% = 93 \text{ kg} \\ \text{Fraction II} = 40\% = 62 \text{ kg} \end{vmatrix}$

(iv) Water

1. for w/c ratio of 0.50, quantity = 25 litres of water.

2. Extra quantity of water to be added for absorption in case of CA, at 0.5 per cent mass. = 0.77 litres

3. Quantity of water to be deducted for moisture present in sand, at 2 per cent by mass. = 1.42 litres

4. Actual quantity of water required to be added

= 25.0 + 0.77 − 1.42

= 24.35 litres.

(i) Actual quantity of sand required after = 71.0 + 1.42

allowing for mass of free moisture = 72.42 kgs.

(j) Actual quantity of CA required

1. Fraction I = 93 − 0.46 = 92.54 kg

2. Fraction II = 62 − 0.31 = 61.69 kg

Therefore, the actual quantities of different constituents required for one bag mix are

Water	:	24.35 kg
Cement	:	50.00 kg
Sand	:	72.42 kg
CA Fraction I	:	92.54 kg
Fraction II	:	61.69 kg

I Trial mix

A typical trial mix test programme is given in Table 11.27.

Table 11.27. Typical Test Results of Trial Mix

	Quantities of material per cubic metre of concrete					Concrete characteristic		
Mix. No.	Cement	Water	Sand	C Type I	A Type II	Workability (CF)	Visual observation	28 days compressive strength
1	2	3	4	5	6	7	8	9
	kg	(l)	(kg)	(kg)	(kg)			N/mm²
1.	383	191.6 w/c = 0.5 (31.5%)	546	712	475	0.80	Under sanded	–
2.	394.6	197.3 w/c = 0.5 (33%)	564	687	458	0.91	Cohesive	28.8
3.	358.7	197.3 w/c = 0.55 (34%)	591	688	459	0.90	Cohesive	26.0
4.	438.4	197.3 w/c = 0.45 (32%)	535	682	455	0.89	Cohesive	31.2

Rapid Method

However, the approach outlined above will need at least 28 days for the trial mix of concrete, and 56 days if cement is to be tested to use Fig. 11.10. This brings out a major difficulty in adoption of design mix concrete in our country. In view of shortage of cement with interrupted supplies, once cement is received at the construction sites, there is a tendency to straightaway use it without waiting for trial mixes. Unless one is in a position to procure adequate quantities of cement and aggregates well in advance, protect and store them at the site, it will be difficult to expect the site-engineer to wait for completing the trial mixes, before using cement in constructions. Variability of materials, on the other hand, will not enable one mix design worked out earlier with one set of material to be applicable in all cases. In other words, another prime requirement for adoption of design mix concrete is to cut down the time required for trial mixes.

In a method developed by erstwhile CRI; now NCBM, where use of accelerated curing method of testing compressive strength of concrete have brought down the time required for mix proportioning to 3 days only. Such methods of accelerated curing of concrete for strength tests are now standardised and covered in IS: 9013–1978. In so far as concrete is concerned, there exists a statistically significant correlation between its 28 days strength and accelerated strength, so much so that the trial of mixes can be related to target 'accelerated strength' rather than the target 28 days strength, with the help of correlation between the two. A typical correlationis shown in Fig. 11.12 which is based on cements from all plants in the country and different grades of concrete, using boiling water method of accelerated curing. The correlation is found to be not affected by the type or characteristics of cement, presumably because they affect both the accelerated and 28 days strength of concrete in a proportionate manner, so that the influence is nullified, when their ratios are compared. Moreover, for individual

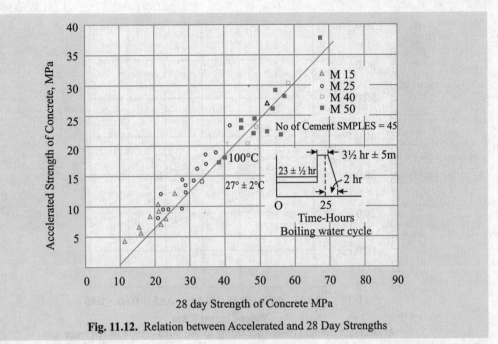

Fig. 11.12. Relation between Accelerated and 28 Day Strengths

applications such correlations can be easily established for the type of materials and mix proportions in hand.

In so far as the compressive strength of cements is concerned, accelerated tests on standard cement mortars (as per IS: 4032–1968) have not given equally reliable results. This problem has been overcome by testing cements also in a 'reference' concrete mix and determining its accelerated strength. The 'reference' concrete mix has w/C = 0.35 and workability = 0.80 (compacting factor). The nominal maximum size of natural crushed aggregate should be 10 mm and fine aggregate conforming to zone II of Table 4 of IS: 383–1970 are used. Typical composition of such a reference concrete mix, per m³ of concrete is

Cement	– 570 kg	
Water	– 200 kg	
Fine aggregate	– 400 kg	⎤
Coarse aggregate	– 1178 kg	⎦ On saturated-surface dry basis

150 mm size cube specimens of such reference concrete mix are made with the cement at hand. From the accelerated strength (boiling water method), the 28 days compressive strength of concrete is obtained and using correlation between cement and concrete strengths of such mix proportions, established by exhaustive tests at CRI, the 28 days cement strength can be estimated. However, for use in field, the relationships given in Fig. 11.10 are recalled in terms of the accelerated strength of the reference concrete mix which is shown in Fig. 11.13.

Steps of Mix Design based on rapid method

(*i*) Determine the accelerated strength (boiling water method) of 150 mm cube specimens of a standard concrete mix, using the cement at hand as per IS: 9013–1978.

(*ii*) Corresponding to the accelerated strength in step (*i*) determine the water cement ratio for the required target strength of concrete mix from Fig. 11.13.

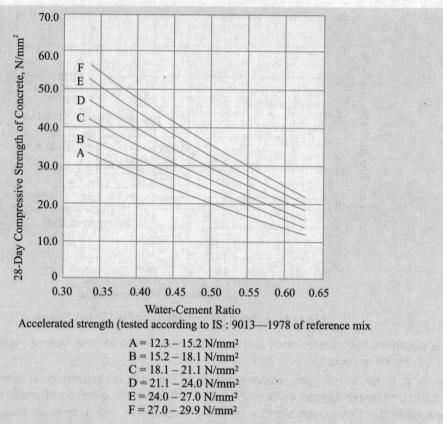

Fig. 11.13. Relation between free Water-Cement Ratio and compressive strength of concrete for different cement strength determined on reference concrete mixes (Accelerated Test-Boiling water mehtod)

Example. Suppose the target 28 days strength of concrete mix to be designed is 30 N/mm², and accelerated strength of standard concrete mix is 18 N/mm². Then from Fig. 11.13 (curve B), the required water-cement ratio is 0.423.

(*iii*) Work out the remaining mix proportions as per the example worked out in preceding pages or by any other accepted method of mix design and check the workability of fresh concrete, against the desired value.

(*iv*) Determine the accelerated compressive strength of the trial mix.

(*v*) Estimate the 28 day compressive strength from the accelerated strength in step (*iv*), using correlations of the type of Fig. 11.12 and check against the target strength.

Sampling and Acceptance Criteria

A random sampling procedure should be adopted to ensure that each concrete batch will have reasonable chance of being tested. It means that sampling and cube casting should be spread over the entire period of concreting. In case of more than one mixing units or batching plants are used for a concrete construction, the sampling should cover all the mixing units.

Frequency of Sampling: The minimum frequency of sampling of concrete of each grade will be as shown in Table 11.28.

Table 11.28. Frequency of Sampling

Quantity of concrete in the work, m³	Number of Samples
1–5	1
6–15	2
16–30	3
31–50	4
51 and above	4 plus one additional sample for each additional 50 m³ or part thereof

Note: At least one sample must be taken from each shift.

Test Specimen: Three test specimens should be made for each sample for testing at 28 days. Additional samples may be required for 7 days strength or for finding out the strength for striking the formwork etc.

Test Results: The test result of sample is the overage of the strength of three specimen. The individual variation should not be more than ± 15 per cent of the overage. If more, the test result of the sample is rejected.

In a major construction site a register is maintained showing the test results of the samples of concrete taken. Possibly samples should denote the time and part of the structure to which the concrete represented by this samples has been used, so that the strength of test specimen and the part of the structure can be matched, if need be. The test register is an important legal document and should be kept in safe custody. When the number of samples tested becomes more than 30 or at a pre determined interval of time, standard deviation is worked out to see that the mix design adopted is neither very conservative nor too liberal. If so, using the standard deviation actually worked out from the kind of quality control exercised at site, a fresh mix design is worked out and the proportions of materials are recast. In other words mix design is not a one time job. It should be reviewed continuously to make the whole concreting operation safe and economical.

Earlier it was said that 5 per cent of test results are allowed to fall below the characteristic strength. But it was not mentioned that this 5 per cent is how much below the characteristic strength. IS 456 of 2000 has simplified the earlier version of acceptance criteria of concrete used in a major work site. The compliance requirement is given in Table 11.29.

Table 11.29. Characteristic Compressive Strength Compliance Requirements as per IS 456–2000

Specified Grade	Mean of the Group of 4 Non-over-lapping Consecutive Test Results in N/mm^2	Individual Test Results in N/mm^2
(1)	(2)	(3)
M 15	$\geq f_{ck} + 0.825 \times$ established standard deviation (rounded off to the nearest 0.5 N/mm^2) or $f_{ck} + 3\ N/mm^2$ whichever is greater	$\geq f_{ck} - 3\ N/mm^2$

M 20 or above	$\geq f_{ck} + 0.825 \times$ established standard deviation (rounded off to the nearest 0.5 N/mm²) or $f_{ck} + 4$ N/mm² whichever is greater	$\geq f_{ck} - 4$ N/mm²

Note: In the absence of established value of standard deviation, the values given in Table 11.22 may be used. And attempt should be made to obtain results of 30 samples as early as possible to establish the value of standard deviation.

Acceptance Criteria

Compressive strength

The concrete is deemed to comply with the compressive strength requirements when both the following conditions are met,

(a) The mean strength determined from any group of four consecutive test results complies with the appropriate limits in column 2 of Table 11.29.

(b) Any individual test result complies with the appropriate limits in column 3 of Table 11.29

Flexural strength

When both the following conditions are met, the concrete complies with the specified flexural strength.

(a) The mean strength determined from any group of four consecutive test results exceeds the specified characteristic strength by at least 0.3 N/mm²

(b) The strength determined from any test result is not less than the specified characteristic strength less 0.3 N/mm²

Inspection and Testing of Structures

Concrete is a very faithful construction material. If care is taken with respect to various constituent materials and workmanship, it, generally, does not fail to give the required results. In case the test results show unacceptable values, the compressive strength can be established from core test and load test.

Core Test

The points from which the cores to be taken can be established from cube testing register. If not possible it can be at the descretion of inspecting authority. The number of test cores will be not less than three which should represent the whole of the doubtful concrete.

The core strength should be converted to equivalent cube strength. If the equivalent cube strength gives at least 85 per cent of characteristic strength of the grade of concrete, and no individual core has a strength less than 75 per cent, the strength of the concrete can be considered adequate.

In case the core test results do not satisfy the requirements or where such core tests have not been done, load test may be resorted to.

Load Tests for Flexural Member

The structure should be subjected to a load equal to full load plus 1.25 times the live load for a period of 24 hours and then the imposed load is removed.

The deflection due to imposed load only is recorded. If within 24 hours of removal of the imposed load, the structure does not recover at least 75 per cent of the deflection under super imposed load, the test may be repeated after a lapse of 72 hours. If the recovery is less than 80 percent, the structure is deemed to be unacceptable.

If the maximum deflection in mm, shown during 24 hour under load is less than $\dfrac{40l^2}{D}$,

where I is the effective span in metre and D, is the overall depth of the section in mm, it is not necessary for the recovery to be measured and the recovery provision mentioned above does not apply.

Non–destructive Tests

Non-destructive tests used for estimation of strength of concrete has been discussed in chapter number 10. Non-destructive tests provide alternatives to core tests for estimating the strength of concrete in a structure, or can supplement the data obtained from a limited number of cores.

Any of the non-destructive methods may be adopted, in which case the acceptance criteria shall be agreed upon prior to the testing.

REFERENCES

11.1 Himsworth F.R., *The Variability of Concrete and its Effect on Mix Design,* Proceedings of the Institution of civil Engineers, March 1954.

11.2 Murdock L.J, *The Control of Concrete Quality,* Proceedings of the Institution of Civil Engineers, Part I Vol. 2, 1954.

11.3 ACI Committee 2111.1–91, *Standard Practice for Selecting Proportions for Normal, Heavyweight, and Mass Concrete,* Part I, ACI Manual of Concrete Practice, 1994.

11.4 Department of the Environment, *Design of Normal Concrete Mixes* (Building Research Establishment, Walford, U.K., 1988.

11.5 Concrete pumping and spraying – A padieal guide by T.H. Cooke – Thomas Telford Ltd., Thomas Telford House, A Heron Quay, London E149 x F.

11.6 Indian Standard Recommended Method of Concrete Mix Design (IS 10262 - 1982)

12

Special Concrete and Concreting Methods

SPECIAL CONCRETE

Light-weight Concrete

One of the disadvantages of conventional concrete is the high self weight of concrete. Density of the normal concrete is in the order of 2200 to 2600 kg/m³. This heavy self weight will make it to some extent an uneconomical structural material. Attempts have been made in the past to reduce the self weight of concrete to increase the efficiency of concrete as a structural material. The light-weight concrete as we call is a concrete whose density varies from 300 to 1850 kg/m³.

There are many advantages of having low density. It helps in reduction of dead load, increases the progress of building, and lowers haulage and handling costs. The weight of a building on the foundation is an important factor in design, particularly in the case of weak soil and tall structures. In framed structures, the beams and columns have to carry load of floors and walls. If floors and walls are made up of light-weight concrete it will result in considerable economy. Another most important characteristic of light-weight concrete is the relatively low thermal conductivity, a property which improves with decreasing density. In extreme climatic conditions and also in case of buildings where air-conditioning is to be installed, the use of light-weight concrete with low thermal conductivity will be of considerable advantage from the point of view of thermal comforts and lower power consumption. The adoption of light-weight concrete gives an outlet for industrial wastes such as clinker, fly ash, slag etc. which otherwise create problem for disposal.

Basically there is only one method for making concrete light *i.e.*, by the inclusion of air in concrete. This is achieved in actual practice by three different ways.

(a) By replacing the usual mineral aggregate by cellular porous or light-weight aggregate.

(b) By introducing gas or air bubbles in mortar. This is known as aerated concrete.

(c) By omitting sand fraction from the aggregate. This is called 'no-fines' concrete.

The Table 12.1 shows the whole ranges of light-weight concrete under three main groups.

Light-weight concrete has become more popular in recent years owing to the tremendous advantages it offers over the conventional concrete. Modern technology and a better understanding of the concrete has also helped much in the promotion and use of light-

Table 12.1. Groups of Light-weight Concrete

No-fines Concrete	Light-weight aggregate concrete	Aerated Concrete	
		Chemical aerating	Foaming mixture
(a) Gravel	(a) Clinker	(a) Aluminium powder method	(a) Preformed foam
(b) Crushed stone	(b) Foamed slag	(b) Hydrogen peroxide and bleaching powder method	(b) Air-entrained foam
(c) Coarse clinker	(c) Expanded clay		
(d) Sintered pulverised fuel ash	(d) Expanded shale		
(e) Expanded clay or shale	(e) Expanded slate		
(f) Expanded slate	(f) Sintered pulverised fuel ash		
(g) Foamed Slag	(g) Exfoliated vermiculite		
	(h) Expanded perlite		
	(i) Pumice		
	(j) Organic aggregate		

weight concrete. A particular type of light-weight concrete called structural light-weight concrete is the one which is comparatively lighter than conventional concrete but at the same time strong enough to be used for structural purposes. It, therefore, combines the advantages of normal normal weight concrete and discards the disadvantages of normal weight concrete. Perhaps this type of concrete will have great future in the years to-come. Out of the three main groups of light-weight concrete, the light-weight aggregate concrete and aerated concrete are more often used than the 'no-fines' concrete. Light-weight concrete can also be classified on the purpose for which it is used, such as structural light weight concrete, non-load bearing concrete and insulating concrete. The aerated concrete which was mainly used for insulating purposes is now being used for structural purposes sometimes in conjunction with steel reinforcement. The aerated concrete is more widely manufactured and used in the Scandinavian countries; whereas in U.K., France, Germany and U.S.A. owing to the production of large scale artificial industrial light-weight aggregate, light-weight aggregates concrete is widely used. In some countries the natural dense graded aggregate are either in short supply or they are available at a considerable distance from the industrial cities. In such cases the use of locally produced light-weight aggregates in the city area offers more economical solutions. These factors have led to the development and widespread use of considerable varieties of industrial light-weight aggregates of varying quality by trade names such as Leca (expanded clay), Aglite (expanded shale), Lytag (sintered pulverised fuel ash), Haydite (expanded shale).

Light Weight Aggregates

Light-weight aggregates can be classified into two categories namely natural light-weight aggregates and artificial light-weight aggregates.

Natural light-weight aggregate	Artificial light-weight aggregate
(a) Pumice	(a) Artificial cinders
(b) Diatomite	(b) Coke breeze
(c) Scoria	(c) Foamed slag
(d) Volcanic cinders	(d) Bloated clay
(e) Sawdust	(e) Expanded shales and slate
(f) Rice husk	(f) Sintered fly ash
	(g) Exfoliated vermiculite
	(h) Expanded perlite
	(i) Thermocole beads.

Natural Aggregates

Natural light-weight aggregates are not found in many places and they are also not of uniform quality. As such they are not used very widely in making light-weight concrete. Out of the natural light-weight aggregates pumice is the only one which is used rather widely.

Pumice

These are rocks of volcanic origin which occur in many parts of the world. They are light enough and yet strong enough to be used as light-weight aggregate. Their lightness is due to the escaping of gas from the molten lava when erupted from deep beneath the earth's crest. Pumice is usually light coloured or nearly white and has a fairly even texture of interconnected cells.

Pumice is one of the oldest kinds of light-weight aggregates which has been even used in Roman structures. Pumice is mined, washed and then used. Pumice may be sintered to the point of incipient fusion when a much stronger aggregate is required. The density and other properties of pumice concrete can be seen from Table 12.3.

Diatomite

This is a hydrated amorphous silica derived from the remains of microscopic aquatic plants called diatoms. It is also known a Kieselguhr. The deposits of this aquatic plants are formed beneath the deep ocean bed. Subsequently when the ocean bed is raised and becomes continent, the diatomaceous earth become available on land. In pure form diatomite has an average weight of 450 kg/m^3. But due to impurities, the naturally available diatomite may weight more than 450 kg/m^3. It has been pointed out earlier that diatomite is used as a workability agent and also as one of the good pozzolanic material. Diatomite or diatomaceous earth can also be sintered in rotary kilns to make artificial light-weight aggregates.

Scoria

Scoria is also light-weight aggregate of volcanic origin which is usually dark in colour and contains larger and irregularly shaped cells unconnected with each other. Therefore, it is slightly weaker than pumice.

Volcanic Cinders

These are also loose volcanic product resembling artificial cinder.

Saw Dust

Sometimes saw dust is used as a light-weight aggregate in flooring and in the manufacture of precast products. A few difficulties have been experienced for its wide-spread use. Saw dust affect adversely the setting and hardening of Portland cement owing to the content of tannins and soluble carbohydrates. With saw dust manufactured from soft wood, the addition of lime to the mix in an amount equal to about 1/3 to 1/2 the volume of cement will counteract this. But the above method *i.e.*, addition of lime is not found effective when the saw dust is made from some of the hard woods. Others methods such as boiling in water and ferrous sulphate solutions also have been tried to remove the effect of tannins, but the cost of the process limits its application. To offset the delay in setting and hardening, addition of calcium chloride to the extent of about 5 per cent by weight of cement has been found to be successful.

The shrinkage and moisture movement of saw dust is also high. The practical mix is of the ratio of 1 : 2 to 1 : 3 *i.e.*, cement to saw dust by volume.

Saw dust concrete has been used in the manufacture of precast concrete products, jointless flooring ad roofing tiles. It is also used in concrete block for holding the nail well. Wood aggregate also has been tried for making concrete. The wood wool concrete is made by mixing wood shavings with Portland cement or gypsum for the manufacture of precast blocks. This has been used as wall panels for acoustic purposes.

Rice Husk

Limited use of the rice husk, groundnut husk and bagasse have been used as light-weight aggregate for the manufacture of light-weight concrete for special purposes.

Artificial Aggregates

Brick Bats

Brick bats are one of the types of aggregates used in certain places where natural aggregates are not available or costly. The brick bat aggregates cannot be really brought under light-weight aggregates because the concrete made with this aggregate will not come under the category of light-weight concrete. However since the weight of such concrete will be less than the weight of normal concrete it is included here. Wherever brick bat aggregates are used, the aggregates are made from slightly overburnt bricks, which will be hard and absorb less water. Brick bat aggregates are also sometimes used in conjunction with high alumina cement for the manufacture of heat resistant concrete.

Cinder, Clinker and Breeze

The term clinker, breeze and cinder are used to cover the material partly fused or sintered particles arising from the combustion of coal. These days the use of these materials as light-weight aggregate in the form of coarse or fine aggregate is getting abated owing to the wider use of pulverised coal rather than lumps of coal. Cinder aggregates undergo high drying shrinkage and moisture movement. Cinder aggregates have been also used for making building blocks for partition walls, for making screeding over flat roofs and for plastering purposes.

The unsoundness of clinker or cinder aggregates is often due to the presence of excessive unburnt coal particles. Sometimes unburnt particles may be present as much as 15 to 25%. This high proportion of coal expand on wetting and contract on drying which is responsible for the unsoundness of concrete made with such aggregate.

Foamed Slag

Foamed slag is one of the most important types of light-weight aggregates. It is made by rapidly quenching blast furnace slag, a by-product, produced in the manufacture of pig iron. If the cooling of the slag is done with a large excess of water, granulated slag is formed which is used in the manufacture of blast furnace slag cement. If the cooling done with a limited amount of water, in such a way as to trip steam in mass, it produces a porous, honeycombed material which resembles pumice. Sometimes, the molten slag is rapidly agitated with a limited amount of water and the steam and gas produced are made to get entrapped in the mass. Such a product is also called foamed slag or expanded slag.

The texture and strength of foamed slag depends upon the chemical composition and the method of production. But in general, the structure is similar to that of natural pumice. The foamed slag must be

(a) Free from contamination of heavy impurities
(b) Free from volatile impurities such as coke or coal.
(c) Free from excess of sulphate.

In India foamed slag is manufactured in many steel mills. In Mysore. Iron and Steel Works at Bhadravati large quantity of foamed slag is being manufactured. Industries have come up near the steel mills to manufacture ready-made building blocks and partition wall pnels. Such prefabricated items being lighter in weight, could be transported at comparatively low cost. Foamed slag is also used for the manufacture of precast RCC lintels and other small structural numbers. By controlling the density, foamed slag can be used for load bearing walls and also for the production of structural light-weight concrete.

Bloated Clay

When certain glass and shales are heated to the point of incipient fusion, they expand or what is termed as bloat to many times their original volume on account of the formation of gas within the mass at the fusion temperatures. The cellular structure so formed is retained on cooling and the product is used as light-weight aggregate. "Haydite", "Rocklite", "Gravelite", "Leca", "Aglite", "Kermazite" are some of the patent names given to bloated clay or shale manufactured in various western countries adopting different techniques.

Central Building Research Institute of India (CBRI) has also developed a process technique for the manufacture of bloated clay for structural use. The experimental building constructed at CBRI using bloated clay as structural light-weight aggregate has been standing well.

Sintered Fly Ash (Pulverised Fuel Ash)

Fly ash is finely divided residue, comprising of spherical glassy particles, resulting from the combustion of powdered coal. By heat treatment these small particles can be made to combine, thus forming porous pellets or nodules which have considerable strength.

The fly ash is mixed with limited amount of water and is first made into pellets and then sintered at a temperature of 1000° to 1200°C. The sintering process is nearly similar to that used in the manufacture of Portland cement. The fly ash may contain some unburnt coal which may vary from 2 to 15 per cent or more depending upon the efficiency of burning. The aim is always to make use of the fuel present in the fly ash and to avoid the use of extra fuel which incidentally improves the quality of sintered fly ash. Sintered fly ash is one of the most important types of structural light-weight aggregate used in modern times. In U.K., it is sold by the trade name "Lytag". It has high strength/density ratio and relatively low drying shrinkage.

Exfoliated Vermiculite

Raw vermiculite is a micaceous mineral and has a laminar structure. When heated with certain percentage of water it expands by delamination in the same way as that of slate or shale. This type of expansion is known as exfoliation. Due to exfoliation, the vermiculite expands many times its original volume. The fully exfoliated vermiculite which may have expanded even as much as 30 times will have a density of only 60 to 130 kg/m^3. The concrete made with vermiculite as aggregate, therefore, will have very low density and hence very low strength. This concrete is used for insulating purposes. It is also used for *in situ* roof and floor screeds or for the manufacture of blocks, slabs and tiles which are used for sound insulation and heat insulation. Vermiculite concrete products can be cut, sawn, nailed or screwed. The prefabricated vermiculite concrete panels can be used for floor sound deadner or wall and partition sound deadner. The hollow blocks made by vermiculite concrete can be used for enacasing pipes carrying steam or hot water. This can also be used as a heat resistant material being non-inflammable. Vermiculite plaster made in conjunction with gypsum is completely incombustible in addition to possessing sound absorption quanlity and thermal insulation characteristics.

In India, Mineral Refining Corporation at Mysore produces vermiculite in many grades for use in concrete industry.

Expanded Perlite

Perlite is one of the natural volcanic glasses like pumice. This when crushed and heated to the point of incipient fusion at a temperature of about 900 to 1100°C it expands to form a light cellular material with density of about 30 to 240 kg/m³. This light material is crushed carefully to various sizes and used in concrete. Due to its very low density this is also used for insulation grade concrete. Table 12.2 gives some of the properties of insulating grade light weight concrete.

Light-weight Aggregate Concrete

Very often light-weight concrete is made by the use of light weight aggregates. We have seen that different light-weight aggregates have different densities. Naturally when this aggregate is used, concrete of different densities are obtained. By using expanded perlite or vermiculite, a concrete of density as low as 300 Kg/m³ can be produced, and by the use of expanded slag, sintered fly ash, bloated clay etc., a concrete of density 1900 kg/m³ can be obtained. The strength of the light-weight concrete may also vary from about 0.3 N/mm² to 40 N/mm². A cement content of 200 kg/m³ to about 500 kg/m³ may be used. Fig. 12.1 shows typical ranges of densities of concrete made with different light-weight aggregates, and Table 12.3 gives the typical properties of light-weight aggregate concrete.

Strength of light-weight concrete depends on the density of concrete. Less porous aggregate which is heavier in weight produces stronger concrete particularly with higher cement content. The grading of aggregate, the water/cement ratio, the degree of compaction also effect the strength of concrete.

Table 12.2. Typical Properties of Common Light-weight Concretes

Sl. No.	Type of Concretes	Bulk density of aggregates kg/m³	Dry density of kg/m³	Compressive strength of 28 days	Drying Shrinkage 10^{-6}	Thermal conductivity Jm/m² 5°C
1.	Sintered fly ash					
	Fine	1050	1500	25	300	–
	Coarse	800	1540	30	350	–
2.	Sintered fly ash with natural sand					
	Coarse	800	1700	25	300	–
3.	Pumice	500–800	1200	15	1200	0.14
4.	Perlite	40–200	400–500	1.2–3.0	2000	0.05
5.	Vermiculite	60–200	300–700	0.3–3.0	3000	0.10
6.	Cellular (Fly ash)	950	750	3.0	700	0.19
	Sand	1600	900	6.0	–	0.22
7.	Autoelaved aerated	–	800	4.0	800	0.25

Most of the light-weight aggregate with the exception of bloated clay and sintered fly ash are angular in shape and rough in texture. They produce a harsh mix. Particular care should be taken to improve workability with the addition of excess of fine material, pozzolanic material or some other plasticizing admixtures. The strength of aggregate will also be influenced by the type of fine aggregates. For increasing the strength, for improving the workability and for reducing the water requirement, sometimes natural sand is used instead

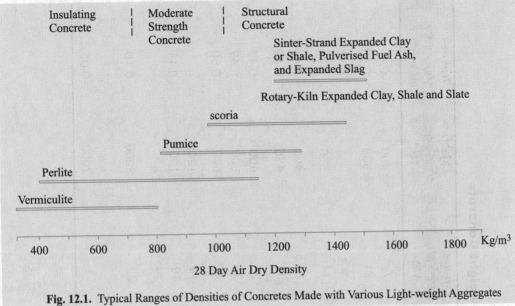

Fig. 12.1. Typical Ranges of Densities of Concretes Made with Various Light-weight Aggregates

of crushed sand made out of light-weight aggregate. Use of air-entrainment will greatly improve the workability, and the tendency for bleeding in the light-weight concrete. But the use of air-entrainment will result in further reduction in strength also.

Most of the light-weight aggregates have a high and rapid absorption quality. This is one of the important difficulties in applying the normal mix design procedure to the light-weight concrete. But it is possible to water-proof the light-weight aggregate by coating it with Bitumen or such other materials by using a special process. The coating of aggregate by Bitumen may reduce the bond strength between aggregate and paste. Coating of aggregate by silicon compounds does not impair the bond characteristics but at the same time makes it non-absorbant.

Light-weight concrete being comparatively porous, when used for reinforced concrete, reinforcement may become prone to corrosion. Either the reinforcement must be coated with anticorrosive compound or the concrete must be plastered at the surface by normal mortar to inhibit the penetration of air and moisture inside. Some of the aggregates like clinker or cinder which has more sulphur in themselves cause corrosion of reinforcement. In such cases coating of steel by corrosion inhibiting admixtures is of vital importance.

Light-weight Structural Concrete convention hall built on the lake at Branson, Missouri, USA.

Table 12.3. Typical Properties of Light-weight Concrete

Type of Concrete		Bulk density of Aggregate kg/m³	Mix Proportion by volume Cement: Aggregate	Dry density of concrete kg/m³	Compressive strengths MPa	Drying shrinkage 10^{-6}	Thermal Conductivity $Jm/m^2 s°C$
Foamed Slag	Fine	900	1 : 8	1700	7	400	0.45
			1 : 6	1850	21	500	0.69
Rotary kiln expanded clay	Fine	100	1 : 11	650–1000	3–4	–	0.17
			1 : 6	1100	14	550	0.31
Rotary kiln expanded slate	Fine	950	1 : 6	1700	28	400	0.61
			1 : 4.5	1750	35	450	0.69
Sintered Pulverised Fuel ash	Fine	1050	1 : 6	1450	28	400	0.47
			1 : 4.5	1500	36	500	0.49
			1 : 3.5	1550	41	600	0.50
Pumice		500–800	1 : 6	1200	14	1200	–
			1 : 4	1250	19	1000	0.14
			1 : 2	1450	29	–	–
Exfoliated Vermiculite		65–130	1 : 6	300–500	2	3000	0.10
Perlite		95–130	1 : 6	–	–	2000	0.05

Structural Light Weight Concrete

The structural light weight concrete is going to be one of the important materials of construction. A concrete which is light in weight and sufficiently strong to be used in conjunction with steel reinforcement will be a material which is more economical than the conventional concrete. Therefore, a concrete which combines strength and lightness will have the unquestionable economic advantage.

Structural light-weight aggregate concrete is a concrete having 28 day compressive strength more than 17 MPa and 28 day air dried unit weight not exceeding 1850 kg/m³. The concrete may consist entirely of light-weight aggregates (all light-weight concrete) or combination of light weight and normal-weight aggregates. For practical reasons, it is common practice to use normal sand as fine aggregate and light-weight coarse aggregate of maximum size 19 mm. Such light-weight concrete is termed as "sanded light-weight concrete", in contrast to "all light-weight concrete".

Workability

Considerable attention is required to be given to the workability aspect for structural light weight concrete. In case of high slump and overvibration, the mortar goes down and aggregate tends to float. This phenomenon is reverse of that of normal weight concrete. In case of floor, or deck slab, the finishing operation will be difficult. To avoid this difficulty it is usual to limit the maximum slump to 100 mm. It should be remembered that there is going to be higher slump loss on account of continued absorption of water by aggregate.

Light-weight concrete exhibits higher moisture movement than the normal weight concrete. Concrete while wetting swells more and the concrete while drying shrinks more. The higher magnitude of drying shrinkage coupled with lower tensile strength makes the light weight aggregate concrete to undergo shrinkage cracks. But the higher extensibility and lower modulus of elasticity help to reduce the tensile cracks.

Since light-weight concrete contains large per cent of air, it is naturally a better material with respect to sound absorption, sound proofing and for thermal insulations.

The coefficient of thermal expansion of concrete made with light-weight aggregate is generally much lower than ordinary concrete. The typical values are shown in Table 12.4.

Table 12.4. Coefficient of Thermal Expansion Made with Light Weight Aggregate

Concrete with light weight aggregate	Linear coefficient of thermal expansion (determined over a range of –22°C to 52°C) 10^{-6} per°C
Pumice	9.4 to 10.8
Perlite	7.6 to 11.0
Vermiculite	8.3 to 14.2
Cinders	about 3.8
Expanded shale	6.5 to 8.1
Expanded slag	7.0 to 11.2

Light-weight aggregate concrete exhibits a higher fire resistance property than the normal concrete. Light weight concrete particularly made with slag or pumice or brick bats as aggregate shows higher fire resistance property.

Design of Light -weight Aggregate Concrete Mix

Mix design methods applying to normal weight concrete are generally difficult to use with light weight aggregate concrete. The lack of accurate value of absorption, specific gravity, and the free moisture content in the aggregate make it difficult to apply the water/cement ratio accurately for mix proportioning.

Light-weight concrete mix design is usually established by trial mixes. The proportions of fine to coarse aggregate and the cement and water requirement are estimated based on the previous experiences with particular aggregate. Various degree of water absorption by different light-weight aggregates is one of the serious difficulties in the design of mix proportions. A reliable information of saturated, surface-dry bulk specific gravity becomes difficult.

Sometimes the aggregate is saturated before mixing so that it does not take up the water used for mixing. The quality of concrete does not get altered on account of absorption by aggregate. It has been seen that the strength of the resulting concrete is about 5 to 10 per cent lower than when dry aggregate is used for the same content and workability. This is due to the fact that in the latter case some of the mixing water is absorbed prior to setting. This water having contributed to the workability at the time of placing gets absorbed later, thus reducing the bad effect of excess of water. Moreover, the density of concrete made with saturated aggregate is higher and the durability of such concrete, especially its resistance to frost is lower. On the other hand, when aggregate with high absorption is used, it is difficult to obtain a sufficiently workable and yet cohesive mix, and generally aggregates with absorption of over 10 per cent are presoaked.

Mixing Procedure

Mixing procedure for light-weight concretes may vary with different types of aggregates. The general practice for structural light-weight concrete is to mix the aggregate and about 2/3 of the mixing water for a period upto one minute prior to the addition of cement and the balance mixing water. Mixing is done continuously as required for homogeneity. Usually 2 or more minutes are required to get uniform mixing. In case of some insulating concrete, the aggregate is added at the end of mixing to minimise degradation.

Mix design data have been prepared for several, proprietary light-weight aggregates available in the United Kingdom. The design charts prepared by Teychenne is reproduced in Fig 12.2. The parameters obtained from these charts cannot be taken as final answers. However, they may give information for first trial.[12.3]

Aerated Concrete

Aerated concrete is made by introducing air or gas into a slurry composed of Portland cement or lime and finely crushed siliceous filler so that when the mix sets and hardens, a uniformly cellular structure is formed. Though it is called aerated concrete it is really not a concrete in the correct sense of the word. As described above, it is a mixture of water, cement and finely crushed sand. Aerated concrete is also referred to as gas concrete, foam concrete, cellular concrete. In India we have at present a few factories manufacturing aerated concrete. A common product of aerated concrete in India is Siporex.

There are several ways in which aerated concrete can be manufactured.

(a) By the formation of gas by chemical reaction within the mass during liquid or plastic state.

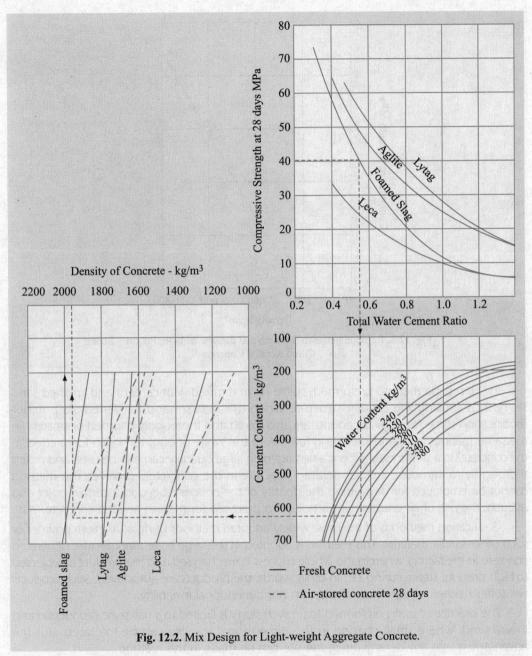

Fig. 12.2. Mix Design for Light-weight Aggregate Concrete.

(*b*) By mixing preformed stable foam with the slurry.

(*c*) By using finely powdered metal (usually aluminium powder) with the slurry and made to react with the calcium hydroxide liberated during the hydration process, to give out large quantity of hydrogen gas. This hydrogen gas when contained in the slurry mix, gives the cellular structure.

Powdered zinc may also be added in place of aluminum powder. Hydrogen peroxide and bleaching powder have also been used instead of metal powder. But this practice is not widely followed at present.

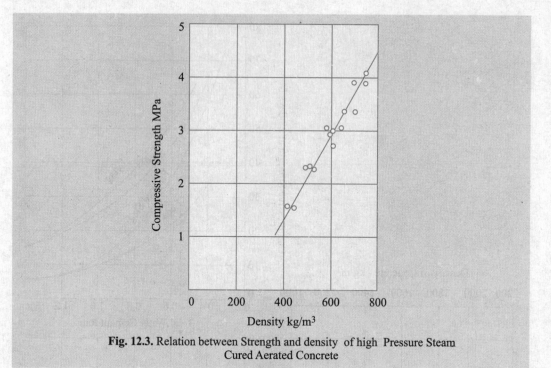

Fig. 12.3. Relation between Strength and density of high Pressure Steam Cured Aerated Concrete

In the second method preformed, stable foam is mixed with cement and crushed sand slurry thus causing the cellular structure when this gets set and hardened. As a minor modification some foam-giving agents are also mixed and thoroughly churned or beaten (in the same manner as that of preparing foam with the white of egg) to obtain foam effect in the concrete. In a similar way, air entrained agent in large quantity can also be used and mixed thoroughly to introduce cellular aerated structure in the concrete. However, this method cannot be employed for decreasing the density of the concrete beyond a certain point and as such, the use of air entrainment is not often practised for making aerated concrete.

Gasification method is of the most widely adopted methods using aluminium powder or such other similar material. This method is adopted in the large scale manufacture of aerated concrete in the factory wherein the whole process is mechanised and the product is subjected to high pressure steam curing *i.e.,* in other words, the products are autoclaved. Such products will suffer neither retrogression of strength nor dimensional instability.

The practice of using preformed foam with slurry is limited to small scale production and *in situ* work where small change in the dimensional stability can be tolerated. But the advantage is that any density desired at site can be made in this method.

Properties

Use of foam concrete has gained popularity not only because of the low density but also because of other properties mainly the thermal insulation property. Aerated concrete is made in the density range from 300 kg/m³ to about 800 kg/m³. Lower density grades are used for insulation purposes, while medium density grades are used for the manufacture of building blocks or load bearing walls and comparatively higher density grades are used in the manufacture of prefabricated structural members in conjunction with steel reinforcement.

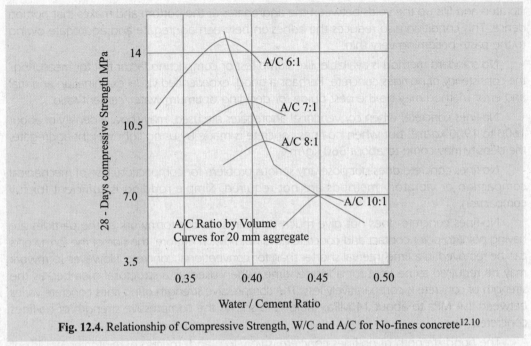

Fig. 12.4. Relationship of Compressive Strength, W/C and A/C for No-fines concrete[12.10]

Figure 12.3 shows relation between strength and density of high pressure steam cured aerated concrete.

No-fines Concrete

The third method of producing light concrete is to omit the fines from conventional concrete.

No-fines concrete as the term implies, is a kind of concrete from which the fine aggregate fraction has been omitted. This concrete is made up of only coarse aggregate, cement and water. Very often only single sized coarse aggregate, of size passing through 20 mm retained on 10 mm is used. No-fines concrete is becoming popular because of some of the advantages it possesses over the conventional concrete.

The single sized aggregates make a good no-fines concrete, which in addition to having large voids and hence light in weight, also offers architecturally attractive look.

Mix-proportion

No-fines concrete is generally made with the aggregate/cement ratio from 6 : 1 to 10 : 1. Aggregates used are normally of size passing through 20 mm and retained on 10 mm. Unlike the conventional concrete, in which strength is primarily controlled by the water/cement ratio, the strength of no-fines concrete, is dependent on the water/cement ratio, aggregate cement ratio and unit weight of concrete. Figure 2.4 shows the relationship of compressive strength, water/cement ratio and aggregate/cement ratio for no-fines concrete.

The water/cement ratio for satisfactory consistency will vary between a narrow range of 0.38 and 0.52. Water/cement ratio must be chosen with care. If too low a water/cement ratio is adopted, the paste will be so dry that aggregates do not get properly smeared with paste which results in insufficient adhesion between the particles. On the other hand, if the water/cement ratio is too high, the paste flows to the bottom of the concrete, particularly when vibrated and fills up the voids between the aggregates at the bottom and makes that portion dense. This condition also reduces the adhesion between aggregate and aggregate owing to the paste becoming very thin.

No standard method is available, like slump test or compacting factor test for measuring/ the consistency of no-fines concrete. Perhaps a good, experienced visual examination and trial and error method may be the best guide for deciding optimum water/cement ratio.

No-fines concrete, when conventional aggregates are used, may show a density of about 1600 to 1900 kg/m^3, but when no-fines concrete is made by using light weight aggregate, the density may come to about 360 kg/m^3.

No-fines concrete does not pose any serious problem for compaction. Use of mechanical compaction or vibratory methods are not required. Simple rodding is sufficient for full compaction.

No-fines concrete does not give much side thrust to the formwork as the particles are having point to point contact and concrete does not flow. Therefore, the side of the formworks can be removed in a time interval shorter than for conventional concrete. However, formwork may be required to be kept for a longer time, when used as a structural member, as the strength of concrete is comparatively less. The compressive strength of no-fines concrete varies between 1.4 MPa to about 14 MPa. Table 12.5 shows the compressive strength of no-fines concrete.

The bond strength of no-fines concrete is very low and, therefore, reinforcement is not used in conjunction with no-fines concrete. However, if reinforcement is required to be used in no-fines concrete, it is advisable to smear the reinforcement with cement paste to improve the bond and also to protect it from rusting.

Drying Shrinkage

The drying shrinkage of no-fines concrete is considerably lower than that of conventional concrete. No-fines concrete made with river gravel, may show a drying shrinkage of the order of 200×10^{-6} which is only about 50% of the conventional concrete. Since there is only a very thin layer of paste existing between aggregates and aggregates, and since the aggregate are having point to point contact, the value of drying shrinkage becomes low. However, the rate of drying shrinkage is generally much higher than conventional concrete. For no-fines concrete 50 to 80% of the total drying shrinkage takes place within about 10 days. The corresponding value for conventional concrete in 10 days is 20 to 30%. Further all the drying shrinkage will get completed in just over a month.

Table 12.5. Compressive Strength of No-fines Concrete Made with Different Grading of Crushed Limestone

Water cement ratio by weight	Aggregate grading	Aggregate cement ratio by weight	Cement content kg/m³	Unit weight of fresh concrete kg/m³	Compressive strength of 150 x 300 mm Cylinders	
					7 days MPa	28 days MPa
0.36	A	8 : 1	359	1910	7.1	8.4
			364	1871	4.8	6.7
			369	1858	5.5	7.5
			368	1813	6.0	5.6
			368	1884	4.7	7.1
0.36	B	9 : 1	360	1820	4.0	5.7
			364	1801	4.4	5.1
0.36	C	7 : 1	361	1877	7.4	8.8
			365	1851	5.4	7.1
			360	1826	5.6	6.9
			368	1826	6.5	6.5

The Thermal Conductivity

The value of coefficient of thermal conductivity of no-fines concrete is much less than conventional concrete. Typical values are shown in Table 12.6.

Table 12.6. Typical values of Thermal Conductivity of No-fines and Conventional Concrete

Type of concrete	Type of aggregate	Thermal conductivity $\frac{k.cal \times m}{m^2 \times hr \times degC}$	Density of concrete kg/m³
No-fines	Conventional	0.74	1760
	Light weight	0.42	1280
Conventional	Igneous	1.28	2540
	Dolomite	3.28	2560
	Light weight	0.12 to 0.52	480 to 1760

Application of No-fines Concrete

No-fines concrete can be used for a variety of purposes. It is used in large scale for load bearing cast in-situ external walls for single storey and multistoreyed buildings. This type of concrete has been used for temporary structures because of low initial cost and also for the ease with which it can be broken and reused as aggregate. Architects consider this as an attractive construction material. Owing to its slightly higher thermal insulating property, it cab be used for external walls for heat insulation. Because of rough texture, it gives a good base for plastering. Even if the outside surface of the no-fines concrete wall is subjected to rain beating, the inside of the wall will be free from dampness because of low capillary action on account of large voids. Where sand is not available, no-fines concrete should become a popular construction material.

High Density Concrete

Density of normal concrete is in the order of about 2400 kg. per cubic metre. The density of light-weight concrete will be less than about density 1900 kg per cubic metre. To call the concrete, as high density concrete, it must have unit weight ranging from about 3360 kg per cubic metre to 3840 kg per cubic metre, which is about 50% higher than the unit weight of conventional concrete. They can, however be produced with the densities upto about 5280 kg per cubic metre using iron as both fine and coarse aggregate. The high density concrete is used in the construction of radiation shields.

The advent of the nuclear energy industry presents a considerable demand on the concrete technologists. Large scale production of penetrating radiaion and radioactive materials, as a result of the use of nuclear reactors, particle accelerator, industrial radiography, and, X-ray, gamma-ray therapy, require the need of shielding material for the protection of operating personnel against the biological hazards of such radiation. Concrete, both normal and high density are effective and economic construction materials for permanent shielding purposes.

Types of Radiation and Hazards

There are two general classes of radiation. They are considered in the design of biological shields:

(a) Electro-magnetic waves,

(b) Nuclear particles.

Of the electromagnetic waves, the high energy, high frequency waves known as X- and gamma rays are only types which require shielding for the protection of personnel. They are similar to light rays but of higher energy greater penetrating power. Gamma-rays are identical with X-rays, except for the source. Both X-rays and Gamma-rays have high power of penetration but can be adequately absorbed by an appropriate thickness of concrete shield.

Nuclear particles consist of nuclei of atoms or fragments thereof. They include neutrons, protons, alfa and beta particles. Of these all but the neutrons possess an electric charge. Neutrons, on the other hand, are uncharged and continue unaffected by electrical fields, until they interact by collision with a nucleus. They have no definite range, and some will penetrate any shield.

Protons, and alfa and beta particles carry electrical charges which interact with the electrical field, surrounding the atom of the shielding material and lose their energy considerably. They generally do not constitute a separate shielding problem, although, accelerated protons at high energy levels may require heavy shielding comparable to that required for neutrons.

The question of shielding resolves into protection against X- and Gamma rays and neutrons. The X- and Gamma-rays are similar except in energy and origin. The biological hazards of radiation arise from the fact that the radiation interacts with human tissues, losing some of their energy in the process. This energy loss is sufficient to ionize atoms in the cells, upsetting the delicate chemical balance and causing the death of the cells. If enough cells are affected the organism dies. Therefore, the radiations must be attenuated sufficiently so that what is left cannot render permanent damage to the persons exposed to it.

Apart from the biological hazards, along with the nuclear reaction very high temperature is also generated and shielding is necessary to protect the electronic and other sensitive equipment in the vicinity.

Shielding ability of Concrete

Concrete is an excellent shielding material that possesses the needed characteristics for both neutron and gamma-ray attenuation, has satisfactory mechanical properties and has a relatively low, initial as well as maintenance cost. Also the ease of construction makes concrete a specially suitable material for radiation shielding. Its only disadvantage is space and weight.

Rajasthan Atomic Nuclear Power Project

There are many aggregates whose specific gravity is more than 3.5 for making a heavy weight concrete. Out of these, commercially employed aggregates are, barite, magnetite, ilmenite, limonite hematite etc. are used. Also available, are steel and iron aggregates in the form of shots, punching scrap for use as a heavy weight aggregate. In determining, which aggregate to use, consideration should be given to availability of aggregates locally and their physical properties.

Kudankulam Nuclear Power Project
Heavy-weight concrete was used for radiation shielding in the above Nuclear Projects.
These days heavy-weight concrete is being used in many major hospitals in India where cancer treatment is carried out.

In general, heavy-weight aggregates should be clean, strong, inert and relatively free from deleterious material which might impair the strength of concrete. Since the capacity of various heavy aggregates to absorb gamma-rays is almost directly proportional to their density, also the heavier elements are more effective in absorbing fast neutrons by inelastic collisions than are the lighter ones, as heavy aggregate, as possible should be used for this purpose.

However, density is not the only factor to be considered in the selection of an aggregate for neutron concrete shield. The desired increase in hydrogen content, required to slow down fast neutrons, can be accomplished by the use of hydrous ores. These materials contain a high percentage of water of hydration. On heating the concrete, some of this fixed water in the aggregate may be lost. Lemonite and goethite are reliable sources of hydrogen as long as shield temperature does not exceed 200°C, whereas serpentine is good upto about. 400°C.

Concrete for Radiation Shielding

It has already been pointed out that the effectiveness of radiation shielding quality of concrete can be increased by increasing the density. Another important requirement of shielding concrete is its structural strength even at high temperature. To produce high density and high strength concrete, it is necessary to control the water cement ratio very strictly. Use of appropriate admixture and vibrators for good compaction are required to be employed. Good quality control be followed.

High density concrete used for shielding differs from normal weight concrete, in that it should contain sufficient material of light atomic weight, which produces hydrogen. Serpentine aggregates are used sometimes, because of the ability to retain water of crystallisation at elevated temperature which assures a source of hydrogen, not necessarily available in all heavy weight aggregates.

High modulus of elasticity, low thermal expansion and low elastic and creep deformations are ideal properties for both conventional and high density concrete. High density concrete, may contain high cement, in which case, it may exhibit increased creep and shrinkage. Because of the high density of aggregates, there will be a tendency for segregation. To avoid this, pre-placed aggregate method of concreting is adopted. Coarse aggregate may be consisting of only high density mineral aggregate or a mixture of mineral aggregate and steel particles or only steel particles. Experiments have indicated that if only smooth cubical pieces of steel or iron are used as coarse aggregate, the compressive strength will not exceed about 21 MPa. cm. regardless of the grout mixture or water cement ratio. If sheared reinforcing bars are used as aggregate, with good grout, normal strength will be produced.

The grout used in high density preplaced aggregate concrete should be somewhat richer than that used in normal density preplaced concrete.

Concreting practice with respect to mixing, transporting, placing as adopted for normal concrete may also be adopted to high density concrete but extra care must be taken with respect to segregation of heavier aggregates from rest of the ingredients. In this regard, higher cement content, better workability may help reducing segregation. Wear and tear of mixer drum may be high. The formwork is required to be made stronger to withstand higher load. Cognisance must also be taken to the strength development of concrete and the dead weight of concrete while removing the formwork.

The Table 12.7 shows the physical properties of high density concrete.

Table 12.7. Physical Properties of High Density Concrete[12.5]

Aggregate	Limonite	Limonite + magnetite	Barite	Barite	Magnetite	Iron limonite
Placement	Conventional	Pre-packed	Conventional	Pre-packed	Conventional	Pre-packed
Density (kg. per m³)	2960	3360	3620	3680	3580	4370
Compressive strength MPa	42.0	33.0	44.0	24.0	41.0	23.0
Modulus of Elasticity GPa	32.0	36.0	31.0	26.0	31.0	39.0
Shrinkage (Per cent)	0.021	0.023	0.029	0.029	0.018	0.013

Table 12.8. Typical Value of Compressive Strength of (50 mm) Moist Cured and Sulphur-Infiltrated Cubes.

Duration of moist curing-hr.	Duration of drying hr.	Age at test hr.	Moist cured Cubes MPa	Compressive strength of sulphur-infiltrated cubes			
				Procedure A		Procedure B	
				Sulphur loading per cent	Mpa	Sulphur loading per cent	Mpa
24	24	54	13.6	9.1	68.0	12.6	108.5

Mix proportions used were: W/C ratio = 0.70

Aggregate/cement ratio = 8.5 : 1

Ratio between C.A. and F.A. = 1 : 1.

Table 12.9. Typical Value of Compressive and Splitting-tensile Strengths of (75 × 150 mm) Moist Cured and Sulphur-infiltrated Cylinders.

Duration of moist curing-hr.	Duration of drying hr.	Age at test hr.	Moist cured cylinders		Sulphur-infiltrated cylinders using procedure B only		
			Compressive strength MPa	Splitting tensile MPa	Sulphur loading per cent	Compressive strength MPa	Splitting tensile strength MPa
24	24	54	9.0	1.9	12.4	72.0	10.5

Mix proportions used were: W/C ratio = 0.70

Aggregate/cement ratio = 8.5 : 1

Coarse Aggregate to fine aggregate ratio = 1 : 1.

Sulphur-Infiltrated Concrete

New types of composites have been produced by the recently developed techniques of impregnating porous materials like concrete with sulphur. Sulphur impregnation has shown great improvement in strength. Physical properties have been found to improve by several hundred per cent and large improvements in water impermeability and resistance to corrosion have also been achieved.

In the past, some attempts have been made to use sulphur as a binding material instead of cement. Sulphur is heated to bring it into molten condition to which coarse and fine aggregates are poured and mixed together. On cooling, this mixture gave fairly good strength, exhibited acid resistance and also other chemical resistance, but it proved to be costlier than ordinary cement concrete.

Recently, use of sulphur was made to impregnate lean porous concrete to improve its strength and other useful properties considerably. In this method, the quantity of sulphur used is also comparatively less and thereby the processes is made economical. It is reported that compressive strength of about 100 MPa could be achieved in about 2 day's time. The following procedures have been reported in making sulphur-infiltrated concrete.[12.6]

A coarse aggregate of size 10 mm and below, natural, well graded, fine aggregate and commercial sulphur of purity 99.9 per cent are used. A large number of trial mixes are made to determine the best mix proportions. A water/cement ratio of 0.7 or over has been adopted in all the trials. A number of 5 cm cubes, 7.5 cm x 15 cm cylinders and also 10 cm x 20 cylinders are cast from each batch of concrete. These samples are stored under wet cover for 24 hours, after which they are removed from moulds and the densities determined. Control specimens are moist cured at 24°C for 26 hours.

Two procedures are adopted. In procedure "A" after 24 hours of moist curing, the specimen is dried in heating cabinet for 24 hours at 121°C. Then the dried specimen are placed in a container of molten sulphur at 121°C for 3 hours. Specimens are removed from the container, wiped clean of sulphur and cooled to room temperature for one hour and weighed to determine the weight of sulphur infiltrated concrete.

In procedure "B", the dried concrete specimen is placed in an airtight container and subjected to vacuum pressure of 2 mm mercury for two hours. After removing the vacuum, the specimens are soaked in the molten sulphur at atmospheric pressure for another half an hour. The specimen is taken out, wiped clean and cooled to room temperature in about one hour. The specimen is weighed and the weight of sulphur-impregnated concrete is determined.

The specimens made adopting procedure A and B are tested by compression and splitting tension tests. It is seen that the compression strength of sulphur-infiltrated cubes and cylinders are enormously greater than the strength of plain moist cured specimen. It is found that when water/cement ratio of 0.7 is adopted an achievement of about 7 fold increase in the strength of the test cube when procedure B is adopted and five-fold increase in strength when procedure A is adopted was obtained. When water/cement ratio of 0.8 is adopted, procedure B gave about a tenfold increase in strength.

Similarly, the sulphur-infiltrated concrete showed more than four times increase in splitting tensile strength when procedure B was adopted.

It was also found that the elastic properties of sulphur-infiltrated concrete has been generally improved 100 per cent and also sulphur-infiltrated specimen showed a very high resistance to freezing and thawing. When the moist cured concrete was disintegrated after about 40 cycles, the sulphur impregnated concrete was found to be in fairly good condition, even after 1230 cycles, when procedure B was adopted and the sample deteriorated after 480 cycles when the sample was made by procedure A. Table 12.8 and Table 12.9, show the typical values of strength test conducted.

The improvement in strength test attributed to the fact that porous bodies having randomly distributed pores have regions of stress concentration when loaded externally. The impregnation of a porous body by some material would modify these stress concentrations. The extent of modification will depend on how well the impregnant has penetrated the smaller pores.

Application of Sulphur-infiltrated Concrete

The sulphur-infiltration can be employed in the precast industry. This method of achieving high strength can be used in the manufacture of pre-cast roofing elements, fencing posts, sewer pipes, and railway sleepers, Sulphur-infiltrated concrete should find considerable use in industrial situations, where high corrosion resistant concrete is required. This method cannot be conveniently applied to cast-in place concrete.

Preliminary studies have indicated that sulphur-infiltrated precast concrete units is cheaper than commercial concrete. The added cost of sulphur and process should be offset by considerable savings in concrete.

The techniques are simple, effective and inexpensive. The tremendous strength gained in pressure application, wherein immersion accompanied by evacuation may also offset the extra cost. The attainment of strength in about two days time makes this process all the more attractive.

Fibre Reinforced Concrete

Plain concrete possesses a very low tensile strength, limited ductility and little resistance to cracking. Internal microcracks are inherently present in the concrete and its poor tensile strength is due to the propagation of such microcracks, eventually leading to brittle fracture of the concrete.

In the past, attempts have been made to impart improvement in tensile properties of concrete members by way of using conventional reinforced steel bars and also by applying

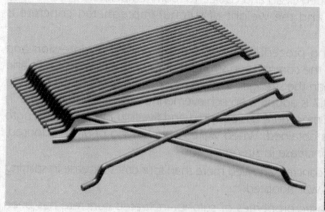

Dramix glued steel fibres. The above fibres were used for casting tunnel segments in the construction of channel tunnel rail link (UK).

restraining techniques. Although both these methods provide tensile strength to the concrete members, they however, do not increase the inherent tensile strength of concrete itself.

In plain concrete and similar brittle materials, structural cracks (micro-cracks) develop even before loading, particularly due to drying shrinkage or other causes of volume change. The width of these initial cracks seldom exceeds a few microns, but their other two dimensions may be of higher magnitude.

When loaded, the micro cracks propagate and open up, and owing to the effect of stress concentration, additional cracks form in places of minor defects. The structural cracks proceed slowly or by tiny jumps because they are retarded by various obstacles, changes of direction in bypassing the more resistant grains in matrix. The development of such microcracks is the main cause of inelastic deformations in concrete.

It has been recognised that the addition of small, closely spaced and uniformly dispersed fibres to concrete would act as crack arrester and would substantially improve its static and dynamic properties. This type of concrete is known as Fibre Reinforced Concrete.

Fibre reinforced concrete can be defined as a composite material consisting of mixtures of cement, mortar or concrete and discontinuous, discrete, uniformly dispersed suitable fibres. Continuous meshes, woven fabrics and long wires or rods are not considered to be discrete fibres.

Fibres Used

Although every type of fibre has been tried out in cement and concrete, not all of them can be effectively and economically used. Each type of fibre has its characteristic properties and limitations. Some of the fibres that could be used are steel fibres, polypropylene, nylons, asbestos, coir, glass and carbon.

Fibre is a small piece of reinforcing material possessing certain characteristic properties. They can be circular or flat. The fibre is often described by a convenient parameter called "aspect ratio". The aspect ratio of the fibre is the ratio of its length to its diameter. Typical aspect ratio ranges from 30 to 150.

Steel fibre is one of the most commonly used fibre. Generally, round fibres are used. The diameter may vary from 0.25 to 0.75 mm. The steel fibre is likely to get rusted and lose some of its strengths. But investigations have shown that the rusting of the fibres takes place only at the surface. Use of steel fibre makes significant improvements in flexural, impact and fatigue strength of concrete, It has been extensively used in various types of structures, particularly for overlays of roads, airfield pavements and bridge decks. Thin shells and plates have also been constructed using steel fibres.

Polypropylene and nylon fibres are found to be suitable to increase the impact strength. They possess very high tensile strength, but their low modulus of elasticity and higher elongation do not contribute to the flexural strength.

Asbestos is a mineral fibre and has proved to be most successful of all fibres as it can be mixed with Portland cement. Tensile strength of asbestos varies between 560 to 980 N/mm^2. The composite product called asbestos cement has considerably higher flexural strength than the Portland cement paste. For unimportant fibre concrete, organic fibres like coir, jute, canesplits are also used.

Glass fibre is a recent introduction in making fibre concrete. It has very high tensile strength 1020 to 4080 N/mm^2. Glass fibre which is originally used in conjunction with cement was found to be effected by alkaline condition of cement. Therefore, alkali-resistant glass fibre by trade name "CEM-FIL" has been developed and used. The alkali resistant fibre reinforced concrete shows considerable improvement in durability when compared to the conventional E-glass fibre.

Carbon fibres perhaps posses very high tensile strength 2110 to 2815 N/mm² and Young's modulus. It has been reported that cement composite made with carbon fibre as reinforcement will have very high modulus of elasticity and flexural strength. The limited studies have shown good durability. The use of carbon fibres for structures like cladding, panels and shells will have promising future.

Factors Effecting Properties of Fibre Reinforced Concrete

Fibre reinforced concrete is the composite material containing fibres in the cement matrix in an orderly manner or randomly distributed manner. Its properties would obviously, depend upon the efficient transfer of stress between matrix and the fibres, which is largely dependent on the type of fibre, fibre geometry, fibre content, orientation and distribution of the fibres, mixing and compaction techniques of concrete, and size and shape of the aggregate. These factors are briefly discussed below:

Relative Fibre Matrix Stiffness

The modulus of elasticity of matrix must be much lower than that of fibre for efficient stress transfer. Low modulus of fibers such as nylons and polypropylene are, therefore, unlikely to give strength improvement, but they help in the absorption of large energy and, therefore, impart greater degree of toughness and resistance to impact. High modulus fibres such as steel, glass and carbon impart strength and stiffness to the composite.

Interfacial bond between the matrix and the fibres also determine the effectiveness of stress transfer, from the matrix to the fibre. A good bond is essential for improving tensile strength of the composite. The interfacial bond could be improved by larger area of contact, improving the frictional properties and degree of gripping and by treating the steel fibres with sodium hydroxide or acetone.

Volume of Fibres

The strength of the composite largely depends on the quantity of fibres used in it. Fig. 12.5 and Fig. 12.6 show the effect of volume on the toughness and strength. It can be seen from Fig. 12.6 that the increase in the volume of fibres, increase approximately linearly, the tensile strength and toughness of the composite[12.7]. Use of higher percentage of fibre is likely to cause segregation and harshness of concrete and mortar.

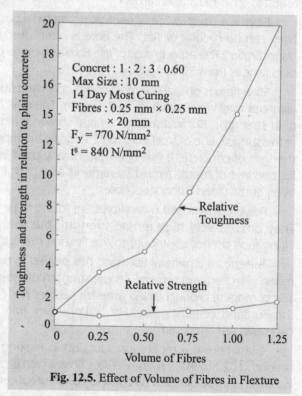

Concret : 1 : 2 : 3 . 0.60
Max Size : 10 mm
14 Day Most Curing
Fibres : 0.25 mm × 0.25 mm
          × 20 mm
F_y = 770 N/mm²
t^s = 840 N/mm²

Relative Toughness

Relative Strength

Volume of Fibres

Fig. 12.5. Effect of Volume of Fibres in Flexure

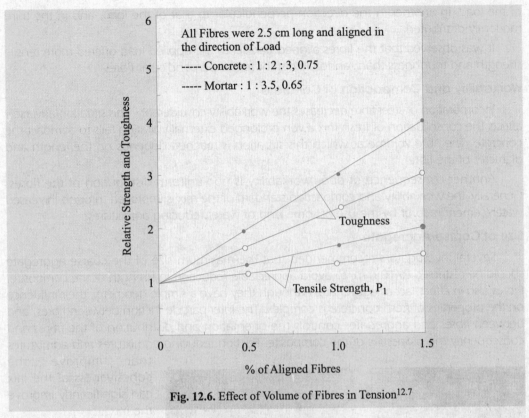

Fig. 12.6. Effect of Volume of Fibres in Tension[12.7]

Aspect Ratio of the Fibre

Another important factor which influences the properties and behaviour of the composite is the aspect ratio of the fibre. It has been reported that upto aspect ratio of 75, increase in the aspect ratio increases the ultimate strength of the concrete linearly. Beyond 75, relative strength and toughness is reduced. Table 12.10 shows the effect of aspect ratio on strength and toughness.

Table 12.10. Effect of Aspect Ratio on Strength and Toughness

Type of Concrete	Aspect Ratio	Relative strength	Relative toughness
Plain concrete	0	1.00	1.0
with	25	1.50	2.0
Randomly	50	1.60	8.0
dispersed fibres	75	1.70	10.5
	100	1.50	8.5

Orientation of Fibres

One of the differences between conventional reinforcement and fibre reinforcement is that in conventional reinforcement, bars are oriented in the direction desired while fibres are randomly oriented. To see the effect of randomness, mortar specimens reinforced with 0.5 per cent volume of fibres were tested. In one set specimens, fibres were aligned in the direction of the load, in another in the direction perpendicular to that of the load, and in the third randomly distributed.

It was observed that the fibres aligned parallel to the applied load offered more tensile strength and toughness than randomly distributed or perpendicular fibres.

Workability and Compaction of Concrete

Incorporation of steel fibre decreases the workability considerably. This situation adversely affects the consolidation of fresh mix. Even prolonged external vibration fails to compact the concrete. The fibre volume at which this situation is reached depends on the length and diameter of the fibre.

Another consequence of poor workability is non-uniform distribution of the fibres. Generally, the workability and compaction standard of the mix is improved through increased water/cement ratio or by the use of some kind of water reducing admixtures.

Size of Coarse Aggregate

Several investigators recommended that the maximum size of the coarse aggregate should be restricted to 10 mm, to avoid appreciable reduction in strength of the composite. Fibres also in effect, act as aggregate. Although they have a simple geometry, their influence on the properties of fresh concrete is complex. The inter-particle friction between fibres, and between fibres and aggregates controls the orientation and distribution of the fibres and consequently the properties of the composite. Friction reducing admixtures and admixtures that improve the cohesiveness of the mix can significantly improve the mix.

Steel wire fibre reinforced shotcrete

Mixing

Mixing of fibre reinforced concrete needs careful conditions to avoid balling of fibres, segregation, and in general the difficulty of mixing the materials uniformly. Increase in the aspect ratio, volume percentage and size and quantity of coarse aggregate intensify the difficulties and balling tendencies. A steel fibre content in excess of 2 per cent by volume and an aspect ratio of more than 100 are difficult to mix. The typical proportions for fibre reinforced concrete is given below:

Cement content	:	325 to 550 kg/m³
W/C Ratio	:	0.4 to 0.6
Percentage of sand to total aggregate	:	50 to 100 per cent
Maximum Aggregate Size	:	10 mm
Air-content	:	6 to 9 per cent

Fibre content   :   0.5 to 2.5 per cent by volume of mix

                               :   Steel —1 per cent 78 kg/m^3

                               :   Glass —1 per cent 25 kg/m^3

                               :   Nylon —1 per cent 11 kg/m^3

It is important that the fibres are dispersed uniformly throughout the mix, This can be done by the addition of fibres before the water is added. When mixing in a laboratory mixer, introducing the fibres through a wire mesh basket, will help even distribution of fibres. For field use, other suitable methods must be adopted.

Applications

Fibre reinforced concrete is increasingly used on account of the advantages of increased static and dynamic tensile strength, energy absorbing characteristics and better fatigue strength. The uniform dispersion of fibres throughout the concrete provides isotropic properties not common to conventionally reinforced concrete. Fibre reinforced concrete has been tried on overlays of air-field, road pavements, industrial floorings, bridge decks, canal lining, explosive resistant structures, refractory linings etc. The fibre reinforced concrete can also be used for the fabrication of precast products like pipes, boats, beams, stair case steps, wall panels, roof panels, manhole covers etc... Fibre reinforced concrete sometimes called fibrous concrete, is manufactured under the trade name "Wirand Concrete". After extensive research, the Wirand concrete is used very extensively in United States. Fibre reinforced concrete in also being tried for the manufacture of prefabricated formwork moulds of "U" shape for casting lintels and small beams.

Glass Fibre Reinforced Cement (GRC)

With the development of alkali resistant glass fibre (by trade name 'CEM-FIL) by the U.K. Building Research Establishment and Pilkington glass, U.K. a wide ranging applications of fibrous concrete is being made in many areas of building construction.[12.9] Glass reinforced cement consists of 4 to 4.5 per cent by volume of glass fibre mixed into cement or cement sand mortar. This glass reinforced cement mortar is used for fabricating concrete products having a sections of 3 to 12 mm in thickness. Methods of manufacture vary and include spraying, casting, spinning, extruding and pressing. Each technique imparts different characteristics to the end product. Spray deposition constitutes a very appropriate and by far the most developed method of processing. In the simplest form of spray processing, simultaneous sprays of cement or cement sand mortar slurry and chopped glass fibre are deposited from a dual spray gun into, or onto a suitable mould. Mortar slurry is fed to the spray gun from a metering pump unit and is atomised by compressed air. Glass fibre is fed to a chopper and feeder unit that is mounted on the same gun assembly. Glass reinforced cement (GRC) has been used for cladding of buildings, permanent and temporary formwork, pressure pipes, doors and doors frames, decorative grills, sun

Typical glass fibre

breakers, bus shelters and park benches. This will find its use in many application as building components.

Current Development in FRC

The following are the three new developments taking place in FRC.
- High fibre volume micro-fibre systems.
- Slurry infiltrated fibre Concrete (SIFCON).
- Compact reinforced composites.

High Fibre Volume Micro-fibre Systems

Micro-fibres are the fibres generally of size about 3 mm long and 5 to 25 μ in cross-section in contrast to macro-fibre of length about 25 mm and cross-section dimension of about 0.5 mm. The specific surface of micro-fibres is more than 200 cm²/gram in contrast to specific surface less than 20 cm²/gm.

Conventional mixing techniques and mix proportions usually lead to fibre balling, improper dispersion and poor workability in micro-fibre cements with large volumes of fiber. Various innovative techniques of mixing in mixers called omni mixer, use of admixtures such as carboxyl methyl cellulose, Silica fume and ground granulated blast furnace slag are practised. The System also requires large dosages of superplasticizers, low sand/cement ratio, longer mixing time and sand particles of size not exceeding one mm.

High fibre volume micro-fibre can replace asbestos fibre with improved properties of high toughness and much greater impact strength. These properties make it attractive for thin precast products such as roofing sheets, cladding panels etc. High fibre volume micro-fibres cement composite will be a very useful material for repair and rehabilitation works.

Slurry Infiltrated fibre Concrete

Slurry infiltrated fibre concrete (SIFCON) was invented by Lankard in 1979. Steel fibre bed is prepared and cement slurry is infiltrated. With this techniques, macro-fibre contents up to about 20% by volume can be achieved, with a consequent enormous increase in both flexural load carrying capacity and toughness. With such high fibre volume, a very high compressive strength is also achieved. SIFCON can be used for blast resistant structures and burglar proof safe vaults in banks and residential buildings.

Compact Reinforced Composites

Compact Reinforced Composites (CRC) is a material consisting of an extremely strong, dense cement matrix, 20 – 30% silica fume by weight of cement, 10 – 20% by volume off conventional reinforcement and 5 – 10% of fine fibres of 6 mm long and 0.15 mm diameter. While such a material is extremely expensive, it exhibits a flexural strength up to 260 MPa and compressive strength of about 200 MPa. It is a material almost as strong as structural steel. Advantage is that it can be moulded and fabricated at site.

Polymer Concrete

Continuous research by concrete technologists to understand, improve and develop the properties of concrete has resulted in a new type of concrete known as, "Polymer Concrete". It is referred time and again in the earlier chapters that the concrete is porous. The porosity is due to air-voids, water voids or due to the inherent porosity of gel structure itself. On account of the porosity, the strength of concrete is naturally reduced. It is conceived by many research workers that reduction of porosity results in increase of strength of concrete.

Therefore, process like vibration, pressure application spinning etc., have been practised mainly to reduce porosity. All these methods have been found to be helpful to a great extent, but none of these methods could really help to reduce the water voids and the inherent porosity of gel, which is estimated to be about 28%. The impregnation of monomer and subsequent polymerisation is the latest technique adopted to reduce the inherent porosity of the concrete, to improve the strength and other properties of concrete.

The pioneering work for the development of polymer concrete was taken up by United States Bureau of Reclamation (USBR). The initial exploratory works carried out at the Brookhaven National Laboratory (BNL) in cooperation with USBR and US in Atomic Energy Commission (AEC) revealed great improvement in compressive strength, permeability, impact resistance and abrasion resistance.

The development of concrete-polymer composite material is directed at producing a new material by combining the ancient technology of cement concrete with the modern technology of polymer chemistry.

Type of Polymer Concrete

Four types of polymer concrete materials are being developed presently. They are:

(a) Polymer Impregnated Concrete (PIC).

(b) Polymer Cement Concrete (PCC).

(c) Polymer Concrete (PC).

(d) Partially Impregnated and surface coated polymer concrete.

Polymer Impregnated Concrete (PIC)

Polymer impregnated concrete is one of the widely used polymer composite. It is nothing but a precast conventional concrete, cured and dried in oven, or by dielectric heating from which the air in the open cell is removed by vacuum. Then a low viscosity monomer is diffused through the open cell and polymerised by using radiation, application of heat or by chemical initiation.

Mainly the following types of monomer are used:

(a) Methylmethacrylate (MMA),

(b) Styrene,

(c) Acrylonitrile,

(d) *t*-butyl styrene,

(e) Other thermoplastic monomers.

The amount of monomer that can be loaded into a concrete specimen is limited by the amount of water and air that has occupied the total void space. It is necessary to know the concentration of water and air void in the system to determine the rate of monomer penetration. However, the main research effort has been towards obtaining a maximum monomer loading in concrete by the removal of water and air from the concrete by vacuum or thermal drying, the latter being more practicable for water removal because of its rapidity.

Another parameter to consider is evacuation of the specimen prior to soaking in monomer. This eliminates the entrapment of air towards the centre of the specimen during soaking which might otherwise prevent total or maximum monomer loading. The application of pressure is another technique to reduce monomer loading time.

Polymer Cement Concrete (PCC)

Polymer cement concrete is made by mixing cement, aggregates, water and monomer. Such plastic mixture is cast in moulds, cured, dried and polymerised. The monomers that are used in PCC are:

(a) Polyster-styrene.

(b) Epoxy-styrene.

(c) Furans.

(d) Vinylidene Chloride.

However, the results obtained by the production of PCC in this way have been disappointing and have shown relatively modest improvement of strength and durability. In many cases, materials poorer than ordinary concrete are obtained. This behaviour is explained by the fact that organic materials (monomers) are incompatible with aqueous systems and sometimes interfere with the alkaline cement hydration process.

Recently Russian authors have reported the production of a superior Polymer cement concrete by the incorporation of furfuryl alcohol and aniline hydrochloride in the wet mix. This material is claimed to be specially dense and non-shrinking and to have high corrosion resistance, low permeability and high resistance to vibrations and axial extension.

Washington State University in cooperation with Bureau of Reclamation tested the incorporation of several monomers into wet concrete for preparing PCC for fabrication of distillation units for water disalination plants. However, it is reported that only epoxy resin produced a concrete that showed some superior characteristics over ordinary concrete.

Polymer Concrete (PC)

Polymer concrete is an aggregate bound with a polymer binder instead of Portland cement as in conventional concrete.

The main technique in producing PC is to minimise void volume in the aggregate mass so as to reduce the quantity of polymer needed for binding the aggregates. This is achieved by properly grading and mixing the aggregates to attain the maximum density and minimum void volume. The graded aggregates are prepacked and vibrated in a mould. Monomer is then diffused up through the aggregates and polymerisation is initiated by radiation or chemical means. A silane coupling agent is added to the monomer to improve the bond strength between the polymer and the aggregate. In case polyester resins are used no polymerisation is required.

An important reason for the development of this material is the advantage it offers over conventional concrete where the alkaline Portland cement on curing, forms internal voids. Water can be entrapped in these voids which on freezing can readily crack the concrete. Also the alkaline Portland cement is easily attacked by chemically aggressive materials which results in rapid deterioration, whereas polymers can be made compact with minimum voids and are hydrophobic and resistant to chemical attack. The strength obtained with PC can be as high as 140 MPa with a short curing period.

However, such polymer concretes tend to be brittle and it is reported that dispersion of fibre reinforcement would improve the toughness and tensile strength of the material. The use of fibrous polyester concrete (FPC) in the compressive region of reinforced concrete beams provides a high strength, ductile concrete at reasonable cost. Also polyester concretes are viscoelastic in nature and will fail under sustained compressive loading at stress levels greater than 50 per cent of the ultimate strength. Therefore, polyester concrete should be considered for structures with a high ratio of live load to dead load and for composite structures in which the polymer concrete may relax during long-term loading. Experiments conducted on FPC composite beams have indicated that they are performance effective when compared to reinforced concrete beam of equal steel reinforcement percentage. Such beams utilise steel in the region of high tensile stress, fibrous polyester concrete (FPC) with its favourable compressive behaviour, in the regions of high compressive stress and Portland cement concrete in the regions of relatively low flexural stress.

Partially Impregnated (or Coated in Depth CID) and Surface Coated (SC) Concrete

Partial impregnation may be sufficient in situations where the major requirement is surface resistance against chemical and mechanical attack in addition to strength increase. Even with only partial impregnation, significant increase in the strength of original concrete has been obtained. The partially impregnated concrete could be produced by initially soaking the dried specimens in liquid monomer like methyl methacrylate, then sealing them by keeping them under hot water at 70°C to prevent or minimise loss due to evaporation. The polymerisation can be done by using thermal catalytic method in which three per cent by weight of benzoyl peroxide is added to the monomer as a catalyst. It is seen that the depth of monomer penetration is dependent upon following:

(a) Pore structure of hardened and dried concrete.

(b) The duration of soaking, and

(c) The viscosity of the monomer.

The potential application of polymer impregnated concrete surface treatment (surface coated concrete, SC) is in improving the durability of concrete bridge decks. Bridge deck deterioration is a serious problem everywhere, particularly due to a abrasive wear, freeze-thaw deterioration, spalling and corrosion of reinforcement. Excellent penetration has been achieved by ponding the monomer on the concrete surface. Due care should be taken to prevent evaporation of monomer when ponded on concrete surface. A 5 cms thick slab, on being soaked by MMA for 25 hours produced a polymer surface coated depth of 2.5 cms. Significant increases in the tensile and compressive strengths, modulus of elasticity and resistance to acid attack have been achieved.

The application of monomer for field application like in bridge decks poses more problems than laboratory application. A typical surface treatment in the field can be done in the following manner.

(a) The surface is dried for several days with electrical heating blanket.

(b) Remove the heating blanket and cover the slab with 0.64 m³ oven-dried light-weight aggregate per 100 sq.m.

(c) Apply initially 2,000 to 3,000 ml of the monomer system per square metre.

(d) Cover the surface with polyethylene to retard evaporation.

(e) Shade the surface to prevent temperature increase which might initiate polymerisation prematurely, that may reduce penetration into the concrete.

(f) Add periodically additional monomer to keep the aggregate moist for minimum soak time of 8 hours.

(g) Apply heat to polymerise the monomer. Heating blanket, steam or hot water can be used for this purpose.

Some of the promising monomer systems for this purpose are:

(a) Methylmethacrylate (MMA), 1% Benzoyl peroxide (BP), 10% Trimethylopropane trimethacrylate (TMPTMA).

(b) Isodecyl methacrylate (IDMA), 1% BP, 10% TMPTMA.

(c) Isobutyl methacrylate (IBMA), 1% BP, 10% TMPTMA.

BP acts as a catalyst and TMPTMA is a cross linking agent which helps in polymerisation at low temperature of 52%C.

Properties of Polymer Impregnated Concrete

Since Polymer impregnated concrete (PIC) is one of the most important category of polymer concrete, the properties of PIC is discussed below.

Stress-Strain Relationship

The stress-strain curve for MMA-impregnated concrete tested to failure is shown in Fig. 12.7. PIC has a nearly linear stress-strain relationship to failure. There is very little departure from linearity upto 90 per cent of ultimate strength and there is no abrupt change at the proportional limit. The stress strain curves for Styrene-TMPTMA impregnated concrete also show the same characteristics as for MMA impregnated concrete. The modulus of elasticity increased from 27 GPa for unimpregnated specimen to 49 GPa for MMA impregnated specimens.

Compressive Strength

The effect of polymer loading on the compressive strength in PIC is given in Fig. 12.8 Using methylemethacrylate as monomer and with a polymer loading of 6.4%, strength of the order of 144 MPa have been obtained using radiation technique of polymerisation. (The

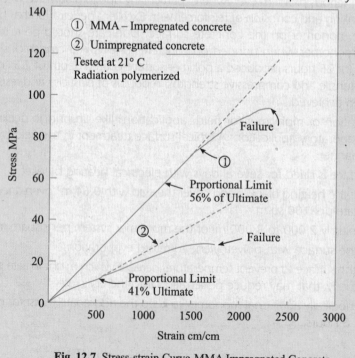

Fig. 12.7. Stress-strain Curve-MMA Impregnated Concrete.

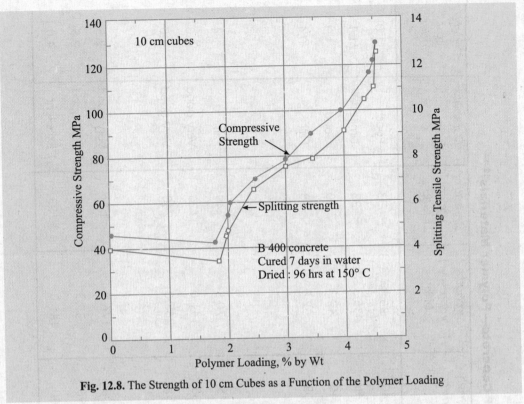

Fig. 12.8. The Strength of 10 cm Cubes as a Function of the Polymer Loading

control specimen had compressive strength of 38 MPa). The compressive strength obtained with thermal catalytic process was 130 MPa.

Styrene impregnated specimens exhibited similar trends, except that the strength levels were somewhat lower. The polymerisation by radiation method produced a concrete of higher strength than that produced by thermal catalytic method.

Perlite concrete impregnated with MMA and polyester styrene have also shown considerable increases in compressive strength. It is found that higher strengths are obtained with MMA impregnated sample than with polyster styrene. The average compressive strength for a 1 : 8 non-air entrained perlite concrete samples, impregnated with MMA was 56 MPa for a polymer loading of 63% compared to a control specimen of compressive strength 1.2 MPa.

Tensile Strength

The increase in tensile strength in the case of PIC has been observed to be as high as 3.9 times that of the control specimen for a polymer loading of 6.4% MMA *i.e.,* impregnated concrete have shown tensile strength of the order of 11.6 MPa compared to the strength of control specimen of 3 MPa using radiation process of polymerisation. Thermal catalytically initiated polymerisation, produced concrete with tensile strength 3.6 times that of the control specimen and 7.3 per cent less than that of radiation produced concrete.

PCC

Polymer cement concrete using polymer latex has given tensile strength of 5.8 MPa with a latex/cement ratio of 0.25; compared to the control specimen of 4.4 MPa strength. The increase in tensile strength is very modest.

Table 12.11. Classification of Concrete—Polymer Materials[12.14]

Type of concrete	Polymer Loading weight % (PMMA)	Density gm/cc	Strength (Compressive) MPa	Strength / Weight ratio	Durability	Benefit/ cost index
1. Conventional concrete control	0.0	2.40	35.3	33	Poor	1.0
2. Surface coating (SC) paint or overlay	0.0	2.40	35.3	33	Limited	1.1
3. Coating in Depth (CID)	1.0	2.40	42.3	40	Good	1.3
4. Polymer Cement Concrete (PCC) premix	35.0	2.08	52.8	58	Fair	0.4
5. Polymer Impregnated Concrete (PIC)						
Standard Aggregate						
a. Undried-dipped	2.0	2.45	70.5	49	Fair	1.4
b. Dried-evacuated-filled	6.0	2.55	141.0	126	Very good	2.0
c. High-Silica steam cured	8.0	2.55	268.0	240	Very good	3.0
Light-weight Aggregate						
a. Structural light-weight concrete	15.0	2.08	176.0	193	Very good	2.5
b. Insulated light-weight concrete	65.0	0.96	35.3	84	Very good	2.5
6. Polymer Concrete (PC) cement-less	6.0	2.40	141.0	133	Excellent	4.0

PC

Polyester resin concrete with binder content varying from 20 to 25% have shown tensile strengths in the range of 9 to 10 MPa at 7 days.

Flexural Strength

Polymer impregnated concrete with polymer loading of 5.6% MMA and polymerised by radiation have shown flexural strength 3.6 times more than that of the control specimen, i.e. the flexural strength was increased to 18.8 MPa from 5.2 MPa.

Polymer Concrete (PC)

Polyester resin concrete has been reported to give flexural strength of the order of 15 MPa at 7 days.

Creep

Compressive Creep deformation of MMA impregnated concrete and styrene—impregnated concrete has been observed to be in direction opposite to that of the applied load *i.e.*, Negative Creep. After the typical initial movement during load application, these concretes expand under sustained compression.

The reason for this negative creep in PIC is not very clear though it may be possible that it is due to residual stresses generated in the concrete after polymerisation of monomers. The increased volume may also be due to phase changes induced by pressure. This behaviour has been noticed at a relatively low loading of 5.7 MPa. Otherwise creep deformation of PIC concrete is generally one-tenth of conventional concrete, when compared on a basis of deformation per unit load. Creep deformation generally stabilises after two to three months.

Shrinking due to Polymerisation

Shrinkage occurs through two stages of impregnation treatment *i.e.*, through initial drying and through polymerisation. The shrinkage through polymerisation is peculiar to PIC and could be several times greater than the normal drying shrinkage.

It has been seen that for the same base material, different monomer systems cause different amounts of shrinkage. It is expected that the shrinkage due to polymerisation will be less for a base that has higher modulus of elasticity.

Durability

The saturation of the hydrated cement with corrosion resistant polymer probably acts as a protective coating and results in excellent improvement in durability.

(a) Freeze Thaw Resistance: Polymer impregnated concrete has shown excellent resistance to freeze-thaw MMA impregnated and radiation polymerised specimens have withstood 8110 cycles of freeze-thaw compared to 740 cycles in case of unimpregnated concrete. Even partially impregnated concrete withstood 2310 cycles.

(b) Resistance to Sulphate Attack: Keeping a failure criteria of 0.5% expansion, it has been observed that there is at least 200 per cent improvement in the resistance of polymer impregnated concrete and 89% improvement in the case of partially impregnated concrete over the conventional concrete.

(c) Acid Resistance: The acid resistance of PIC has been observed to improve by 1200 per cent, when exposed to 15% HCl for 1395 days.

Water Absorption

A maximum reduction of 95 per cent in water absorption has been observed with concrete containing 5.9 per cent polymer loading.

Co-efficient of Thermal Expansion

Polymer impregnated concrete has higher co-efficient of thermal expansion compared to conventional concrete. Compared to the unimpregnated concrete having a value of 4.02 x 10^{-6}, a 5.5% MMA, radiation polymerised concrete has a co-efficient of thermal expansion of 5.63 x10^{-6} and styrene impregnated specimens have shown a value off 5.10 x 10^{-6}.

Resistance to Abrasion

Polymer impregnated concrete has shown appreciable improvement in resistance to abrasion. A 5.5% MMA impregnated concrete has been found to be 50 to 80 per cent more resistant to abrasion than the control specimen. Even surface impregnated concrete slabs have shown an improvement of 20 to 50%.

Wear and Skid Resistance

Though there may be apprehension that polymer filled voids in polymer concrete might produce a slippery surface, on actual wear track test, it was found that the treated surfaces show excellent skid resistance compared to the unimpregnated surfaces. The wear after 50,000 simulated vehicular passes has been less than 0.025 cm.

Fracture of Polymer Impregnated Concrete

Polymer impregnation of concrete changes its microstructure radically resulting in a change in the cracking behaviour of the impregnated concrete under load. Impregnation improves the strength of the mortar matrix and also the strength of the paste-aggregate interface by elimination of microcracks. Polymer probably enters the aggregates also and forms a network of polymer fibres across the interface, thus strengthening it.

Radiographic studies have shown that microcracking starts first around 70 to 80% of the ultimate load, very often in the mortar phase. When an advancing crack reaches an aggregate, it does not follow the aggregate boundary as in ordinary concrete, but usually propagates through the aggregate. This indicates that the paste aggregate interface bond is significantly improved by polymer impregnation.

It has been observed that PIC indicates nearly linear behaviour to failure, which is typical of brittle material. The brittle nature of PIC presents a severe design limitation. It would be ideal to produce a material with the slow failure mode of normal concrete while retaining the high strength and modulus of elasticity of PIC.

One method to achieve this ideal is to adjust the paste aggregate bond so that the failure mode is through the interface like in ordinary concrete. In principle this can be achieved by using a very strong and tough aggregate, so that the advancing crack is diverted round to the paste-aggregate interface.

The fracture mode of PIC can also be altered by incorporating a small quantity (1% by volume) of fibres in the matrix. The fibres do not affect the modulus of elasticity of concrete due to their low concentration, but serve to inhibit crack propagation through the mortar by acting as crack arrestors. Table 12.11 shows properties of various type of polymer modified concretes.

Application of Polymer Impregnated Concrete

Keeping in view the numerous beneficial properties of the PIC, it is found useful in a large number of applications, some of which have been listed and discussed below:

(a) Prefabricated structural elements.

(b) Prestressed concrete.

(c) Marine works.

(d) Desalination plants.

(e) Nuclear power plants.

(f) Sewage works—pipe and disposal works.

(g) Ferrocement products.

(h) For water proofing of structures.

(i) Industrial applications.

(a) *Prefabricated Structural Elements:* For solving the tremendous problem of Urban housing shortage, maintaining quality, economy and speed, builders had to fall back on prefabricated techniques of construction. At present due to the low strength of conventional concrete, the prefabricated sections are large and heavy, resulting in costly handling and erection. These reasons have prevented wide adoption of prefabrication in many countries.

At present, the technique of polymer impregnation is ideally suited for precast concrete. It will find unquestionable use in industrialisation of building components. Owing to higher strength, much thinner and lighter sections could be used which enables easy handling and erection. They can be even used in high rise building without much difficulties.

(b) *Prestressed Concrete:* Further development in prestressed concrete is hindered by the inability to produce high strength concrete, compatible with the high tensile steel available for prestressing. Since PIC provides a high compressive strength of the order of 100 to 140 MPa, it will be possible to use it for larger spans and for heavier loads. Low creep properties of PIC will also make it a good material for prestressed concrete.

(c) *Marine Works:* Aggressive nature of sea water, abrasive and leaching action of waves and inherent porosity, impair the durability of conventional concrete in marine works. PIC, possessing high surface hardness, very low permeability and greatly increased resistance to chemical attack, is a suitable material for marine works.

(d) *Desalination Plants:* Desalination of sea water is being resorted to augment the shortage of surface and ground water in many countries. The material used in the construction of flash distillation vessels in such works has to withstand the corrosive effects of distilled water, brine and vapour at temperature upto 143°C. Carbon steel vessels which are currently in use are comparatively costly and deteriorate after prolonged use. Preliminary economic evaluation has indicated a savings in construction cost over that of conventional concrete by the use of PIC.

(e) *Nuclear Power Plants:* To cope up with the growing power requirements for industrial purposes, many countries are resorting to nuclear power generation.

The nuclear container vessel (pressure vessel) is a major element which is required to withstand high temperatures and provide shield against radiations. Another attendant problem of nuclear power generation is the containment of spent fuel rods which are radioactive over long period of time to avoid radiation hazards. At present heavy weight concrete is being used for this purpose, which is not very effective. PIC having high impermeability coupled with high strength and marked durability provide an answer to these problems.

(*f*) Sewage Disposal Works: It is common experience that concrete sewer pipes deteriorate due to the attack of effluents and when buried in sulphate infested soils. Further, in the sewage treatment plant, concrete structures are subjected to severe attack from corrosive gases particularly in sludge digestion tanks. Polymer-impregnated concrete due to its high sulphate and acid resistance will prove to be a suitable material in these situations.

(*g*) Impregnation of Ferrocement Products: The ferrocement techniques of construction is being extensively used in the manufacture of boats, fishing trawlers, domestic water tanks, grain storage tanks, manhole cove, etc. Ferrocement products are generally thin (1 to 4 cms) and as such are liable to corrode. Application of polymer impregnation techniques should improve the functional efficiency of ferrocement products.

(*h*) Water Proofing of Structures: Seepage and leakage of water through roof and bathroom slabs, is a nagging problem and has not been fully overcome by the use of conventional water proofing methods. The use of polymer impregnated mortar should solve this problem.

(*i*) Industrial Applications: Concrete has been used for floor in tanneries. Chemical factories, dairy farms and in similar situations for withstanding the chemical attack, but performance has not been very satisfactory. The newly developed PIC will provide a permanent solution for durable flooring in such situations.

SPECIAL CONCRETING METHODS

Cold Weather Concreting

The normal procedure adopted for concreting in fair weather will not be valid for concreting when the temperature is low or below the freezing point. In India, such areas are fairly small when compared to fair weather regions. The production of concrete in cold weather introduces special and peculiar problems, such as delay in setting and hardening, damage to concrete in plastic condition when exposed to below freezing point owing to the formation of ice lenses. Therefore, it is essential to maintain the temperature of the concrete positively above 0°C, possibly at much higher temperature.

Effects of Cold Weather on Concrete

(*a*) Delay in setting and hardening: Rate of hydration depends upon the temperature. If temperature is low, concrete takes a long time to set and a longer time to harden *i.e.*, for the development of strength. Fig. 12.9 shows the effect of ambient temperature on setting time. The delay in setting time makes concrete vulnerable to frost attack and other disturbances. Delay in hardening period does not facilitate removal of formwork in a short period. Also the rate of progress of work will be very slow, all of which affects economy.

(*b*) Freezing of concrete at early age: When the temperature goes below freezing point, the free water contained in the plastic concrete freezes. Freezing of water, not only prevents the hydration of cement but also makes the concrete expand. This expansion causes disruption of concrete due to which irrepairable loss of strength and quality takes place.

(*c*) Freezing and Thawing: It is likely that due to varied behaviour of climatic conditions in the cold weather regions, the fresh concrete or hardened concrete gets subjected to freezing and thawing cycles. The durability of concrete gets greatly impaired due to this alternate freezing and thawing. Freezing and thawing may also exert fatigue in the concrete.

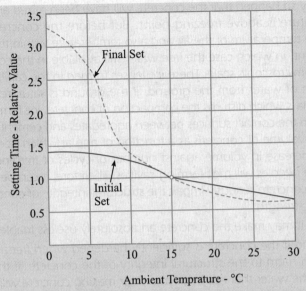

Fig. 12.9. Setting time of Ordinary Portland Cement at Different Temperatures
as a Proportion of Setting time at 15°C

In dealing with the aspect of cold weather concerting, the following conditions may be discussed.

(a) Low temperature, but above 0°C at the time of concreting and later during hardening period.

(b) Low temperature at the time of concreting but below 0°C during the hardening period.

(c) Temperature below 0°C at the time of concreting and during hardening period.

(d) Hardened concrete subjected to alternate freezing and thawing.

It is necessary to deal with the above four conditions to understand the behaviour of concrete clearly and to take appropriate steps to offset the harmful effects of such conditions for the successful placing of concrete.

Low Temperature but above 0°C

If the temperature is only low but always above the freezing point, it only retards the rate of development of strength as shown in the maturity equations stated earlier. There is no other bad effect on the fresh concrete or hardening concrete. As a matter of fact, the ultimate strength of the concrete cured at 9°C has been found to be of a higher order than that of the concrete cured at higher temperature. This may be due to the surperiority of gel structure on account of slow growth. No other precautions are necessary except recognition of the fact of delayed strength for stripping the formwork or for putting the concrete into service.

Low Temperature at the Time of Concreting but Below 0°C after Concreting

The first condition has been discussed in the above para. But after concreting, if the temperature falls below 0°C, it is again necessary to view the conditions under the following two catagories:

(a) Temperature falling below 0°C when the concrete is still green.

(b) Temperature prevailing below 0°C after the concrete is sufficiently hardened.

Many times it may so happen that the concrete will have been mixed and placed when the ambient temperature is above freezing point. But before the concrete has attained sufficient strength, the temperature of the air and also temperature within the concrete may fall below freezing point, in which case the free water still available in the concrete to freeze and form ice lenses in microscopic scale. These ice lenses formed in the capillary cavities may cause capillary suction of water from the ground, if the ground is saturated, and become bigger to disrupt the mass which disturbs the compaction of concrete. Ice formations may also appear as ice needles in the contact surfaces between aggregates and cement paste. Fig. 9.18 shows the increase in volume of concrete as a function of age at which freezing starts. Fig. 9.19 also shows the increase in volume against number of cycles of freezing and thawing. After thawing these ice needles will melt forming cavities. Therefore, it can be concluded that freezing of freshly laid concrete seriously impair the structural integrity of concrete and results in considerable loss of strength.

In extreme cases, it may make the concrete an absolutely useless friable mass.

On the other hand if the concrete is sufficiently hardened when freezing takes place, there will not be much harm to the structural integrity of the concrete. If the concrete has sufficiently hardened, the water that has been mixed for making concrete will have been lost either being used up in hydration process or lost by evaporation. Due to the formation of cement gels, the capillary cavities also will have been very much reduced, with the results that there exists very little of free water in the body of concrete to freeze. Therefore, firstly the magnitude of volume change due to the formation of microscopic ice lens is much less. Secondly, the concrete at this stage is strong enough to resist whatever osmotic pressure resulting from the freezing. Therefore, there is no immediate danger to the concrete.

Temperature Below 0°C at the Time of Concreting and During Hardening Period

Certain precautions are absolutely necessary for concreting when the temperature is below 0°C, so that the fresh concrete does not get frozen. The consequences of freezing of fresh concrete and the effect of sub-zero temperature on the hardened but not fully matured concrete has been explained in the above para. Precautions to be taken and methods for carrying out concreting operations will be explained later.

Hardened Concrete subjected to Alternate Freezing and Thawing

Concrete pavements constructed at high altitude is normally subjected to alternate freezing and thawing. The interval of cycles may be between season to season or between day and night or even a couple of times in a day. It has been found that the durability of hardened concrete is reduced to 1/3 to 1/7 when it is subjected to alternate freezing and thawing depending on the quality of concrete.

It is to be noted that concrete is a pervious material. Degree of porosity is depending upon the Gel/space ratio. A concrete member is likely to get saturated due to the absorption of moisture from surface or from bed. The free water that has filled the capillary cavities of concrete will get frozen with the fall of temperature. Subsequently when the temperature goes above 0°C, the ice lens melts. Due to this alternate freezing and thawing, concrete is subjected to distress and surface scaling. The distress of concrete can be measured by the loss of weight against number of cycles of freezing as shown in Fig. 5.18.

Concreting Methods at Sub-zero Temperature

Having discussed the effect of sub zero-temperature on fresh concrete, hardening concrete and hardened concrete, it is clear that fresh concrete should not be subjected to freezing condition till such time it attains a certain amount of strength. This time interval is known as 'Pre-hardening Period'. The recommended pre-hardening period as recommended by IS 7861 (Part-2)—1979 is given in the following table:

Table No. 12.12. Time Taken by Different Grades of Concrete

Specified minimum strength at 28 days for ordinary Portland cement MPa	Requisite Pre-hardening period			
	At any concrete temperature above freezing in units of maturity °C hr	At stated conctrete temperature in hours.		
		20°C	10°C	5°C
M 20	1050	35	53	70
M 25	780	26	39	52
M 30	660	22	33	44
M 40	480	16	24	32

The precautions to be taken and methods adopted for concreting in sub-zero temperature is listed below:

(a) Utilisation of the heat developed by the hydration of cement and practical methods of insulation.

(b) Selection of suitable type of cement.

(c) Economical heating of materials of concrete.

(d) Admixtures of anti-freezing materials.

(e) Electrical heating of concrete mass.

(f) Use of air-entraining agents.

An enormous quantity of heat is generated in the hydration of cement. If this heat is preserved within the body of the concrete for a duration equal to the prehardening period, it can do the useful job of offsetting the harmful effect of low temperature. To conserve the heat the concrete can be insulated by a membrane, burlap, saw dust or hessain cloth. In case of beams and columns, keeping the formwork without stripping is a good step to conserve the heat, in concrete. In case of very low temperature, it is very necessary that the insulation of concrete be so efficient as to keep the surface temperature of concrete higher than 0°C during pre-hardening period.

Certain type of cement, hydrates fast, in turn gives out much larger quantity of heat and develops early strength. The pre-hardening period for such a cement will be about 40 to 50% of the normal Portland cement. Such cement contains higher percentage of tricalcium silicate (C_3S) and comparatively lower percentage of dicalcium silicate (C_2S). Rapid hardening cement is one such cement that can be used. Extra rapid hardening cement. High Alumina cement or mixture of ordinary Portland cement and high alumina cement in certain proportions can also be used for this purpose. All the above will only reduce the time for which the concrete is vulnerable to frost attack.

Preheating of the materials of concrete is one of the methods very commonly employed in sub-zero temperature concreting. Heating of water is the easiest to be adopted. If the ambient temperature is not very low, heating of water alone will be sufficient, if the aggregates and cement are not in frozen condition. The Figures 12.10, (a), 12.10 (b) and 12.10 (c) show

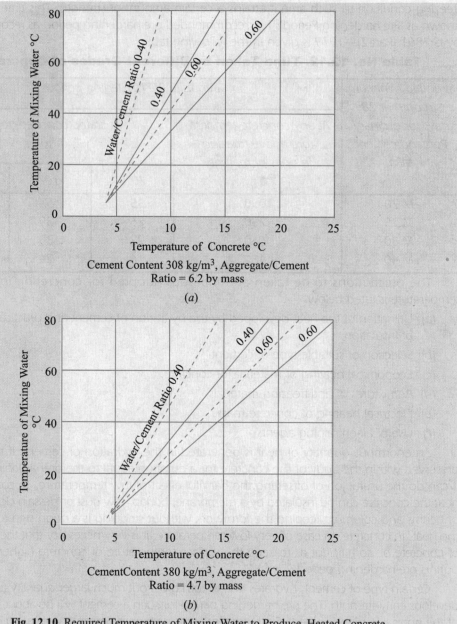

Cement Content 308 kg/m³, Aggregate/Cement
Ratio = 6.2 by mass

(*a*)

CementContent 380 kg/m³, Aggregate/Cement
Ratio = 4.7 by mass

(*b*)

Fig. 12.10. Required Temperature of Mixing Water to Produce Heated Concrete.

the temperature to which the water should be heated to maintain the temperature of the resultant concrete at a stipulated temperature for different aggregate/cement ratio and cement content. As can be seen for the figure, the desirable concrete temperature can be achieved by heating water alone provided the aggregates are free from ice and the formwork and top surface are properly insulated. In case of very low temperature or if it is estimated that a good amount of heat is lost in transportation and placing, the heating of mixing water alone may prove to be inadequate to maintain the required temperature in concrete. In such cases, aggregate is also heated either by closed steam coils under the stock piles or by injecting live steam into the stock piles or by hot air blowers. Fine aggregate can also be heated on hot plates. Overheating of aggregates should be avoided. Cement should never be heated.

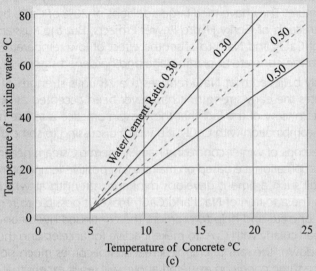

Fig. 12.10. Required Temperature of Mixing Water to Produce Heated Concrete.

Note: — Moisture content of fine aggregate 4 per cent and that of coarse aggregate 1 per cent (damp)
          — Moisture content of fine aggregate 8 per cent and that of coarse aggregate and 2 per cent (wet)
          — Temperature of aggregate and contained moisture = 1°C
          — Temperature of cement = 5°C.

To maintain the prehardening temperature, electrical heating of the entire mass of concrete may be adopted where plenty of cheap power is available. Only alternating current should be used for this purpose. Electricity is conducted through mats or reinforcing bars. Sometimes special electrodes are carefully positioned in such a way that uniform heat is generated. In order to protect the workers, only low current should be used. The heating has to be designed very carefully including the voltage, the type and location of the electrodes as well as heating for each element. Evaporation of the mixing water has to be restricted by covering the entire surface effectively with vapour tight memberane.

Inspite of these precautions it is found that the strength of electrically heated concrete is about 20% less than normally cured concrete because of water loss and temperature stresses caused by the cooling of the heated concrete. Electrical heating is justified only in very cold climatic conditions where cheap power is available, but it has the disadvantage of high cost of installation, power consumption and loss of strength. In Sweden, Russia, and Japan electrical curing is being used quite extensively for protecting concrete from frost.

One of the widely adopted practices in winter concreting is the use of accelerating admixtures which incidentally works as antifreeze also. The most commonly employed material is calcium chloride. There are divergent views about the quantity of calcium chloride to be admixed for optimum results. Many specifications do not permit the use of more than 3% $CaCl_2$ by weight of cement for fear of flash set and loss of long term strength. However, there are other reports that the $CaCl_2$ can be used in much higher quantity where the temperature is very low, without any fear of retrogression of strength or corrosion of reinforcement. But the use $CaCl_2$ may cause some increase in volume change, greater tendency for alkali aggregate reaction and lower resistance to sulphate attack.

It is reported that in Russia the use of chlorides are extensively employed for concreting at subzero temperature. They have tried large additions of 20% of $CaCl_2$ by weight of mixing water in the construction of Gorky Hydro Power Projects. But the Russian practice is to use the combination of $CaCl_2$ and $NaCl$ to offset the effect of low temperature and also to give optimum benefit to the concrete at plastic stage and hardened stage.

It is commonly believed that $NaCl$ reduces the 28 days strength of concrete by 12% though it accelerates the early strength. It has never been accepted as one of the standard accelerating agent. In view of the fact that the Russian practice is to use high concentration of $NaCl$ or $NaCl$ in combination with $CaCl_2$, it is worth discussing to some detail in this regard.

All existing methods of winter concreting namely thermos, steam heating, electric heating or their combined application are based on maintaining positive temperatures during the early age of concrete, till such a time it develops minimum strength at which freezing has no detrimental effect. The addition of $NaCl$ and $CaCl_2$ makes it possible to regulate the freezing point of water in concrete and help to promote the continued hydration. $CaCl_2$ forms high hydro-complexes particularly with C_3A, to make it active for accelerating the hydration. As the temperature goes down, the rate of chemical reaction becomes much slower. If $NaCl$ alone is added, almost the same condition as stated above will result except that it exhibits a better plasticising properties. But it is found that if a combination of $CaCl_2$ and $NaCl$ is used, the concrete will show quicker hardening property, a much higher frost resistance property and also better placeability characteristics.

The suggested quantities of the salt mixture is shown in Table 12.13.

It was seen that very little corrosion has taken place in the reinforcing bars even with large addition of salts, when the concrete is compacted well. The corrosion problems become serious only in the case of insufficient compaction and lack of cover for reinforcing steel.

Till recently concrete technologists were of the view that durability of concrete is dependant upon the compressive strength only. But with the innovation of air-entrained concrete, the opinion got reversed. It is now known that weaker concrete with air-entrainment is more durable under freezing condition than that of strong concrete without air-entrainment. The superiority of air-entrained concrete over plain concrete is shown in fig. 5.18. In general the entrainment of air will increase durability to the extent of about 3 to 7 times of that of ordinary concrete.

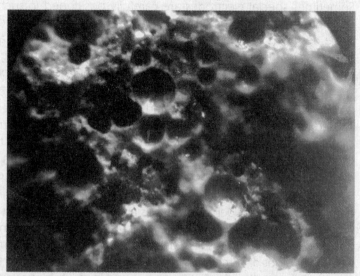

Photograph (25 times magnification) showing the presence of air-entrainment in hardened concrete, generated by Ritha powder as air-entraining admixture. *(source M.E. Dissertation work of M.S. Shetty —1964)*

Table 12.13. Addition of the appropriate quantity of CaCl₂ and NaCl in winter concreting

Open Air temperature	Percentage contents of salts per degree fall of temperature by weight of mixing water	Quantity of CaCl₂ and NaCl by weight of mixing water
From 0°C to −5°C	1.3	3% CaCl₂ + 3.5% NaCl or 6.5% NaCl or 6.5 CaCl₂
From −6°C to −10°C	1.2	4% CaCl₂ + 8% NaCl or 12% NaCl or 6% CaCl₂ + 6% NaCl
From −11°C to −15°C	1.1	10% CaCl₂ + 6% NaCl or 8% CaCl₂ + 8% NaCl
From −16°C to −20°C	1.0	15% CaCl₂ + 5% NaCl or 10% CaCl₂ + 10% NaCl

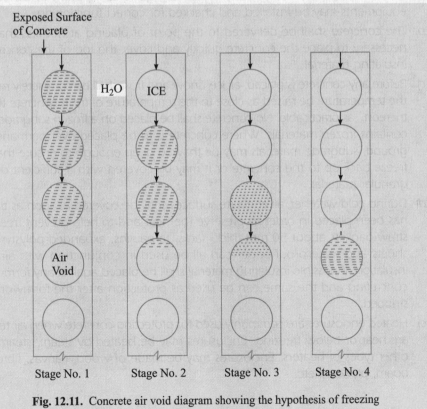

Fig. 12.11. Concrete air void diagram showing the hypothesis of freezing

Modification of pore structure caused by air-entrainment is believed to be responsible for the marked improvement in resistance to frost attack. The hypothesis as to how the air-entrainment enhances the resistance of concrete to freezing and thawing is shown in Fig. 12.11. It is assumed that the concrete member is wet and quick freezing occurs. The surface is immediately sealed due to the freezing of water at the surface and when freezing continues ice crystals are formed inside the voids. Since the volume of ice is 10% more than that of water, only 90% of water in the voids will turn into ice. The excess of water is forced out through the capillary channels into the adjoining lower air-voids, and the pressure is relieved. Stage No. 3 and 4 show progressive freezing and relief of pressure in the interior of concrete. If sufficient water free voids are available, pressure build up will not occur and the eventual disruption of the concrete will not take place.

The reduction in water cement ratio that might be permitted by the use of air entrainment in concrete may also account for the greater resistance to freezing and thawing action.

From the above discussion, it can be seen that the use of air-entraining admixtures in concrete is positively useful in increasing the durability of concrete in very cold regions.

To summerise, the following general precautions may be observed in cold weather concreting:

(a) Preparation for concreting in cold weather may be completed well in advance of severe conditions. Wind breakers shall be erected to shield the mixing and batching plants; tarpaulins, plastic sheets and other covering and insulating materials may be made available at the site and the steam generating plant or other necessary equipments may be installed and checked for correct functioning.

(b) The concrete shall be delivered to the point of placing at not less than 5°C. It is necessary to place the concrete quickly and cover the top of the concrete with an insulating material.

(c) Before any concrete is placed, all ice, snow and frost shall be completely removed and the temperature be raised as close to the temperature of fresh concrete to be placed thereon, as practicable. No concrete shall be placed on a frozen subgrade or on that contains frozen materials. Where concrete is to be placed over permanently frozen ground, subgrade materials may be thawed deep enough to ensure that it will not freeze back up to the concrete or it may be covered with a sufficient depth of dry granular material.

(d) During cold weather, all concrete surfaces shall be covered as soon as the concrete has been placed in order to preserve the heat and to help prevent freezing. Clean straw bankets about 50 mm thick, sacks, tarpaulins, expanded polystyrene, plastic sheets and waterproof paper can all be used in conjunction with air gap as an insulation. If possible insulating material shall be placed against any formwork before concreting and the same can be used as protection after the formwork has been stripped.

(e) Heated enclosures are commonly used for protecting concrete when air temperatures are near or below freezing. Enclosures may be heated by steam, steam pipes and other types of heaters. Enclosures may be made of wood, canvas, fibre insulation board, plywood etc.

(f) During placement of unformed concrete, tarpaulins or other readily movable coverings supported on frame work shall follow closely the placing of concrete, so that only a small area of finished slab is exposed to outside air at any time.

Such tarpaulins shall be used so that hot air can be circulated freely on the slab. Layers of insulating materials placed directly on the concrete are also effective in protecting the concrete.

(g) During periods of freezing or near-freezing conditions, water curing is not necessary as the loss of moisture from the concrete by evaporation will be greatly reduced in cold air conditions.

(h) For concrete cast in insulated formwork it is only necessary to cover the member completely in order to retain sufficient water for the hydration of cement. On removal of the formwork and insulation, the member shall immediately be covered with plastic sheet or tarpaulins, properly lapped and made air-tight. On no account should such concrete, just released from insulated formwork, be saturated with cold water. When protective measures are to be discontinued, the surface temperature of the concrete shall be gradually adjusted to the air temperature.

(i) Low pressure wet steam provides the best means of both heating the enclosures and for moist curing the concrete. Early curing with liquid membrane forming compounds may be followed on concrete surface with heated enclosures. It is better to cure first with steam curing during the initial period of protection and then apply a curing compound after the protection is removed and the air temperature is above freezing.

(j) Forms shall not be released until the concrete has achieved a strength of at least twice the stress to which the concrete may be subjected at the time of removal of formwork. In the normal circumstances where ambient temperature does not fall below 15°C and where OPC cement is used and adequate curing is done, the striking period as shown in Table.12.14 is a satisfactory guideline. For other cements and lower temperature, the stripping time recommended in Table 12.14. may be suitably modified.

(k) In cold weather protection offered by formworks other than of steel, is often of greater importance. With suitable insulations, the forms, including those of steel, in many cases will provide adequate protection without supplementary heating. Therefore, it is often advantageous not to remove forms until the end of a minimum period of protection or even later.

(l) During cold weather, inspection personnel should keep a record of the date, time, outside air temperature, temperature of concrete at the time of placing and general weather (calm, windy, clear, cloudy, etc.). The record should also include the temperature at several points within the enclosure and on the concrete surface, corners and edges in sufficient number to show the highest and lowest temperatures of the concrete.

Thermometers should be inserted in those parts of the concrete where maximum stresses will appear at removal of forms.

To control the hardening process, it is necessary to measure the temperature of concrete at placing, at the time of applying the protection and three times each day until resistance to freezing has been obtained.

Concreting in winter times, requires that the quality control of concrete is carried with great care. The test results should be used for fixing the time of removal of insulations and formwork. Control test specimens should also be cast and cured in a standard way to indicate the potential strength properties of the mix.

In addition to the control test cubes, it is necessary to cast a number of specimens, the curing conditions of which are maintained in the same way as that of the actual structure. These specimens are tested before stripping the formwork to indicate the strength development of the actual structures.

Hot Weather Concreting

Normal methods of mixing, transporting and placing of concrete discussed in Chapter No. 6, will not be exactly applicable to extreme weather conditions. Special problems are faced in making, placing and compacting concrete in hot weather and in cold weather. In India most of the areas are in tropical regions and some areas in extremely cold weather regions. Therefore, it is necessary for us to be aware of the special problems faced in making concrete structures in both hot weather and cold weather regions. The procedure of concreting in such a situation is set out in IS 7861 (Part I) ans IS 7861 (Part II).

Table No. 12.14.

Recommended Minimum Time Limits for stripping Formwork to Normal Structural Concrete when the Member is carrying only its own Weight as per IS 456 of 2000.

Type of Formwork	Minimum Period Before Striking Formwork
(1) Vertical formwork to Columns, Walls, Beam	16 – 24 hours
(2) Soffit formwork to slabs (Props to be refixed immediately after removal of formwork)	3 days
(3) Soffit formwork to Beams (Props to be refixed immediately after removal of formwork)	7 days
(4) Props to Slabs	
(a) Spanning up to 4.5 m	7 days
(b) Spanning over 4.5 m	14 days
(5) Props to Beams and Arches	
(a) Spanning up to 6 m	14 days
(b) Spanning over 6 m	21 days

It is difficult to define what is hot weather condition. However, just for convenience it is regarded that the concrete placed at an atmospheric temperature above 40°C is considered as hot weather concreting. At this temperature certain special problems are usually encountered. They are:-

(a) Rapid rate of hydration of cement, quick setting and early stiffening.

(b) Rapid evaporation of mixing water.

(c) Greater plastic shrinkage.

(d) Less time for finishing.

(e) Reduced relative humidity.

(f) Absorption of water from the concrete by the subgrade and formwork.

(g) Difficulty in continuous and uninterrupted curing.

(h) Difficulty in incorporation of air entrainment.

The effect of the above situations on the production of quality concrete is required to be fully identified and care must be taken to make the concrete strong and durable.

(a) Rapid rate of hydration: It is brought out in chapter one that the rate of hydration depends upon the temperature. At high ambient temperature the setting time of the cement is reduced considerably. It must be remembered that the setting time as discussed earlier pertains to a temperature range of 27 ± 2°C. At a higher temperature, naturally setting time will be reduced with the result that early stiffening takes place which makes the concrete lose the workability. Partially set concrete may reduce the bond between the successive lifts more than anticipated.

This is also pointed out that the quality of gel and gel structure formed at higher temperature in the early period of hydration is of poor quality. Concrete placed in hot weather no doubt develops high early strength, but it will suffer certain loss of long term strength. Fig. 12.12 shows the effect of curing temperature on one day and 28 days compressive strength.

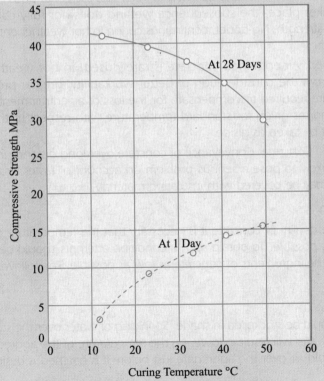

Fig. 12.12. Effect of curing temperatures on 1-day and 28-day compressive strength of concrete

(*b*) Rapid evaporation of mixing water: Hot weather condition is normally associated with relatively lower relative humidity. On account of this, the water mixed with the concrete to give the required workability will be lost. The concrete turns to be unworkable with the result, inordinate amount of compacting effort is required to compact concrete fully. If this is not forthcoming, large voids will remain in the concrete, which are responsible for all the ills in concrete.

(*c*) Greater plastic shrinkage: The rate of evaporation of water from the surface of the concrete will be faster than the rate of movement of water from the interior to the surface. As a result, a moisture gradient will be set up which results in surface cracks known as plastic shrinkage cracks. The plastic shrinkage is more pronounced, in case of floors, roads and pavement concrete where the surface area exposed is more when compared to depth.

(*d*) Finishing time: In hot weather, finishing must be done as early as possible after placing. In certain cases if early finishing is not possible due to faster stiffening and quicker evaporation of water, the quality of finishing will be of poor standard. Usually extra fresh mortar is required to be used for finishing which results in poor performance.

(*e*) Absorption of water by subgrade: In hot weather regions the subgrade is normally dry and absorptive. The subgrade or surface of formwork is required to be wetted before placing the concrete. If this is not done carefully with proper considerations, the water in the concrete may be lost by absorption by the surface in contact with concrete making the contact zone poorer in quality.

(*f*) Curing: In hot weather comparatively early curing becomes necessary, particularly where 53 grade cement is used. Hot weather requires a continuous effort for curing. If there is any lapse, the concrete surface dries up fast and interrupts the continuous hydration. Once the interruption takes place, the subsequence wetting does not fully contribute to the development of full strength. No doubt, continuous curing in hot weather entails greater cost of water and labour.

(*g*) Air-Entrained: Air-entrained concrete is rarely used in hot weather conditions. However, if used from the consideration of better workability, greater proportion of air-entraining agents are required to compensate for the loss of air-entrainment due to higher temperature. The norms given for standard temperature with respect to the per cent air-entrainment cannot be taken as guide.

(*h*) Ready Mixed Concrete: Conveyance of concrete over long distance in case of Ready Mixed Concrete is likely to pose a serious problem on account of faster loss of slump. The transit mixer drum may be covered with insulating material.

Precautions Taken

To improve the quality of concrete it is necessary that the temperature of the concrete should be as low as possible. To obtain such a condition attempts should be made to keep the temperature of the ingredients of concrete as low as possible. The following precautions could be taken.

Aggregates

Aggregates should be stockpiled in shade. Sprinkling of water over the stockpile and the evaporation of this water will result in lowering the temperature of the aggregate. If possible heavy spraying of cold air over the aggregate just before it is batched is desirable.

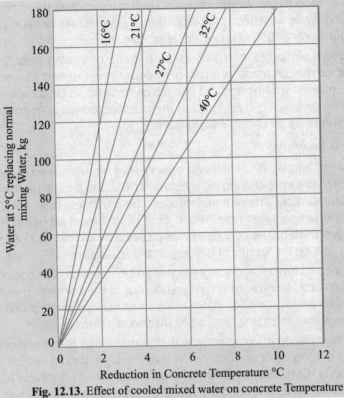

Fig. 12.13. Effect of cooled mixed water on concrete Temperature

Water

The temperature of the mixing water has the greatest effect on the temperature of concrete. In practice the temperature of water is easier to control than that of the other

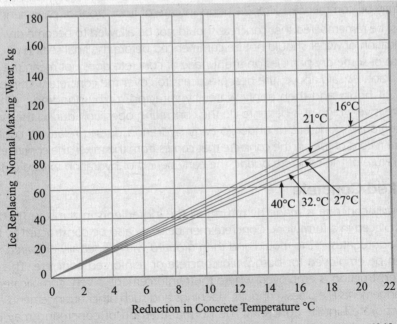

Fig. 12.14. Effect of ice in mixing water on concrete Temperature[12.15]

ingredients. Even though the weight of water used is lesser than the other ingredients, the use of cold mixing water will effect good reduction of concrete temperature. Fig. 12.13 shows the effect of cold water at 5°C on concrete temperature.[12.15]

If the ambient temperature is very high, the use of cooled water may not be fully effective. Use of ice may be made as a part of mixing water. Crushed ice can be incorporated directly into the mixer. It shall be ensured that ice crystals should be completely melted by the time mixing is completed. Fig. 12.14 shows the possible reduction in concrete temperature by the substitution of ice as part of mixing water.

Production and Delivery

Temperature of aggregates, water and cement shall be maintained at the lowest practical level so that the temperature of concrete is below 40°C at the time of placement. Some works demand the maximum placement temperature to be much less than 40°C. The concrete is mixed to the minimum required time. When ice is used it must be mixed to such an extent that all the ice gets melted. The concrete mixer must be positioned as close to the final place of deposition to reduce the length of delivery to the minimum.

Reinforcement, formwork and subgrade should be sprinkled with cooled water just prior to placing the concrete. Reinforcement projecting out of the concrete should be covered or kept cooled by any practical means. More number of masons are required to be employed to finish the concrete at the same rate as the placing of concrete.

The concrete is placed in comparatively thin layers so that the time interval between the successive lifts is reduced. It should be noted that the layer should not be so thin as to get dried up very early. Concrete on finishing must be covered effectively to prevent loss of moisture from the concrete. Covering the top of concrete by wet gunny bag or hessain cloth is desirable. Precautions should be taken to squeeze the gunny bag fully so that water does not drip into the fresh concrete. Covering of finished floor by wet gunny bags may not be very suitable for flooring where surface finish is of primary importance. Wet curing must be commenced at the earliest possible time. If the concrete is effectively moist covered, the ponding may be commenced after 24 hours in case of floor, roof or pavements.

It must be remembered that concrete should not be allowed to become dry. At the same time, application of water should not be commenced before the final setting of cement also. Appearance of some dry particles on the surface of concrete does not mean the final setting has taken place. As said above, the best practice is to cover the concrete with moist covering for about 24 hours and then apply water by spraying, or by ponding., When the day temperature is very high, it is better to do the concreting operation during the evening time, leaving the young concrete to undergo early hydration during relatively cooler night. A temperature record of the air, the concrete that comes from the mixer, the concrete placed and the temperature of the concrete during the early period of hydration will be of help.

Pre-Packed Concrete

Generally concrete is made by mixing all the ingredients in a mixer. Then the mixed concrete is placed in a formwork. Concrete member may also be constructed by first placing the coarse aggregates in the mould and then grouted with a specially prepared mortar. This process can be employed for both plain concrete or reinforced concrete. This method of concrete construction is employed where the reinforcement is very complicated or where certain arrangements like pipes, conduits, openings and such other arrangements are required to be incorporated in the concrete. The normal method of concreting may disturb the preplanned fitments. This method is also employed in mass concreting, in bridge abutments and piers, well steining etc. This is one of the practicable methods of concreting under water, wherein aggregates are placed in water and subsequently mortar is grouted in, to displace the water.

There are many proprietary methods in vogue. They are called, intrusion grouting, grouted concrete, pre-packed concrete colcrete process etc.

The advantages of pre-packed concrete are that it undergoes little drying shrinkage. As the aggregates are in point contact with each other and the grout only fills the voids, the concrete as a whole does not undergo much drying shrinkage. Vibrating the aggregate before grouting makes the quality of concrete better. Both single sized or graded aggregates can be used without much difficulty.

The essential requirement is that the grout should fill the voids fully and develop full bond with the aggregate. The right extent of pressure is applied so that the grout, just fills the aggregate, but does not disturb or lift up the aggregate. Sometimes, the workability agent or expanding admixture such as aluminium powder are also added. The grouting pressure is changed depending upon the depth at which the injection of grout is done. The grout mixture should be sufficiently fluid for pumping. The fairly thick grout, well mixed in high speed machine, which has got a pumpable consistancy is referred to as colloidal grout. Such grout can travel uniformly into the aggregate voids. The fluidity of grout and keeping its identity while pushing the water out in case of underwater grouting, is the property to be looked for in the grout.

In the Colcrete process, the mortar grout is made in a special high speed, double drum type of mixer in which cement and water are mixed in one drum and the sand is added and mixed with the cement slurry in the second drum. The high speed action of the mixers produce a very intimate mix, which is more fluid than a normal grout and is comparatively immiscible with water. The ratio of the grout may range from $1 : 1^1/_4$ to $1 : 4$, the rich being used for underwater work or for grouting prestressed concrete members.

Grouting is done by there methods:

(a) Grout mixture is poured on the packed aggregate and allowed to penetrate downwards. This method is normally adopted for thin concrete members, such as, road pavement slabs and floor slabs. If the depth of the aggregate bed is thicker, it cannot be assumed that the grout has completely traversed through the entire thickness.

(b) The mould is partially filled up with grout over which the aggregates are deposited. Vibration at this stage would help distributing sinking and smearing of paste over the aggregate.

(c) The grout is pumped into the prepacked aggregate at the bottom of the mould. The injection pipe full of perforations, one or more in number distribute the grout into the concrete. This injection pipe is extracted upwards by a certain distance and again the grout mixture is sent. In this way the entire depth of the concrete member is concreted. It should be noted that less pressure is to be used to inject the grout into the top layers of concrete.

Alternatively perforated horizontal pipes are embedded in the prepacked aggregate at different levels. Grout may be sent through these pipes. Finally, it is possible to withdraw the pipe or the pipe may be left in the concrete.

Sometimes, if the grout is forced at a high pressure without any regard to the over burden pressure of packed aggregate, the pressure may cause dislodging of the aggregate with the result that excess of grout may be consumed. Therefore, the pressure at which the intrusion of grouting is to be used, will be decided carefully. This aspect needs particular care when grouting near the top surface. Sometimes, a plywood covering is fixed to the top to obviate the floating effect of the aggregate in the event of high pressure and low viscosity of the grout.

Vacuum Concrete

It has been amply brought out in the earlier discussion that high water/cement ratio is harmful to the overall quality of concrete, whereas low water/cement ratio does not give enough workability for concrete to be compacted hundred per cent. Generally, higher workability and higher strength or very low workability and higher strength do not go hand in hand. Vacuum process of concreting enables to meet this conflicting demand. This process helps a high workable concrete to get high strength.

In this process, excess water used for higher workability, not required for hydration, and harmful in many ways to the hardened concrete is withdrawn by means of vacuum pump, subsequent to the placing of the concrete. The process when properly applied, produces concrete of quality. It also permits removal of formwork at an early age to be used in other repetitive work.

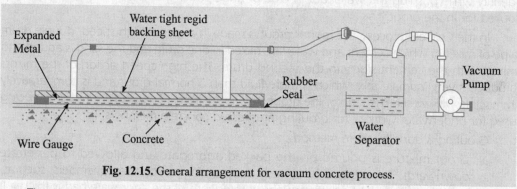

Fig. 12.15. General arrangement for vacuum concrete process.

The equipment is shown in Figure 12.15. It essentially consists of a vacuum pump, water separator and filtering mat. The filtering consists of a backing piece with a rubber seal all round the periphery. A sheet of expanded metal and then a sheet of wire gauge also forms part of the filtering mat. The top of the suction mat is connected to the vacuum pump. When the vacuum pump operates, suction is created within the boundary of the suction mat and the excess of water is sucked from the concrete through the fine wire gauge or muslin cloth. At least one face of the concrete must be open to the atmosphere to create difference of pressure. The contraction of concrete caused by loss of water must be vibrated.

The vacuum processing can be carried out either from the top surface or from the side surface. There will be only nominal difference in the efficiency of top processing or side processing. It has been seen that the size of the mat should not be less than 90 cm x 60 cm. Smaller mat was not found to be effective.

Rate of Extraction of Water

The rate of extraction of water is dependent upon the workability of mix, maximum size of aggregate, proportion of fines and aggregate cement ratio. In general, the following general tendencies are observed:

(a) The amount of water which may be withdrawn is governed by the initial workability or the amount of free water. A great reduction in the water/cement ratio can, therefore, be obtained with higher initial water/cement ratio.

(b) If the initial water / cement ratio is kept the same the amount of water which can be extracted is increased by increasing the maximum aggregate size or reducing the amount of fines in the mix.

(c) Although the depression of the water/cement ratio is less, the lower the initial water/cement ratio, the final water/cement ratio is also less, the lower the initial value.

(d) The reduction in the water/cement ratio is very slightly less with mixes leaner than 6 to 1, but little advantage is gained with mixes richer than this.

(e) The greater the depth of concrete processed the smaller is the depression of the average water/cement ratio.

(f) The ability of the concrete to stand up immediately after processing is improved if a fair amount of fine material is present, if the maximum aggregate size is restricted to 19 mm and if a continuous grading is employed.

(g) Little advantage is gained by prolonging the period of treatment beyond 15 to 20 minutes and a period of 30 minutes is the maximum that should be used.

It is found that there is a general tendency for the mix to be richer in cement near the processing face. This may be due to the fact that along with water, some cement gets sucked and deposited near the surface. It is also found that the water/cement ratio near the surface will be lower in value, anything from 0.16 to 0.30, than the original water/cement ratio. Because of the above reasons the vacuum processed concrete will not be of uniform strength. The simultaneous vibrations or the subsequent vibrations will reduce this shortcoming to some extent and also increase the strength of the concrete. If vibration is not done, the continuous capillary channels may not get disturbed and the strength would not be improved in relation to decreased water/cement ratio. Table 12.15 shows the comparisons of strength of processed and unprocessed cubes.

Table 12.15. Comparison of Strength of Processed and unprocessed cubes having the same water/cement ratio

Initial water/cement ratio of processed cubes	0.74	0.71	0.65	0.60
Average final water/cement ratio of processed cubes	0.68	0.59	0.57	0.55
Strength of unprocessed cubes of the same water/cement ratio as the initial water/cement ratio of the processed cubes MPa	18.0	15.3	19.1	30.1
Strength of fully vibrated processed cubes and increase of strength due to processing (per cent) : MPa	23.3 30	22.6 48	27.5 43	33.4 11
Strength of unprocessed cubes of the same water/cement ratio as the average final water/cement ratio of the processed cubes and in-				

crease of strength due to the reduction in water/cement ratio				
MPa	24.9	33.7	36.5	39.4
(per cent):	38	74	91	30
Increase in strength due to the reduction of water/cement ratio according to Road Note No. 4				
(per cent):	20	44	27	16

Vacuum Dewatered Concrete

It has been stressed time and again that adoption of low water cement ratio will give alround improvement in the quality of concrete, but satisfactory workability is the essential requirement for placing concrete. One solution to this problem is the use of superplasticizer and the other solution is the adoption of vacuum dewatering of concrete. For the last about ten years vacuum dewatering technique is fairly widely used in the construction of factory floors. The techniques have been adopted in a big way for the construction of DCM Daewoo Motors at Delhi, Whirpool factory construction near Pune, Tata Cummins at Jamshedpur, Fiat Ltd. etc. amongst hundreds of other factory floors.

The process is equipment oriented. It requires formwork in the form of channels, internal vibrators, double beam screed board vibrator for the full width, bull float, filter pads, vacuum pump, disc floater, and power trowel.

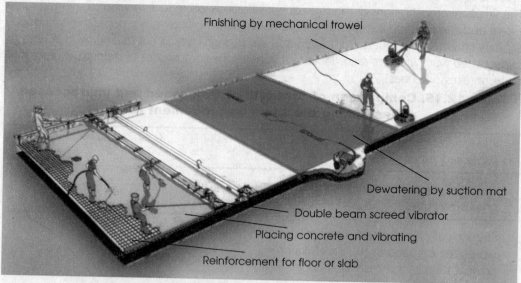

Finishing by mechanical trowel

Dewatering by suction mat

Double beam screed vibrator

Placing concrete and vibrating

Reinforcement for floor or slab

Schematic sketch showing method of vacuum dewatering system.

First, concrete with relatively higher w/c to facilitate full compaction with needle vibrator, is poured. Then the concrete is further compacted by double beam screed vibrator. This makes the surface smooth. Filter mat is placed and it is pressed on all the four sides and effectively sealed. Within about 30 minutes, the vacuum pump is started which sucks the unwanted water, what could be termed as "water of workability" from the concrete and is thrown out.

Vacuum pump is run for about 20 to 30 minutes depending upon the thickness of concrete floor. Vacuum dewatered concrete becomes stiff and walkable. The top surface may undergo a depression of about 3 per cent, with loss of about 20% of original water. Then the concrete is skimfloated and further power trowled and finished. Often surface hardners are used in

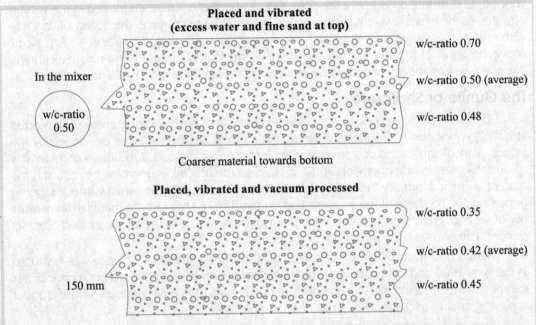

Fig. 12.16. W/c ratio is changed from an average of 0.50 in the mixer to 0.70 in the top part of the slab in normal concrete before vacuum dewatering. Vacuum dewatering rectifies the water-cement ratio to an ideal level. The illustration is based upon research reports from the Cement and Concrete Institute in Stockholm, Sweden.

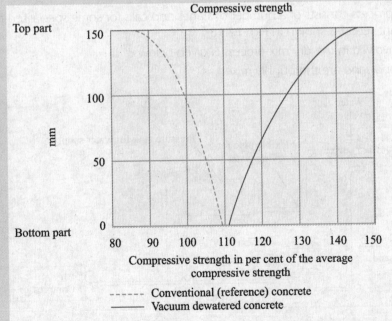

Fig. 12.17. Test carried out at the Cement and Concrete Institute, Stockholm, Sweden, evidences that the strength of a concrete plate is increased through vacuum dewatering.

conjunction with dewatering process. After vacuum dewatering, it gives the ideal condition for application of surface hardners in powder form. With the combined effect of vacuum dewatering and application of floor hardners a very good abrasion resistant factory floor may be constructed. The application of disc float and power trowelling may act like revibration of concrete to eliminate or segment the continuous capillaries or channels formed in the suction of water. As the effective w/c is comparatively lower at the top surface, the quality of concrete with respect to strength and abrasion resistance will be better. Fig. 12.16 and   Fig. 12.17 show the result of the test carried out at the Cement and Concrete Institute, Stockholm, Sweeden, who is the supplier of vacuum dewatering equipment by trade name "Tremix".

The Gunite or Shotcrete

Gunite can be defined as mortar conveyed through a hose and pneumatically projected at a high velocity on to a surface. Recently the method has been further developed by the introduction of small sized coarse aggregate into the mix deposited to obtain considerably greater thickness in one operation and also to make the process economical by reducing the cement content. Normally fresh material with zero slump can support itself without sagging or peeling off. The force of the jet impacting on the surface compact the material. Sometimes use of set accelerators to assist overhead placing is practised. The newly developed "Redi-set cement" can also be used for shotcreting process.

There is not much difference between guniting and shotcreting. Gunite was first used in the early 1900 and this process is mostly used for pneumatical application of mortar of less thickness, whereas shotcrete is a recent development on the similar principle of guniting for achieving greater thickness with small coarse aggregates.

There are two different processes in use, namely the "Wet-mix" process and the "dry-mix" process. The dry mix process is more successful and generally used.

Dry-mix Process

The dry mix process consists of a number of stages and calls for some specialised plant. A typical small plant set-up is shown in Fig. 12.18.

The stages involved in the dry mix process is given below:

(a) Cement and sand are thoroughly mixed.

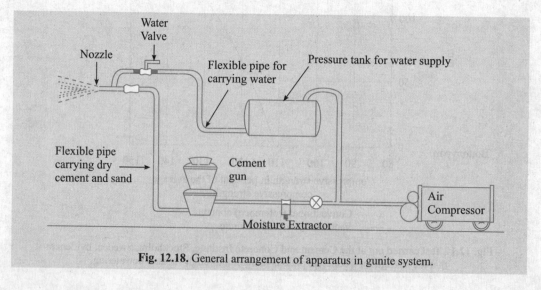

Fig. 12.18. General arrangement of apparatus in gunite system.

(b) The cement/sand mixture is fed into a special air-pressurised mechanical feeder termed as 'gun'.

(c) The mixture is metered into the delivery hose by a feed wheel or distributor within the gun.

(d) This material is carried by compressed air through the delivery hose to a special nozzle. The nozzle is fitted inside with a perforated manifold through which water is sprayed under pressure and intimately mixed with the sand/cement jet.

(e) The wet mortar is jetted from the nozzle at high velocity onto the surface to be gunited.

The Wet-mix Process

In the wet-mix process the concrete is mixed with water as for ordinary concrete before conveying through the delivery pipe line to the nozzle, at which point it is jetted by compressed air, onto the work in the same way, as that of dry mix process.

The wet-mix process has been generally discarded in favour of the dry-mix process, owing to the greater success of the latter.

The dry-mix methods makes use of high velocity or low velocity system. The high velocity gunite is produced by using a small nozzle and a high air pressure to produce a high nozzle velocity of about 90 to 120 metres per second. This results in exceptional good compaction. The lower velocity gunite is produced using large diameter hose for large output. The compaction will not be very high.

Advantages of Wet and Dry Process

Some of the advantages and disadvantages of the wet and dry processes is discussed below. Although it is possible to obtain more accurate control of the water/cement ratio with the wet process the fact that this ratio can be kept very low with the dry process largely overcomes the objection of the lack of accurate control. The difficulty of pumping light-weight aggregate concrete makes the dry process more suitable when this type of aggregate is used. The dry process on the other hand, is very sensitive to the water content of the sand, too wet a sand causes difficulties through blockade of the delivery pipeline, a difficulty which does not arise with the wet process. The lower water/cement ratio obtained with the dry process probably accounts for the lesser creep and greater durability of concrete produced in this way compared with concrete deposited by the wet process, but air-entraining agents can be use to improve the durability of concrete deposited by the latter means. Admixtures generally can be used more easily with the wet process except for accelerators. Pockets of lean mix and of rebound can occur with the dry process. It is necessary for the nozzelman to have an area where he can dump unsatisfactory shotcrete obtained when he is adjusting the water supply or when he is having trouble with the equipment. These troubles and the dust hazard are less with the wet process, but wet process does not normally give such a dense concrete as the dry process. Work can be continued in more windly weather with the wet process than with the dry process, Owing to the high capacities obtainable with concrete pumps, a higher rate of laying of concrete can probably be achieved in the wet process than with the dry process.

General Use of Shotcrete

The high cost of shotcrete limits its application to certain special circumstances where considerable savings are accrued and where its peculiar adaptability and technical advantages render it more suitable than conventional placing methods. Shuttering and formwork need be erected only on one side of the work and it does not have to be so strong as the shuttering for poured concrete. The saving in shuttering costs makes it particularly applicable for thin sections and although there is no technical reason why unlimited thicknesses cannot be deposited in horizontal and vertical work. The cost generally limits it to a thickness of 200 mm. The possible rate of application is low particularly with the dry process. Normally not more than 80 mm thickness can be deposited in overhead work in one day and the possibility of this will depend on the use of a suitable accelerator.

The fact that it can be conveyed over a considerable distance in a small diameter pipe makes this process suitable for sites where access is difficult. The other method that can be adopted in such situation is pumping techniques. It cannot, however, be used in confined spaces as the expansion of the compressed air will cause air turbulences which make accurate placing difficult. Sufficient room is required to hold the nozzle, say 1 m from the work. To accommodate a large radius bend of the delivery hose also requires considerable space. It will bond extremely well to the existing concrete, to masonry and to exposed rock. Suitably prepared steel surface also can be covered with gunited concrete.

The quality of the finished product is liable to be variable and particularly in the dry process the quality is very much dependent on the skill of the nozzleman. Quality control is very difficult and it is not possible to cast reliable test cubes or cylinders. The only way of testing the strength of the work deposited is by taking drill cores or by making a parallel slab by guniting with identical mix. It is difficult to remove rebound material as this tends to collect inside corners and behind reinforcing bars or other obstructions. Pockets of rebound formed as above and due to lack of skill of the nozzleman form weak and porous patches in the finished work. The proportions of the concrete deposited are affected by variation of the water supply and variations in the amount of rebound caused by this and other reasons. Too low an air pressure and surges in the air and water supply also can cause patches of relatively dry material. Defects of this type can result in porous concrete and also contribute to high permeability.

The amount of rebound greatly affects the economics of the shotcrete process as it has all to be discarded and involves labour in collection and disposal. The area surrounding the work will be heavily coated with mortar particularly in windy weather.

It is difficult to obtain a satisfactory surface finish with Shotcrete, particularly with the dry process, because it is almost impossible to trowel due to the low water content. Often it becomes necessary to apply a screed of about 2 cm over the gunited surface.

The application of the shotcrete process is limited to exceptional areas and that too when good nozzleman having the required skill are available. The nozzleman's job is a very strenuous one. It is, therefore, necessary to have relief nozzlemen and for high rates of application some mechanical means of holding the nozzle is required.

The maximum rate of deposition is about 15 m³. hr for the dry process but this can be exceeded with the wet process.

The low water/cement ratio, the thinness of the section deposited and the fact that normally only one side of the concrete is covered, necessitates careful attention to curing more than with normal concrete.

The normal specifications with respect to cement, aggregate and water, also apply for shotcrete but it is desirable that the aggregate should be rather harder than normal to allow for attrition due to the action of the process. Any cement, provided it does not set too quickly, can be used.

Admixtures can be used in shotcrete to produce the same effects as in ordinary concrete. They should be added to the water in the dry process, but some difficulty may be experienced in obtaining correct proportioning due to variations in the rate of feed of the dry materials. On account of the difficulty of precise control, admixtures whose effects are very sensitive to the proportion added should not be used. Great caution should be exercised in using accelerators in the wet process but accelerators causing an initial set within 30 seconds are used in the dry process. This enable the process to be used in very wet conditions and for sealing leakages. But deficulties have sometime been experienced in obtaining adhesion of the concrete to very set surfaces and these very rapid accelerators are very expensive.

There is not much information on the drying shrinkage and creep of shotcrete. The drying shrinkage will depend on the water content and may, therefore, be expected to be fairly low for the dry process. The creep of dry shotcrete is similar to that of high quality normally placed concrete. But shrinkage and creep of wet shotcrete is likely to be high.

The durability or resistance to frost action and other agencies of dry shotcrete is good. It is not so good for wet shotcrete but can be improved to a satisfactory degree by the use of air-entraining agents. About half of the entrained air is likely to be lost while spraying.

Concluding Remarks on Shotcrete

There has been considerable increase in the use of shotcrete in Europe and U.S.A. during the last 15 years because of the good performance of many shotcrete applications. (Strictly speaking, guniting applications). Stiff, well-compacted concrete of the type used in shotcrete is a good structural material. A well designed and well executed job makes a satisfactory work.

It has been well established that the strength and other properties of shotcrete are the same as those of conventional mortar or concrete of the same proportion and water content. Shotcrete is a mix with high cement content and very low water/cement ratio. Normal shotcrete mixes applied by qualified personnel under favourable conditions are capable of strengths above 35 MPa. One of the strong points of shotcrete is its excellent bond with old concrete, rock face and even with metal sheet. The shotcrete applied as overlay to old concrete slab is found to have good bond strength at the interface. The shotcrete applied as ground support worked very well with or without rock bolting as additional support. The use of shotcreting is very frequently adopted for tunnelling operations.

Shotcrete for ground support generally should have quick setting properties in order to permit a rapid build up of the shotcrete section,

Shotcreting with steel reinforcement for slope protection.

develop very early strength and seal off seepage where existing. These properties are usually obtained by the use of powerful accelerators in the mix. These accelerators should be compatible with the cement and concrete with respect to durability and stability.

It has been reported by Corps of Engineers, USA, that in one of the recently completed large shotcrete tunnel support job in California, there was an apparent saving of about two million dollars by using shotcrete in lieu of steel supports. They also reported that obtaining

Shotcreting for slope protection by Robot Jet Machine at central secretariat, Delhi Metro.

strength more than 28 MPa requires very rigid quality control at great cost and as such, strength exceeding 28 MPa should not be specified.

Recent Studies

Use of fibre reinforced shotcrete is one of the recent innovations. In this, steel fibres of about 30 gauge and 20 mm long is mixed with the shotcrete and then pneumatically applied in the usual manner. It is found that such a fibre reinforced shotcrete process increases the tensile strength of the shotcrete considerably.

Another important innovation made is the polymer shotcrete. In this, aggregate and monomer are mixed together and then this mixture is pneumatically applied in the same manner as shotcrete. The principal difference between Polymer Shotcrete and Conventional shotcrete is that a polymeric binder is used in lieu of Portland cement and water. The developmental results of polymer shotcrete indicate a potential use of this material because of its high strength and excellent durability.

Ferrocement

Ferrocement techniques though of recent origin, have been extensively used in many countries, notably in U.K., New Zealand and China. There is a growing awareness of the advantages of this technique of construction all over the world. It is well known that conventional reinforced concrete members are too heavy, brittle, cannot be satisfactorily repaired if damaged, develop cracks and reinforcements are liable to be corroded. The above disadvantages of normal concrete make it inefficient for certain types of work.

Ferrocement is a relatively new material consisting of wire meshes and cement mortar. This material was developed by P.L. Nervi, an Italian architect and engineer, in 1940. It consists of closely spaced wire meshes which are impregnated with rich cement mortar mix. The wire mesh is usually of 0.5 to 1.0 mm dia wire at 5 mm to 10 mm spacing and cement mortar is

Small diameter wires and chickenwire mesh reinforcement used in casting ferrocement water tank

Ferrocement water tank 1000 litre capacity — thickness 15 mm.

Ferrocement boat floating on water— thickness 25 mm.

of cement sand ratio of 1 : 2 or 1 : 3 with water/cement ratio of 0.4 to 0.45. The ferrocement elements are usually of the order of 2 to 3 cm. in thickness with 2 to 3 mm external cover to the reinforcement. The steel content varies between 300 kg to 500 kg per cubic metre of mortar. The basic idea behind this material is that concrete can undergo large strains in the neighbourhood of the reinforcement and the magnitude of strains depends on the distribution and subdivision of reinforcement throughout of the mass of concrete.

Ferrocement is widely accepted in U.K, New Zealand and U.S. as a boat building material. It has also found various other interesting civil engineering applications. The main advantages are simplicity of its construction, lesser dead weight of the elements due to their small thickness, its high tensile strength, less crack widths compared to conventional concrete, easy repairability, noncorrosive nature and easier mouldability to any required shape. There is also saving in basic materials namely, cement and steel. This material is more suitable to special structures like shells which have strength through forms and structures like roofs, silos, water tanks and pipelines.

The material is under active research in various countries and attempts are being made to give a sound theoretical backing to establish the material behaviour. This is a highly suitable material for precast products, because of its easy adaptability to prefabrication and lesser dead weight of the units cast. The development of ferrocement depends on suitable casting techniques for the required shape. Development of proper prefabrication techniques for ferrocement is still not a widely explored area and gap needs to be filled.

Ferrocement plank 3000 x 300 x 25 mm, bends like a bow when supported as shown above

Sample of ferrocement manhole covers

Casting Techniques

There are four methods of casting. They are:

(a) Hand plastering,

(b) Semi-mechanised process (using hand plastering),

(c) Centrifuging and

(e) Guniting.

(a) Hand plastering (without using any formwork): In this system a reinforcement cage is made using small diameter steel rod reinforcement bent to the required shape, say cylindrical in shape. Usually this frame provides the rigidity for the whole structure before plastering. Then the required number of wire mesh layers are securely tied to the reinforcement cage, the mortar is dashed from outside against a plain curved G.I. sheet held on the other side. The flexible curved G.I. sheet moved allround and from outside the mortar is dashed. Continuing this procedure the whole cylindrical tank is built-up. Closely spaced wire mesh helps adhering of mortar when dashed. The whole thickness is built-up gradually in two or three consecutive dashing of mortar and then both inside and outside are rubbed smooth. Hand plastering results in slightly increased thickness of ferrocement member.

For thin cylindrical units of about I metre diameter, 6 mm diameter mild steel rods at 15 cms spacing are used to make a cage of cylindrical shape and then chicken mesh or woven mesh is tied to the cage and plastered. Use of chicken mesh in this type of construction may not be advisable as it is very flexible and plastering over chicken mesh (without inner mould) may not be satisfactory. Woven mesh and welded mesh are superior and more suitable than chicken mesh. In this method the control of thickness is difficult and the minimum thickness of section that can be cast works out to about 2 cms. Because of lesser control, the thickness of units cast by this method becomes more. The greater thickness not only makes it uneconomical but also makes it lose some of the technical advantages. The strength obtained by this system will be lower compared to other methods as the compaction is by hand and since no inner form or mould is used, the hand pressure applied is relatively less. Less pressure is required to be applied to prevent the distortion of the shape of cage. However, the units can be cast by this process and used in situations where the facilities for other improved methods do not exist. These units can be used for pipes, storage structures and gas holder units. This type of casting suits cylindrical units of size approximately 60 cms in diameter and above and also for other irregular shapes for which mould is difficult to make. Only the engineer's imagination is the limit to cast sections of any given shape by this process. It is advisable to give a water proof coating on the surfaces, as hand plastering is unlikely to result in a water tight structure.

(b) Semi-mechanised process (using hand plastering over formwork): A semi-mechanised process has been developed at SERC, Roorkee, for casting thin ferrocement cylindrical units. In this system an inner cylindrical mould is provided over which one layer of wire mesh is wound. Over this layer, 4 mm wire is tied at a spacing of 15 cm in both the directions. Over this one more layer of chicken wire mesh is wound. This forms the complete wire mesh system of reinforcement. The cement plastering is then done layer by layer. As the mesh is tightly wound round the formwork the thickness of unit is reduced. With this system, units with thickness upto a minimum of one cm. can be cast containing two layers of wire mesh in that thickness. This system is termed as semi-mechanised because the mould can be rotated to facilitate dashing of mortar.

Ferrocement garden umbrella
thickness 20 mm.

Ferrocement, "W" shapped folded
plate roof for span 3.5 m.
Thickness of plate is 20mm.

This system is better than the earlier system as better compaction could be obtained by means of a straight edge pressed against inner mould. The uniformity of thickness obtained in this system is also better than of the earlier system. The wire mesh can be tightly wound over the mould and can be tightened during the casting process. This helps in avoiding any looseness in the mesh and uneven thickness.

The advantages of this system are that it does not require any sophisticated enquipment or electricity, the skill can be easily acquired by local people, and it can be adopted at rural areas with ease. This system is convenient for cylindrical units of size about 1.0 m and above.

This system can be further improved by mechanising the rotation of mould and using a spray technique for mortar application. This requires synchronisation between the speed of the mould and rate of spray. Mortar spray guns of lower pressure of application of mortar than the guniting equipment may be better suited for this purpose.

(c) Centrifuging: The centrifuging process is commonly adopted for the fabrication of concrete cylindrical units. Because of the high first crack strength of ferrocement compared to reinforced concrete, the pipe thickness can be reduced thus, resulting in lesser dead weight. In the existing centrifuging process, the mild steel reinforcement cage is replaced by wire mesh layers cage. The trial casting of pipes by centrifuging done at SERC Roorkee has indicated that this method could well be adopted for casting ferrocement units. Because of good compaction, the ferrocement pipe cast by centrifuging can be used as pressure pipes.

Outer shell of this car is made up of ferrocement.

(*d*) Guniting: The process of guniting can be adopted for applying the mortar to the wire mesh system. This process, applied properly with experienced gunman can give good compact and uniform surface. This appears to be suitable process for mass production of ferrocement prefabricated units. A continuous process of layer guniting with an interval of about an hour will yield good results.

Application

Ferrocement has been successfully used for casting domestic over-head water tanks. The tank being light and flexible can be transported and hoisted without much difficulty. Inlet and outlet connections can also be easily done with the help of a modern adhesive like "m-seal". The ferrocement tank will be cheaper than any other competitive materials

Similar tanks or slightly modified tanks can be used as grain silos in villages. The tank can be made with hopper shaped bottom with simple arrangements for drawing the grains. The ferrocement tank will help in preserving the grain uneffected by moisture and rodents.

Similar ferrocement container can be used as gas holder unit in 'Gobbar gas" plants With a few modifications, ferrocement tanks can also be used as septic tank units.

The properties of ferrocement make it an ideal material for boat building. It has been reported that ferrocement boats 14 metres long weighs only 10 per cent more than wooden boats and the same is 300 per cent cheaper than fibre reinforced concrete boats, 200 per cent cheaper than steel boats and 35 per cent cheaper than timber boats. Many countries notably China are manufacturing ferrocement boats and fishing trawlers in large scale.

Ferrocement manhole cover is becoming very popular to replace cast iron manhole cover over sewers around domestic building where they are not subjected to heavy vehicular traffic. Owing to the reason that the cost of ferrocement manhole cover is only about 1/10 of the cost of cast iron manhole cover, and that it can be manufactured readily, it makes a good substitute for cast iron manhole cover.

Ferrocement is becoming a popular material for prefabricated roof units. Ferrocement folded plate being light, could be used advantageously as prefabricated roof units for garrages and storage sheds. A 3 cm thick ferrocement folded plate with two layers of chicken wire mesh can be used over a span of 3.5 metres. It can also be used for prefabricated channel units for roof construction.

Ferrocement is a suitable material for pressure pipes. It will be much lighter compared to normal reinforced concrete pipes. Suitable techniques like centrifuging and guniting can be used for mass production in a factory.

Ferrocement is found to be a suitable material for casting curved benches for parks, garden and open-air cinema theatre.

It is also an ideal material for making tree guards which can be cast in two parts to facilitate its removal at a later date.*

Roller Compacted Concrete

Roller Compacted Concrete (RCC) is a recent development particularly in the field of dam construction. Roller compacted concrete is a lean no slump, almost dry concrete that is compacted by Vibratory Roller. A mixture of aggregates, cement and water are mixed in a conventional batch mixer or in other suitable mixers. Supplementary cementing material, such as fly ash can also be used. In some cases high volume fly ash to the extent of 60% by weight of cement has been used. The cement content ranges from 60 to 360 kg/m³.

Roller compacted concrete is placed in layers thin enough to allow complete compaction. The optimum layer thickness ranges from 20 to 30 cm. To ensure adequate bonding between the new and old layer or at cold joint, segregation must be prevented and a high plasticity bedding mix must be used at the start of the placement. A compressive strength of about 7 MPa to 30 MPa have been obtained.

For effective consolidation, roller compacted concrete must be dry enough to support the mass of the vibrating equipment, but wet enough to allow the cement paste to be evenly distributed throughout the mass during mixing and consolidation process.

The first RCC dam was taken up during 1978 and completed during 1980 in Japan. A number of other dams quickly followed. By end of 1985, seven RCC dams have been completed, and this method of construction technology has been accepted. In the next seven years (1992) the number of dams constructed by this techniques rose to 96 in 17 different countries mainly in USA, Japan, Spain etc.

In India Roller Compacted Concrete has been used as a base concrete in the construction of Delhi-Mathura concrete road construction project. Similarly RCC has been used as base course concrete in Pune - Mumbai express highway construction. In both the projects the RCC was referred as "Dry Lean Concrete. The grade of concrete was M 10, thickness 15 cm. Such a concrete was thoroughly compacted by vibratory roller over which Pavement Quality Concrete (PQC) of grade M 40, 35 cm thick was laid.

Self-compacting Concrete (SCC)

Self Compacting Concrete (SCC)

Making concrete structures without vibration, have been done in the past. For examples, placement of concrete under water is done by the use of tremie without vibration. Mass concrete, and shaft concrete can be successfully placed without vibration. But the above examples of concrete are generally of lower strength and difficult to obtain consistent quality. Modern application of self-compacting concrete (SCC) is focussed on high performance, better and more reliable and uniform quality.

Recognising the lack of uniformity and complete compaction of concrete by vibration, researchers at the University of Tokyo, Japan, started in late 1980's to develop SCC. By the early 1990's, Japan has developed and used SCC that does not require vibration to achieve full compaction. By the year 2000, the SCC has become popular in Japan for prefabricated products and ready mixed concrete. The Fig. 12.19 shows the amount of SCC used in Japan 12.17.

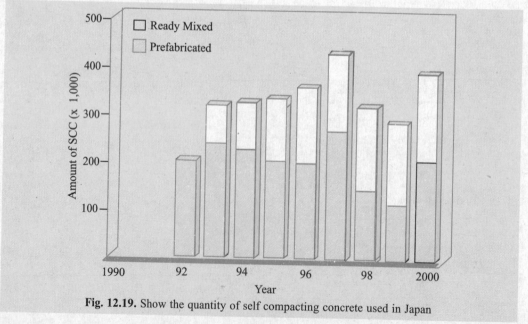

Fig. 12.19. Show the quantity of self compacting concrete used in Japan

Several European countries recognised the significance and potentials of SCC developed in Japan. During 1989, they founded European federation of natural trade associations representing producers and applicators of specialist building products (EFNARC) 12.18.

The utilisation of self-compacting concrete started growing rapidly. EFNARC, making use of broad practical experiences of all members of European federation with SCC, has drawn up specification and guidelines to provide a framework for design and use of high quality SCC, during 2001. Most of the information particularly test methods given in this chapter is based on specification and guidelines for self-compacting concrete given by EFNARC.

Self-compacting concrete has been described as "the most revolutionary development in concrete construction for several decades". Originally developed in Japan to offset a growing shortage of skilled labour, it has proved to be beneficial from the following points.

- Faster construction
- Reduction in site manpower
- Better surface finish
- Easier placing
- Improved durability
- Greater freedom in design
- Thinner concrete sections
- Reduced noise level
- Safer working environment

Material for SCC

Cement : Ordinary Portland Cement, 43 or 53 grade can be used.

Aggregates : The maximum size of aggregate is generally limited to 20 mm. Aggregate of size 10 to 12mm is desirable for structures having congested reinforcement. Wherever possible size of aggregate higher than 20mm could aslo be used. Well graded cubical or rounded aggregates are desirable. Aggregates should be of uniform quality with respect to shape and grading.

Fine aggregates can be natural or manufactured. The grading must be uniform throughout the work. The moisture content or absorption characteristics must be closely monitored as quality of SCC will be sensitive to such changes.

Particles smaller than 0.125 mm i.e. 125 micron size are considered as FINES which contribute to the powder content.

Mixing Water : Water quality must be established on the same line as that for using reinforced concrete or prestressed concrete.

Chemical Admixtures : Superplaseizers are an essential component of SCC to provide necessary workability. The new generation superplasticizers termed poly-carboxylated ethers (PCE) is particularly useful for SCC.

Other types may be incorporated as necessary, such as Viscosity Modifying Agents (VMA) for stability, air entraining agents (AEA) to improve freeze-thaw resistance, and retarders for Control of Setting.

Mineral Admixtures:

Fly ash: Fly ash in appropriate quantity may be added to improve the quality and durability of SCC.

Ground Granulated Blast Furnace Slag (GGBFS) : GGBFS which is both cementitious and pozzolanic material may be added to improve rheological properties.

Silica Fume : Silica fume may be added to improve the mechanical properties of SCC.

Stone Powder : Finely crushed lime stone, dolomite or granite may be added to increase the powder content. The fraction should be less than 125 micron.

Fibres : Fibres may be used to enhance the properties of SCC in the same way as for normal concrete.

The approximate compositions of traditional concrete and SCC are shown below.

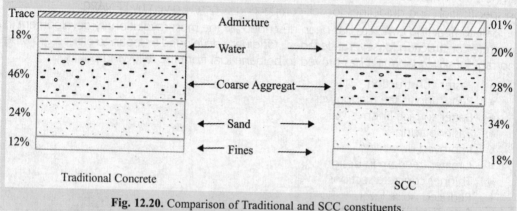

Fig. 12.20. Comparison of Traditional and SCC constituents.

The SCC mixes are designed and tested to meet the demands of the projects. It is reported that SCC for mass concrete was designed for pumping and depositing at a fairly high rate in the construction of the anchorages of the Akashi-Kaikyo batching plant and pumped through a pipe line to the location of anchorages 200 m away. The SCC was dropped from a height of 5 m without segregation. For mass concrete, the maximum size of coarse aggregate was as large as 50 mm. The SCC construction reduced the construction time for the anchorages from 2.5 years to 2 years. The coarse aggregate size for reinforced concrete generally varies from 10 mm to 20 mm.

Examples of SCC Mixes

There are three ways in which SCC can be made
(*i*) Powder Type
(*ii*) VMA Type
(*iii*) Combined type

In powder type SCC is made by increasing the powder content. In VMA type it is made by using viscosity modifying admixture. In combined type it is made by increasing powder content and using VMA. The above three methods are made depending upon the structural conditions, constructional conditions, available material and restrictions in concrete production plant etc. The following table gives an idea about the three methods and a feel for how SCC mixes differ from normal concrete mixes and from each other mixes.

Table 12.16. Shows Typical SCC Mixes in Japan 12.17

Ingredient	Powder Type	VMA Type	Combined Type
Water kg/m³	175	165	175
Cement kg/m³	530	220	298
Fly ash kg/m³	70	0	206
GGBFS kg/m³	0	220	0
Silica Fume kg/m³	0	0	0
F.A. kg/m³	751	870	702
C.A. kg/m³	789	825	871
High, Range Water reducing admixtures kg/m³	9.0	4.4	10.6
VMA kg/m³	0	4.1	0.0875
Slump flow test dia. of spread mm	625	600	660

Requirements for self-compacting concrete

The main characteristics of SCC are the properties in the fresh state. The mix design is focussed on the ability to flow under its own weight without vibration, the ability to flow through heavily congested reinforcement under its own weight, and the ability to retain homogeneity without segregation. The workability of SCC is higher than "very high" degree of workability mentioned in 15 456 : 2000.

A concrete mix can only be classified as self-complicating if it has the following characteristics.

- Filling ability
- Passing ability
- Segregation resistance

Several test methods have been developed in attempts to characterise the properties of SCC. So far no single method or combination of methods has achieved universal approval to include in national or international organisations. However, the Table   12.17 gives the list of test methods for workability properties of SCC based on EFNARC specification and guidelines.

Table 12.17. List of test methods for workability properties of SCC

Srl No.	Method	Property
1.	Slump flow by Abrams cone.	Filling ability
2.	$T_{50 cm}$ Slump flow	Filling ability
3.	J-ring	Passing ability
4.	V-funnel	Filling ability
5.	V-funnel at T_5 minutes	Segregation resistance
6.	L-box	Passing ability
7.	U-box	Passing ability
8.	Fill-box	Passing ability
9.	GTM Screen Stability Test	Segregation resistance
10.	Orimet	Filling ability

For the initial mix design of SCC all the three workability parameters need to be assessed.

Table 12.18. The workability properties of SCC and alternative test methods.

Property	Test Methods Lab mix. design	Field quality control	Modification of test according to max. size agg.
Filling ability	slump flow T_{50} cm slump flow V-funnel orimet Orimet	slump flow $T_{50\,cm}$ slump flow V-funnel Orimet	None None Max. 16 mm
Passsing ability	L-box, U-box Fill-box	J-ring	Different opennings in L-box and J-ring
Segregation resistance	GTM test V-funnel at T_5 min.	G.T. test V-funnel at T_5 minutes	None

For site quality control, two test methods are generally sufficient to monitor production quality. Typical combinations are slump-flow and V-funnel or slump-flow and J-ring. With consistent raw material, even a single test method carried out by trained and experienced technician may be sufficient.

Workability Requirement for the fresh SCC

The following requirements are to be fulfilled at the time of placing. Any changes in workability during transport and other delay should be taken into account in production.

Table 12.19. The typical acceptance criteria for SCC 12.18.

Srl No.	Method	Unit	Typical ranges of values Minimum	Maximum
1.	Slump flow by Abrams cone.	mm	650	800
2.	$T_{50\,cm}$ Slump flow	sec	2	5
3.	J-ring	mm	0	10
4.	V-funnel	sec	8	12
5.	V-funnel at T_5 minutes	sec	0	+3
6.	L-box	(h_2/h_1)	0.8	1.0
7.	U-box	(h_2-h_1)mm	0	30
8.	Fill-box	%	90	100
9.	GTM Screen Stability Test	%	0	15
10.	Orimet	sec	0	5

Initial Mix composition

In the design of mix, the relative proportions of the key components may be considered by volume rather than by mass. Indicative proportions of materials are shown below for self compactability.

- Water/powder ratio by volume is to be 0.80 to 1.00
- Total power content to be 160 to 240 litres (400-600 kg) per m³
- The sand content may be more than 38% of the mortar volume
- Coarse aggregate content should normally be 28 to 35% by volume of the mix
- Water/cement ratio is selected based on strength. In any case water content should not exceed 200 litres/m³.

One must bear in mind that there is going to be some variation in raw material quality and variation in moisture content in aggregates.

After laboratory trials, the mix should be tested at full scale at the concrete plant or site. In the event of not getting satisfactory performance, the mix should be readjusted in respect of type and quantity of filler material, proportions of F.A. or C.A., dosage of superplasticizer and VMA. Try also alternative type of superplaticizer which may be more compatible.

Production and Placing

Aggregates : Aggregate should come from same source. There should not be much variations in size, shape and moisture content.

Mixing : Any suitable mixer could be used - Generally, mixing time need to be longer than for conventional concrete. Time of addition of admixture is important. A system should be established for optimum benefit during trial itself.

In the beginning there may be fluctuations in the quality of freshly mixed concrete. It is recommended that every batch must be tested until consistent and compliant results are obtained. Subsequently, checking could be done "by the eye" and routine testing is sufficient.

Placing: Formwork must be in good conditions to prevent leakage. Though it is easier to place SCC than ordinary concrete, the following rules are to be followed to minimise the risk of segregation.

- limit of vertical free fall distance to 5 meter.
- limit the height of pour lifts (layers) to 500 mm
- limit of permissible distance of horizontal flow from point of discharge to 10 meters.

Curing: On account of no bleeding or very little bleeding, SCC tends to dry faster and may cause more plastic shrinkage cracking. Therefore, initial curing should be commenced as soon as practicable. Alternatively the SCC must be effectively covered by polyethylene sheet. Due to the high content of powder, SCC can show more plastic shrinkage or creep than ordinary concrete mixes. There are disagreements on the above statement. These aspects should be considered during designing and specifying SCC. It should also be noted that early curing is necessary for SCC.

Mix Design

Procedure : The following sequence is followed
- Determine the desired air content
- Determine the coarse aggregate volume
- Determine the sand content
- Design the paste composition
- Determine the optimum water to powder ratio and superplasticizer dosage in mortar
- Finally the concrete properties are assessed by standard tests.

Air Content: Generally air content may be assumed to be 2%. In case of freeze-thaw conditions in cold weather concreting higher per cent of air content may be specified.

Determination of Coarse Aggregate Volume : Coarse aggregate volume is defined by bulk density. Generally coarse aggregate (D > 4.75) should be between 50% and 60%. Optimum coarse aggregate content depends on the following parameters.

- The lower the maximum aggregate size, the higher the proportion.
- The rounded aggregate can be used at higher percentage than crushed aggregates.

Determination of Sand Content: Sand, in the context of mix design procedure is defined as all particles bigger than 125 micron and smaller than 4.75 mm. Sand content is defined by bulk density. The optimum volume content of sand in the mortar varies between 40-50% depending on paste properties.

Design of paste composition: Initially the water/powder ratio for zero flow (β_p) is determined in the paste; with chosen proportion of cement and additions. Flow cone tests with water/powder ratios by volume of e.g. 1.1, 1.2, 1.3 and 1.4 are performed with the selected powder composition. Fig. 12.21 shows the typical results. The point of intersection with "Y" axis is the β_p value. This β_p value is used mainly for quality control of water demand for new batches of cement and fillers.

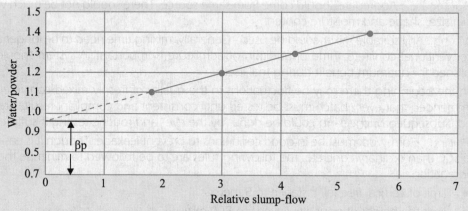

Fig. 12.21. Determination of water/powder ratio b_p for zero slump flow.

Determination of Optimum Volumetric Water/powder ratio and Superplasticizer dosage in mortar :

Tests with flow cone and V-Funnel for mortar are performed at varying water/powder ratios in the range of (0.8 to 0.9) β_p and dosages of superplasticizer. The superplasticizer is used to balance the rheology of the paste. The volume content of sand in the mortar remains the same as determined above.

The target values are slump flow of 24 to 26 cm and V-funnel time of 7 to 11 seconds.

At target slump flow, where V-funnel time is lower than 7 secs, then decrease the water/powder ratio. For largest slump flow and V-funnel time in excess of 11 seconds water/powder ratio should be increased.

If these criteria cannot be fulfilled, then the particular combination of materials is inadequate. One can also change the type of superplasticizer. Another alternative is a new additive, and as a last resort is to change the cement.

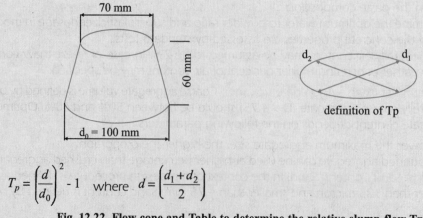

$$T_p = \left(\frac{d}{d_0}\right)^2 - 1 \quad \text{where} \quad d = \left(\frac{d_1 + d_2}{2}\right)$$

Fig. 12.22. Flow cone and Table to determine the relative slump-flow Tp

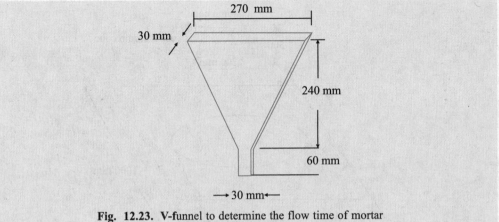

Fig. 12.23. V-funnel to determine the flow time of mortar

Tests on Concrete: The concrete composition is now determined and the superplasticizer dosage is finally selected on the bases of tests on concrete.

Guideline for mix composition

Coarse aggregate < 50%
Water/powder ratio = 0.8 to 1.0
Total powder content = 400–600 kg/m^3
Sand Content = < 40% of the mortar (by volume)
Sand = < 50% of paste volume
Sand = > 50% by weight of total aggregate
Free water < 200 litre.
Paste > 40% of the volume of the mix

With the above parameters conduct the workability tests and see whether you get the following results. If not adjust the parameters to get the following test results.

Slump flow by Abrams cone.	650 to 80 mm
$T_{50\ cm}$ Slump flow	2 to 5 sec
J-ring	0 – 10 mm
V-funnel	8 – 12 sec
V-funnel at T_5 minutes	+3 sec
L-box	H_2/H_1 = 0.8 to 1.0
U-box	$H_2 – H_1$ = 30 mm (Max.)
Fill-box	90 to 100%
Screen Stability	0 – 15%
Orimet	0 – 5 sec

Test Methods :

It is important to mention that none of the test methods for SCC has yet been standardised and the tests mentioned below are not yet perfected. They are mainly adhoc method which have been devised for SCC.

Slump flow Test

The slump flow test is done to assess the horizontal flow of concrete in the absence of obstructions. It is a most commonly used test and gives good assessment of filling ability. It can be used at site. The test also indicates the resistance to segregation.

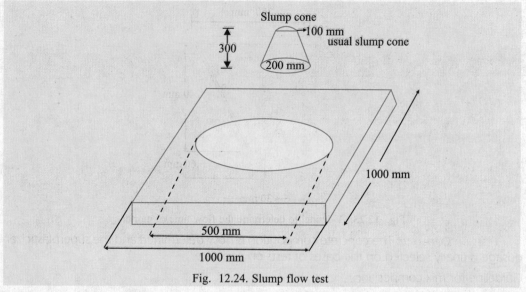

Fig. 12.24. Slump flow test

Equipments : The usual slump cone having base diameter of 200 mm, top diameter 100mm and height 300mm is used.

● A stiff base plate square in shape having at least 700 mm side. Concentric circles are marked around the centre point where the slump cone is to placed. A firm circle is drawn at 500 mm diameter
  ● A trowel
  ● Scoop
  ● Measuring tape
  ● Stop watch

Procedure : About 6 litre of concrete is needed for this test. Place the baseplate on level ground. Keep the slump cone centrally on the base plate. Fill the cone with the scoop. Do not tamp. Simply strike off the concrete level with the trowel. Remove the surplus concrete lying on base place. Raise the cone vertically and allow the concrete to flow freely. Measure the final diameter of the concrete in two perpendicular directions and calculate the average of the two diameters. This is the slump flow in mm. Note that there is no water or cement paste or mortar without coarse aggregate is seen at the edge of the spread concrete.

Interpretation: The higher the flow value, the greater its ability to fill formwork under its own weight. A value of at least 650 mm is required for SCC. In case of severe segregation, most coarse aggregate will remain in the centre of the pool of concrete and mortar and paste at the periphery of concrete.

T_{50} **Slump Flow Test** : The procedure for this test is same as for slump flow test. When the slump cone is lifted, start the stop watch and find the time taken for the concrete to reach 500 mm mark. This time is called T_{50} time. This is an indication of rate of spread of concrete. A lower time indicates greater flowability. It is suggested that T_{50} time may be 2 to 5 secs.

J-Ring Test : J-ring test denotes the passing ability of the concrete. The equipment consists of rectangular section of 30 mm x 25 mm open steel ring drilled vertically with holes to accept threaded sections of reinforcing bars 10 mm diameter 100 mm in length. The bars and sections can be placed at different distance apart to simulate the conjestion of reinforcement at the site. Generally these sections are placed 3 x maximum size of aggregate. The diameter of the ring formed by vertical sections is 300 mm and height 100 mm.

Equipment :
- slump cone without foot pieces.
- Base plate at least 700 mm square
- Trowel
- Scoop
- Tape
- J-ring-rectangular section 30mm

x 25mm planted vertically to form a ring 300 mm dia generally at a spacing of 48 ± 2mm.

Procedure : About 6 litres of concrete is

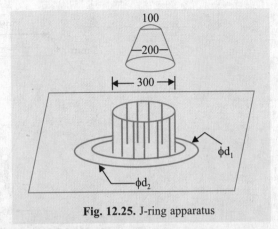

Fig. 12.25. J-ring apparatus

You can see unsegregated and cohesive concrete coming out of J-ring.

Courtesy : Hindustan Construction Company

needed for the test. Moisten the inside of the slump cone and base plate. Place the J-Ring centrally on the base plate and the slump cone centrally inside the J-ring. Fill the slump cone with scoop. Do not tamp. Simply strike off the concrete level with trowel. Remove all surplus concrete. Raise the cone vertically and allow the concrete to flow out through the J-ring. Measure the final diameter in two perpendicular directions. Calculate the average diameter. Measure the difference in height between the concrete just inside J-Ring bars and just outside the J Ring bars. Calculate the average of the difference in height at four locations in mms. Note any border of mortar or cement paste without coarse aggregate at the edge of the concrete. The acceptable difference in height between inside and outside should be between 0 and 10 mm.

V-Funnel test and V-Funnel test at T_5 min.

This test was developed in Japan. The equipment consists of a V-shaped funnel shown in Fig. 12.26. The V- Funnel test is used to determine the filling ability (flowability) of the concrete with a maximum size of aggregate 20 mm size. The funnel is filled with about 12 litre of concrete. Find the time taken for it to flow down.

After this the funnel can be filled with concrete and left for 5 minutes to settle. If the concrete shows segregation then the flow time will increase significantly.

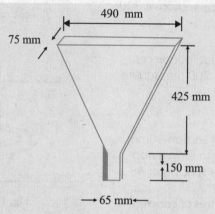

490 mm

75 mm

425 mm

150 mm

65 mm

Fig. 12.26. V-Funnel Test Equipment

Equipment
- V-funnel
- Bucket 12 litres
- Trowel
- Scoop
- Stopwatch

Procedure : About 12 litre of concrete is needed for the test. Set the V-funnel on firm ground. Moisten inside of the funnel. Keep the trap door open to remove any surplus water. Close the trap door and place a bucket underneath. Fill the applaratus completely with concrete – No compaction or tamping is done. Strike off the concrete level.

Open within 10 seconds the trap door and record the time taken for the concrete to flow down. Record the time for empltying. This can be judged when the light is seen when viewed from top. The whole test is to be performed within 5 min.

Observing the time of emptying of concrete from V-funnel.

Procedure for flow time at T_5 mm : Do not clean or moisten the inside surface of the funnel. Close the trap door and refill the V-funnel immediately after measuring the flow time. Place the bucket underneath. Fill the apparatus completely with concrete without tamping or tapping. Strike off the concrete level with the top by trowel. Open the trap door after 5 minutes after the second fill of the funnel and allow the concrete to flow. Calculate the time taken for complete discharge. It is called the flow time at T_5 min. For V-funnel test the flow time should be between 8 and 12 secfonds. for V-funnel flow time at T_5 min. + 3 seconds is allowed.

L box test method. This test is developed in Japan. The test assesses the flow of concrete, and also the extent to which the concrete is subjected to blocking by reinforcement. The apparatus is shown in Fig. 12.27.

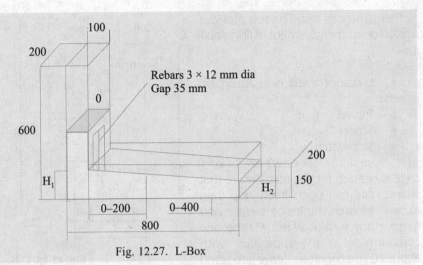

Fig. 12.27. L-Box

Concrete flowing through L-Box
Courtesy : Hindustan Construction Company

Procedure : About 14 litres of concrete is required for this test. Ensure that sliding gate can open freely and then close it. Moisten the inside surface, remove all surplus water. Fill the vertical section of the apparaturs with concrete. Leave it standing for 1 minute. Lift the sliding gate and allow the concrete to flow out into the horizontal section. Simultaneously start the stopwatch and record the time taken for the concrete to reach 200 and 400 mm marks. When the concrete stops flowing, the height H_1 and H_2 are measured. Calculate, H_2/H_1 , the blocking ratio. The whole test has to be performed within 5 minutes.

Interpretation of result: If the concrete flows as freely as water, at rest it will be horizontal. Therefore H_2/H_1 will be equal to 1. Therefore nearer the test values, the blocking ratio, is to unity, the better the flow of concrete. The European union research team suggested a minimum acceptable value of 0.8. T_{20} and T_{40} time can give some indication of ease of flow, but no suitable values have been suggested.

U-box test method:

Introduction. The test was developed in Japan The test is used to measure the filling ability of self com,pacting concrete. The apparatus consists of a vessel that is divided by a middle wall into two compartments shown by R_1 and R_2 in Fig.12.28.

An opening with a sliding gate is fillted between the two compartments. Reinforcing bars with nominal diameter of 13 mm are installed at the gate with centre to centre distance of 50 mm. This creates a clear spacing of 35 mm between the bars. The left hand section is filled with about 20 litres of concrete. The gate is then lifted and the concrete flows to the other section. The height of concrete in both the sections is measured.

Asessment of test: This test provides a good direct measurement of filling ability.

Equipment

- U-box of a stiff non absorbing material
- Trowel
- Scoop
- Stopwatch

Procedure : About 20 litre of concrete is needed for this test. Ensure that sliding gate can open freely and then close it. Moisten the inside surface and remove any surplus water. Fill the one compartment of the apparatus with about 20 litre concrete. Leave it to stand

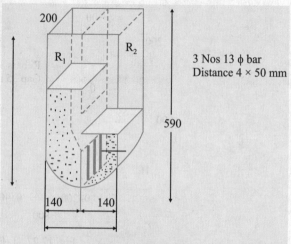

3 Nos 13 φ bar
Distance 4 × 50 mm

Fig. 12.28. U-box

Concrete passing through U-Box
Courtesy : Hindustan Construction Company

for 1 minute. Lift the sliding gate and allow the concrete to flow to the other compartment. Once the concrete has come to rest, measure the height of the concrete in the second compartment in two places. Calculate the mean. Let it be H_2. The height of concrete in the 1st compartment be H_1.

Calculate $H_1 - H_2$ the filling height. The whole test has to be completed within 5 minutes.

Interpretation of result : If the concrete flows as freely as water, at rest it will be horizontal, so $H_1 - H_2 = 0$. Therefore the nearer the test value, the filling height, is to zero, the better the flow and passing ability of the concrete. The acceptable value of filling height is 30mm maximum.

Fill box test

Introduction : This test is also called "Kajima test". The test is used to measure the filling ability of self compacting concrete with the maximum aggregate size of 20 mm. The apparatus consists of a container (transparent) with a flat and smooth surface. In the container there are 35 obstacles made of PVC with a diameter of 20mm, placed at centre to centre distances of 50 mm. At the top side is put a filling pipe 100 mm diameter 500 mm high with a funel 100 mm high. The container is filled with concrete through the filling pipe and the difference in height between two sides of the container is a measure for the filling ability.

Assessment of test : This is basically a laboratory test. It gives a good impression of the self compacting characteristics of the concrete. The apparatus is shown in Fig. 12.29.

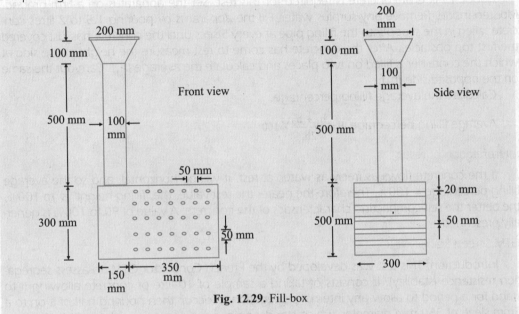

Fig. 12.29. Fill-box

Detail of the Fill-Box empty and filled with concrete.
Courtesy : Hindustan Construction Company

Equipment :

> Fill box of a stiff transparent, non-absorbing material
> Scoop 1.5 to 2 litre capacity
> Ruler
> Stop watch

Procedure

About 45 litre of concrete is required for this test. Set the apparatus on a firm ground. Moisten inside. Remove any surplus water. Fill the apparatus by pouring 1.5 to 2 litres concrete taken in the scoop into the filling pipe at every 5 secs until the concrete has just covered the first top obstacle,. After the concrete has come to rest measure the height at the side at which the container is filled on two places and calculate the average (h_1). Carryout the same on the opposite side (h_2).

. Calculate the average filling percentage.

Average filling percentage $F = \dfrac{h_1 + h_2}{2h_1} \cdot 100$

Interpretation of result :

If the concrete flows as freely as water, at rest, it will be horizontal, and so the average filling percentage = 100%. Therefore the nearer the test value, the "filling height" is to 100%, the better the self compacting characteristics of the concrete. A value of 90 to 100% is generally prescribed.

GTM Screen Stability test:

Introduction: This test was developed by the French Contractor GTM, to assess segregation resistance (stability). It consists of taking a sample of 10 litre of concrete allowing it to stand for a period to allow any internal segregation to occur, then pouring half of it on to a 5mm sieve of 350 mm diameter, which stands, on a sieve pan on a weigh scale. After two minutes, the mortar which passed through 5 mm sieve is weighted; and expressed as a percentage of the weight of the original sample on the 5mm sieve.

Assessment of the test:

Practising engineers who have used this test method are of the opinion that it is an effective method for assessing the stability of SCC. Though simple, it is not a rapid test and needs accurate weighing which may make it difficult to adopt at the site.

Equipments

- 10 litre bucket with lid
- 5 mm seieve 350 mm diameter
- Seive pan
- Balance, accuracy 20 gm minimum capacity 20 kg
- Stop watch

Procedure:

About 10 litre of concrete is needed. Allow the concrete to stand in a bucket for 15 minutes. Cover the concrete with the lid. Determine the weight of empty seive pan. Inspect the surface of concrete if there is any bleeding water and note it. Pour the top 2 litre or approximately 4.8 ± 0.2 kg of concrete into a pouring container. Determine the weight of the filled pouring container. Determine the weight of the empty seive pan. Pour all the concrete from the pouring container on to the seive from a height of 500 mm in one smooth continuous movement. Weigh the empty pouring container. Calculate the weight of concrete poured onto seive, Ma (*i.e.* the difference between the weight full and empty). Allow the mortar fraction of the sample to flow through the seive into the seive pan for a period of 2 minutes. Remove the seive and determine the weight of filled seive pan. Calculate the weight of sample passing seive, M_b, by substracting the empty seive pan weight from the filled seive pan weight.

Calculate the percentage of the sample passing seive, the segregation ratio is $\dfrac{M_b}{M_a} \cdot 100$

Interpretation of result:

Empirical observation suggest that if the percentage of mortar which has passed through the seive, the segregation ratio, is between 5 and 15% of the weight of the sample, the segregation resistance is considered statisfactory. Below 5% the resistance is excessive, and likely to affect the surface finish. Above 15% and particularly above 30% there is strong likelyhood of segregation. The suggested value is 0–15%.

Orimet test

Introduction:

Orimet test was developed at the University of Paisley as a method for assessment of highly workable, flowing fresh concrete mixes on construction sites. The orimet consists of a vertical casting pipe filled with a changeable inverted cone shaped orifice at its lower end, with a quick release trap door to close the orifice. Usually the orifice has 80 mm internal diameter for 20 mm maximum size of aggregate. Orifices of other sizes, usually from 70 mm to 90mm can be fitted instead.

Operation consists simply of filling the orimet with concrete, then opening the trap door and measuring the time taken for emptying it.

Assessment of test:

This test is able to simulate the fresh of fresh concrete during actual placing at site. It is a rapid test. This test has the useful characteristics of being capable of differentiation between

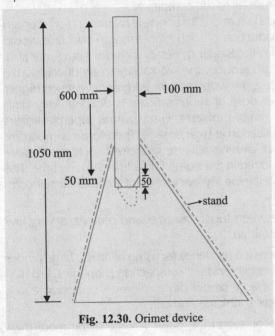

Fig. 12.30. Orimet device

Concrete flowing through Orimet device

highly workable, flowing mixes, and might therefore useful for compliance testing of successive loads on site. Orimet device is shown in Fig. 12.30.

Equipment:

- Orimet device of a stiff non-abosrbing material
- Bucket Appx. 10 litre
- Trowel
- Scoops
- Stopwatch

Procedure:

About 8 litre of concrete is needed for the test.
Set the orimet on a firm ground
Moisten the inside of pipe and the orifice
Keep the trap door open to drain of surplus water
Close the trap door and place a bucket underneath
Fill the apparatus completely. Do not compact or tap the pipe. Strike off the concrete level with the top by trowel. Open the trap door within 10 seconds after filling and allow the concrete to flow out. Find the time taken for complete discharge (Flow time). The whole test has to completed within 5 minutes.

Interpretation of Result

This test measures the ease of flow. Shorter duration indicate greater flowability. For SCC a flow time of 5 seconds or less is considered apporpriate. The inverted cone shape of the orifice restricts the flow, and prolonged flow time may give some indication of the susceptibility of the mix to blocking and/or segregation.

Complexities Involved in Making SCC:

Normal strength concrete itself is a complex material. High strength and high performance concrete with low water/binder ratio adds to the complexity. Making self compacting concrete, particularly of high strength, adds further to the complexity.

Generally self compacting concrete is used in situations for concrete requiring high strength say over 40 MPa upto 100 MPa or more. Production of such high strength concrete would require the use of relatively low water/binder ratio. Binder generally includes silica fume also. Use of silica fume while increasing the strength reduces the workability to an unacceptable level for self compacting requirements. To restore the workability or even to have much higher level of workability needed for SCC, a higher dose of superplaticizer is needed. Very high dosage of superplasticizer could lead to two major problems. Firstly, all the superplasticizers available in the market are not suitable for application at high dosage. Therefore it is important to choose the one that could be used without causing adverse side effect such as excessive retardation, at the sametime the one that could retain the slump for sufficiently long time. The superplasticizers based on Naphthalene or Melamine are generally not suitable for self compacting concrete requiring very high strength.

Initial trial for finding the compatibility between superplasticizer and cement, at very low water/binder ratio is also required to be ascertained.

Another point for consideration is that, there is a tendency for using relatively large binder paste volume in order to achieve both high strength and self compacting properties. From all round performance point of view, the use of a large binder paste volume is undesirable as it would lead to higher heat of hydration, greater shrinkage and creep.

EFNARC specification and Guideleines recommend the paste volume to be more than 40% of the volume of the mix. But other authorities have recommended that the paste volume not to be more than 35% for concrete to be considered as high performing. The above brings more complexities. It is to be pointed out that although, on the face of it, higher paste volume may result in higher shrinkage and creep in SCC, the comparativestudy conducted by Persson B. as reported in Cement and concrete Research vol 31, 2001, the mechanical properties such as strength, elastic modulus, creep and shrinkage of SCC and conventional concrete did nto show significant difference, when the strength was kept the same.

New Generation Plasticizers :

From various studies for production of SCC it was found better to use poly-carboxylate based superplasticizer (PC). This next generation superplasticizer or what is sometimes called hyperplasticizer is more efficient than naphthalene or melamine based superplasticizer with respect to plasticizing property and slump retention property. They cause dispersion of fine particles more by steric hindrance of many side long chain of PC than only by Zeha potential of naphthalene based or melamine based plasticizers. Such polycarboxylate based (PC), Multicarboxylatethers (MCE) or carboxylic acrylic ester (CAE) etc. are avaialble in India.

Viscosity Modifying Agent:

Another important material required for production of SCC. is Viscosity Modifying Agent (VMA). One of the methods of improving the stability of flowing SCC is to increase the paste content by using large amount of filler active or insert. Of late, however attempts are being made to reduce the fines content (the paste content) with a view to reduce shrinkage and creep by using VMA for stability.

VMAs have been in use for long time for under water concreting in the past. Now their use is extended to SCC. Most VMAs contain polysaccharides as active ingredient. Some starches could also be used for control of viscosity. Diutan gum and welan gum are often become part of certain viscosity modifying admixture. It is claimed that such VMA becomes compatible with all superplasticizers.

One must be careful about the sequence of addition of VMA and superplasticizer into SCC. VMA should be added after superplasticizer is added and mixed with cement particles. If VMA is added before superplasticizer, it swells in water and dispersion of superplasticizer in concrete becomes difficult. Usually VMA is added in a small dose of 0.2 to 0.5 per cent by weight of the binder content.

Availability of New generation Superplasticizer and VMA in India for SCC

The following table gives the brand names of new generation superplasticizer and VMA available in India.

Table 12.20 Brand names of new generation plasticizers and VM³A

S.No.	Names of chemical admixtures manufacturing Companies	New Generation Superplasticizers for SCC	VMA for SCC
1.	MC Bauchemie (Ind) Pvt. Ltd.	Muraplast FK 63 FK 61	Centrament Stabi 510 (non-organic base)
2.	Degussa MBT	Glenium 51 Glanium B 233	Glanium Stream - 2
3.	Fosroc	Structuro	—
4.	Sika	VISCO Crete–1	Sika Stabilizer 229
5.	Burgin And Leons Agenturen Pvt. Ltd	—	Kelco-crete 200 (containing Diutangunm)

Indian Scenario of SCC

In India, during the last few years, attempts were made in the laboratories and in the field to develop and use SCC. However, large scale uses have been rare. Some pionering efforts have been made in Delhi Metro projects in association with L&T and MBT. Nuclear Power Corporation, Gammon India, Hindustan Construction Company have made large scale laboratory trials and on the ground Moch up trials. Laboratory studies conducted at SERC Chennai, Indian Institute of Technologies at Madras, Roorkee and other places have given enough inputs and confidence to adopt SCC in India.

Experience at Delhi Metro Project

Of all the places Delhi Metro Project have used SCC in large scale for dome construction, tunnel lining, column casting etc. About 10,000 m³ of SCC has been used in as many as forty locations during the year 2004, This is by far the biggest use of SCC in India.

Hindustan Construction Company have also carried out considerable studies on the use of High Volume Fly ash self compacting concrete for domes, walls in turbine building in Rajasthan Power Project, and Concrete for Piers in Bandra-Worli Sea Link Projects. Based on their extensive trials, they used High Volume Fly ash self compacting concrete in the above projects and in many other works.

Experiance of SCC at Delhi Metro Project. (12.19)

Table 12.21 gives the mix proportions adopted at Delhi Metro Project.

Table 12.21. Mix Proportions adopted at Delhi Metro Project For 35 MPa SCC

Sl.	Materials	For Retardation time 90 mm	For Retardation time 120 mm	Volume litres
1.	Water (kg)	163	163	163
2.	Cement kg	330	330	105
3.	20 mm (kg)	455	455	169
4.	10 mm (kg)	309	309	115
5.	Sand kg	917	917	354
6.	Fly ash kg	150	150	68.5
7.	Glenium 51 (litre)	2.4	3.12	–
8.	Glenium stream 2 (litre)	0.96	1.3	–
9.	Possolith 300 R(litre)	0.66	0.99	–
10.	Fresh density (kg/m³)	2340	2337	
11.	Quantity of fines	525 kg*		
12.	Water/Powder ratio	0.85%		
13.	Paste Content by (vol)	36%		
14.	Sand Content by vol.	35%		
15.	Coarse Agg. by vol.	28%		

Note : 1. Entrapped air at 2% assumed
2. Sand contains 5% fives (< 125 micron)

SCC poured at Rotary Dome at central secretariat station – Delhi Metro Project

Table 12.22 shows the Trial Results of SCC at Delhi Metro as against EFNARC recommended values.

Table 12.22. Trial Result at Delhi Metro Project

Table 12.22 Shows the Trial Result of SCC as against EFNARC Values

Method	Property	Unit	Min	Max	Trial Result
Slump flow	Filling ability	mm	650	800	680
V-Funnel	Filling ability	Sec	8	12	8
L-Box	Passing ability	mm	8	1.0	0.91
U-Box	Passing ability	%	0	30	15
V-Funnel at 5 min	Segregation	sec	0	+3	+2

The strength of SCC poured at Delhi Metro, on the basis of Cube strength was between 44 and 49 MPa at 28 days. The target mean strength was 43 MPa for the characteristic strength of 35 MPa.

Experience of Mock-up Trials conducted at Tarapur Atomic Power Project [12.20]

Based on EFNARC guidelines, extensive trials were conducted to select the ingredients for SCC to be used in underground pump house wall. As per the designer's requirement, they used micro silica. The following are the mix proportions adopted based on laboratory trials for 40 MPa SCC

Cement	300 kg
Fly ash	200 kg
Micro silica	25 kg
Water	175 kg
Coarse aggregate	664 kg
Fine aggregate	976 kg
Superplasticizer	12.60 kg (2.4% by wt. of cementitious material)
VMA (Powder)	52.5g (0.03% by wt. of water).

The following laboratory trials were carried out for final acceptance of the three SCC mixes.

- Slump flow by Abrams cone.
- $T_{50\,cm}$ Slump flow
- J-ring
- V-funnel
- V-funnel at T_5 minutes
- L-box
- U-box
- Fill-box
- GTM Screen Stability Test
- Orimet
- Unit weight
- Air Content
- Initial and Final Setting time
- Compressive strength of 7, 28, and 56 days.

Having successfully conducted the laboratry trials, they used the selected SCC mix for the mock–up trials for the construction of 12 m long beam with two column junctions. The width of beam was 300 mm and the depth was 750 mm. The beam had highly conjected reinforcements, especially at the column junctions.

At Tarapur, they have also used SCC for construction of three walls of a pump-house. The hight of the wall was 14.4 m and it was done in 5 pours.

If this is the situation, what else is possible except self compacting concrete ? Above shows the mock-up trial of SCC at Kaiga Nuclear Power Project, (Karnataka).

Use of SCC in nuclear power plants–Laboratory and Mock-up trials at Kaiga (12.21)

Nuclear power plants are designed with higher safety factors particularly in case of seismic loadings. This results in higher percentage of steel which leads to conjestion of reinforcement, particularly at a column-beam junctions. In addition, there are number of inserts which add to the difficulties for normal method of compaction.

At Kaiga, SCC of characteristic strength 30 MPa was used in the two Mock-up structures one being heavily reinforced column with two beams passing through it and the other being a thin wall (140 mm thick). The conjested reinforcement is shown in Fig. 12.32.

The mix proportions adopted is shown in table 12.23.

Table 12.23. Mix proportions adopted at Kaiga Mock up trial

Cement kg/m³	Fly ash kg/m³	Water kg/m³	20mm C.A. kg/m3	10mm F.A.kg/m³	River sand kg/m³	Crushed sand kg/m³	Super plasticizer kg/m³	VMA kg/m³
225	225	165	354	354	288	684	1.80	1.35

The trial mix data of self compacting concrete (Seven Samples) are Shown in table 12.24

Table 12.24. Trial mix data of self compacting concrete (7 samples)

Mix identification no	GTM 29	GTM 30	GTM 31	GTM 32	GTM 33	GTM 34	GTM 35
Fresh concrete properties							
Flow, mm							
"0" min	690	710	700	675	670	680	710
"60" min	640	665	680	660	650	645	690
Flow T50, s							
"0" min	2.00	2.50	2.00	2.00	2.50	2.00	2.00
"60" min	2.50	3.00	2.50	2.50	2.50	2.00	2.50
V-Funnel T '0' min,s							
"0" min	8.00	9.00	7.00	8.00	8.00	9.00	8.00
"60" min	8.50	10.00	8.00	8.00	8.50	10.00	9.00
V-Funnel T'5' min,s							
"0" min	+0	+0.5	+0	+0.5	+0.5	+0	+0
"60" min	+1.0	+0	+0.5	+1.0	+1.0	+.05	+0.5
L-Box (h2/h1)							
"0" min	1.00	0.98	1.00	1.00	0.98	0.98	1.00
"60" min	0.96	0.93	1.00	0.96	0.96	0.94	0.96
U-Box ($h_1 - h_2$)							
"0" min	2.00	3.00	3.00	5.00	2.00	5.00	3.00
"60" min	5.00	5.00	3.00	8.00	5.00	7.00	7.00
Fill box							
"0" min	100	100	100	100	100	100	100
"60" min	98	95	100	96	95	98	94
Air content, percent	1.6	1.8	1.2	1.3	1.3	1.3	1.2
Unit, weight, kg/m³	2298	2308	2312	2332	2290	2312	2304
Setting time, h							
Initial	10.00	9.50	8.55	10:15	9:15	9:00	10:30
Final	11:35	12:00	10:05	12:50	11:55	11:05	12:20
Strength data							
Compressive strength, MPa							
3-day	12.36	14.80	12.86	13.31	11.03	11.35	13.79
7-day	18.36	20.22	22.43	19.05	22.21	20.62	23.04
28-day	43.20	49.60	39.80	40.49	38.85	37.97	40.42
56-day	54.20	52.40	49.80	55.80	50.46	48.88	53.20
90-day	58.20	57.64	53.50	61.93	54.49	54.70	58.52
Split tensile, MPa							
7-day	2.64	2.44	2.64	2.06	2.33	2.45	2.61
28-day	3.92	3.62	3.35	3.77	3.92	3.77	4.18
Flexural strength, MPa 28-day	4.44	4.85	4.48	4.35	4.55	4.12	4.33
Permeability (DIN), min	Nil	Nil	Nil	Nil	Nil	Nil	Nil

In the trial diutan gum as VMA showed excellent result but it delayed the setting time too much. Therefore they had to go for VMA with Synthetic polymer base. VMA dose of 0.8 per cent by weight of mixing water was used. Though the dosage of VMA with synthetic polymer base in liquid form is comparatively higher than diutan gum it was preferred for the following reasons.

- it facilitated easy disperson of VMA during large scale production of SCC at batching plant

- In case of diutan gum, not only it delayed the setting time, weighing and dispersion of a very small quantity (30–35 gm/m³) in powder form in a batching plant was found to be difficult.

Rapid chloride penetration test (RCPT) conducted on SCC showed an average charges passed was only 599 coulombs. Whereas the RCPT test on control mix showed 5040 coulombs. The surface finish of SCC both in case of column and wall was found to be excellent.

Trials at structural engineering research centre (SERC) Chennai [12.22]

Structural Engineering Research Centre at Chennai conducted some trial on SCC regarding structural behaviour and compared the same with conventionally vibrated concrete (CVC) of same strength (70 MPa). Reinforced Concrete (RC) beams of size 150 mm x 400 mm x 3000 mm with similar concrete shrength and identical reinforcement were cast and tested in flexure. They compared the structural behaviour such as load-deflection characteristics, crack widths, spacing of cracks, number of cracks, crack pattern, ultimate load carrying capacity, moment-curvature relationship, longitudinal strain in both concrete and steel for SCC and CVC.

The mix proportions of SCC and CVC are given in table 12.25

Table 12.25. Details of SCC and CVC mixture

Mix binder	Cement kg/m³	Fly ash kg/m³	Sand kg/m³	Coarse aggregate kg/m³	Water kg/m³	Water/binder ratio	Superplasticizer by weight of
CVC	450	50	775	950	186	0.37	0.6
SCC	490	160	790	700	220	0.34	0.4

Table No. 12.26. Shows the Mechanical properties of SCC and CVC

Properties	Age, days	SCC	CVC
Compressive Strength MPa	1	18.3	19.3
	3	39.8	37.1
	7	54.2	46.8
	28	72.1	69.4
Split tensile Strength MPa	1	1.9	2.0
	3	4.7	4.6
	7	5.5	5.2
	28	6.2	5.8
Flexural strength MPa	28	7.6	7.1
Modulus of Elasticity GPa	28	37.5	38.9
Bond Strength MPa	28	18.6	17.6

From the study at SERC it was observed that although the SCC and CVC have defferent mode of compaction, both mixes yielded similar strength at ages 1, 3, 7 and 28 days. Besides, compressive strength, split tensile, flexural and bond stregth of both mixcs were found to be similar. In view of the assured self compactability property, SCC can be adopted for any structural applications especially when there is conjested reinforcements.

Studies at Hong Kong

An interesting study has been conducted in Hong Kong by Albert K.H. Kwan and Ivan Y.T. NG and this has been reported in Hong Kong Institution of Engineers Transactions (12.24). The study involves self compacting concrete of grade 80 to 100 MPa.

Structural Engineering Research Centre, Chennai Study, as reported in table 12.26, indicated that the strength parameter of self compacting concrete is slightly higher than conventionally vibrated concrete (CVC), it is intended to take one more view in this respect from the study carried out at Hong Kong.

It has been realised that it is not easy to achieve both high strength, which demands a low water/binder ratio, and high workability, which demands a high water content without increasing the binder paste volume, which may lead to thermal and shrinkage cracking problems. In the study at Hong Kong they investigated the feasibility of producing high strength (80 to 100 MPa), self compacting concrete with a binder paste volume of not more than 35%. They used Poly carboxylate-based (PC) superplasticizer. A total of 18 trial mixes were made in the study. The mix proportions are shown in table 12.27.

Table 12.27. Mix Proportions of the Trial Concrete Mixes. (12.24)

Mix no.	W/B ratio	PFA %	PFA %	CSF %	Material kg/m3 Cement	PFA	CSF	Weight of Water	PC
1			0		435	145	0	139	18.3
2	0.24	25	5	3	401	143	29	137	18.0
3			10		367	141	57	136	17.8
4			15		335	140	84	134	17.6
5A			0	3	421	140	0	146	17.7
5B			0	4	421	140	0	146	23.6
5C	0.26	25	0	5	421	140	0	146	29.5
6			5	3	388	139	28	144	17.5
7			10	3	356	137	55	142	17.2
8			15	3	325	135	81	141	17.0
9					408	136	0	152	17.1
10	0.28	25		3	376	134	27	150	16.9
11					345	133	53	149	16.7
12					315	131	79	147	16.5
13					395	132	0	158	16.6
14	0.30	25		3	365	130	26	156	16.4
15					335	129	52	155	16.2
16					306	127	76	153	16.0

Note : W/B ratio stands for water/binder ratio
PFA stands for pulverised fuel ash (fly ash)
CSF stands for Condensed Silica fume
PC stands for polycarboxylate based superplasticizer

Table 12.28. Shows the workability results of the Trial Concrete Mixes [12.24]

Mix no.	W/B ratio	CSF %	PC %	Slump (mm)			Flow (mm)		
				0 min	30 min	60 min	0 min	30 min	60 min
1		0		205	185	185	420	395	363
2	0.24	5		240	235	235	545	513	513
3		10	3	205	205	210	465	435	428
4		15		225	225	220	480	500	445
5A		0	3	220	215	215	620	585	525
5B		0	4	255	235	225	725	650	620
5C	0.26	0	5	240	230	230	770	710	660
6		5	3	220	220	205	518	495	450
7		10	3	220	220	215	525	510	425
8		15	3	230	240	230	555	560	510
9		0		235	235	220	663	640	595
10	0.28	5	3	250	240	230	660	645	620
11		10		225	185	185	580	415	400
12		15		220	185	190	530	445	410
13		0		225	215	220	670	565	505
14	0.30	5	3	235	235	240	660	600	600
15		10		225	225	225	620	585	555
16		15		230	235	230	600	540	540

Table 12.29. Shows Strength Results of the Trial Mixes [12.24]

Mix no.	W/B ratio	CSF %	PC %	Compacted Cube Strength MPa			Uncompacted Cube Strength MPa	Strength ratio
				3-day	7-day	28-day	28-day	
1		0		67.7	80.2	98.1	83.3	0.85
2	0.24	5	3	70.4	88.1	109.1	109.0	1.00
3		10		70.1	89.0	114.6	107.8	0.94
4		15		70.1	94.6	116.6	113.4	0.97
5A		0	3	65.9	78.2	98.0	86.0	0.88
5B		0	4	64.6	77.5	101.2	97.4	0.96
5C	0.26	0	5	51.6	65.6	84.6	80.8	0.96
6		5	3	65.1	82.6	107.9	102.4	0.95
7		10	3	60.6	85.3	107.2	105.8	0.99
8		15	3	57.2	85.0	109.0	105.4	0.97
9		0		61.7	74.6	96.1	94.1	0.98
10	0.28	5	3	58.4	74.6	101.4	99.6	0.98
11		10		57.0	81.4	108.5	102.7	0.95
12		15		55.2	84.2	109.0	101.7	0.93
13		0		50.1	63.3	81.6	81.5	1.00
14	0.30	5	3	58.6	77.1	102.7	99.1	0.96
15		10		51.1	73.1	104.8	100.4	0.96
16		15		49.8	75.8	106.0	98.8	0.93

Note : The strength ratio is the ratio of the 28 day Uncompacted Cube Strength to the corresponding 28 day Compacted Cube Strength.

The table 12.28 shows that the polycarboxylate-based (PC) superplasticizer can produce self compacting concrete of grade 80 to 100 MPa with not more than 35% binder paste volume. Not only that, the PC superplasticizer could retain the required slump for 60 minutes.

Out of 18 mixes, 11 mixes have given more than or equal strength ratio of 0.95 at 3% superplasticizer dosage. Point to note is that the study carried out at Hong Kong, the self compacting concrete did not give higher strength than conventionally compacted concrete, as reported by SERC study at Chennai.

How Economical is Self Compacting Concrete ?

There is a feeling that cost of SCC is much higher than that of the corresponding normal stregth or high stregth concrete. It is seen that the cost of materials of SCC is about 10 – 15 percent higher. If one takes the other components of costs such as cost of compaction, finishing, etc, then one would realise that SCC is certainly not a costly concrete for comparable stregth.

Table No. 12.30 and Table 12.31 give comparision of cost of SCC and control concrete of similar stregth.

Table 12.30. Cost analysis of SCC and control concrete of similar stregths [12.23]

		Control Concrete		SCC	
	Rate Rs.	Quantity/kg	Amount Rs.	Quantity kg	Amount Rs.
Cement	3000/ton	450	1350	400	1200
Fly ash	1500/ton	–	–	175	263
Natural sand	900/ton	627	564	225	203
Crushed sand	850/ton	267	227	680	578
Course Aggregate					
20 mm	370/ton	510	189	405	150
10 mm	370/ton	430	159	330	122
Water	–	–	–	–	–
PCE – based admixture	140/l	–	–	5.175	725
Superplasticizer	33/l	11.25	371	–	–
Retarder	50/l	1.35	68	1.725	86
VMA	40/l	–	–	0.575	23
Total			**2928**		**3350**
Cost over control					**16.05 %**

Another example of cost analysis of SCC and control concrete of approximatly 40 MPa strength is given in Table 12.31 [12.23].

Table 12.31. Cost analysis of SCC and control concrete of approximately 40 MPa strengths

Material	Control concrete		SCC		Difference
	Quantity	Rate Rs.	Quantity	Rate Rs.	Rs.
Cement kg	395	3000/ t	300	3000/ t	– 285
Fly ash kg	130	1500/ t	170	1500/ t	+ 60
20 mm aggregate kg	639	370/ t	842	370/ t	+ 75
10 mm aggregate kg	462	370/ t	0	370/ t	– 171
Crushed sand kg	0	850/ t	235	850/ t	+ 200
Natural sand kg	660	900/ t	745	900/ t	+ 76.5

Admixture PCE /	–	140/ /	4.23	140/ /	+ 592
Admixture VMA /	–	40/ /	1.41	40/ /	+ 56.4
Admixture SNF /	5.25	33/ /	–	33/ /	– 173.0
Net					**+ 430.9**

∴ Cost above control = 16.8%

From the abvoe two examples it can be inferred that the material cost of SCC will be about 16 to 17% higher than ordinary concrete. But if one takes into considerations like savings in labour cost, rate of pouring, savings in repair work etc, the cost of SCC will be comparable with that of conventional concrete.

Bacterial Concrete [12.25]

Natural process, mainly weathering, deteriorates concrete by creating cracks, fractures and fissures, which result in reducing service life of structures. Even historical monuments built in stone also develop cracks and fissures. Grouting with epoxy or other cementitious materials are often adopted for remediating such defects.

Ramakrishan et al of South Dakota School of Mines and Technology have experimented a novel technique for remediating cracks and fissures in concrete structures by employing a selective microbial agency. In their attempt to seal cracks in concrete they used common soil bacteria called "Bacillus pasteruii" which during the process of their metabolic activities secrete or precipitate calcite $(CaCO_3)$ which is responsible for sealing the cracks. Calcium Carbonate is a natural calcareous cementing material and a bonding agent which is environmental friendly unlike other bonding materials, like epoxy or calcium silicate hydrates (C–S–H gel) resulting from hydration of cement.

The idea was taken from earlier paper on consolidation of sand by using similar bacteria. Earlier similar technique was also employed for sealing cracks and fissures in oil wells. From earlier studies it was found that an average crack width of 2.7 mm in granite rock was remedied with a mixture of sand and silica fume by using same kind of common soil bacteria.

Experimental Investigations [12.25]

In the South Dakota School of Mines, the effectiveness of microbiologically induced caleite $(CaCO_3)$ precipitation in remediating cracks in concrete was evaluated by comparing the compressive strength and stiffness of cracked specimens treated with bacteria and with those of the control specimens (without bacteria).

For studying the above, cement mortar beams of size 152 x 25.4 x 25.4 mm were prepared. The specimens were cured in water for 28 days and then kept exposed to air for another 3 months. Artificial cracks were cut. The width of the cracks were 3.2 mm for all the 10 specimens and the depth of cracks were 3.2 and 9.5 mm. The first 5 specimens were used as control without any filling in the cracks and were left exposed to air. The craeks in the remaining 5 specimens were filled with a mixture of sand and B. Pasteurii Bacteria. The final concentration of bacteria in the sand is of the order of 6.2×10^{10} cells per ml. is forced into the crack by knife edge. Then the beams with bacteria in their cracks were placed in a tray containing urea – $CaCl_2$ medium as food for bacteria and cured for 28 days. The medium was replaced after 14 days. Extreme care was taken not to disturb the precipitation of the calcium carbonate during change of the medium.

The control beams and those of beams with bacteria were tested for their stiffness after 28 days. It was found that stiffness value of beams whose cracks were filled with bacteria and sand were higher than those of control specimens. This was also true for beams with both crack depths. But the beams with deeper cuts showed comparatively lower stiffness value than the beams with shallower cuts, meaning thereby the bacterial action and precipitation did not reach to the full depth of deeper cuts. Shallow cut beams showed improvements of stiffness by 23.9% while the deep cut beams showed an improvement of 14% over control specimens.

Appropriate and similar investigations were also conducted with respect to the following

● The effect of microbial calcite precipitation to various depth of cracks on the compressive strength of cement mortar cubes.

● The effect of different concentration of bacterial cells for cracks remediation, on the compressive strength of cement mortar cubes.

● The effect of B. Pasturii with various concentration on the modulus of rupture of the cracked cement mortar beams.

The experimental results showed that the microbial remediation increased the compressive strength by approximately 80%, when compared to that of control specimens.

The cracked beams with bacteria showed 57% greater modulus of rupture than that of cracked specimens without bacteria.

Investigations on Durability Characteristics

Recently Ramakrishnan et al investigated the durability aspects of cement mortar beams made with different concentration of bacteria. The main objective was to determine whether the beams with bacteria performed better, when subjected to alkaline, sulphate and freeze-thaw attack.

They used Scan Electron Microscope (SEM) which is one of the most versatile instruments available for examination and analysis of micro structural characteristics of solids.

From the detail investigations they concluded that microbial culture generated in the cracks of mortar beams increased the compressive strength, stiffness and modulus of rupture. It was also found that the durability characteristics improved with the addition of bacteria. SEM examination established the fact that the calcite precipitation inside cracks has been responsible for the improvement in mechanical properties and permeability characteristics for enhancing the durability.

When bacterial concrete is fully developed, it may become yet another alternative method to replace OPC and its hazardous effect on environmental pollution.

Zeopolymer Concrete [12.26]

The emission of CO_2 coupled with non absorption of the same on account of deforestation etc has caused tremendous environmental pollution leading to global warming and other bad effects. It is estimated that about 7% of greenhouse gas is being emitted into the atmosphere annually on account of production of OPC alone.

Therefore, it is necessary to reduce the emission of CO_2 into atmosphere by reducing the cement production and consumption.

It is suggested that consumption of cement could be reduced by three ways.

● Through economical mix design

● By replacing cement with fly ash by adopting high volume fly ash concrete (HVFC) or by using other supplementary cementitious materials.

● By using alternate binding materials for concrete such as Bacterial concrete or Geopolymer concrete. (no cement in concrete)

Geopolymer Concrete

The term "Geopolymer" was coined by Davidovits in 1978. Geopolymer is an inorganic alumino-silicate polymer, synthesized from predominantly silicon and aluminium material such as fly ash. Alkaline solutions are used, to induce the silicon and aluminium atoms; in the source materials (fly ash), to dissolve to form gel. The polymerisation process may be assisted by applied heat followed by drying. The Geopolymer gel binds the loose coarse and fine aggregates to form geopolymer concrete. Geopolymer gel replace the C–S–H gel in cement concrete. Chemical reaction period is substantially fast and the required curing period may be within 24 to 48 hours.

Davidovits claimed that the Egyptian pyramids were built by casting geopolymer on site. He also reported the geopolymer possesses excellent mechanical properties, does not dissolve in acidic solutions, and does not generate any deleterious alkali-aggregate reaction even in the presence of high alkalinity. Some applications of geopolymer concrete are for marine structures, precast concrete products such as railway sleepers, sewer pipes etc.

B.V. Rangan et al of Curtain University of Technology, Perth, Australia [12.25] have carried out pioneering experimental work for the production of geopolymer concrete with a view to develop optimum mix design process and to establish the engineering properties such as compressive and tensile strengths, stress-strain relations, modulus of elasticity etc. The studies undertaken by them also aimed at establishing shrinkage, creep and durability properties, in particular, the corrosion resistance. The information given under geopolymer concrete in this book is freely drawn from the article published by RV Rangan et al in the proceedings of the seminar, INCONTEST 2003 held at Coimbatore, India.

In the experimental work low calcium (Class F) fly ash has been used. Sodium hydroxide in flake form Na(OH) with 98% purity and sodium silicate solutions (Na$_2$O = 14.7%), SiO$_2$ = 29.4% and water 55.9% by mass) were used as alkaline activators. To improve the workability of fresh concrete, a commercially available naphthaline based superplasticizer was used. Four types of locally available aggregates (at Perth, Australia) were mixed together.

Aggregates and the fly ash were mixed dry in a pan mixer for 3 minutes. The alkaline solutions and the superplasticizer were mixed together, and then added to the solid particles and mixed for another 3 to 5 minutes. The fresh concrete had a stiff consistency and was glossy in appearance. The mixture was cast in 100 x 200 mm cylinder in three layers. Each layer was tamped 60 times and vibrated for 10 seconds on a vibrating table. Five cylinders were prepared for each test variable.

Immediately after casting, the samples were covered by a film to avoid the loss of water due to evaporation during curing at an elevated temperature. After being left in room temperature for 30 – 60 minutes, the specimens were cured in an oven at a specified temperature for a period of time in accordance with the test variables selected.

Numerous trial mixes of geopolymer concrete were made and tested. The data collected from these studies indicated that the salient parameter affecting the compressive strength of geopolymer concrete are listed below :

● Silicon oxide (SiO2) to aluminum oxide (Al$_2$O$_3$) ratio by mass in fly ash should preferably be in the range of 2.0 to 3.5 to make good concrete.

● Activator liquid to source material (fly ash) ratio by mass

● Concentration of sodium hydroxide NaOH liquid measured in terms of Molarity (M) in the range of 8 to 16 M.

● Sodium silicate to sodium hydroxide liquid ratio by mass. The effect of the parameter depends on the composition of the sodium silicate solution.

- Curing temperature in the range of 30° to 90°C
- Curing time in the range of 6 to 48 hours.
- Water content in the mixture.

Table 12.32. Effect of Parameter on Compressive strength

Mix	Concentration of NaOH liquid in Malarity (M)	Sodium Silicate / (NaOH) liquid ratio by mass	7 day compressive strength after curing at 60°C for 24 hours MPa
A1	8 M	0.4	17.3
A2	8 M	2.5	56.8
A3	14 M	0.4	47.9
A4	14M	2.5	67.6

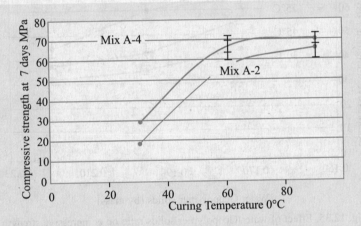

Fig. 12.33. Shows the Effect of curing temperature on compressive strength

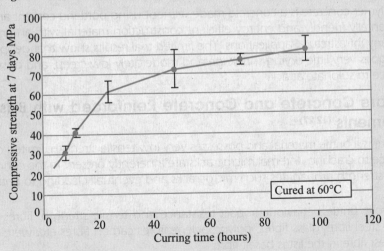

Fig. 12.34. Influence of curing time on compressive strength for Mix A2.

Effect of water contents in the Mix

In order to study the effect of water content on the compressive strength of geopolymer concrete several tests were carried out. The dose of superplasticizer to the mass of fly ash was taken as 1.5%.

The effect of water contents is shown in Fig. 12.35 by plotting the compressive strength versus water to geopolymer solid ratio by mass. For a given geopolymer concrete the total mass of water in the mix is taken as the sum of the mass of water in the sodium silicate solution plus the mass of water in sodium hydroxide solution plus the mass of extra water, if any, added to the mixture. The mass of geopolymer solids is the sum of the mass of fly ash, the mass of sodium hydroxide flakes and the mass of sodium silicate solids.

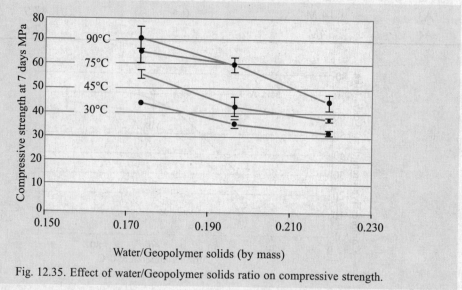

Fig. 12.35. Effect of water/Geopolymer solids ratio on compressive strength.

Concluding Remarks

Geopolymer concrete is a concrete made without using portland cement and as such it is environmentally friendly and energy efficient construction material with an enormous potential in many infrastrctural applications. The limited trial results show that geopolymer concrete undergoes very little drying shrinkage and moderately low creep, and possesses excellent resistance to sulphate attack.

Basalt Fibre Concrete and Concrete Reinforced with Basalt Fibre Reinforcements (12.27)

Concrete is a brittle material and possesses very low tensile strength; limited ductility and little resistance to cracking. Internal microcracks are inherently present in the concrete and its poor tensile strength propagates such microcracks and eventually leading to brittle failure of concrete.

To improve brittle behaviour, impact resistance and tensile strength, fibres of different kind such as steel fibre, glass fibres, polypropylene fibres carbon fibres etc. were used in the past. The latest fibre in the list is basalt fibre.

One of the causes of failure of reinforced concrete structures is due to corrosion of steel reinforcement. It was reported that about 40 per cent of failure of RCC structures was due to corrosion of reinforcement. Use of nonferrous fibre-reinforced polymer (FRP) reinforcement bars making use of glass fibres or carbon fibres etc. in conjunction with suitable resins have been used to mitigate chloride induced corrosion and to impart many better mechanical properties to reinforced concrete. The latest one in this direction is the basalt fibre reinforcement bars in concrete.

Basalt Continuous Fibers

V. Ramakrishnan and others in South Dakota school of Mines and Technology have investigated, for the first time in the world, the use of basalt fibres and use of basalt fibre reinforcement in concrete. They used both plain bars and modified bars with corrugation and indentation bars. The result of the investigations showed that the rebars made from basalt fibre is a viable alternative to the conventional steel reinforcement as it is found to be superior in many respects.

Basalt fibres are manufactured in a single-stage process by melting naturally occurring pure basalt rock. They are abundantly available, environmentally safe, nontoxic, non corrosive, non-magnatic, possess high heat stability and insulating characteristics. The tensile strength of continuous basalt fibres is about twice that of E-glass fibres and modulus of elasticity is about 15 to 30 % higher. Basalt fibres in an amorphous state exhibit higher chemical stability than glass fibres. When exposed to water at 70°C basalt fibres maintain their strength for 1200 hours, whereas the glass fibres do so only for 200 hours.

Basalt fibre concrete [12.27]

Investigations were carried by Ramakrishan et al to find out the following :

- The properties of fresh concrete with and without basalt fibres
- The properties of hardened concrete such as compressive strength, static modulus,

Basalt Fibres

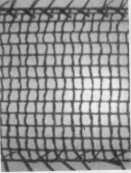

Basalt Fibres
Reinforcement Mesh

Woven Fabrics made
from Basalt Fibres

static flexural strength, unit weight and impact strength.

● The toughness indices by ASTM method with the help of load deflection curves.

● The flexural toughness factor and equivalent flexural strength by the Japanese standard method.

The investigation involves making 5 mixes and the dosages of basalt fibres added to the concretes were 0.1, 0.25, 0.4 and 0.5 by volume. One control mix was also done. The mix proportions are given in table 12.33.

Table 12.33. Mix proportions for Basalt fibre Concrete For 0.057 cubic metre

| Mix designation | Water/ Cement Ratio | Fibres | | Weight in kg | | | |
		Kg	Vol. %	Cement	coarse Agg.	Fine Agg.	Water Kg.
B1	0.5	–	–·	20.85	53.1	53.1	10.25
B2	0.5	0.68	0.5	20.85	53.1	53.1	10.25

For 0.071 cubic metre

B3	0.5	0.5	0.4	25.68	66.5	66.5	12.83
B4	0.5	0.43	0.25	25.68	66.5	66.5	12.83
B5	0.5	0.17	0.1	25.68	66.5	66.5	12.83

Basic mix proportions for 1 m3 of concrete

Cement Kg	Water Kg	Coarse Agg Kg	Fine Agg. Kg	Water/ Cement Ratio
361.9	.188	937.4	937.4	0.5

Plastic Properties

The freshly mixed concrete was tested for slump, air content, unit weight, concrete temperature, Vee-Bee time etc.

In all the tests the basalt fibre reinforced concrete did not differ much from plain concrete accept that slump and Vee-Bee slump decreased with the addition of fibres, and Vee-Bee time increased with the addition of fibres.

Test for hardened Concrete

For hardened concrete, compressive strength test, static modulus, flexural strength test, behaviour of load-deflection and impact test by drop weight test method, were conducted. In all these tests much desirable properties were exhibited by basalt fibre concrete than the plain concrete.

Conclusions.

● Satisfactory workability can be maintained with the addition of basalt fibres up to 0.5 % by volume. A higher % of fibres could be used without causing any balling or segregation.

● Compared to the control concrete, there was considerable increase to the toughness and impact strength for the basalt fibre concrete.

● The most important contribution due to the addition of basalt fibre in concrete is the change of mode of failure from a brittle to ductile failure, when subjected to compression, bending and impact.

● Based on earlier research conducted with other fibers in concrete, it is suggested that the length of the fibres could be increased from 25 mm to 50 mm for better performance.

Concrete Reinforced with basalt fibre reinforcement

Basalt composite rebars are made by utilising basalt fibres and epoxy resin binder. They are non corrosive and consist of 80% fibres. They have tensile strength three times that of the steel rebars. Wherever the corrosion problem exists, basalt fibre composite rebars have the potential to replace steel bars in reinforced concrete structures. Currently the FRP rebars available in the market are made of E-glass fibre and they suffer from lack of durability under extreme alkaline environments and are costly.

Modified basalt fibre reinforcement

Other advantages are that the basalt rebars weighs only one-third of the steel rebars. Thermal coefficient of expansion is very close to that of concrete. The high mechanical performance to price ratio of basalt bars, combined with corrosion resistance to alkaline attack are further justification for the use of basalt bar in place of steel bars.

To evaluate the properties of concrete reinforced with basalt fibre reinforcements, studies were conducted by Ramakrishan et al at South Dakota school of Mines and Technology in five phases.

In phase I they directed their studies to flexure test using plain basalt bars as reinforcement in concrete beams. In phase II they conducted flexure test of plain basalt bar reinforced concrete beam, concrete 3-dimensionally reinforced with basalt fibres. In phase III they conducted bond test on basalt rebars and cables. In phase IV they conducted investigation for determination of cracking and ultimate loads for extremely under-reinforced beams and in phase V the trials were conducted to determine cracking and ultimate loads for five under-reinforced beams.

The results obtained from Phase I and II revealed that the actual ultimate failure moments of basalt rebar reinforced concrete beams were less than the theoretically calculated ultimate moments. This was due to bond failure between rebars and concrete. To avoid this type of failure, they developed basalt cable with corrugations and rods with slots, barriers and anchors; for improving the bond between the bars and the concrete. In phase III to V, they studied the bond between modified basalt rebars and concrete. The photographs of the modified basalt rebars are shown in fig. 12.36.

Results of the investigations

Phase I

● The beams reinforced with plain basalt bars failed in flexure, due to inadequate bond between the rod and the concrete. All the actual ultimate moments were much less than the calculated ultimate moments due to the bar pullout failure.

Phase II

- The beams with 3D-fibres and rebars exhibited a primary failure in flexure and shear followed by a secondary failure on splitting.
- The 3D-fibres caused a ductile failure of the beam and also increased the actual cracking moment capacity of the beam.
- All the actual ultimate moments were much less than the calculated ultimate moments due to bar pullout failure.

Phase III to V

- The bond between all the modified basalt rebars and concrete was extremely good
- The experimental ultimate moments nearly matched or exceeded the calculated moments for all the beams tested.
- The experimental ultimate moment was much higher than the first crack moment in all the beams tested, indicating a good bond between rebar and concrete.
- The deflections were considerable, indicating adequate ductility.
- All the beams had primary flexural failure and a few beams had secondary shear failure.
- There was no slip of the rebars in any of the beams tested and there was no evidence of bond failure between the concrete and the modified basalt rebars and twisted cables.
- In general, the basalt rebars are suitable for use in reinforced concrete structures.

Basalt continuous fibres are manufactured, apart from other places, at kottingbrunn, Austria, in the patented name of BaXalt Technologie GmbH, established during 2003. A cooperative union has been formed with the South Dakota School of Mines (Prof Ramakrishnan) and with the Vienna Technical University for process engineering (Prof Marini) BaXalt Technologie, by way of passionate innovative strategies will revolutionize the fibre industries.

The market has not seen this magnitude of cutting edge technology since 1940's when fibre glass was first invented.

Basalt continuous fibres will fill the niche between fibre glass and carbon fibres. Subsequently basalt exhibits a vital competitive edge due to higher Modulus of elasticity, chemical consistency, temperature stability and low cost raw material.

REFERENCES

12.1 Cement and Concrete Association, *An Introduction to Light-weight concrete, Fourth Edition* 1970.

12.2 Valore R.C. *Insulating concrete, ACI Journal*, Nov. 1956.

12.3 Teychenne D.C., *Light-weight Aggregate, their properties and use in the United Kingdom, Proceedings of the First International Congress on Light-weight concrete London*, May 1968.

12.4 Short and Kingburgh W., *The Structure use of Aerated Concrete, The Structural Engineer, London,* Jan. 1961.

12.5 American Concrete Institute, *Concrete for Radiation Shielding compilation No. 1*, 1962.

12.6 Malhotra V.M., *Development of Sulphur-unfiltrated High strength concrete, ACI Journal*, Sept. 1975.

12.7 Surendra P. Shah and Vijaya Rangan B, *Fibre Reinforced Concrete Properties, ACI Journal*, Feb 1971.

12.8 Majumdar A.J., *Fibre Cement and concrete, Building Research Establishment, Current Paper*, March 1975.

12.9 Pilkington Cem-fil, *Alkali-resistant glass fibre for Glass reinforced Cement-Technical literature.*

12.10 Mackintosh R.H. Bolton J.D. and Miur, *No-Fines concrete as a structural Material, Proceedings, Institution of Civil Engineers*, No 1966.

12.11   Malhotra V.M., *No-Fines Concrete—Its Properties and applications, ACI Journal*, Nov. 1916.

12.12   De Pug G.W. and Dikeou J.T, *Development of polymer Impregnated concrete as a construction Material for Engineering Projects, ACI Publication SP 40*, 1973.

12.13   Solper B, Fiorato A.E. and Lenschow R., *A study of partially Impregnated polymerised concrete specimens, ACI Publication SP 40*, 1973.

12.14   Meyer Steinberg, *Concrete Polymer Materials and its world wide Development, ACI Publication SP 40*, 1973.

12.15   Indian standard code of practice *for extreme weather concreting* IS 7861—1971.

12.16   Thomas J Reading, *Corps of Engineers Studies of Shotcrete, ACI Publication SP* 45.

12.17.   Application of self compacting concrete in Japan, Europe and United States

12.18.   Specification and Guidelines for self-compacting concrete - EFNARC, Association House, 99 West Street, Farnham, Survey GU9 7EN, U.K.

12.19.   Vachhani S.R. Rajeev Choudhary, SM Jha, Innovative use of self compacting concrete in Metro construction. Indian concrete Institute Journal.

12.20.   Amit Mittal, M.B. Kaisare and R.G. Shetti, use of SCC in a pump House at TAPP 3 and 4, Tarapur Indian concrete Journal, June 2004

12.21.   S.G. Bapat, S.B. Kulkarni, K.S. Bandekar, Using SCC in Wuclear power plants – Laboratory and Mock-up Trials at Kaiga, Indian concrete, Indian concrete Journal, June 2004.

12.22.   J. Annie Peter et al, Flexural behaviour of R.C. beams using self compacting Concrete, Indian concrete Journal, June 2004.

12.23.   B.V.B. Pai, How economic is self compacting concrete ? Indian concrete Journal, June 2004.

12.24.   Albert K.H. Awan and Ivan YTNG, Grade 80-100 self-consolidating concrete for Hong King, The Hong Kong Institution of Engineers Transactions, Volume II, Number 2.

12.25.   V. Ramakrishan et all Bacterial concrete school of mies and Technology.

12.26.   Djwantoro Hardjito et al Geopolymer concrete : turn Waste into Environmentally Friendly concrese. Proceeding of International Conference on Recent Trends in Concrete Technology and structure, Red al coimbatore.

12.27.   V. Ramakrishna et all, performane characteristics of 3D and 2D reinforced Basalt Fibre concrete composits proceedings of International Conference on Recent Trends on concrete Technology and structure, held at Coimbatore.

GENERAL REFERENCE BOOKS

Sl. No.	Author	Title	Publisher
1.	Amerongen, CV	Dictionary of Cement	BGW, Germany Oxford 1967
2.	—	Proc 3rd Int. Symp. on the Chemistry of Cement in 1952	BR S & CACA UK 1954
3.	—	World Cement Directory	Cembureau
4.	Czernin	Cement Chemistry and physics for Civil Engineers	—
5.	Lea, FM	Chemistry of Cement and Concrete	Edward Arnold UK — 1970
6.	Taylor, HFW	Chemistry of Cements Vol I	Academic Press UK
7.	—do—	Chemistry of Cements Vol II	and USA 1964
8.	Bogue, RH	Chemistry of Portland	Cembureau 1959
9.	—	On the Testing of Cement	Cembureau
10.	Fintel	Hand Book of Concrete Engg.	Vannostrand 1974
11.	Lalonde	Concrete Engg. Hand Book	McGraw. Hill USA 1961
12.	Orchard D.F.	Concrete Technology Vol I	Applied Science UK 1973
13.	— do —	Concrete Technology Vol II	Applied science UK 1973
14.	— do —	Concrete Technology Vol III	Applied Science UK 1976
15.	Singleton-Green	Concrete Engg. Vol I— Practical Concrete	Charls Griffin Co UK 1935
16.	Singleton-Green	Concrete Engg. Vol II — Properties of Concrete	Charls Griffin Co. UK. 1934
17.	Tattersall	Workability of Concrete	A viewpoint pub UK 1976
18.	—do—	Concrete Manual	USBR 1972
19.	Figg-JW and Bowden SR	Analysis of Concrete	HMSO UK 1971
20.	Neville	Properties of Concrete	FLBE 1977
21.	Powers	Properties of Fresh Concrete	J.Wiley and sons USA 1968
22.	Troxell and Davis	Composition & properties of concrete	McGraw Hill USA 1956
23.	Whitehurst	Evaluation of Concrete properties from Sonic tests ACI Monographs No. 2	ACI USA 1967
24.	—	Computer applications in Concrete Design & Technology ACI SP—16	— do —
25.	—	Fatigue of Concrete ACI SP—41	ACI, USA 1974
26.	—	Durability of Concrete ACI SP—47	— do — 1975

Sl. No.	Author	Title	Publisher
27.	—	RILEM Symp on durability of Concrete	*Checkoslovak Academy of science*
28.	Woods	Durability of Concrete ACI SP— 4	*ACI USA 1968*
29.	—	Concrete Hand Book	*Concrete Association of India 1969*
30.	Petzold & Rehrs	Concrete for High Temperature	*Elservier Publication 1970*
31.	Ramchandran VS	Calcium Chloride in Concrete	*Science and Technology Applied Science UK*
32.	Steward DA	Design and Placing of High Quality Concrete	*E & FN Spon Ltd UK 1962*
33.	Thursby H	Controlling Concrete on the site	*Cement and Concrete Association UK 1976*
34.	Tretyakav A	Concrete and concreting	*Mir Pub Moscow, 1968*
35.	Waddell JJ	Concrete Construction Hand Book	*McGraw Hill 1968*
36.	Woddell JJ	Practical Quality Control for Concrete	
37.	Wals HN	How to make good Concrete	
38.	—	Concrete Hand Book	*ACI Publication 1969*
39.	—	Recommended practice for cold weather concreting	*ACI Publication 1966*
40.	—	Recommended practice for selecting proportions for structural light weight concrete	*ACI 1967*
41.	—	Manual of concrete Inspection	*ACI SP-2, 1967*
42.	—	Proceedings of symposium on shotcreting	*ACI SP-14 1966*
43.	—	Causes Mechanism and Control of cracking in concrete	*ACI SP-20 1968*
44.	—	Concrete for Nuclear Reactor Vol I Vol II Vol III	*ACI SP-34 1972*
45.	—	Use of shotcrete for undergoing structural support	*ACI SP-45, 1974*
46.	—	Corrosion of Metals in Concrete	*ACI SP-49 1975*
47.	—	Roadways and Airport Pavements	*ACI SP-51*
48.	—	Insulating Concretes	*ACI Publication*
49.	—	Recommended Practice for Design of Concrete pavements	*ACI Publication*
50.	—	Selection and use of Aggregates	*ACI Publication*
51.	—	Guide for use of Epoxy compounds with Concrete	*ACI Publication*
52.	Preschke B	Concrete construction	*Asia Publishing House*

Sl. No.	Author	Title	Publisher
53.	Biczok	Concrete corrosion and concrete protection	*Alkademiai, Kaido Hungary*
54.	Hurd MK	Formwork for Concrete	*ACI SP-4, 1963*
55.	—	Light weight Aggregate concrete Technology & word application	*Cembureau France 1974*
56.	Short, Andrew Kenniburg	Light weight concrete	Asia Publishing House Bombay— India 1963
57.	Spratty BH	Structural use of light weight aggregate concrete	*Cement and Concrete Association UK 1974*
58.	Erntroy HC Teychenne DC Franklin RE	Design of Normal Concrete Mixes	*HMSO Publication UK 1976*
59.	—	Road Note No. 4, Design of Concrete Mixes	*HMSO—1965*
60.	Lyndon FD	Concrete Mix Design	*Applied Science UK 1972*
61.	Krishna Raju, N	Design of concrete Mixes	*M/s Sehgal Faridabad India —1975*
62.	Shacklock BW	Concrete constituents and Mix proportions	Cement and concrete Association UK 1974
63.	Richardson JG	Precast concrete Production	*CACA—UK—1973*
64.	Gerwick BC	Construction of Prestressed concrete construction	J.Wiley USA—1971
65.	Akroyd	Concrete properties and Manufacture	
66.	—	Proceedings of Rilem symposium on winter concreting—1956	Danish National Institute of *Building Research Copenhagen —1956*
67.	—	Polymers in Concrete	*ACI SP—1940*
68.	Malhotra VM	Testing of Hardened concrete nondestructive Methods	*ACI Monograph series No. 9*
69.	—	Polymers in Concrete	*Concrete Society UK—1976*
70.	Blank R.F. Kennedy HL	Technology of Cement and Concrete	*J.Wiley—1955*
71.	Murdock	Concrete Materials and Practice	*Edward Arnold Ltd. London—1960*
72.	Elvery RH	Concrete Practice Vol I Vol II	*Asia Publishing House—1963*
73.	Meintosh JD	Concrete and Statistics	*CR Books Ltd. London 1963*
74.	Illingworth JR	Movement and Distribution of concrete	*Mcgraw-Hill UK—1972*
75.	Rixom MR	Chemical Admixtures for concrete	*E & FN Spon Ltd London—1978*

Sl. No.	Author	Title	Publisher
76.	—	Structure of Concrete, Proceedings of an International Conference	*Cement and Concrete Association London—1965*
77.	—	Performance of Concrete Proceeding of a Symposium	*University of Toronto Press, Canada—1968*
78.	—	Proceedings of Rilem Symposium on Fibre Reinforced Cement Concrete Vol II	*The Construction Press Ltd —1976*
79.	—	Concrete and Concrete making materials	*ASTM Special Technical Publication No. 169-A 1966*
80.	—	Tests and Properties of Concrete and Concrete Aggregates	*ASTM STP No. 169*
81.	—	Fibre Reinforced Concrete	*ACI — 44*
82.	—	ACI Manual of concrete Practice Part I Part II Part III	*ACI —1979*
83.	A.M. Neville J.J. Brooks	Concrete Technology	*ELBS with Longman 1987*
84.	A.M. Neville	Properties of Concrete Fourth Edition	*Longman 1995*
85.	Steven H. Kosmatka and William C. Panarese	Design and Control of Concrete Mixture	*PCA 1988*
86.	P. Kumar Mehta Paulo J.M. Monteiro	Concrete Micro-structure, Properties and Materials	*Prentice Hall INC & McGraw Hill, USA*

LIST OF INDIAN STANDARD SPECIFICATIONS AND CODE OF PRACTICES, RELATED TO CEMENT AND CONCRETE

SI No.	IS Number	IS Codes and specifications for Cement and Concrete	Date Reaffirmed
1	IS 269:1989	Specification for ordinary Portland cement, 33 grade (fourth revision)	Sept-98
2	IS 383:1970	Specification for coarse and find aggregates from natural sources for concrete (second revision)	Feb-97
3	IS 455: 1989	Specification for Portland Slag cement (fourth revision)	Mar-00
4	*IS 456 : 2000	Code of practice for plain and reinforced concrete (third revision)	Aug-00
5	*IS 457 : 1957	Code of practice for general construction of plain and reinforced concrete for dams and other massive structures	Mar-00
6	*IS 516 : 1959	Method of test for strength of concrete	Jan-99
7	IS 650 : 1991	Specification for standard sand for testing of cement (second revision)	Jan-99
8	*IS 1199: 1959	Methods of sampling and analysis of concrete	Jan-99
9	**IS 1343: 1980	Code of practice for prestressed concrete (first revision)	Jan-99
10	*IS 1344: 1981	Specification for calcined clay pozzolana (second revision)	Jan-99
11	IS 1489(PT1): 1991	Specification for Portland Pozzolana Cement Part I Flyash based (third revision)	Mar-00
12	IS 1489(PT2): 1991	Specification for Portland Pozzolana Cement Part II calcined clay based (third revision)	Mar-00
13	IS 1727 : 1967	Methods of test for pozzolanic materials (first revision)	Jan-99
14	IS 2386(PT2): 1963	Methods of test for aggregates for concrete Part 1 Particle size and shape	Sept-97
15	IS 2386(PT2): 1963	Methods of test for aggregates for concrete part 2 estimation of deleterious materials and organic impurities	Feb-97
16	IS 2386(PT3): 1963	Methods of test for aggregates for concrete Part 3 specific gravity, density, voids, absorption and bulking	Feb-97
17	IS 2386(PT4): 1963	Methods of test for aggregates for concrete : Part 4 Mechanical properties	Feb-97
18	IS 2386(PT5): 1963	Methods of tests for aggregates for concrete : Part 5 Soundness	Feb-97
19	IS 2386(PT6): 1963	Methods of test for aggregates for concrete : Part 6 Measuring mortar making properties of fine aggregates	Feb-97
20	*IS 2386(PT7): 1963	Methods of test for aggregates for concrete : Part 7 Alkali aggregate reactivity	Feb-97
21	*IS 2386(PT8): 1963	Methods of test for aggregates for concrete : Part 8 Petrographic examination	Feb-97
22	IS 2430: 1986	Methods for sampling of aggregates for concrete (first revision)	Mar-00
23	*IS 2502: 1963	Code of practice for bending and fixing of bars for concrete reinforcement	Jan-99
24	IS 2505: 1980	General requirements for concrete vibrators	Jan-99
25	IS 2506: 1985	General requirements for screed board concrete vibrators (first revision)	Mar-00
26	*IS 2645: 1975	Specification for integral cement waterproofing compounds (first revision)	Jan-99
27	IS 2770(PT1): 1967	Methods of testing bond in reinforced concrete Part 1 Pullout test	Feb-97
28	IS 3085: 1965	Methods of test for permeability of cement mortar and concrete	Feb-97

SI No.	IS Number	IS Codes and specifications for Cement and Concrete	Date Reaffirmed
29	*IS 3370(PT1): 1965	Code of practice for concrete structures for the storage of liquids : part 1 General requirements	Jan-99
30	*IS 3370(PT2): 1965	Code of practice for concrete structures for the storage of liquids : Part 2 Reinforced concrete structures	Jan-99
31	IS 3370(PT3): 1967	Code of practice for concrete structures for the storage of liquids : Part 3 Prestressed concrete structures	Jan-99
32	IS 3370(PT4): 1967	Code of prctice for concrete structures for the storage of liquids : Part 4 design tables	Jan-99
33	IS 3466: 1988	Specificaation for masonry cement (second reivision)	Jan-99
34	IS 3535: 1986	Methods of sampling hydraulic cement(first revision)	Jan-99
35	IS 3558: 1983	Code of practice for use of immersion vibrators for consolidating concrete (first revision)	Jan-99
36	IS 3812: 1981	Specification for fly ash for use as pozzolana and admixture (first revision)	Jan-99
37	IS 4031(PT1): 1996	Methods of physical tests for hydraulic cement: Part 1 Determination of fineness by dry sieving (second revision)	
38	IS 4031(PT2): 1999	Methods of physical tests for hydraulic cement: Part 2 Determination of fineness by specific surface by Blaine air permeability method (second revision)	
39	IS 4031(PT3): 1988	Methods of physical tests for hydraulic cement : Part 3 Determination of soundness (first revision)	Mar-00
40	IS 4031(PT4): 1988	Methods of physical tests for hydraulic cement : Part 4 Determination of consistency of standard cement paste (first revision)	Mar-00
41	IS 4031(PT5): 1988	Methods of physical tests for hydraulic cement : Part 5 determination of initial and final setting times (first revision)	Mar-00
42	IS 4031(PT6): 1988	Methods of physical tests for hydraulic cement : Part 6 determination of compressive strength of hydraulic cmt (other than masonry cement) (first revision)	Mar-00
43	IS 4031(PT7): 1988	Methods of physical test for hydraulic cement: Part 7 Determination of compressive strength for masonry cement (first revision)	Mar-00
44	IS 4031(PT8): 1988	Methods of tests for hydraulic cement: Part 8 determination of transverse and compressive strength of plastic mortar using prism (first revision)	Mar-00
45	IS 4031(PT9): 1988	Methods of physical tests for hydraulic cement : Part 9 Determination of heat of hydration (first revision)	Mar-00
46	IS 4031(PT10): 1988	Methods of physical test for hydraulic cement : Part 10 Determination of dring and shrinkage (first revision)	Mar-00
47	IS 4031(PT11): 1988	Methods of physical tests for hydraulic cement : Part 11 Determination of density (first revision)	Mar-00
48	IS 4031(PT12): 1988	Methods of physical tests for hydraulic cement: Part 12 Determination of air content of hydraulic cement mortar (first revision)	Mar-00
49	IS 4031(PT13): 1988	Methods of physical tests for hydraulic cement : Part 13 Measurement of water retentivity of masonry cement (first revision)	Mar-00
50	IS 4031(PT14): 1989	Methods of physical test for hydraulic cement Part 14 Determination of false set	Mar-00
51	IS 4031(PT15): 1991	Methods of physical test for hydraulic cement Part 15	Mar-00

SI No.	IS Number	IS Codes and specifications for Cement and Concrete	Date Reaffirmed
		Determination of fineness by wet sieving	
52	IS 4032 : 1985	Method of chemical analysis of hydraulic cement (first revision)	Mar-00
53	IS 4305 : 1967	Glossary of terms relating to pozzolana	Mar-00
54	IS 4634 : 1968	Methods for testing performance of batch-type concrete mixer (first revision)	Mar-00
55	IS 4845 : 1968	Definitions and terminology relating to hydraulic cement	Jan-99
56	*IS 4926 : 1976	Specification for ready mixed concrete (first revision)	Jan-99
57	IS 5512 : 1983	Specification for flow table for use in tests of hydraulic cements and pozzolanic materials (first revision)	Jan-99
58	IS 5513 : 1996	Specification for vicat apparatus (second revision)	
59	IS 5514 : 1996	Specification for apparatus used in Le-Chatelier test (first revision)	
60	IS 5515 : 1983	Specification for compaction factor apparatus (first revision)	Jan-99
61	IS 5516 : 1996	Specification for variable flow type air-permeability apparatus (Blaine type) (first revision)	Jan-99
62	IS 5525 : 1969	Recommendations for detailing of reinforcement in reinforced concrete works	Jan-99
63	IS 5536 : 1969	Specification for constant flow type air-permeability apparatus (Lea and Nurse type)	Mar-00
64	IS 5816 : 1999	Method of test for splitting tensile strength of concrete (first revision)	
65	IS 6452 : 1989	Specification for high alumina cement for structural use	Mar-00
66	IS 6461 (PT1): 1972	Glossary of terms relating to cement concrete : Part I Concrete aggregates	Feb-97
67	IS 6461 (PT2): 1972	Glossary of terms relating to cement concrete : Part II Materials	Feb-97
68	IS 6461 (PT3): 1972	Glossary of terms relating to cement concrete : Part III Concrete reinforcement	Feb-97
69	IS 6461 (PT4): 1972	Glossary of terms relating to cement concrete : Part IV types of concrete	Feb-97
70	IS 6461 (PT5): 1972	Glossary of terms relating to cement concrete : Part V Formwork for concrete	Feb-97
71	IS 6461 (PT6): 1972	Glossary of terms relating to cement concrete : Part VI Equipment tools & plant	Feb-97
72	IS 6461 (PT7): 1973	Glossary of terms relating to cement concrete : Part VII Mixing, laying, compaction, curing and other construction aspects	Feb-97
73	IS 6461 (PT8): 1973	Glossary of terms relating to cement concrete : Part VIII properties of concrete	Feb-97
74	IS 6461 (PT9): 1972	Glossary of terms relating to cement concrete : Part 9 Structural aspects	Feb-97
75	IS 6461 (PT10): 1973	Glossary of terms relating to cement concrete : Part 10 tests & testing apparatus	Feb-97
76	IS 6461 (PT11): 1973	Glossary of terms relating to cement concrete : Part 11 Prestressed concrete	Feb-97
77	IS 6461 (PT12): 1973	Glossary of terms relating to cement concrete : Part 12 Miscellaneous	Feb-97
78	IS 6491 : 1972	Methods of sampling fly ash	

SI No.	IS Number	IS Codes and specifications for Cement and Concrete	Date Reaffirmed
79	IS 6909 : 1990	Specification for supersulphated cement	
80	IS 6923 : 1973	Methods of test for performance of *screed board* concrete vibrators	Jan-99
81	IS 6925 : 1973	Methods of test for determination of water soluble chlorides in concr. admixture	Jan-99
82	IS 7246 : 1974	Recommendations for use of table vibrators for consolidating concrete	Jan-99
83	IS 7320 : 1974	Specification for concrete slump test apparatus	Jan-99
84	IS 7325 : 1974	Specification for apparatus for determining constituents of fresh concrete	Jan-99
85	IS 7861 (PT1): 1975	Code of practice for extreme weather concreting Part I Recommended practice for hot weather concreting	Feb-97
86	IS 7861(PT2): 1981	Code of practice for extreme weather concreting : Part II Recommended practice for cold weather concreting	Feb-97
87	IS 8041: 1990	Specification for rapid hardening Portland cement (second revision)	Mar-00
88	IS 8042: 1989	Specification for white portland cement (second revision)	Mar-00
89	IS 8043: 1991	Specification for hydrophobic Portland cement (second revision)	Mar-00
90	IS 8112: 1989	Specification for 43 grade ordinary portland cement (first revision)	Mar-00
91	IS 8125: 1976	Dimensions and materials of cement, rotary kilns, components and auxiliaries (dry process with suspension preheater)	Jan-99
92	IS 8142: 1976	Method of test for determining setting time of concrete by penetration resistance	Feb-97
93	IS 8229: 1986	Specification for oil-well cement (first revision)	Jan-99
94	IS 9012: 1978	Recommended practice for shotcreting	Feb-97
95	IS 9013: 1978	Method of making, curing and determining compressive strength cured concrete test specimen	Feb-97
96	IS 9103: 1999	Specification for admixtures for concrete (first revision)	
97	IS 9142: 1979	Specification for artificial lightweight aggregates for concrete masonry units	Feb-97
98	IS 9284: 1979	Method of test for abrasion resistance of concrete	Feb-97
99	IS 9376: 1979	Specification for apparatus for measuring aggregate crushing value and ten per cent fines values	Jan-99
100	IS 9376: 1979	Specification for apparatus for aggregate impact value	Jan-99
101	IS 9399: 1979	Specification for apparatus for flexural testing of concrete	Jan-99
102	IS 9459: 1980	Specification for apparatus for use in measurement of length change of hardened cement paste, mortar and concrete	Jan-99
103	IS 9799: 1981	Specification for pressure meter for determination of air content of freshly mixed concrete	Jan-99
104	IS 10070: 1982	Specification for machine for abrasion testing of coarse aggregates	Jan-99
105	IS 10078: 1982	Specification for jolting apparatus for testing cement	Jan-99

SI No.	IS Number	IS Codes and specifications for Cement and Concrete	Date Reaffirmed
106	IS 10079: 1982	Specification for cylindrical metal measures for use in tests of aggregates and concrete	Jan-99
107	IS 10080: 1982	Specification for vibration machine for casting standard cement mortar cubes	Jan-99
108	IS 10086: 1982	Specification for moulds for use in tests of cement and concrete	Jan-99
109	IS 10262: 1982	Recommended guidelines for concrete mix design	Jan-99
110	IS 10510: 1983	Specification for vee-bee consistometer	Jan-99
111	IS 10850: 1984	Specification for apparatus for measurement of water retentivity of masonry cement	Jan-99
112	IS 10890: 1984	Specification for planetary mixer used in tests of cement and pozzolana	Jan-99
113	IS 11262: 1985	Specification for calorimeter for determination of heat of hydration of hydraulic cement	Jan-99
114	IS 11263: 1985	Specification for cylinder measures for determination of air content of hydraulic cement mortar	Jan-99
115	IS 11389: 1986	Methods of test for performance of concrete vibrators : Immersion type	Jan-99
116	IS 11993: 1987	Code of practice for use of screed board concrete vibrators	Jan-99
117	IS 12089: 1987	Specification for granulated slag for manufacture of Portland slag cement	Jan-99
118	IS 12119: 1987	General requirements for pan mixers for concrete	Jan-99
119	IS 12269: 1987	Specification for 53 grade ordinary portland cement	Jan-99
120	IS 12330: 1988	Specification for sulphate resisting portland cement	Mar-00
121	IS 12423: 1988	Method for colorimetric analysis of hydraulic cement	Mar-00
122	IS 12468: 1988	General requirements for vibrators for mass concreting : Immersion type	Mar-00
123	IS 12600: 1989	Specification for low heat portland cement	Mar-00
124	IS 12803: 1989	Method of analysis of hydraulic cement by X-ray fluorescence spectrometer	Jan-99
125	IS 12813: 1989	Methods of analysis of hydraulic cement by atomic absorption spectrophotometer	Jan-99
126	IS 12870: 1989	Methods of sampling calcined clay pozzolana	
127	IS 13311(PT1): 1992	Methods of non-destructive testing of concrete : Part 1 Ultrasonic pulse velocity	Jan-99
128	IS 13311(PT2): 1992	Methods of non-destructive testing of concrete : Part 2 Rebound hammer	Jan-99
129	IS 14345 : 1996	Specification for autoclave apparatus	
130	IS 14687 : 1999	Guidelines for falsework for concrete structures	
131	SP: 16(S&T): 1980	Design for reinforced concrete to IS 456: 1978	
132	SP: 23(S&T): 1982	Handbook on concrete mixes (Amendment No. 1)	
133	SP: 24(S&T): 1983	Explanatory handbook on Indian Standard code of practice for plain and reinforced concrete (IS 456: 1978)	

SUBJECT INDEX